A CENTURY OF AUTOMOTIVE STYLE

100 YEARS OF AMERICAN CAR DESIGN

BY MICHAEL LAMM & DAVE HOLLS

To Mac
(Strother MacMinn)

Lamm-Morada Publishing Company Inc.
Post Office Box 7607
Stockton, California 95267
Phone (209) 931-1056
Fax (209) 931-5777

™

© Copyright 1996-97

Second printing Sept. 1997

Printed in Hong Kong

Library of Congress card catalogue number 96-094154

ISBN 0-932128-07-6

A CENTURY OF AUTOMOTIVE
STYLE
100 YEARS OF AMERICAN CAR DESIGN

BY MICHAEL LAMM & DAVE HOLLS

TABLE OF CONTENTS

SIDEBARS

There is now no question, 100 years after the beginning, that the art and science of automotive *styling*—what today we call automobile *design*—has had a tremendous impact on this nation's economy. To understand the dollar importance of styling--ignoring aesthetics for the moment--think first about all the money that's been pumped through the American economy during the past century just by the sale of new automobiles. It's staggering. The total runs well beyond the limits of ordinary imagination; far beyond what now constitutes the $3.5 trillion national deficit.

Consider further, over the span of those same 100 years, how many times the *individual* sale of each automobile must have been prompted by the way it looked: its first impression in the showroom, its lasting image, how the new owner saw himself or herself driving and owning that particular make and model. Survey after survey has shown that styling outranks all other considerations as *the* prime motivator of most new-car purchase decisions.

Styling began to take on fiscal importance as early as 1901, long before the motorcar had an established shape or enough mechanical reliability to be trusted as a fairly friendly contraption. Even at that primitive stage of the motorcar's development, the wealthy turn-of-the-century car buyer thought carefully about how his newest toy might look in the family driveway, how it complemented his personality, how it fit his status in the community and business, and whether it matched his other possessions and preoccupations.

Styling, that one simple and complex factor—the overall shape, ornamentation and resulting aura of any automobile—has moved so much money through the national economy that the wonder isn't its longterm financial effect but rather the question: *Why has so vital and pervasive a topic as automobile design never been examined as the history of a commercial or industrial artform?* Isn't it every bit as much a national treasure as those commercial arts that *have* been so thoroughly scrutinized: architecture, furniture and interior design, clothing fashion, textiles, jewelry, ceramics, etc.?

Too little has been written about the value of automotive styling, either from an economic or a marketing or an aesthetic or an evolutionary viewpoint. That oversight in itself comes as a something of a shock. It's an oversight we hope to remedy in some small measure with this book.

--Michael Lamm & Dave Holls

CHAPTER 1

ROOTS

Andrew F. Johnson spent the better part of his life—half a century, from 1892 to 1943—teaching carriage and automobile design. What makes Johnson loom large in the history of motorcar design is that he inspired and encouraged his students to make the transition from designing horsedrawn vehicles to designing automobile bodies. And he did this at a time when America was very much in a quandary about that change.

Some 2300 students eventually graduated from Johnson's technical school, many of whom went on to become giants in the automobile business. Among them were William C. Durant, Charles W. Nash, Frederick B. Judkins, John Dobben (of Judkins), Raymond H. Dietrich, Hermann A. Brunn, George J. Mercer and three of the seven "Body by Fisher" Brothers.

Today, Andrew F. Johnson remains virtually unknown, even within the modern design community. But he did and still does rank as the pioneer, the Grand Old Man, the Mr. Chips, the maestro, the person who laid the foundation that brought auto design from its infancy to its present state of significance. Johnson shaped the first generation of men who shaped the first generation of automobiles. He did for autobody design what Henry Ford did for the motorcar itself: If Ford put the nation on wheels, Johnson gave those wheels style.

In 1927, on the occasion of his 35th year as a teacher, 300 of his former students—his "boys" as he called them—honored Johnson at a banquet in Detroit. Following the speeches and toasts, the three Fisher Brothers who'd attended the technical school—Fred, Alfred and Edward—stood up and made an announcement. In recognition of their former teacher's generosity, his inspiration and high standards, the influence he'd had on their lives and the lives of all those present, General Motors was pleased to present Mr. Johnson with a brand-new automobile: a maroon 1927 Pontiac four-door sedan.

The gift came as a complete surprise to Johnson, and he nearly blacked out when he heard the news. Tears welled up in his eyes, and he could only whisper his thanks.

Johnson lived at that time, as he would for many years more, in the tiny hamlet of Gray, Maine, in a house from which, since 1921, he'd offered his autobody design courses by mail. Many of his students had gotten their educations by correspondence.

All seven Fisher Brothers had agreed among themselves beforehand that their venerated teacher had no real need of a car, because he didn't know how to drive and wasn't likely to learn. But what Johnson did need in 1927 was money. And since the Fisher Brothers knew he wouldn't accept a check or cash, they gave him the Pontiac instead. They reasoned that Johnson would sell the car. In any case, they wanted to present him with this token of their gratitude; this automobile that he'd given them the ability to design and manufacture.

As the Fishers suspected, Andrew F. Johnson never did learn how to drive. But he never sold the Pontiac either. How could he, a gen-

Andrew F. Johnson, the father of American automobile design. Photo from around 1900.

tleman from the old school, sell a gift so generously given by some of his most illustrious students? Johnson continued to walk, even during the coldest Maine winters, to and from the Gray post office, where he personally picked up and delivered his lessons. And after he passed away in 1943 at age 89, the 1927 Pontiac, still virtually new but with four long-flat tires, was sold to a citizen of Gray named Warren Libby.

Over the course of his lifetime, Andrew F. Johnson had become a major contributor to the origins and the later orderly development of automobile body design. He was born in 1854 in Nova Scotia and left home at 16 to seek his fortune in the United States. He found his first job as a woodworker in Gray, Maine, with a company called Smith & Leslie, that built carriages and sleighs. While working there, young Andrew Johnson fell in love with, wooed and soon married the boss's daughter, Agnes Leslie.

At that time, the world's great carriage designers and builders were French and British. The French, especially, set the styles and published the important books about carriagemaking. Garsault's *Traite des Voitures (Treatise on Carriages)* appeared in Paris in 1754 and, in 1771, A.J. Roubo finished his comprehensive three-volume *L'Art du Menuisier (The Art of Woodworking)*. These works set the international baselines for carriage fashion and technology, and France continued to lead right up until 1789 and the French Revolution. At that point, everything Gallic that smacked of aristocratic frivolity, including coach and carriage design, came to an abrupt halt. The British then took the lead for a time, but the French made a rapid recovery and, by the mid-19th century, France again led the carriage fashion parade.

Here in the U.S., we didn't even join that parade until the last part of the 19th century, and then only because a few families found themselves with enough money to afford custom-built carriages. Common folk, like farmers and merchants, might own wagons, and if crops and business went well, they might even buy a buggy or a runabout. But only the upper classes could treat themselves to anything as luxurious as a carriage. And since carriages were strictly for the trade that bore the name, they were never so common in this country as in Europe. Europe had its ruling elite plus an established class of landowners, wealthy bankers and businessmen, so the carriage trade thrived overseas.

After the Civil War, a few U.S. carriagemakers did come into prominence, notably Brewster & Co. in New York and the Frederick Wood Co. of Bridgeport, Connecticut. These firms and a few more like them, mostly along the eastern seaboard, were able to design and build carriages to European standards and styles. They owed much of this ability to U.S. trade magazines like *The Hub* and *The Carriage Monthly*, which published "fashion plates" of the latest continental body types. (Fashion plates were side-view drawings of stylish carriages and buggies. Today, of course, we use the term to describe a person rather than a sketch.)

Brewster, in particular, made an effort to keep up with European carriage styles. For a time, Brewster had a reciprocal agreement with the French luxury coachbuilder Kellner & Freres: an exchange program by which employees for one company could go abroad and work for the other. Henry Brewster's son, William (Willie), apprenticed for a time at Kellner's in Paris, and Kellner's son came to New

John Gribbon, right, explains to two of his students how to loft a carriage. Photo is from around 1885.

Early American carriage designers might be anyone who happened to be able to sketch—a draftsman, say, or the shop foreman. Designers were often called "delineators," meaning simply the artists who could make professional-looking presentation sketches to show to prospective customers.

Slowly, though, over time, the more successful American coachbuilders recognized that a good staff designer helped bring in business. The designer, often working directly with clients, became especially important at that crucial selling stage when a sketch meant so much to both the patron and the shop itself.

As designers proved their dollars-and-cents value, it became apparent to the more prestigious coachbuilding houses, in the U.S. as well as in Europe, that the world didn't really have enough qualified, trained people who could design and style carriages. To overcome this shortage, the French established, around 1860, three small schools in Paris that trained young men who wanted to go into carriage design and drafting. One such school was sponsored by the *Chambre Syndicale de Carrosserie,* a national coachbuilders' trade union.

American carriagemakers knew about these schools, because they'd been making annual pilgrimages abroad to view the *concours d'elegance* and other carriage competitions and sometimes, like Brewster, to take part in them. At these expositions, American carriage engineers, shop foremen, designers and draftsmen could catch up on the latest

York to study Brewster's methods. Brewster & Co. also regularly entered European coachbuilding competitions and won, among many prizes, the French Legion of Honor in 1873.

Carriage design was a respected occupation in Europe, but in this country, designers weren't usually even recognized as such.

It All Goes Back to Shipbuilding

It's no big secret that a lot of early motorcars took their body design from carriages. But it's less obvious that carriage design evolved from shipbuilding. As with so many other arts and crafts, it all began with the Greeks.

In the 19th century, archeologists discovered mysterious lines scribed on the floors of Roman temples. What did these odd lines mean? The scholars discovered that they were the outlines of huge Roman ships, drawn in plan view (plan view means "as seen from directly above"). The smooth temple floors made an ideal surface to loft a ship's hull full size.

The Greeks, Norsemen, Southeast Islanders and even some tribes of American Indians used a variation of this same idea. They would draw a full-sized hull outline on a sandy beach, plant sticks around the perimeter, and then connect the sticks with thongs. Finally they'd string more thongs diagonally across the hull to indicate the ship's ribbing. The resulting "blueprint," crude as it was, became the working drawing for a trireme, a packet or a war canoe.

These techniques worked well enough for the ancients, but as ships grew larger and more complicated, the blueprints had to be refined. For one thing, a simple plan-view drawing gave the shipwright only a two-dimensional, incomplete map to work from. What he really needed was a set of plans that showed all three dimensions, with curves and surfaces recorded in a way that workmen could read and follow.

So in the 1600s, European ship designers came up with a system for representing all three dimensions on a flat sheet of paper. This system involved basic geometry. Automobile stylists still use it today to map out autobody surfaces, but they now let computers do the

Wooden half models were carved in layers, then taken apart and scaled up in three dimensions.

mathematical calculations.

Once a ship's designer had the ability to indicate to the carpenter or shipwright exactly how the finished hull ought to be constructed, style started to enter the picture. Ships evolved from the tall, ungainly craft that sailed the ocean blue in 1492 to the sleek clipper ships of the mid-1800s. Amazingly, in that transformation, the fundamentals of shipbuilding didn't change. What did change was that the ship designer--call him "stylist"--could and did get involved in the building process.

It's easy enough to see that the design system that evolved for ships' hulls carried over first into carriage-building and then into autobody design. In the 18th and 19th centuries, the first step in designing a ship's hull meant carving a scale "half model" from wood. A common scale was one inch to four feet, or 1/48. And the half model was exactly what it sounds like: not a representation of the entire hull but just half of it, split vertically down the middle and flat from the keel line up. This half-hull model was usually carved from a stack of planks, or layers. The planks fit tightly together, one atop the other, and they were held in place with tapered pegs that fit into vertical holes. The model did not have masts or sails.

Once this scale half model was approved, the master builder would take the half-model planks apart and use the individual slices to make sectional full-sized drawings. In other words, the separate sections (planks) were all scaled up, or "lofted," to full size. (The verb "to loft" grew out of shipyard parlance, because the only place where a shipbuilder's shop had enough room to lay down the scaled-up outlines of a full-sized ship's hull--enough clear floorspace, as in those Roman temples--was usually in the loft: the attic above the boatworks. This was also the area where, at other times, most of the sails were cut and sewn.)

In the shipyard loft, the "loftsman"--the person in charge of scaling up the half-hull model--would first draw out the lines of each hull section and then, from those drafts, make full-sized templates, or "molds." The ship's carpenters and craftsmen in the shop below then used these templates to cut and size the wooden beams that formed the ship's

continental construction techniques and styling advances.

In 1878, the French put on a huge and, as it turned out, important international carriage show. Some 400 vehicles were entered from 12 countries, including the U.S. This exhibition received worldwide attention, especially after Brewster & Co. won another important gold medal. The resulting publicity made the American carriage industry take note of its place in the world, and George Houghton, editor of *The Hub,* stayed in Paris for three months during the ongoing 1878 exhibition and sent back information and engravings that showed the subtle differences between U.S. and European designs.

The upshot of all this was that American carriage manufacturers agreed that they all faced a similar shortage of trained, qualified designers. As a result, John W. Britton, Brewster's shop foreman, began to lobby his U.S. colleagues for the establishment of a school. The school, he felt, should be patterned after the successful French schools then in existence.

In 1879, Henry Killam, incoming president of the Carriage Builders National Association, the industry group that represented most major U.S. vehicle manufacturers at that time, recommended funding a carriagebuilding school to be headquartered in New York City. This school was duly commissioned late in 1880. Its classroom was inside the Metropolitan Museum on Fifth Avenue. The headmaster was John D. Gribbon, a carriagemaker who'd previously worked for both Brewster and Frederick Wood. As part of his own education, Gribbon had studied drafting and freehand drawing at the Dublin Society of Fine Arts in Ireland.

Known formally as the Technical School for Carriage Draftsmen and Mechanics, Gribbon's evening classes at the museum met three times a week. Twenty-two students enrolled that first year, most of them working as apprentices during the day and attending school at night. Tuition was mostly paid for by sponsoring companies or by the association itself. To broaden the school's reach into the hinterland, where so many carriagemakers had their shops and factories, Gribbon established a correspondence curriculum in 1884 that offered instruction based on his regular classroom work.

The previous year, 1883, Andrew F. Johnson had left Smith & Leslie and had gone to New York to work for Brewster & Co. He also enrolled in Gribbon's night school. Johnson applied himself with such zeal that he graduated at the head of his class, and Gribbon recommended him for an industry scholarship called the Paris Prize. In 1885, the Carriage Builders National Association sent the 31-year-old Johnson to France for five months to continue his education under Albert Dupont of the Dupont school in Paris.

Albert Dupont needs a bit of limelight here, too, because he, like Gribbon and Johnson, contributed a great deal to carriage- and, later on, to autobody design. Dupont owned a carriagebuilders' trade journal in Paris called *Le Guide de Carrossier.* One day he met a young man who'd been let go from a French carriage factory. The young man had later taken a job in Marseilles at a shipbuilding yard. It was here that he noticed the curious fact that ship-hull designers could somehow describe, on paper, the subtle three-dimensional surfaces and transitions that ships' carpenters transformed into huge, actual forms: the wooden hulls of ocean-going vessels. In this young man's experience in carriage shops, draftsmen supplied only two-dimensional drawings—usually full-scale side views—and the workmen had to transform these two-dimensional body drafts into three-dimensional carriages.

---

main framework. By using the same templates first on one side of the hull and then the other, the two halves of the finished framing came together as mirror images.

Now it's important to recognize that any mistake the hull designer or the master builder might have made in his original scale model got magnified, often by a factor of 48 or more, when that model was lofted full size. And since any scale model always did contain surface flaws, it was up to the loftsman to "fair" the full-sized representations. Fairing meant, first and foremost, making an ungainly or flawed design efficient as it moved through the water. Fairing meant smoothing the surface, sculpting the lines, reshaping, streamlining the hull...because a smooth, streamlined hull made the ship go faster, and speed meant money. Speed made the ship more profitable. So profit became the main motive for fairing a hull.

But fairing also had an aesthetic component. The art of fairing meant that the loftsman had the authority to change the full-scale drawings and templates so the lines looked "right;" so that the hull had what was generally accepted as a "proper" shape. The hull should look pleasing; it should look graceful and "fair," as in "a fair young maid." A good loftsman had an eye for fairing, and his aesthetic sense was as critical to the design process as his ability to make the hull efficient. Fairing, then, became the act of combining efficiency with beauty.

And now we make that leap that allows us to recognize that the same techniques and processes used in ship design carried over into horsedrawn vehicles. Carriages, like

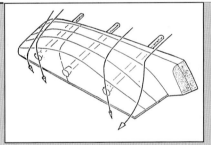

ships, needed to be efficient, but efficiency in this case didn't mean streamlined; it meant lightweight. A carriage had to be light. That's because there was only from one to four horsepower to pull it.

Unlike ships' hulls, the designing of carriages was almost never preceded by a scale model. It's possible that a few carriagemakers did use models, perhaps made of wood or sculptors' clay, to help customers visualize what they were buying. But models weren't

Sections were taken at specific intervals and transferred to full-sized drawings on floor of shipbuilder's loft (below).

common in carriage design, even in Europe. Rather, what carriagebuilders did was to first make detailed sketches, usually in 1/10 or 1/12 scale, and then loft those sketches full size on big, upright wooden panels.

To save space, the technique of lofting a carriage involved drawing a side view and then also superimposing half of a plan view on top of it. Both views were crammed onto the same board, and the drawings were kept separate and readable by being done in different colors. Offsets were called out on separate sheets of paper, and sometimes templates were made for the carriage body, but mostly not. This same technique evolved into the design and construction of automobile bodies and was used well into the 1980s.◆

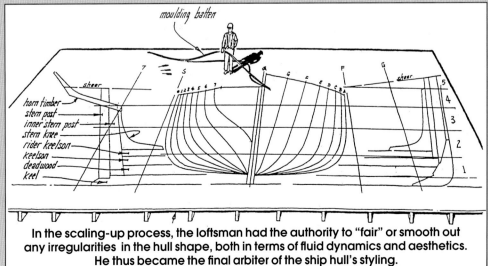

In the scaling-up process, the loftsman had the authority to "fair" or smooth out any irregularities in the hull shape, both in terms of fluid dynamics and aesthetics. He thus became the final arbiter of the ship hull's styling.

The ship-design process remained a mystery to the young man until he finally went to his yard's design loft and learned the "secret" of hull design. The secret consisted basically of plotting the incremental intersections of the ship hull's three axes or planes: horizontal, vertical and end-view. The surface points, arrived at by geometric calculations, were called "keys." When he heard about this wonderful system of defining three-dimensional shapes, Dupont wrote about it in his magazine. His carriagebuilding readers wanted to learn more, so Dupont and a partner, Brice Thomas, opened a school in Paris. They applied this system of surface description specifically to carriage design and taught it in their school. No longer was the translation of two-dimensional drawings left to the buggyshop craftsmen. Now every inch of the body surface, no matter how subtle, could be set down mathematically in keys and numerical tables called "offsets." Offsets consisted of a series of numbers that described, in millimeters or inches and fractions, exactly where any point on the body surface had to be. Offsets could also be used to make templates.

The system that Dupont taught, and which Americans soon copied, was called "the French Rule." John Gribbon had brought the French Rule to this country when he opened the first U.S. technical school. Young Johnson now studied under Dupont directly and took, in effect, a postgraduate course from the master himself, especially in the use and application of the French Rule.

In 1892, John Gribbon died suddenly, and Andrew F. Johnson was named the technical school's new principal. Johnson continued in that capacity through World War I, and he applied the same zeal and care to his teaching that he had to his studies. His own students apparently received more than mere technical training, because many of them later wrote to tell Johnson what an inspiration he had been. He would interlace his lectures with quotations from Shakespeare and the great poets, use objects of fine art as examples of good design, show examples from nature to illustrate the appropriateness of color and form, and he generally combined a great deal of enthusiasm and personal warmth with his strict observance of craftsmanship and the 19th-century insistence that things be done properly. He must have been, judging by the letters, lessons and drawings now contained at the National Automotive History Collection at the Detroit Public Library, a most extraordinary man.

In the early 20th century, as the demand for horsedrawn vehicles waned and the acceptance of the automobile rose, Johnson quietly switched the technical school's emphasis to the design of motorcar bodies. The school's name, too, changed. It now became the New York Technical School for Carriage and Automobile Body Designers and Draftsmen, headquartered at the Young Men's Institute, 222 Bowery.

Johnson's wife, Agnes, died in 1917, and by 1918 the outdated Carriage Builders National Association had stopped underwriting the technical school. Despite these tremendous upsets in his life, Johnson felt a responsibility to his students, especially those who'd already paid their tuition for the correspondence portion of the curriculum. As a result, he decided to continue the school on his own. He at first moved to Detroit and offered courses not only by correspondence but also directly through Detroit's Cass Technical High School. Then in late 1920, he returned to Gray, Maine, where his wife's family still lived. He'd long been an active member of Gray's Universalist movement, and he served for 20 years as a trustee of the Pennell Institute, a private high school. It was from Gray that Johnson continued his correspondence courses.

When asked philosophically, in 1928, about the education of automobile body designers, Johnson wrote, "...a good sense of artistic forms and proportions must enter into its successful practice. The eye must be trained to see, and the hand to make, lines of beauty and utility, and the color sense must be cultivated.... If these things are absent in the creation of [an automobile] body, it may, when finished, be a useful thing, but it will never reach the dignity of a masterpiece." Johnson's goal was always to teach and inspire his students to create

Andrew F. Johnson, far left, taught early auto design to some 2300 students in the course of his career. This was his classroom in the Bowery section of Manhattan in 1912-13.

masterpieces. Many of them, of course, did.

In 1939, after another alumni dinner where his boys honored him, the Society of Automotive Engineers made Johnson a lifetime member. During that ceremony, Otto Graebner, chief body engineer of the Murray Corp. of America, rose and said of Johnson: "You might say that he designed every automobile body on the street, because we all learned the business from him."

Andrew F. Johnson continued to teach by correspondence nearly until the day he died. His inspiration radiated out from Gray, Maine, into a national classroom, and his students, some of whom he never met personally, wrote years later to tell him that they were buoyed by his dedication and always looked forward to his thoughtful and beautifully handwritten letters. He passed away at his home two days before Christmas 1943. ◆

Early cars were horseless carriages quite literally. The 1905 Columbia Electric (left) amounted to an electrified hansom cab, with coachman seated where he'd always sat. The 1911

International "panel express" was a farm wagon converted to internal combustion, its body lowered thanks to Ackerman steering. This vehicle still used high, old-fashioned wagon wheels.

CHAPTER 2

ON THE ROAD

Merri Ferrell, associate curator of the carriage collection at the Museums of Stony Brook on Long Island, reminds us that without the horse, the design of a carriage didn't look finished. The horse gave the carriage a harmony and a wholeness that it didn't have without one.

She points out that carriage designers usually drew presentation sketches on translucent paper. That way, she says, they could slip a picture of a horse underneath, ahead of the carriage sketch, and show customers not only the carriage but the total ensemble: carriage plus horse.

"The flow of the horse's shoulders, its rump line, the whole conformation affected the look of the carriage. People wanted to see the horse out front." The horse served an aesthetic function, but even beyond that, the horse symbolized power and speed. It gave life to an otherwise static and incomplete design.

It's no surprise, then, that when the first automobiles came chugging out of the late 19th century, they just didn't look right; not to the average citizen. Something was missing. The auto-

mobile's horselessness went against all established design formats. Besides which, no one—least of all carriage designers—had the foggiest notion what a motorcar should look like. There'd been no precedent. Most early auto engineers and designers simply took an existing vehicle, a buggy or a carriage, and motorized it. Then around 1905, a few put engines into buggies and farm wagons and turned them into what came to be known as *motor buggies, motor wagons* and *highwheelers*.

Still others, including Henry Ford, borrowed bicycle technology. Ford's first self-propelled motorcar, the 1896 "quadricycle," was basically a four-wheeled bicycle, just as the earliest German Benz and French De Dion-Bouton had been motorized tricycles.

But keep in mind that bicycle technology probably suited the automobile better in those days than carriage technology. Safety bicycles of the 1890s—that is, bikes with equal-sized wheels—were state-of-the-art and extremely popular. Many fledgling automakers therefore adopted a number of innovations from the bicycle, among them lightweight seamless-steel tubing for the frame, wire-spoke wheels, pneumatic tires, roller-chain or shaft drive, band brakes, Ackerman steering (from early three- and four-wheeled cycles) and the differential. Also, bicycle manufacturers had the skills and equipment to make entire cars, whereas carriage-makers could build only the bodies.

The bicycle led more directly into the motorcycle, but what's important here is the bicycle's impact on early auto-

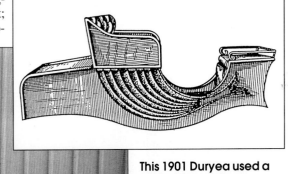

This 1901 Duryea used a body style originally designed for carriages. Fish motif had a symbolic Christian significance.

mobiles because: 1) a number of major bicycle manufacturers began to make automobiles, and 2) the safety bicycle gave Americans a taste of the open road. The bicycle soon prepared middle-income citizens not only to accept but to clamor for inexpensive cars like the Curved Dash Oldsmobile and the Model T Ford.

Among bicycle manufacturers who switched to making motorcars were the Duryea Brothers and Col. Albert A. Pope. The Pope Mfg. Co. of Hartford, Connecticut pioneered safety bicycles but also built the 1898 Waverly and 1899 Columbia electric automobiles and went on to produce the Pope-Hartford, Pope-Toledo and Pope-Tribune motorcars. The Cleveland Bicycle Co. spawned the Winton automobile, and another bicycle manufacturer, Gormully & Jeffrey, gave birth to Rambler, Jeffrey and Nash automobiles. The George N. Pierce Co. made bicycles before producing Pierce-Arrow cars. Henry Leland, godfather of both Cadillac and Lincoln, began his career machining bevel gears for shaft-driven bicycles. So we shouldn't think of early automobiles simply as buggies gone horseless. Like the airplane, the motorcar owed a lot to the bicycle.

But when we look at this turn-of-the-century transition from buggies and bicycles to motorcars, we're initially led to believe that early automobiles were designed wholly along mechanical lines and only by engineers. That's partly true but not entirely. Some early cars

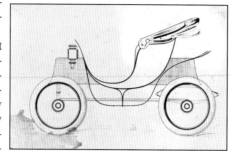

Early design sketch by Willoughby dates from 1901, shows an attempt to style a carriage as an automobile.

were consciously and intentionally *styled*. As evidence, witness some early design sketches donated to the Henry Ford Museum in Dearborn, Michigan by the estate of Henry Austin Clark Jr.

These early autobody presentation sketches date back to 1901 and were made by Willoughby & Co., a carriagemaker in Utica, New York (see page 64). Willoughby, who later enjoyed success as a custom automobile coachbuilder and remained in business through July 1938, was building mostly carriages at the turn of the century. The company also produced bodies for Col. Pope's 1899 Columbia electric automo-

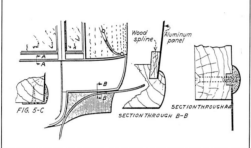

1905 Quinby aluminum bodies necessitated filling seams between panels with wooden moldings.

biles. The Willoughby sketches leave no doubt that carriagemakers included motorbody designs in their presentation portfolios along with carriage designs.

The Willoughby autobody designs might have amounted to early dreamcars. Whether any of the earlier ones were actually built we don't know. But in the broadest possible terms, the Willoughby sketches clearly tell us that automotive fashion and style were selling points as early as 1901, a fact that wasn't generally known or appreciated until these drawings came to light in 1992.

Turn-of-the-century automobile bodies followed carriage practice by being made almost entirely out of wood.

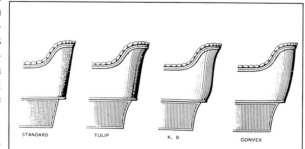

These are four seat styles common in early automobiles. The King of Belgium type stands second from the right and enjoyed great popularity for a time.

Sheetmetal didn't arrive generally until around 1903, and then largely in answer to a fashion established by King Leopold II of the Belgians. The king was an ardent motorist, but car seats were often too narrow to fit his rather ample royal posterior. So his mistress, Cleo de Merode (so goes the story), suggested that His Majesty have

a special Mercedes built with rear seats patterned after the overstuffed chairs in the palace guest room. These chairs bulged out in the seat area and had an ogee curve at the back—an elongated, S-shaped profile. The Mercedes coachbuilder copied the palace chairs, including the ogee section, and this style spread like wildfire across Europe. In fact, the ogee rear body profile soon came to be known as the *Roi des Belges* shape. By 1903, the *Roi des Belges* concept had arrived in this country, but here we translated the name as the "King of Belgium" or "K.B." style.

To shape the K.B. ogee in wood took considerable doing: steaming the wooden body panels and pressing them over special forms. As a result, European bodymakers soon began to use hand-hammered aluminum panels for the outer body corners, with more gently curved wooden surfaces between them. In 1902, J.M. Quinby & Co. of Newark, New Jersey sent a young designer named Herbert T. Strong to Europe to study the making of aluminum automobile bodies. Strong visited the coachbuilding shops of Kellner, Rothschild, Labourdette and Muehlbacher. He brought back his report, and Quinby soon patented a process for making composite aluminum-over-wood automobile bodies, their specialty being the K.B. rear section. For several years, Quinby ranked as a leading manufacturer of quality motorcar bodies.

In 1905, Quinby offered several set body types, among them a runabout, a limousine, a landaulet and variants of what the company called its "standard" body. The standard body came with four choices for the rear-seat profile: straight-back, convex, K.B. and "tulip." The tulip body had a slightly concave bustle. All these shapes involved fairly subtle differences, but again, the differences obviously mattered to the now-fashion-conscious American car buyer.

NDAULETTE   DRAWING NO. 76

Quinby pioneered the blending of sheetmetal and wood by cleverly hiding and waterproofing the inter-panel seams under strip moldings. The first of these moldings was wood. George J. Mercer, one of Andrew F. Johnson's former students and later chief body engineer for the Saxon Motor Car Co., published his six-part *History of Automobile Body Building* in *Autobody* magazine in 1925-26. Here he wrote, "[Quinby's] aluminum panel was set in a groove [in the wood], and a wooden spline forced the panel tightly against the molding to prevent the entrance of water." A few years later, Quinby's moldings were made of bronze. In both cases, the moldings were predrilled, then nailed through the body sheetmetal and into the structural wooden framework beneath. The nailheads were ground flush with the molding surface before the body was painted.

Aluminum was easy to form, and that's why early bodymakers liked it so much. Craftsmen could form aluminum skins into complex shapes with handtools as simple as a mallet and a bag of sand. But power hammers soon replaced human muscle. With a power hammer, the metalman would position his aluminum sheet between the convex head of the hammer and a concave dolly beneath it. He controlled hammer speed with a foot pedal and moved the sheet back, forth and sideways until it took the shape he wanted. He also made beads for fender and door edges by using a beading machine, which had special grooved rollers

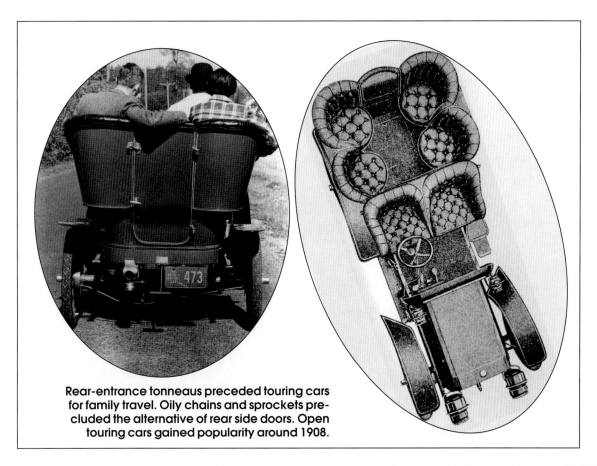

Rear-entrance tonneaus preceded touring cars for family travel. Oily chains and sprockets precluded the alternative of rear side doors. Open touring cars gained popularity around 1908.

that folded the sheetmetal back on itself.

But aluminum had some disadvantages, too. It tended to be expensive and to dent easily. Also, paint didn't like to stick to it. So around 1906, sheet steel started to replace aluminum as the body material of choice. Sheet steel, however, like aluminum, added almost no torsional strength to the body. For rigidity, bodymakers still relied on the main wooden body framework. A carbody, therefore, was only as rigid as its frame and no better than the metal-reinforced joints, screws and glue that held the internal framing together (see sidebar *When Wood Was Good,* page 35).

Body framing was an evolving science. Automobile bodies obviously had different requirements from carriage bodies: They needed greater stiffness because they hit road bumps at higher speeds, and vibrating engines tended to shake the frame joints the way a pitbull shakes a rag

doll. Anyone who's watched a Model T idle can appreciate the intensity of those early engine vibrations.

The typical automobile at the turn of the century was open, had no top or windshield, no bumpers, often no fenders and usually came without front doors. Body styles with rear seats had either token rear side doors or one door at the very back. Bodies with doors at the very back were called "rear-entrance tonneaus." This body style had seats on either side of a central aisleway.

The rear-entrance tonneau enjoyed a brief vogue—brief for reasons that had to do with women's fashion. Early chain-drive cars had greasy sprockets that stuck out from both sides of the chassis. These sprockets made it hard for women to climb into the rear seat through a side entrance without soiling their long skirts. The folding top on a rear-entrance tonneau, when it had one, presented another problem.

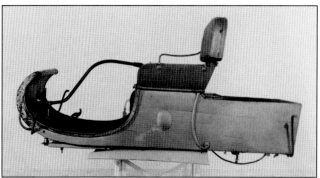

Curved Dash Oldsmobile of 1901-05 borrowed styling elements from both sleighs and carriages. Its had no real frame but instead used full-length leaf springs and counted on the stiffness of the wooden runabout body to give structural rigidity. The shield with decal beneath the seat plus the scroll that came down from the seatback were subtle design elements that helped people bridge the awkward stylistic transition from horsedrawn conveyances to motor vehicles.

Climbing through the back door, you had either to lift the rear edge of the top or duck down under it.

A less challenging body type in those days was the two-passenger runabout, the most popular example being the 1901-05 Curved Dash Oldsmobile. Part of the Curved Dash Olds' attraction was its price, $650 at a time when most other cars sold for well over $1000. But the CDO also charmed buyers with its appearance, especially the curved dashboard. No one seems to remember who designed the CDO, but whoever laid out the runabout body understood the importance of carrying over as many traditional styling cues as possible. The CDO blended carriage and sleigh design—especially the sleigh's swan-neck profile—with the necessities of the motorcar. To the average person, the CDO's overall lines and shape looked familiar and non-threatening, but the design still had enough verve in the

The Engineer as Designer

We certainly don't mean to minimize the engineer's contributions to automobile design. Technical feasibility has always opened the door to styling innovation. Technical feasibility sometimes preceded and sometimes followed the styling concept, but that concept would never have gone on the road without the engineer.

The idea of connecting the front and rear fenders with a runningboard, for example, was just an idea until an engineer solved the structural problems of attaching the runningboard to the frame, and doing it cheaply. The same process applies to every other styling nuance that's come along since. So while engineers and stylists have often been at odds, and while they've sometimes disagreed strongly about matters of technical feasibility, they've always had to work together for the commercial success of their cars.

Note, too, that any number of early engineering advances started out having nothing to do with style but ended up being styling determiners anyway. Many, in fact, became unexpected gifts to the stylist. Among the less obvious is Ackerman steering. Ackerman steering's importance to auto design lies in lowering the carbody. Unlike center-pivot axles used on horse-drawn vehicles, Ackerman steering didn't need a "cut-under" beneath the driver's seat.

Another early styling determinant was seat height. At the turn of the century, seats were nearly always the highest points on any vehicle, cars as well as carriages. In carriages a high seat was good, because it helped the driver see over the horse. But in early runabouts the seats perched above the engine, which meant that even though cars were lower than carriages, people sat literally on the summit of the body and certainly not inside it, as they would later.

Which leads us to a third important styling determiner: engine placement. Before 1900, most American cars tucked the engine under the seats. The more advanced automakers of Europe, though, were already putting the engine under a hood ahead of the passenger compartment. According to Randy Mason, former transportation curator of the Henry Ford Museum in Michigan, around 1893-94 the French automaker Panhard et Levassor began mounting the engine up at the front of a dedicated chassis frame. French engines were bigger and more powerful than ours, and all that horsepower no longer fit under the seat.

It took American automakers several years to catch up with the "French arrangement," but in 1901, when French race cars started outrunning everything on the road, European cars with front-mounted engines and hoods became all the rage among wealthy Americans. So U.S. automakers quickly added hoods to existing designs. A hood didn't mean there was an engine underneath it; most American carmakers kept stuffing their engines up under the seat. But starting around 1902-03, the majority of U.S. cars had something like a simple, upturned box ahead of the dashboard. The resulting "French hood" gave American cars the look of European racers, sort of.

Many of these *faux* hoods were louvered, and some appeared to be real enough. A few hid tanks for water, oil and gasoline, others contained a small storage compartment. But with the coiled-tube radiators of that day standing ahead of the French hood, heat made this an impractical place to store anything. The false hood, however, again showed that fashion was taking hold as a selling point.

It wasn't long before American engineers followed European practice and moved the engine out to the front of the car. The hood really did have a purpose now, and it also became visually important, partly because it led to that final, vital automotive styling determiner: the upright honeycomb radiator.

The idea for the honeycomb radiator again came from Europe, where the race-winning 1901 Mercedes used one to reduce weight. The honeycomb radiator offered a number of technical advantages over the earlier coiled-tube type. Its core was more compact, needed less surface area and less water per unit of cooling, thus it weighed less. It also mounted higher than the coiled-tube radiator, so it wasn't so vulnerable to rocks and ruts in the roadway.

All of its technical advantages might not have put the honeycomb radiator across had it not, in one swift stroke, totally changed the automobile's appearance. The upright radiator immediately became the motorcar's single most recognizable and important design feature. Again, what began as an engineering advance became a styling determiner. The upright radiator at the front of the hood finally said: *This is an automobile; this is not a horseless carriage.*

1903 Cadillac still placed engine beneath seat but used a coiled-tube radiator ahead of front axle. Such radiators were inefficient and easily damaged by flying rocks and deep ruts.

Building on that essentially automotive design format, the designer now took the honeycomb radiator and used it to put a face on the motorcar. He made the radiator, usually in combination with two large headlamps, the car's primary focal point. We mentioned "face" before, and that's exactly what this became. The ensemble of radiator, headlamps and front fenders served the same visual function that a human face serves in the recognition and appreciation of a specific person. It's also most often the first point of eye contact, both among people and between person and car.

The early automobile stylist, body designer, draftsman, body engineer—whoever on the staff made fashion decisions—immediately recognized the impact of the automotive face and took advantage of it in several ways. He first encased the radiator core in a plated metal shell: initially brass, later nickel and, starting in 1926, chromium (*see below*). The bright surface drew even more attention to the car's face. In many cases the designer gave the radiator shell an identifying shape: square-shouldered, round-cornered or a lapped leading edge; ox-yoke shoulders in Packard's case, an oval grille in Brewster's and an infinite variety in between.

Mercedes soon veed the radiator core, giving it a prow effect and curved dashboard to give it some romance.

Designer, instructor and auto historian Strother MacMinn makes another point here. He feels that the Curved Dash Oldsmobile shows distinct elements of *art nouveau*. "The influence of *art nouveau* dominates that particular vehicle," he contends. "The curved, scrolled dash is a feature of *art nouveau* profiling, as is the decorative wooden molding that runs down below the seat, with the scrolled knob at the bottom. Those elements, in the popular aesthetic of the day, made the car quite acceptable. It looked like a complete vehicle, as opposed to most others of that day, which were simply horseless buggies with straight leather dashes. The person who did the Curved Dash Oldsmobile had the courage to invent a dynamic style."

The CDO also contained another appeal-

(continued on page 19)

Faux hood of 1904 Peerless (top) hid tanks for water and oil. Peerless race car (above) pioneered prow radiator.

a more "streamlined," wind-splitting look. The veed radiator was soon copied by a number of auto manufacturers in this country. Despite the wide range of radiator shapes both here and abroad, Herbert Hosking, writing in 1930, felt that all American radiators to that time took their themes from just three cars, all of them European: Mercedes for the prow front, Fiat for the flat front and Minerva for the rounded front. (It was also Hosking who reminded us, "A quarter of an inch difference in the length of Cleopatra's nose would have changed the course of...history....")

And now that automakers were identifying their cars with radiator shapes, pirating became a concern. Brewster, for instance, was not the only automaker to use an oval grille. The 1904-07 Hill, 1906-10 Franklin, 1906 Ariel, 1907 Cosmopolitan, 1909-13 Kearns and the 1922 Electrocar taxi also had oval radiators. The 1904 Wright, 1905 Grout, 1905-07 National and 1907 Continental had perfectly round ones. These makes coexisted amicably enough, but it wasn't long before U.S. carmakers began to fight to protect their distinctive radiator shapes. The 1910 Lexington's radiator borrowed Packard's ox-yoke shoulder, as did Buick in 1924-28. Packard wasn't pleased but didn't sue. In 1915, American Fiat did sue Oldsmobile, Daniels and SGV for pirating its radiator design. And from 1916 through 1929, Roamer and Moon used an exact copy of the Rolls-Royce radiator, but Rolls-Royce

of America Inc. apparently didn't care enough to challenge them.

As an identity reinforcement, many early automakers, including Ford, emblazoned their names in sheet brass across the front of the radiator. These brass nameplates soon gave way to subtler cloisonne radiator emblems. In the 1920s and '30s, a number of carmakers added identifying hood ornaments to radiator caps: archers, cormorants, greyhounds, flying ladies, "donut chasers" and other figures that provided part of the entertainment of later auto design.

Since early brass and nickel brightwork tended to tarnish easily and needed constant polishing, the industry eventually turned to chromium plating. Elwood Haynes had tried early in the century to find a cheap way to electroplate chromium, but chrome remained more expensive than brass or nickel and wasn't used much on motor vehicles until 1916-17, when Pancho Villa became a problem for General Blackjack Pershing. Pancho and his men created a need for U.S. armor-plated scout cars, and that gave rise to chrome-nickel armor sheet to ward off the *bandito's* bullets. Pershing's mechanics soon discovered that the tough, shiny chrome-nickel plate also resisted rust and looked like a mirror when buffed.

Engineer W.M. Phillips at Oldsmobile refined the three-step process of electroplating copper, nickel and chromium onto sheet steel and made it inexpensive enough for mass production. Olds replaced nickel brightwork with chromium for the hubcaps, bumpers and radiator shells on all its 1926 models, and this marked the first widespread use of chrome in the American auto industry. In addition to helping identify a car, the radiator served another styling function by determining, to some extent, the shape of the hood. At first, the trailing edge of the hood butted against a flat wooden dashboard, and since the earliest cars had no upright radiator, the hood could be any shape the designer wanted. Suddenly, though, with a stylized grille shell to contend with, the designer had to make the hood conform to the radiator shape. (Interestingly, *dashboard* is one of the few words that's come down to us from horsedrawn car-

Henry Ford wanted flat hood surfaces, so the Model T grille shell ended up with angular shoulders. T's upright wooden dashboard rose straight up into the 2-pane windshield.

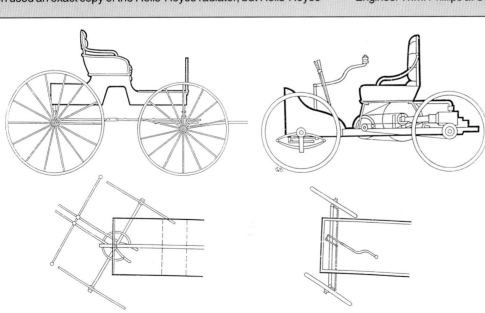

Ackerman steering became one of the stylist's best friends. It did away with the "cut-under" of horsedrawn carriages (left). Henry Ford's 1896 Quadricycle (right) used Ackerman steering, the result being a considerably lower body. This is an example of engineering helping styling.

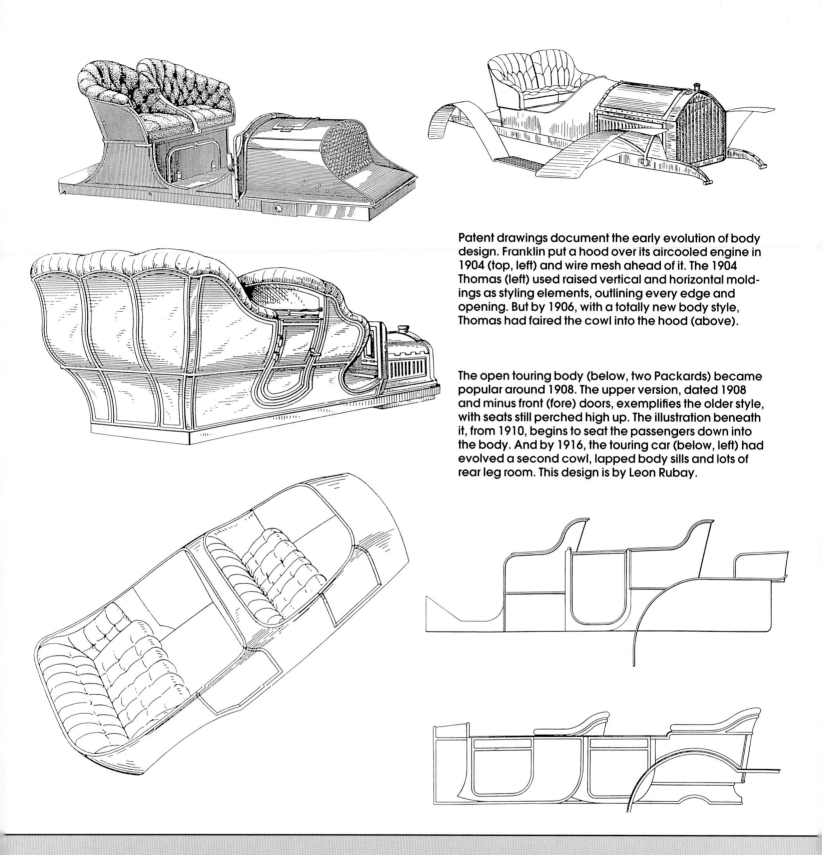

Patent drawings document the early evolution of body design. Franklin put a hood over its aircooled engine in 1904 (top, left) and wire mesh ahead of it. The 1904 Thomas (left) used raised vertical and horizontal moldings as styling elements, outlining every edge and opening. But by 1906, with a totally new body style, Thomas had faired the cowl into the hood (above).

The open touring body (below, two Packards) became popular around 1908. The upper version, dated 1908 and minus front (fore) doors, exemplifies the older style, with seats still perched high up. The illustration beneath it, from 1910, begins to seat the passengers down into the body. And by 1916, the touring car (below, left) had evolved a second cowl, lapped body sills and lots of rear leg room. This design is by Leon Rubay.

riages. In carriages, the dashboard was a vertical front panel, usually leather, that protected the passengers from mud and road splash being "dashed" up on the vehicle by the horse. Early automobile dashboards were also upright panels, usually wooden, that separated the engine compartment from the passenger area. It sometimes supported the windshield and carried the cowl lamps. Today, we often use the word *dashboard* interchangeably with *instrument panel*. In some cases, including the engineer-styled Model T, the early Ford's flat hood panels determined the radiator shape, not vice versa. But where designers took a hand and asked for a bit more sophistication, the tops of hoods became rounded or vaulted. Finally, in 1907-08, the hood began to blend back into a sheetmetal cowl structure. The metal cowl at first flared outward and upward behind the wooden dashboard; later, the radiator, hood, and cowl began to flow together into a single unit, in time fairing more and more smoothly into the passenger compartment. The "through," horizontal line that ran straight back along the top of the hood from the radiator to the instrument cowling didn't appear generally until around 1914-15, although the Harkness racing car had it as early as 1903. So did the 1908 Jewel roadster, but cyclecars, which enjoyed a brief vogue in 1913-15, pioneered the horizontal, straight-through hood/cowl line and, by the end of World War I, the straight hood/cowl line was nearly universal. ◆

(continued from page 17)

ing but more subtle design touch: the red/gold/black Oldsmobile crest, which the designer placed on an oval wooden shield at each side of the seat stanchion. The crest, like a cameo, gave the CDO a finished look. There's no doubt that style, whatever its source, helped make this early automobile the commercial success it became.

By the time of the Curved Dash Olds, style and fashion had probably taken on as much importance in carbody design as it ever had for horsedrawn vehicles. Even engineers began to notice that style helped sell their machines. And fledgling body designers paid careful attention to the impact their work was having on the buying public.

Early design patents reinforce this notion that auto manufacturers made style a priority. The 1904 Thomas body drawing, registered by James R. Koen and E.R. Thomas, shows the whole menu of what designers considered significant and advanced at that time. This 1904 Thomas had a stylized radiator shape, a coved, metal-shrouded cowl and a King of Belgium side-entrance tonneau passenger

compartment with ornamental moldings. Moldings here didn't merely hide body seams; they'd already become a form of decoration. As they would in the future, the Thomas' horizontal moldings added to the illusion of body length, while the moldings surrounding the doors and seats lent interest.

The aircooled 1904 Franklin runabout body had a simpler design than the Thomas, but it, too, was highly stylized, with a coved grille (no radiator, of course) and a graceful base for the two seats. A few early designs, like the Cadillac body designed in 1905 by Alanson P. Brush, showed just shapes and sweeps, with the merest hint of a solid body. The Brush patent drawing was almost an abstract.

Howard Coffin, who soon became one of the co-founders of the Hudson Motor Car Co., designed another Thomas runabout, this one receiving a design patent in 1907. Being primarily an engineer, Coffin included practical details like spring hangers, fender braces, brackets and grab handles. The coved, sheetmetal cowl hid the wooden dashboard in Coffin's design.

Wraparound sheetmetal cowls, which swept downward and back along both sides of the passenger compartment appeared in 1907 on such cars as the Oldsmobile roadster, Colt runabout, BLM roadster, and the 1908 Tincher and Dragon roadsters. Flat-faced, wooden dashboards were still the order of the day, however, and wouldn't disappear until around 1913.

Russell Huff's design for the 1908 Packard placed emphasis on fender contours and, again, on moldings. Sidney Waldon's ideas for the 1911 Packard did the same. By now, though, Packard was offering four doors. Front doors on roadsters and touring cars began to

appear between 1910 and 1912 on any number of American cars. Front doors were also called "fore" doors, as opposed to "aft" doors.

The general configuration of Waldon's 1911 Packard started to show the lines of the traditional touring car. By 1913, O.E. Hunt, who later became Chevrolet's chief engineer and then vice president of engineering for GM, took Waldon's Packard lines and carefully modernized them. Hunt kept Waldon's earlier theme but placed the passengers down lower inside the body instead of making them sit on top of it, as in the past. Four doors and higher body sides became keys to the evolution of the touring car. The inexpensive, open, four-door touring car now began to replace the tonneau and runabout as America's favorite body style, and it predominated until the early '20s, when closed coaches began to sell for nearly the same price.

The flush-sided body, without all those fussy moldings, originated in England around 1906-07, when the British developed a way to butt-weld sheetmetal body panels. Welding meant that moldings weren't needed to hide the seams. Weld joints were covered by spreading molten solder with a wooden paddle, a process called "leading." Here in the U.S., Chalmers picked up this idea and added the overlapping door panel, where the outer door skins extended out beyond the openings. These were all important fashion advances that swept through the industry.

By World War I, body moldings began to be considered old-fashioned, and from 1916 through about 1923, a lot of bodies, especially open touring cars, were totally without them. Decorative moldings made a strong comeback in the mid 1920s, especially double belt moldings on closed body styles (coupes, coaches and sedans). Here, the lower of these parallel double moldings picked up the hinge line on each side of the hood and followed it back around the body. The upper belt molding, meanwhile, encircled the body just beneath the beltline. As more ductile steels became available, moldings were stamped right into the metal and were usually pinstriped or painted a contrasting color.

Most fenders were at first made of wood or leather and were thus often flat. When bodymakers switched to metal fenders, these might have an ogee sweep, but viewed side-on, their cross section was again essentially flat. It wasn't long before a few manufacturers gave their fenders some depth by hanging shallow valances down around the edges. These valances sometimes even

And yet the automobile had a hard time shedding its carriage ancestry. The 1908 Welch (above) shows its carriage heritage in spades, as does the 1911 Willoughby center-door coach (below).

formed duckbills at the front. In time, as diework became more common, fenders received raised moldings and, in some cases, shallow central crowns. These moldings and crowns became more pronounced as time went on. Their function was not only aesthetic but also to make the fenders more rigid; harder to bend and dent.

Windshields, of course, always played a role in autobody design. Early cars, if they had windshields at all, used towering sheets of plate glass, often in horizontally split double or triple frames. Windshields were made up in sections for several reasons. First, if one section broke, it was easier and cheaper to replace that part alone than the windshield as a whole. Second, the upper pane had a hinge along the top and could be pushed outward for ventilation and vision. Automatic wipers weren't yet invented, so anyone driving in rain or snow usually swung open the upper glass in order to see the road. If water or snow swept in, well, that was the way it was.

Early windshields were often held upright by stays anchored to the front frame horns. Slowly, as bodies became lower, so did glass height, and by 1917 it was common to see a few windshields raked back at very mild angles. This rake was mostly intended to mitigate headlight glare from cars following behind, but designers thought it looked rakish (thus the term), and the tipped windshield became another styling consideration.

In early touring cars and roadsters, there was also a trend toward

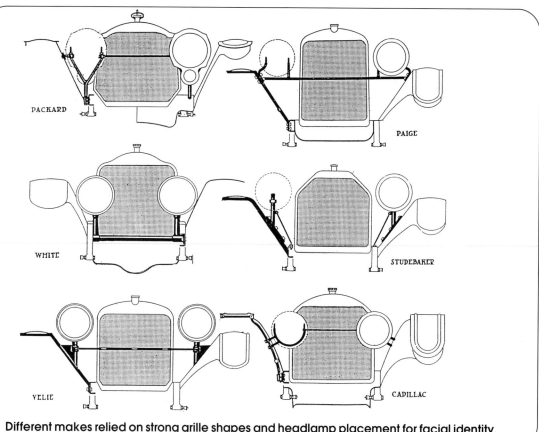

Different makes relied on strong grille shapes and headlamp placement for facial identity.

rolling the beltline up and over into the body cavity to make a rounded sill around the entire passenger compartment. The cowl flange ran across the top of the instrument panel, swept back in a beautiful curve into the tops of the doors and extended back just past the seats. A few body designers gave this lapped surface a beveled, hard edge, but most made it a gentle roll. The French named these flush-sided bodies the "torpedo" style, one of many applications of that name. The flush-sided torpedo style with overlapping doors and cowl marked one more step toward fully integrated bodywork.

Closed bodies were rare and expensive in the early days of the automobile and, for a lot of people including Henry Ford, they held some terror. "Who'd want to ride around inside all that glass?" Ford once asked. Safety glass was still 25 years in the future. But

Blended hood and cowl arrived around 1907-08. Hinge became a body molding.

by 1903, some customers were ordering closed bodies, particularly doctors and businessmen who had to use their cars in all types of weather.

B ody design, it seems, has always been governed—at least to some extent—by guidelines and rules. These rules tended to change from one era to another, but all contemporary designers knew them, discussed them and usually took them seriously. As a result, rules were often talked about or written up in the trade literature.

Two such guidelines that affected fashion in early closed bodies were "belling the top" and "arching the roof." Belling the top meant that the typical closed autobody, when viewed from behind, had the general shape of an upside-down bell. The widest part of the body was the roof. Then, as the body lines cascaded down, they curved inward toward the bottom. This general rule for the shape of closed cars was widely followed through the early 1920s.

Arching the roof meant putting a slightly raised section over the rear doors. This might be anything from a gently lifted sweep along the top of the roof to an actual vaulted peak above the rear door. The

tallest part of early closed bodies, generally speaking, consisted of this arched roof area about three quarters of the way back from the windshield. Belling the top and arching the roof derived from carriage practice, and both served to keep rainwater from dripping down onto the rear passengers as they stepped out of the vehicle. These early closed cars were mostly chauffeur-driven, so the rear passengers were usually the owners.

Another guideline handed down from carriage practice was the "cheat line." Rules governing cheat lines changed over time as autobodies became lower and less angular. Designers concerned themselves with different sets of rules about cheat lines in different eras. But one of the earliest cheat lines, according to George Mercer, came at the rear corner pillar. Here, the designer/draftsman would pick up the shape of the body pillar ahead of it but would draw a cheat line that tilted inward slightly at the bottom, usually about 5/8 inch on each side. This narrowed the rear bottom portion of the body and made it look better, or so decreed the rule of the day.

Early doors also demanded very subtle cheat lines. Doors should appear square or rectangular, said the rules, but if they actually were square or rectangular, they wouldn't look it, due to the slightly barrel-sided nature of the typical touring body. So as in Greek architecture, there needed to be a little fudging, like the different distances between inboard and outboard temple columns*. To make car doors look square, you made them 3/8 inch wider at the bottom than at the top. The human eye translated that shape into perfect squares or rectangles.

Those were just a few of the subtleties of early automobile design. Not only were most turn-of-the-century styling conventions carried over from carriages, but U.S. designer/delineators were led by the ideas and tastes of Europe. A distinctively American automotive fashion still lay some years ahead. ◆

---

*Spacing between the columns of each corner of a Greek temple were slightly wider than those in between. Corner columns also bowed outward slightly to compensate for an optical illusion that otherwise—if all spacing were equal and the columns were perfectly straight—would make them look unequal, a phenomenon called entasis.

CHAPTER 3

THE NUTS & BOLTS OF EARLY AUTOMOTIVE FASHION

Bear in mind that very few U.S. automakers produced their own bodies in the early years. At the turn of the century and for a decade after that, bodies were most often made to order by carriagemakers or former carriagemakers. A car manufacturer would usually design a body, then hand the drafts and specifications to the bodymaker. The bodymaker might add a few touches and would most often deliver one preliminary sample body—a single finished prototype. In addition to the sample body, he might provide a disassembled wooden frame, each member numbered to correspond to the full-sized body draft.

At this point, the client auto manufacturer might dissect the sample body to check fits. Or the bodymaker might suggest ways to make it easier to build. Or make it more durable or comfortable. Once all the bugs had been worked out and the client approved the sample, the bodymaker would build however many copies the manufacturer wanted.

The autobody industry soon factored itself into three basic types of producers: mass, custom and those in between. In time, five bodymakers became giants: the C.R. Wilson Co., Fisher Body, Briggs Mfg. Co., Murray Corp. of America, and the Edward G. Budd Mfg. Co. These companies had the capacity to produce thousands of bodies a day, and in good economic times they did.

At the other end of the scale, the custom coachbuilders made bodies one at a time. These relatively small shops designed and built high-grade, high-fashion bodies for private individuals or sometimes as styling and working samples for client automakers. The custom coachbuilders clung to traditional, labor-intensive ways long after the bigger producers had gone to more advanced and efficient methods.

Individual custom bodies were, by nature, far more expensive than those that were mass produced or built in small lots. These smaller batches were termed "series customs," "semi-customs" and "catalogue customs," which usually meant quantities ranging from five to 100 (versus thousands from the big producers).

A few of the better-known shops that designed and built custom bodies, although by no means just custom bodies—and this is not a complete list—included Brewster, Derham, Fleetwood, Brunn, Judkins, Dietrich, LeBaron, Willoughby, Walter M. Murphy, Rollston and Holbrook (see pages 38-71).

The most crowded category, though, consisted of the medium-sized bodymakers, names like Seaman, Walker, Biddle & Smart, Union, Springfield, Ames, Hayes, J.C. Widman,

Towson, J.W. Murray and scores more. These mid-sized firms usually turned out bodies for the smaller independent automakers. This meant, first of all, that they were locked into shorter runs, because the small independents didn't usually sell many cars. Second, the mid-sized bodymakers often found themselves the bag holders in bankruptcies and defaults, because the smaller automakers tended to go out of business more easily than the majors, and eventually all of the independents did. Third and as a result of the first two circumstances, the financing of these medium-sized bodymakers was usually stretched thinner than either the large producers or the custom shops. Mid-sized bodymakers had less capital to invest in plant modernization, process revision and automation. So by the 1930s, the mid-sized bodymakers simply weren't able to compete with the giants like Briggs and Murray, who could outbid them on nearly any job that came along. But throughout the boom years of the auto industry, 1909-29, all three categories thrived.

There was some overlap among the three

sizes of automobile bodymakers. Biddle & Smart, a medium-sized company, built production bodies for Hudson and became one of Hudson's main suppliers during the 1920s (see page 65). At the same time, Biddle & Smart also produced custom and series bodies for Hudson, Rolls-Royce and other automakers. Walker was another mid-sized body producer with a dual role. Franklin counted on Walker as its primary bodymaker, but Walker also made short runs of semi-custom bodies. Among the dedicated coachbuilders, Judkins, Brunn and Willoughby commonly built up to 100 identical or similar "catalogue" bodies for Lincoln during the late 1920s and early '30s. Dietrich later did the same for Packard.

It's not commonly recognized that the coachbuilders who became so well known for their work during what we now call the classic period—roughly 1925-39—had been designing and building automobile bodies from the very beginning of this century. Most coachbuilders got their start making buggies and carriages, and a good number were founded before 1900. Many, in fact, began producing

motorcar bodies between 1887 and 1907: Judkins in 1887, Willoughby in 1899, Brewster and Biddle & Smart in 1905, Derham and Fleetwood in 1907 and Brunn & Co. in 1908. By 1910, the majority of these and other coachbuilders were out of the carriage business and entirely into designing and making bodies for automobiles.

Automotive coachbuilders became tastemakers to the motorcar industry. They took on that role because, before about 1910, only the rich and the moderately rich could afford motorcars. Fashionable autobodies of that day were custom designed and built to order. The moderately wealthy bought American cars, and the super-rich bought mostly big, expensive, impressive, mechanically advanced foreign cars: Darracq, Renault, Fiat, Berliet, Daimler, Mercedes, Minerva, Rolls-Royce, Isotta-Fraschini and so forth.

From roughly 1900 through 1925, America's mecca of both wealth and automotive fashion was not Detroit; it was *New York City*. The typical, well-to-do, urbane New Yorker ordered an imported chassis and commissioned a custom body to be built for it. These handcrafted creations, like the prestigious chassis that carried them, had a continental flavor, because it was actually Europe that set most of the automotive fashion trends during those years.

Early European luxury cars became so popular along the eastern seaboard—in New York, Boston, Philadelphia and Washington—that a number of French, British, Italian and German manufacturers allowed their chassis to be built in this country. Early captive imports—U.S. versions of the De Dion (1900-01), Mercedes (1905-07), Napier (1905-12), Berliet (1906-08), Mors (1906-09), Fiat (1910-18) and Rolls-Royce (1921-35)—were all manufactured and bodied here in America under license.

The latest insights into fashion and automotive styling were gleaned from the exhibitions that took place each year in Europe. To gather ideas, as in carriage days, it was common for U.S. autobody designers, draftsmen and fabricators, large and small, to make annual pilgrimages to Europe's three major motor exhibitions: Paris, London and Berlin. American coachbuilders freely brought back the ideas they found abroad. People from the giant body suppliers, like Fisher and Briggs, also made these voyages of discovery and engaged in similar borrowings. Those who couldn't or didn't want to travel overseas attended the shows in New York and kept up with fashion by reading articles and studying pictures in trade magazines.

You're the Top, You're a Brewster Body

The leading coachbuilder before World War I was unquestionably Brewster & Co. (see page 38). If you wanted the very finest automobile possible, you bought a European chassis and had Brewster design and build a custom body for it. By the turn of the century, Brewster had become a carriagebuilding institution, the traditional choice of old money. When Brewster switched to building automobiles and custom autobodies, the name continued to mean luxury without ostentation, a car designed to the highest standards, workmanship without parallel. A Brewster body, as Cole Porter said in his song, was the top. And Brewster remained at or near the top well into the 1930s. ◆

So for the first quarter of this century, the styling advances—the influential design ideas that found their way into American production automobiles—most often originated in Europe, especially in France. They arrived via New York and subsequently spread to the rest of the country. There were two reasons New York became and remained America's fashion center: First, most of the great coachbuilders were clustered along the eastern seaboard, principally in and around Manhattan but also in Amesbury, Massachusetts, Boston and Philadelphia. Second, the big, influential coachbuilding exhibitions took place in Manhattan at the beginning of each season.

There were actually two important U.S. automotive fashion events staged in New York each year, and both contributed mightily to domestic style for the upcoming season. The most prestigious, called the Automobile Salon, was held in late November or early December and was limited to coachbuilt cars only; no production bodies. The earliest salon, according to designer George Hildebrand, took place in 1904 on the top floor of Macy's department store in New York. At that time these events were called Foreign-Car Exhibitions and were limited strictly to the display of imported marques. In 1905, the Foreign-Car Exhibition moved to an unspecified building in or near Herald Square, then later to the Hotel Astor through 1919 and finally, now officially called Salons, to the Hotel Commodore from 1920 through 1931.

Salons amounted to very chic trade shows where luxury automakers and coachbuilders released their designs, much like Paris *haute coutures* presenting next season's clothing fashions. Until the U.S. entered World War I in 1917, the Foreign-Car Exhibitions refused to allow any domestic chassis to be shown. American coachbuilders could display *bodies*, but only on foreign chassis. The idea was to promote and extend the early tradition and exclusivity of the big, expensive imports.

Then in 1917, with war raging in Europe and very few imports coming into this country, sales agents for the heavier domestics—Packard, Peerless, Stearns-Knight, Marmon, Locomobile, Cadillac, Cunningham, Daniels, Pierce and so forth—began lobbying for equal display space in the same hotels as the foreign makes. This led to the replacement of the Foreign-Car Exhibitions by the annual Salons.

In the beginning, promoter Emil (Pop) Lacaris ruled entries with a gloved fist. He had that power because Salons became the point of sale for new coachbuilt bodies. At the same time, Salons were crucial to the presentation and dissemination of autobody knowledge and fashion, a significance they continued to hold until the Depression ended them after 1931. (A short-lived Importers Show, held at New York's Astor during the mid-1920s, preceded each salon and, for a time, tried to revive the Foreign-Car Exhibitions.)

Entry into each year's salon was by invitation only, both for those who exhibited and those who came to see the cars. Entrants felt honored to be invited, and they gladly paid the required $500 per display stand. Each entrant could place four cars on a stand and was given a fixed number of engraved invitations to send out to customers. In New York,

Show-and-sell atmosphere of Salons allowed coachbuilders to display and market their latest creations and, incidentally, to help establish automotive fashion for America's mass producers. New York Auto Show of 1908 (top) contrasts with the elegance of Locomobile and Pierce stands at 1925 New York Salon (right). Packard boattail speedster highlighted 1930 Commodore exhibit (above, center), while Chrysler showed off 1932 Imperials at Grand Central Palace (above).

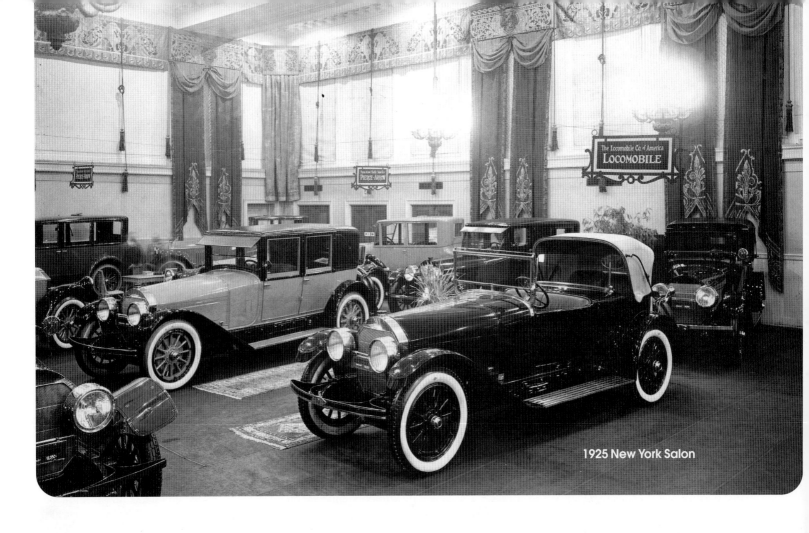

1925 New York Salon

cars were shown in the Commodore ballroom, sometimes spilling out into the hotel lobby. After a week at the Commodore, each year's salon moved to the Drake Hotel in Chicago in January, the Los Angeles Biltmore in February, and sometimes to the Palace in San Francisco in the spring. Cars participating in different Salons were usually, but not always, the same group. Many were *driven,* not trucked, across the country from show to show. And some were repainted in brighter colors for display on the west coast.

The most important exhibit was always at the Commodore. Salons had the effect of crystalizing and introducing future fashion and styling themes and became, in effect, the magnets that drew together auto manufacturers, designers, coachbuilders, major body producers, engineers, chassis sales agents, paint suppliers, trim vendors, leather dealers, fabric houses, chauffeurs and wealthy patrons. All came to ogle, critique, buy and sell the latest and most elegant cars for the next season. Those in the business regarded the Salons as opportunities to see and be seen, to network, to talk shop and often to look for a better job.

Inside the Salon

Salon promoter Emil (Pop) Lacaris always reserved the day before each New York Salon's formal opening for industry insiders. Men like Henry and Edsel Ford, Walter Chrysler, GM's Alfred Sloan, Packard's Alvan Macauley and the Fisher Brothers might roam the carpeted aisles chatting with coachbuilders Willie Brewster or Hermann Brunn or James Derham. Everyone knew everyone. And no gentleman would be seen in anything less than a tuxedo.

That evening, all would gather for a gala dinner in the glittering Commodore dining room, with champagne, caviar and the finest cigars. This preview dinner came to be a highly ritualized, very exclusive, yet strangely relaxed affair and, as a result, business did get transacted.

Next day the Four Hundred began to arrive. Salons, especially in New York, were eagerly attended social events. Many of the invited public preferred to visit the Salon on a Friday or Saturday evening between dinner and the theater. Again, everyone dressed to the nines.

One mid-week afternoon of the Salon was set aside for chauffeurs, because some families preferred to let their chauffeurs choose and do the dickering for next season's cars. The chauffeur, according to coachbuilder Hermann C. Brunn, played an important role in selecting chassis and custom bodywork for the families who employed them. The chauffeur was, after all, a modern extension of the traditional coachman, and good chauffeurs knew a lot more about cars than did their employers.

Brunn, in his reminiscences, mentions the J.P. Morgan family and their chauffeur, Charles Robertson. Robertson had Mr. Morgan's complete confidence and dealt with automotive vendors of all types, including Brunn. Coachbuilders and chauffeurs were usually on friendlier terms than coachbuilders and patrons due to their closer social rank.

Agents competed for sales to chauffeurs, and they did this by offering "commissions." The standard commission was 10%, a figure that by no means encouraged moderation in either sellers or chauffeurs. It was often the coachbuilder offering the most expensive car and thus the highest commission who landed the sale. Employers, of course, knew all about these fees. They also realized it was they who were paying them and occasionally asked their chauffeurs to hand the commissions back.

Salons, it turns out, were the forerunners of that great American institution, the annual model changeover. By 1930, common folk were doing on a vastly larger and more democratic scale what New York's Four Hundred had been doing at the Salons: They were going to local auto dealerships to inspect the coming year's attractions. Salons were also the precursors of GM's Motorama displays of show- and concept cars that attracted so many millions of visitors during the 50s and '60s (see page 113). ◆

Cars of the teens stood tall and upright, the above two being representative of the common shapes and lines of that era. The 1916 Chalmers sedan (left) illustrates a point Stutz president Fred E. Moskovics made to the Society of Automotive Engineers in 1928: "Let us ask ourselves honestly," he said, "how many of us designed a chassis primarily to take a closed body, or whether we have simply placed a closed body on a chassis as it then existed.... We simply took an existing type of chassis that was not low, added four or five feet on top of it...and tried to make it artistic. The chassis and the body (did) not blend particularly well." The 1914 Locomobile (right) looks austere, top-heavy and totally without flair.

S ix to eight weeks after each annual salon came the National Automobile Show. The National Automobile Show was open to the public and differed from Salons by exhibiting both production and coachbuilt cars. For many years, this larger display took place at New York's Grand Central Palace but moved, in 1924-25, to the Bronx Armory, then back to the Palace in '26 and for a number of years afterward. At the Palace, the coachbuilders' exhibits were usually found on the third floor.

And in 1922, the Automobile Body Builders' Assn. launched an additional annual event called the Body Builders' Show. This exhibit really *was* a trade show, its purpose being more to introduce accessories, parts and services than to present style or styling ideas. The Body Builders' Show completed New York's "Automobile Week," which usually consisted of the salon, the Body Builders' Show, plus meetings, dinners, sales presentations and festivities put on by the car manufacturers for their distributors and dealers. As a sustained event, Automobile Week drew thousands of industry insiders from all over the country.

Each year's shows, of course, were written up in all the trade magazines, but not necessarily as straight photo reports. Instead, the magazines often published *styling critiques,* much like today's film reviews. George Mercer contributed design evaluations to *Autobody* and *Automotive Industries* magazines. John Jay Ide, who'd advocated streamlined cars as early as 1912 and served as a U.S. military aeronautical attache in Europe after World War I, wrote for *Scientific American. Horseless Age* had a critic known simply as "Autocraft." These authors reviewed body design with a keen eye, carefully noting new styling nuances and trends but at the same time giving thumbs up or thumbs down to the latest fashion ideas.

Nor were they shy about expressing personal opinions and pointing out the mistakes they felt the coachbuilders had made in their designs or execution. For example, Ide wrote in the Jan. 2, 1915 edition of *Scientific American,* "The [Packard] body...has quite pleasing proportions, but is slung far too high above the ground. I well remember that at the last Paris Salon the exhibitor of this make had cleverly arranged ramps approaching the car from the sides, so that would-be purchasers accustomed to low-hung European productions would not be overwhelmed." Autocraft talked in 1917 about body proportions and even suggested different formulas for cars with short and long wheelbases.

For the most part, then, fashion for the general industry was set by the coachbuilders. These smaller shops became important beyond their size and the number of cars they produced, because they led in bringing style not just to their own creations but to the American automobile in general. Coachbuilders weren't alone in that mission, but they often pioneered or catalyzed, and they did this on a scale grander than their larger cousins—at least for the first quarter of the century. The makers of production bodies—the giants and medium-sized body suppliers—took the greatest number of their styling ideas either directly or indirectly from the coachbuilders. And the coachbuilders, as we've seen, got a lot of their ideas overseas.

G iven that background, then, why, during that growth period from 1900 to 1925, were there no standout examples of influential styling, no milestones, no memorable masterpieces of American automotive art, surely nothing like the designs that soon followed: the 1929 Cord L-29, 1932 Graham Blue Streak, 1933 Pierce-Arrow Silver Arrow, so many of the traditional classics, then the untraditional classics like the 1936 Cord, 1940 Lincoln Continental and finally the postwar landmark designs like the 1947 Studebaker, 1948 Cadillac, 1953 Studebaker Starliner coupe, 1955 Thunderbird, 1963 Buick Riviera and dozens of other beautiful and influential automobiles?

Somehow, no home-run designs emerged from those first 25 years; nothing that takes your breath away or ever did; nothing that we now hold up as remarkable or especially influential. We can point to any number of *unusual* designs, like the 1912 Scripps-Booth Bi-Autogo and the 1914 Tiffany Electric. But when it comes to agreeing on the worthiness or the inherent beauty of any specific early automobile body, we don't seem to be able to find any. Or at least not many. Why?

There appears to be no single answer. Randy Mason blames it on the "formative nature of the period, when automotive fashion was finding itself and the real emphasis was on making cars reliable, durable, useful and comfortable."

Then, too, as some body types and styling developments advanced in the early days, others regressed. Regressive styles included the high-wheelers, most electrics and the colonial coach styles. And the motoring public, despite a certain fashion *consciousness,* was basi-

Designer of 1914 Tiffany electric had no engine to worry about, so he let his whimsy go wild. Door cut and downward-thrusting roof were very advanced and unusual.

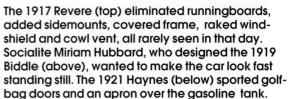

The 1917 Revere (top) eliminated runningboards, added sidemounts, covered frame, raked windshield and cowl vent, all rarely seen in that day. Socialite Miriam Hubbard, who designed the 1919 Biddle (above), wanted to make the car look fast standing still. The 1921 Haynes (below) sported golf-bag doors and an apron over the gasoline tank.

Two of the more notable designs from the teens include the American Underslung (top), designed by engineer Fred Tone, and the Mercer Raceabout. In the Underslung's case, Tone turned frame upside down and hung it from the axles. Mercer became revered as one of America's great early sports cars.

cally conservative. American automakers recognized this, and those who didn't follow the latest styling trends, who held back a little, probably ended up selling more cars than those on the leading edge.

For years, Packard, to mention one of the most consistent practitioners of slow styling evolution, walked that very fine line between the new and the traditional. Its customers apparently appreciated Packard's conservatism, because most didn't want to risk endorsing a fad. Ford, too, probably profited—surely for a while—by keeping the Model T several years behind trendy fashion. Henry Ford's own thoughts on styling mirrored that of his mostly rural and small-town customers. And yet automakers who prided themselves on innovation, like Auburn and Franklin, never really joined the mainstream.

Yet we can't overlook some of the more significant and interesting cars from that early period. The "underslungs," for instance, including the 1907-14 American, 1910-11 Cavac, 1911-12 KRIT and the 1912 Norwalk, pioneered the long, low look. They drew people's attention to styling that *could* be; the possibilities that lowness offers a car. It's fair to say, then, that the underslungs accelerated public awareness and acceptance of a lower silhouette—something stylists have consistently advocated since carriage days.

The American Underslung needed huge wheels for ground clearance, and Fred Tone, its designer, took advantage of that fact by aligning the tops of the fenders with the top of the hood. So the device of big wheels combined with the parallel lines of the fenders and hood accentuated what was already a very low silhouette for that day. The overall effect was to help speed the trend toward bringing down the height of American automobile bodies in general.

And then there were cars like the 1911-16 Mercer Raceabout, the 1912-16 Stutz Bearcat, the 1919 Biddle roadster, the 1919-28 Kissel Gold Bug series: two-seaters that gave the motoring public an appreciation of personal sports cars and made them aware of the raciness that could be expressed in autobody design. Cunningham, National, Simplex, Locomobile, McFarlan, Templar, Haynes and a handful of other pre-1925 cars showed consistently *decent* body styling, yet there wasn't anything especially outstanding among them. Perhaps that's because the American auto industry was still following European fashion and not yet creating trends or leading the world. Then, too, perhaps we lacked standouts because style was still evolving on a *component* level, in small, incremental ways. We were making specific advances, like adding front doors, figuring out how to form flush body sides, cowled dashboards, overlapped door panels, lower windshields, roll-up windows, crowned fenders and inexpensive closed bodies.

That first quarter century amounted basically to the American car designer's *apprenticeship* period. We were still learning from Europe. But the student was about to become the master. ◆

CHAPTER 4

THE MASS PRODUCERS

One of Detroit's earliest important quantity producers of automobile bodies was the C.R. Wilson Co., founded in the 1870s as the Wilson Carriage Co. Charles R. Wilson, owner of the company, became friends with Henry Ford when Wilson built the seat for Ford's 1896 quadricycle.

By 1902, the C.R. Wilson Co. claimed to be the world's largest maker of buggy and carriage bodies, a pronouncement also made by Studebaker. Unlike Studebaker, though, Wilson, in 1903, began building autobodies almost exclusively and supplied them to Oldsmobile, Cadillac, Ford, Elmore and Peerless, among other carmakers.

Many examples exist of Detroit's small-townishness, but the Fisher/Briggs link makes one of those classic stories of Detroit's working and social relationships intertwined. If ever the characters for a television mini-series existed in real life, here they were.

The seven Fisher Brothers grew up in Norwalk, Ohio, and all of them apprenticed in their father's carriage factory. As they became adults, each brother left home to seek his fortune. The eldest, Fred Fisher, studied business for two years in Sandusky. Then, at age 24, Fred became the first of the brothers to venture to Detroit. He got a job there in 1902 with the C.R. Wilson Co. as a draftsman, earning $20 a week,

Woodworkers at Fisher Body set pre-cut pieces into jigs, then glued and screwed the frame members together.

The C.R. Wilson Co. quickly became one of those pivotal, central Detroit meeting places where future industry leaders bumped into each other. Henry Ford and Fred Fisher met there when Fisher worked as a Wilson draftsman. Other notable Wilson drop-ins included Ransom E. Olds, Henry M. Leland, Charles W. Nash and Walter P. Chrysler. Detroit was still small enough, population 285,000 in 1903, that nearly everyone in the auto business knew everyone else, both professionally and socially. Paradoxically, it's still that way today.

The C.R. Wilson Co. dominated the body business for several years, and then the Fisher Brothers and Walter Briggs took over. Fisher and Briggs were joined a few years later by the Edward G. Budd Mfg. Co. and the Murray Corp. of America.

and he soon enrolled in Andrew F. Johnson's Technical School and began taking lessons by mail.

Within months, Wilson put Fred Fisher in charge of the entire drafting room. In 1904, Brother Charles (Charlie) Fisher joined Wilson, and everything went along fine until four years later when Charlie got married and needed more money. One morning, Charlie told Fred he planned to ask Mr. Wilson for a $5-a-week raise. Fred warned Charlie that he didn't think Mr. Wilson would give it to him. They agreed, though, that if Charlie didn't get his raise, both would leave. Wilson didn't give Charlie his raise, so the two brothers quit.

Their safety net was Uncle Albert A. Fisher, who owned a huge wagon factory in Detroit. Albert lived comfortably and, coincidentally, had already built some 50 automobile bodies for Henry Ford. The year was 1908, Ford was about to launch his Model T, William C. Durant incorporated General Motors that September, and if ever the auto industry had a ground floor to get in on, this was it. Uncle Albert and the two senior Fisher Brothers seized the moment and, with Uncle Albert putting up $30,000 in cash, they organized the Fisher Body Co. Timing was perfect. The autobody business boomed right on schedule, and the Fishers' earliest customers came flocking in: Ford, Cadillac, Oldsmobile, EMF and Herreschoff.

It now happened by the purest chance that directly across the hall from Charlie Fisher and his new bride, in a modest boarding house near downtown Detroit, lived another young couple, the Walter O. Briggses. The Briggses and Fishers met and soon discovered that they had a lot to talk about. In 1904, Walter Briggs had started working as an upholsterer in Barney Everitt's carriage trim shop. Briggs quickly rose through the shop ranks and was running the place by 1905. Everitt made him president in 1906.

At the boarding house, the Briggses and Fishers used to play whist to while away the evenings. Between hands, the two men would compare notes and talk about the autobody business. It wasn't long before they discussed going out on their own. In 1908, the two Fisher Brothers did just that, and two years later, so did Walter Briggs. Briggs bought Barney Everitt's trim factory, which by that time was building complete wooden bodies not only for EMF but also for Ford (everybody built bodies for Ford), Paige, Abbott and Chalmers. Then, immediately after taking over Everitt, Briggs landed a juicy contract to supply Ford with 10,000 Model T bodies.

In 1910, Walter Briggs changed the name of his company to Briggs Manufacturing Co. and settled in to become a major Ford body supplier. That same year, Cadillac placed an order with Fisher for 150 *closed* bodies, and that marked the beginning of Fisher's important relationship with Cadillac.

Briggs and the Fisher Brothers were now in direct competition. But the auto industry needed so many bodies that neither thought of the other as a rival. Both of their companies flourished, and the Fishers and Briggses remained close friends all their lives. By 1916, Fisher Body Co. was turning out 370,000 bodies a year, and by 1925, Briggs Mfg. Co. was delivering 500,000 bodies annually (compared with 1.3 million for Fisher).

By the mid teens, Fisher and Briggs were the undisputed giants of bodymaking, and to show how intertwined the two families had become: In the early 1920s, Walter Briggs and Charlie Fisher built large, imposing, luxurious homes next to one another on West Boston Blvd., in a fashionable Detroit subdivision developed by automaker Childe Harold Wills. A few years later, Charlie Fisher's son, Charles Jr., married Walter Briggs' daughter, Elizabeth Jane, and eventually Charlie Fisher Jr. served on the Briggs Mfg. Co. board of directors. Soon afterward, a second Briggs daughter, Susan Ann, married another Fisher son, Everell. But we're getting ahead.

In 1912, a third Fisher Brother, Lawrence P. (Larry), who later became president of Cadillac, joined the Fisher Body Co. as superintendent

of paint and trim. Next year, fresh from the Andrew F. Johnson Technical School in New York, Edward F. and Alfred J. Fisher came into the business, each working for several months in every department of the main Fisher plant before moving on to more permanent duties. Eventually all seven Fisher Brothers came to Detroit, and when they all worked together, it was in unison. "When one cut himself shaving," said Charlie's son Thomas K. Fisher, "they all bled."

The Fishers had a strong sense of family and adhered to an ethic that honored mature wisdom.. The younger Fisher Brothers deferred to their older siblings without question. At the outset, this meant that Fred Fisher ruled. For years, all seven brothers sat down to lunch together, with

Sheetmetal bodysides were moved around the assembly floor on dollies. The sides were pre-assembled, all framed and ready to mate with cowls and end stampings. This photo was taken in one of the Fisher plants around 1914.

Early Sheetmetal Presses

By 1910, a few bodymakers, including C.R. Wilson and Fisher, were starting to use primitive drop presses to make sheetmetal stampings. These presses consisted of a semi-steel female die and a lead male punch. The punch usually took its shape directly from the female die. Large loops were cast into the top surface of the lead punch, and it was lifted to the ceiling by ropes. Channels guided the punch to direct its drop into the female die.

To make the actual stamping, workmen heated large sheets of steel in a gas furnace. When the metal was red hot, they used tongs to hold the cherry-colored sheet over the female die. The male lead punch was then dropped from the ceiling and forced the sheetmetal into the female die.

The quality of sheet steel varied widely in that day, and it wasn't unusual to have the stamped piece split as it took shape. Metal lubricants, more ductile steels and more consistent quality arrived with the advent of larger hydraulic and toggle presses (see sidebar, page 101). ◆

Fred at the head of the table and the younger six seated down both sides in descending order of age. Discussions were usually democratic, but when it came to a close call, Fred had the final say. When Fred passed away in 1941, Charlie, the next-oldest brother, moved to the head of the table, and so on until the last four Fisher Brothers retired in 1944. In defense of this system, it did discourage squabbling and intra-family rivalry and politics.

After the brothers' father died in 1921, their mother, Margaret Fisher, came to Detroit to be nearer her sons. The brothers bought her a comfortable house and were absolutely devoted to her. Mrs. Fisher suffered a stroke in 1925, and from that day until she passed away in 1936, Margaret Fisher never had dinner alone or spent an evening without one of her sons at her side. Fred would assign turns and see to it that, each evening, at least one of the brothers made time to be with Mrs. Fisher.

The Fisher Brothers were fortunate to have, as an early partner and financial advisor, architect Louis Mendelssohn. Mendelssohn had

The seven Fisher Brothers, with Fred, the eldest, in the middle, pose during groundbreaking ceremonies for the Fisher Building, across the street from the GM Building in Detroit.

bought out Uncle Albert in 1913 and soon organized many of the brothers' business expansions. In time, Louis worked out the details of selling the Fisher Body Co. to General Motors. GM, of course, did not want to be beholden to an independent source for its bodies, so it bought what the corporation considered to be its biggest and best supplier.

The sale took place in two stages. The first consisted of a 60% buyout, completed in late 1919, and then GM bought the remaining 40% in 1926, paying a grand total of $234.7 million. GM president Alfred P. Sloan Jr. made Fisher Body a semi-autonomous division and asked the Fisher Brothers to stay on. All seven did and held responsible positions both within Fisher Body and in the larger corporation. By 1927, Fisher had 71 plants in the U.S. plus one in Walkerville, Ontario.

The Briggs Mfg. Co., meanwhile, went public in 1924 and immediately declared a 200% dividend on that year's $11 million net profit, 60% of which went into Briggs' personal bank account. Walter's game, though, wasn't finance or even bodymaking; it was *baseball*. In 1927, he owned a half interest in the Detroit Tigers, the other half belonging to Frank J. Navin. Navin had won his initial 10% in a poker game in 1904, then bought the other 40% in 1909. Briggs and Navin worked out a deal that whoever outlived the other would inherit the Tigers. Navin passed away in 1935, and Briggs lived until 1952, so Briggs owned the Tigers alone for 17 years. He also owned Briggs Stadium, and he scheduled his plant shifts so workers could attend the Tigers' afternoon games. Briggs hired Mickey Cochran as his manager, and the Tigers won the American League pennant for 1934 and the World Series in 1935.

Briggs' main customer had always been Ford. Henry Ford prided himself on paying his own workers well (at least for a time), but by playing his suppliers off against each other, he kept them on *extremely* tight leashes. During Model A days, 1928-31, Ford bought approximately $167 million worth of bodies each year from Briggs and fought over every penny. According to Ford company records, Briggs typically received $229.71 for a 1929 Model A town sedan body, versus $237.98 for a Murray version of the same.

At one point, Ford's tightfistedness became so oppressive that Briggs and Murray held secret talks aimed at a merger. When Henry Ford heard about this, he threatened to take his business away from both companies and parcel it out among the medium-sized bodymakers like Midland Steel, Ames and Hayes. Understandably, Briggs

In the 1920s and '30s, Briggs Mfg. Co., largest of the independent bodybuilders, produced hundreds of thousands of carbodies each year. Above, a workman shapes an early '20s cowl on an English wheel. Others add roof framing (center) and perform metal finishing (top right). At immediate right is the line that produced the all-steel 1934 Chrysler Airflows.

Bringing the Motoring Family in From the Cold

The touring car was by far the most popular body style of the teens and early 1920s. Touring bodies were popular mostly because they were relatively easy to build, thus cheap. They were also versatile. Touring cars could carry a family of five to church on Sunday, a load of chickens to town on Monday, and fence posts to the back 40 on Tuesday.

Yet, popular and handy as they were, they were cold in the winter, hot in summer, and owners fought the balky canvas top constantly. Worse were the sidecurtains. Once in place,

1917 Studebaker came with a factory California top. This was essentially an open touring car with a bolt-on rigid roof. It still used sidecurtains.

they leaked. Within a couple of seasons they'd become brittle, cracked, and no one could see out through them. So despite the versatility of touring cars, they were by no means loved.

Drivers of touring cars soon came to envy people who drove sedans and coaches. Closed body styles, though, were expensive, often costing half again as much as a touring body on the same chassis. A 1921 center-door Model T sedan, for example, cost $934 versus $644 for the same year's Ford touring car.

The first step toward providing closed-car comfort in a touring car came from California, according to P.W. Steinbeck, chief body engineer for the coachbuilder H.H. Babcock Co. of Watertown, New York. Speaking before the York chapter of the Society of Automotive Engineers in Jan. 1922, Steinbeck said that the California top originated around 1915 in response to the big differences in that state's daytime and nighttime temperatures. To keep from forever wrestling with canvas tops and sidecurtains, some motorists began to make and install rigid, wood-framed hardtops on their touring cars. The earliest were crude, cobbled affairs, but it wasn't long before California tops were being made commercially and sold on the aftermarket. Some became quite sophisticated.

The typical California (also known as "all-seasons") top had a wooden frame covered with some type of waterproof fabric. Wooden door sills were screwed onto the body top rail, and this formed the foundation for mounting the top. Each top was made to fit a specific make of touring car. Tops manufactured in volume for popular cars like Ford, Willys-Overland, and Chevrolet naturally cost less than those built in smaller batches. In some cases, auto

dealers offered California tops as new-car accessories so that customers could buy both at the same time.

Early aftermarket California tops still had flexible isenglass or Xylonite curtains that rolled up like window shades and stored under the roof, above each door. These, though, tended to mildew when rolled up wet, and they had the same drawbacks as regular sidecurtains. The next step was to make the side and rear windows out of glass. In 1919, a company called Gould introduced a California top with glass windows that slid horizontally in wooden channels. When open, all glass panes slid to the back of the top and stored side by side in the sail-panel area. Other types of glass windows lifted out and tucked into pouches behind the front seat. And Studebaker, from 1925 through 1927, offered what they called the "Duplex" style: a touring car body with a steel, bolt-on, factory-built hardtop that was intended to remain permanently in place.

Slowly, though, the price of closed bodies came down as demand increased. Ford kept offering the least expensive closed body styles, but the breakthrough arrived in late 1921 when Hudson announced that its moderately priced Essex line would offer a two-door coach for $1495, only $300 more than the open Essex touring car. By July 1922, the price had dropped to $1295, then $1145 by 1923 and $795 in 1925. Due to the inexpensive

1922 Essex coach revolutionized bodymaking--in addition to family motoring. It made the closed car affordable. The revolution had to do with the body's modular assembly.

coach, Essex became a tremendous bestseller and totally changed the public's priorities and preferences in body styles. A closed car with more amenities and prestige than the Model T had suddenly become as affordable to the middle-income motorist as the touring car.

The closed car quickly made the touring car obsolete, and by 1925—for the first time in history—Americans were buying more closed than open body styles. Conversely and rather amazingly, by the late 1920s, open body styles—convertible sedans, phaetons, convertible victorias, and roadsters—came to be considered sporty and luxurious. Open body styles were viewed in a new light. By 1929, the public held open-bodied phaetons,

roadsters and speedsters in high regard as the pleasure craft of the wealthy and sports minded.

The question remains: How did Hudson manage to make the 1922 Essex coach so inexpensively? Actually, Hudson had the good sense not to rely on its own body engineers alone. Hudson consulted with Budd on making the sheetmetal stampings and with Briggs on whittling expenses for the wood framing. Briggs, which sharpened its own skills and pared its costs while making closed bodies for Ford, suggested to Hudson that the 1922 Essex use as many straight-cut wooden frame members as possible. Only two wooden pieces were cut on an arc—those at the sides of the "trunk." In contrast, the 1919-22 Model T sedan body called for curved pieces in nearly every part of its wooden framing.

Briggs further suggested that the Essex body be made modularly. The roof, for example, became one of several subassemblies. Workmen stretched the top fabric over the outer surface and tacked the headliner in place underneath before installing the complete roof on the body pillars.

Two other economies helped keep the Essex's price down: the use of two doors with identical outer skins and equal-sized glass in all four side windows.

The 1922 Essex body, built in Hudson's up-to-the-minute Gratiot plant, contained few amenities and wasn't a particularly handsome car, yet it did provide the comfort and weather protection denied owners of touring cars. As a result, the Essex sold extremely well.

So while 99% of all American cars made in 1916 had been open-bodied, by

1929 nearly 90% were closed. Around 1927, Hudson managed to lower Essex closed-car prices so much that the difference between a new coach and a touring car came to just a few dollars. Basically, then, it was Essex that launched the technology and competitive edge that brought the average motorist in from the cold. ◆

and Murray broke off their talks, and Edsel Ford installed his old tutor, Clarence Avery, as Murray's president.

During the Depression, Ford shaved Briggs' profits so thin that Briggs workers, who'd already taken pay cuts, staged several protest strikes. One 1933 strike in particular shut down not only all Briggs plants for a month but also Ford, Chrysler, Hudson and a number of their major suppliers. The upshot was that Ford lost more money in missed sales than he would have if he'd been more generous with the bodymakers in the first place.

Soon afterward, Briggs branched out into bathroom fixtures and garden furniture. Eventually Briggs' Ford business tapered off, and the company's contracts with Chrysler and Packard increased. In 1953, following Walter Briggs' death, Chrysler bought all of Briggs' body plants and leased one to Packard: the old Conner Avenue plant in which Packard finished out the rest of its life.

In their heyday, even though Fisher and Briggs remained the industry giants, they eventually did feel some competition from the Murray Corp. of America and the Edward G. Budd Mfg. Co.

The Murray Corp. of America took shape as an autobody con-

glomerate dreamed up by Allan Shelden, an entrepreneur with a vision. In the early 1920s, Shelden was on the board of the mid-sized Murray Body Corp., a company known throughout the industry as the "King of the Stampers." Shelden talked Murray's owner and a banker named Keane into helping him buy up a number of small body man-

Fisher had body plants all over the country plus one in Canada. Large stampings were often shipped "knocked down" and nested, then assembled onsite (left). At right are Briggs presentation models and sketches made in 1939 in an attempt to bring in more carbody business. Headed by Ralph Roberts and John Tjaarda, Briggs' styling staff was one of the largest and finest in the nation.

ufacturers in an effort to form one big integrated combine. Together they bought the old C.R. Wilson Co. and then the Towson Body Co. Towson was a major supplier of bodies to Lincoln and also built a few for Packard. Shelden soon added J.C. Widman & Co., which specialized in door glass and windshields.

The resulting, much-expanded Murray Body Corp. immediately

The sturdiness of Dodge's all-steel body spoke for itself.

had more business than it could handle. Then, within eight months, it went into bankruptcy due to underbidding too many jobs. The company quickly reorganized and emerged from bankruptcy long enough for Allan Shelden to hire Ray Dietrich and establish Dietrich Inc. as its coachbuilding arm in Feb. 1925 (see page 51). Murray then proceeded to fall into receivership a second time late that year. Finally, in a legal maneuver that only bankers and lawyers can appreciate, the Murray Body Corp. came out of receivership partly by changing its name to Murray Corp. of America.

Murray sometimes did approach Briggs in volume but never in financial stability. Murray built a lot of bodies, though, and for a time enjoyed the distinction of being Ford's principal body supplier. That came about partly because, in August 1927, after the secret merger talks between Murray and Briggs collapsed, Henry Ford installed Clarence W. Avery to run Murray, and Avery became president in 1929 when the court receiver finally left.

Avery turned out to be one of the best things that ever happened to Murray. He'd been a close friend and teacher of Edsel Ford and, in 1913,

Impatience with Paint

By 1920, the Fisher Brothers, Briggs and other major autobody manufacturers had the ability to assemble a body in four to five hours. But it still took them three to eight weeks to paint it. Paint technology hadn't kept up with mass production at all; in fact, the paint area in a body factory was like a big swamp at the end of the assembly line. Before 1924, when DuPont introduced Duco nitrocellulose lacquers, nothing held back auto production like paint. Paint was the anchor, the iron boot of the auto industry.

For the first quarter of this century, most cars were painted by hand, with brushes. Painters came from the time-honored, time-consuming tradition of carriagemaking and, as a carryover, preferred to finish carbodies with varnish. This process involved brushing on several color coats and then topping those with clear varnish. You have to appreciate their skill and craftsmanship, but the process was literally as slow as watching paint dry. Techniques varied from man to man and company to company, but basically here is what the typical varnish job entailed.

Any paint area had to be clean and bright to begin with. It usually had a concrete floor with a central drain so it could be hosed down periodically. Walls and ceiling were often covered in light-colored tile for good illumination and washability. There was usually a series of drying ovens—huge, heated rooms, actually—off to one side.

After a thorough cleaning, the unmounted body-in-white came into this area on a wheeled dolly and first went into the drying room to remove solvents and moisture. (The term "body-in-white" means an unpainted body with a light-colored primer coat to keep it from rusting.) Some drying rooms could hold up to 150 bodies at a time. Filtered air, warmed to 120°-150°F, got pumped in at one end and pumped out at the other.

After drying, the bodies were rolled into the paint rooms, where four to six coats of primer, or so-called "rough stuff," were brushed onto the body with two- to three-inch-wide brushes. To hide the brush strokes, each coat was applied at 90° to the one before it. To speed drying, the body went back into the drying room for 60 to 90 minutes between primer coats.

After primering, the body was totally covered with a coat of yellow ochre paint. By dry-sanding this coat, high and low spots showed up on the body. High spots were tapped down and low spots got puttied. The sanding process also smoothed brush marks from the primer coats. When the ochre had been sanded off and all body surfaces felt smooth, it was time to apply two "ground coats." These were again primer coats that served as a base for the color coats. The ground coats were put on with a two-inch camel-hair brush, then dried for several hours, after which each body was rubbed down with fine pumice on a felt or rubber pad. The second ground coat had a little color in it, but this was the first stage where any color showed up. Until now, the entire process involved nothing but surface preparation.

After another few hours in the drying room, the body was finally ready to be varnished. Here came the critical part. At this stage, to keep down lint and dust, painters often wore no shirts. Instead, they covered their chests and arms with linseed oil. The paint area, too, had to be as clean as a hospital.

Finely ground pigments were now mixed into clear varnish to give it color. The finest varnish bases came from England, and these were what the coachbuilders used. Color varnish was applied by master painters in four to six thin coats, then topped by one or two coats of thick, clear varnish.

For the color varnish process, most master painters used two badger-hair brushes: one 2.5 inches wide to apply the varnish and

Before 1924, it commonly took master painters 6-8 weeks to varnish a body. This scene from 1908 shows workmen applying the undercoat "rough stuff."

he'd helped Charles E. (Cast-Iron Charlie) Sorensen set up Ford's moving assembly line. Avery maintained excellent relations with both Edsel and Henry, and immediately after his arrival at Murray, a fire shut down one of Briggs' biggest plants. So Murray took up the slack and became Ford's main body supplier for early Model A production.

In addition to Ford, Murray supplied bodies to Lincoln, Packard, Hudson, Willys-Overland, Hupmobile, Reo, Graham, Marmon and (later) Mercury. In 1934, when Hupmobile seemed moribund, Avery arranged to have that year's Ford sedan bodies modified to become the 1934 standard-series Hupp 417-W, thus saving Hupmobile the cost of tooling up new bodies. And as Briggs concentrated more on Chrysler business, Murray's share of the Ford pie increased. In 1936, Ford was buying 22.6% of its bodies from Murray, a figure that rose to 48.1% in 1939. That year, too, Murray picked up Mercury and Crosley as customers.

But Clarence Avery realized that all car companies would eventually build their own bodies, just as GM was doing through Fisher. At one point, Avery suggested to Henry Ford that he put little *Body by Murray* tags on all his cars, but Ford refused. During the 1930s, Murray

a smaller brush to pick off the dust and lint, which they called "lice." Despite all precautions, there were always lice in the air. The best master painters could apply varnish without leaving brush marks. Between color coats, the body was rubbed down with ever-finer grades of pumice and then re-dried. After all the color coats had been applied—and this might include several different two-tone treatments plus pinstriping—the master painter flowed on one or two final coats of clear varnish. These last coats had the consistency of molasses, and each coat took two weeks or longer to air dry. If heat-dried, these clear coats tended to check or crack.

As mentioned, early varnishing processes took from three to eight weeks. Timing depended on weather, humidity, work hours, scheduling of the various rooms, the number of painters available, etc. In the early 1920s,

dous depth; almost a glow. But within a year or so, varnish would go dark due to oxidation and irreversible chemical changes. Colors became obscured, clear sealer coats turned yellow, and the surface would start to crack. Raindrops acted as tiny magnifying lenses that left permanent sun spots. Bird droppings were worse. That's why wealthy owners of custom bodies often took their cars back to the coachbuilder every year for revarnishing.

The fastest-drying varnish was black. That's part of the reason Ford offered "any color you want so long as it's black" from 1914 through 1925. Black (and other dark colors) absorbed more heat and therefore dried faster than lighter hues. Black varnish, which used a carbon base, also resisted the sun's ultraviolet rays and lasted longer than other colors. Finishing a carbody in black varnish took about a week. This was still too long for Ford, so he kept look-

fired in a gas oven at 450°F for 4.5 hours, a temperature that would burn or split the wood framing. So only those body parts that had no wood could be finished in baked enamel: fenders, hoods, splash aprons, radiator shells, etc. This explains why those components were black on so many early cars. (It was possible, however, to treat an assembled wooden body frame so it *could* withstand the 450°F bake oven. This involved dipping the frame in Gilsonite and then baking the wood itself for four hours at 250°F. The treatment allowed a common ash body frame to withstand the 450°F heat of the gas-fired baking oven. Although theoretically possible, the Gilsonite wood treatment proved too expensive, risky and time consuming for most makers of composite bodies to bother with. Very few ever resorted to it.)

Touring cars with all-steel bodies, though, like the 1915 and later Dodges, *were* painted

These scenes show various aspects of the varnishing process at Hudson in 1917. Below, finished bodies are rubbed out with rough stuff and sanded with leather-backed pumice.

a body supplier capable of building 1000 bodies a day had to store 20,000 in various stages of painting (assuming a five-day work week and four weeks of drying time). This, of course, presented tremendous logistical problems. Fisher, Briggs and Murray could each build thousands of bodies a day up to a point, but every body had to wait for the paint to dry before it could be mounted. When Hudson introduced the inexpensive Essex coach for 1922 (see sidebar, page 29), its sales literature boasted, "The finish has not been slighted as there are 25 paint operations, this being fully up to the normal number."

And after all that work and painstaking care, a varnish job lasted only two to three years at best. Freshly applied, it had tremen-

ing for more rapid finishing methods.

One way around the varnish problems—slow drying times and short lifespan—was to use baked enamel. Bicycle manufacturers had been applying baked enamel since about 1896, maybe earlier, and automakers started using it around 1908. Baked enamel could be flowed or sprayed onto metal, it was tough, had good luster and dried in less than a day.

Why, then, wasn't Ford and everyone else using baked enamel? Well, Henry did, but this type of finish presented a few problems of its own. For one, baked enamel came only in black, because only Gilsonite, a fossil asphalt pigment, could withstand the heat needed to bake it. The other problem was the heat itself. A carbody painted with baked enamel had to be

entirely in black baked enamel. Each Dodge body took as little as one day to finish. By 1923, Ford had removed much of the wood from his open body styles, so he ordered his body suppliers to also use black baked enamel. Since Model T bodies still had *some* wood in them—tacking strips, etc.—Ford avoided the 450°F ovens by specifying six thin coats of baked enamel instead of one heavy one, and each coat was fired at 165°F instead of 450°F. Finishing time now took about three days.

In April 1923, *Autobody* magazine explained that, "Ford cars are now finished in several coats of baked enamel. The paint is flowed on [sprayed with a hose], which insures freedom from brush marks, and the body passes through a huge conveyor oven, 100 ft. long,

branched out by making Eljer bathroom fixtures, steel beer barrels and household appliances for Montgomery Ward & Co.

During World War II, Murray employed a record 13,500 workers and, with its military contracts, turned profits during every year of the conflict. After the war, with Ford's old guard gone, Murray supplied only stampings to Ford, not entire bodies. A brief uptick followed in the 1950s when Murray helped engineer and then built bodies for the compact Hudson Jet and Aero Willys. But after that, Murray quietly left the autobody business. In 1955, Murray sold its chassis plants to Dana Corp. and its appliance facilities to Wallace-Murray, which at that time made everything from bicycles to superchargers.

This left The Budd Co. as the only surviving independent manufacturer of automobile bodies. To begin at Budd's beginning: In 1912, Edward Gowen Budd had been working for Hale, Kilburn & Co. in Philadelphia when Hupmobile asked them to supply steel body panels for their cars. Hupp's order gave Mr. Budd the idea of fabricating automobile bodies *entirely* from steel, a very odd notion at the time. So in 1912, he and 13 other former Hale, Kilburn employees, including engineer Joseph Ledwinka, left to set up their own business. Their plan was to eliminate the heavy wooden framing used in automobile bod-

heated to 165 deg. After emerging from the other end of the oven, the body is rubbed down, a second coat is given, and it then makes a return trip through the oven. This cycle of operations is repeated until six coats have been given." In 1923, too—although Ford still offered only black—the bakeable enamel spectrum was broadened to include a popular orange red and several other colors.

Ford and a few other automakers used another quick painting method called "japanning." This involved dipping a sheetmetal part, like a fender, into a vat of paint or flowing the paint on with a hose. The part was then hung up to air-dry. A worker came along after a certain time and razored off the half-dried drips and runs.

The breakthrough finally came in 1924 when General Motors and DuPont announced Duco nitrocellulose "lacquer." Duco wasn't re- ditional colors for 1925, and by 1926 DuPont had made Duco available to the entire auto industry.

Soon after Duco arrived, a competing finish, another nitrocellulose lacquer called pyroxylin, also came on the market. Pyroxylin was sprayable, just as fast-drying as Duco, and had much the same properties. Acme, later absorbed into Sherwin-Williams, made a popular pyroxylin lacquer, as did Ditzler and other paint suppliers.

A number of coachbuilders stayed with varnish for a time, but by 1929 most had switched. "Lacquer finish was general," said *Autobody* in its review of the 1929 New York Salon, "and so well executed that only expert examination would have detected any difference between the finish at this Salon and that of the pre-lacquer Salon of, say, 1923, at which no custom builder would admit the possibility of this new ing became the last step in the process except for the pinstriping, which went on afterward and was done strictly by hand and eye.

Henry Ford reluctantly adopted Duco in 1927 but wasn't pleased to pay for anything developed by General Motors and DuPont. So by 1929, Ford began using an alkyd enamel, which DuPont countered with a similar enamel called DuLux. Both finishes took longer than Duco to dry but didn't need buffing.

Also in the late 1920s, Ford launched a research program to make paints from plant products, notably soybeans. He eventually managed to make a synthetic baked enamel in 1934 that contained 35% soy oil, and the next year he was using a million gallons to paint Ford cars.

Mica flakes had been added to color varnishes as early as the teens. The early flakes were relatively large and had to be applied by brush. Then around 1930, finely ground alu-

Another picks out the "lice" while a third touches up blemishes.

Before okaying the application of final color coats, an inspector checks for flaws.

ally a lacquer but amounted instead to a solvent-based, liquid celluloid, with the same basic chemistry as early movie film. Duco absolutely revolutionized the auto industry, mostly because it dried quickly and cut painting time from weeks to days. In addition, you could apply Duco with a spray gun instead of a brush. Other advantages: It came in bright colors, didn't fade or yellow, was more flexible than varnish, yet didn't need high-temperature ovens. As a result of the manhours saved, Duco cost less than baked enamel and involved just a fraction of the handwork of varnish. The first production car to use Duco was GM's 1924 Oakland. The Oakland came in a satin-finish "true blue," but with baked-enamel black fenders and aprons. Chevrolet offered Duco in several ad- finish ever displacing the old-time varnish "for cars of this class."

Not that applying Duco was any picnic either. In 1927, GM's Fisher Body Div. reported that their system of painting meant first washing the body with acidic water and boiling it back off in a 190°F oven before spraying on an initial coat of red iron-oxide primer. The oxide got baked at 185°F for 3.5 hours, after which body dents were puttied. Five additional coats of primer were sprayed on, each oven dried and sanded. The final primer contained a touch of the eventual hue. Then four to six coats of the colored Duco lacquer were sprayed on. Each was wet sanded and oven dried. And while varnishes and baked enamels didn't require final buffing, Duco lacquers did, so buff- minum powder began to appear in various types of sprayable paints. Graham offered "opalescent" metallic colors in 1932 but wasn't the first to do so.

Paint technology changed in the 1950s, when acrylic lacquers with more stable pigments became available. Acrylic enamels followed in the late 1960s. In the 1970s, auto companies began trying to use more environmentally friendly paints. This led to the less-than-successful waterbased varieties with electo-deposition primers. The primers actually improved corrosion resistance, but with some colors the top coats tended to flake off. Then in the 1980s, bright, low-volatility basecoat/clearcoat finishes arrived.

In the 1990s, the Big Three automakers

ies and replace it with pressed steel. An all-steel body, they reasoned, could be lighter, stronger, more uniform, more quickly made and painted, therefore cheaper than a composite body. This seemed a radical idea in 1912 and very much against the tradition of that day's wood-based body industry.

The E.G. Budd Mfg. Co. began to build all-steel touring-car bodies in late 1912, Oakland and Garford being their first customers. Budd also produced pressed-steel body panels that year for Ford, Willys-Overland and Buick. In late 1914, the Dodge Brothers gave Budd an order to make 5000 all-steel bodies for their new touring car. Edward Budd, the Dodge Brothers and Joseph Ledwinka all contributed to the design of the 1915 Dodge. The relationship between Budd and Dodge lasted until the Dodge Brothers' widows sold out to the New York investment house of Dillon, Read & Co. in 1925.

One advantage of the Dodge all-steel body was that Budd could paint it in just one day (see sidebar, page 31), a feat unheard of in 1914-15. Every other manufacturer took from three to eight *weeks* to paint a carbody. While other bodymakers had to hand varnish their bodies and store them for weeks on end while they were drying, Budd sprayed the Dodge bodies each with one heavy coat of black Gilsonite enamel and then baked it at 450°F in a gas-fired oven for a few hours. The body emerged shiny black and ready for the road in only one eighthour shift (and in only that one color). The reason composite bodies couldn't be finished in baked enamel was because the oven's heat would split or burn the wood framing. So all-steel bodies held a tremendous logistical and price advantage over composite bodies.

To get production of their 1915 body started, the Dodge Brothers paid $25,000 toward Budd's tooling and diemaking costs, and Budd ultimately charged Dodge $42 for each finished body plus another $2 for a set of fenders. The 1915 Dodge became an immediate hit and, by 1916, Budd was building 500 bodies a day for Dodge. That year Budd also began making detachable steel tops for Dodge Brothers touring cars. And formed the Budd Wheel Co. to produce wire wheels. And Budd would soon make steel disc wheels under license from the French company, Michelin. By 1919, Budd was likewise producing *mostly* steel bodies (with some wood still in them) for the nation's two

biggest automakers, Ford and Willys-Overland.

In 1920, Budd started production of all-steel *sedan* bodies for Dodge, but that year's recession plus the sedan's fairly steep price kept it from selling in quantity. It wasn't until 1921, when Budd was asked by Hudson to help design the inexpensive Essex coach body, that closed cars started coming into their own. By this time, Budd's customers included Ford, Dodge, Willys-Overland, Studebaker, Hudson and Chalmers.

Budd held patents on the technology and machines needed to make steel car bodies. In 1916, the company offered these patents, usually for a nominal licensing fee, to anyone who wanted to make use of them. Budd licensed Citroen in France and Morris in England to make all-steel bodies in 1924-25. In 1926, Budd established Ambi-Budd of Germany and Pressed Steel of Great Britain. By this time, advances in welding and presswork made all-steel bodies even less expensive than they'd been for Dodge, but even so, since diemaking took a bigger investment than the then-common machinery used to work wood, it wasn't always economical to tool up an all-steel body unless the automaker expected to sell *a lot* of identical cars. This limitation made Budd an unsuitable supplier for small- and medium-sized body customers. In addition, since Budd had its main stamping plant in Philadelphia, shipping usually added to the cost of Budd bodies and components.

Budd helped engineer a great number of smaller pressed-steel parts which the company then sometimes made and supplied to specific automakers and sometimes didn't. Budd carried out body engineering work, both major and minor, for the 1929 front-drive Ruxton, the 1934 Chrysler Airflow, the 1936 Lincoln Zephyr, the unit-bodied 1941 Nash 600, the 1948 stepdown Hudson, the 1951 Aero Willys, the 1953 Studebaker and both generations of 1955-60 Ford Thunderbirds. Thunderbird bodies, in fact, were almost totally built by Budd during those years, as were some parts for the Aero Willys.

In its early years, Budd maintained a tiny styling staff under Joseph Ledwinka. This department turned out styling and engineering presentations for a number of customers and potential customers. Budd,

---

formed the Low Emissions Paint Consortium and explored powder coatings. Powder coatings could be applied dry, electrostatically, with virtually zero emissions. But the initial problem with powder coatings was a lack of surface gloss. In an attempt to solve that, Ford installed a pilot program in its Wixom plant in 1995 to test a new type of powdered clearcoat.

All three U.S. automakers are spending millions on developing workable powder paint systems.

Meanwhile, the future promises an eye-popping range of new special-effect, or "chameleon," colors. These range from irridescents through candyapples to holographic finishes. BASF is working on a paint whose color can be

changed not by varying its basic chemistry but by simply tossing in different-colored flakes. In other words, instead of having to go through the expensive process of mixing a new batch of paint for every color, the basic solvent remains the same. What changes is the addition of colored, microscopic flakes of mica or aluminum. And these flakes give the finish an irridescence that's fast becoming popular.

DuPont, meanwhile, is experimenting with what it calls "holographic" paints. These give a total color shift as the angle of viewing changes. A portion of a car body might look green in one angle of sunlight and then purple in another. As the car moves and the body surface changes highlights, the colors constantly dart around the rainbow. Again, the finish has an irridescent sheen plus the tiny points-of-light brilliance of a metalflake. Such paints are still very expensive, but as development continues, prices promise to come down. ◆

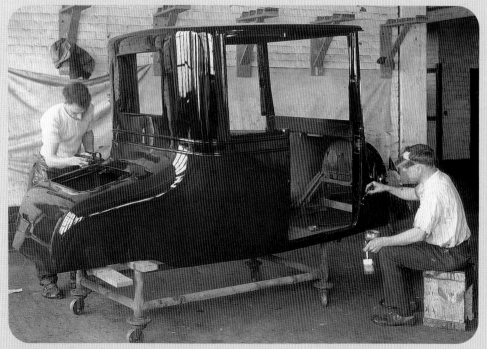

Master painters brushed on final color coats of varnish, then sealed them with 2 to 3 coats of clear. They left no brush marks, used a second brush to remove airborne lint and "lice" that inevitably landed on the slow-drying finish. Photo depicts Fisher Body scene circa 1920.

When Wood was Good

The earliest automobile bodies followed carriage practice and were made mostly of wood. The 1903 Winton's body, for one, was totally wood, right down to the fenders. Wood was not only traditional but, in those days, plentiful and inexpensive.

All major car and body manufacturers, including Ford, Fisher, Briggs, Murray and Hayes, owned huge tracts of timberland and were committed to using wood on a large scale. Fisher, for example, had hardwood forests in upper Michigan and Arkansas, sawmills in Louisiana and a huge woodworking plant in Memphis.

From 1905 through the mid-1930s, most car bodies were framed in wood and covered with sheetmetal skins. This type of construction was called "composite." Most bodymakers preferred ash for the main, structural framework, luxury coachbuilders often specifying second-growth ash because it had a longer grain and held screws better. Ash was relatively lightweight, cured rapidly, was easy to saw and shape, and resisted warpage.

But by 1923, ash had become over-harvested and costly. So mass producers like Fisher and Briggs switched from ash to maple and elm for primary frame members. Maple was less shock-absorbent than ash, took longer to season properly and didn't hold screws quite so well. And elm generally showed more variation than either ash or maple. Yet maple and elm accounted for 51% of all types of wood used in automobile bodies by 1923. Oak was next at 10% and was found mainly in commercial and truck bodies.

Unlike all-steel bodies, whose shapes were hard to revise because they required expensive dies and presswork, the styling of wood-framed bodies could be changed fairly easily by redesigning and reshaping the wooden frame members and then re-forming the sheetmetal over them. For mass production, wooden pieces could be gang-sawed and shaped either by hand or with simple milling machinery. Jigs were made so that larger individual body parts, like roofs and door framing, could be built up as subassemblies. Complicated shapes, like rear wheelhouses, were sometimes made up from as many as 10 individual pieces of wood, which had to be glued and screwed together in special jigs. These subassemblies came together in ever-bigger jigs until they formed the framing for an entire automobile body.

Not only was the process of woodworking time consuming and labor intensive, but wood was heavy and difficult to store and ship. It took months to cure properly: 90 days in the open air, then various periods in special kilns. By 1927, Fisher kept a permanent stock on hand of 21 million board feet in its curing yards plus another four million in its kilns. Moisture content was reduced from 31% to 5% (or from 45% to 5% by the "oven-dry" method of calculating).

Even when properly seasoned, screws and glue would loosen. "Squeaks and rattles," wrote George Mercer in 1926, "will to some extent be noticeable with any known method of body construction; to reduce to a minimum the cause for same is all that the manufacturer can expect." Composite bodies tended to become loose and flexible with age. As the wood degenerated, doors would commonly sag on their hinges.

Another problem with wood was wastage. The Forest Products Laboratory estimated in 1924 that nearly 50% of all wood that entered an automobile body plant left as scrap. Henry Ford tried to put some of the waste to use by converting wood scraps into charcoal briquets and selling them to weekend barbequers (the "Ford" in Kingsford-brand charcoal traces its name back to that effort).

Two factors eventually made composite bodies obsolete. The first was baked enamel, which dried quickly but required temperatures that set wood ablaze. The second involved a rising public awareness that all-steel bodies were frankly

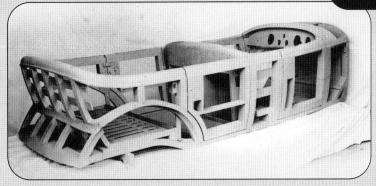

Wooden body framing got heavier as cars evolved. Relatively lightweight framing from 1908 (top left) contrasts with the heavier members used to frame the 1920 Premier (left). Second-growth ash was the preferred wood, but automakers soon used it all up. Many body- and automakers owned huge tracts of timberland.

better—more rattle- and squeakfree, safer and longer-lasting—than composite types. And as production runs grew larger, the costs of dies, tools and presswork for steel bodies could be amortized over more and more units, so steel bodies eventually became less expensive than composite ones.

General Motors (Fisher) was the last major U.S. holdout to use composite body construction. The Fisher Brothers, of course, had grown up in the tradition of woodworking, which probably had a lot to do with their conservatism.

GM launched several propaganda campaigns during the late 1920s and early '30s to show that carbodies needed both steel and wood for maximum strength and durability. They used as their illustration a wooden dowel tightly wrapped in a thin sheet of steel. Alone, the steel tube could be easily bent and the wooden dowel was easy to snap. Together, they reinforced each other and were nearly impossible to break. This made a convincing, graphic illustration.

What GM didn't mention was that a steel dowel inside a thin steel tube, or two steel tubes, were even stronger. General Motors kept building composite bodies until the 1937 model year. ◆

Budd championed all-steel automobile bodies and pioneered them with such cars as the popular 1915 Dodge (top left). One benefit of getting the wood out was that it allowed the use of baked enamel, which cut painting time to one day. Budd also helped Dodge design its bodies, as evidenced by the 1925 scale clay coupe (above) and the full-sized sedan half model (left). In 1930, Budd tried to sell Plymouth on a lower, more stylish sedan (below), with a raked windshield and more integrated cowl. Photo shows Budd's proposal behind a production 1930 Plymouth sedan.

for example, tried to take some of Chrysler's business away from Briggs in 1930 by building a spec body for the 1931 Plymouth. This Plymouth proposal was approximately four inches lower than the 1930 Plymouth and considerably more advanced and modern looking. Budd made the same sort of presentation—successful this time—to Citroen on the first *traction avant* (front-wheel-drive) model.

Budd also hired Gordon Buehrig in late 1936, after the Cord empire collapsed, and asked him to create a modern styling studio in Detroit. Buehrig did and then hired a small staff of designers, who turned out a number of auto and truck proposals for Budd, including an easy-to-build economy compact called the "Wowser." But due to disagreements and political problems with Budd's sales vice president, none of Buehrig's designs was ever shown to potential customers, so Buehrig resigned in late 1938. At that point, Joseph Ledwinka resumed control of Budd's styling section and continued to make spec body proposals, one of which became the 1941 Nash 600. (Ledwinka's brother, Hans, was chief engineer of the Czech automaker, Tatra. Neither

brother showed any fear of radical engineering. Both aggressively promoted such concepts as front-wheel drive and rear engines.)

During the 1930s, Budd diversified into aircraft and railcars, building thousands of stainless-steel railway passenger cars. After World War II, the company formed divisions that made highway trailers, wheels and brakes, industrial and automotive plastics, high-tech measuring equipment, components for communications satellites, plus products for the nuclear and aerospace industries.

Budd also continued to make autobody parts. In the 1970s, they supplied Ford Motor Co. with major stampings for Lincolns and Marks; also Chrysler Corp. with body panels for Dodge vans. But Budd's automotive customers were by then building most of their own bodies, and in 1978 Budd was acquired by the German conglomerate Thyssen AG. The Budd Co., now headquartered in Troy, Michigan, supplies mostly frames for trucks and utility vehicles, stampings for cars and vans, molded plastic exterior body panels, plus wheels, hubs, brake parts and foundry products. ◆

CHAPTER 5

THE COACHBUILDERS

Brewster chief designer Beck goes over a full-sized chalk drawing of a 1930 Rolls-Royce towncar with a client inside the company's Long Island plant.

From the very beginning, of course, coach-builders catered to clients who, above all, valued distinctiveness and craftsmanship. By 1916, the well-to-do were ordering custom automobile bodies almost as nonchalantly as custom-tailored suits. Special bodies had become *de rigueur* among society's upper strata, especially in the more style-conscious cities from New York to San Francisco.

Donald McLeod Lay wrote in *The Automobile* in 1916 that, "There is a large class in the United States that prides itself upon its fastidious tastes in every phase of existence. It aims to be distinctive, individual, and to have everything in life correspond. Clothes must be smart, elegant and well tailored; homes must be artistic backgrounds for personalities; food must be dainty and delicately prepared and must represent the most exquisite dishes money can buy; and...throughout the establishment, everything must be in keeping with these standards.

"To-day the number of firms designing and building [automobile] bodies for the custom trade is growing almost from day to day. New concerns are springing up in all parts of New York City and neighboring districts, while old established coachmakers find that the...bulk of their trade [is now] in special bodies for automobiles.

"From present indications it would seem that the American custom body trade is graduating from a mere local occupation of negligible importance to a branch of the great automobile industry which will be national in scope, and involving thousands of men and immense capital.... The accelerated activity in the custom body field in New York City is significant of what may be expected, though probably to a lesser degree, first in the other large centers of population and later in the smaller communities."

The archetypal coachbuilder, the Grand Mother of that tightly knit trade, the revered name from the golden days of carriagemaking was undoubtedly Brewster. The Brewster magic continued into the 1930s, and to understand the firm's significance in the overall scheme of design and craftsmanship, we need to take a short course not only in Brewster history but in the history of all the significant east- and west-coast coachbuilders. ➜

Brewster & Co.

Founder James Brewster was descended from Elder William Brewster, who came over on the Mayflower in 1620. James started a carriage factory in 1810 in New Haven, Connecticut and soon became that city's most respected volume and quality carriagemaker.

James Brewster had two sons, James B. and Henry, and for a time each son acted as manager of Brewster's branch offices in New York City and Bridgeport, Connecticut. After working for their father for a few years, both sons decided to strike out on their own. Suddenly there were three carriagemaking Brewsters, each competing for the name and the Brewster reputation. The prestige of the Brewster name went to Henry's company when, in 1878, it won international acclaim at the Paris carriage exposition. Henry Brewster's 13 entries received the highest honors and a gold medal.

The family's infighting eventually cooled, and Henry's son, William (Willie) Brewster, inherited Brewster & Co. Willie began making automobile bodies in 1905 and had stopped building carriages by 1911. Willie recognized that carbodies held far greater potential than carriages, so he moved the Brewster plant from midtown Manhattan to much larger quarters in Long Island City, just over the Queensboro bridge.

Brewster & Co. had been an early American sales agent for the French automaker Delaunay-Belleville. In 1914, they switched to the Rolls-Royce franchise. Under this arrangement, Rolls-Royce sent chassis over from England, and Brewster added custom bodies here. Brewster designed and built 46 bodies for Rolls-Royce customers between mid 1914 and America's entry into World War I, when chassis shipments stopped. Brewster bodies were very much to Rolls-Royce standards and specifications; no surprise because Brewster had been the standard of American coachbuilding long before Rolls-Royce began producing automobiles.

Brewster maintained a fair-sized design and drafting department, and among those who worked there in the late teens and early '20s were Ray Dietrich, Tom Hibbard, George Snyder, Henry Crecelius, Eugene T. (Bob) Gregorie, Philip Brostom and J.J. St. Croix. Dietrich and Hibbard founded LeBaron Carrossiers in late 1920. Henry Crecelius moved to Lincoln to become chief body engineer under Edsel Ford. George Snyder later went to General Motors and Ford. Bob Gregorie became Edsel Ford's mentor and design chief in 1932, and Brostom and St. Croix are noteworthy because both won top honors and cash prizes in the 1922 Body Builders' design competition.

According to Francis N. Howard, writing in the Rolls-Royce Owners' Club's *Flying Lady,* "Most of the prominent people in those days owned one R-R chassis and two bodies, a closed one for winter and an open one for summer. The bodies were usually painted in special family colors. Some used the color schemes of their horseracing silks. J.P. Morgan's was dark bottle green. The Vanderbilts had a special maroon, and the Astors and Stevenses had special blues.... Most of their cars had black tops and undercarriages. Some families had two sets of colors, a darker one for the winter car and lighter, cooler-looking ones for the touring cars used in summertime."

The trick for Brewster was to add colors for new customers without offending established clients. Brewster ground and mixed its own pigments and kept a roomful of elaborate color matches. "The extent," said *Autobody* magazine in Dec. 1921, "to which the demands for exclusive family colors is carried can best be appreciated by a visit to their [Brewster's] grinding room where there are on exhibition several thousand small panels, each bearing the color of some customer, differing at least in shade from that of any of its neighbors. Many Brewster automobile bodies today carry the same colors as the ante-bellum carriages of the owners' ancestors." The "several thousand" panels would imply at least half that number of clients.

Bamboo canework was another of Brewster's fortes. They had master craftsmen who did canework in the painstaking "French style." This meant mixing a cane-colored, paste-like, slow-drying paint that an artisan applied layer over layer through a self-feeding tube. This was a time-consuming, tedious process that often took weeks to finish (on top of the weeks it took to hand-varnish the entire body; see sidebar on page 31). But Brewster liked the French style better than the faster fabric back-ed canework that was glued on over the finish. Fabric-backed caning had a tendency to chip and flake after a few seasons. French canework, on the other hand, became tougher and more attractive as it aged.

One of the services Brewster and other coachbuilders offered was the storage and maintenance of customers' off-season bodies. These rested side by side in long rows on the fifth and sixth floors of Brewster's Long Island body plant. A crew of maintenance workers dusted the stored bodies daily, chamoi-

Brewster specialized in conservative towncars before being bought out by Rolls-Royce in 1925. The oval radiator was a Brewster hallmark.

sed them weekly, and painters would refinish any that looked less than perfect. When the seasons changed, there would be a flurry of chauffeurs bringing their employers' cars in for the installation of next season's bodies.

When planning new custom coachwork, Brewster went so far as to measure patrons and their chauffeurs to get seating dimensions right. Seat springs could be ordered soft, medium or firm. Special bamboo canework beneath the seats allowed them to "breathe." Brewster pioneered such innovations as roll-up windows, the "retreating" windshield to counter glare and reflections, and disappearing jumpseats.

Brewster manufactured its own cars from 1915 (1916 models) to 1925, again and always to the very highest standards. Brewster automobiles were recognizable by their oval radiator. Bodies were mostly towncars, and many mechanical components, like brakes and suspension, were copied from Rolls-Royce. Brewster built not only their own bodies but also their own Knight sleeve-valve engines under license.

In 1919, Rolls-Royce of America Inc. opened offices and manufacturing facilities in Springfield, Massachusetts. Rolls-Royce built complete chassis in this country, but the company also realized the need

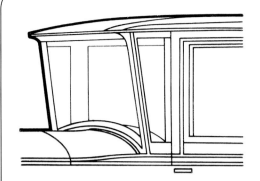
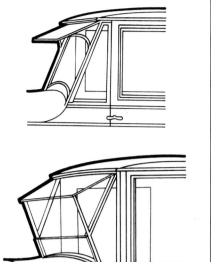

Another Brewster hallmark was the retreating "clear vision" windshield (above). The idea was to make the pillars thin without compromising roof strength. Other automakers introduced variations on the clear-vision theme throughout the late teens and 1920s (right).

Initially owned by industrialist/playboy Tommy Manville, Rolls-Royce "windblown" coupe (top left), was built for the 1930 New York Salon. Aluminum-bodied 1929 York roadster (top right) and Derby tourer (center left) sport Brewster wheel discs plus coved, buffed belt molding. Brewster towncar (center right) featured hand-applied canework, carriage lamps, severe razor-edge styling. (Bottom) In 1935, actress Constance Bennett bought a 1930 Rolls-Royce and had Brewster rebody it with this swoopy towncar. She and her car were smash hits at that year's Academy Awards.

After Rolls-Royce cast Brewster loose, John Inskip kept the company going by creating coachbuilt bodies on mostly Ford and Buick chassis. What gave these cars personality were their heart-shaped grilles and flying fenders.

Brewster *continued*

for a range of standard bodies. These were supplied by a number of coachbuilders under the name "Rolls-Royce Custom Coach Work." The major body suppliers, then, were Merrimac, who built mostly open bodies; Willoughby and Holbrook, who specialized in limousines; and the company's own Waltham Avenue works. A number of additional independent east-coast coachbuilders also built custom bodies for Rolls-Royce, among them the Springfield Body Co., Biddle & Smart and Brewster.

In Oct. 1925, Rolls-Royce bought Brewster & Co. outright, and after that approximately 425-430 American Rolls-Royce were fitted with Brewster bodies. John S. Inskip, who became president of Rolls-Royce of America around 1930, received credit for designing the Ascot and Derby series plus a number of individual bodies. Inskip and others on Brewster's staff, notably George Snyder, designed perhaps the most strikingly exquisite custom bodies of their day. A few, like the Constance Bennett car, were surprisingly, unusually daring, especially considering Rolls-Royce's reputation for conservatism. And quality, without question, remained a given.

American Rolls-Royce bodies were built in Brewster's Long Island plant, but instead of shipping them to Springfield to be mounted, a factory chauffeur would test-drive each bare chassis

down to Long Island City, and the bodies were installed there. Since most Rolls-Royce were sold from the company's showroom on Fifth Avenue at 53rd Street, factory chauffeurs usually took the train from Long Island City back to Springfield.

Rolls-Royce of America Inc., stopped manufacturing chassis in 1931, but Brewster continued to build bodies. Brewster sought new business among old customers by offering to rebody cars that were five years old or older, and the rebody program included fabricating new fenders, updating accessories like lamps and adding more modern bumpers.

The company went into receivership in 1934 and reorganized as the Springfield Manufacturing Co., with John Inskip again as president. Rolls-Royce was now out of the picture, but Inskip kept Brewster, at least in name, as a maker of custom bodies on less expensive chassis. Starting in 1934, Brewster bodies, designed by Inskip, appeared mostly on Ford and Buick chassis. A few were also built with Lincoln and Cadillac mechanicals. It was Inskip, in fact, who designed the flying fenders and heart-shaped grille that gave the 1934-36 Brewsters their identity and flair. The idea behind these moderately priced luxury towncars, convertible sedans and convertible coupes was to provide wealthy customers with inexpensive yet stylish and well-built substitutes for the huge, highly visible vehicles they'd come out of. But the latter-day Brewster, too, faltered and, in 1938, the company went out of business. ◆

LeBaron Carrossiers

Another important early body design firm, coachbuilder and an indirect descendant of Brewster was LeBaron. Ray Dietrich and Tom Hibbard formulated plans for LeBaron in 1919 while they worked at drafting tables across the aisle from each other in Brewster's Long Island design department.

Their initial concept was simple. They would provide a design service; would design and engineer automotive coachwork the way architects design homes. This was not an altogether new idea: From 1909 to 1918, George Mercer had an office in New York, listing himself as an independent autobody designer, draftsman and consultant. The sign on Mercer's door read "Automobile Body Architect." And freelance designer George P. Harvey also opened a Manhattan office in 1916 for the same purpose.

Like Mercer and Harvey, Dietrich and Hibbard would design carbodies but wouldn't build them. For that, they would contract with independent coachbuilders. And their customers needn't be just private individuals. They might also be the agents who sold luxury cars or, in time, the auto manufacturers themselves.

While still with Brewster, Dietrich and Hibbard spent many a lunch hour talking

and working out the details of their idea. Their boss, Willie Brewster, heard rumors, called Dietrich into his office, and asked if the tales were true. Dietrich conceded they were, whereupon Willie said he was sorry to hear it, because Dietrich and Hibbard might steal some of Brewster's designs. Besides, it smacked of insubordination and disloyalty. After telling Ray that an independent design business didn't stand a chance (a statement perhaps based on Mercer's earlier experience), Brewster fired both Dietrich and Hibbard.

So in the spring of 1920, these two young men, all of 26 and 22 respectively, found themselves out on their own. Needed immediately were a prestigious address and a French-sounding name. For the name, legend has it that they consulted the Manhattan phone directory. Wanting the name to sound very, very French, they quickly settled on LeBaron and added the French word for coachbuilders: Carrossiers.

LeBaron Carrossiers soon found space at #2 Columbus

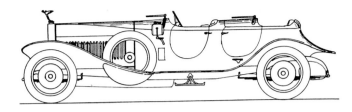

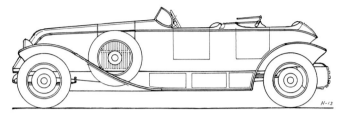

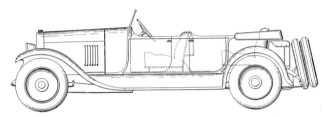

That's LeBaron's catalogue logo on the opposite page. On this page, the sketches above are typical of those LeBaron produced on spec and sold for $25 apiece to dealers and distributors in and around New York in the early 1920s. That's a 1924 Isotta-Fraschini at the top, a 1925 Renault sport phaeton beneath it and a 1926 Cadillac phaeton just above. The 1931 Stutz (below) was masterfully rendered by Roland Stickney and appeared in LeBaron's catalogue that season. Briggs acquired LeBaron in 1927.

Edsel Ford kept close tabs on all custom Lincolns, including the austere, molding-less 1929 Lincoln LeBaron towncar (top). As part of Briggs, Ralph Roberts and LeBaron's styling staff also submitted body designs to production automakers. Two LeBaron-designed production cars were the 1931 Marmon V-16 (above) and 1934 Franklin V-12 (below). Franklin's and Imperial's hoods flowed back over the cowl.

Collectors agree that the 1931-33 Chrysler Imperials have to be among LeBaron's most beautiful designs.

LeBaron *continued*

Circle, in the same building as Fleetwood's New York sales office. These digs were far too expensive, Dietrich recalled later, but LeBaron could not skimp on this most essential part of their image.

Dietrich, in his autobiography in *The Classic Car,* vividly recounts living on bologna sandwiches in the early days of LeBaron. The fledgling design firm had no customers at first, so Dietrich and Hibbard filled their time knocking out office walls, sanding the floor, remodeling and painting. They also made complete sets of sweeps so they could later use them for both scale and full-sized drawings. They went around to all the New York automobile agencies, showing their portfolios to the sales managers and trying to sell their services. For what seemed like the longest time, no one responded.

LeBaron's first customer was Grover C. Parvis, the Packard branch manager in New York. Parvis commissioned a design of a seven-passenger Packard limousine. LeBaron provided full-sized working drawings and charged Parvis $50 for all rights to the design plus $400 for the working drawings. Fleetwood built the body.

When word got out that Parvis had bought designs from LeBaron, other car agents suddenly became interested. Dietrich and Hibbard then retraced their steps, this time offering pre-drawn designs for $25 each. These were 1/12-scale, pen-and-ink side views—original sketches—that the agency sales people could show to potential body clients. If a customer liked a particular design, LeBaron would provide color renderings. LeBaron was also able to put the job out for bid and offered to send working drafts to the commissioned coachbuilder. As a result of their door-to-door campaign, the New York Lincoln dealer ordered three body styles from LeBaron in late 1921: a roadster, a dual-cowl phaeton and a berline, all to be built in groups of 10.

With business finally coming alive, Dietrich and Hibbard took in Ralph S. Roberts as a third LeBaron partner. Roberts, who'd always had a burning desire to become an auto designer, had visited Hibbard previously at Leon Rubay in Cleveland. Hibbard had given Roberts, a Dartmouth student at the time, the grand tour of Rubay's body plant. After Roberts graduated, he wrote Hibbard for a job. Dietrich and Hibbard agreed

that they could use a business manager, so they offered Roberts not just a job but a full partnership, with a 1/3 interest in the business. Roberts borrowed $700 from his mother to buy in.

Because several coachbuilders had misinterpreted LeBaron's early designs—by accident or on purpose—Dietrich and Hibbard soon made it a habit to visit each bodyshop to ensure that their ideas were being executed properly. This involved travel time, but everyone agreed that the extra effort paid off.

The height of each year's coachbuilding season was the annual round of automobile Salons (see page 23). In the early 1920s, firms like LeBaron counted on a good number of sales at America's three major Salons: New York, Chicago and Los Angeles. Dietrich, in his autobiography, mentioned how pleased he was in 1922 when LeBaron, only two years old, was asked to take part in the Hotel Commodore Salon. Unfortunately, LeBaron's first Salon car, an Isotta-Fraschini convertible four-door cabriolet built by Derham, contained a terrible mistake. The rear window frames, which folded inward and down flush with the insides of the doors, were square and larger than the rounded door cutouts. So they wouldn't let the doors open or close with the window frames folded. LeBaron showed this car the only way possible, with the top and window frames up. Luckily, the woman who bought this ill-fated Isotta asked that the top be made stationary, and that solved the problem.

By this time, the LeBaron partners had deals going with any number of Manhattan sales agents. Wealthy New Yorkers still loved the big imports, so foreign-made cars were selling well. Each imported chassis brought with it the opportunity to design and market special coachwork. The

sales agents quickly recognized that the coachbuilders, including LeBaron, could, with a little grease, steer sales their way. So LeBaron was now designing bodies for the agencies that handled Mercedes-Benz, Rolls-Royce, Minerva, Delage, Fiat, Hispano-Suiza, Isotta-Fraschini and Renault. Agents with American franchises included Packard, Lincoln, Locomobile, Pierce-Arrow, Cadillac and LaFayette.

In 1922-23, LeBaron landed two factory assignments. The first was to design eight body styles for Henry M. Crane's new Crane-Simplex, a short-lived car for which very few bodies were actually built. The second contract called for seven body types for W.C. Durant's newest and most prestigious acquisition, Locomobile. The Locomobile job required sample bodies to be designed by LeBaron and built by different coachbuilders: Brewster, Demarest, Ostruk, McFarlan and Locke. (Durant also asked LeBaron to submit production-body designs for his new Flint and Princeton lines. Durant asked J. Frank de Causse to likewise submit designs for the Flint, and Durant ultimately chose de Causse's designs over LeBaron's. Later Flint production bodies were designed by George S. Daniels.)

LeBaron's problem #1 with the Locomobile assignment: a tight deadline. Problem #2: Dietrich now needed to create and submit different types of drafts for the Locomobile bodies to conform with each builder's special manufacturing methods. Problem #3: Dietrich had to cover considerable distance driving from one coachbuilder's shop to the other to keep tabs on construction. And problem #4: LeBaron was also anxious to expand into France.

So 1923 became the year when Tom Hibbard left for Europe, ostensibly to set up a LeBaron office in Paris. But once there, Hibbard set himself up with another

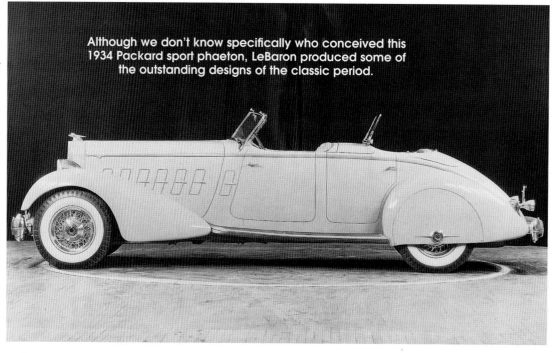

Although we don't know specifically who conceived this 1934 Packard sport phaeton, LeBaron produced some of the outstanding designs of the classic period.

American, Howard A. (Dutch) Darrin, perhaps partly because Dietrich had spread himself so thin with the Locomobile account. Another factor that might have contributed to Hibbard's leaving LeBaron: Behind what looked like a prosperous venture, the company wasn't really doing that well. Whatever the reasons, Hibbard sold his LeBaron stock to the other two partners and stayed in Paris with Dutch Darrin.

LeBaron had done design work for the Leland Lincoln and for several Lincoln agents but nothing yet for Edsel Ford.

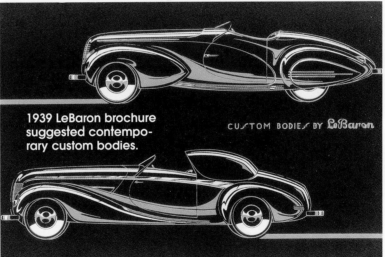

1934 Packard LeBaron roadster complemented sport phaeton opposite and fastback coupe on page 221.

1939 LeBaron brochure suggested contemporary custom bodies.

CUSTOM BODIES BY LeBaron

In Dec. 1923, Dietrich got a call to meet Edsel at the Commodore Salon. The two men toured the exhibits together and immediately struck up a friendship, in part because Edsel impressed Dietrich with his knowledge of design and body construction. Edsel confided his dream to make the Lincoln America's premier luxury car, and would LeBaron help him? Dietrich wrote later that he felt very flattered by Edsel's request.

Meanwhile, in addition to Locomobile, LeBaron began picking up more car companies as clients, including Packard. Packard had resisted LeBaron's sales efforts for some time, but several custom Packards that LeBaron had designed were so successful and in such demand that Packard agreed to include LeBaron designs in its dealer catalogues. Orders for LeBaron designs began to pour in to Packard headquarters.

LeBaron also "ghosted" for Fleetwood. Fleetwood, being in the same building as LeBaron on Columbus Circle, commissioned specific designs, then built them and took full credit. LeBaron didn't mind. In addition, according to Ralph Roberts, LeBaron ghosted for Demarest and Locke, and Franklin and Rolls-Royce contracted with LeBaron to provide designs for their production and custom bodies.

Even with all this work in hand, LeBaron still wasn't showing a profit. And then an opportunity arose in late 1923 that would let Roberts and Dietrich improve the firm's financial picture. Clarence W. Seward and James H. Hinman, owners of the Bridgeport Body Co. in Bridgeport, Connecticut were willing to let LeBaron become their design partners in exchange for stock. This arrangement looked good to all concerned. It would give Bridgeport an

up-and-coming design staff and, at the same time, would benefit LeBaron by allowing it to go into the coachbuilding business. LeBaron would no longer just design bodies and farm them out. Through Bridgeport, LeBaron would share in the profits of fabrication. Why pass that income along to outside coachbuilders?

Another consideration that made the new partnership appealing: Roberts and Dietrich often had a hard time, especially before a salon, finding independent coachbuilders who could turn out LeBaron's custom designs on a tight deadline. Too often, the good shops around New York were already busy with other rush jobs.

So on Jan. 7, 1924, LeBaron merged with the Bridgeport Body Co. The resulting company was renamed LeBaron Inc., the principal shareholders being Roberts and Dietrich with 105 shares each, and Seward and Hinman owning 100 shares apiece. Seward became LeBaron's president, with Hinman as company treasurer. Dietrich held the title vice president, and Roberts became LeBaron Inc.'s secretary.

Now, with its Bridgeport affiliation, LeBaron Inc. began to build the bodies that Dietrich designed. Roberts says that at that point he managed the office but did no designing. This meant Dietrich spent considerable time traveling to and from the plant, which again had the effect of spread-

ing him thinner than was comfortable. So LeBaron Inc. hired Roland L. Stickney and Werner Gubitz as delineators and illustrators. Both had worked previously for Frank de Causse at Locomobile, and Gubitz would later become top man on Packard's small design staff. Hinman and Seward, meanwhile, ran the Bridgeport body plant and oversaw the 50 or so craftsmen working there.

At that point, Lincoln became LeBaron's biggest customer, thanks to the relationship forged when Edsel Ford met Ray Dietrich at the 1923 New York Salon. Edsel, in fact, now wanted LeBaron to become a part of the Murray Corp. of America, the company that built most of Lincoln's production bodies. So in 1925, Edsel asked Murray president Allan Sheldon to try to get the LeBaron partners to relocate to Detroit. It made sense to have LeBaron's design staff in the same city as Lincoln and Murray. LeBaron might, in time, become Lincoln's exclusive design studio and even the foundation of some future Ford design staff. With Edsel's backing, Shelden made the LeBaron partners an offer for 51% of their shares.

Both Roberts and Dietrich were basically willing to sell and come to Detroit, but only if they could keep control of LeBaron. They'd part with 49% of LeBaron Inc. but not 51%. Then, too, there was the problem of Hinman and Seward in Bridgeport. Their partnership was so new that, as Roberts put it in a letter to Shelden, "...both Mr. Dietrich and I have decided that we should not care to climb, no matter to what heights, by stepping on [Seward's and Hinman's] shoulders, and we are certain that you and your associates will agree with us, Mr. Shelden, that ours would be a weak foundation if laid on the ruins of those who have helped us." Roberts mentioned in the same letter that, "...they [Seward and Hinman] have tided us over a crisis that otherwise would probably have put us out of business."

Shelden now invited Dietrich and Roberts to Detroit, ostensibly to inspect Murray's facilities, but everyone knew it was to make a final offer for LeBaron Inc. Roberts was sick in bed with the flu, but Dietrich wanted to go. Before Dietrich left,

Roberts said to him, "Ray, just promise me you won't sign anything.... You can look and talk, but don't sign." Ray agreed not to.

"Very soon thereafter," according to Roberts, "I got a telegram. It said, 'Sorry, I've accepted this proposition for myself.' That was kind of a tough one. I've had other experiences that disappointed me, but this was one of them...." Roberts said that he and Dietrich had been like brothers.

What happened: When Dietrich arrived in Detroit, Shelden told him that Edsel Ford wanted his design talent more than LeBaron Inc. Shelden proposed to Dietrich that Murray set him, and him alone, up as their custom body designer and coachbuilder. Murray would give Dietrich 50% of a new corporation to be called Dietrich Inc., and would provide him with a separate, dedicated manufacturing plant.

The offer overwhelmed Dietrich. In Feb. 1925, he sold his stake in LeBaron to his other three partners and moved his family to Detroit; moved, in fact, right across the street on Jefferson Avenue from Edsel Ford's house. Ray Dietrich and Edsel Ford would soon be taking long evening walks together, chatting as they strolled the neighborhood.

LeBaron, despite dire predictions, seemed to get along fine without Dietrich and Hibbard. Ralph Roberts and artist Roland Stickney worked well together. Roberts became the idea man and Stickney put those ideas on paper. Roberts could phone Stickney from a client's office, outline his thoughts and, by the time he reached his own office, Stickney would have a rough sketch waiting. Roberts kept up LeBaron's contracts and turned out a succession of very good designs.

In 1927, with merger fever in the air, Walter Briggs approached Roberts and asked if he and the Bridgeport partners would be willing to sell LeBaron. The Briggs proposal seemed too good to pass

up, and Roberts, speaking for Hinman and Seward, said yes. Stickney, though, who refused to travel anywhere west of the Hudson River, wasn't interested in going to Detroit. He went first to Judkins, then did illustrations for Rollston and Brewster, and later worked for Henry Dreyfuss.

The Briggs deal called for Roberts to move to Detroit and continue to manage LeBaron. LeBaron would be Briggs' in-house custom body design center and coachbuilder, just as Dietrich Inc. was now Murray's. Briggs soon also hired John Tjaarda, who'd worked at Locke and GM Art & Colour. Roberts and Tjaarda were given roughly equal status and responsibilities, Roberts having more say in design and Tjaarda overseeing experimental body engineering and prototypes. (For detail on Briggs' styling services, see page 157.)

Briggs sold its body manufacturing plants, along with the LeBaron name, to Chrysler Corp. in 1953. Chrysler still used the name in 1994. Fleetwood and LeBaron were the only names of classic coachbuilders that survived into the 1990s. ◆

Hibbard & Darrin

LeBaron, in 1923, produced a spinoff, Hibbard & Darrin, which also proved influential in American car design although the company was based in Paris. And here we have to backtrack a bit.

Fresh out of high school, Thomas L. Hibbard went to work for French-born auto designer/coachbuilder/manufacturer Leon Rubay in early 1916. Rubay had been hired a few years earlier by White in Cleveland to style and build their production bodies (see page 72). He hired Hibbard on the strength of Hibbard's masterfully rendered car sketches.

The next year, the C.P. Kimball & Co. in Chicago hired Hibbard away from Rubay and gave him free rein as a designer. As one of his duties at Kimball, Hibbard took his portfolio on the road and became something of a door-to-door salesman. He sold Kimball's custom bodies to midwestern auto dealers and wealthy private customers. Hibbard was still with Kimball when he enlisted in the Army Signal Corps and was shipped off to France. It was there that he learned French. After the war, the Paris coachbuilder Kellner et Freres offered Hibbard a job, but the army wouldn't release him, and he had to go back to the U.S. to muster out.

Discharged in early 1919, Hibbard took a job as a designer/draftsman with Brewster & Co. in New York. At the drawingboard next to him sat Ray Dietrich, who'd already been with Brewster for a number of

years. The two young men became friends, and during shared lunches, Hibbard and Dietrich both decided to leave Brewster. When Willie Brewster heard about Dietrich and Hibbard's plans, he fired them both (see page 40), whereupon they established LeBaron Carrossiers.

How Dutch Darrin initially met Hibbard remains unclear. In his *The Classic Car* autobiography, Ray Dietrich said that Hibbard and Darrin had known each other in Europe during the war. Hibbard, however, contended that it was in the LeBaron offices that he first met Darrin. According to Hibbard, Darrin came in one day and proposed the idea of having American-designed custom bodies built in Europe and shipped here. At that time, European chassis cost less overseas, and overseas coachbuilders also charged considerably lower labor rates.

Ralph Roberts, however, mentioned that Darrin had been working with a fellow in New York named "Tiny" (Roberts couldn't remember Tiny's last name). Tiny bought and sold used luxury cars, and Darrin helped him. It was in that capacity that Darrin

Hibbard & Darrin patented the fully enclosed torpedo phaeton design, seen here on a 1928 Cadillac. V-shaped center pillars snapped in place.

In 1928, General Motors asked Hibbard & Darrin to submit five concept designs for possible production. H&D not only designed the cars but also built sample bodies. This was their proposal for a LaSalle sedan.

visited the LeBaron offices, but he never commissioned any custom automobile bodies.

In 1923, Paul Ostruk, the sometime coachbuilder and New York Minerva agent, asked LeBaron to design two bodies for him. The LeBaron-designed Ostruk bodies were to be built in Brussels, where coachbuilding rates were far lower than here, and then shipped to New York. Since Hibbard spoke French and had no

expensive on the continent than in America, because U.S. importers, including Paul Ostruk, shamelessly doubled and tripled wholesale prices. Better yet, none of Europe's luxury carmakers produced factory bodies. Customers had to contract for coachwork with independent builders. So Hibbard did find an address for LeBaron, in the Rue de Berg near the Champs Elysees, and LeBaron went so far as to print new letterhead with *New York and Paris* on it.

But at that point, Hibbard somehow bumped into Dutch Darrin in Paris. Roberts felt they probably just ran into each other at the Ritz bar, that famous watering hole where Americans wet their whistles. Roberts speculated that they started talking and Darrin, accomplished salesman that he was, convinced Hibbard to leave LeBaron and go into business with him.

The two Americans soon rented a showroom across the Champs Elysees from Kellner et Freres and started the same type of design business in Paris that LeBaron was doing in New York. LeBaron itself never did open a Paris office and eventually used its *New York and Paris* letterhead as scrap paper.

The firm of Hibbard & Darrin, meanwhile, took on the Minerva franchise in Paris. In their Minerva salesroom, the two designers could show potential customers original sketches, and they sometimes rendered these as part of their sales presentations. Generally speaking, rich Europeans accepted radical styling far more readily than their American counterparts.

H&D contracted initially with two Belgian coachbuilders, Van den Plas and d'Ieteren, to build Minerva custom bodies to their

Duesenberg towncar used H&D's patented Sylentlyte alloy construction. Doors and all major body skins were made of cast aluminum.

family commitments, it made sense to send him to Brussels to oversee construction of the Ostruk bodies. Roberts, in fact, remembered buying Hibbard a third-class steamship ticket and explained that money was still tight at LeBaron at that time.

The LeBaron partners decided that while Hibbard was overseas anyway, why not open a branch office in Paris? The plan was threefold: 1) to have Tom check out the possibility of saving money on coach-built bodies in Belgium, 2) to see whether there was a demand for independent design work in Europe and 3) to find a Paris address for LeBaron as prestigious as #2 Columbus Circle. Hibbard left for Paris in the spring of 1923.

Hibbard found that conditions overseas looked amazingly good. Europe was revitalizing after World War I, and wealthy Europeans needed new cars. Hibbard also found that chassis like Rolls-Royce, Hispano-Suiza and Minerva were considerably less

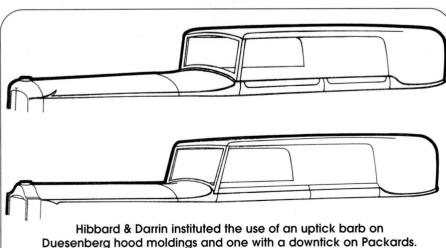

Hibbard & Darrin instituted the use of an uptick barb on Duesenberg hood moldings and one with a downtick on Packards. Packard received permission to use the H&D arrow in production.

Typical of the flair that Hibbard & Darrin put into their designs, the 1929 Stutz Blackhawk (above) advanced bold torpedo fender forms taken from the streamlined "wheel pants" of racing aircraft. Dutch Darrin, when he returned to the United States, designed and built Rolls-Royce towncar (right) in the European style.

specifications. Business was soon going nicely, and Hibbard recalled later that nearly half of all their cars were sold to wealthy North and South Americans passing through Paris. These travelers took out customs permits that somehow exempted them from paying duties.

Minerva's fortunes, however, soon began to sag, so H&D sold the franchise and opened a body operation of their own in the industrial Paris suburb of Puteaux. The Puteaux "plant" occupied an open quadrangle inside a huge apartment complex, and H&D

at one point employed as many as 200 workers. All were skilled panel beaters, sometimes hammering away on as many as 50 cars at a time. Hibbard said that the noise was horrible. Many of H&D's designs went to French auto dealers, and Paris had agents who not only handled the top European makes like Rolls-Royce, Mercedes and Hisso but also American luxury nameplates such as Duesenberg, Packard, Lincoln and Cadillac.

The flamboyant Dutch Darrin and the quieter, more reserved Tom Hibbard were held in high esteem by the French, partly because of their exotic American backgrounds and partly through their success in the system of French *concours d'elegance*. *Concours* were especially popular with young continental

More than One Way to Skin a Car

If there's another way to skin a car, bodymakers will find it. Through the years, they've tried a spreadable plaster made from sawdust and glue, *papier mache*, plywood, leather, various types of leather-like fabric and, in more recent times, fiberglass and plastics. All these materials were envisioned, at one time or another, as substitutes for sheet aluminum and steel.

In 1914, the French developed a method for making automobile bodies using conventional wood framing and then covering it with a rabbit-wire screen mesh and troweling on a wood plaster. The plaster was made of sawdust in a glue matrix. This was called the Botiaux process. No one ever found out what the mysterious glue consisted of. The Botiaux people pointed out that their body material went on like wall plaster. It dried in 24 hours, could be planed, sanded and painted; wasn't affected by temperature or humidity; didn't burn and couldn't rust. Weight was about the same as a steel-skinned body, and doors could be formed separately or cut out of the finished body with a saw, using the inner framing as a guide. Both surfaces, inside and out, could be smoothed and finished.

Benjamin Briscoe developed his 1914-15 cloverleaf roadster along French lines. Briscoe roadsters came with two unusual features: a single cyclops headlight sunk into the top of the radiator shell and a main

body section made of thick, pressed *papier mache*. This material again promised light weight, flexibility (considered vital to a good ride at the time), rust resistance and general economy. The *papier mache* was treated inside and out with waterproofing, then var-

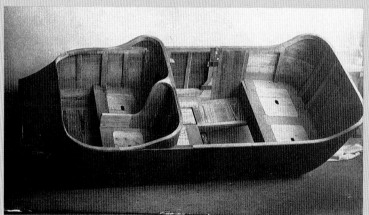

Haskelite plywood construction promised inexpensive, lightweight monocoque bodies. However, problems with wrapping the wood around corners and flaws in the finish kept this process from becoming popular.

nished in the usual way. It held up amazingly well but didn't gain many advocates. Briscoe went to normal composite bodies in 1916.

In 1922, a Chicago company call Haskelite began promoting plywood as a body material. Engineer Armin Elmendorf pointed out that Haskelite plywood skins, glued and screwed firmly to conventional

wooden body framing, made what amounted to a monocoque shell ("monocoque" means that the skin is a load-bearing part of the structure). The plywood didn't shift on the wooden framing the way steel skins did. And since the plywood added strength, the framework could be made lighter, so the body weighed less.

But two problems with plywood kept it from being widely accepted. First, the surface finish could never be gotten as smooth as sheetmetal, and glossy paint only showed up the flaws. Second, plywood was difficult to bend smoothly around corners. Elmendorf suggested covering compound curves with fabric or leather, but those materials cost more than paint. Although Brunn, it seems, built a few plywood Haskelite bodies and covered them with fabric, the idea didn't catch on with automakers.

A number of companies, both here and abroad, began to offer fabric-skinned bodies in the early 1920s. At that time, one of the great advantages of fabric bodies was that they didn't need to be painted. Body fabrics came in a variety of colors, and not having to go through the tedious process of painting saved tremendous amounts of time and hand labor.

Best known among fabric body licensors was the Charles T. Weymann Co., headquartered in Paris. Weymann bodies boasted, above all else, light weight and silence. Weymann licensed its patents throughout Europe, including to some 30 bodymakers in England. Several British auto manufacturers offered Weymann bod-

owners themselves. Owners often asked coachbuilders to design and construct bodies specifically for a given concours, and these were mostly done on short deadlines. The *grand prix* winners—necessarily wealthy and usually widely known—were admiringly photographed and talked about in the European press. Europe's prestigious concours served as models for our current concours d'elegance for collectible cars.

Hibbard & Darrin's clientele included such notables as Marion Davies, Gloria Swanson, movie heroine Pearl White, model Kay Aldridge, Hope Hampton, the Lazard banking family, Spain's King Alphonse XIII, Patino the Bolvian tin king plus the usual royalty, career diplomats, magnates and entertainers.

Hibbard & Darrin had a flair for developing new and widely

When he returned from Paris in 1937, Dutch Darrin opened a shop in Santa Monica. There he designed and built the early Packard-Darrins and also customized other cars, including Fords (above). Tom Hibbard came back to the States in 1931 and did some freelance designs (right). Hibbard later rejoined GM and eventually worked at Ford.

socialites. These events were held throughout the 1920s and '30s in places like Nice, Cannes, Monte Carlo and Paris. Judges awarded gold, silver and bronze medals on the basis of design excellence and craftsmanship.

Entrants were not usually the coachbuilders but rather the car

ies as standard equipment.

Weymann bodies were designed to remain flexible, to absorb noise and shock. They were said to weigh about 25% less than steel-skinned composite bodies. One test, in which a Weymann body and a conventional body were both dropped from a height of 60 feet, showed less damage to the fabric body.

Special lightweight wooden framing had to be made for Weymann bodies. This framework consisted mostly of a series of parallelograms. Part of the Weymann system included an assortment of metal plates, brackets and reinforcements that held the wooden frame members slightly apart so they didn't touch or rub. Everything was calculated to keep down weight, squeaks and road rumble.

Once framed, a tough, leather-like fabric called Zapon was stretched over a multi-layered base of padding. Zapon came in a number of colors and textures, including a glossy surface that was virtually impossible

to tell from painted sheetmetal. The base beneath the Zapon fabric consisted first of canvas duck, then cotton bat, then curled horsehair to fill out the contours and finally wadding or rubber pads in areas that might rub. Aluminum corners underlay the more complicated body curves. Special door latches and window regulators were designed to take a minimum of physical effort to operate.

In 1926, Weymann established a U.S. subsidiary, the Weymann American Body Co., at the former National automobile plant in Indianapolis. The first Weymann bodies were produced there in early 1927 for Weymann's main customer, Stutz. Weymann also built bodies on many other chassis plus a few metal bodies, notably the 1934 "baby Duesenberg" running prototype that evolved into the 1936 Cord 810 (see pages 239-40).

The Indianapolis plant was run by Charles Weymann's cousin, H. Steinbrugge. Both Weymann and Steinbrugge had

American fathers and French mothers, who were sisters, and both grew up and went to school in France. Charles Weymann developed an early interest in aviation and flew the American plane that won one of the early Bennett Cup races. When the judges handed young Weymann his trophy, he could only thank them in French. Weymann later won a chestful of French medals in World War I as a pilot. After the war, both he and his cousin fell in love with cars, and they went into the accessory business together in France. Weymann, in fact, invented an improved vacuum fuel tank that was widely used in Europe. He and Steinbrugge then developed their system for the fabric body, based on aircraft technology, sold licenses in Europe, and eventually set up their outpost in Indianapolis.

Five years before Weymann built bodies in Indianapolis, Kenneth L. Childs devised a similar soft-body system here in America. His overall idea was similar to Weymann's, but simpler. He used a wire-

Charles Weymann developed a sophisticated fabric-over-wood body construction technique that kept frame members from touching each other. Drawing shows the metal joints, hinges and reinforcements.

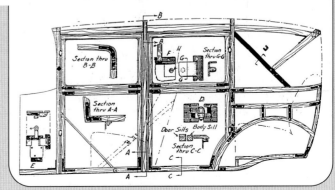

Hibbard & Darrin   *continued*

copied body innovations. One was an applied aluminum body molding that swept back from the front of the hood through to the back of the cowl, where it split, one branch lapping up and over ahead of the windshield and the other continuing along the doors, finally wrapping around the rear of the body. H&D received a European design patent on this molding, and General Motors later used it on some of its European cars, apparently without permission. In 1932, after Hibbard & Darrin had gone out of business and perhaps as an informal out-of-court settlement (this is speculation), GM gave Tom Hibbard a two-year contract to work in Art & Colour, while Darrin apparently took cash and stayed in Paris.

One detail of the H&D hood molding was that with Duesenbergs and a few other cars, the leading point just behind the radiator shell had a little upward barb. This barb became an H&D hallmark, as did the molding itself. On Packards, the barb projected downward and had the shape of half an arrowhead. Packard executives liked this so much that, in 1930, they began making the half arrowhead a hood-side feature of their production cars. Darrin said later that a Packard representative had

approached him in Paris and admired the barb. He asked whether Hibbard & Darrin would sell Packard rights to the design. "If you like it," Darrin told him, "you take it for Packard and use it. We don't want any money for it. It's yours."

Another of H&D's innovations was what Darrin called the "torpedo" body. This was a handsome, barrel-sided, dual-cowl phaeton that had a snug-sealing fabric top. The top was unusual in that it used V-shaped flaps over the centerposts and small, trapezoidal side windows. With roll-up windows, this top design transformed the dual-cowl phaeton from what was usually a drafty rain barrel into a livable body type. H&D again took out a design patent, this time worldwide, and licensed rights to Derham in the U.S., Castagna in Italy and Gill in England. Other coachbuilders soon offered H&D's torpedo phaeton, too, but without authorization.

H&D's most spectacular idea had to do with making complete bodies from thin-wall aluminum castings. The framework for these bodies was cast integrally with the skins. Hibbard felt that the wooden framing in custom bodies made most coachbuilt cars far too heavy. Excess weight handicapped performance. He admired Weymann's fabric bodies for their silence and lightness and Lancia's unitized, all-steel, monocoque construction

for its strength. So he and Darrin, along with a financial partner named William Brokaw, decided to offer what they called "Sylentlyte" bodies. The idea wasn't entirely new. Pierce-Arrow had offered cast-aluminum bodyskins as early as 1910, but these still used a wooden framework, although the wood was generally lighter than in steel-skinned composite construction (see page 229).

Hibbard & Darrin's Sylentlyte bodies were made up of 10 individually cast Alpax aluminum sections. Since most large European and American cars of the late 1920s were similar in size, one set of castings, with minor alterations, would fit all. The trick to mounting these bodies on a variety of chassis was to use a sandwich of long wooden slats, or shims, between the frame rails and the bottom of the aluminum body sections. These shims were hand shaped to conform to the different, irregular top surfaces of various chassis frames. Long, L-shaped aluminum strips covered the wooden shims and hid them from sight.

H&D's 10 main castings formed an open four-door convertible body. For the normal cloth top, H&D used hollow metal bows instead of the conventional but heavier wooden ones. The partners also offered a closed Sylentlyte four-door sedan body style. For this, they cast a separate roof

---

mesh or metal-lath base. The mesh could be stretched and nailed over the same wooden framing used for regular composite bodies. The outer fabric, called Meritas, sometimes carried an embossed, repeating pattern, like wallpaper, and went on over a layer of cotton padding.

Childs licensed his patents to the Fabric Body Corp., and Meritas-covered bodies were shown on a Peerless and several other chassis at the 1923 salon in New York. The Mengel Body Co. in Louisville, Kentucky mass produced aftermarket Model T Ford fabric Childs bodies in 1924, and Apperson made Meritas-covered coupe bodies standard in 1926. Fabrics similar to Meritas were sold under the names Fabrikoid (DuPont), Regaleather and Duratex. All competed with Weymann and Childs.

In 1922, George Mercer calculated that a fabric-covered automobile body cost 26¢ per square foot to build, compared with 30¢ for sheet aluminum and 7¢ for sheet steel, all with similar wood framing. Fabric bodies could be made more quickly in small quantities, but in small quantities only. They

Fiberglass held great promise after WW-II. Here, a 1953 Motorama Corvette front end emerges from its female mold.

required no painting, thus no paint booths or baking ovens, and were easy to repair if ripped. It was no more expensive to reskin a body, said Childs and Weymann, than to repaint it.

One major drawback, however, kept fabric-covered bodies from being more widely accepted: The hand labor of applying the fabric made them too costly for mass production. As the demand for custom bodies dropped during the early Depression, the Weymann and Childs systems lost favor. Weymann stopped promot-

ing fabric automobile bodies altogether when the parent company in Europe merged with a builder of commercial vehicles.

Fiberglass, or more correctly GRP (glass reinforced plastic), was developed in 1944 by Owens-Corning. One of the first cars to have a fiberglass body was the 1946 Stout Project Y sedan, designed by Gil Spear and built in conjunction with Kaiser-Frazer. While a number of small U.S. companies offered fiberglass body kits after World War II, the 1953 Corvette had the first fiberglass body produced in quantity. It was initially made by Molded Fiber Glass Body Co. of Ashtabula, Ohio via the vacuum-bag method, but later Corvettes used steel dies.

Many different types of SMC (sheet-molded compound) and other hybrid plastics have been used for automobile body skins and components since the late 1960s. In addition to the Corvette, the Pontiac Fiero used SMC skins starting in 1984, and more recently the Saturn, GM's F-Cars and some minivans have plastic skins over a full metal framework. ◆

assembly that bolted to the main body section. The cast roof had a fabric top insert.

H&D's Sylentlyte bodies held several advantages over composite construction. They were lightweight, didn't creak or rattle and couldn't rust. On the minus side, patterns and molds were excruciatingly difficult to make, and some of the thin, large castings often contained flaws. To complicate matters, H&D sometimes had to match cowl or front-door castings to pre-existing hood shapes. Front doors sometimes had to be made longer or shorter, depending on the chassis. Custom front doors necessitated forming sheet aluminum over a wooden framework, meaning that some of the advantages of Sylentlyte were lost. Nor did paint adhere well to the aluminum. Besides, Sylentlyte bodies were very expensive to manufacture. So after considerable development work but few actual sales, the project was abandoned.

At Puteaux, Hibbard & Darrin also made a line of aluminum wheelcovers that fit over wire wheels. These had a raised circular molding halfway out from the center. Chauffeurs loved these wheelcovers because they were much easier to keep clean than wire wheels. H&D wheelcovers could be polished to a high luster and soon became popular in all countries. Rival coachbuilders often bought them and added them to their own catalogues. Other items that H&D designed and manufactured included outside door handles, spare-tire mirror attachments, and a five-sided lug nut to prevent the theft of expensive wheels.

One crusade H&D advanced on the concours circuit was the use of lighter colors for formal body styles. This went against common practice, and H&D had only partial success. They particularly promoted a grey-green, called almond, plus shades of beige, yellow and a roof-tile red. These stood out from the traditional drab blacks, dark blues, greens, and dusky greys that were usually seen at *concours*.

In a 1966 article, Tom Hibbard wrote in *The Classic Car*: "The transformation from paint and varnish to [nitro]cellulose lacquer came after we opened our body shop [in Puteaux]. Cellulose lacquers saved us time and money and gave the buyer a more durable finish, but it could never approach the rich color and depth of finish we had obtained with paint and varnish. To do a good job with the latter material required from two to three weeks, because much time was needed to dry the successive coats. After the color coats were applied over the base coats, the car was varnished. Several days were required for the varnish to dry and harden. When the process was complete (if the job had been done with the best materials and skill), the resultant finish was deep and lustrous. It was much richer looking than the finishes on the production cars today, where the color is just on the surface, with no effect of depth."

Dust was always a problem when varnishing a car. H&D set up their paint room so it was completely sealed and tiled on all walls, ceiling and floor. This way it could be washed down regularly. Hibbard also reported that they used nothing but the finest British coach varnish. Some of the finishes they offered were early versions of metallics, with large metal flakes too big to pass through the nozzle of a paint gun. With varnish, though, this was no problem, because it was always brushed on. Hibbard reports, too, that Barker & Co. in England would sometimes woodgrain the entire exterior surface of some cars for an odd but very striking effect.

In the late 1920s, H&D's reputation was such that production carmakers began asking them to design and build sample bodies that could be mass produced. Among those for whom H&D provided design services and sample bodies were Moon, General Motors, Stutz, Auburn, Dodge, Renault and Armstrong-Siddeley. For Moon Motors Corp., H&D designed the entire 1929 Windsor White Prince line. In the case of General Motors, in 1928 H&D's showroom received a visit from no less a trio than GM board chairman Alfred P. Sloan, Jr., Chevrolet president William S. Knudsen and Harley J. Earl, head of Fisher Body's fledgling Art & Colour section. Sloan and Knudsen commissioned H&D to design, style and build five sample bodies: one Chevrolet, two Cadillacs, a LaSalle and either a Pontiac or an Oldsmobile (memories differ). During this visit, Earl quite naturally felt left out. Many years later, Tom Hibbard confided that Earl took him aside and told him not to spend too much time on this assignment. And although the five sample bodies were quickly designed, built and delivered, GM never used any of H&D's styling ideas.

In its June 1929 issue, *Autobody* magazine reported

Dutch Darrin (left) stands behind his first Packard-Darrin of 1937. Actor Dick Powell bought this car. The series was so successful that Packard included Darrins in its catalogue and, in 1940, Darrin began building them in Connersville, Ind.

that, "The success of Hibbard & Darrin is not based merely on designing ability, but is the result of a combination of experience, organization and experimentation. Their designing ability we need say nothing of, as their work is known all over the world. Regarding their organization, they have an entire building...in the artistic center of Paris, in which they employ numerous designers, sculptors and draftsmen for the interpretation of their creations. Working for a worldwide clientele and with the important automobile factories of Europe and America, the scope and character of their work is necessarily extremely broad. Probably the greatest factor in their success in the creation of workable and practical designs has been their large experimental facilities. Hibbard & Darrin built last year over a $1 million worth of samples in special bodies, and even large manufacturers do not generally have the organization necessary for similar experimentation."

In late 1929, Hibbard & Darrin considered opening a branch office in New York. But the Sylentlyte project and H&D's New York representative were taking great amounts of money, and then came Black Tuesday. Hibbard & Darrin's financial partner in France, William Brokaw, refused to extend the two active partners more credit, and the firm folded in 1931. Its unfinished commissions were carried out by Felber Freres of Paris.

Tom Hibbard and Dutch Darrin stayed in Paris for a time, operating a moviehouse that showed American films. In late 1931, Hibbard returned to the U.S. and worked under Harley Earl at a salary of $20,000 a year (roughly $340,000 in 1994). This seems to have been part of GM's design patent settlement, and the $20,000 was probably more than Earl himself made at the time. Hibbard came into Art & Colour as head of the Cadillac studio and, perhaps due to Earl's animosity and lack of cooperation (Hibbard never said), the arrangement at GM didn't work out. Hibbard opened his own consulting office, Hibbard Inc., in 1934 and did some designs for Studebaker and race-car engineer Harry Miller. He worked for Fiat in 1938 and designed armored cars in 1939, then returned to GM briefly in 1940 as an advisor and finally went to work for Ford in 1941. He stayed with Ford until 1948 and even served for a short time as head of Ford design when E.T. (Bob) Gregorie left (see page 139). ◆

FERNANDEZ & DARRIN

Darrin, meanwhile, remained in Paris. In late 1931, at a *concours,* he ran into M. Fernandez. Fernandez's main interests had to do with finance and banking, but he also owned factories that built furniture and custom automobile bodies. His hobby was car design. Chit-chat followed, and Darrin talked Fernandez into becoming his backer and partner.

According to Dutch Darrin, Fernandez already had a well-equipped body plant plus two luxurious showrooms in Paris, one at the front of the factory and another on the Champs Elysees, across from Kellner et Freres. Darrin, it seems, ran the Fernandez & Darrin coachbuilding operation pretty much by himself. At its height,

F&D employed 200 workmen, the same number as Hibbard & Darrin, and finished an average of three cars every two weeks.

Unlike H&D, F&D bought new chassis outright. Darrin then added the body and sold the entire car, usually before it was finished. Principal chassis suppliers included Rolls-Royce, Mercedes, Isotta, Packard, Duesenberg, Voisin, Maybach, Bentley, Delage, Hispano, Panhard, Renault and Delahaye. Most F&D cars remained in Europe; few were ever brought to this country, but Americans did feel the influence of Fernandez & Darrin.

Fernandez & Darrin designs generally continued the spirit and types of bodies built by Hibbard & Darrin, but with even more flair and flamboyance. F&D received a design patent in 1933 for under-cowl steering and popularized applied moldings made from brass. They often used Brazilian ash for the main body framing,

Fernandez & Darrin built torpedo-fendered 1933 Duesenberg convertible victoria for Greta Garbo.

Major U.S. Coachbuilders and Bodymakers

Firm name	Dates	Primary Customers
New York City & vicinity		
-Brewster & Co.	1810-1938	Brewster, Rolls-Royce, Ford, Buick
-Brooks-Ostruk Co.	1910-1932	Minerva, Rolls-Royce
-Chupurdy & Co.	1912-1926	
-The Clayton Co.	1915-25	
-Demarest & Co.	1908-30	
-Flandreau & Co.	1895-1912	
-Holbrook Co.	1908-1931	Lincoln, Packard, Franklin
-Hurner-Binder Co.	1918-??	
-J.R. Inskip Inc.	1932-39	Rolls-Royce, Ford, Packard
-LeBaron Carrossiers	1920-23	various clients
-LeBaron, Inc.	1923-27	Packard, Chrysler,Lincoln,Stutz,Pierce,Marmon
-Locke & Co.	1902-1932	Chrysler, Franklin, Lincoln, Packard
-Moore & Munger Co.	?? teens	K-D
-Paul Ostruk Co.	??	Locomobile
-Rollston Co.	1921-38	Packard, Stutz, Duesenberg (reorganized as Rollson)
-Rollson Inc.	1938-42	Packard
-F.R. Wood & Son	1880?-1939	Panhard, E.V., Crane, Rolls-Royce, Mercedes
New York State & Connecticut		
-American Body Co.	1919-1925	(Buffalo NY) Lincoln
-H.H. Babcock	1845-1926	(Watertown) Babcock, Dodge Bros., Franklin, Duesenberg
-Blue Ribbon Body Co.	1890?-1925	(Bridgeport CT)Locomobile, Packard, Willys-Knight
-Bridgeport Body Co.	1910-1924	(Bridgeport CT) Locomobile
-Bridgeport Body Co.	1934-1938	(Bridgeport CT) Packard
-Brunn & Co.	1908-1941	(Buffalo NY) Lincoln, Pierce-Arrow, Stearns
-Buffalo Auto Body	1897-1915	(Buffalo NY)
-Jas. Cunningham & Sons & Co.	1890?-??	(Rochester NY) Cunningham, Ford
-H.F. Holbrook-Henry Brewster Co.	1926-1928	(Bridgeport CT)
-New Haven Carriage Co.	1880?-1924	(New Haven CT) Locomobile, Rolls-Royce, Columbia
-Seabrook & Smith Carriage Co.	1890?-1915	(New Haven CT)
-Willoughby & Co.	1903-1938	(Utica NY) Lincoln, Cole,Wills-Ste. Claire
Amesbury & Merrimac, Mass.		
-Amesbury Metal Co.	1907-1921	sheetmetal work
-Amesbury Splty. Co.	1915-1923	interior trim

Firm name	Dates	Primary Customers
-Auto Body & Finishing Co.	1906-??	
-Biddle & Smart Co.	1882-1930	Hudson, Rolls-Royce
-Briggs Carriage Co.	1876-1923	
-Bryant Body Co.	1919-1925	(absorbed by Walker) Jordan
-Currier-Cameron Co.	1870?-1920	Locomobile, Stanley
-Hollander & Morrill	1909-1925	(absorbed by Biddle & Smart)
-Hume Co.	1857-1925	Marmon
-John B. Judkins Co.	1857-1941	Lincoln, Packard, Pierce, Cadillac
-Merrimac Body Co.	1918-1933	(started by Judkins; specialized in open bodies) duPont, Packard
-S.C.Pease & Sons	1861-1922	
-Walker Body Co.	1920-1933	Franklin
-Witham Body Co.	1922-1925	(absorbed by B&S) Stearns-Knight
Other Massachusetts & Rhode Island		
-Bela Body Co.	1916-1922?	(Framingham) Franklin, Hudson
-Osgood Bradley Co.	1920-1927	(Worcester)
-Farnham & Nelson	1905-1930	(Roslindale) Locomobile
-Geo. W. McNear	1920-1940	(Springfield)
-Springfield Metal Body	1902-1927	(Springfield) Rolls-Royce
-Waterhouse & Co.	1928-1933	(Webster) Marmon, duPont, Lincoln, Packard, Chrysler, Pierce-Arrow, Rolls-Royce
-Woonsocket Mfg. Co.	1921-1929	(Woonsocket) Dagmar
Philadelphia & vicinity		
-Auto Top & Body Co.	1906-1915	
-Edw. G. Budd Mfg. Co.	1912-46	Dodge, Ford, Studebaker, Ruxton, Erskine, Jordan
-The Budd Co.	1946-present	T-Bird, components
-Derham Body Co.	1884-1971	Packard, Duesenberg, Locomobile, Pierce-Arrow, postwar customs
-Floyd-Derham Co.	1928-29	
-Hale, Kilburn & Co.	1911-1930	Trumbull, Stutz
-Jacques Mfg. Co.	1920-25	Lexington
-Alexander Wolfington's Sons & Co.	1880?-1950	Duesenberg
Other Pennsylvania bodymakers		
-Banker Brothers & Co.	1906-16	(Pittsburgh) Pierce-Arrow, Stevens-Duryea
-Fleetwood Metal Body Co.	1909-1925	Stutz, Packard,Cadillac
-Reading Metal Body Co.	1905-1912	(Reading)
-C. C. Schuette Body Co.	1910-1926	(Lancaster) Franklin, Marmon, Packard, Olds, Wescot, Cadillac
-E.J. Thompson Co.	1907-1927	Dodge Bros.

covered with either sheet steel or aluminum. After the mid-1930s, slow business convinced Fernandez & Darrin to close shop and part company.

Darrin returned to the U.S. in 1937, settled in California and soon produced his series of Packard-Darrin convertibles. These became quite successful and, as a result, Packard asked him to contribute to the design of the 1941 Clipper. After the war, Darrin consulted for Kaiser-Frazer, oversaw the creation of their 1947-50 models, styled second-generation Kaisers, did the Kaiser-Darrin and tried several times to launch various small car- and coachbuilding ventures of his own. These met with mixed success, but Darrin remained active until his death in Santa Monica on Jan. 4, 1982. ◆

DIETRICH INC.

Ray Dietrich worked from age 12 until he was 16—1906 to 1910—for the American Bank Note Co. in lower Manhattan. He earned $3 at first for a 60-hour week. It was at American Bank Note that Ray first saw artists engrave the precise artwork for stock certificates and the paper money the company printed for China, Mexico, Germany, etc. According to American Bank Note's Aurelia Chen, someone in the company's art department apparently took Ray under his wing, because Ray mentioned in his autobiography that he did some vignettes for bills or stock certificates even at that tender age.

When he was 16, Dietrich went to the David Schmidt Co., which made wooden hammers for Steinways and other pianos. He now earned $18 a week. Big, strapping, good-looking, he discovered he had a talent for pitching a baseball, and he loved the game. So for extra income he found work as a semi-professional baseball pitcher. When his team won, Ray made $100 and when it lost, $50. He spent part of his new-found wealth on formal art classes.

What Ray Dietrich really wanted to do, though, was to design cars. In 1913, he applied to Brewster & Co. Brewster was just then poised to take on the New

New Jersey

-D.B. Dunham & Son	1863-1923	(Rahway) Richelieu
-Fitzgibbon & Crisp Carriage & Auto Body Co.	1890?-1915	(Trenton) Mercer, Packard, Crane-Simplex
-Healey & Co.	1890?-1926	(Keyport) Cadillac, Packard, Stevens-Duryea
-J.M. Quinby & Sons	1834-1917	(Newark) various (taken over by Crane-Simplex in 1922)

Detroit & vicinity

-Briggs Mfg. Co.	1909-1953	Ford, Chrysler, Packard, Studebaker, Lincoln, Hudson, Willys-Knight
-Detroit Carriage Co.	1898-1910	Oldsmobile
-Dietrich, Inc.	1925-1937	Lincoln, Packard, Franklin, Chrysler
-Erdman-Guider Co.	1913-1926	Sheridan, Columbia
-Fisher Body Co.	1908-1987	Ford, Packard, GM, Chrysler
-Griswold Motor Body Co.	1909-193?	Palmer, Graham-Paige, Auburn Cabin Speedster
-LeBaron-Detroit Co.	1927-1941	Owned by Briggs Mfg.
-Murray Corp. of Amer.	1913-195?	Ford, Lincoln, Hupmobile, Packard, Jordan, Reo
-Towson Body Co.	1922-1925	(acquired by Murray) Packard, Velie, Davis
-Trippensee Closed Body Co.	1923-1925	Rickenbacker, Essex, Chevrolet, Saxon, Chalmers
-C.R. Wilson Body Co.	1873-1927	(acquired by Murray) Ford, Lincoln, Packard
-J.C. Widman Co.	1920-1925	(acquired by Murray) Jewett, Franklin, Chalmers

Other Michigan bodymakers

-Auto Body Co.	1908-1926	(Lansing) Durant, Star, Oldsmobile, Locomobile
-Pontiac Body Co.	1905-1915	(Pontiac) Oakland
-Hayes Body Co.	1890?-1935	(Grand Rapids) Marmon, Peerless
-Limousine Body Co.	1915-1936	(Kalamazoo) ACD, Gardner, Moon

Chicago & vicinity

-R.W. Graff & Co.	1907-1935	
-C.P. Kimball & Co.	1877-1929	
-Lehmann-Peterson Co.	1925-70	limousines
-Limousine & Carriage Manufacturing Co.	1905-1915	
-Pullman Co.	1870-1925	Moon, Packard

Other Illinois bodymakers

-Henney & Co.	1915-present	(Moline) hearses

Ohio bodymakers

-Baker, Rauch & Lang	1916-??	(Cleveland) Steams-Knight, Peerless
-Bender Body Co.	1910?-1930?	(Cleveland)

-Dayton Folding Tonneau Co.	1907-1927	(Dayton)
-Frantz Body Co.	1898-1930	(Akron)
-Hess & Eisenhardt	1930?-present	Cincinnati) stretch limos
-Lang Body Co.	1917-1927	(Cleveland) Lincoln, Stutz, Dodge Brothers
-Milburn Wagon Co.	1890?-1920?	(Toledo)
-Ohio Body & Blower Co.	1902-1927	(Cleveland) Moon, Jordan
-Phillips Custom Body Co.	1923-1928	(Warren; acquired by Briggs Mfg. Co.) Stutz, Pierce-Arrow, Franklin, Stearns-Knight, Wills Ste. Claire
-Leon Rubay & Co.	1916-1923	(Cleveland) White, Leon Rubay, Pierce-Arrow

Indiana bodymakers

-Central Mfg. Co.	1908-1948	(Connersville) ACD, early Packard-Darrin, Jeep
-LaGrande	1930-1937	(Union City) custom name for Union City Body Co., Duesenberg
-McFarlan Automobile Co.	1886-1928	(Connersville) Auburn, HCS, Locomobile, Lexington
-Millspaugh & Irish	1915-1928	(Indianapolis) Duesenberg, Dodge Brothers
-Robbins Body Co.	1906-1928	(Indianapolis) Stutz, Premier
-Studebaker Corp.	1840?-1964	(South Bend) Studebaker
-Union City Body Co.	1903-1937	(Union City) Auburn
-Weymann American Body Co.	1926-1931	(Indianapolis) Stutz

West Coast bodymakers

-Advance Auto Body Co.	??	(Los Angeles)
-Geo. R. Bentel Co.	1916-1919	(Los Angeles) Mercer, Simplex, Jordan
-Bohman & Schwartz	1932-1961	(Pasadena) movie stars
-Coachcraft Ltd.	1940-1966?	(Los Angeles) postwar customs
-Earl Automobile Works	1908-1919	
-J. Gerard Kirchhoff	1926-1931	(Los Angeles)
-Larkin & Co.	1880?-1930	(San Francisco)
-Don Lee Coach & Body Works	1907-1925	(Los Angeles) Cadillac
-Walter M. Murphy Co.	1921-1932	(Pasadena) Duesenberg, Lincoln, Packard

Bodymakers, other states

-Blakeslee Vehicle Body & Seat Co.	1905-1915	(Kansas City MO)
-R.N. Collins Vehicle Woodwork Co.	1890?-1923	(St. Louis MO) Dorris
-Thomas Connolly Carriage Works	1890?-1910	(Dubuque IA)
-Seaman Body Corp.	1910-1938?	(Milwaukee WI) Locomobile, Lozier, Dorris, Packard, Cadillac, Kissel, Moline, Velie, Nash

Dietrich Inc. *continued*

York Rolls-Royce agency. Willie Brewster hired Dietrich as an apprentice body draftsman at exactly half what he'd been making at the David Schmidt Co.

Dietrich, in recounting his days with Brewster, said he always felt extremely fortunate to begin his automotive training there, because it gave him such good grounding in the art and craft of bodymaking. The working drafts he made were almost crude at first, he later recalled, because the craftsmen who built the bodies

were so good at their jobs. Most were older men who'd come to this country from carriage shops in Germany, France and Austria. Dietrich's drafts typically contained a full-sized side view, a halfbody plan view with as few sweeps as possible (to keep construction simple) and sometimes end elevations. "It was unnecessary to show any developed surfaces," he wrote in 1958 in *The Classic Car*, "as they [the artisans] would 'prick off' with dividers the required twists of the wood parts which were to form the body construction."

Brewster's craftsmen worked on commission and would bid against each other on given body jobs. They were employed by Brewster, and Brewster would tack its own commission onto the winning craftsman's bid, but in actuality they all worked for themselves. Each master craftsman—and there were 10-12 at Brewster when Ray got there—had his own staff of assistants and apprentices. These assistants would do the rough work, including the basic hand-shaping of wooden parts and panels. The master craftsman would then finish the body, often in some hidden area or room where no one could see his methods and secret techniques. The masters weren't anxious to teach these skills to their underlings or even to each other. Ray says that these men didn't take his body drafts very seriously. They trusted their own judgment and fairing skills much more than a draftsman's ability to lay down an accurate map. "The standard of quality," recounts Dietrich, "was perfection."

After a few years with Brewster, the company sponsored Dietrich at the Andrew F. Johnson Technical School. Once enrolled, regular attendance was mandatory, but Ray sometimes fell victim to his love of baseball and played hooky. Johnson sent reports of Ray's non-attendance directly to the sponsor, in this case to Willie Brewster, who soon called Ray on the carpet. "Study or you're out!" said Brewster. Dietrich now worked 60 hours a week in the Brewster drafting room and spent an addi-

tional 12 evening hours a week at school, often returning home at midnight. He graduated in 1917.

Almost immediately after graduation, Dietrich left Brewster to work as an assistant body engineer for Chevrolet. This was just before W.C. Durant sold Chevrolet to General Motors. Chevy at that time had a development center in midtown Manhattan, in a building on West 56th Street. They even had a test track on the second floor, and Dietrich says the boards creaked and groaned when a car circled the huge, open room. After GM took over Chevrolet, the New York development group disbanded and, in late 1918, Dietrich rejoined Brewster. It was here that he met Tom Hibbard and the two formulated plans that eventually led to the founding of LeBaron (see page 40).

Fast forward now to Feb. 1925. After selling his interest in LeBaron to Ralph Roberts and leaving New York, Dietrich arrived in Detroit as a 50% partner in Dietrich Inc. The other half was owned by Murray Corp. of America. Murray, as mentioned, was a major body supplier to Lincoln, Ford, Reo, Hupmobile, Hudson and others.

Murray already had at least two good designers: Amos E. Northup and Jules Andrade. So Murray wasn't interested in Dietrich as a designer of production car bodies. What Ray Dietrich and Dietrich Inc. would do was design, produce and sell

Ray Dietrich began his career with Brewster and is shown here at his desk at LeBaron in the early 1920s. He was an excellent draftsmen as well as a talented designer, doing not only coachbuilt customs but also production body designs, among them the 1927 Studebaker Erskine (below).

custom and semi-custom bodies, primarily for Lincoln at first and later for Packard and others. Edsel Ford had discussed the Lincoln connection in a casual way when he and Dietrich first met at the New York Salon in 1923.

Dietrich's immediate problem in Detroit was to find good artisans. He ultimately talked two of Brewster's former master craftsmen, John Wasserman and a Mr. Keubler,

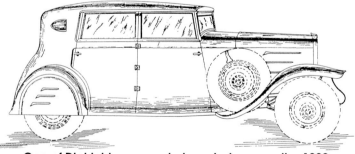

One of Dietrich's more notorious designs was the 1929 Franklin Pirate. Flared door extensions covered running-boards; rear fenders were skirted. Walker built nearly 100 Pirates in sedan, coupe and open 4-door forms.

into coming to Detroit, and these two formed the nucleus of Dietrich's new staff. Wasserman and Keubler would soon train additional craftsmen through the apprentice system. Dietrich also brought along Werner Gubitz as a designer and watercolorist, and Gordon Buehrig joined Dietrich in Jan. 1926 (for a year). So after luring metalworkers and others away from rival coachbuilders, Dietrich soon had his new facilities humming.

In addition to custom and series-custom Lincoln bodies,

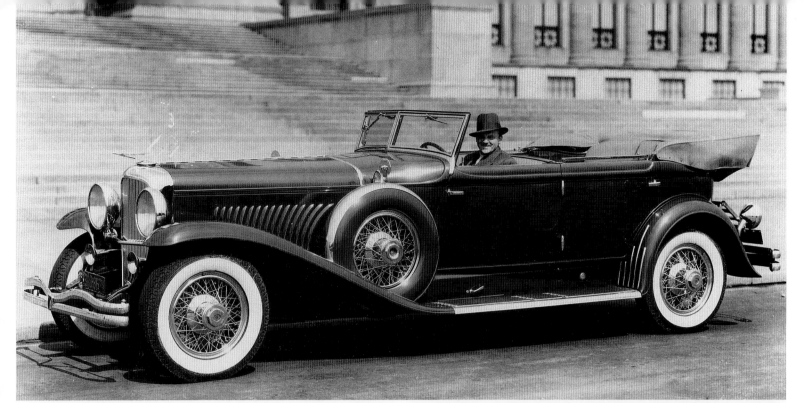

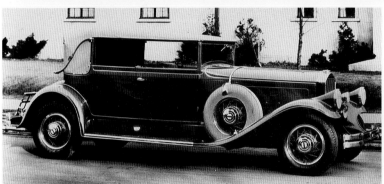

Hollywood bad guy Jimmy Cagney (top) seems to have been thoroughly pleased with his Dietrich-bodied Duesenberg. For 1930, Pierce-Arrow offered a long-wheelbase convertible victoria (above left), and for '31 Packard buyers could order this stylish Deluxe Eight sport phaeton by Dietrich on the 147-inch chassis.

Dietrich Inc. began doing work for a number of Packard agents and a few of LeBaron's former clients. Prospects looked good, but to make them even better, Dietrich hired Gordon C. (Jack) Parvis, a friend of Packard's soon-to-be design chief Ed Macauley. Parvis had 15 years of Packard sales experience and immediately brought in a tremendous amount of new business, putting Dietrich into the happy position of having to move to larger quarters. It was Edsel Ford, in fact, who offered Dietrich the empty Leland Lincoln manufacturing plant and rented it to him for a very reasonable price.

In 1926, Dietrich Inc. designed and built three custom Packards: a coupe, a convertible sedan and a sport sedan. To publicize and sell these cars, sales manager Jack Parvis took them on tour. Parvis, along with two uniformed chauffeurs, drove all three cars around the country. It turned out to be like a series of small, private salons. Parvis showed the cars first in New York, then in Boston, Washington D.C., St. Louis, Chicago and finally in Los Angeles and San Francisco.

Before arriving in each city, he would send out advance notice and then put the cars on display in hotel lobbies or dealer showrooms. Invitations to wealthy socialites went out from dealers and agents. At each showing, Parvis took orders for copies of these three showcars and also quoted prices to dealers and distributors for runs of series customs. At the end of the six-week tour, Parvis had deposits on 150 semi-custom Packards. Luckily, Dietrich had anticipated the success of Parvis' sales junket and had already built 10 copies of each body style.

It wasn't long before Packard president Alvan Macauley heard about Parvis' aggressive and highly successful nationwide tour. After a quick conference with his staff, Macauley, Col. Jesse Vincent and Packard sales manager Doc Hill drove over to the Leland Lincoln plant to visit Dietrich. Dietrich thought they'd come just to ogle the three tour cars, but instead Macauley personally placed an order for 175 additional bodies of the same three types. Immediately afterward, Packard sent 175 bare chassis over. This marked the beginning of an association between Dietrich Inc. and Packard that resulted in hundreds of custom and semi-custom factory bodies being designed and built. Ray Dietrich for a time became Packard's "body critic" and one of its principal stylists of the late 1920s and early '30s (see pages 218-19).

By the end of 1926, Dietrich Inc. was turning out 18-25 bodies a week. Lincoln, meanwhile, signed Ray Dietrich up as a styling consultant. In July 1927, Dietrich began an additional consultancy for Studebaker. It was Ray who designed the first Studebaker Erskine, yet for reasons not clear, Studebaker body engineers decided to shorten and narrow the body. Dietrich also designed bodies for Franklin, including the controversial and sinister-looking 1927-32 Pirate series. These were four-door sedans and phaetons with skirted rear fenders, low windshields and flared door bottoms that hid the runningboards. Dietrich took the idea for the hidden runningboards from a French Bugatti.

In 1927, Dodge likewise hired Dietrich as a consultant. As with Franklin, Dietrich Inc. designed and built sample bodies for Dodge. And when Chrysler Corp. bought Dodge in 1928, Dietrich began designing and producing series customs for Chrysler, too. Despite what might seem like wild conflicts of interest, Dietrich continued some of these consultancies for years. They came initially in response to Fisher Body setting up Harley Earl at GM Art & Colour.

Due to the growing volume of series bodies for Lincoln, Packard, Pierce-Arrow and now Chrysler, Dietrich Inc. enjoyed the stature of being the country's largest producer of non-production bodywork. Dietrich customs won gold medals at the 1927 Paris and Monte Carlo *concours d'elegance,* and Dietrich designs

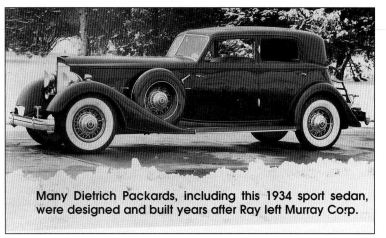

Many Dietrich Packards, including this 1934 sport sedan, were designed and built years after Ray left Murray Corp.

became the hit of several salon seasons, notably 1928-29-30. The company's volume continued to grow right up to the end of 1929, but at that point the Depression brought about a vertical plunge. By 1931, business had fallen off so badly, both at Murray and at Dietrich Inc., that the partners decided to fold the coachbuilding enterprise.

The last year that Ray Dietrich worked as an active coachbuilder was 1931. Murray president Clarence Avery, who'd never gotten along with Ray, forced Dietrich out of the partnership and replaced him with L. Clayton Hill as head of Dietrich Inc. Ray remained a principal shareholder, but his shares were quickly dwindling in value. Dietrich Inc. was now largely a shell. Murray did, however, continue to use the Dietrich name and coachbuilder's logo as late as 1937.

The Artisan Craftsman

"Carriage-body makers have told me that formerly it was customary, when the body was finished and had received the first coat of lead, to have it returned to the body shop while drying so that the man who made it could have the satisfaction of showing his friends what a good piece of workmanship he was capable of turning out. I know of two successful carriage builders who determined the size of a piece of wood or steel for special jobs simply by feeling them. One of these men made a national reputation as a sulky builder, and his judgement was wonderfully accurate in determining the sizes of stock on racing sulkies and sleighs. He...was guided entirely by his eye and by the feel of the piece of stock in his hand."
—*George J. Mercer, September 1920*

In 1932, Ray Dietrich was having a beer and munching a cheese sandwich at the Detroit Athletic Club when Walter P. Chrysler came over and clapped him on the shoulder. "I heard what happened," he told Dietrich, and in the course of conversation, Chrysler offered Dietrich a job. Dietrich went to work for Chrysler Corp. in 1932 and stayed there until 1940.

At the beginning of Dietrich's tenure at Chrysler, he occupied a position equal to that of Herbert V. Henderson, who had charge of Chrysler Art & Colour. Henderson's staff added ornamental styling details, designed interiors and chose trim. Most of the exterior sheetmetal, however, was designed by Chrysler body engineers under Oliver H. Clark (see pages 153-54).

At first, Dietrich had a small room to himself at Chrysler, but no staff. One of his early assignments was to create facelifts for the post-1934 Chrysler and DeSoto Airflows. His front ends for the 1935-37 Airflows took their cues from the Airstream series. The Airstreams had been created by Phil Wright at Briggs (see page 80). Dietrich

Ray Dietrich worked at Chrysler after leaving Murray. His first assignments were to restyle the front ensembles of the slow-selling Airflows, among them this 1936 DeSoto coupe.

was also asked to teach classes at the Chrysler Institute for body draftsmen—classes much like those he'd attended at the Andrew F. Johnson school.

Henderson left Chrysler in 1935, and at that point Dietrich took responsibility for the company's exterior design activity. He wasn't a forceful manager, however, and despite his friendship with Walter Chrysler, Ray could never overcome the powerful influence of corporate body engineers. He and Oliver Clark rarely saw eye to eye on anything. A.B. (Buzz) Grisinger, who also joined Chrysler in 1932 as a young designer, remembered that the engineering department simply wore Dietrich down. Ultimately, Dietrich lost interest. He became, in Grisinger's words, "...lackadaisical, indifferent to the job." On occasion, Dietrich would disappear for days at a time. Eventually, in 1940, four days after Walter Chrysler died and due to pressure from engineering, the company let Dietrich go.

He founded Ray Dietrich Inc., his own design and fabrication firm in Grand Rapids, and ran it from 1949 to 1953. It was here that he built the 1950 Presidential Lincoln parade limousine for the Truman administration. In 1953, Dietrich began consulting for Checker Cab in Kalamazoo, Michigan. After a series of later projects, which included designing electric guitars, Dietrich retired to Albuquerque in 1969 and passed away in 1980. ◆

THE DERHAM BODY CO.

Joseph J. Derham set up his Rosemont Carriage Works along Philadelphia's Main Line in 1887. It was generally agreed that Derham carriages were equal to Brewster's in terms of quality and style, their main difference being reputation.

Derham built its first autobody in 1907, this for a local woman named Pansy Griscom. Ms Griscom wanted a closed limousine body to complement the open touring-car body she already owned. Derham built the new body, and each half year thereafter, they removed and revarnished one body while Ms Griscom was driven around in the other. Ms Griscom continued as a Derham customer until 1960.

Joseph Derham had four sons. The youngest, Enos, soon supervised the Rosemont plant, and it was under Enos that Derham began building series-custom automobile bodies. Enos foresaw a market among those who wanted something more than a production body but who couldn't comfortably afford a one-off custom. For those customers, he contracted with east-coast Packard and Hudson dealers and, through them, sold series-custom bodies. The Rosemont plant turned out from five to 40 copies of specific designs, the number depending on dealer orders. The resulting mini assembly lines in Rosemont enabled Derham to charge considerably less than for individually crafted bodies. Because of the quantities involved, Derham also had the luxury of making or ordering special hammer forms for door skins, cowls, hoods, quarter panels, etc.

In 1916, Derham bought a former truck plant in downtown Philadelphia and moved its coachbuilding activity there. Another brother, James, had charge of the downtown operation. The Rosemont facility, still under Enos, now operated mostly as a showroom and refurbishing shop. The downtown plant allowed Derham to complete as many as one body a day, and by 1920, with a workforce now numbering nearly 200 men, Derham was producing 250 cars a year. Nearly all of these went to dealers and sales agents as series customs, but a few dozen were also built for individuals. During the 1920s and early 1930s, Derham produced bodies for everything from Rolls-Royce and Duesenbergs to a Model T Ford town-car.

Joseph J. Derham, the company's founder, passed away in 1927, and at this point the sons started to bicker. James and Enos kept the old business, but brother Phillip, who'd been the company's sales manager, formed a rival company called Floyd-Derham Body Co. Floyd-Derham took away some of Derham's key workmen and customers, but after only about a year, Floyd-Derham had caused so much ill will and made so many mistakes that it went out of business. These problems had the effect of tarnishing the reputation of the Derham Body Co. But despite the Floyd-Derham disaster and the stock-market crash in late Oct. 1929, the Derham Body Co. continued to flourish and was one of the few coachbuilders who survived not just the Depression but also World War II.

Derham didn't immediately feel the effects of Black Tuesday. Through the year 1930, Derham kept busy filling orders for custom and semi-custom bodies on Duesenberg, Packard, Lincoln, Stutz, Pierce and Franklin chassis. That year, too, Edsel Ford contracted for a number of Derham Lincoln roadsters. And hoping to stimulate sales for 1931, Derham outdid itself for that season's New York Salon. Hit of the show was the "Derham Tourster," Derham's $15,000 1931 Duesenberg SJ dual-cowl phaeton with a roll-up rear windshield. Gary Cooper bought one, as did comedian Joe E. Brown and Johnny (Tarzan) Weismuller. In all, five copies of that style were built and sold.

A Derham Packard four-door hardtop

Film star Gary Cooper had his Duesenberg Derham tourster finished in primrose yellow with green fenders. Joe E. Brown and Johnny Weismuller also owned Derham tourster phaetons.

Derham licensed Hibbard & Darrin's torpedo phaeton style, seen here on a DuPont. In this car, top could be partially folded into a towncar position.

Derham Body Co. *continued*

sedan, with folding cast-bronze center pillars and roll-up side windows, looked extremely sporty, especially among conventional sedans of that era. Franklin commissioned Derham to design and build a sportsman's close-coupled coupe, whose rear seats folded against the back wall to make room for guns, animal carcasses, etc. Not many sportsmen stepped forward to buy this body style, however.

What kept Derham afloat during the Depression was service and maintenance business. With so many loyal local customers in the Philadelphia/Main Line area, the Derham shops stayed busy remounting old bodies on newer chassis, re-doing worn or tatty interiors, constructing new bodies along modern lines for traditional customers, and revarnishing existing bodies on a seasonal basis. As a sideline, Derham produced a few inexpensive towncars during the early 1930s by purchasing leftover, unsold 1929 Model A towncars from Ford dealers, removing the bodies and remounting them on 1933-34 Ford and Plymouth chassis. Meanwhile, a few conventional custom orders did trickle in throughout the Depression.

From roughly 1938 to 1952, Derham took on a DeSoto-Plymouth franchise and found itself in the healthiest position of all established coachbuilders. Except for Brunn, Derham's rivals had largely disappeared, and Brunn would soon go, too. Ironically, Derham took on a few more custom body orders, mostly on Chrysler chassis, as war broke out in Europe. During WW-II, Derham built cafeteria trailers for the Navy, tanks and floats for the Air Force, and various parts for Vickers, the British/Canadian aircraft maker.

After the war, Derham's coachbuilding business resumed in dribs and drabs. The company built two 1946 Chrysler Imperial "Continentals," customized Raymond Loewy's 1941 Lincoln Continental coupe (to Loewy-approved designs), produced a limited series of 1953 Packards, made convertible versions of the 1956 Continental Mark II, stretched a Corvair and turned out a number of other customs. In the 1960s, Derham's business consisted mostly of adding armor plate and converting cars for handicapped customers. In 1964, the east-coast Ferrari distributor, Albert A. Garthwaite, purchased Derham and made it part of Algar Enterprises Inc. Derham continued in business on a very limited basis through 1969 and closed its shops permanently in 1971. The Derham Co. files and records are now stored at the Gilmore/CCCA Museum in Hickory Corners, Michigan. ◆

Derham turned quite a few Fords into towncars, starting in Model T days. At top is an example from 1936. Custom Studebaker President convertible sedan (center), built by Derham, played a starring role in the 1940 auto shows. The coachbuilder customized the impressive 1947 Packard convertible limousine (above) for a private client.

1942 Chrysler might be suspected of borrowing the "Darrin dip," but Derham built a similar 1935 Bentley that used an identically dipped beltline.

J.B. JUDKINS CO.

Judkins started in 1857 as a carriage shop in Amesbury, Massachusetts. The company went through several early name and partnership changes and made its first automobile bodies in 1897. That year, Judkins received an order to design and build 20 brougham-like cab bodies for the Electric Vehicle Co. of Hartford, Connecticut. These were huge battery-powered vehicles, and the driver sat in a little open "balcony" behind the tall, glass-enclosed passenger compartment. He steered with a wheel.

By 1905, the J.B. Judkins Co. was building or had built bodies for Locomobile, Peerless, White, Morse, Winton, Alco, Stevens-Duryea and others. The company's last horsedrawn vehicle left the factory in 1910, and after that Judkins concentrated wholly on automobile bodies. Most were closed styles, designed and tailored for individual clients on large, expensive chassis such as Peerless, Pierce-Arrow, Mercer and Renault.

Judkins' chief designer was John Dobben, a Dutchman whose father had been a coachmaker for Queen Wilhelmina. Dobben and one of the Judkins founder's sons, Frederick, had both attended the carriagebuilders' technical school in New York. Dobben remained with Judkins well into the 1930s and, along with Edsel Ford, designed most of its Lincoln-based products. During the teens, though, the company's large, closed bodies were not what you'd call beautiful. They were skillfully wrought and solidly impressive, like all luxury cars of that day, but too tall and fussy to have lasting appeal. Dobben did design a couple of radical bodies: a round-backed 1915 Locomobile sedan that was 15 years ahead of its time, and the 1927 Lincoln coaching brougham, introduced on the Judkins stand at that year's New York Salon.

Judkins enjoyed its greatest sales during the 1920s, when its biggest customer was Lincoln. During a 20-year association with Lincoln (1921-41), Judkins produced a total of 5904 Lincoln bodies, all of them custom or series-custom.

The earliest Leland Lincolns were beautifully engineered and mechanically ahead of their time but tremendously tall and out of fashion. Ray Dietrich called the Leland Lincolns "Noah's arks" and said, "Wearing a topper, you could just about stand up in any one of them."

Runningboards stood 21 inches above the roadway.

A Boston Lincoln dealer, who recognized the negative value of the factory body, ordered the first Judkins Lincoln body, a four-place sedan with a partition window. Judkins called it a "berline." This dealer then drove the Judkins berline to Detroit to show to the Lelands. Along with Lincoln sales manager Ralph C. Getsinger, the Boston dealer held forth and finally convinced Henry Leland that Lincoln needed lower, more modern-looking bodies. In July 1921, Leland gave Judkins an order for 50 copies of the Judkins berline.

When Henry Ford bought Lincoln in 1922 and put Edsel in charge, the relationship with Judkins continued. Edsel soon came to rely on four major independent coachbuilders to supply Lincoln with most of its custom bodies: Judkins, Brunn, Willoughby and LeBaron. To minimize overlap, each firm was assigned specific body types, and Judkins ended up specializing in closed bodies: berlines, sedans, limousines and coupes. Edsel worked very closely with Judkins and the others on body details and overall styling. Most Judkins Lincolns were built in batches of from five to 100. Each year, Lincoln dealers received lavish catalogues that showed body selections from all four coachbuilders. Dealers used these catalogues to help sell local customers custom and semi-custom Lincoln bodies, hence the term "catalogue customs."

Not all of Judkins' business, though, had to do with Lincoln. The company also built bodies throughout the 1920s for Packard, Cadillac, Duesenberg, Marmon, Pierce, Locomobile and others. Many of these were again catalogue customs ordered by dealers or the factories, but a few were also for private individuals.

All Judkins Lincolns of the 1930s were beautifully designed and impeccably crafted. Among the best were the three-window coupes of the mid to late 1930s and the 1938 two-door touring fastback that John Judkins designed and built for himself.

By 1938-39, with virtually no more demand for coachbuilt automobile bodies, Judkins looked into the possibility of manufacturing aluminum caskets. The company already had the metalworkers and trimmers, so the casket business seemed a natural. But the competition was so firmly entrenched that Judkins couldn't break in. Instead, Judkins entered into the fabrication of aluminum house trailers, commercial display trailers and modular aluminum diners. They sold these on credit and carried their own paper. Too many customers, though, defaulted. As a result, Judkins closed its doors in 1941. ◆

Judkins Lincoln coaching brougham (top) took inspiration from Concord coaches, debuted at 1927 Commodore Salon. While Judkins built mostly Lincolns, the firm did do a few Duesenbergs (center page). 1938 Lincoln touring coupe (below) was John Judkins' personal car until 1946.

BRUNN & CO.

One confusion about Brunn's history is that there were two Hermann Brunns, father and son. Hermann A. was the father and company founder, and Hermann C. was his son.

The elder Brunn started in 1898 as an apprentice at his uncle's carriageworks in Buffalo, N.Y. After jobs with the New Haven Carriage Co. and the H.H. Babcock Co., Hermann A., in 1908, set up his own company, also in Buffalo, specifically to design and build custom automobile bodies. He'd graduated from the Andrew F. Johnson Technical School in New York, and among his first customers was Leslie Carter, the red-haired actress, who ordered two extremely yellow bodies on Thomas chassis ("I want them *yellow, yellow, yellow*," she shouted). Brunn also built early bodies for aircraft manufacturer Glenn Curtiss and Mary Roberts Reinhart, the mystery writer. When the Leland Lincoln arrived in Sept. 1920, its coachwork was gener-

ally considered so ugly, old-fashioned and noisy that prospective buyers used to get out halfway through a demonstration ride and walk back to the showroom. These inaugural Lincoln bodies were designed by Henry Leland's son-in-law, a man named Woodbridge. Woodbridge was, according to Hermann C. Brunn, a milliner and certainly no body designer. After Lincoln's embarrassing debut, a business friend of Brunn's, William R. Laidlaw, a large supplier of automotive upholstery fabrics, suggested to the Lelands that Hermann A. become Lincoln's styling and body consultant. Brunn was offered a $50,000 retainer to design 12 different body styles for the Leland Lincoln, which Hermann A. dashed off in his little home studio. His associate, Victor Lang, drew up the full-sized drafts. Sample bodies of all 12 designs were made by the Anderson Body Co. in Detroit and the American Body Co. in Buffalo.

When Ford took over Lincoln in 1922, Hermann A. Brunn, who was already friendly with Henry Ford, met Edsel Ford, and the two of them hit it off famously. As a result, Brunn continued to design custom bodies for Lincoln. Short-run customs were built in Brunn's Buffalo shops, but the longer series, including some of the catalogue customs, were farmed out to Anderson (later taken over by Murray) and other medium-sized bodymakers. Brunn, at the peak of production, employed 150 workmen and produced 20 or so bodies a month, most of which were shipped directly to the Lincoln plant for mounting. Sometimes, though, a dealer or a private customer would send Brunn a chassis and have the body built and mounted in Buffalo.

During a trip to Detroit in 1924, Hermann A. suggested to Edsel that he let Brunn & Co. build a special custom body specifically for him. "Funny you should say that," replied Edsel, "because I recently took delivery of a new Hispano-Suiza chassis, and I had it sent over to your plant for bodywork. When it gets there, let me know, and we'll talk

Brunn added a clear-vision windshield to early 1920s Packard (left). Sugar king Adolph Spreckels purchased one of Brunn's two 1932 Lincoln Doublentry sport sedans (below). Doors on both sides opened from either end. The 1934 Lincoln KB convertible victoria (bottom) stood on a 145-inch wheelbase, weighed 5171 pounds, cost $5700.

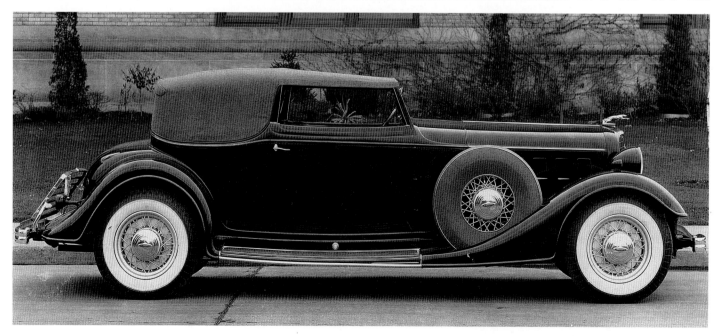

about the details." Brunn designed and built a very lovely, quite modern, dual-cowl, beavertail-back phaeton for Edsel Ford.

Brunn, being in Buffalo, also produced bodies for his neighbors at Pierce-Arrow. One of Brunn's most notorious Pierces was a towncar for the Shah of Iran. This had 18-carat gold-plated interior fixtures plus gold brocade upholstery. All exterior trim was also gold-plated: the grille shell, hubcaps, headlight rims, windshield frame, door handles and bumpers.

Instead of sending his only son to college, Hermann A. Brunn arranged for young Hermann C. to go to Paris and apprentice with Kellner, as Willie Brewster had done. When Hermann C. returned one year later, he joined his father and, although he was never given control, took an increasing role in the business.

Just as Edsel Ford asked Judkins to specialize in custom Lincoln berlines and coupes; and Willoughby to concentrate on limou-

sines; and LeBaron to make convertible sedans, he now assigned Brunn the task of designing and building mostly Lincoln towncars and convertible body styles: soft-top broughams, cabriolets, victorias and dual-cowl phaetons. Lincoln towncars, in particular, spread the Brunn name. They showed up in all major cities and were greatly admired, not only by their owners but also by interested observers. Chauffeurs, too, expressed their fondness for Brunn towncars, because Brunn was among the first to offer a folding canopy, or "tendelet," over the driver's compartment. When not in use, the canopy rolled up and stowed inside the hollow header behind the chauffeur. Later towncars even had roll-up windows for the chauffeur's compartment.

In the late 1920s, Hermann A. Brunn and Victor Lang designed and engineered production bodies for Dodge and Jordan. And in the early 1930s, a few of Brunn's custom bodies were recognizable by a sweep that picked up the windshield angle and continued it down to the bottom of the cowl. The hood then stretched all the way back to this line, which was sometimes highlighted with a raised, bright molding that served to separate contrasting paint colors.

1937 Lincoln Brunn touring cabriolet (above) had header "lights," chromed wire wheels, while 1940 Zephyr's front roof section lifted off to convert it into a towncar (below).

Brunn & Co. also prided itself on a manganese bronze windshield casting that weighed about 60 pounds. Manganese bronze was a common material for cast body parts, but this particular windshield frame, when polished, sparkled like gold. Once, at a meeting with Cadillac president Larry Fisher and some regional salespeople, a New York Cadillac dealer commented on the Brunn windshield. "Considering what Brunn charges for it," said the dealer, "the windshield might as well *be* gold!" Whereupon Hermann quietly replied that anyone else who built the same windshield frame to the same high standards would have to charge just as much. Fisher concurred and awarded Brunn some showcar contracts.

In 1932, Brunn & Co. championed the so-called Doublentry door. This was an extra-long side door that could be opened from either end. It had two handles and two sets of hinges. Turning one handle locked pins in the hinges at the opposite end, so the door couldn't accidentally be opened on both ends at the same time. With the trailing edge open, rear passengers could enter and exit easily, and front

Brunn often blended the traditionally severe towncar roof profile into the highly "streamlined" main body section, in this case on a 16-cylinder 1935 Cadillac 154-inch chassis.

passengers could do the same when they opened the leading edge. Brunn designed several different body styles with Doublentry doors, including four-place, close-coupled sedans and convertible victorias.

Brunn continued to supply custom bodies to Lincoln throughout the 1930s. Dealers for Packard, Pierce-Arrow and Cadillac occasionally ordered Brunn bodies during the Depression. Brunn's private customers included such notables as W.H. Annenberg, Adolph Spreckels, the Edsel Ford family and Joseph E. Widener.

In 1939, Buick general manager Harlow Curtice decided to offer

catalogue customs in the 1941 Limited 90 series. Curtice approached Fleetwood (Fisher Body) to build custom Buicks, but Cadillac objected, so Buick's chief engineer, Ed Ragsdale, offered the job to Brunn. Brunn had cut his workforce to 50 people by that time but eagerly took on the commission. Only five Brunn Buicks had been built when GM ordered Curtice to cancel the project. He was stepping on Cadillac's toes. (Actually Curtice did a bit more toe-stepping than that. Buick had 15 more horsepower in 1941 than Cadillac and five more than Packard.)

Brunn outlived most coachbuilders and continued to build custom bodies for Lincoln as late as 1941. Brunn also built the famous "Sunshine Special," the 1936 Lincoln K designed for Franklin D. Roosevelt and used by the White House until 1951. ◆

FLEETWOOD METAL BODY CO.

Fleetwood began in 1909, not from carriage origins but as a dedicated manufacturer of custom automobile bodies. Founder and former blacksmith Harry C. Urich had earlier founded another autobody company, the Reading Metal Body Co., which he sold. After Urich sold Reading, he and some business partners immediately started Fleetwood. They decided to name the company after the tiny borough near Reading that Fleetwood now called home.

Fleetwood immediately found itself with more work than it could handle, even with a staff of 375 and a series of additions to the plant. By 1920, 80% of Fleetwood's bodies were built on Packard chassis, 10% on Pierce-Arrow, 5% on Cadillac and the rest on various other makes. The coachbuilder's customers ranged from Rudolph Valentino, Theda Bara and Mary Pickford to the Vanderbilts, the Rockefellers and Andrew Carnegie.

Fleetwood's designs tended toward the conservative side, but not always. Valentino's Isotta-Fraschini, in unpainted aluminum, had a certain distinctive flashiness. Fleetwood bodies were always solid and beautifully crafted. Ironically, the company's New York sales and design offices were in the same building as LeBaron's, at #2 Columbus Circle. In fact, during the early 1920s, LeBaron's Ray Dietrich created some of Fleetwood's designs, which Fleetwood represented and built as its own.

In 1925, the Fisher Brothers approached Fleetwood and bought the entire operation. Although now owned by General Motors, Fleetwood continued to build bodies on non-GM chassis. Fleetwood turned out a good number of production bodies for Chrysler during 1926-27. Also, according to Richard Burns Carson, Fleetwood kept a modest catalogue-custom program going on the early Imperial 80 chassis. Fleetwood's "stationary cabriolet" on the Imperial E-80 127-inch chassis graced the Fleetwood stand at the 1927 New York Salon. Fleetwood additionally continued to build custom bodies for Stutz up to 1929. Packard and Lincoln, though, stopped patronizing Fleetwood after Fisher took over.

The reason Fisher chose Fleetwood rather than, say, Brunn, Derham, Judkins or one of the other coachbuilders, might have had to do with Fleetwood's fairly conservative, mainstream nature. Carson suggests that Fleetwood was a "business" rather than a "family" enterprise, thus the Fisher

Before GM bought Fleetwood, the coachbuilder built bodies on all makes of chassis, including this upstanding 1924 Lincoln limousine.

Brothers might have felt it was more approachable.

In Dec. 1930, Fisher closed the Pennsylvania plant, moved Fleetwood's sales office from New York to Detroit, where they gave Fleetwood two Fisher plants and relocated those Pennsylvania employees who wanted to come to Detroit. Apparently not many did. But Fleetwood's president Ernst Schebera and designer Jules Agramonte made the move, and Agramonte soon became a member of Harley Earl's styling staff at GM Art & Colour.

From Jan. 1, 1931 until Apr. 1, 1934, according to Alfred Sloan, Earl's entire operation came under the aegis of Fisher Body. One reason was to make all Fleetwood employees members of the Art & Colour staff, a move intended to simplify Fleetwood bookkeeping and salaries. It also gave Earl a pool of highly skilled artisans for special jobs and low-volume custom bodies. During the Depression, with very few orders coming in for coachbuilt bodies, Fleetwood craftsmen at Art & Colour stayed busy with projects like fabricating the Cadillac Aerodynamic Coupe for the 1933 Chicago World's Fair. Their steadiest job was hand-welding the deep-draw, multi-panelled fenders for 1934 Cadillacs and LaSalles.

The sudden abandonment of Fleetwood's Pennsylvania plant in Dec. 1930 left that community reeling through the worst of the Depression. Fleetwood Metal Body Co. had been the town's biggest employer. The residents who stayed in Fleetwood,

Fleetwood's sporty 1924 Packard 4-passenger phaeton on the Twin Six chassis used an extreme windshield rake and stood very low for that day.

After Fleetwood became part of General Motors, it moved to Detroit and built fewer and fewer cars on non-GM chassis. Soon Cadillac remained its only "customer," and Harley Earl's new Art & Colour section did all Fleetwood styling. The

1929 Cadillac transformable town cabriolet was the last to use the sweepside hood/cowl treatment (left). In 1930, the Cadillac V-16 reigned at GM, and Fleetwood created an elegant catalogue full of customs like this canework towncar.

Pennsylvania began to shun General Motors and for many years refused to buy GM cars, even though the only dealer in town sold new Chevrolets.

As for the Detroit operation, after 1931, the Fleetwood name was applied more and more to Art & Colour-designed, Fisher-built custom and semi-custom Cadillac coachwork. However, bodies for the 1948-49 and 1972 Fleetwood Cadillacs were unique, unshared with other styles. And the 1955-56 Fleetwood models used longer wheelbases and different roofs from standard bodies. Cadillac reserved the Fleetwood name for special C-bodied Cadillacs through 1992, and for 1993 they switched it to the rear-drive Brougham, which was discontinued in 1996. ◆

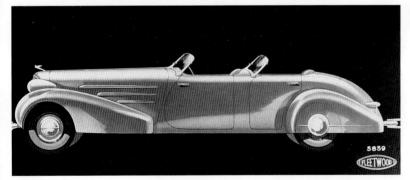

Rear windshield folded on 16-cylinder 1931 Cadillac dual-cowl phaeton (top), and a styled canvas boot fit over top. Subtle but important changes in rocker sills, clamshell fenders, headlamps and grille shape distinguish 1932 Cadillacs, including all-weather phaeton (above). The 1934 Fleetwood catalogue drawing (left) eliminated runningboards, used biplane bumpers, skirted rear fenders and two veed windshields. It seems even more advanced than 1936 Fleetwood convertible sedan below.

LaGrande

Duesenberg president Harold Ames made up the name LaGrande in 1930, the year LaGrande became Duesenberg's in-house carrossier. According to Duesenberg historian and restorer Randy Ema, LaGrande was nothing more than a name. It was never a real company. LaGrande had no letterhead, no headquarters or employees and was never an official business other than Duesenberg Inc.

Harold Ames probably used LeBaron as his inspiration for the name LaGrande. LaGrande bodies were built for and most often sent to Duesenberg in the white by three suppliers. One was the A.H. Walker Body Co. Albert H. Walker had been Weymann American's shop foreman in Indianapolis. Bodies supplied by A.H. Walker later became known as "Walker-LaGrandes," although a body tag with that name never appeared on any Duesenberg. In fact, only one or two Duesenbergs ever had tags that even said "LaGrande." Most LaGrande tags on restored cars today were installed by the restorers. A.H. Walker, by the way, had no relationship with the Walker Body Co. of Amesbury, Massachusetts.

Other suppliers of LaGrande bodies were the Union City Body Co., and the Central Manufacturing Co. Central was owned by the Cord Corp. and built mostly Auburn bodies. Auburn was also Union City's best customer, but Union City did make bodies for other manufacturers. And all three had special sections in their plants where they constructed LaGrande bodies for Duesenberg.

LaGrande bodies were designed by Gordon Buehrig and Herb Newport. The first LaGrande body was a Duesenberg phaeton ordered on May 19, 1930. It was finished a mere 45 days later, on July 3. It's estimated that a total of 29 LaGrande-designated bodies were built in all. Chassis production stopped in 1933 and the last LaGrande-bodied Duesenbergs were sold in 1936-37.　　　　　　◆

La Grande, Duesenberg's in-house coachbuilder, turned out a variety of bodies and body styles, including (top to bottom) an L-29 Cord victoria, one of two built. Gordon Buehrig designed the 1931 Duesenberg sweep-panel dual cowl phaeton and 1933 SJ boattail speedster, which Weymann constructed in metal. Buehrig later used this car as the styling basis for the 1935 Auburn boattail. La Grand produced five torpedo phaetons (below) in 1934 and three convertible coupes. Herb Newport styled coupe (left), used 1934 LaSalle bumpers and nonstandard grille. Roadster's hidden top (bottom left) cranked up by hand.

ROLLSTON/ROLLSON

The Rollston Co. began building custom bodies in 1921 and, although it remained small, was soon known for extremely high construction and trim standards. Rudy Creteur came over from Locke in 1927 to be Rollston's sole designer and sometime draftsman. According to Creteur, Rollston built 218 bodies between mid 1927 and mid 1931, an average of 54 a year. During the Depression, between 1931 and Rollston's demise in 1938, the company averaged only 22 bodies per year.

Five months after Rollston went into receivership in Apr. 1938, its president, Harold Lonschein, and three partners, including Rudy Creteur, founded Rollson Inc. (no "t" this time). Rollson designed and built bodies almost exclusively on Packard chassis, producing 50 custom Packards between Sept. 1938 and the U.S. entry into World War II. Rollson also built one Duesenberg all-weather convertible cabriolet and one Ford V-8 formal brougham. After Pearl Harbor, the company made parts for aircraft, submarines and even missiles. Rollson continued to make furnishings for ocean-going ships through the 1960s. ◆

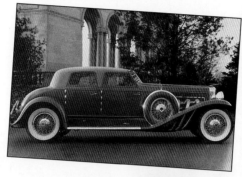

(Top to bottom) Rollston built 1932 Stutz convertible victoria plus several similar Packards. Rollston's Duesenberg Twenty Grand took its name from its price and bowed at 1933 Chicago Worlds Fair. Its coupe-like rear deck might have inspired similar trunk on 1938 Cadillac 60-Special. During Depression's depth, several coach-builders put patrician body types on plebeian chassis, in this case a Rollston 1934 Ford towncar. Rudy Creteur designed and Rollson finished Duesenberg JN convertible sport sedan at right in 1936 and convertible towncar below in 1940. The 1940 town-car was one of the last genuine coachbuilt Duesenbergs produced. Screened hood side invited passers-by to peer into the engine compartment.

WILLOUGHBY CO.

R.M. Bingham began making carriages and sleighs in Rome, New York in the late 1800s. Bingham's carriage factory burned to the ground in 1897, so he bought the Utica Carriage Co. in Utica, New York and named his son-in-law, Edward Willoughby, president. Willoughby and a partner, W.H. Owen, formed a separate company and began building bodies for the Columbia Electric in 1899.

Edward Willoughby later manufactured electrics under his own name and, in 1903, formed the Willoughby Co. to design and build automobile bodies. Six years later, Willoughby's son Francis came into the business.

As a coachbuilder, Willoughby always enjoyed the highest reputation. Willoughby supplied at least five cars to the White House (during the Coolidge and Hoover administrations) and others to the Rockefellers, Joe Louis, New York mayor Jimmy Walker and

automaker Horace Dodge. Lincoln and Packard became Willoughby's main customers, but the company also built one-off and series bodies on Wills Ste. Claire, Rolls-Royce, Duesenberg, Pierce-Arrow, Marmon, Cadillac, Cole, Studebaker, Chandler and Hudson chassis.

At its peak, Willoughby employed 300 craftsmen and, as the Depression wore on, Francis Willoughby refused to compromise his standards and perhaps felt too reluctant to let his people go. Finally, in 1938, he ran out of money and closed his doors for good. ◆

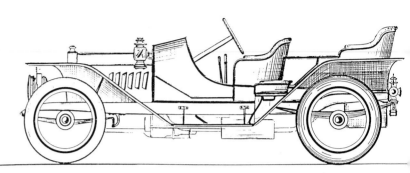

Willoughby began styling and making automobile bodies in 1899. By 1909, the former sleigh- and carriagemaker was designing sophisticated body types, like the 4-place sport tourer above. Lincoln became one of Willoughby's sustaining customers, sometimes with standing orders for 25-50 series customs. At right is a 1931 Lincoln towncar, formally called a panel brougham. The 1937 K towncar (directly below) was one of four built, and the 1936 sport sedan (below right) sold 11 copies. Lincoln's catalogue for 1937 offered a Willoughby convertible sedan (bottom) of which seven were built.

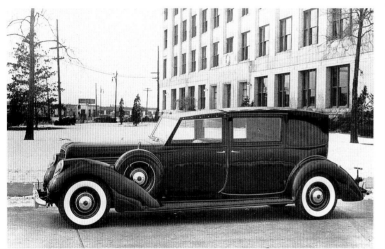

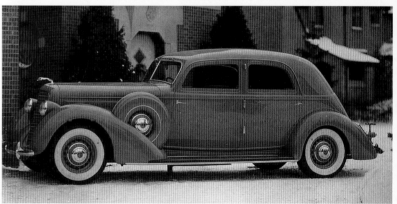

THE AMESBURY GROUP

It's remarkable that in the 1920s, the small North Shore town of Amesbury, Massachusetts could sustain eight well-known coachbuilders and two medium-sized autobody producers. There were body plants, large and small, all over what used to be called Carriage Hill, the industrial section of Amesbury where buggy-makers had flourished during the last quarter of the 19th century.

In those days, Amesbury used to make some of the finest carriages and buggies in the country. Each year, the town held a huge exhibition and carriage sale. These annual events became like the later coachbuilders' salons. People would arrive from all over the east to inspect and buy Amesbury's stylish, beautifully made carriages.

Amesbury's first autobody customer was the Electric Vehicle Co., who contracted with Judkins in 1897. Around 1903, Locomobile asked the Briggs Carriage Co. (no relation to Detroit's Briggs Mfg. Co.) to bid on a certain new style of body. Briggs' bid was so low that Locomobile voluntarily doubled the estimate "to assure good quality," and awarded Briggs the contract.

Amesbury craftsmen not only built the bodies but also had the skills to varnish them.

Briggs subcontracted the wood framing to Currier-Cameron, the result being that Locomobile was more than satisfied with the job. Soon other auto manufacturers sought out Amesbury carriagemakers to build bodies for them. The timing was perfect, because without automobile customers, Amesbury's carriagemakers would have gone out of business.

By 1919, Biddle & Smart had become Amesbury's largest auto-body producer, and four years later they owned nine plants in town. They were followed in size by the Walker Body Co. with five plants and the Bryant Body Co. with three. Other Amesbury bodymakers included Hollander & Morrill, Shields, Witham, Judkins and Judkins' subsidiary, the Merrimac Body Co. (Technically, Judkins and Merrimac were in the adjoining town of Merrimac, which was actually West Amesbury with a new name.)

Amesbury also played host to a number of support businesses and suppliers who specialized in such things as plating, metal and woodworking machinery, metal castings, window channels, regulators, glass, fasteners, springs, seats, trim, lamps and wheels. Gray & Davis, the lampmaker, had a plant in Amesbury, as did the Pettingell Machine Co., which made power hammers for the industry, including hundreds purchased by Fisher Body. In short, there was nothing that had to do with automobile bodies that couldn't be made or purchased in Amesbury.

Biddle & Smart, due to its production volume, fit into the category of medium-sized bodymakers that included Hayes, Ames, Seaman and Walker. The story of Biddle & Smart gives some insight not only into Amesbury but also into series body production.

The Biddle & Smart Co. began building carriages in 1882 and soon became one of the east coast's largest producers of buggies, wagons, carts and other horsedrawn vehicles. The company started making carbodies in 1905, the year William E. Biddle Jr.

assumed the company presidency. W.W. Smart died in 1897, and Biddle Sr. passed away in 1907, but the business continued to grow under Biddle Jr.

Biddle & Smart reached its peak in the mid 1920s, when its customers included Hudson, Rolls-Royce, Lincoln, Peerless, Mercer, White, Chalmers, Speedwell and Haynes. Its biggest account was Hudson and its busiest year ever was 1929, when the Essex ranked #3 in national new-car sales, behind Ford and Chevrolet.

Hudson initially contracted with Biddle & Smart in 1922 to produce aluminum bodies for its seven-passenger sedan, switching to five-passenger sedans in 1923. Biddle & Smart supplied Hudson with aluminum bodies only. They had no presses to form steel, nor did any other company in Amesbury. In 1925, Biddle & Smart also began making bodies for Rolls-Royce, and by March 1926 their Amesbury holdings had grown from nine shops to 41 scattered around town. Some were quite small, but together they were turning out 400 bodies a day. Biddle & Smart's piecemeal facilities amounted to a cottage industry. Bodies were dollied from place to place and put through individual departments for framing, metalworking, painting, trimming, etc. The Italian coachbuilders evolved a similar system after World War II.

Hudson bodies were sent by rail from Amesbury to Detroit in special train cars. Biddle & Smart shipped 41,000 bodies in 1926, and employment rose to 4700, this according to Hudson historian John Conde. By this time, Biddle & Smart had absorbed several other Amesbury body firms, among them Witham, Hollander & Morrill and Auto Body & Finishing Co. (At the height of Amesbury's productivity, most body-makers used two shifts. Oldtimers recalled that both shifts passed through Market Square in the town's center each workday at five in the afternoon. The traffic jams were horrendous.)

Hudson contracts sustained Biddle & Smart throughout the rest of the decade. During the latter half of the 1920s, the Walter M. Murphy Co. in Pasadena, California provided designs and working drafts for some of Hudson's production bodies. These were then built by Biddle & Smart and shipped to the Hudson plant in Detroit. Several of Murphy's Hudson designs became Biddle & Smart semi-customs.

Murphy at times designed cars with lower roof lines than Hudson management deemed acceptable. The general public, so claimed Hudson's body engineers, would never buy cars with roofs that low. The 1928 Hudson convertible sedan became a case in point. Unbeknownst to Murphy, Hudson decided to raise the roof three inches, and that's how the car came out. By the time Murphy discovered the change, it was too late to say anything. The car wasn't a big seller but probably wouldn't have been even if it were lower.

Hudson had been manufacturing most of their own bodies at the Gratiot plant in Detroit and contracted others out to Briggs and Murray, both of whom were much nearer Hudson. Transportation charges to and from Amesbury made Biddle & Smart too expensive for Hudson to continue using. Also, as Amesbury historian Charles R. Yeaton has pointed out, the community couldn't keep up with the rapidly evolving technology of

A drying room inside one of the Amesbury bodymakers' plants.

Amesbury Group *continued*

bodymaking. It didn't have the modern presses and machine tools to form deep-draw steel panels like roofs and fenders. "Draw depths, contours and radii that had previously been available only in handformed aluminum," said Yeaton, "were now practical on a production basis in much less expensive C-1010 and C-1020 drawing steels."

With the Depression worsening and Hudson turning more body business over to nearer suppliers, Biddle & Smart found themselves without a major Detroit customer. B&S tried for a time to manufacture aluminum boats, but this venture failed, and B&S soon shut their doors. The loss of Biddle & Smart dealt a terrible blow to Amesbury, but Walker and Judkins managed to survived through 1933 and 1941 respectively. ◆

Around 1919, Amesbury bodymaker Walker, whose main customer was Franklin, built a center-door hardtop sedan on what seems to be a Jeffrey chassis (above). This was not a California top but a true hardtop. Companies like Biddle & Smart set up systems whereby large numbers of similar assembly operations took place simultaneously (above right). In other Amesbury shops, cars and bodies went together one at a time (right). Biddle & Smart supplied Hudson with thousands of production bodies each year throughout the 1920s. Most were aluminum, as in the case of 1926 Hudson sedan (below) and 1928 victoria coupe (below right).

EARL AUTOMOBILE WORKS AND DON LEE COACH & BODY WORKS

In 1908, the Earl Carriage Works, founded by Jacob William (J.W.) Earl in 1889 in downtown Los Angeles, left buggymaking and began to produce accessory windshields, tops and then entire motorcar bodies. By 1910, J.W. had changed the name of his company to the Earl Automobile Works. The Earl coachworks became significant not so much for their famous customers or the cars they produced but because this was where J.W.'s son, Harley J. Earl, began his career. As we'll see in Chapter Seven, Harley Earl became the single most important figure in American automobile design.

The Earl Automobile Works was absorbed into the pre-existing Don Lee Coach & Body Works in 1919. Don Lee had been selling Cadillacs since 1906 and, in 1919, in addition to buying out J.W. Earl, had become Cadillac's official west-coast distributor. His dealerships already blanketed the state from Los Angeles and Pasadena to Fresno, San Francisco, Oakland and Sacramento. Don Lee was now Cadillac's answer to Packard's prestigious Earle C. Anthony distributorship and would, in less than a year, also compete with Walter M. Murphy's west-coast Lincoln franchise.

On July 13, 1919, the *San Francisco Chronicle* announced that, "...[Don Lee has acquired]...the largest plant of its kind west of Chicago, and for several years Earl's has been one of the six largest builders of custom bodies in the United States. J.W. Earl...will continue in active charge, and his son, Harley Earl, will continue as chief designer.

"It is Don Lee's intention to turn out the very best coach work obtainable anywhere. With this idea in view, he will send one of his designers to New York twice a year, and as soon as European manufacturers are once more in production, a Don Lee designer will make a yearly trip abroad.... Harley Earl will leave this week for a trip to the Eastern factories to ascertain the trend of the enclosed car styles for the coming fall and winter. Immediately upon his return, construction will be started on several types of the newest enclosed car designs."

In Tom Hibbard's estimation, the custom bodies Harley Earl designed at Don Lee were "striking in appearance," but at the same time, "were what we Easterners considered flamboyant," which was probably Earl's intent. In 1926, when Harley Earl left Los Angeles permanently to work for General Motors, Don Lee shut down his custom body operation, and this left the field wide open for Walter M. Murphy. ◆

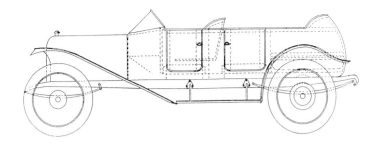

J.W. Earl most likely designed 1911 sport tourer at left, apparently with a wraparound windshield. His son, Harley, adapted a similar windshield to his 1918 sedan sketch. This and similar sketches appeared in coachbuilder's brochure. Earl, at Don Lee, designed and produced Jack Pickford's 1920 Cadillac towncar (below) and 1920 roadster. Earl's daring caught the attention of A.P. Sloan and Larry Fisher at GM, who asked him to design first LaSalle.

WALTER M. MURPHY CO.

Walter Montgomery Murphy grew up in Detroit, graduated from Detroit University and afterward spent two years in the family lumber business. According to Strother MacMinn writing in *Automobile Quarterly*, the Murphy family made its fortune in Michigan lumber. Walter's uncle, William H. Murphy, had helped bankroll Henry Ford's 1899 automobile company and, in 1903, befriended Henry Leland when Leland carved Cadillac from yet another Ford venture.

Around 1904, the young and entrepreneurial Walter moved to Pasadena, California, where he began to mass produce millwork for the booming Los Angeles housing market. But in 1916, Murphy sold his woodworking shops and opened a Locomobile and Simplex dealership in downtown Los Angeles. He arranged with east-coast coachbuilders to supply custom bodies for his agency's cars.

When Henry M. Leland announced his new Lincoln in 1920, it's likely but not documented that Uncle William arranged for Walter to become Lincoln's California distributor. Recognizing Lincoln's immediate need for more appealing bodywork and knowing the California market, Walter M. Murphy organized his own coachbuilding enterprise in Pasadena and hired George R. Fredericks away

Los Angeles, met pilot and flying enthusiast Frank S. Spring and hired him as an efficiency consultant. Spring came from a wealthy family and had grown up in France; had, in fact, graduated from the polytechnic in Paris. So he wasn't just a pilot but also a practicing auto engineer. He knew a great deal about cars, motorcycles and aircraft, especially European makes, and had been chief engineer of the short-lived 1923 Courier.

After Fredericks drowned, Murphy asked Spring to take over as manager of the coachbuilding operation, with J. Gerard Kirchhoff as shop supervisor. In late 1926, Murphy traded his Lincoln franchise for rights to distribute Hudson and Essex motorcars throughout southern California. In Murphy's eyes, Hudson had a better future than Lincoln. Through this new distributorship, Murphy and Spring became acquainted with Hudson's management, and Hudson became interested in using the Walter M. Murphy Co. to design its custom and semi-custom bodies, which were then being

Second custom body built by Murphy was this 1921 Lincoln roadster for Maj. Max Fleischman. Murphy made first Lincoln roadster for himself.

1921 Lincoln sedan shows windshield and general conformation similar to Earl designs. This particular Murphy body was painted in tones of magenta , with a striped Boyriven broadcloth interior in two hues of henna.

built by Biddle & Smart. Murphy designed a low, handsome 1928 Hudson convertible sedan, which Biddle & Smart built (but three inches taller). Each of these Biddle & Smart bodies carried a cowl tag that announced *Designed by Walter M. Murphy, Coachbuilders, Pasadena.*

In the meantime, Murphy managed to bring together some of the finest young design talent on the west coast. Wellington Everett Miller, as a mere lad of 16, began his apprenticeship as a part-time artist under Murphy staff designer George McQuerry Jr. Miller had seen the new Murphy-bodied Lincolns at the 1920

from Healey & Co. in New Jersey to manage it. Fredericks brought with him Chris Bohman and other capable craftsmen, and the Walter M. Murphy Co. began to produce custom-bodied Lincolns in August 1920. Murphy retained his sales agency, which by then had switched from Locomobile and Simplex to Lincoln.

Murphy's second custom Lincoln went to Major Max Fleischman (Murphy built the first one for himself), and from then on the company's patrons included the luminaries of Hollywood and the west-coast business community. Meanwhile, Murphy's sales agency had expanded and, by 1923, was selling Lincolns, Fords and Fordson tractors in Los Angeles, Pasadena, San Francisco, Oakland and Fresno. Also during 1923, Murphy agreed to supply Abner Doble with bodies for Doble's luxurious steam-powered automobiles, although in very small numbers as it turned out. But the Murphy shops were soon providing bodies for more than just Lincolns. Customers began rolling in with Mercer, Packard, Mercedes-Benz, Rolls-Royce, Minerva, Auburn, Hudson and other chassis.

Unfortunately, Murphy's manager, George Fredericks, drowned while trying to rescue a company secretary at a Fourth of July beach party in 1924. The secretary somehow made it to shore but Fredericks didn't. Just before the tragedy, Walter Murphy, in the process of developing a small airport in Whittier, southwest of

Thin clear-vision A-pillars graced Murphy 1928 Cadillac convertible sedan. Murphy applied same design to Auburn, Packard and Rolls-Royce. Designers Frank Hershey and Phil Wright joined Murphy that year.

Los Angeles Auto Show and immediately made up his mind that car design would be his life. Which it duly became.

Two other marvelously gifted young designers who started with Murphy were Franklin Quick Hershey and Philip O. Wright. Tall, lanky, energetic Frank Hershey arrived at Murphy's in 1928, and the more reserved Phil Wright joined later that year. Wright had almost no use of his left arm and also suffered with breathing problems, but he played a lively right-hand-only piano and had a great ear. Hershey and Wright learned from each other, Wright teaching Hershey a watercolor illustrating technique that Frank eventually did as well as Phil. Both contributed to the coachbuilder's greatest designs during that golden age when Murphy put more bodies on Model J and SJ Duesenberg chassis than any other bodymaker in the nation. Hershey's low, luscious designs on the L-29 Cord included the sweepside dual-cowl phaeton (three built), and Wright designed a pair of L-29 towncars for Lola Montez and John Barrymore, plus several other magnificent L-29 Cords.

Spring and Murphy were now family, related through their wives, and in this less formal atmosphere, Frank Spring suggested to Walter Murphy that they become involved in the Guggenheim competition to build a small "safety" airplane; one that any automobile driver could fly. At the time, Guggenheim offered $100,000 to anyone who could come up with a winning entry. Murphy poured at least $100,000 into the Guggenheim project but then abandoned it as the Depression deepened. By 1930, it had become obvious that there wouldn't be an immediate market for a small safety airplane, and even coachbuilt cars were beginning to seem iffy.

The movie colony still did commission a few coachbuilt cars, so around 1930, Murphy launched an ambitious engineering program to build all-steel custom automobile bodies. Murphy thus became one of very few American coachbuilders to even consider steel as a replacement for traditional wood framing. The company fabricated several all-steel Duesenberg bodies in 1930-31

and at least one on a Bentley chassis.

About this time, a number of independent automakers, in addition to Hudson and Auburn, began asking Murphy to submit design proposals for their production cars. The heartbreaker was Peerless which, in 1931, commissioned Murphy to style and build either one or two (accounts differ) aluminum sample bodies for an ambitious 16-cylinder sedan. Peerless president James Bohanon saw the luxurious V-16 as his company's salvation.

Frank Hershey received the assignment to design what he said were two versions of a long, low four-door body, one with five windows and the other with seven. The doors curved up into the roof. For the seven-window sedan, which was built and delivered, Hershey made a full-sized side-view cutout—a two-dimensional approximation of a clay model—and used it to show proportion and scale, particularly height. Peerless went out of the car business (into beermaking) soon after Murphy finished the two V-16 bodies, and it's not known whether Peerless ever paid Murphy.

In 1931, Frank Spring saw the handwriting and took a job in Detroit as Hudson's director of styling (see page 190). The Guggenheim safety plane, along with losses from Walter Murphy's Hudson-Essex distributorship, caused Murphy to sell his coachworks to Kenneth McKay in 1932 while the company still had a few contracts. Just before McKay took over, Murphy burned hundreds of photos and negatives, all body drafts and shop records. McKay limped along for another six months and then folded. Walter Murphy also closed his Hudson business in 1932. He founded the Murphy Petroleum Co. the next year and became a products distributor for Standard Oil of California. ◆

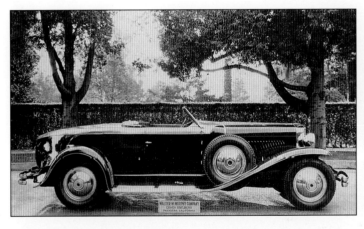

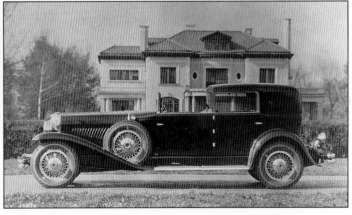

(Above) Boattail 1929-30 Murphy Duesenberg "torpedo convertible coupe" had a polished aluminum upper deck that swept forward along the beltline and onto the hood. Murphy turned out more custom-bodied Duesenbergs than any other coachbuilder. Among them were the 1929 towncar (above right) and 1929 sedan (below left). The sedan's graceful upper combines the thin A-pillars of the clear-vision windshield with semi-oval rear side windows for a strikingly light

look. The applied belt moldings wrapped ahead of windshield in Hibbard & Darrin fashion. One of Murphy's most famous creations was the 1932 Peerless V-16 sedan designed by Frank Hershey (below right). All four doors wrapped into roof, and delicate fender edgings consisted of thin, polished aluminum strips. Even before Murphy closed its doors in 1932, company manager Frank Spring was offered --and accepted--a position as Hudson's styling director.

BOHMAN & SCHWARTZ

Bohman & Schwartz made two similar 1935 Duesenberg SJ convertibles. One, built over an older cowl, belonged to Clark Gable (right). Woolworth heiress Barbara Hutton then commissioned the other, with a different front, new cowl and on a new chassis, and presented it to her husband, Prince Serge M'Divani, as a gift.

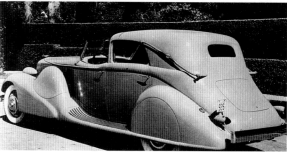

Herb Newport designed the Bohman & Schwartz 1935 Duesenberg towncar above for candy heiress Ethel Mars. And 57-Varieties heir Rust Heinz commissioned B&S to build 1938 Phantom Corsair (left) on a Cord 812 platform. Heinz designed the low fastback coupe himself and hoped to interest investors in series production. He was killed in a car accident before he could realize that dream, but the Phantom Corsair survives.

Bohman & Schwartz 1940 Cadillac convertible (below) made use of the Darrin dip. The Pasadena coachbuilder also fabricated the 1937 Topper car, used in movie versions of the Thorne Smith novels.

Two smaller coachbuilders rose up from the Murphy ashes: Bohman & Schwartz and Kirchhoff. Chris Bohman came to Walter M. Murphy from Healey & Co. W.E. Miller said later that Bohman was one of Murphy's earliest employees and was brought along by Murphy manager George A. Fredericks.

Maurice Schwartz learned coachbuilding in his native Austria, starting in 1904, and worked for Don Lee in the late teens and early 1920s under Harley Earl. In 1924, Schwartz also joined Murphy. After Murphy went out of business in 1932, Bohman & Schwartz teamed up and continued to build custom bodies in Pasadena on a very limited basis. Everett Miller contributed some of the designs and layouts. Bohman & Schwartz did the Ethel Mars 1935 Duesenberg, the Topper movie car, and a number of other customs for motion-picture stars and film companies. Maurice Schwartz died in 1961, but Chris Bohman kept the company alive for a number of years after that. ◆

COACHCRAFT LTD.

In early 1940, Rudy Stoessel, Paul Erdos and Burt Chalmers opened a small shop on Melrose Avenue in Hollywood called Coachcraft Ltd. Coachcraft immediately began building custom bodies for movie stars and wealthy Angelinos.

Stoessel, the primary partner, had worked in Pierce-Arrow's experimental shops from 1926 to 1929, then came west and took jobs with J. Gerard Kirchhoff and Dutch Darrin in the 1930s. It was Rudy who made the casting patterns for the early Packard-Darrin's aluminum cowl, bronze windshield frame, door pillars, top bows, etc. Stoessel and Paul Erdos were Coachcraft's craftsmen. Erdos had been a metalshaper for the Bender Body Co. in Cleveland in the 1920s and formed most of the body skins at Coachcraft.

Burt Chalmers, the third partner, was the company's salesman and promoter. He'd sold menswear in New York, then came to Los Angeles to sell French cars and Packard-Darrins. It was through Dutch Darrin that Chalmers met Stoessel and Erdos. When Darrin left L.A., the three partners formed Coachcraft Ltd.

Among Coachcraft's customers were Preston Foster, Charles (The Durango Kid) Starrett, Bill Holden, Henry Ford II, Liberace, Mrs. Morgan Adams, Huntington Hartford III, gangster Mickey Cohen and auto designer Peter Stengel. Among other designers who penned some of Coachcraft's creations were Phil Wright and Strother MacMinn.

The Peter Stengel car was a sedanca de ville based on a 1941 Mercury, chopped and channeled, with the front fenders extended into the doors, a padded deauville roof and blacked-out headlamps. For Charles Starrett, Coachcraft built a 1941 Cadillac station wagon along the lines of the 1941 Chrysler Town & Country. Their two-passenger formal coupe for Morgan Adams used a shortened 1949 Cadillac chassis, and the body had subtly muted rear fenders that kept the stock Cadillac tail lamps but not the fins.

When things got slow in the shop, Coachcraft marketed a line of continental kits, roof racks and mufflers. In 1959, Rudy Stoessel bought out Erdos and Chalmers and dropped "Ltd." from the company name. Some of Coachcraft's later business included restorations and body creations for Harrah's Automobile Collection. Coachcraft survived until 1966. ◆

Coachcraft's channeled 1940 Ford convertible had a removable hardtop, belonged for a time to cinema photographer James Wong Howe, who drove it until 1952. George Barris once credited Coachcraft for inspiring the sorts of custom cars he created just after World War II.

Peter Stengel commissioned Coachcraft to build 1941 Mercury sedanca de ville. He reportedly sold it that year to Mrs. Huntington Hartford III for $20,000 but repurchased it in 1953. Designer was Buzz Petersen of Lockheed.

Coachcraft put "through" fenders on a number of cars, among them this 1941 Cadillac. Other Coachcraft hallmarks were the rolled, simple beltline and steeply raked, veed windshield.

CHAPTER 6

EARLY CORPORATE DESIGN ACTIVITIES

Both Locomobile and White officially had body designers on their payrolls as early as the 1910s. Locomobile hired Frank de Causse in 1914 to head that company's custom body department, and White employed Leon Rubay that same year to style its production bodies. In 1916, Studebaker set up a custom body division headed by J.H. Bourgon, previously with Brewster, Willoughby and Pierce-Arrow. Studebaker's idea was to have Bourgon design and oversee construction of a line of medium-priced, semi-custom bodies; sort of a middle-class version of catalogue customs. Studebaker built and trimmed these bodies in a special area in their South Bend, Indiana plant and sold them for much less than coachbuilt bodies. By sidestepping the independent *carrossiers,* Studebaker passed the saving along to their dealers and customers.

Nor were these the first or only corporate styling departments in the industry. We mention them mostly to show that General Motors didn't suddenly conceive the nation's first-ever corporate styling operation when they formed their Art & Colour section in 1927. By that time, dozens of automakers already had one- or two-person styling staffs. Very few records exist, so figures are hard to come by. But in addition to the stylists employed by the various automakers, nearly all established coachbuilders also had designers and delineators on their payroll.

Two auto-design pioneers—at least two who left their marks plus some record of their existence—were Leon Rubay and Frank de Causse. And since we can tell you a little about them, we'll do that before taking up the weightier topic of GM Art & Colour and

the establishment of the nation's other principal corporate styling staffs.

Both Rubay and de Causse came to the U.S. from Paris, a distinction that probably gave them a fashion edge in selling their ideas and services to American automakers. Rubay's original surname might have been Rubé, with an accent over the "e." If so, he Anglicized it for obvious reasons when he came to New York in 1902 or '03 and started the Leon Rubay Corp., which sold French electrical equipment, tires and auto accessories. His company went bankrupt in 1908, whereupon Rubay took a job with the coachbuilder Rothschild and, in 1911, with Holbrook.

In 1914, Rubay became manager of the White Motor Co.'s automobile department in Cleveland. During his two years with White, Rubay designed all of its "pleasure-car" bodies (as opposed to trucks). In late 1916, the White Motor Co. reorganized and helped set Rubay up in his own body company nearby.

Rubay continued to manufacture production and custom bodies for White, at the same time designing (and sometimes building) coachwork for several other automakers: Henry A. Lozier's prestigious 1917-18 HAL V-12, the 1921-22 Duesenberg Model A, Franklin, Roamer, Locomobile, Marmon and Cole.

In 1920, Rubay received a design contract from Pierce-Arrow, who wanted to reduce the number of its body styles from 60-odd to 10. Those 10, though, had to be every bit as attractive and laden with image as the previous 60-plus. In addition, Pierce insisted that Rubay design around the existing aluminum castings the company was using for wheelhouses and window frames. Rubay

LeBaron designers, working on the top floor of Briggs' main office building on Mack Av. in Detroit, had a separate area that took advantage of space and natural light. Along the windows, front to rear, are designers Jim Wilson, Hugh Galt and Phil Wright. At the fourth drawingboard is Ralph Roberts talking with Al Prance. Name of the clay modeler at left is unknown, as is date.

complied with all of Pierce's requests and delivered his designs on time. Meanwhile, he'd also hired Tom Hibbard as a sketch artist, effectively launching Hibbard's career. Rubay worked, too, with Amos Northup (see page 76), who at that time was with Pierce-Arrow. Northup's name appears on catalogue renderings of the 1923 Leon Rubay automobile.

Ralph Roberts of LeBaron met Rubay in the late teens and remembered him as "French through and through." Rubay's reddish-blond hair, mustache and goatee earned him the nickname "Pink Whiskers" around the White plant. Rubay's wife, Germaine, suffered a fatal stroke in 1920, "and then a very strange thing happened," Roberts told one of the authors in 1993. "When Mr. Rubay's wife died suddenly, he went back to France, married her identical twin sister, returned with her to this country and continued right on!"

In 1923, Rubay launched an automobile under his own name. The 1923 Leon Rubay was almost as French as its namesake and, like Rubay himself, had a European accent but much smaller specifications than competitive, high-priced American makes. The 1923 Leon Rubay stood on a 118-inch wheelbase, versus 138 inches for the 1923 Stevens-Duryea, had a tiny engine—only 97.5 cubic inches—with an overhead camshaft and four cylinders. As for coachwork, Rubay tried to tempt high-end buyers with simple, tasteful, European lines. His car's steep price, $5100-$5300, its small size and lack of power, though, didn't bring customers running, and Rubay stopped production late in 1923. The failure of this venture had a profound psychological effect on Rubay. He became deeply depressed and returned to France permanently with his new wife. His body plant was purchased by Baker-Raulang in 1924.

The other notable Franco-American designer of that era was J. Frank de Causse (rhymes with *rose*). According to his principal biographer, Walt Gosden, de Causse studied art, architecture, design and art history in his native France. As a teenager, de Causse became interested in cars and took a job as a drafting apprentice with Kellner, the Paris coachbuilder. Here he soon found himself involved not only with making body drafts but also with designing, and he discovered a knack for presenting his designs to Kellner's customers. It was by combining these three skills—designing, drafting and salesmanship—that de Causse became an assistant manager in 1904.

In 1914, the Locomobile Co. of Bridgeport, Connecticut decided to offer its own line of custom bodies. To start the project, Locomobile needed a custom body designer, someone with experience and a name, preferably French. To find such a person, Locomobile sent a representative

to the Paris Salon, the purpose being to interview designer candidates. De Causse was hired and arrived at Locomobile's New York office in the autumn of 1914. Here he soon built up a small design staff, which included the superb watercolorist, Roland L. Stickney. Stickney turned out to be no mean designer himself. He later went to LeBaron and did catalogue illustrations not only for LeBaron but also for a number

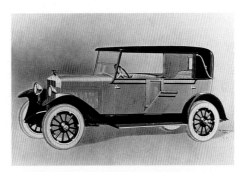

The short-lived 1923 Leon Rubay, styled by designer of same name, copied French luxury format. Touring car had California top and a compartment between doors to store sidecurtains. Realistic rendering carries logo of Amos Northup Studio, Buffalo.

Dealers complained that Franklins looked too unusual, so company hired Frank de Causse to style its 1925 Series 11. De Causse designed a formidable "radiator" with focal circle at bottom.

of automakers and other coachbuilders.

Locomobile's "custom department" commissioned only about 40 or so cars a year, none actually built by Locomobile. De Causse created many of the designs, which Stickney rendered and Locomobile published in catalogue form. Agents sold specific designs to customers from these catalogues, and de Causse then farmed the work out to independent coachbuilders in and around Manhattan, notably Healey, Locke, Demarest and Holbrook. Whether de Causse became involved in making presentations to individual clients we don't know, but that era's Locomobile owner list read like the Social Register: the Vanderbilts, the Carnegies, the Wanamakers, Chicago chewing-gum magnate William Wrigley and even General "Black Jack" Pershing.

The first de Causse-created Locomobile bodies appeared on the Healey stand at the

1916 New York Salon. Here de Causse introduced one of the earliest examples (perhaps *the* earliest) of a dual-cowl, double-windshield phaeton. Later, de Causse also designed Locomobile's production bodies. But when Locomobile went into receivership in 1922, de Causse found himself without a steady income. (By 1923, W.C. Durant had taken over Locomobile, and LeBaron's Ray Dietrich designed a number of Locomobile's custom bodies. These were built by Demarest, Brewster and Locke. Four LeBaron bodies went on display at the 1923 Importers Show at the Hotel Astor.)

By this time, LeBaron Carrossiers was doing business in New York as an architectural autobody design firm. After Locomobile let him go, de Causse decided to open an office based on the same idea. He would design but not build custom bodies for private individuals and corporate customers. Like LeBaron, de Causse rented offices in midtown Manhattan, and like LeBaron, too, he sold many of his designs to factory sales agents. Taking one final cue from LeBaron, de Causse arranged with local coachbuilders to put his designs on wheels. Among his first customers was the New York agent for Benz automobiles, for whom de Causse designed four different and distinctive body styles. Tom Hibbard used to run into de Causse at the New York Salons and later described him as "cordial but aloof."

In 1923, de Causse received a frantic phone call from Franklin. The company's sales people were all upset because several dealers had threatened to give up their franchises if Franklin's future air-cooled cars didn't show a more conventional "radiator" design. Franklin management, prodded by their influential Southern California distributor, asked for styling proposals from the Walter M. Murphy Co. in California and from J. Frank de Causse in New York. Franklin ended up choosing the de Causse design, and de Causse ended up reshaping not just the grille, with its distinctive circle at the bottom, but the entire line of bodies for the 1925 Series 11 Franklins.

Concurrently, W.C. Durant hired de Causse to style a new Flint automobile. Durant had by then taken over Locomobile and, when he heard about de Causse working for Franklin, told de Causse that he was still under exclusive contract to Locomobile. Not at all, said de Causse, and these two very strong personalities got into a lively argument, which de Causse eventually won.

H.H. Franklin, who'd suddenly become an enthusiastic convert to the idea that "style sells," asked de Causse to create additional custom designs for his company as well as several for production. De Causse was given a small studio inside Franklin's Syracuse engineering offices,

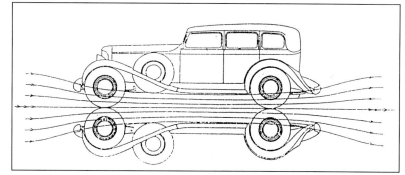

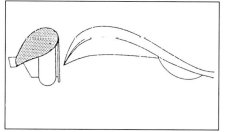

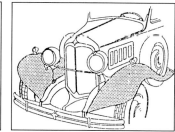

Amos Northup and Jules Andrade at Murray Corp. of America styled the 1931 Reo Royale. This car was revolutionary because the designers rounded what had formerly been sharp body edges and blended body parts that had previously been separate. During development, they tested scale plaster models in a windtunnel and made adjustments based on aerodynamic observation. Sketches at right were used in an SAE talk to illustrate airflow and how the designers faired in various components.

where he worked with Franklin's manager of its custom division, Kent C. Haven. It wasn't long before Franklin was offering boat-tail speedsters and other much more sporting designs than the company ever had before.

Meanwhile, de Causse kept his New York office going and did additional designs for various private individuals. He also arranged for special-bodied Franklins to have their coming-out at the more prestigious North American salons: New York, Chicago and Los Angeles. He later traveled to the European motorshows on Franklin's behalf. And in 1926, de Causse took on Locke & Co. as a client and made up all of Locke's full-sized body drafts.

Things were going well, but late in 1926 or early '27, Frank de Causse was diagnosed with throat cancer. He traveled to Paris for treatment, but nothing helped. He passed away, aged 48, on May 10, 1928. Walt Gosden wrote de Causse's epitaph in *Automobile Quarterly*: "His was an age of grace, of elegant automobiles that were made of wood, bronze, alloy, steel and tender loving care."

DeCausse passed away too soon, because this was precisely the time when the business of automobile design went from a low-priority occupation—one that hardly even existed in a formal sense—to one with high priority and tremendous potential. And here's why.

First, the auto companies, prompted by their own sales people, suddenly realized, or at least acknowledged, that physical appearance—good looks, glamor, verve, flair, color, snap, sexiness, sportiness; call it what you will but just be sure the product has it—could help sell cars. Style, fashion, color, appearance became recognized as important factors in bringing customers into the showroom. Now that cars ran fine and stayed put together, the major differences in each price class became looks.

As a result of this dawning realization by the major automakers, the citadel of style and fashion began to shift, starting around

1926, from New York to Detroit. The eastern establishment's salons were still important, but they were beginning to give way to Detroit's embryonic production studios.

And as Detroit began to look seriously at appearance as a sales stimulant, styling would soon become competitive, as in, "Our car has to look better than their car." So from 1925 to 1930, design studios began popping up all over the industry. The east-coast *carrossiers* would still influence production design to some extent during those years, but less and less. And it's likely that the coachbuilders' influence would have declined even if there'd been no Great Depression.

Between 1925 and 1930, Detroit's rising interest in style swiftly prompted Fisher, Briggs, Murray and Hayes (but not Budd) to add custom body departments to their operations and then, just as quickly, to hire production-body design staffs: people who could help style salable cars for their present and future customers. During this period, the autobody industry saw an unprecedented number of styling-related mergers, buy-outs and takeovers as the big bodymakers began to compete for the nation's relatively small pool of known talent.

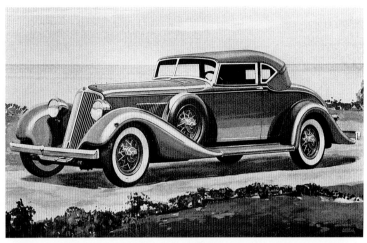

Northup and Andrade followed up Royale with trendsetting 1932 Graham Blue Streak (above). The Blue Streak's valanced front fenders, raked grille and integrated lines

were highlighted with monochromatic paint schemes. Bel Geddes' 1928 brass model (below) of a 1933 car missed the mark but came fairly close on the grille and organic shape.

We mentioned in Chapter 5 that Murray Corp. of America lured Ray Dietrich away from LeBaron in 1925 and created Dietrich Inc. as their in-house coachbuilder. In a similar move, Fisher Body bought Fleetwood, also in 1925, taking on Fleetwood's good name and prestige. Briggs responded in 1927 by purchasing LeBaron Inc. and moving Ralph Roberts to Detroit. Not to be outdone by the big independents, the Hayes Body Corp. of Grand Rapids hired Count Alexis W. de Sakhnoffsky, the White Russian nobleman who'd worked in Brussels for Van den Plas. Hayes announced in Jan. 1929 that Sakhnoffsky would become its "art director," and his services would be available to all clients.

The major independent body suppliers and Fisher had two motives for acquiring coach-building satellites. The first was image: By designing and fabricating custom bodies, the mass body producers were able to display them at the Salons, and this put them on shoulder-rubbing terms with the social elite. Without this, constructors of production car bodies had the status of blacksmiths.

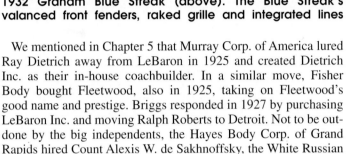

Second, the major body suppliers hoped to generate more business by making ideas and themes from their custom designs available for use on their mass-produced bodies. They saw this as a customer service, reasoning that the fashions, shapes and nuances they created at the high end would filter down into the customers' standard lines. These standard lines would then sell better, resulting in more body orders. At the same time, new production-body customers would be attracted by the bodymaker's ability to style and, as a result, help sell more cars.

The idea made sense, but things didn't work out as hoped. The big body suppliers soon discovered, first, that custom bodies didn't bring in much money, especially compared to production bodies; second, that while a few touches from custom designs did trickle down into production, the presentation of those ideas was neither forceful or focused enough to generate much additional business nor to bring in new customers.

But then they all realized, pretty much simultaneously, that what their carmaker customers really needed and wanted were the services of production-oriented stylists who could design modern, attractive, salable cars. Body manufacturers who could provide that service would, as planned, help their customers sell more cars, thus creating more body business. This also looked like a much better way to tailor presentations to prospects directly. So staff stylists were set up in production design studios on the body-makers' premises, and this had a much more positive effect than the trickle-down theory of coachbuilding.

Thus, toward the end of the '20s, Briggs, Murray, Fisher and Hayes began putting together production design studios and staffing them with the best talent they could find. Murray hired

Amos E. Northup in 1927 as their chief designer of production bodies. Also in 1927, GM called on Harley Earl to organize and head their Art & Colour section. Briggs now put Ralph Roberts in charge of both production and LeBaron designs. And as mentioned earlier, Briggs hired John Tjaarda in 1932 to oversee its experimental body department. Roberts and Tjaarda had equal authority at Briggs but with different responsibilities and separate staffs.

Due to the commercially competitive nature of these newly established styling groups, industry emphasis started to shift even further away from custom design and much more toward production design. If the major body suppliers, including Fisher, could add to their clients' profits by designing and making more stylish and marketable bodies, it followed that they'd increase their own profits through greater production volume.

Again, production studios sounded great in theory, but it took some time to get them accepted. These newly added styling studios started out as tiny islands in great oceans of an older order. Designers often had to learn chains of command and internal politics by bitter experience. Then came the traditional and expected battles with the engineering and marketing establishments. The task of creating and shepherding style through these mazes seemed almost too formidable at times. Here was "styling," whatever that meant: an activity with no ground rules, no set way to do business, no job descriptions, very little credibility and much more resistance than acceptance.

And that's why those styling departments within the big, independent body suppliers—like Briggs and Murray—might have had an easier time getting started and being accepted than those in the big auto companies, like GM, Ford and Chrysler. Easier start-up and speedier acceptance might also explain why two of the earliest influential production designs came from Amos Northup's small studio at Murray Corp. of America.

The significant and trendsetting cars that Northup and his assistant, Julio (Jules) Andrade, designed were the 1931 Reo Royale and the 1932 Graham Blue Streak. Both these cars went one step beyond anything done to that time. In each case, Northup and Andrade blended and shaped the previously separate body elements into a harmonious, integrated whole.

The 1931 Reo Royale had no sharp angles. Northup and Andrade flowed the veed grille into the hood, then the hood into the cowl, the cowl into the windshield pillars, and the pillars up into roof. The roof then wrapped down into the windows and doors, and the rear deck flowed out over the fuel tank. In the case of the Royale coupe and cabriolet, the deck had no side moldings and swept cleanly down into the rear quarter panels.

The leading edges of the Royale's front fenders formed a vee, like a bird in flight, and the wings cascaded down into the radiator pan. The Royale wasn't a radical departure from the norm, but it did have enough visual differences so that everyone noticed and admired the car.

The Royale's initial concept, according to a retired Reo employee named George Svede, came from Fabio Segardi, designer of the earlier Reo Flying Cloud series. Ray Dietrich also claimed to have had a hand in the Royale's design. But from all reports, Northup and Andrade did most of the detail work, including the final sculpting.

Andrade told the Society of Automotive Engineers that he and Northup believed in styling cars initially in clay and later in pen and ink. Clay allowed the shapes to come alive in three dimensions. Andrade also said that he and Northup tested plaster scale models of the Royale in a small windtunnel at the University of Detroit, in tests performed by a Professor Altman. These tests led to changes in the curvature of the Royale's windshield header and the sedan's swept-out rear body panel, modifications that reduced turbulence in both areas.

In Nov. 1930, *Automobile Topics* published a detailed account of the Reo Royale's body evolution. "Those who have studied Northup's work," wrote the anonymous author, "may trace back several years...leading up to the Reo design; a growing impatience with unnecessary emphasis of angles, a fondness for well rounded curves, the continued effort to erase the last vestiges of that sharp break where, in the conventions of carriage design, the dashboard used to be. But up to now, he has not entirely let himself go."

Northup let himself go a bit more with his next major project at Murray, the 1932 Graham Blue Streak. Graham-Paige's Graham Brothers might have been Indiana

Amos E. Northup

Amos Northup was born Oct. 23, 1889 in Bellevue, Ohio and attended the Cleveland Polytechnic Institute, where he studied design under Henry G. Keller. He began his career in 1908 as a designer of furniture,

home interiors and draperies. In 1918, he joined Pierce-Arrow as its truck designer and soon helped select Pierce's paint colors and interior trim. He also created some wonderfully lively, colorful artwork that Pierce used in its advertising.

Northup left Pierce around 1921, opened his own art studio in Buffalo and continued to do ads, illustrations and custom auto designs for, among others, Pierce-Arrow. He also provided artwork to Leon Rubay and production body designs to Wills Ste. Claire. He's credited, in

fact, with designing all 1924 and later Willses.

In 1927, Murray Corp. of America hired Northup as its chief designer. But he felt Murray wasn't paying him enough, so he left again in Mar. 1928 to join one of Murray's larger customers, Willys-Overland in Toledo. At Willys, Northup had charge, according to a company news release, of "all body styles, color combinations, upholstery, decorative work and appointments." While in Toledo, Northup styled the 1930 Willys-Overland 66B series, including that year's very striking plaid-side roadster. He also redid Willys' low-priced Whippet line.

When Northup went to Willys, he hired Jules Andrade as his assistant. Andrade had previously been chief designer for Chandler-Cleveland Motors, which had been absorbed by Hupmobile in 1928. A year or so after Northup left Murray, though, Allan Sheldon wanted him back and offered him more money than Willys-Overland. Northup accepted and was reinstated as chief designer, and he brought Andrade along as his assistant. Andrade stayed with Murray for another year and then moved on to a long career with General Motors, under Harley Earl.

LeBaron's Hugo Pfau said long ago that Northup never followed fashion; he set it. During his decade with Murray, Amos

Northup generated designs, complete or partial, for practically all of Murray's customers. He's credited with the 1930 Hudson, several Hupmobiles, the 1930-32 Ford A/B-400 convertible victorias, the compact 1933 Willys 77, the entire Willys

line through 1938, plus others. In 1935, Northup designed a luxury ocean liner and a streamlined locomotive. He was developing the 1938 Sharknose Graham when he died.

Northup was a short man,

Northup conceived the 1930 Plaidside roadster (top) while at Willys-Overland and the 1933 Willys 77 (above) and Sharknose 1937 Willys during his employment at Murray Corp. of America.

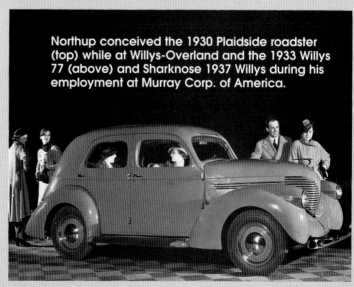

farmboys, but they surely had an eye for style. The first (1928) Graham-Paige cars were designed by LeBaron. Then, in 1928, the Grahams commissioned Norman Bel Geddes, the industrial and stage-set designer, to project five years into the future and come up with five scale models, each one suitable for the years 1929 through 1933. The Grahams were asking Bel Geddes, in effect, to shine up his crystal ball, something unusual at that time but soon an industry commonplace.

Bel Geddes cast his five year-by-year projections in brass. The first brass model looked fairly conventional, but the fifth model—the 1933 projection—seemed jar-

ring in 1928. As it turned out, Bel Geddes wasn't far off with his 1933 model, but even so, the Graham Brothers felt that the 1933 proposal would be too far-out to sell. And they weren't all that sure about those in between. So the Grahams paid off Bel Geddes and turned to their body supplier, Murray, and asked Northup and Andrade to style their 1932 line.

Like the Reo Royale, the 1932 Graham Blue Streak sedan still had that era's two-box shape. But Northup and Andrade had once again rounded all corners, smoothed the edges and blended all body surfaces so the car came out looking like one solid, organic whole. The concept that really set

the Blue Streak apart, though—that wowed the public and sent designers back to their boards—was the valanced front fender. Valances extended and draped the fender sheetmetal down behind the wheel, hiding the spatter that had been visible underneath previous fender styles. By 1933-34, there wasn't a U.S. car in the showroom that didn't have front- and sometimes rear-fender valances.

Another idea that set the Blue Streak design apart was Northup's use of one single color for the body, fenders, radiator shell, headlamp buckets, everything. That's not to say that all Blue Streaks were blue. Graham offered a number of colors,

---

just over five feet tall, and he had an unusually large head. On Saturday morning, Feb. 13, 1937, he left his home in Pleasant Ridge, Michigan and walked down the street to buy a newspaper. The sidewalk was icy. Northup slipped, fell and cracked his skull. He died two days later in Harper Hospital. At the time of his death, the 1938 Graham, a design he'd begun in 1935, wasn't yet finished. Northup originally meant the Graham's front fenders to be

skirted and to flow back into the front doors, like the 1941 Packard Clipper. Someone else—probably Graham-Paige chief body engineer William Nealey, according to Jeff Godshall—finished the Sharknose Graham, adding the square headlamps and the front fender creases. But the overall result was just as original as the rest of Northup's work. Designers called him a designer's designer, and he had more impact on the industry than he's ever been given credit for. ◆

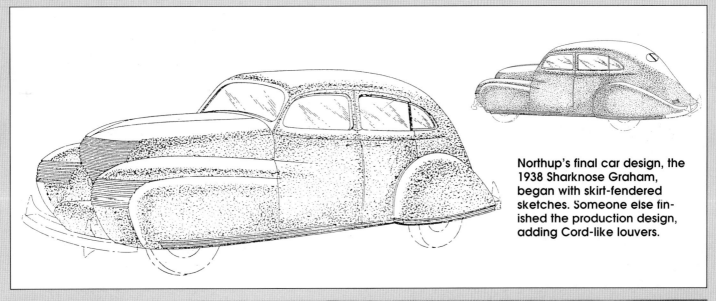

Northup's final car design, the 1938 Sharknose Graham, began with skirt-fendered sketches. Someone else finished the production design, adding Cord-like louvers.

including metallics. But very few other cars were monochromatic in that day. The public was taken with the overall effect of the 1932 Graham and, while they mightn't agree today, people referred to the Blue Streak as "streamlined."

Carmakers got the message that stacking one low, smaller rectangle ahead of a taller, bigger rectangle wasn't likely to please the public much longer, nor was it the correct way to slice through the air. However, they had no idea at first which aerodynamic ideal—bird, fish, egg, teardrop, airplane, boat or dirigible—

fenders and faired-in shock absorbers, all much like a small monoplane.

There's some question as to who actually designed the 1929 Auburn Cabin Speedster. The design patent credits race driver Wade Morton, but it's unlikely that he really had much to do with it. Alan H. Leamy, the Auburn-Cord staff designer, couldn't have done the car either, because he arrived at Auburn too late. An R.H. Robinson from Indianapolis took credit in a 1955 issue of *Road & Track*, and it's also possible that Robert Grimshaw, chief designer for Detroit's Griswold Body Co., designed the Auburn Cabin Speedster.

source for production-car design, especially the low and jewel-like front-drive machines built by Harry Miller. Miller's rwd Golden Submarine of 1917 probably helped to inspire the Auburn Cabin Speedster to some extent. And after Maj. H.O.D. Seagraves drove his aerodynamic Sunbeam to 203.79 mph at Daytona Beach in early 1927, streamlining got another boost. Maj. Seagraves' twin-engined monster had an aluminum envelope body with flush sides but open wheel cuts and full wheelcovers. Through the use of scale models and a windtunnel, the Sunbeam at 200 mph ended up with 400 psi of frontal

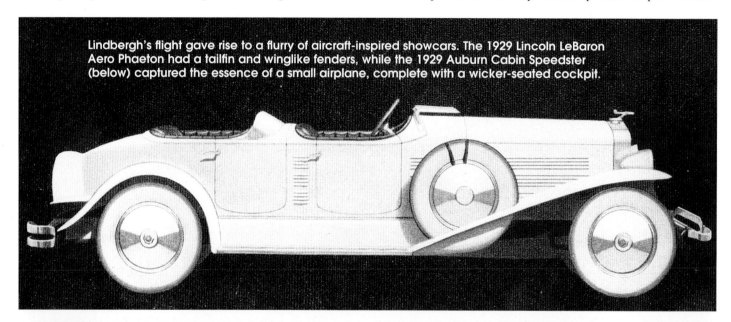

Lindbergh's flight gave rise to a flurry of aircraft-inspired showcars. The 1929 Lincoln LeBaron Aero Phaeton had a tailfin and winglike fenders, while the 1929 Auburn Cabin Speedster (below) captured the essence of a small airplane, complete with a wicker-seated cockpit.

would make an aesthetically pleasing and practical alternative. They simply knew that the shape of cars had to change.

Soon after Lindbergh's flight, designers began putting aircraft themes into automobiles. Among the first were showcars like the 1929 Auburn Cabin Speedster and LeBaron's 1929 Lincoln Aero Phaeton. The Auburn had an aluminum body without runningboards, a two-place "cockpit" with wicker seats, a veed and steeply raked windshield, "periscope" backlight, cycle

There's no doubt that Griswold did build it.

As for the 1929 Lincoln LeBaron Aero Phaeton, it had a central tailfin plus winglike front fenders and several aircraft-inspired gauges. Publicity stated that it and the Auburn Cabin Speedster would be built in limited numbers, but neither was. The one-off Auburn Cabin Speedster, in fact, burned and melted into a puddle of aluminum during the fire that ravaged the Los Angeles auto show on Mar. 5, 1929.

Race cars became another inspirational

downforce and 200 psi of lift at the tapered tail. From a styling standpoint, the Sunbeam's most important contribution was its envelope body, which was easily 20 years ahead of its time.

Briggs Mfg. Co. had considerable styling impact on the auto industry of the late 1920s and early 1930s. Between them, Ralph Roberts and John Tjaarda managed to hire the absolute cream of designers and clay modelers: men like Phil

Tjaarda's initial droop-nosed Zephyr prototype influenced the shape of Porsche's Volkswagen, which began to take form in Jan. 1934.)

Briggs' LeBaron studios designed and built concept cars for Chrysler in 1941: six Newport parade phaetons (far left) and six Thunderbolt retractable hardtops. That's Ralph Roberts beside a Thunderbolt, with his wife and mother sitting inside.

successful, thanks in part to Bob Koto's and Bob Gregorie's addition of the prow grille and fender-mounted headlamps. (Ferdinand Porsche visited Briggs in 1933 and saw the Lincoln Zephyr in some stage of development. It's likely, although not certain, that

Ralph Roberts, starting in 1932, had been spending a good deal of time in England, helping set up Ford's major body supplier in Dagenham, Briggs Ltd. Roberts kept going back and forth from England to Detroit until the outbreak of World War II. He usually returned to the U.S. two or three times a year and stayed a month

European aerodynamicists experimented more seriously than we did with truly streamlined bodies. In Berlin, Dr. Edmund Rumpler built a series of 1921-28 cars along aircraft principles. In plan view, they looked like teardrops, with curved windshields and straight, horizontal fenders. Then, too, an Austrian-born aerodynami-

cist, Paul Jaray, received U.S. patents on 12 claims of a basic streamlined autobody shape in 1927. Jaray licensed his patents to automakers worldwide and established a subsidiary in the U.S. When Chrysler got interested in building an aerodynamic car, the Jaray Corp. of America made an aerodynamic running 1931 Chrysler prototype based on Jaray's body ideas. After the Airflow came out in 1934, Jaray sued Chrysler for patent infringement and eventually settled out of court.

Jaray-bodied cars were designed for both racing and passenger use. Among European automakers who took Jaray's aero principles seriously were Maybach, Adler, Ley and Wikov. The shape that Jaray advocated consisted of two teardrop forms, one atop the other. The roof was teardrop-shaped as seen in plan view. In side view, the roof tapered downward into a low tail,

and another teardrop formed the main body section as seen from the side.

By the mid 1930s, several U.S. visionaries began to build cars that lifted aerodynamics over styling: the 1933-34 Dymaxions by Buckminster Fuller, William B. Stout's 1936-46 Scarab series, W.E. Miller's Arrowhead Spring Water car (inspired by a Radebaugh sketch on a MoToR annual cover), plus a flurry of concept proposals from GM, Chrysler, Bel Geddes and others. Their ideas seemed too far out for most people, and yet cosmetically "streamlined" body shapes continued to sell well. Henry Crane was right when he said in 1939: "Appearance is based on what is commercially known as streamlining, with practically no consideration for the real implication of this word."

After World War II, Nash and a few other car companies ran windtunnel tests on scale styling models, and the 1949 Nash Airflyte did end up with modifications suggested by aero results, notably its enclosed front wheels and tapering bustle. But the auto-design industry didn't pay much attention to true aerodynamics until the early 1970s when OPEC cut oil shipments to the U.S. After that, the windtunnel became an extension of the design studio. Today, no carbody goes into metal (or plastic) until it's been extensively tested in the windtunnel. ◆

Aircraft and auto engineer William B. Stout, who designed the Ford Tri-Motor among others, built several streamlined Scarabs (above) in the 1930s. George Walker envisioned the future in his 1941 patent below.

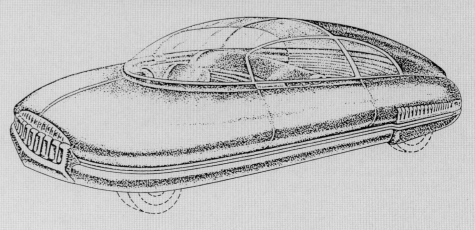

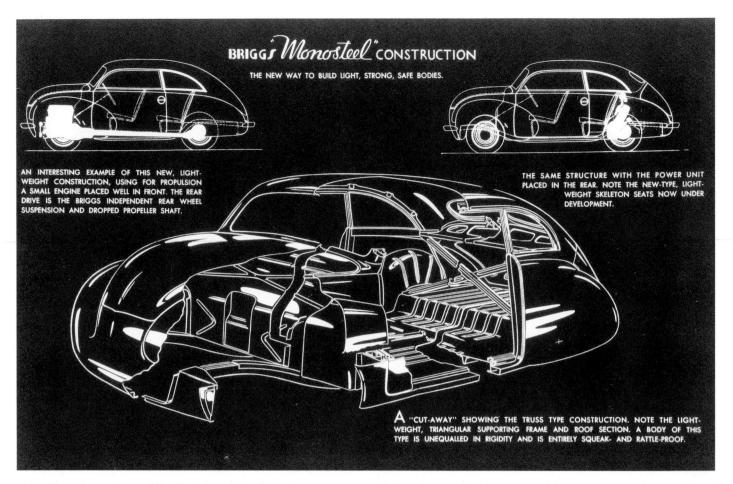

BRIGGS "Monosteel" CONSTRUCTION

THE NEW WAY TO BUILD LIGHT, STRONG, SAFE BODIES.

AN INTERESTING EXAMPLE OF THIS NEW, LIGHT-WEIGHT CONSTRUCTION, USING FOR PROPULSION A SMALL ENGINE PLACED WELL IN FRONT. THE REAR DRIVE IS THE BRIGGS INDEPENDENT REAR WHEEL SUSPENSION AND DROPPED PROPELLER SHAFT.

THE SAME STRUCTURE WITH THE POWER UNIT PLACED IN THE REAR. NOTE THE NEW-TYPE, LIGHT-WEIGHT SKELETON SEATS NOW UNDER DEVELOPMENT.

A "CUT-AWAY" SHOWING THE TRUSS TYPE CONSTRUCTION. NOTE THE LIGHT-WEIGHT, TRIANGULAR SUPPORTING FRAME AND ROOF SECTION. A BODY OF THIS TYPE IS UNEQUALLED IN RIGIDITY AND IS ENTIRELY SQUEAK- AND RATTLE-PROOF.

John Tjaarda at Briggs tried to interest body customers in a "world car" in 1939. He proposed all-steel unitized construction and engineered his vehicle so engine could be placed either front or rear. Tjaarda later went out on his own and pitched his world car concept to a number of established automakers, including Ford and Willys-Overland. His ideas got more consideration after the war, when all domestic car manufacturers experimented with small, inexpensive cars.

or two each time to keep tabs on contracts and customers. In his absence, John Tjaarda had charge of Briggs' production body designers, the LeBaron operation and his own experimental body department. Briggs' main customers before the war were Ford, Chrysler, Hudson and Packard, and most of them made use of Briggs' design services.

Briggs published a large-format book in 1939 that showed not only a number of interesting production design proposals—with details like through fenders and grille spinners—but also LeBaron custom towncars and sport roadsters, interiors and instrument panels. John Tjaarda had a page with phantom views of a fully unitized small car with thin seats and front or rear engine placement. So Briggs was definitely in the styling and engineering forefront at that time.

One of LeBaron's last coachbuilding assignments came from Chrysler president K.T. Keller. Keller wanted Briggs to design and build a dozen showcars that Chrysler could send around to dealers to display during the introduction of Chrysler's 1941 models. This resulted in six copies of the 1941 Thunderbolt retractable hardtop convertible and another half dozen of the Newport dual-cowl phaeton. Of the two, the Thunderbolt was the more significant. Designed by Alex Tremulis along true aerodynamic principles, the Thunderbolt had a radiator air intake under the bumper and a raked, curved windshield. Ralph Roberts is credited with the Newport, which he designed as a parade phaeton with flat-glass windshields that could be tilted forward or back. Both designs pointed toward future developments, especially in their carefully sculpted through fenders and full envelope bodies.

At Hayes, Count Sakhnoffsky styled production bodies for the 1930 Marmon 78. The Marmon body dies were used concurrently by Peerless. Sakhnoffsky also designed the DeVaux, the Continental and restyled the tiny British Austin, transforming it into the 1930 American Austin. In addition, he designed a number of remarkable customs, including the *concours*-winning L-29 Cord coupe and a 1931 Marmon V-16 four-passenger victoria. His 16-cylinder Marmon had a very light roof treatment and a pennant-like paint scheme that began at the hood ornament and ended just ahead of the rear bumper.

Sakhnoffsky pioneered common window reveals that joined the side apertures together visually. After he left

Count Sakhnoffsky's sketching technique was ideally suited to advertising. Auburn commissioned him to illustrate its ads in 1935, as did White trucks. He later became a regular contributor to *Esquire*.

Sakhnoffsky, as art director for the Hayes Body Co. in Grand Rapids, Mich., earned valuable publicity for himself and his employer by showing his rendition of the Cord L-29 at various European styling competitions. His design won Monte Carlo's grand prize and placed well at Paris.

Alexis de Sakhnoffsky became a master in the rendering technique using wax-based, colored pencils on dark cover stock. He learned it from W.E. Miller at Packard. Sakhnoffsky's 1938 Bantam (left) illustrates the tempera highlights and spiral swirls that marked virtually all of his work.

Hayes, Sakhnoffsky consulted for Budd for a short time, where he helped design the 1934 Nash. In 1932, as a freelance designer and artist, he also consulted for Studebaker and Packard and, in 1940, built a Nash convertible with cutdown doors, much like the Packard-Darrin. He hoped that his Nash design would lead to limited production.

What Sakhnoffsky became famous for, though, was an illustration technique that he'd learned at Packard from W.E. Miller. Strother MacMinn said that Miller introduced Sakhnoffsky to the potential of wax-based, colored pencils on dark cover stock, Mi-Teintes or Canson illustration paper. This combination plus a dab of white tempera gave bright, flaring highlights to an automobile sketch—more dramatic and active than anything seen to that time. Most designers soon picked up this technique, but Sakhnoffsky mastered it like no one else. He added spiral-nebula swirls coming off the car, and these became his trademark. With such drawings, he created some gems of advertising art, including ads for

the 1935 Auburn and the 1938 American Bantam, which he also styled. *Esquire* magazine hired him to do sketches and articles on product design, as did other magazines.

The major body producers like Briggs, Murray and Hayes weren't the only ones to provide design services to U.S. automakers. Several suppliers also helped customers with styling ideas, notably Ditzler, the paint manufacturer. Around 1934-35, Ditzler asked Buzz Grisinger from Chrysler's Art & Colour staff to moonlight, and Grisinger created a number of 1/8-scale clay models that Ditzler painted, used in ads and showed around to the automakers.

Such supplier-maintained styling departments still exist today (1996). According to Chrysler designer Jeff Godshall, the Prince Corp. styles and supplies many Chrysler Corp. headliners, sunvisors, overhead consoles, etc. Johnson Controls Inc. likewise has an internal styling section that designs seats and associated hardware for various car manufacturers. ◆

CHAPTER 7

MISTERL

It was one of those sparkling May weekday mornings in 1926, decades before smog. Harley J. Earl, 33, was out on the golf course at the Los Angeles Country Club. The clubhouse phone rang. Long distance from New York City: a Mr. Sloan calling. Could Mr. Earl come to the phone, please? Earl was easy to spot on the links: a big man, six-foot-four-and-a-half, great tan, snappy dresser.

When Earl got to the clubhouse, he mostly listened while the president of General Motors spoke. Sloan was calling from his Manhattan office. He had Fred and Larry Fisher in the room with him. The three had talked earlier about the fine job Earl had done styling the 1927 LaSalle. That started them wondering whether Harley could be persuaded to come back to Detroit to help choose colors and submit styling ideas first for Cadillac and then perhaps for all GM car lines.

Sloan was no designer, but he did have a strong design sense and realized how much appearance and style contributed to the sale of new automobiles. He hadn't really formulated Earl's role at General Motors but was considering what he called an "art and color section." Fisher Body's Ternstedt Div. already had an Art and Colour department that styled trim items, door handles, hood ornaments, etc. Sloan foresaw creating a larger color and styling department and making its services available to all General Motors car divisions.

Earl might start by working for Larry Fisher and dressing up the 1928 Cadillac. Then in a year or so, maybe he could get involved with the styling of all of GM's different lines; not just Cadillac but Buick, Oldsmobile, Pontiac and Chevrolet. If the idea appealed to Earl, Sloan wanted him to come to New York as soon as possible so they could discuss the details.

Next day, Harley Earl boarded Santa Fe's *California Limited.* After an uneventful four-day trip, he arrived at Mr. Sloan's desk, where he, Sloan and the Fisher Brothers talked about how this new styling department might work: how to set it up and how it could help Fisher Body and GM's various car divisions. It sounded like a fantastic idea to Harley. "Then we'll do it," said

Harley J. Earl circa 1930.

Mr. Sloan, and he flashed an odd facial expression that passed for the Sloan smile.

Basically that's how General Motors touched off the most important, influential automotive styling section the world has ever known. GM's was by no means the first corporate styling department, just the most significant. "Art & Colour," as Sloan named it, soon became the mother church of auto styling, the university that graduated design vice presidents for nearly all other U.S. car companies. Harley Earl was their professor.

He also at times became their bogeyman, the boss who gave auto designers the work they loved and then made them keep at it through 80-hour weeks; who drove them nuts, drove them to drink, drove them to the divorce court; who threw lavish annual picnics and Christmas parties where the designers' wives—those still riding out their marriages—would meet this towering ogre and then return to their husbands and mew, "Ohhh, but he seems so *nice!"*

Harley J. Earl still casts the longest shadow in the auto-design field. He's by far the greatest figure in the industry, the giant among giants, super ego among sizable egos, larger than life, legendary; the man who gave form and order to an activity profoundly lacking in organization; lacking, in fact, even a satisfactory name.

His younger brother, Art, once said of Harley that he grew up too fast. He reached his mature height by age 13. Harley, said Art, felt awkward at school proms, because his dance partners had to look straight up at him. Although he was always a good athlete and very popular, he never became a comfortable dancer.

As an adult, in conversation Harley would often lean forward at the waist so he didn't appear too daunting. He could be very thoughtful and charming, and he often was. Yet he had a brusque, rough, profane side, and many of the people who worked with and for him came to view Harley Earl with a mixture of fear and grudging respect. Dick Teague, later chief stylist for Packard and styling vice president of American Motors, worked for Earl in his younger years. "He had charisma in spades," said Teague. "Everyone called him Misterl, all one word. You never called him Harley to his face."

Earl had a tremendous conviction about how cars should look, and that conviction locked him into a crusade to see his visions put on the road. The courage of his convictions helped give him a tremendous selling ability, and he needed it daily to convince GM's divisional general managers ("presidents" they were called

in the early days) and engineers that his designs would help sell cars. And he was nearly always right.

Crusaders and people who end up being right, though, never have it easy. While Earl's knowledge of tact and diplomacy would have served a Machiavellian prince, his short fuse didn't always allow him to exercise those graces. There's no doubt, especially after listening to some of his former designers, that Harley Earl could be maliciously cruel. He had the ability to shred an employee with a snarl or to burn a hole through him with his laser-like glare. He often fired people in the heat of passion and then had to have someone chase after them, apologize and rehire them. Leonard McLay, Earl's mechanic, said he counted on getting fired at least once a year.

Earl could direct his tirades just as easily at those higher on the org chart as at people on his own staff. He feared no one. Earl once told Chevrolet chief engineer Jim Crawford to go to hell for refusing to lower a roof line. He had a command of profanity that made division managers blanch, and if opinion went too much against him, he'd pick up a telephone and say to whoever disagreed with him, "Well, let's see what Alfred thinks about this." Rarely did he have to actually talk to Sloan in such instances.

Harley Earl was born in Los Angeles in 1893 and grew up in Hollywood long before anyone in that farm community ever cranked a movie camera. He spent a normal, happy childhood among three brothers and one sister, all of whom were raised by loving parents in a rambling three-story house on five acres of citrus at the corner of Hollywood and Bronson, four streets west of Hollywood and Vine.

When Harley graduated from Hollywood High in 1912, his father, J.W. Earl, wanted him to become a lawyer and perhaps enter politics someday. An uncle had been mayor of Los Angeles—quite successfully so—and Harley shared a lot of his uncle's qualities: bright, good-looking, outgoing. People seemed to want to please him; enjoyed being with him.

So at his dad's insistence, Harley enrolled at USC, where he spent most of his time playing football and running track. He even set a pole-vaulting record. After a year, though, Harley quit USC and went to work in his father's shop, the Earl Automobile Works, nominally as chief designer and superintendent.

In 1916, J.W. again urged Harley to study law and this time sent him away to Stanford. Again, though, Harley preferred track and rugby, and he cartooned his way through classes.

His youngest brother, Bill, fondly remembered that, "I was four or five years old when Harley came home from his freshman year at Stanford.... This was during the Christmas holiday. We had this great big old house with a tremendous pantry. The cabinets went all the way to the ceiling. Harley was dating Sue, but he spent two hours entertaining me.

"In those days in California, we didn't use paper money. A dollar coin was a 'cartwheel.' Anyway, like every Stanford freshman, Harley had learned a few card tricks, sleights of hand...and he must have hidden two or three silver dollars in every cabinet in the kitchen. He showed me magic tricks and then would boost me up to any cabinet I wanted to point to, and no matter which one it was, he'd pull out a silver dollar. Of course, I was completely flabbergasted.

"Then, to top it off, my Christmas present from Harley was a billfold with a paper dollar in it. I'd never seen a paper dollar before. I've always been impressed with that holiday after noon and felt it was so typical of Harley; thoughtful and amusing."

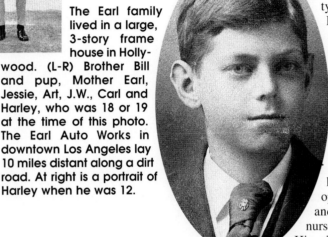

The Earl family lived in a large, 3-story frame house in Hollywood. (L-R) Brother Bill and pup, Mother Earl, Jessie, Art, J.W., Carl and Harley, who was 18 or 19 at the time of this photo. The Earl Auto Works in downtown Los Angeles lay 10 miles distant along a dirt road. At right is a portrait of Harley when he was 12.

At Stanford, Harley joined a fraternity, became more involved with rugby, and one afternoon got cleated in the leg. He developed an infection, and the infirmary nurse sent him home. His sister Jessie said Harley's leg looked so awful that the doctors told him he ought to have it amputated. Harley laughed and wouldn't let them, but being sent home pretty much ended his college career. Stanford eventually gave him credit for two years of undergraduate pre-law.

Harley recovered and returned to work at the shop, which his father now talked about selling to Don Lee, the Cadillac distributor down the street. Harley also took up golf and became serious about Sue Carpenter, his high-school sweetheart.

By this time, Hollywood had grown into a style-conscious, high-living movie colony. Film producers and stars were building homes in and around Hollywood and ordering fancy cars. Cecil B. DeMille lived a few houses down from the Earls. All this new money created a market for custom, coachbuilt automobiles, and Don Lee bought the Earl Automobile Works in 1919 to cash in on that demand. Lee put Harley in charge of designing and selling his custom bodies, and the outgoing Earl soon found himself on first-name terms with Mary Pickford, Douglas Fairbanks, Wallace Reid, Tom Mix, Mary Miles Minter, Fatty Arbuckle, Pauline Fredericks, director Henry Lehrman and others, all of whom were customers of Don Lee.

Even during the time he worked for his father, Harley Earl had put some of his styling ideas across by making scale clay models of auto bodies. Some designers design better in three dimensions than two, and Earl was one of them, at least during that period. Harley sculpted scale models for prospective customers to show them what their cars would look like. Customers could, at that point, ask for changes, and they were delighted to be given the opportunity.

Clay remained a fairly unusual styling and demonstration medium at that time. Most designers preferred to make side-view renderings. But modeling appears to have been Harley's forte. He probably used sketches, too, and some of his early designs were subsequently re-rendered by artists at GM, although none of his originals seem to have survived.

Harley's interest in clay modeling most likely went back to the camping holidays he and his family took at Bailey's Ranch in the Tehachapi Mountains north of Los Angeles. Years later, Harley's brother Art talked about one such vacation when the rains came to Bailey's Ranch. "This would be about 1910," Art recalled in a

On one of the Earls' vacations at Bailey's ranch in the Tehachapis, Harley and his brother, Art, sculpted little cars out of riverbank clay.

1980 interview. "Harley was 16 and I was 14. We were up at Bailey's Ranch, camped in this canyon. It started to rain, and we ended up having this big flood. The whole canyon flooded, and it filled up this hollow with clay.

"Harley and I made little saws out of wood, and we went over to the clay, and Harley started designing cars out of clay way back then; clay that he took right out of the ground. He'd pick up a big chunk of clay and would work it down to the sort of car he wanted. I guess we had 20 or 30 of these little cars of different shapes: roadsters and touring cars.... But [then] it started to rain again. We got two more inches of rain in about half an hour, and it melted all our clay cars. They all turned back into mud."

Harley had initially caught car fever from his father. In 1911, the year after the floods at Bailey's Ranch, J.W. Earl bought himself a flame-orange Mercer roadster, one of the liveliest, snazziest, fastest cars on the road. Harley learned to drive the Mercer and took it out every chance he got. There are several versions of this story, but one weekend after Harley had borrowed the roadster, J.W. noticed the speedometer pegged at the top indicated reading, 80 miles per hour. When asked for an explanation, Harley said he must have hit a bump and knocked something out of kilter.

That Monday, a customer came into J.W.'s shop and congratulated him on his son's driving skill. "What are you talking

about?" asked J.W. "Haven't you heard?" said the customer. "Harley won a race in your Mercer roadster this weekend." J.W. hadn't heard, and he exchanged a few choice words with his son, but he couldn't stay mad at Harley for long. Harley, by the way, never lost his love of auto racing, an interest he later passed along to his own sons.

By the time Don Lee bought the Earl Automobile Works in 1919, J.W. had turned over responsibility for the shop almost entirely to Harley. Harley had married Sue Carpenter in 1917, they'd had one child, Billy, and they'd bought a house on Los Feliz Boulevard. Under the Don Lee Cadillac banner, some of Earl's body designs began to show up at east-coast salons. It was in the early 1920s when General Motors people like Alfred Sloan

Earl admired Hispano-Suiza and patterned first LaSalle after it. This 1926 cabriolet had a British Hooper body, belonged to film actor Carlyle Blackwell (shown).

and the Fisher Brothers first noticed Earl's work at the Commodore and Plaza hotels in New York and Chicago. Earl's cars were flashier, more colorful, more imaginative than the stolid designs from the east-coast coachbuilding establishment.

As to how he came to Detroit, Earl said in a 1954 interview with writer Stan Brams that in 1922, the eldest Fisher brother,

To design 1927 LaSalle, Earl and his assistants used clay over a wood-and-metal armature. Photos show details of 1927 LaSalle sedan clay model, but whether it's one of the four that Earl presented to Sloan and the Fisher Brothers isn't certain.

At top, more views of clay 1927 LaSalle, probably inside the Cadillac experimental shops. Earl was on leave from Don Lee and was hired by Cadillac president Larry Fisher as a consultant. The 1927 LaSalle became an instant success, largely by virtue of its European styling. As a result, General Motors president Alfred P. Sloan Jr. hired Earl full-time and asked him to contribute to the styling of all GM car lines. (Above right) Harley Earl at the wheel of a 1927 LaSalle roadster.

Fred, began taking yearly vacations in Los Angeles. Fred would stay for five or six weeks at a stretch and was often joined by a friend from Toledo, a Chevrolet dealer named Jimmy Baldwin. Baldwin's son, Andy, had been a Stanford collegemate of Earl's, and all three families—Earl, Fisher and Baldwin—belonged to the Los Angeles Country Club.

One day the phone rang at Harley's Don Lee office. It was Andy Baldwin suggesting they have lunch together and then play golf. Andy mentioned that they'd be joined by another golfer, but he wouldn't say who it was. "He's a competitor of yours from back east." Yes, but who, asked Earl. "Well, you'll see when you get out there," replied Andy.

It turned out that his "competitor" and soon-to-be golf partner was Fred Fisher. After that, whenever Fisher vacationed in Los Angeles, he and Harley would team up on the golf course. It got so they'd play two or three times a week, a routine and a very comfortable partnership that lasted for several years.

Through Fred, Harley met Larry Fisher, the playboy of the Fisher clan who, in 1925, became president of GM's Cadillac Motor Car Div. Larry and Harley also became chums, and just before Christmas 1925, Harley received a phone call from Larry Fisher in Detroit. Larry explained that his Cadillac body designers and the Fisher people had been trying to come up with a companion car for the Cadillac, essentially a less expensive, more youthful luxury car to compete with the Packard Six. Several styling teams had failed to impress Fisher with an acceptable design and did he—Harley—want to take a crack at it?

So on Jan. 6, 1926, Harley Earl left for Detroit for the first time and spent the next three months in the experimental body shops of the Cadillac plant on Clark Avenue. Joseph D. Thompson worked in that area and remembered later that Cadillac assigned three men to help Earl: Ralph Pew, Dave Anderson and Jack Parks. Pew was a Cadillac body engineer, as was Anderson, and Jack Parks was a master woodworker and clay modeler.

Earl took inspiration for his 1927 LaSalle design from his favorite European marque, the Hispano-Suiza, and he made no bones about it. He'd admired Hissos during his several trips to the Paris Salon in the late teens and early 1920s, and he later told Barbara Holliday of the *Detroit Free Press*, "The Hispano-Suiza was the apple of my eye. All the chic people who appreciated cars drove Hispanos. They were very light as against the heavier models American companies were making, and every line meant something." An Earl-designed, custom Pierce-Arrow that Don Lee rebodied for Fatty Arbuckle in 1920 already showed a strong Hisso influence, especially in the grille and hood louvers. Earl, in fact, kept a Hispano-Suiza radiator in his office for many years after the LaSalle's success, and a number of his early 1930s cars—particularly Cadillac—also borrowed the Hispano grille shape and ornamentation.

For now, though, to add drama to his LaSalle presentation and to help sell his ideas to Sloan and the Fisher Brothers, he did something unexpected: He asked Pew, Anderson and Parks to make four full-sized, clay-over-wood models of his proposed LaSalle design. Whether Earl wielded any of the clay-modeling tools himself we don't know.

Earl's LaSalle clays consisted of four different body styles: a rumbleseat roadster, a coupe, a four-door sedan and a touring car. "We coated the models with non-pareil japan [black enamel] and then lightly sprayed them with Duco," Earl told the *Detroit Free Press* many years later. "Larry and Fred Fisher came over and looked at the models. Then the executive committee came in: Mr. Sloan, Mr. Raskob, John Thomas Smith, Kettering, George

Clay, Yesterday and Today

Precisely what type of clay Harley Earl used in 1926 for his four full-sized LaSalle models remains something of a mystery. It surely wasn't the water-based natural clay he'd found at Bailey's Ranch.

Extruder heats clay to 125°F, then forces it out in long strips. It might have been a strip of this type that led Frank Hershey to create Pontiac silver streak.

Although potters use natural clay, in large lumps the surface tends to dry out and crack.

Earl might have used sculptor's clay, which is what he probably did his scale models in at Don Lee. Sculptor's clay has an oil base, so it doesn't dry out. However,

it's more likely that for his full-sized LaSalle models, Earl used some type of wax-based modeling clay from France or Germany. The wax content of these imported clays made them soft when heated in an oven. At room temperature, they solidified but could still be sculpted with special handtools. Today's styling clays retain these same characteristics.

Joseph D. Thompson, who worked in Cadillac's experimental body department when Earl arrived in 1926, mentioned in an interview with Cadillac historian Roy Schneider that the Mullins Body Co. offered a clay sculpting service to carmakers as early as 1912. Mullins, according to Joe Thompson, would make full-sized clay models over box-like wooden bucks. Mullins offered this service to help bring in new body customers.

Thompson also wrote in his autobiography that modeling clay had been used by body-design engineers at both Packard and Cadillac as early as 1916. Vincent D. Kaptur Sr.,

Vince Kaptur Sr. (shown) pointed out that Packard was using clay to make accurate scale body models as early as 1916.

who started at Packard in 1916 but went to GM in 1928, recalled that at Packard it was common to make quarter-scale models out of clay. For full-sized body mockups, however, Packard used mostly wood.

Writing in the *Journal of the Society of Automotive Engineers* in 1920, George Mercer described the use of clay for full-sized body modeling. The bodymaker

would set up the usual wooden framework as though he were building a custom body. Then, instead of skinning the exterior with aluminum or sheet steel, he would trim back half an inch or so from the outside of the wooden frame ribs, tack on a lattice-work of thin wooden strips and cover these with clay. The clay, he said, when warmed, went on like plaster. Once applied, it could be shaped, then dressed and painted. "When the design has been approved," wrote Mercer, "the wax [he called it 'wax,' the common term for industrial modeling clay at the time] is removed, changes are made in the framing if needed, the entire assembly is covered with metal panels, and the result is a quickly-built experimental body."

A brochure published by Fisher Body in 1927 shows a process identical to the one described by Mercer. Fisher used a matrix of thin wooden slats over standard composite body framing, with a clay/wax material as the sculpting medium. So Fisher was probably using clay even before Harley Earl began doing his LaSalle models in early 1926. Despite the common misconception, full-sized clay models were not new or particularly novel when Earl unveiled his 1927 LaSalle designs to Sloan and the Fisher Brothers.

In fact, applying clay over a relatively finished version of the body's final wooden framing had the advantage of presenting the bodymaker with a set of patterns for most of the wooden parts he'd need for mass production. That's one reason why the 1927 LaSalle and other cars of that era could be finished and produced so quickly after being styled. We have evidence that the 1932 Graham went into mass production at Murray only nine months after the Graham Brothers approved Northup's scale clay models. Coachbuilt bodies were usually done in three to four months and could, if rushed, be finished in less than two.

In Joe Thompson's autobiography, he mentioned that just after GM hired Harley Earl full-time, Earl sent a sample of the styling clay then being used by Art & Colour (A&C) to GM's research labs for chemical analysis. That particular clay, German in origin, consisted of about 10% powdered natural clay, 30% wax and 60% filler, the filler being mostly sulphur. With this formu-

In the 1950s, modelers applied clay over wooden armatures, smoothed all surfaces by hand in interpretation of the designers' sketches, then covered the approved clay with vinyl Di-Noc films. The results looked extremely realistic.

Whitney, Charlie, Fred, and Larry Fisher. They walked around and around the models, and finally Mr. Sloan said, 'Get Earl over here so everyone can meet him.' Then he announced, 'Earl, I thought that you'd like to know that your design has been accepted!'"

Harley said afterward that the news made him feel like a freshman quarterback who'd just thrown a touchdown pass. With the LaSalle models approved, Mr. Sloan turned to Larry Fisher and remarked, "Larry, I think we should send Earl to the Paris auto show," and Fisher replied, "Mr. Sloan, I already have his ticket!"

Sloan and Earl, along with Chevrolet president William S. (Big Bill) Knudsen, traveled to France together and, aboard ship, became solid friends. In Paris they visited the Hibbard & Darrin showroom and shops, where Sloan commissioned the five sample bodies that GM never used (see page 45).

On his return from Paris, Earl checked with Larry Fisher to see how the LaSalle was progressing. It wouldn't make the New York Salon, said Larry, but its formal unveiling was slated for the Boston auto show on Mar. 5, 1927. The 1927 LaSalle turned out to be an immediate hit and soon won a number of design awards. The public responded by making the LaSalle an instant bestseller.

Alfred Sloan, in 1963, wrote in his book, *My Years With General Motors,* "I was so impressed with Mr. Earl's work that I decided to obtain the advantages of his talents for other General Motors car divisions. On June 23rd, 1927, I took up with the Executive Committee a plan to establish a special department to study the question of art and color combinations in General Motors products. Fifty persons would make up the department, ten of them designers, and the rest shop workers and clerical and administrative assistants. I invited Mr. Earl to head this new staff department, which we called the Art & Colour Section. Mr. Earl's duties were to direct general production body design and to conduct research and development programs in special car designs."

If the above date is correct, Sloan had already made up his mind to set Earl up as head of Art & Colour, because Earl had gone on the GM payroll nine days earlier, on June 14. So the executive committee's approval of Art & Colour, if Sloan sought it at all, must have been a rubber-stamp formality.

But there's a continuing question of dates during this transitional period, because in later accounts Earl had several different stories when he described the beginnings of Art & Colour (A&C). He also left out an entire year. Piecing together the chronology from interviews, newspaper and magazine accounts, company records and oral reminiscences, here's a time line of what probably happened.

Going back to the original LaSalle assignment: In Dec. 1925, Earl received the first phone call from Larry Fisher. Earl asked for and was granted a three-month leave of absence from Don Lee. On Jan. 6, 1926, he went to Detroit for the first time, designed the LaSalle and was home by the end of March 1926.

Earl resumed work at Don Lee but then, only two months later, in May, got Sloan's phone call at the Los Angeles Country Club. He went to New York and returned home later that same month (May 1926). At that point, Earl asked for a second leave of absence from Don Lee, this time for six months. Granted that second leave, he

lation, Earl contacted Chavant Inc. of Red Bank, New Jersey and asked it to supply him with a similar formulation. Chavant soon became the major supplier of styling clay to the auto industry and remains so today. The other major source is the American Art Clay Co. Inc. of Indianapolis.

To make clay models look more realistic, they were sometimes painted in the early days. The clay surface was coated with a casein (milk-based) sizing, or "feather fill," and the paint sprayed over that. More recently, a thin, flexible plastic film called Di-Noc,

Fred Hoadley, GM used a red-tinted clay and Ford used a natural grey-green. Eventually all styling clay evolved into a tan color. And as composite bodies gave way to all-steel construction, greater amounts of clay were applied over generic wooden or Styrofoam armatures. Slight differences in clay formulations remain even today for the various car companies. Ford's clay is slightly harder than GM's, and Chrysler's softens at a lower temperature (Chrysler's primary supplier is American Art Clay).

Also, due to the use of modern electronic equipment in today's

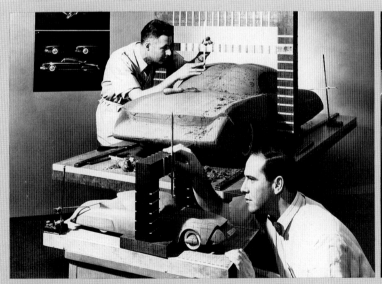

Before committing to the work and expense of full-sized clay models, modelers sculpted scale versions. In 1953, Ford used styling bridges in 1/20 and 1/5 scale (left) to hold side-to-side accuracies, while GM used a system of dowels (right).

made by 3M Co., is carefully applied over the clay model to represent painted or glass surfaces. Di-Noc comes in a range of colors. Modelers use metal foil over bumpers and grilles to mimic chrome, and they also use Safalloy, a low-melting-point metal, to quickly make diecast trim parts. Safalloy can be buffed to a silvery gloss.

During the 1930s, according to retired Ford master modeler styling studios, much of the sulphur has been taken out of modeling clay. Sulphur has always been hard on modelers' noses, eyes and skin, but in recent times the fumes have tended to corrode the electrical contacts in nearby computers and clay milling machines. So clay suppliers have had to come up with other mineral fillers. Specific clay formulations remain closely guarded secrets. ◆

packed up Sue and son Billy and moved to Detroit. Don Lee, according to his company magazine, *Don Lee Spirit*, expected Earl back in November, but it didn't turn out that way. Instead, the Earl family remained in Detroit for the next 31 years.

The question comes up at this point: What did Harley Earl do between his second arrival in Detroit in June 1926 and his official installation as head of GM A&C nearly a year later? In his recorded reminiscences and all histories of A&C, Earl glosses over this period. He either repressed or forgot it, because according to his own account, he launched A&C immediately after his second arrival in Detroit. But it simply didn't happen that way. The year-long gap did exist and needs filling.

Earl undoubtedly spent his first few weeks in Detroit settling Sue and Billy into Larry Fisher's top-floor suite at the Whittier Towers. Fisher lent them this luxurious apartment until 1933. In 1933, the Earls moved into a rented house on Seminole Av. in Detroit, and in 1941 they bought a home in Grosse Pointe. Earl's consultancy fee during this period was paid by Cadillac, not by the corporation, so he worked that first year for Cadillac and Larry Fisher.

Joe Thompson remembered that Earl spent a good deal of the lost year in the shop area at the rear of the Cadillac plant, near Thompson's own office in the experimental body department. Earl said later that he had a major hand in designing the 1928 Cadillac, something Sloan mentioned, too. We assume Earl again had men like Pew, Anderson and Parks helping him, but we can't be sure. Nor do we know the actual extent of Earl's contribution to the 1928 Cadillac.

This is speculation, but Earl might have started drawing up new designs for Fleetwood during this period. Fleetwood already had an excellent staff designer named Jules Agramonte. Agramonte worked in New York at that time, in Fleetwood's sales office, but it's possible that even as early as 1926, Earl and Agramonte got together and talked about future Fleetwood designs. Whether Earl had much to do with the veed windshields introduced on the 1928 Cadillac Fleetwood towncars isn't recorded, but knowing his interest in windshields, *vis-a-vis* his Don Lee days, he probably did.

Earl and Agramonte also might have worked together on some of Cadillac's 1928-29 Fleetwood catalogue customs, notably the 1929 All-Weather phaeton. Earl did oversee the entire line of Fleetwood V-16s for 1930, especially the wonderful Madam X series with its slim windshield pillars. According to his reminiscences, Earl built the first Madam X for Larry Fisher on a LaSalle chassis, and the Fleetwood Madam X Cadillac series followed. Madam X's can be recognized by the 72° rake of their thin windshield pillars. Incidentally, the name Madam X came from the Broadway play starring Pauline Fredericks. Earl and Fredericks had had dinner together the previous evening when someone asked him what Cadillac should call the Fleetwood series with the clear-vision windshield pillars. Earl replied without hesitation: *Madam X,* and the name stuck.

Most 1930 Cadillac V-16 bodies with veed windshields seem to have been built in Pennsylvania, and all flat-windshield V-16s that year were probably built in Detroit. After Fisher closed Fleetwood's Pennsylvania plant and brought the custom operation to Detroit in late 1930, Agramonte joined Earl in Art & Colour and became head of the Cadillac design group.

As we say, that's mostly speculation (except for the part about Fleetwood and Agramonte), but it seems a reasonable explanation to fill Earl's lost year. Then, on June 14, 1927, Earl got Sloan's official nod to start the A&C section. He was now on GM's payroll, not Cadillac's.

Art & Colour initially occupied the 10th floor of the General Motors Building on Grand Boulevard in the New Center area of Detroit. Earl said that those first few months on the 10th floor weren't easy. Sloan supported him but gave him no instructions, no assignments, no blueprint for how A&C was supposed to operate. Sloan did this on purpose, trusting Earl to improvise and find his way.

In an unpublished typescript written for him in 1954 by Stan Brams, Earl claims that he sat in his 10th-floor office and, for his first three days as head of A&C, didn't have a single visitor. As he explained to Brams: "It took a little while for us to get acquainted. You see, I didn't know anybody except the Cadillac group.... Mr. Sloan never gave orders that you had to do anything. That was his way of operating. And he made it very clear to me that he would give me a good recommendation, but from there on I was on my own. And it might take several years to get all the divisions into the fold, but not to be discouraged...that it was a pretty tough assignment. These people [the car divisions and Fisher Body engineers] kind of liked the idea of doing it [designing] themselves, and they liked the secrecy of having it up there in their respective divisional engineering departments.

"Well, O.E. Hunt was chief engineer of Chevrolet at that time [Hunt had previously been with Packard], and Mr. Sloan was very fond of Mr. Hunt, and I presume in talking to him he said, 'Well, gee, it'd be nice if you would kind of be the bell cow and go up and give him a little encouragement.'

"So first thing I knew, O.E. Hunt came up and asked us to go to work on the next year's Chevrolet. Well, it wasn't a com-

Ternstedt's Art & Colour Department

The Ternstedt Mfg. Co. was founded in 1917 as a joint venture between Fisher Body and inventor Alvar K. Ternstedt. Alvar Ternstedt held a number of patents on window regulators. Ternstedt Mfg. Co., as an operating unit under Fisher Body, set up an Art & Colour section in the early 1920s and called it by that name. The Ternstedt Mfg. Co. was soon designing and supplying automotive hardware—door and window handles, lamp bezels, hood ornaments, robe rails, etc.—not only for all General Motors cars but also to other auto manufacturers.

Ternstedt's A&C section existed even when Harley Earl arrived in Detroit in 1926 to design the first LaSalle. Early that same year, Ternstedt had hired Wilhelm (William) N. Schnell as chief designer of their A&C department. Schnell had been a German jewelry designer, silversmith and diemaker. He introduced a number of modeling processes to Fisher Body: lost wax and other techniques for making high-fidelity castings, molds and dies for these small, mostly cast parts. Schnell also assembled a staff of artists, modelers, toolmen, chasers and foundry personnel, some of whom he brought with him from Germany and Scandinavia.

In 1930, Ternstedt was commissioned to design a new "archer" hood ornament for the 1931 Pierce-Arrow. Bonnie Lemm, a woman designer on Ternstedt's staff, received the actual assignment. For a live model, Schnell asked Albert J. Gonas, a newly hired apprentice, to strip to the waist and pose for Lemm. Gonas thought Schnell was joking and refused to strip, but after being convinced, he enrolled in an archery school and learned how to hold a bow correctly so he could pose realistically. Pierce-Arrow approved Bonnie Lemm's archer, and Ternstedt produced the hood ornament from 1931 through 1934, after which another company took over production. ◆

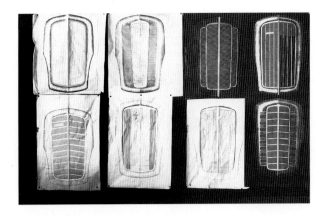
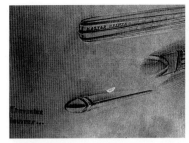
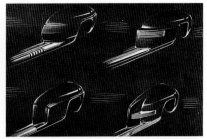

Newcomers to GM's Art & Colour section were asked to create details: grilles, lamps, fender shapes, etc. Once drained of their best ideas, Earl would often let all but most promising go again.

plete car, it was sort of a facelifting. So we worked, and O.E. Hunt was very nice, very helpful, and we got away to a nice start....

"Then Mr. W.A. [Bill] Fisher...who was president of Fisher Body, heard that I was down in my office. His brothers had told him, so he dropped down to visit me, and he said, 'How are you getting along?' And I said, 'Well, I don't know who to call; I don't know a soul in the building; certainly happy you dropped in.'

"'Well,' he said, 'I have a man working for me that goes between plants. He's been doing it for a couple of years, and he's a very smart young fellow and knows everybody...at the divisions and in our plants and subsidiaries. He knows where to find everybody, and his name is Howard O'Leary. I'll send down a letter to you, sealed, and you tear it open and read it and ask him some questions, and if you like him, just write *Yes* on the paper, and seal it, and bring it back up, and I'll take care of it. So that's how O'Leary came to work for me."

Howard O'Leary joined Art & Colour six days after Earl and immediately became Earl's right hand; his administrative assistant. O'Leary was also A&C's second employee, Earl being the first. He had a degree in law but never used it. What his duties had been with Fisher isn't clear, but Howard O'Leary became a godsend to Earl because, as Bill Fisher had said, he knew everyone at GM's five car divisions, from the president on down, and everyone liked him. O'Leary immediately became the introducer, the opener of doors between Earl and the auto divisions.

O'Leary was a man of average height and build. According to those who knew him, he had a wonderful sense of humor, told marvelous stories, was bright, efficient, extremely loyal to Earl and, unlike Earl, *tactful*. And he had a great fondness for people. O'Leary was no designer, nor did Earl expect him to be, but O'Leary soon became the one person who would interview prospective designers and hire them (plus most other A&C employees). He remained in charge of the day-to-day administration of A&C from Mar. 16, 1928 until his retirement in May 1954, after which he took over a Cadillac dealership in Grosse Pointe, Michigan.

Howard O'Leary in the 1950s

O'Leary and Earl immediately began the task of putting together a design team. Of the 50 employees Sloan envisioned in A&C's charter, only 11 had been hired by the end of the first six months. Among them were Ralph Pew, who'd helped Earl on the 1927 LaSalle and who now came to A&C as a design engineer. He was officially listed as Earl's third employee, but he'd probably been with Earl at Cadillac before O'Leary arrived.

Fisher Body woodcarver and patternmaker John Lutz Sr. became Earl's first clay modeler. Lutz was followed to Art & Colour by the legendary Miss Ramshaw. Her first name was Loretto, not Loretta, and she was tall, slim, regal, cool, efficient and either loved or hated you. She eventually became an alcoholic (as did O'Leary) but remained Earl's executive secretary until 1951.

Next came Frank Humer, designer and the best body layout man

in the business; then two draftsmen: Joe Pizzo and E.E. Harshman. O'Leary hired Mike Bogre as head of the woodshop, Herman Jensen as chief of the metalshop, and John S. Parks, another oldtimer from Earl's LaSalle experience. Parks came in as chief of the drafting room.

Earl now had the beginnings of a design staff, but he still had to convince GM's auto divisions that he could help them sell cars. O'Leary did some proselytizing and introduced Earl to those divisional chiefs, engineers and marketing people who counted. And Earl took it from there.

Earl's earliest problems had to do with Fisher Body's engineering fortifications. Fisher engineers didn't like to be told how to bend sheetmetal. They'd done nicely before Earl got there and didn't see much need for him now. So when Earl suggested styling changes, like increasing the crown of a fender or the rake of a windshield, Fisher's engineers could easily show the division how such things would add to production costs. It took Earl a while to learn the game, and some of the lessons were hard.

Earl told Brams that the earliest GM production bodies he helped design were the 1928-29 Cadillac and the 1929 Chevrolet. What he forgot to mention was the 1929 Buick. The Cadillacs and Chevrolet went through Fisher's drafting and engineering processes without much change, but the '29 Buick became a monumental fiasco. Earl blamed Fisher, and several conflicting legends grew up concerning who spoiled the 1929 Buick's styling.

What made the 1929 Buick look different from other cars of that day was a bulging beltline. (The beltline is that horizontal area of the body under the windows.) The 1929 Buick sedan and coupe both had puffy little rolls around their middles. Seeing either car today, most people probably wouldn't notice any difference between it and other sedans or coupes of that era. But in 1929, the puffed-out beltline hit the public like the brick bouncing off Krazy Kat's head.

Christy Borth, writing in *Ward's AutoWorld* in 1969, claimed that when Walter Chrysler got his first glimpse of the 1929 Buick, he immediately said that the car looked "pregnant." Within two weeks, the entire country called it the Pregnant Buick, this at a time when refined people didn't whisper that word. Buick sales plunged from 222,000 in 1928 to 162,000 in '29, and the division lost its #3 sales status (behind Ford and Chevrolet) to Hudson/Essex. This was serious business, because Buick had been GM's #1 moneymaker, ahead even of Chevrolet!

Designer/author Jeff Godshall, in a recent interview, felt that Harley Earl did, in fact, design the 1929 Buick pretty much as it came out. Earl said later that Fisher had changed his body drafts, so it was Fisher's fault that the car arrived looking pregnant. Earl even told Borth that Fisher Body's chief engineer, Glen Simpson, wanted to put more hip space into all GM bodies and, in Simpson's sincere desire to make General Motors cars roomier, he picked the 1929 Buick as his first attempt. Simpson ordered the redrawing of A&C's Buick drafts to give more cross-body space,

Pontiac was about to go belly up in 1932 when Frank Hershey (above) arrived at GM A&C from Hudson. He was immediately assigned to design a new 1933 Pontiac, because no one liked the then-current proposal (top center and right). Hershey borrowed his grille shape from the British Bentley, added valanced fenders with press-in speed streaks, and that was basically how the 1933 Pontiac came out. Frank's design and a new Straight 8 engine revitalized the marque.

and that gave the car its beltline roll.

Another designer, Richard H. Stout, recalled seeing photos of the 1929 Buick's original design in 1948. Stout said the beltline roll already existed on the Art & Colour body draft. He added that Earl's initial concept of the 1929 Buick included slightly keystone-shaped B-pillars with

curved drip moldings that swept down from over the windows and touched the beltline. The windows were arched, as they ended up in production.

Designer Frank Hershey further felt that Fisher raised the Buick's roof about two inches over what Earl had called for. Fisher probably eliminated the curved drip mold-

ings at the same time, substituting conventional B-pillars.

Whatever happened, Fisher Body could not have made any changes without Buick's approval. Buick president Ed Strong and his sales staff had to okay the beltline, the roof height and the pillar changes, so by rights they should have got-

Beginning around 1932, Earl regularly staged design competitions among his stylists to bring out their best ideas. This 1934 contest focused on a small fastback sedan. Earl and the Fisher Brothers judged these competitions, and winners were often awarded expense-paid vacations.

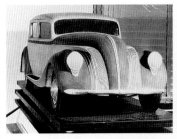

In the early 1930s, Harry Shaw had charge of A&C's advanced design. Scale models above were all done under Shaw in 1933 and show tremendous diversity, probably because no one knew at the time which direction future auto design would take. Slope-nosed model at far left echoed what Briggs was doing with Lincoln Zephyr prototype, while design at far right anticipated production 1936 Zephyr. Fastback above presages Cadillac's suitcase fenders.

During that period, full-sized body mockups were laboriously carved from wood and then scrimmed (see *Scrimming* sidebar, page 99). Tom Hibbard's Cadillac group proposed uninspired 1934 LaSalle at the left, while Jules Agramonte submitted the LaSalle-saving style above. British "beach racers" inspired 1934 LaSalle's tall, slender radiator grille, and contemporary aircraft evoked the "biplane" bumpers. Round hood louvers were added by Jack Morgan.

ten the blame. But it landed on Earl instead, partly because he now had overall corporate design responsibility and partly because he couldn't accuse Fisher Body or Buick of any wrongdoing. If anything, the Pregnant Buick showed how little authority Harley Earl had at that time.

Not for long, though. The Buick fiasco, whatever actually happened, did bring about two important changes in the way A&C interacted with Fisher Body and the divisions. First, Earl started insisting that Fisher show him all major styling changes for his staff's approval. Second, Earl decided he needed his own body engineer to anticipate the "can't-be-done" or "too-expensive" objections that Fisher Body brought up to the divisions. So in 1928, O'Leary hired Vincent D. (Kap) Kaptur Sr., 33, who'd been a body designer and engineer with Packard for 12 years. Kaptur became A&C's supervisor of body development and *the* major liaison between A&C and Fisher Body.

Also brought aboard in 1928 were John Tjaarda, the Dutch engineer/designer who'd previously been with Locke; and Gordon Buehrig, formerly with Gotfredson Body Co., Dietrich Inc. and Packard. Both

Harley Earl got blamed for the 1929 "pregnant" Buick. Its beltline rolled upward and made the body look fat.

designers stayed at General Motors for only a short time. Tjaarda served briefly as Earl's chief designer before moving to Briggs. And Buehrig went on to an illustrious career with Auburn-Cord-Duesenberg (see page 233).

Meanwhile, to fill out A&C's styling staff, O'Leary placed ads in the *New York Times* and other U.S. and European newspapers soliciting applications from anyone interested in automobile design. He had in mind commercial and advertising artists, interior decorators, architects, yacht designers, colorists, jewelry designers, etc. As a result, an army of hopefuls began marching through O'Leary's office, most of whom he hired on a trial basis. Many soon washed out again, but a number stayed.

By mid-1928, Earl's staff numbered near the 50 Sloan had anticipated. Among them were blackboard men, clay modelers, wood- and metalshop craftsmen and office personnel. A&C moved from the 10th floor of the GM Building to a large, open room on the third floor. It was here that the entire design activity—the auto design industry, in fact—began to take form.

Earl was still many years away from putting the different design groups into separate studios. Walled studios wouldn't arrive until 1937, the same year that the name "Art & Colour" got changed to "General Motors Styling." In the beginning, Earl evolved a system of segregating groups of designers and clay modelers by setting up movable blackboards between them. These seven-foot-tall, wheeled blackboards were used to draw full-sized side views of cars. The workspaces between blackboards became informal studios. And although designers and modelers could hear each other in adjoining areas and could listen to Earl talking to other groups, they couldn't actually see what was going on next door. If they wanted to sneak a peek, they had to spy into the neighboring area and that, by Earl's edict, was *verboten*, because Earl wanted each group to be original.

Earl was still experimenting, though; feeling his way. For a short time in the early 1930s, he tried another arrangement. He moved the blackboards to the sides of the open room and placed his desk at one end. He had his designers set up their

Compare shape of 1931 Madam X (above) with "stream-lined" Cadillac Aerodynamic Coupe of only two years later. Sleek 16-cylinder coupe was GM's showcar at the 1933

Chicago Century of Progress and proved so popular that Fleetwood offered it in limited production (20 built). It pioneered all-steel Turret Top and No-Draft ventipanes.

THE MOST
BEAUTIFUL THING
ON WHEELS

Frank Hershey again led team that came up with 1935 Pontiac. Its hallmark silver streak ran up grille and along hood, then down the decklid (not shown on early mockup above right). Hershey's design grew from a 1933 contest

model, and it's possible that the silver streak came about when someone laid a ribbed, extruded strip of clay on the model's hood. Clay ribbing reminded Frank (center, top left photo) of finned oil coolers sticking out from race-car hoods.

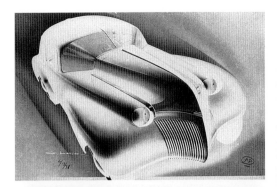

In the mid 1930s, Harley Earl started saving his designers' more notable sketches in a series of large scrapbooks. He used these to capture ideas and explorations for possible future reference. Earl also had files set up at Art & Colour that contained photos and drawings taken from architecture, aircraft and ship design, nature, commercial and fine art, etc. Although he rarely suggested specifics, he occasionally brought these out to exemplify what he had in mind.

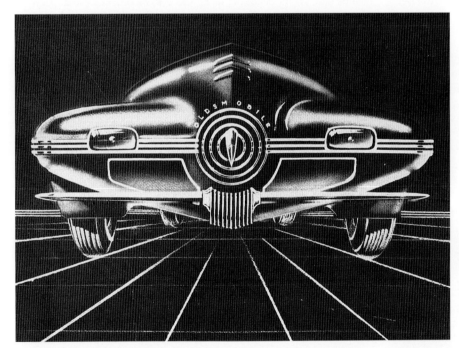

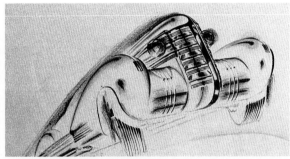

The Harley Earl scrapbooks showed a tremendous diversity of styles and ideas, from the car based on a locomotive--by future Edsel designer Roy Brown (upper left)--to the very modern spinner-nosed Oldsmobile done by Art Ross in 1939 (above). George Lawson and Bill Mitchell rarely sketched cars that stood still; they always put motion into their artwork (above right). Earl's genius consisted of organizing all these ideas and steering them toward a salable synthesis.

easels or drawingboards in a fan-like pattern, with everyone facing Earl. The idea was to run Art & Colour like a newspaper. Earl was the managing editor, so to speak, and the designers were his reporters. They could approach his desk with sketches or to talk. That experiment, though, failed miserably, and Earl soon rearranged the room with blackboard dividers.

Harley recognized the value of publicity, and one way he got his people known within GM was to dress them in uniforms.

For a time, designers wore white cotton smocks with dark collars and epaulets. Modelers wore darker smocks minus epaulets. Earl had a wonderful flair for showmanship, and the uniforms were one early expression of that. They made A&C personnel highly visible as they moved around the GM Building and thus became walking advertisements for Earl's department. After the uniforms had served their publicity purpose, Earl scrapped them again.

As he settled into his work, Earl developed ways for getting the most from his designers. For example, he rarely dictated and never gave clear, precise instructions. He purposely kept his suggestions vague. This seemed terribly aggravating and illogical to some, but his sharpest people soon figured out what Earl was doing. If he dictated, his designers would get to know what Earl wanted and would tailor their designs to suit his tastes. By remaining vague and ambivalent, though, and by changing direction often and unexpectedly, Earl gave his designers the greatest possible latitude to use their imaginations. He realized that by committing himself, he ran the risk of stifling creativity. That might be one reason he never tried to model clay or sketch, even to explain a rough idea.

Another reason, according to retired GM design executive Stanley R. Wilen, might have been that Earl knew his limits. He realized he couldn't draw nearly so well as some of the people under him, so he didn't try to compete. Rather than do a sketch clumsily, said Wilen, Earl would direct designers verbally and by handwaving.

But Earl also had trouble articulating. He stuttered. It wasn't severe; just enough to make him self-conscious. Earl usually spoke in a soft voice and battered the language doing it. *Chromium* became "chronium," *narrow* was "nare," and he pronounced *LaSalle* "L'Sawl." Earl could also, of course, offer up some very salty, colorful language at times, and in later life he shied away from speaking in public.

Another of Earl's strategems: He had no qualms about lifting design ideas from one group and carrying them over to another. He might like a grille sketch that the Oldsmobile studio had done, would take it to Chevrolet and ask the Chevy designers to use either that idea or to work up variations.

It's said, too, that Earl would hire young designers, assign them to do details sketches, assume that their best ideas would show up in their earliest work and then, after they'd produced, let them go again. This got to be common practice before World War II, and many designers called it Mr. Earl's or Mr. O'Leary's "revolving door policy."

Technical stylist Orval Selders worked in the Oldsmobile studio in the 1950s and spent most of his time doing full-sized blackboard drawings. "When Mr. Earl entered the studio," recalled Selders, "he'd first go where we were doing the full-sized line drawings on these huge blackboards. Everyone in the studio

would follow him and converge on that area. Mr. Earl would walk over, pick up one of the new Bertoia wire-mesh chairs and walk toward the board, holding the chair cupped around his rear end. He would sit down about 10 feet from the board and would direct me to move the lines up or down as he chose, sometimes only 1/8 inch. As he was directing the placement of these lines, he would often also be pointing with the toe of his shoe."

Earl could sit by the hour and watch a drawing or clay model take shape. In the case of clay models, he usually *would* make suggestions. He might order a modeler to raise a molding by a fraction of an inch, then lower it again, move it up, now down, and this might go on for a long time until, in Earl's estimation, the model finally looked right. The studios had a saying, according to former GM designer John Barclay Foster: "Mr. Earl wants it raised down a 1/64 inch."

As Selders mentioned, Earl would often sprawl in a chair and point or motion with the toe of his very expensive shoe. What many designers called "handwaving" more commonly became footwaving. And no one, according to designer J.S. (Steve) McDaniel, ever left a studio before Earl did. Earl was a workaholic. Most mornings he'd arrive around seven and stay until nine in the evening, sometimes take a few hours off, go home or catch a meeting and finally return again late at night. Some designers put their best sketches on the studio walls after 10:00 p.m., because they knew Earl would be passing through around midnight.

When he wanted to see a project finished, or when one of his groups had a tight deadline, designers and modelers were expected to spend their weekends on the job. They sometimes stayed around the clock and slept at their drawingboards or on seats in the studios. Later, Earl would issue scrip that allowed studio personnel to order dinners at the coffee shop on the lower concourse of the GM Building. Or sometimes he allowed them to order out and have gourmet meals delivered: shrimp, roast beef, cham-

Planned Obsolescence

Sloan's timing for GM Art & Colour couldn't have been better. After 1925, the center of American autobody design shifted steadily from New York to Detroit. East-coast coachbuilders still had *some* influence on production design during the late 1920s, but production studios, especially those at Briggs, Murray, Hayes and GM, were now taking fashion leadership away from the *carrossiers*. And due to the more aggressive nature of the production studios and the huge amounts of money generated by the yearly styling changes of mass-produced automobiles, the fashion leadership of coachbuilders would probably have gone away even if there'd been no Great Depression.

When Detroit's marketers realized they could draw millions of Americans into dealer showrooms every year by first piquing their curiosity with teaser ads and then unveiling the newest forms of rebent sheetmetal, that's exactly what they did. The carmakers managed, in fact, to sustain this tradition not just for years but for decades. The ritualized trip to the local dealership became one of this country's favorite forms of free family entertainment.

"The present-day motorist takes the excellence of the chassis for granted but satisfies his individual taste by shopping for the body he likes," wrote *Automotive Industries* in 1923. "It is conceded that a line of bodies may make or break an automobile company."

The annual visits to local showrooms became events that Henry Crane and Alfred Sloan noticed and capitalized on. Crane was Sloan's technical advisor, and the insights he passed along to Sloan went beyond engineering and production topics but also

dealt with what the public wanted and would buy. In a talk before the Society of Automotive Engineers in New York, Crane said, "To many people, the automobile is their most outstanding personal possession. This is why appearance is so important, and a continual modification of appearance is equally important. The tag of up-to-dateness is practically essential.... I think that you will realize from the foregoing remarks that I believe wholeheartedly in change for the sake of change.... Car owners have shown over and over again that they will accept a certain degree of discomfort in payment for what they consider, at the time, to be more attractive appearance."

Sloan wholeheartedly agreed. In 1963, he wrote in *My Years With General Motors*: "The degree to which styling changes should be made in any one model run presents a particularly delicate problem. The changes in the new model should be so novel and attractive as to create demand for the new value and, so to speak, create a certain amount of dissatisfaction with past models as compared with the new one, and yet the current and old models must still be capable of giving satisfaction to the vast used-car market."

This was basically Sloan's blueprint for planned obsolescence, and that's where Harley Earl came in. Earl and other designers, those at rival car companies and at the major body suppliers, would see to it that automotive shapes would mutate more quickly and more radically in the decade between 1930 and 1940 than at any time since the turn of the century. That was basically what Sloan launched when he gave Earl free rein in 1927. ◆

pagne, the works.

When it came to styling judgements, Harley Earl designed totally by intuition. He said in any number of interviews and articles that he always believed what he liked would please everyone. Yet if he designed basically to please himself—and chances are he really *didn't*—his knowledge of the market was so sharp that he had the ability to empathize with the typical new-car buyer. He obviously understood—somehow miraculously fathomed—those things that interested the majority of GM customers. And for that reason, Earl never put much stock in market research or outside opinion.

He believed in long, tall hoods, because a massive hood implied power. He had a profound appreciation for the entertainment value of glitter and chrome. Earl developed a theory of the "light value" of chrome trim; that it should capture the maximum brightness and throw it directly into the eye of the beholder. To make this happen, Earl constantly urged his designers to bevel or tilt chrome trim at 45° to the horizon so that reflections would bounce up into the viewer's face. And he liked automotive jewelry—cloissone badges, hood ornaments, spears, finned wheelcovers, etc.—that flashed and glittered in the sunlight. As Strother MacMinn put it, "Harley Earl designed so you could walk around a car and be entertained the whole trip."

According to GM designer William L. Porter, Earl had elaborate "highlight rules" as well. He assigned one of his modelers, Jack Wylie, to go around to all the studios with a highlight gauge—a little angle device with a leveling bubble in it—to make sure Earl's highlight rules were being followed. Late in Earl's career, James McCormack, a man who could design as well as sculpt and model, was put in charge of training all newly hired modelers. New hirees at that time had to have college degrees in sculpting, and some even had master's degrees. "McCormack's conception of form was much more sophisticated than the normal modeler's, and for many years the high level of artistry in the modeling of GM cars was widely admired throughout the industry," noted Porter.

Earl also insisted on making all of his cars recognizable by small children from a block away. Each car should be so distinctive that any American six-year-old could call out its name as it hove into view.

Earl's over-riding philosophy, though—his supreme effort throughout his 31 years as head of GM's styling activity—had to do with making cars look *lower* and *longer*. He did this in part by physically

lowering them, an effort that represented a constant battle with GM managers and engineers. But he also did it with cheat lines and styling tricks that fooled the eye: horizontal moldings, longer windows, wraparounds, fender skirts, increased overhangs and massive bumpers.

One of the earliest instances of Art & Colour influencing the industry as a whole came when Kap Kaptur suggested GM's A-B-C body plan. At that time, Kaptur, Earl's body-development supervisor and Fisher liaison, was one of the few people who had access to all areas of A&C. One day in 1931, Kap happened to be checking body sizes and noticed that the standard bodies for Chevrolet, Pontiac and the small Oldsmobile were nearly identical. Dimensions were within fractions of an inch. Likewise the big Olds, the standard Buick and the small Cadillac: all very close dimensionally.

"I traced up three different cars on one set of vellum overlays," Kaptur said in a 1980 interview, "lined them up at the firewall and the sill, and from there you could see the variations. When I showed that to Harley, I says, 'God, look at that! There's the wheelhouse. Everybody makes his own wheelhouse, but there's only a quarter inch difference. Why not make them all the same? And the door sizes. Such small dif-

ferences: a quarter, three-eighth, half an inch. You can't even detect those things by eye.' I says, 'Why couldn't it all be the same? All that money spent on separate dies for each division...think how much money we'd save!'"

Harley Earl showed Kaptur's conclusions to Fisher Body and suggested that all GM cars share four basic body shells. He designated these A-B-C-D. The A-body would be used for the Chevrolet, standard Pontiac and small Oldsmobile. The large Pontiac, mid-sized Oldsmobile and small

Buick would use the B shell. The C-body accommodated the big Olds, big Buick, LaSalle and small Cadillac. And all Cadillac and Buick limousines used the D-body. Kaptur mentioned in his interview that the A-B-C-D idea saved GM hundreds of millions of dollars over the years, and that's likely a conservative assessment. The A-B-C-D body system became one of A&C's great early contributions to General Motors' profitability, and the corporation continues to use an expanded version of the same idea today, as do all other U.S. automakers. (As of 1994, Detroit's Big Three used alphanumerical platform instead of body designations. GM's 16 platforms were still coded A-Z, but the corporation was trying to replace letters with codes like GM-20. Chrysler used a combination of letters—LH and SR, for instance—or letters plus numbers, like H24S. Ford's platform codes carried a mix of letters and numbers: DN5 for Taurus.)

With the A-B-C-D body system in place, it was up to GM A&C to make the standardized core bodies take on styling identities by giving them different grilles, different fender lines, hoods, lamps, moldings, wheels, hubcaps, accessories, ornamentation, instrument panels, upholstery and other details. That became and remained one of Harley Earl's biggest challenges through the years.

Earl believed mightily in entertaining the spectator during the entire trip around a car. Earl's personal convertible, the 1938 Buick Y Job, makes a good example.

One way he tackled the challenge was to have incoming designers work on small, isolated parts of a car, not the overall design. One young stylist might be assigned to sketch nothing but hood louvers day after day for a week. Or tail lights. Or hubcaps. The work became terribly tedious, but it showed Earl whether the designer had the grit and patience to stick with a project. It also gave Earl a reservoir of usable ideas, because some of these detail designs were quite good.

General Motors soon developed a corpo-

Harley Earl gave GM cars a corporate look. Here we see noticeable similarities between the 1932 Cadillac (right) and the 1932 Chevrolet. Edsel Ford pioneered this trickle-down idea when he made the 1928 Model A look like a baby Lincoln (see page 123).

rate look, an identity that made it obvious that Chevrolet, Pontiac, Oldsmobile, Buick and Cadillac all belonged to the same family. Occasionally, Earl would make one of GM's lower-priced makes look like a smaller version of a more expensive one. He might have taken this idea from Ford, who styled the 1928 Model A to look like a baby Lincoln (see page 123).

In GM's case, it happened for the first time with the 1932 Chevrolet. The '32 Chevy had all the cues and attributes of the 1932 Cadillac, particularly in the hood doors, grille shape, fine-mesh grille texture and headlamps. Even the central body contours were very similar, just scaled down. (In fact, all 1932 GM cars looked very similar.) Earl didn't do this consistently, but for 1939 the Chevrolet again looked a lot like a smaller 1939 Cadillac, and for 1940 it looked like a miniaturized 1940 Buick.

Additional examples of styling crossover are the prow-nosed 1939 Cadillac and 1939 Chevrolet at top and the 1940 Buick and 1940 Chevy above and right. Earl's philosophy was to let the prestige of GM's up-market cars rub off on the less expensive makes.

The Great Depression took a terrible toll on General Motors, just as it did on other U.S. automakers. During 1932-33, GM seriously considered dropping both Pontiac and LaSalle. Pontiac sales had fallen 80% between 1929 and 1932, and LaSalle's were down 85% for the same period.

Pontiac's fate rested with the 1933 model, because the division had an all-new Straight Eight engine ready to launch that year. Unfortunately, Harley Earl's Pontiac design group wasn't coming up with styling to match the new engine.

Frank Hershey, formerly with Walter M. Murphy (see page 68), worked for GM briefly in 1928, then went back to California and finally followed Frank Spring to Hudson in Detroit in late 1931. Howard O'Leary phoned Hershey at Hudson, offered him the Pontiac studio at GM Art & Colour, and Hershey took it.

His second day on the job, Earl called Hershey up to his office and told him to drive out to Pontiac, Michigan and look at a wooden mockup that was then being considered for the 1933 car. Hershey reported back to Earl the next day, saying that in his opinion, the mockup looked too much like the 1932 Pontiac. "If that's all you're going to do to it," said Hershey, "you might as well leave it alone." Whereupon Earl told him, "All right, you've got two weeks to come up with something better."

Hershey got to work and, in two weeks, had a full-sized 1933 Pontiac clay ready for inspection. "Just before that," recalled Hershey many years later, "I'd gone down to a private showing of the new 1932 Graham, the Blue Streak, and this car had front fender valances and rounded lines: a very, very far-out car, and beautiful. It was like a shot in the arm.'"

Hershey's proposed 1933 Pontiac shared Chevrolet's A-body, but the two cars looked entirely different. The Pontiac used front and rear valances like the Graham's but with speed streaks pressed into all four fenders. The new car also had wide hood louvers and more streamlined headlamps. But the kicker was the radiator grille, which turned out to be a blatant copy of the British Bentley design. "I was in love with Bentleys," confessed Hershey, "and I'd designed custom bodies for Bentleys at Murphy's, so I decided to do a Bentley front end on this Pontiac."

Hershey's 1933 Pontiac design did everything Earl and Knudsen had hoped for. Earl felt the car looked modern and handsome, and so did Knudsen, who now made decisions for both Chevrolet and Pontiac. The public enthusiastically agreed. Buyers saw great style and value in the 1933 Pontiac. Sales doubled that year, leading GM to reprieve Pontiac. Hershey, in effect, had saved the marque.

The LaSalle's fate hung in a similar balance that next year, 1934. Again, there were insider rumors that Cadillac couldn't afford to keep its companion car. Other GM makes had already dropped their companions: Buick the Marquette and Olds the Viking. Pontiac's parent make, the Oakland, was also discontinued. But it bothered Earl to hear talk of scuttling the LaSalle; the 1927 model had been his baby.

As with the 1933 Pontiac, Earl's Cadillac/LaSalle group under Tom Hibbard wasn't coming up with anything that would breathe new life into the LaSalle. Even at this critical moment, Harley Earl decided to leave for Europe to make his usual rounds of the Paris Salon and other major shows. In Earl's absence, Harry Shaw was left in charge of GM's design activity.

With Earl gone, Jules Agramonte, the former Fleetwood designer, made a full-sized airbrush rendering on black paper of the front of a car with a tall, slender radiator grille. The grille took its inspiration from that day's track and beach racers. According to Strother MacMinn, Harley Earl talked in 1939 about some of the cars that gave rise to the 1934 LaSalle front end. Earl described the narrow radiator opening as coming from "...those English beach racers." This Mac interpreted to be the four-liter Sunbeam in which Sir Malcolm Campbell made his early record runs on the Pendine sands in Wales. The Sunbeam had an extended, tapered nose cowling to cut down the volume of incoming air. There were other cars with similar slit-like nostrils, among them Oliver Bertram's special eight-liter Bentley and the Pacey/Hassan Bentley.

In Agramonte's rendering, the headlights stood off the hood on stalks, the front bumper had double blades like the wings of a biplane, and the catwalks—the areas between the grille and front fenders—were very low. Little chromed chevrons served as ornaments on the front-fender noses. Agramonte's drawing looked sensational, and he showed it to Harry Shaw, mentioning that it might make a good LaSalle. Shaw didn't agree and told Agramonte to roll up the drawing and put it away.

When Earl got back from Europe, Shaw left on vacation, and Agramonte took out his LaSalle drawing, unrolled it and put it back on the board. According to Gordon Buehrig, "Earl came in and got terribly excited about it, and they were working on it night

and day from then on...." John R. (Jack) Morgan added the round hood louvers. After that, all other elements seemed to fall into place naturally. Earl ordered up a sample body of Agramonte's proposed 1934 LaSalle made from scrimmed wood and metal, completely trimmed and accurate in every detail.

When General Motors' executives assembled in the GM auditorium to look at Art & Colour's 1934 styling proposals, Earl had the LaSalle mockup onstage, alone, with the curtains drawn. As he rose to make his presentation, he said, "Gentlemen, if you decide to discontinue the L'Sawl, this is the car you're not going to build." The curtains parted, and there stood the wooden mockup of the 1934 LaSalle (see photo, page 93). The audience sat silent for a moment and then came to life. Everyone liked the design, and GM quickly approved it.

From the very beginning, Earl had put emphasis on "advanced" or future designs. He'd assigned several stylists, under Harry Shaw, to produce an on-going series of scale clay models of styles that might spur ideas for future production. He also began staging contests—idea starters—among the various other design groups.

Design competitions weren't new. The French and British had been holding contests for years, and here in this country, the Automobile Body Builders Assn. sponsored a number of competitions during the 1920s, usually offering cash prizes. Earl often rewarded his winners with expense-paid vacations.

Each of the GM contest groups consisted of two to four designers plus one or two clay modelers. Each contest focused on a specific "package," meaning a given set of dimensions in a certain body style. Earl's contests usually filled slow times in the work schedule, and they served a number of purposes. They made designers think competitively and let them focus on future designs. They occasionally led to production designs, as in the

Scrimming

The compound-curved surfaces of carriage bodies were often built up from "walls" of little wooden cubes that filled the voids between ribs. These cubes were glued together like tiny bricks. The surface was then sanded smooth and "scrimmed." Scrimming meant dipping cheesecloth in hot vegetable glue and placing it over the surface of the wooden blocks. It was like an early version of fiberglassing. When the scrim dried, it could be sanded, primed and varnished.

The wood-and-metal body mockups that GM Art & Colour and other automakers built in the early 1930s used scrimming on many of the compound-curved surfaces. According to Strother MacMinn, some of the artisans at A&C had learned their scrimming skills in carriage days and carried them over into the making of sample bodies. Scrimmed carbodies looked entirely real. They had glass in all windows, handmade grilles and plated brightwork, and their

interiors were usually trimmed just like the real thing. Doors opened and closed, so you could climb inside and sit in the car. Everything looked functional. It's estimated that even in the 1930s, one of these scrimmed wooden mockups cost approximately $100,000 to build. ◆

Full-sized styling mockups of the 1930s were typically built up of small blocks of wood, glued together and then covered with glue-saturated cheesecloth. The doors opened, and these prototypes looked real inside and out.

case of the 1935 Pontiac, and they also allowed Earl to evaluate each designer's skills and leadership potential.

Gordon Buehrig recalled a contest in 1933 in which he led one team, Frank Hershey another, Jack Morgan a third and Tom Hibbard a fourth. The assignment was to design a two-year-ahead, full-sized sedan. On Hershey's team were Steve McDaniel and ex-Murray designer Jules Andrade. Chevrolet-Pontiac president Bill Knudsen judged this contest and declared Morgan's team the winner. Morgan and his mates were given an all-expense trip to the 1933 Century of Progress World's Fair in Chicago.

Earl didn't say anything, but he wasn't pleased with Knudsen's choice. Instead, he favored the Hershey team's clay, which represented a 1935 Pontiac. Hershey had again created a bold design. His model had no runningboards, used fender skirts over the rear wheels, headlights were blended into the fenders, and the most distinctive feature was what later became known as the "Pontiac silver streak"—a broad, fluted band of bright metal running up the car's nose, along the top of the hood and down the decklid. After Knudsen left, Earl ordered the Hershey/Andrade/McDaniel model scaled up full size. Pontiac soon released a very similar version as their 1935 car, complete with the silver streak, a hallmark that continued to identify Pontiac through the 1956 model year.

In a second 1933 contest, Gordon Buehrig designed a model that, after he left GM, he developed into a small Duesenberg and then into the 1936 Cord 810 (see page 239). Still later, in yet another contest, Virgil Exner and Clare Hodgman won an all-expense vacation to New York, where they were put up at the Waldorf-Astoria. "It was a very nice thing which Harley Earl instigated," Hodgman said in a 1980 interview. Contests continued periodically after that, and Earl's successor, William L. (Bill) Mitchell also held them on occasion.

The immensely popular Chicago World's Fair, known as the Century of Progress, opened in May 1933, and General Motors set up one of the biggest and most impressive pavilions on the site. Chevrolet, for example, kept a small assembly line going that actually built cars. And as A&C's contribution, Harley Earl provided his first publicly shown dreamcar: the 1933 Cadillac V-16 Aerodynamic Coupe (photos on page 94). This long, lithe, gloss-black fastback captured the attention of everyone entering the GM pavilion.

Impressive as it was, the 1933 Cadillac Aerodynamic Coupe faced stiff competition from other Century of Progress dreamcars. The Briggs rear-engined prototype by John Tjaarda—a precursor of the 1936 Lincoln Zephyr—was more radical (page 127), and the 1933 Pierce Silver Arrow by Phil Wright, with its "through" front fenders, ended up having a much greater effect on future car design (page 231). The Cadillac V-16 Aerodynamic Coupe, however, did foretell two GM advances: No-Draft ventilation for 1933 and the all-steel roof, or Turret Top, for 1935.

After 1933, Fleetwood offered a very similar Cadillac Aerodynamic Coupe as a limited-production model. Twenty were built, if we include the Century of Progress showcar, and Bill Knudsen took delivery of the first production coupe when the fair closed for the season in Nov. 1933. The fair reopened in May 1934, but by that time the Aerodynamic Coupe was generally regarded as just another custom Fleetwood body style and not a dreamcar.

By now, A&C enjoyed a tremendous degree of acceptance within General Motors. Through Earl's hard work and as a byproduct of his personality and skill, the department had a definite measure of indispensability. No division president or general manager would ever after consider planning future models without first talking to Earl and his top designers.

On Oct. 23, 1933, Harlow Curtice took over the presidency of Buick, and he immediately made an appointment to see Earl. Curtice introduced himself and explained that, with his accountancy background, he needed not only styling help with Buick, which was ailing at the time, but also a quick course in automotive design.

Earl liked Curtice's candor and responded by showing and explaining how his department worked and what it could do for Buick. The two men formed a lasting bond, and Curtice, for his part, quickly developed an appreciation for the benefits of sophisticated styling. Earl worked closely with Curtice on his first car, the 1936 Buick and, as a result, Buick sales rose nearly 400% between 1933 and the end of 1936. So Curtice, an excellent businessman, nurtured a feel for cars.

The relationship between Earl and Curtice evolved to such a degree after Larry Fisher left Cadillac in mid 1934 that Earl began to favor Curtice and Buick in the same way he'd favored Larry Fisher and Cadillac previously. When Curtice asked Earl in 1936 what make of car he drove, and Earl replied, "Cadillac," Curtice urged him to switch to Buick, and Earl did.

By 1935, nearly all domestic automobiles had gone to the more curvilinear forms, the more rounded and deeper-drawn fenders, domed all-metal roofs and the punched-through windows that characterized the American "streamlined" look. It was at this

Since General Motors assembled cars in farflung body plants, it was important to stamp large pieces, like roofs and hoods, from single sheets of steel; also to design them so they nested for shipment. These were technical considerations stylists had to keep in mind.

point that Detroit design began to lead the world. And GM, due to its size and consistently good car sales, began to lead the U.S. industry in styling.

GM's 1935-36 Oldsmobile, 1936 Chevrolet and 1936 Buick had what came to be known as the "fencer's mask" grille: bright, oval, protruding shapes that fit the rounded noses of the rounded bodies themselves. Earl remained a firm advocate of cast, rather than stamped, grilles, because chromed castings gave a sharper edge and a richer, brighter reflection than stainless-steel or chrome-plated stampings. Ford used the lighter stampings for its grilles through 1937; GM favored cast potmetal grilles.

Earl's successor, William L. Mitchell, looking back at GM's early Turret Top bodies, said that he and the other designers at that time hated the compromises involved in accommodating the all-steel roof. GM's 1935-37 cars got to be awfully "fat," he said, and he explained that they got all that visual weight because Fisher's body engineers insisted on overcrowning the roofs to prevent drumming. The designers then had to work with round window openings to go with the rounded door cuts.

GM's leadership position at that time prompted most other U.S. automakers to follow the "fat" format, complete with small, rounded windows and bulging sides. So the Turret Top, while it benefitted car owners, was not an innovation that the designers liked, at least not in the early years of the all-metal roof.

For the 1937-38 model years, General Motors abandoned wood body framing, which they'd slowly been phasing out anyway, and began to produce nothing but all-steel bodies. GM's A and B bodies went to all-steel in 1937, and the bigger cars lost their wood for 1938. This changeover meant a huge capital outlay. It also meant much greater complexity in terms of engineering each individual body. Some degree of body strengthening now came via pressed-in ribs, creases and moldings as, for example, in the front face of a cowl or the "speed crease" stamped into the cowl and front door of the 1937-38 Chevrolet. The crease was put there to add strength to these panels and to prevent drumming. To that extent, it became both a styling and an engineering consideration.

Another styling/engineering consideration had to do with the stacking or nesting of fenders, roofs, cowls, and other body panels, especially for Chevrolet. These parts had to be designed to nest so that more could fit into a railcar for shipment to outlying Fisher assembly plants. The ability for components to nest, of course, affected styling.

And it was basically the all-steel body that made lead times so much longer than they'd been in the days of composite bodies. Steel structures required more engineering, more precise jigs and more machine- than hand labor. It now took an average of 27

Bigger and Better Stamping Presses

You'll recall that early drop presses worked by gravity (page 27), and sheet steel at that time had to be heated red hot because otherwise it would tear when drawn or bent. By the early 1930s, though, there had been tremendous advances in the technology of alloying sheet steel, so with the help of lubricants, it could be rolled and pressed cold.

Stamping presses had also been greatly improved, and what made them so impressive (wups) was their size, speed and the pressures they generated. Fisher Body's Turret Top, for example, became possible in 1935 for a number of reasons. More ductile steels now came in a 110-inch width instead of the earlier 72-, and the larger presses could stamp a roof from a single 110-inch sheet. It actually took four strikes through four separate presses to make all the Turret Top contours, flanges, rails and trims. For this, Fisher used two toggle presses each weighing 500 tons and exerting nearly 2000 tons of pressure plus two tandem slide presses weighing about 400 tons each and exerting 650 tons of force.

Fisher's outlay for presses to stamp 1935 Turret Tops amounted to some $25 million. Then GM's decision to convert to all-steel bodies for 1937 cost Fisher roughly that much again. So you can understand why Fred and Charlie Fisher weren't anxious to abandon composite construction. And it's significant that GM decided to go to all-steel bodies only after both founding Fisher Brothers had retired.   ◆

Huge GM/Fisher stamping press turned out Pontiac inner doors in the 1950s.

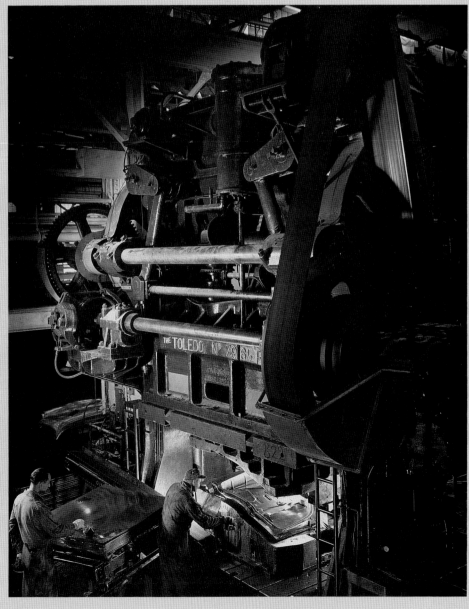

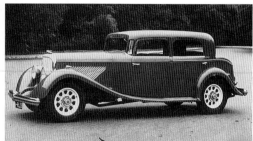

William L. (Bill) Mitchell had wanted to design Buicks, because his father had been a Buick dealer. But Earl put Mitchell into the Cadillac studio (top left) in 1935, and Mitchell was running it by 1936. Earl recognized Mitchell's talent early on, assigned him to do a smaller, more youthful Cadillac, the 1938 60-Special. This car began as a LaSalle, with a narrow grille and suitcase fenders. The upper was inspired by the French Panhard Panoramic sedan (top right).

months from concept to Job One, whereas in 1931 it had taken only nine months.

On Jan. 3, 1937, Art & Colour was renamed "General Motors Styling," and on that date it moved again, this time to the top four floors of GM Research Annex B, behind the General Motors Building and across Milwaukee Avenue. Styling's 125 employees now occupied the eighth through the 11th floors of Research Annex B, and design teams were given separate rooms, or "studios," for the first time.

From the beginning, these studios were kept locked, and only a few people had keys: Earl, O'Leary, Kaptur and the studio chiefs. Locking the studios was meant to discourage espionage by other car companies and also to prevent any unauthorized exchange of ideas between styling groups. Earl wanted complete control. Elevators stopped just on the eighth and 11th floors, and workers on the ninth and 10th floors entered and exited Styling only from the 11th floor. Earl posted a "timekeeper" at the elevator, a Mr. White, and Mr. White not only wrote down the names of those who came in late but had the authority to inspect anyone's packages going in or out. Harry Bradley, who had polio as a child, said that even years later, the only way he could smuggle his own sketches out of the design building was to roll them up very tightly and stuff them into the hollow ends of his crutches.

Dick Teague recalled that Earl, "...had a habit of wandering around at unexpected times. I think he did that on purpose, because we'd kind of track him through the studios. When he'd come back from Florida with his white Palm Beach suit and this terrific tan, the drumbeats would start in the studios. Miss Ramshaw was pretty good about alerting the troops.... We'd kinda track him like on a radar screen. That's when we'd be all asses and elbows....

"[One day in Bob Lauer's Pontiac studio] word was out that Misterl was on his way, and you could hear the key fumbling in the door, which was the signal for the head of the studio to walk up and open it. And here he was: white suit, glistening tan, pale blue eyes, six-foot-eight or seeming that...and here were Lauer and us guys standing almost at attention. Misterl looks across at this clay model of a Pontiac and stares at it for a moment, and finally he says, 'No, Bob. It's two or three years from now and you're out in Pasadena or wherever, and this little old lady comes into the showroom, and she's standing about this distance from the car, and she'll look it over, and do you know what she'll say?'

"Lauer says, 'No, Misterl, I don't know.'

"She'll say, 'I wouldn't buy that sono-fabitch!'

"That's typical Harley Earl, because he'd just shred you with that sort of remark. So you'd go back to the oven with this clay, and you'd start all over."

In its new quarters, GM Styling had access to a second elevator—a large one that was used to carry full-sized clay models or wooden mockups up onto the roof of the building. The idea was to view models in natural sunlight. This gave a more real-world appearance and showed off highlights better than the artificial illumination of the studios. (Earl once asked General Electric to develop a bulb or a system of lamps that duplicated sunlight, but he and his designers always preferred the real thing.)

The 11th floor of Styling's new premises contained an auditorium built specifically for model presentations, and it also housed Harley Earl's private office. By this time, Earl had occupied at least three different offices, two in the GM Building and now

1938 Cadillac 60-Special used 2-piece doors and narrow chromed channels around side windows. Coupe trunk on a sedan set the car apart, and typical Mitchell "creased pants" windsplits adorned fenders. Cord 810 inspired the hood louvers, and 60-Special's runningboard-less style soon led into General Motors' 1940 "torpedo" C-bodies.

this third in Research Annex B. All three had a similar floorplan—long and narrow—and some of his staff felt that Earl laid out his offices to intimidate, or at least to overwhelm, those who entered. Earl and his decorator, William Wright, preferred dark-panelled walls; a high, elaborate, handcarved, beamed ceiling with touches of gilt; deep oriental carpets; lots of leather and heavy, muted drapes. At the far end of the office, on a raised dais, stood Earl's massive, handcarved, oak desk.

Frank Hershey remembered how it felt when Miss Ramshaw ushered him into Earl's office for the first time. She opened the door, and Hershey saw Earl sitting there on the dais at the far end, waiting silently behind his desk. The walk toward the desk seemed endless, especially as the young designer tried to take in all the Jacobean details. By the time he finally arrived at the desk, Hershey noticed that his and Earl's eyes were meeting on the same level, even though Earl was sitting and Hershey was standing. This, recalled Hershey in a videotaped interview, made him feel about two feet tall, and then it dawned on him that Earl was using his office to its fullest effect.

Earl also dressed to make an impression, and he rarely failed. He might typically come to work wearing a white linen suit that set off his tan, and with that he'd wear a yellow silk shirt, sky blue tie with handkerchief dyed to match, and white suede shoes. He had an identical set of clothes hanging in his office closet, and on hot, clammy Detroit summer days, he'd change at noon and would look beamingly unruffled while everyone around him wilted. He had his clothes tailored by Basil Durant in New York and Schmidt

of California. His shoes came from England. Earl, by virtue of all this sartorial splendor, stood out considerably from the common GM executive, who usually wore dark suits and neutral ties.

Earl's new styling auditorium on the 11th floor now gave him full control of his design presentations. In one presentation in the mid 1930s, Earl wanted to show how to lower a car without sacrificing headroom. Alfred Sloan was in the audience along with the Fishers and others. Sloan wrote later that, "[Mr. Earl] made one of the most dramatic demonstrations I have ever witnessed. He had a Cadillac...on the stage before us. There were a number of workmen who, after lifting the [unattached] body from the chassis, proceeded to cut the chassis frame apart with acetylene torches. Proceeding very quickly, they welded the frame back together in such a way as to lower its height by a good six inches. When they replaced the body on the makeshift frame, Mr. Earl had proved a point—not only could the body be lowered but, in its revised form, it looked 100% better."

In Dec. 1935, O'Leary hired a dynamic young man named William L. Mitchell. Mitchell was 23 when he arrived in Detroit, and he got the job on the strength of a portfolio he'd put together of racing sketches done while working at the Barron Collier advertising agency in New York. The Collier Brothers were dilettante auto racers, and they admitted young Mitchell into their private club, ARCA, the Auto Racing Club of America. Mitchell developed a flair for capturing on his sketchpad not just the race action but the unmistakable identities and details of the cars themselves. The ARCA logo, which Mitchell designed, showed a supercharged Bentley lunging at the viewer and about to run him down (see page 176).

Mitchell, like Earl, loved car racing. When O'Leary showed Earl Mitchell's portfolio of race sketches, Earl told Mitchell to submit some original designs. Mitchell's designs were so good and so dynamic that Earl hired Mitchell right away. A year or so later, Earl named Mitchell head of the Cadillac studio. And Earl immediately put Mitchell to work on a design that turned into the 1938 Cadillac 60-Special (60-S).

Harley Earl initially wanted the 60-S to be another LaSalle. In the back of his mind, he envisioned the third rebirth of his beloved marque (1927 and 1934 being the LaSalle born and reborn). Inspiration for the LaSalle 60-Special came from France. Earl and Big Bill Knudsen had been to the 1934 Paris Salon, where Knudsen fell head over heels in love with the Panhard 6 CS Panoramic. Knudsen especially liked the Panoramic's upper treatment: a roof and window theme inspired by that era's posh French passenger trains. French luxury railcars used arched windows with delicate, bright metal surrounds. The 1934 Panhard roof, like the railcar (and somewhat like the Hibbard & Darrin "torpedo" phaetons), had an extension of the roof surface flowing down the B-pillar to the beltline. This slightly veed B-pillar separated the frameless, chrome-edged glass of the front and rear doors.

Knudsen wanted to buy a Panoramic, but Earl assured him he could do that same roof better, and he brought the Panhard idea back with him to Bill Mitchell's Cadillac studio. Mitchell now did several clays with versions of the five-window roof, the two-piece doors and the thin chrome window frames rising from a rolled, molding-less beltline, much like the 1929 Buick's and the 1936

Cadillac considered a full line of body styles on 60-Special format, including a 3-window coupe (left) and convertible

sedan in Cadillac's 1938 lineup. Since Earl was having a hard time selling Dreystadt, he now offered the 60-S roof and window treatment to Chevrolet and Buick. Neither of those divisions, though, showed any interest.

Finally, according to Frank Hershey, "I remember they had it [the 60-S] all finished and were showing it in the auditorium and had the board and all the division heads there. Harley had to sell it to the board of directors, and he wasn't getting very far. The car was a little too radical.... Sloan was supposed to be there, too, but he wasn't for some reason. They all knew, though, that Sloan and Knudsen liked it. Out of desperation, Earl turned, put his hands on his hips...looked down at everybody and said, 'What will I tell Mr. Sloan when he asks me?' And that sold it in five minutes!"

The Cadillac 60-Special influenced the entire auto industry, because General Motors sedans, starting with the 1940 C-body, adopted the 60-S's five-window roof. Club coupes from Mercury and Chrysler Corp. copied the 60-Special's two-piece doors and thin chrome window surrounds (bodies by Briggs and Hayes, repectively). The 1941 Packard Clipper also took some of its

sedan. Earl's accident occurred in a convertible sedan. In the end, Cadillac brought out only the 4-door 60-S sedan.

Cord's. The earliest 60-S clays wore LaSalle badges and had no runningboards. In time, the Cadillac studio developed not just the sedan but also a coupe and a four-door convertible version of the 60-Special. Four examples of the 60-S convertible sedan were built, one of which Harley Earl was riding in when it got T-boned in 1938. Earl spent two weeks in Harper Hospital with broken ribs and bruises.

Even so, according to Mitchell, Earl directed this particular design with even more care and attention than usual. As it progressed, the sedan's trunk kept getting longer and longer, ending up like the sloping decklid of a coupe. A coupe trunk on a sedan seemed an unusual idea, but it looked great. The window treatment and the sloping deck became two of the 60-S's most original and striking features.

Around front, Mitchell designed a massive and formal grille. He rejected the normal Cadillac eggcrate texture and substituted a grille composed of chromed, horizontal blades that he stacked from bumper to beltline. In plan view, the grille followed the vee of the hood, but it then flared out in "wings" behind the headlights. The hood louvers picked up this same texture. Mitchell then added suitcase fenders—those long, rectangular shapes with the knife-blade trailing edges. GM designers had been sketching and modeling suitcase fenders since at least 1933, but this time they *worked;* in fact, worked stunningly well.

As noted, Larry Fisher had left Cadillac by this time, and Nicholas Dreystadt, a former Mercedes mechanic, had replaced him on June 1, 1934. Dreystadt had come to the U.S. from Prussia in 1912 and had risen through the Cadillac ranks from salesman to factory service manager, then works manager and finally to division president. Due to Cadillac's weak sales in 1933-34, Dreystadt was given the Cadillac presidency with a mandate to cut expenses, which he did with full Prussian efficiency. While Dreystadt got along fine with Earl, his mandate made him considerably more conservative than the flamboyant Larry Fisher. He was also less style conscious and saw no need for a new, sporty, five-passenger

styling cues from the GM C-body. And the 1941 Nash and Studebaker both came out with C-body lookalikes.

At the same time Mitchell and Earl were wrestling with the 1938 Cadillac 60-Special, Earl was also directing a project he referred to as the "Y-Job." Earl called it the Y-Job after the designation for prototype aircraft. The Y-Job started out as an idea car, funded by Harlow Curtice and taking shape in the Buick studio under designer Paul Meyer; a "Car of the Future," as *Life* magazine would later call it. The Y-Job certainly did provide ideas that Buick used in later models, but more important to Earl was that,

America's Taste in 1934-38 Cars

In Dec. 1937, *Sales Management* magazine published a list of the public's opinion on the best- and worst-looking cars of 1934 through 1938. The Market Research Corp. of America surveyed people each year at the New York Auto Show. Here are the results of those five surveys.

Year	Worst-looking	Best-looking
1934	Chrysler	Chrysler
1935	Willys	Packard
1936	Willys	Buick
1937	Willys	Buick
1938	Willys	Buick

The winner: 1938 Buick

Interesting how the Chrysler Airflow received the most votes for both best- and worst-looking car of 1934. The Market Research Corp. interpreted those figures by saying that people either loved or hated the Airflow at first sight. Oldsmobile, by the way, was judged the runner-up for best-looking in 1936 and '37, Buick in 1935 and Packard in 1934. ◆

In its pre-war iteration (top left and above), Harley Earl's Y-Job lacked fender skirts. After the war, Earl had skirts, different bumpers, wheelcovers and pushbutton door handles installed (left).

with Curtice's and Sloan's consent, this large, low, ultra-sleek, shiny, black, boattail convertible would serve as Earl's own personal car. Even beyond that, the Y-Job was going to be Earl's answer to Edsel Ford at Lincoln and Ed Macauley at Packard, the two other corporate design executives who mattered to Earl. Edsel and Macauley both drove around in company-built, special-bodied, sporty boattail roadsters: common sights on the streets of Grosse Pointe and Dearborn.

Sloan had hired Earl partly because he recognized Earl's eagerness to be first in everything, particularly in fashion. Earl *consciously* tried to lead the American automobile industry in styling and did throughout most of his career. His competitiveness extended to the automobiles he drove, and with the Y-Job, his personal car became an extension of himself and his wardrobe.

Edsel Ford and Ed Macauley had similar fashion urges. Throughout the 1930s, Edsel Ford, whose competitive streak was subtler and less aggressive than Earl's, owned a number of two-place V-8 roadsters. Craftsmen at the Lincoln plant built him a 1932 Ford V-8 boattail as well as a number of other speedsters and estate vehicles, almost as toys (see page 125). Edsel's masterpiece—his greatest personal car—would be the 1939 Lincoln Zephyr Continental, but that still lay ahead. Meanwhile, Packard's chief stylist and the company president's son, Ed Macauley, like

Earl's own Styling craftsmen hammered out the body, which was so flawlessly smooth that Earl had it repainted gloss black nearly every year. He drove the Y-Job to work and as everyday transportation until his next personal convertible, the LeSabre Motorama showcar, became functional in 1951.

Nothing topped the Y-Job for mechanical innovation: hidden headlamps, built-in tail lights, a power top that stowed under a hinged metal panel behind the seats, front fenders that flowed back into the doors, a grille design and hood ornament that foretold the 1942-46 production Buicks, electric window lifts, flush outside door handles and banks of delicate, parallel chrome streaks on all four fenders. It stood out as the car Earl could be proud to drive because, after all, he'd designed it.

The Y-Job received a facelift in 1947 that included adding rear fender skirts. On a vacation, driving the Y-Job down to Florida, Earl had a rear tire go flat near Washington, D.C. No one, including the D.C. Buick dealer, could figure out how to remove the fender skirt to get the tire off. Finally, according to designer Richard Stout, Earl wired Buick studio chief Ned Nickles in Detroit. Nickles made three detail sketches showing how to pull the skirt, and he shipped these to Earl by special courier.

The 1939 Buick came out with what's now called the "harp" grille. Paul M. Browne, whom Strother MacMinn refers to as the

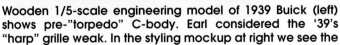

Wooden 1/5-scale engineering model of 1939 Buick (left) shows pre-"torpedo" C-body. Earl considered the '39's "harp" grille weak. In the styling mockup at right we see the

beginnings of GM's 1940 C-torpedo body plus attempts to make harp grille bolder; also to eliminate applied headlamps and to extend front fenders back onto the doors.

Edsel, also commissioned and drove an evolving series of boattail Packard speedsters and sporty convertibles throughout his career.

Earl's idea was to top them both, and it's safe to say that neither Edsel's nor Macauley's specials could touch the Y-Job for style and sophistication. Curtice sent over a Buick chassis, and the Y-Job used Buick hubcaps and had a Buick badge on the hood.

star of the Buick studio, greatly admired the cloverleaf grille shape and texture of the 1937 Mercedes Grand Prix racing car. Brown had been sketching variations of that grille since Dec. 1936. It's possible and likely that Harley Earl wanted a low grille for the 1939 Buick in answer to Bob Gregorie's extremely successful grille on the 1938 Lincoln Zephyr.

Schools for Auto Designers

George J. Mercer, who'd been Andrew F. Johnson's student turned autobody consultant/critic/author, tried throughout the 1920s to raise money for a Detroit school of auto design and drafting, but without success. For many years, Johnson's correspondence course from Gray, Maine was the only formal program available for aspiring auto designers.

Then in 1928, the Chicago Industrial Arts School offered a short-lived course in industrial clay modeling. Harley Earl was one of the speakers at that school's first fund raiser. The school soon dropped the course, however.

In 1932, Chrysler set up its own body-design course at the Chrysler Institute. This came under the direction of Chrysler engineering, and for several years Raymond H. Dietrich taught the class. Dietrich was an expert in, among other things, making full-sized body drafts.

Pratt's School of Design in Brooklyn, New York started offering industrial-design courses around 1932, under James C. Boudreau. In 1935, Pratt received a $20,000 scholarship grant from General Motors. Alexander Kostellow, a Pratt professor of industrial design, had solicited Harley Earl directly. Pratt set up a special course within the industrial-design department, taught by Kostellow and Donald Dohner, aimed at producing auto designers. Among students taking the Pratt course were Richard Arbib and Homer LaGassey.

Soon afterward, GM also made scholarship funds available to the Art Center School in Los Angeles. Founded in 1930 by Edward A. (Tink) Adams, Art Center at first taught only advertising and photography, then added industrial design in 1931.

in on Adams and his staff to admire their students' work. That's when GM began organizing Art Center scholarships. Ford later became a major contributor also.

In 1946, Art Center moved to new quarters on West Third Street in Los Angeles. The new campus had been a large estate that later became a private girls' school. Postwar classes began that year with eight students and 12 part-time professionals from different areas of the commercial arts. Enrollment grew steadily, as did grants from Detroit's automakers and other firms who needed designers. In 1976, Art Center College of Design, as it was renamed, moved to its present hillside campus in Pasadena. Its teachers of automobile design and modelmaking have included George A. Jergenson, Strother MacMinn, Harry B. Bradley, Keith Teter, Ron Hill and Joseph D. Thompson.

Art Center opened a second campus in Switzerland in 1986 but closed it again in 1996. At that time, enrollment was approximately 1500. A strong bond exists between the world's auto companies and Art Center. By 1990, graduates of the college headed 10 of Southern California's auto-design studios (see page 290).

But GM also had its own design school for a time. Harley Earl, while acknowledging Pratt and Art Center, felt that he needed an in-house training center in addition, so in 1938 he established the Detroit Institute of Automobile Styling (DIAS; also at times called the Detroit Institute of Automotive Design). Like Andrew Johnson's earlier school of carriage and autobody design in Manhattan, Earl's had a classroom facility, where students trained under some of GM's best designers. The man initially in charge was a former illustrator, painter and art instructor named Reginald (Reg) Bennett. "He came from Oklahoma," recalled Homer LaGassey, one of his students, "the quiet cowboy type." Coursework even-

advertised in *Popular Mechanics* and similar magazines. Each candidate had to submit art samples and references. Many already had training and experience as fashion, theater-set and furniture designers and advertising illustrators. Early students included Richard Arbib, Gene Bordinat, Joe Oros, Elwood Engel, Richard Hitchcock, Homer LaGassey, Irv Rybicki and Frank Bianchi. The DIAS later offered a three-month correspondence course administered by Richard Arbib.

At first, the classroom was in the General Motors Building. GM paid students $75 a month (not vice-versa) to attend the one-year course. Every three months, though, each student was evaluated and the weak ones were asked to leave. Those who stayed received a $10-a-month raise and another three months' training. On graduation, GM offered the student a job at $150 a month and put him to work in an industrial design or special developments studio. Later, graduates usually interned in one of GM's advanced studios. The DIAS was interrupted by the war but restarted in 1945. The postwar school became part of the Harley Earl Corp. (see page 112), with the classroom at 40 Milwaukee. Earl discontinued the DIAS around 1948.

Another important school for auto designers began in 1959 at what was then known as the Art School of the Detroit Society of Arts & Crafts. Homer LaGassey, previously a student at Pratt and DIAS and later a designer with GM (1942-55), Chrysler (1955-60) and Ford (1963-80) founded and chaired Arts & Crafts' four-year degree program in transportation design. LaGassey, who styled the Ford Le Mans J-Car, among others, brought in working Detroit designers as instructors. Between them they gave their students professional coursework in exterior and interior automotive design. LaGassey also established a training program for clay modelers underwritten by the Big Three automakers. LaGassey says proudly that 98% of his students found jobs in the industry. Arts & Crafts changed its name to the Center for Creative Studies (CCS) in 1975, and the transportation design program was taken over in 1987 by Carl Olsen. CCS and Art Center are by far the most important auto-design schools in the world. Their graduates now work for every major car company in America, Europe and Japan.

Since the late 1960s, Japanese and European automakers have been sending more and more of their young design students to Art Center and the Center for Creative Studies. In addition, several other schools have also contributed to the education of automobile designers through the years, among them the Cleveland Institute of Art, Cranbrook Academy, Rhode Island School of Design, Cincinnati State University, Georgia Tech and the Illinois Institute of Technology. ◆

In the early 1950s, students at Art Center College of Design enjoyed outdoor classes on its old Third Street campus in Los Angeles.

Classes were held in a rented shopping complex near MacArthur Park. Harley Earl, who occasionally stayed at the nearby Ambassador Hotel on Wilshire, would drop

tually blended general auto design with full-sized blackboard layout work, sketching and clay modeling.

At first, to attract students, Bennett

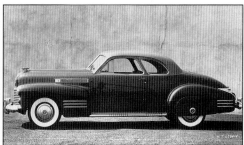

General Motors made a huge stylistic leap with its "torpedo" C-body for 1940. All GM divisions except Chevrolet used the new C-body, which drew inspiration from the Cadillac 60-Special. Most other automakers, especially Studebaker and Nash, copied the C's fuller, rounder lines.

Earl had seen a photograph of the 1938 Zephyr while he was in Europe, and the horizontal nature of its low catwalk grille frankly shocked and puzzled him. The '38 Zephyr, as we'll see in Chapter Eight, served as a predictor of that monumental shift from vertical to horizontal grilles—a trend no one could see clearly at that time. In his frustration, Earl's response to the 1938 Zephyr front end became Browne's 1939 Buick harp grille, which went against all of Earl's precepts. It had too fine a texture to reflect much light, and the thin vertical bars looked weak. The 1940 and '41 Buicks had much bolder grilles with heavier horizontal bars. The 1940-41 grille shape remained similar to the 1939 harp grille but was much more forceful.

One of GM's most successful prewar body types was the "torpedo" style introduced as the C-body of 1940. We mentioned earlier that the C-body took its overall shape from the Cadillac 60-S, and it wasn't just the five-window roof. The five-window roof became an important 60-S legacy, one that set a pattern for GM sedans for at least a decade. But the 60-S also lent the C-body sedan its coupe trunk which, in side view, projected out beyond the rear fenders.

Another striking feature of GM's 1940 C-body was the fact that the bottom of the body ahead of the rear bumper wrapped back under the car in a curve that followed the bottom edge of the rear fenders. This gave the rear a much more finished look. The C-body borrowed the 60-S's puffed beltline and its basically softer, more Rubenesque form. GM's torpedo C-body was available for 1940 with or without runningboards; same price either way. And it became available in all GM lines except Chevrolet, offered as a sedan, coupe, convertible coupe and convertible sedan. GM continued the 1939 B-body into 1940-41, but for 1941 they made the C-body dominant and limited the B to fastback body styles only. The more modern-looking C-body sold infinitely better than the B.

One battle Earl didn't win, at least not right away, had to do with the placement of headlights. As early as 1933, Earl and his designers were making proposals with flush headlights. These mounted either in or on the fenders or, sometimes, were faired into the hood sides. Bill Knudsen and some of GM's engineers, though, favored pod- or stalk-mounted headlamps, contending that any fender bender would throw integrated headlights out of adjustment.

Nearly all other U.S. automaker had fender-mounted headlights long before GM did, and Earl tried for years to convince Knudsen that GM was falling behind. Even the 1939-40 headlights on some GM cars—those mounted on the tops of the fenders—represented a compromise and a holdover from earlier style. Knudsen and some of the other GM brass finally saw it Earl's way with the 1940 C-body, the first year the corporation adopted fender-mounted headlamps.

On Sept. 3, 1940, the General Motors executive committee voted to make Harley J. Earl a corporate vice president. The announcement came as a surprise to rival car companies, all of whom still considered stylists little more than cake decorators. Chrysler's designers were very much under the thumb of engineering, and Ford's Bob Gregorie held no formal title at all. So Earl's sudden vice presidency gave a boost to his already considerable authority, especially since it marked the first time any major U.S. automaker had ever given a designer such high corporate status.

It was rumored at the time that GM made Earl a vice president to keep him from going over to Ford. Sue Earl and Eleanor Ford, Edsel's wife, played bridge together, and it's possible (but never confirmed) that Ford hinted at hiring Earl.

General Motors brought out two more noteworthy designs just before World War II: the 1941 Cadillac, with its tombstone grille and beautiful jewelry, and the through-fendered 1942 Buick.

The '41 Cadillac came from Bill Mitchell's studio, and this design became important because it took the horizontal grille several steps beyond anything produced to that time. While it's true that the 1938 Zephyr pioneered the low horizontal grille and that cars like the 1939 Buick, 1939 Studebaker and 1940 Hudson picked it up soon afterward, no one had run the grille across the front of a design the way Cadillac did in 1941. The 1941 Cadillac's tombstone grille was the first to emphasize the horizontal and de-emphasize the vertical aspect of a front end. From that example and with very few exceptions, U.S. cars switched forever to predominantly horizontal grilles.

In a 1976 interview, Mitchell credited Arthur (Art) Ross with the Cadillac tombstone grille and its rich eggcrate texture, commenting, "Art Ross...made the sketch that really turned our heads

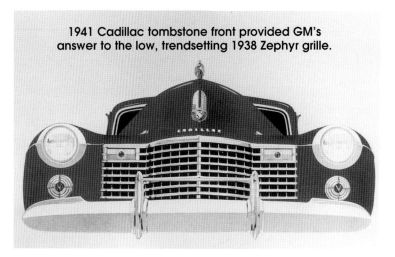

1941 Cadillac tombstone front provided GM's answer to the low, trendsetting 1938 Zephyr grille.

around. At the time, he made a straight-on front view, and actually it shocked us. [The front ensemble looked] like a tombstone, especially after we'd been doing those pointed front ends. Then Mr. Earl got interested in this one, and he was a master of making 180° turns; changes that would sort of surprise you. Most of us didn't realize how serious he was; couldn't do that jump at first. But we did it, and then it was Lincoln that turned around and followed us."

Mitchell's contention about Earl's 180° turns was quite correct. Earl would follow a trend for a certain distance, in this case copying the 1936 and '38 Lincoln Zephyr prow grilles and adapting them to all 1939 and some 1940 GM cars. But then he'd suddenly see a new direction and would zig when everyone else was still zagging. That's one way he competed and stayed ahead.

Strother MacMinn pointed out other aspects of the 1941 Cadillac design, and this applies to a number of cars—other makes as well as GM—back into the early to mid 1930s. "The big trend affecting car designers at that time," said Mac, "was *art moderne*, in which parallelism was very important. You remember the Paris exposition with the skishkabob skewers and parallel planes superimposed? It was that kind of era, but actually all this design was very architectural; done by people who'd had architectural training.

"They also had a sense of form. This taking a bullet shape and squeezing it and stretching it and flattening it, doing various things to it sculpturally and then superimposing the trim to accent certain character lines; this was the generic kaleidoscope from which all this design emanated.

"Well, I think the 1941 Cadillac became obviously architectural. The grille is a Wilshire Boulevard building...and then [they trimmed] it with the hard quality of diecastings to get the detailing like jewelry...." The jewelry consisted of such touches as the letter-by-letter **CADILLAC** across the hood, the Egyptian wings lifting up from the traditional cloisonne Cadillac crest, the vees within the concentric target castings beneath the headlamps, chrome speed streaks along the hood sides and fenders, the fuel filler hidden under the left rear finlet, the raised ribs on the horizontal center of the rear bumper—all those details load themselves into the viewer's eye, one right after the other, to give the 1941 Cadillac a very rich, elegant look. The 1941 Packard and 1941 Lincoln Custom seemed almost spartan alongside that year's Cadillac. More important, the 1941 Cadillac, and especially the tombstone grille, carried over into—and set the tone for—Cadillacs long after the war.

As for the 1942 Buick and its "Airfoil" through front fenders, Earl had offered them to Cadillac at first. He reasoned that fenders had been stretching farther and farther back into the front doors, and it seemed natural that the final iteration—the through

GM Art & Colour began experimenting with the "through" fender in 1941. At left is a Buick proposal from '41, and the 1941 Cadillac below was built for the Duke of Windsor.

Notes on the Postwar Cars

After World War II, GM facelifted its 1942 models and began producing them in late 1945. Most other U.S. automakers also warmed over their '42 designs for the 1946 model year. The American public, denied new vehicles during the 3 1/2 years of war, went on a buying spree after VJ Day and, from 1946 though 1950, eagerly accepted anything Detroit had to offer, no matter what it looked like.

Today, in retrospect, it's obvious that most American auto manufacturers began producing their rebodied postwar cars two to three years sooner than necessary. Some manufacturers, like Kaiser-Frazer, had no choice; K-F didn't have prewar designs to warm over. But Studebaker, which introduced new-bodied cars in Apr. 1946 as 1947 models, certainly could have postponed the huge expense of retooling by simply continuing to sell nothing but facelifted versions of their 1942 models.

No Detroit automaker really *needed* to produce any new styles until 1950. Yet they all did, most starting in 1948. The competitive "newness" turned out to be a vanity. Postwar automobile sales didn't need stimulation.

Hardest hit were the independents. Packard introduced what came to be known as the "pregnant" Packard in 1949—a well-fed version of the 1941 Clipper. The pregnant Packard ended up being a triple mistake: First, the public didn't find the bulkier body especially appealing. Second, Packard now had nothing new to celebrate the company's golden anniversary in 1950. And third, the older Clipper would have sold just fine until 1951.

Meanwhile, Hudson's new "stepdown" body style, introduced for 1948, marked a similar marketing mistake (easy to say now but hard to see at the time). By introducing its new body for 1948, Hudson locked into

six years of one basic body style when the company could just as successfully have brought out the stepdown body three years later, for 1951. Hudson could then have given the car a major restyling for 1954, thus getting in synch with Detroit's common three-year styling cycle.

Interestingly, rebodied postwar cars fell broadly into two categories: those with defined ("applied") rear fenders and those without. Studebaker, GM, Tucker and Chrysler Corp. all chose to follow the applied-rear-fender approach. The other automakers—Kaiser-Frazer, Ford, Mercury, Lincoln, Hudson, Nash and Packard—opted for the full envelope body that gave no illusion of having a separate rear fender. Postwar cars like Nash, Hudson and Kaiser seemed to be headed toward a more truly aerodynamic form, but GM's market share convinced the entire industry to forgo aero and fall in line behind Harley Earl. ◆

GM put the through fender into production on the 1942 Buick Super and Roadmaster. By this time, all auto plants were being converted for the war effort, and there wouldn't be many more cars built for a while.

version—should appear first on GM's highest car line. But Nick Dreystadt wasn't buying, saying it was too expensive to produce.

Whereupon Earl offered the idea to Buick and Harlow Curtice. Curtice jumped at it, and the through fender appeared on two Buick models for 1942: the Roadmaster and the Super two-doors. The technical feasibility that made the through fender possible involved Fisher Body figuring out how to engineer the hidden hinges. For 1946, unlike earlier through fender designs as on the Pierce Silver Arrow, Buick's four doors all opened at the rear, and that presented a greater hinging challenge than hanging all doors off the centerpost.

World War II reduced GM Styling from about 100 designers to 35. Some, like Frank Hershey, volunteered for military

service even though Harley Earl didn't like to see them go. Yet he helped others, like Bill Mitchell, to get commissions. He also requested deferments for a number of designers who stayed.

GM had no immediate need for new car designs, so emphasis shifted to war work, and Earl's staff did provide some valuable military services. Big Bill Knudsen, now one of the chiefs of war production in Washington, D.C., pushed several contracts toward General Motors. One of them, early in the war, had to do with designing new types of camouflage. Harley Earl converted the Styling auditorium, with its tennis-court-sized stage, into a huge studio. The designers made a gigantic scale-model layout of a city and developed different types of camouflage to hide it. The camouflaged city was ringed with tall stepladders, and the designers would perch atop these, peering down through reducing glasses to check what pilots might see from high altitudes. The program ended abruptly when U.S. Intelligence learned that the enemy was using infrared to distinguish camouflage from the real thing.

Another wartime project at GM Styling had to do with illustrating manuals and guides for the military. Steve McDaniel, Earl's chief interior designer, had charge of what came to be known as the Wartime Production Illustration studio. McDaniel and his staff turned out thousands of drawings, cutaways, exploded views, diagrams, airbrush renderings and other illustrations for the military. Homer LaGassey, fresh out of Harley Earl's design school in 1942, recalled that McDaniel's group did pre-production illustra-

  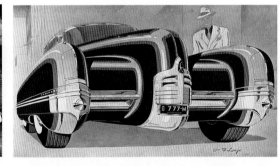

Throughout the war, GM stylists worked mainly on military projects, but the reduced studio staffs were also able to sneak in some postwar concepts. Aircraft evoked the ideas

of spinner grilles, panoramic windshields, all-glass roofs, enclosed pontoon fenders and tailfins. The envelope-bodied, tri-hull Oldsmobile above was done by Bill Lange in '41.

Tailfins and vertical air intakes in the leading edges of applied rear-fenders (right) were old hat by 1942. The Cadillac-like model above, done in 1944 by Frank Hershey, carried a Vauxhall badge on the decklid.

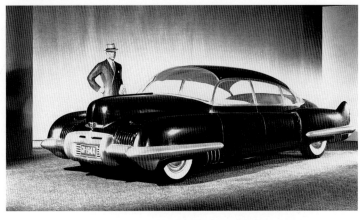

In 1946, before plunging into tailfins and the trendsetting styling cycle of 1948, Cadillac briefly considered this design, the C.O. It embodied much of what all designers saw for the postwar car: rounded, pudgy forms, wraparound glass and bumpers. Earl, in typical fashion, decided he didn't like the C.O. and revived Hershey's 1944 tailfin Vauxhall design.

tions for the Norden bombsight, a Howitzer gun mount plus all sorts of aircraft.

Olds studio chief Art Ross went so far as to design the Wildcat tank destroyer. His concept sketch, which came strictly from Ross' imagination, caught the eye of a visiting armaments officer. The concept made it up through the ranks to acceptance. Not only did Ross' tank destroyer go into production (in Buick's Flint plant), complete with his ideas for a pivoting gun turret, but during the Wildcat's field trials at Ft. Hood, Texas, a general phoned Earl to ask whether Styling could come up with a shoulder patch for his unit. Henry Lauve drew a sinister, scowling black panther whose jaws were crunching a German tank, and that was it.

GM Styling also became involved in technical drawings for converting the Douglas B-19 and Boeing B-29 aircraft to Allison 24-cylinder engines. At one point, the staff even sculpted a full-sized clay model of a proposed Fisher P-75 Eagle pursuit plane—a huge undertaking. The war ended, though, before the P-75 could be considered for production.

Between military assignments, designers managed to turn out sketches and scale models of possible postwar cars. Much of this wartime automobile work took place at 40 W. Milwaukee Av., also known as Studio 40 or Studio 4-F, a building just down the street from Styling. Since no one knew when the war would end and GM had no plans to produce any of these proposed cars, the designers could go pretty wild.

The pillbug shapes of these wartime styling studies pointed toward what *all* designers of that era—not just those at GM—thought cars of the future would look like. Many took the Briggs/Chrysler Thunderbolt approach but applied it to sedans. These often had fully enclosed wheels, domed glass greenhouses, wraparound windshields and hidden headlamps. But other wartime designs, unlike the Thunderbolt, showed aggressive, leaping

fenders and bold, aircraft-inspired round grilles with big propeller spinners.

One idea that kept popping up on these wartime studies was tailfins. Just before the war, Harley Earl took his studio chiefs on a field trip to study the lines of the then-new P-38 twin-boom fighter plane. Aircraft with single tails were old hat and not all that inspiring, but the designers got all excited about the P-38, especially since they could see its twin tails as extensions of a car's rear fenders. They went back to their studios and started doing sketches of cars with tailfins. The P-38 also prompted other aircraft motifs: Plexiglas canopies, various types of air intakes, grille spinners and bumper bullets.

Fins and spinners became wildly popular during and immediately after the war, first with designers and then with the general public. Tailfins appeared in production for the first time on the 1948 Cadillac and spread like dandelions to nearly every other car made in America. (It should be noted that automotive tailfins weren't altogether new. Land-speed record cars had them before the war and, by 1946-47, Giovanni Savonucci made fins a prominent feature of his trendsetting Italian Cisitalia.)

The 1948 Cadillac's particular fin configuration as seen in side view—the sculpting of the kicked-up lens and L-shaped chrome bezel base—came out of Frank Hershey's special-projects studio, where he and Ned (Nick) Nickles worked on just that sort of thing. Hershey, the young designer who'd helped save Pontiac in 1932, had become supervisor of this studio shortly after he got a medical discharge from the service in late 1944.

In early 1945, with Bill Mitchell still away in the Navy, Hershey was called on briefly to head the Cadillac studio. He remained Cadillac's active studio chief until May 14, 1945 when Art Ross took over and filled in until Mitchell returned on Nov. 12, 1945. At that point, Hershey was made head of GM's "special car design and export car design" studio. Here his job was to come up with proposals for GM's

postwar British Vauxhall and German Opel plus to work on "special projects."

Before that, though, while Hershey was interim head of the Cadillac studio, he'd designed what came to be called the "Cadillac C.O." The C.O. was very much an expression of what GM had envisioned a postwar car to be: rounded, high, fat beltline, pontoon fenders, wraparound windshield, coved headlights. In 1946, Cadillac made a running metal prototype of the C.O. and tested it at the GM proving grounds near Milford, Michigan. While C.O. performed well, Harley Earl and the Cadillac people weren't at all taken with the styling. What Earl didn't like was the high beltline. It made the body look overweight and bulky. According to Bill Mitchell as interviewed by C. Edson Armi, Earl came in one day and said, "To hell with that big, blown-up thing [meaning the C.O]," and he started in a totally different direction. "If he [Earl] saw something wasn't going," Mitchell told Armi, "he wasn't a diehard."

Earl's solution to the C.O. beltline dilemma borrowed from the 1942 Buick. On the 1942 Buick, the top of the front fender extended back along the bodyside and formed a second roll independent of the beltline. On the 1948 Cadillac (and the 1948 Olds 98, too), Earl used this same idea of a second body roll along the top of the fenderline. But instead of sloping downward as on the 1942 Buick, the Cadillac's front fender ran back in an almost horizontal line and formed a roll *just below* the beltline. The Cadillac's entire through front fender ultimately slipped beneath the applied rear fender and disappeared, as on the 1947 Studebaker.

The 1948 Cadillac beltline now became a wraparound extension of the relatively high hood and cowl. So with the horizontal fender roll beneath it, the beltline didn't end up being one fat roll, as on the C.O. Instead, it could have a fairly flat, shallow section, because the fender top now formed a secondary roll. This softened the beltline, and the double roll also added the illusion of length and lightness. Meanwhile, the applied rear fender made the back of the car look muscular, like the rear haunch of a crouching animal getting ready to leap. After 1948, Earl adapted this same side configuration to all GM cars.

And now we come to several different legends about how the 1948 Cadillac got its tailfins. Hershey claimed he kept working on fins in his own special studio when, suddenly, the United Auto Workers called a strike and locked everyone out of GM. The lockout lasted 113 days, during which time designers couldn't get into their studios. So Hershey invited the Cadillac group out to his farm north of Detroit, and they continued to work on scale clay models of the 1948 Cadillac, all of them with tailfins. Harley Earl would drive out to Hershey's farm in his Y-Job two or three times a week to check progress.

According to Hershey, after the strike ended, he returned to the Cadillac studio and put fins onto the developing 1948 Cadillac full-sized clay. Cadillac general manager Nick Dreystadt didn't like them at first, and Earl wasn't too keen on them either, but GM president Charles E. Wilson felt they gave Cadillac the same strong identity symbol at the rear that the eggcrate grille did up front, and that pretty much ended the argument.

Another version tells of Bill Mitchell returning from the military in Nov. 1945 and resuming his duties as head of the Cadillac studio the next month. It's true that Dreystadt didn't care for the fins, but on June 5, 1946, John F. Gordon replaced Dreystadt as Cadillac general manager, and Edward N. Cole came in as Cadillac's chief engineer. Both men were much younger and more forward-looking than Dreystadt, and Cole particularly liked the idea of tailfins. Tom Christiansen, who became Harley Earl's technical secretary in Feb. 1946, related that Gordon and Cole came into Mitchell's studio soon after their new appointments. Mitchell introduced them to his full-sized clay model with tailfins, and Gordon sat on an upturned wastebasket for 10 minutes, staring at the fins. He didn't say anything but finally started shaking his head no. "Too tall," he said, and Gordon suggested dropping the tops of the fins down about 3/4 inch.

Gordon then left the studio, but Cole stayed, and he and Mitchell agreed that the fins on the clay were just right. So Mitchell asked his clay modeler to make the far fin an inch or so taller than the one nearer the viewer. Next day when Gordon returned,

General Motors' postwar designs, particularly the 1948 Cadillac and Oldsmobile (below), led the industry away from the full envelope body by emphasizing applied rear fenders. This was slightly retrograde, yet Earl felt applied fenders gave the rear a crouching, ready-to-leap look. He also favored a secondary beltline created by extending the fender tops parallel to the primary belt.

he said, "See, didn't I tell you it looks better lower like that?"

So in the final analysis, there's no doubt that Frank Hershey put finned rear fenders very much like the 1948 Cadillac's on several Vauxhall models. Photos of Hershey's tailfin Vauxhalls still exist, dated 1944. Those fins entered Mitchell's studio and were ultimately released for production on the 1948 Cadillac.

In all his postwar design efforts, Earl, who before the

1949 Buick hardtop arrived mid-year along with sweep spear. Portholes, though, became Buick's predominant identifier.

war had relied on "faces" to identify the different GM makes, now realized that longterm identity symbols—or "signatures"—like Pontiac's silver streak—could benefit all five car lines. He still wanted the five makes to be instantly recognizable from a block away, but he found a different, more positive way to make that possible. As primary identifiers, Cadillac took on fins and the eggcrate grille for 1948. Buick had vertical chrome teeth in a horizontal grille and adopted portholes and the sweepspear for 1949.

Designer George Snyder gave Oldsmobile its so-called "fishmouth" grille for 1946 and then refined it for 1948. Olds

capitalized on that fundamental front-end shape for a decade. Olds also got its chrome globe in 1948 and the rocket in 1949 as primary symbols. Earl figured that Chevrolet needed no specific signature, because the car was so popular that everyone recognized it anyway.

There were also secondary identifiers that Earl carried through from year to year to reinforce the primary ones: Buick's cigar-in-a-hoop hood ornament, Pontiac's Indian head and round tail lamps, Cadillac's chrome V on the hood and decklid, and Oldsmobile's rocket-shaped tail light lenses.

The postwar Cadillac had some of the

LeSabre capsulized everything Earl wanted in a car, both stylistically and technically. It soon replaced his Y-Job.

production. Buick, which had responsibility for the front-fender dies, already had them finished. But Curtice demanded portholes, so the die shop duly reworked the dies, and portholes remained Buick's hallmark for decades.

Another major contribution from Nickles was the "hardtop convertible" that appeared for 1949. That again, according to Nick, had its beginnings in the special studio. By this time, Hershey had left the special studio, and Jules Andrade had taken his place. Nickles and Andrade made a 3/8-scale model of a pillarless coupe. Buick chief engineer Ed Ragsdale caught

strongest identity symbols in the industry. In time, Cadillac's symbols all got copied: the chrome vees, the fins, the rear-fender "airscoop," the entire Cadillac look. And Buick, under Curtice, also tried to come up with a look. Ned Nickles, who'd been made head of the Buick studio in May 1947, always drove a new Buick convertible. Just after he'd bought a maroon 1948 Roadmaster convertible, one of his modelers, Joe Funk, suggested that Nickles let him install three flashing lights along each side of both front fenders. Funk had already put similar lights on his brother's car. Nick saw and liked them, so he told Funk to install a set.

Funk drilled three three-inch holes into both front fenders of Nick's Roadmaster, finished them off with chromed bathroom pipe rings from a plumbing store and put colored lights in the centers. The lights flashed in sequence when the spark plugs fired. Nickles loved the effect. Harlow Curtice saw Nick's car one evening after

Earl eventually put some 45,000 miles on the LeSabre.

work and insisted that chrome-ringed portholes be put on all 1949 Buicks. (Portholes also weren't a new idea. The 1910 Chadwick Great Six had them, as did the 1919 Biddle, 1919 Greyhound speedster and the 1926 Shaw runabout.) Problem was, by that time the '49 Buick was not only designed but effectively released for

sight of it and enthused, "Boy, would my wife love that!" Mrs. Ragsdale liked the sporty look of a convertible but never put the top down, because she didn't want her hair mussed.

Again, the hardtop idea wasn't new, but GM made it the postwar body style everyone had to have. The concept went back at

Harley Earl's Design Firm

Loewy a run for his money," referring to the famous private industrial designer. But critics pointed out that Mitchell had an advantage over Loewy, because any supplier wanting to sell to General Motors would naturally choose Earl's company over other design firms.

Earl received a number of perks and privileges from General Motors that no one before him had ever gotten. His corporate vice presidency in 1940 might have been one, but in 1945 GM allowed him to set up a private industrial-design firm. He called his company the Harley Earl Corp. (HEC).

GM employees simply did not have outside businesses at that time. Sloan might have allowed Earl to establish his own company to make up for Earl's missing out on a special class of GM stock, this according to Earl's son, Jim. It's also possible that Sloan made the concession to keep Earl from leaving GM. Earl had apparently had another offer from Ford after the war, this time from Henry Ford II. In letting Earl set up HEC, Sloan did stipulate that Earl couldn't compete with GM; couldn't design any vehicles or kitchen appliances.

In the beginning, designer Richard Arbib ran HEC. The firm's office was on Woodward Av., 12 blocks from the GM Building. Jim Earl feels that Arbib did a fine job as a designer but didn't like Detroit and yearned to go to New York. On Apr. 18, 1949, Earl replaced Arbib with then-Cadillac studio head William L. Mitchell. Mitchell mentioned later that he wasn't pleased to be away from cars, but his experience at HEC taught him how to sell. Mitchell brought in Hamilton-Beach, Parker Pens, Clark Equipment Co. and Westinghouse. Mitchell boasted later that he "gave Raymond

Mitchell mentioned in a 1977 interview that Earl let him keep 10% of HEC's gross income, which was more than he made when he returned to GM Styling in June 1953. From 1953 to 1958, designers Jim Balmer and Bill Armstrong ran Harley Earl Corp. Under their leadership, HEC began doing work for 3M, Bissell, Tappan, Burroughs Corp. and U.S. Rubber. HEC, in fact, designed the popular narrow-whitewall tire for U.S. Rubber.

People close to Harley Earl felt he'd originally founded HEC for his two sons, Jim and Jerry Earl. They took over the company in 1958, renaming it Harley Earl Associates. Jim stayed aboard for 14 years, until 1972, and Jerry worked at HEA for 11 years. Both agreed that the design business never really suited them. When Jerry left, he became a Pontiac dealer in Florida, and Jim went into commercial film production in Colorado.

In 1964, HEA merged with Walter Buhl Ford Associates. Wally Ford, husband of Edsel Ford's daughter, Josephine (Dody), had been an industrial interior designer and a good friend of Jim Earl's. With Wally Ford's arrival, the company changed its name again, this time to Ford & Earl Associates Inc. Ford & Earl still exists in Troy, Michigan. ◆

A Gallery of GM Motorama Stars

1951 Buick XP-300

1953 Chevrolet Corvette

1956 Buick Centurion

1954 Oldsmobile Cutlass

1954 Pontiac Bonneville

1954 Cadillac El Camino

1955 Pontiac Strato Star

(Left) 1955 Buick Wildcat III

(Below) 1955 Waldorf Nomad

1956 Pontiac Club de Mer

1955 Oldsmobile Delta

1956 Oldsmobile Golden Rocket

least to 1918, when Dodge received two design patents on pillarless hardtops. California tops for touring cars of the 1920s also belonged in this category, and Chrysler built seven Town & Country hardtop coupes in 1946. The 1949 Buick Roadmaster Riviera, 1949 Cadillac Coupe de Ville and Olds 98 Holiday became GM's first mass-produced hardtops, and all three were such resounding commercial successes that all other U.S. automakers scrambled to catch up with GM.

In 1947, Harley Earl had some mechanical work done to his Y-Job and, at the same time, gave the car a minor facelift. He also began to think about replacing the Y-Job altogether. He'd been driving it, after all, for nearly 10 years. After talking with Harlow Curtice and Buick's new chief engineer Charles Chayne (pronounced *Chain*), Earl decided to make his next personal car as state-of-the-art and advanced mechanically as it would be in appearance.

Earl proposed building two two-passenger convertibles, one for himself and one for Chayne. He asked Chayne to project as far as practical into the future and fabricate two identical chassis. Earl would create two equally futuristic bodies: similar but not identical. The rationale was to show off Buick's and General Motors' engineering and styling leadership, after which Earl and Chayne would take the cars for their own use.

Charles Chayne put nearly every known

Relief Valves

The business of auto design can be a pressure cooker. But designers always seem to have found ways—good, bad, and silly—to defuse workaday tensions.

Eraser wars used to break out in the early days of GM Styling when tempers wore thin. Designers would rip apart rubber art-gum erasers and throw the pieces at each other. This was all great sport and a good antidote for stress. Harley Earl once walked into a studio where an eraser war had stopped just as the combatants heard his key click in the door. Bits of rubber were still bouncing around on the floor. Earl immediately sized up the situation, turned and left again. He didn't say a word, probably realizing that eraser wars were good for relieving tensions.

In 1939, Joe Oros, fresh out of the Harley Earl design school, worked as a junior designer in Bill Mitchell's Cadillac studio. The studio had a bald blackboard man named Matty Schumer. One of the designers airbrushed "hair" on Matty and laid tape down the center of his scalp as a "part." Matty went into the studio next door to see whether anyone would recognize him. Nobody did.

Strother MacMinn tells about the ritualized way the small Hudson design studio relieved tension when he worked there in 1938. Once a month or so, the designers would play what they called "Indianapolis." This was an enactment, largely unrehearsed but becoming more ritualized each time they played it, of the warhorse plot of a typical movie or radio show that had a motor-racing theme.

"There's this brand-new prototype race car with a special secret carburetor," Mac-Minn recounted in his Ford Archives oral reminiscenses, "and it goes out for testing on the track. It's an erratic car. Now each of us in the studio had a role to play in this drama. When the car started, one guy would do the grinding noise of the starter, and the next guy would pick up the sputtering of the exhaust as the engine warms up; he does its initial revs and then makes the sounds as the car takes off down the track. This was all taken, of course, from radio recordings that we've all heard.

"So we get the car, and then Earl Hovey, whose idea this was in the first place, played the announcer. 'There it goes, ladies and gentlemen. It's off down the track going through the south turn, coming around, looking very smooth, coming up

When Adam (Batman) West visited GM Design Staff, some of the studio guys tricked out design director Chuck Jordan's Corvette to look like the Batmobile.

the backstretch at incredible speed, going into the dangerous north turn,' and so we'd do these dramatics.

"My role, besides doing the tire squeals as the car goes out of control in the dangerous north turn, was to hold up an old hubcap. This was a large hubcap full of nuts and bolts and a pair of pliers. I'd stand on a little ladder in the studio and then, at the right moment, as the announcer screamed into the microphone, 'I'm sorry, ladies and gentlemen, it's terrible! This car is out of control!' And then I'd drop this hubcap, and there'd be an awful crash: clatter, bang, bang, bang, and tinkle, tinkle.

"Well, next door in the Hudson accounting department, where it was always tick-tick-tick because these girls were running the calculators and typewriters, when we'd finish this little episode, there'd be dead silence. Finally, the accounting supervisor would simply open the door. He was into the routine, and he'd say, 'Was anybody hurt?' and he'd close the door and go away."

Ray Dietrich was another designer who enjoyed a lifetime of highjinx and constantly got in trouble as a result, first at Brewster and later at Chrysler. He'd been a professional baseball pitcher in his teens and liked to toss things to people at quiet times, all in fun. At Chrysler, where the engineering staff had little love for Dietrich, he once tossed an apple to designer Herb Weissinger, expecting Herb to catch it. Herb, who wore thick glasses, missed, and the apple spattered against an artboard and ruined some drawings. At that moment, engineering vice president Fred Zeder walked into the studio. Zeder was a large, imposing, no-nonsense kind of guy. Zeder said nothing, but this became one more strike against Dietrich. In 1940, four days after Walter Chrysler passed away, the engineering staff engineered Dietrich's departure.

Stanley R. Wilen, former executive designer at General Motors, recalled some of the stress-busting moments of his career. Soon after he arrived in Bill Lang's orientation studio as a freshman stylist, one of designers had caught a live fly. This designer proceeded to make up a tiny banner out of tissue paper, then plucked a hair out of his own head and attached it to the fly's body with rubber cement. He glued the other end of the hair to the banner, then turned the fly loose. The other designers watched as the fly frantically buzzed itself into exhaustion, towing this tiny tissue banner around the room.

On another occasion, Stan returned to the Oldsmobile studio and, to his horror, saw the division's top brass standing just inside the door, watching barefoot modelers skateboarding around a slalom course they'd set up among the full-sized clays. "The looks on the Olds guys' faces was unforgettable," said Wilen. At the same time, the designers had set up platform angles and a crossbar and were kicking field goals from the middle of the room. "Now these were the people," smiled Wilen, "that Olds relied on to direct $40 million worth of design work."

Another bit of fun involved blowing pencil shavings from one studio into another with a paper cone attached to the rubber hose used for airbrush work and spotting the models. Shavings and powered graphite would rain down for half an hour. This diversion stopped abruptly one day when the shavings came drifting down on Mr. Earl and some visiting Cadillac dignitaries.

Finally, Homer LaGassey told of a fun-loving modeler named Fritz Wagner. Fritz could capture a mouse in a wastebasket, then would make a little parachute and toss the rodent out the 11th-story window of the GM Research Annex. Air currents would lift and drop the mouse, and sometimes people on the lower floors could watch the mouse hover for quite some time. "On one occasion," said Homer, "the mouse drifted three blocks from the styling building—a new record—and the bets were collected." ◆

---

innovation into what Earl coded the XP-8 and XP-9 (XP stood for "experimental pursuit" in aircraft parlance, a designation used for fighter aircraft through the late 1940s). Both convertibles began to take shape in 1947 in a small, off-site studio a block away from Styling's normal activities. Only Earl and a handful of designers and clay modelers had any knowledge of the XP-8 and XP-9, and Earl swore them all to secrecy.

The more exotic XP-8 took its cues from the jet aircraft that began to appear toward war's end. It had a high "grille" that concealed the headlamps, an air inlet beneath the grille, wing-like fenders and side sweeps, twin front bumper spinners, wraparound windshield, a cockpit-like interior, tapering decklid with jet-nozzle tail and central antenna. The car was also aircraft-like in the way everything fit together so seamlessly: bumpers blending into

Engineer/designer Bob McLean stands with GM's three Firebird gas-turbine cars. All had aircraft attributes. 1954 Firebird I (left) crashed during testing. 1956 Firebird II could carry 4 passengers. Double-bubble 1959 Firebird III boasted 3 fins and 4 skegs.

body, wheelcovers into tires, grille into nose, fenders skirts into body sides and so forth.

Among other concepts, the XP-8 body was meant to be a rolling laboratory of advanced body materials, most of which proved far too expensive for production. To keep weight down, the floor was made of laminated aluminum honeycomb. All major body panels were cast magnesium: the cowl, door lock pillars, the doorskins themselves, hood, rear deck and front fender valances. Some of these massive but intricate castings had to be remolded several times to get the fits right. The rest of the body consisted mostly of handformed aluminum.

Earl renamed the XP-8 "LeSabre" and made its existence public for the first time in *Life* magazine in Dec. 1950. In Mar. 1951, the LeSabre appeared on the cover of *Motor Trend*. The published photos, though, were of a plaster model, not the finished car. What impressed 1950-51 readers was, first, the LeSabre's extreme lowness—overall height was only 50 inches, versus 64 inches for the average 1950 car; second, its wraparound or "Panoramic" windshield; and third, the busy detailing. The cockpit alone took half an hour of study to sort out.

Mechanical marvels (and here we're listing only the highlights) included a 335-horsepower, supercharged aluminum hemi V-8, aluminum driveshaft, rear-mounted automatic transmission (the only production part in the car), de Dion rear axle, inboard rear drum brakes, 13-inch wheels, four built-in hydraulic jacks, fuel cells in both rear fenders, single-leaf rear springs, 12-volt electrical system with two batteries, a full hydro-electric servo system, automatic power top mechanism with rain detector, semi-bucket seats, console, rear-projection speedometer that turned different colors at various speeds, remote-scanning rearview mirror—and on and on. How much the LeSabre cost to build is anyone's guess, but educated estimates put the tab at over $500,000 in 1951, which translates roughly into $5 million today (1994). Bill Mitchell once called the LeSabre Harley Earl's masterpiece and, in terms of artistry, it probably was.

The LeSabre came with its own mechanic, the oft-fired Leonard McLay, who accompanied the car wherever it went. So complicated were the various subsystems that the LeSabre broke down constantly. One time, the rain detector didn't work, and the cockpit flooded in a downpour. Another time, on the day before a big road race at Watkins Glen, New York, Earl got the LeSabre airborne going over a railroad crossing and, when the car landed, the impact bent the driveshaft. McLay and his aides stayed up all night fixing the car and had it ready the next morning. According to Tom Christiansen, Earl paced Watkins Glen in the LeSabre as though nothing had happened.

Charlie Chayne's version of the LeSabre, the XP-9, was rechristened "XP-300" for its public unveiling, but its

shape and detailing weren't nearly so impressive as the LeSabre's, so it came as something of an anti-climax. Chayne wasn't even especially eager to drive it, being much more involved with his own Bugattis and personal sports cars. While Earl put some 45,000 miles on his LeSabre, the XP-300's odometer shows only about 10,000 miles even today. Both cars are now retired in Michigan museums.

One of the LeSabre's serendipitous side effects had to do with its success and the public's craving for more dreamcars like it. This demand soon led Earl's staff to supply GM's Motoramas with a steady flow of show- and concept cars, starting in 1953. GM's Motoramas grew out of Alfred P. Sloan Jr.'s yearly industrialists' luncheons. The earliest was held in 1931 at the Waldorf-Astoria in New York. Sloan would make corporate policy announcements at these luncheons, and the invited financial community could also inspect GM's latest cars, trucks and appliances. These luncheons evolved after WW-II into a 1949 extravaganza that told the GM story to the press and public under the title *Transportation Unlimited*. The name was later changed to *Motorama*, and the last one was held in 1961. By that time, Motoramas had become huge and elaborate traveling exhibits, shuttled around the country in as many as 143 trucks and buses. Motoramas visited a number of major cities each year: New York, Chicago, Miami, Dallas, Los Angeles and San Francisco.

The Motoramas' main attractions were the GM dreamcars along with Broadway-like stage revues that featured singers, dancers and a full orchestra. GM never charged admission, and all expenses were written off to publicity. In the eight years that Motoramas were held, total attendance came to just under 10.5 million. As for the impact Motoramas had on GM's production cars, the 1953 Chevrolet Corvette came directly from a showcar, as did the 1957 Cadillac Eldorado Brougham. And a great number of futuristic details also made their public debut in Motorama exhibits.

One of the most commercially successful Motorama "ideas"

In 1951, GM began to replace wooden full-sized mockups with fiberglass models. This 1952 Chevy's body panels were all fiberglass.

Motorama payoffs included wraparound windshield, seen here on the 1954 Oldsmobile 98 Holiday coupe and 1955 Chevrolet. Bold 2-tone paint schemes were the order of the day, and in 1955, the Chevy again amounted essentially to a baby Cadillac, down to the V-8. That's Ed Cole (right), who engineered both the 1949 Cadillac and the 1955 Chevrolet.

was the Panoramic windshield. GM put it into production in 1953-55. Harley Earl had pursued the elusive wraparound windshield even in his Don Lee days, when he tried to have a San Francisco company form curved glass for a custom car he designed in the early 1920s. That attempt, though, failed, and Earl had to content himself with small wrapround insets at the corners of a normal, flat windshield.

Not that making a wraparound windshield proved much easier 30 years later. Two problems plagued the project from the start: 1) visual distortion due to sharp bends in the glass and 2) producing sharply curved windshields in quantity. Earl wanted to keep development secret, so he told GM's glass suppliers that these were to be aircraft windshields. Then he and Charles Kettering of GM Research Labs enlisted the help of an opthamologist at Cornell University to solve the distortion problem. While they never licked it entirely, they came pretty close.

Meanwhile, both Libby-Owens-Ford and Pittsburgh Plate Glass were working on mass production techniques and, after eight months, LOF finally came up with a solution. LOF laid semi-molten glass over a steel form, and the ends draped down by gravity. This way, GM's Panoramic windshield was hardly more expensive to form than one with a gentler curvature.

By 1955, Ford, Chrysler and other U.S. automakers had copied GM's wraparound windshield, although Chrysler and Studebaker used raked A-pillars to reduce the chance of people hitting their knees when getting into and out of the front seat. GM, meanwhile, introduced an even more swept-back pillar in 1957 and a compound-curved wraparound windshield for 1959. (The Imperial used a compound-curved windshield in 1957, as did all Chrysler Corp. cars in 1958.)

Another important advance shown at the 1953 Motorama was fiberglass. Back around 1951, GM Styling had started experimenting with fiberglass and had even built a fully operational Chevrolet convertible with a stock-looking body made entirely of fiberglass. After Earl's production people taught themselves to lay up fiberglass by hand, he ordered the replacement of traditional wooden full-sized styling mockups, which were tremendously heavy and expensive, with fiberglass mockups.

Steve McDaniel noted that fiberglass forever changed the way GM made styling presentations. "Mockups before then had to be made of wood. Wood wasn't stable, because I can remember a wooden model going up on the roof one cold day, and then when we brought it back inside, the hood, which was solid poplar, split right down the middle; sounded like a cannon shot. But fiberglass meant you could make a patch overnight, change the shape of a fender or do whatever you wanted. And we at GM did as much as anybody in the country to make today's modern fiberglass technology available to the industry as a whole."

Earl recognized fiberglass as the ideal body material for his Motorama showcars, one of the first being the 1953 Motorama Corvette. Earl initially conceived the Corvette with his two college-age sons, Jim and Jerry, in mind. This was a time when MG-TDs and Jaguars XK-120s were all the rage, and U.S. kit-car manufacturers were beginning to make fiberglass roadster bodies available to shade-tree mechanics. Earl thought that if General Motors could make a good-looking $1800 American sports car on a production chassis, there'd be a market for it. And there would have been. Chevrolet rushed the Corvette into production in late 1953, and everything came out as planned except the price. The first Corvette cost $3513 instead of $1800. Yet, despite poor sales, Chevrolet now couldn't abandon the Corvette. To do so would have left the field wide open to Ford's Thunderbird (see page 143), which insiders knew was due out in Sept. 1954.

The Motorama years put a tremendous strain on everyone at GM Styling because, in addition to designing or facelifting each year's production cars, every studio had to work nights and weekends on dreamcars. According to Tom Christiansen, the man who succeeded Howard O'Leary, "I remember once before a Motorama, we were having a terrible time. It looked touch and go for the final week: People were working around the clock, napping in the stu-

GM customers and corporate insiders felt that Harley Earl might have gone a little too far with the 1958 models, particularly the 1958 Buick (left) and Oldsmobile. Earl's designers wondered whether he was losing his touch. He ordered chrome trim by the pound, and the shapes of GM cars had become bloated and overweight. Something had to give.

The proposals Earl put forward for GM's 1959 models continued the fat forms and heavy ornamentation of his '58s. Earl even ordered a sedan front based on the 1951 Motorama LeSabre (top right). When he left for Europe, his studio chiefs launched work on a series of slimmer, more angular clays (see pages 178-79).

dio or back in the trimshop, sleeping inside cars or on seats. Well, Mr. Earl called me up to his office and said, 'I want you to get Al Greene, the restaurateur, and have him set up a cafeteria in the auditorium. I want him to serve meals so that anytime someone wants to come down to get dinner he can.' Well, we did that, and Al had standing rib roast, shrimp, anything anybody wanted; as much roast beef as anyone could eat; just unbelievable."

Bill Mitchell added about the Motorama days, "We worked our tails off. My God, we had 15-18 cars going at a time. He never knew when to quit."

Designer Duane (Sparky) Bohnstedt remembered that, "...when I first came here [in 1951], I worked for 40 days straight, nonstop. I'd go home, take a shower, put on a clean shirt and I'd come back. I've seen guys in the shop so tired that they'd sit down on a bench, go to sleep and fall off on the floor. It was just a tremendously driving, exciting time, but it was hard on people; really hard...." And according to designer Henry Lauve, "We'd work Saturdays, Sundays, nights, holidays, Christmas...but it wasn't unusual for Mr. Earl to be there until midnight or two in the morning himself."

Virgil Exner, who started his design career at GM in late 1934, said in a 1969 letter to author Christy Borth, "An incident occurred in my early years at GM which has remained indelible in my association with Harley. He had selected a front-end design sketch of mine to model in full-scale clay. This had to be done on a crash basis. He and I, along with a modeling man, worked on this all night until 5:00 a.m. At this time Harley called a halt, whereupon we 'retired' to an adjoining drafting room and slept on drawingboards until 7:30. We then arose, had a cup of coffee and finished the job for a meeting of Buick executives at 11:00 a.m."

Just before WW-II, Sloan, Kettering and Earl talked about GM building an entirely new and separate set of buildings to house the company's ever-expanding engineering and styling activities. Earl realized he'd soon outgrow the four top floors of Research Annex B. Tom Christiansen noted that, "We were running out of space...and had to go over into Plant 8 to set up the paintshop, trimshop and eventually the plastershop over there; also the truck studio and some of the advanced studios. Plant 8, which some people liked to call 'Planet 8,' was about six blocks south and four long blocks east of the GM Building, so it wasn't a handy place to get to. Also, Plant 8 had been an old Fisher Body paintshop. It was four stories tall and the floors were two inches thick with dried lacquer and varnish. If that place had ever caught fire, it'd be gone in an hour. Even with Plant 8, things at Styling got so crowded that we had to go down Cass Avenue and rent an old Nash dealership. We put our industrial design group down there. So we were bursting at the seams."

Kettering presented a plan for a "technical center" to GM's administrative committee in 1945. GM searched Detroit's northern suburbs for a good railhead and settled on 990 acres in the township of Warren, Michigan, 10 miles north of the New Center area and the General Motors Building. Here GM decided to build the ambitious, campus-like General Motors Technical Center.

Harley Earl's involvement included finding an architect. In the beginning, GM considered five candidates, three from New York, one from Chicago and a local firm called Saarinen & Swanson. GM chose Saarinen & Swanson, whose most recent work included various buildings at Cranbook Academy in Bloomfield Hills, the Smithsonian Gallery of Art in Washington and the Kleinhaus Music Hall in Buffalo. Eliel Saarinen, who'd trained in Finland, directed the Cranbrook Academy of Art, and his son, Eero, graduated from Yale and had won several architectural competitions. J. Robert F. Swanson handled the business side of the firm and did most of the fieldwork.

According to retired GM designer George Moon, Saarinen quickly came back with his first concept drawings and plans, whereupon Kettering immediately objected, saying the buildings were too "beautiful" and "frivolous." Then, because of the UAW strike of 1945-46, GM froze its budget of $20 million for the new Technical Center (named that by Sloan) and stopped all work. Earl suggested to Sloan that GM reconsider the project after Kettering retired in 1947. By that time, though, the tab had shot up to $125 million. GM went ahead anyway, handing the contract to Eero Saarinen, Eliel's son, who at that time was unproven and had no individual designs to his credit. Construction began in 1949, the GM Technical Center was officially declared finished on Sept. 15, 1955, the day Styling moved to its new quarters. The official dedication took place May 16, 1956.

Even today the Tech Center looks amazingly modern. The use of open space and glass walls filled Styling's new studios with light. The Styling auditorium was (and is) a dome adjacent to a huge, high-walled courtyard. The courtyard is where full-sized clay models and fiberglass mockups are viewed under natural light.

Harley Earl had a different idea in mind for his own office this time. It wasn't the long, chute-like hallway as in the past; rather it ended up as a large, square room at the front of the building, overlooking the Tech Center's manmade lake. The visitor had to come through Earl's secretary's office, so the approach to his desk again held an element of surprise. The desk, along with an adjoining counter area and interconnected sofas and tables, rambled around the room and formed one huge freeform sculpture carved out of laminated cherrywood. Long seating areas against the walls repeated the voluptuous forms, again in laminated, layered cherrywood. The layers, all slightly different in hue, ran horizontally throughout the ensemble.

In the words of Charles M. (Chuck) Jordan, who occupied Earl's office from 1986 through 1992, "Mr. Earl wanted his desk and the interconnected furniture to simulate rounded, wooden die models." At that time, full-sized wooden models were used to master the stamping dies of sheetmetal presses so, in effect, the furniture contained the massive, rounded autobody shapes Earl liked so much. Because General Motors treats the entire Technical Center as a historic architectural preserve, Earl's office remains very much the same today as it was in 1956.

Earl eagerly took part in the Firebird gas-turbine program of 1953-58. Gas turbines were seen at that time as the next logical step after the piston engine, particularly by Chrysler Corp. When Chrysler started developing roadable turbine cars, General Motors and Ford felt they had to keep up. Unlike Chrysler, though, GM decided to make their turbine cars styling exercises as well as technical tours de force.

The resulting three GM Firebird turbine cars shared a look, but each body was totally different. Firebird I, capable of 200 mph, became a single-seater and looked like a jet without wings. On a shakedown run at GM's Milford Proving Ground, engineer Charles L. McCuen lost control of the 1953 Firebird I, crashed and severely injured himself.

The 1956 Firebird II, with seating for four, was designed to become a long-distance luxury car, so it ended up much larger and heavier than the Firebird I. Like the Firebird I, though, the II had a tubular body with modified aircraft styling. And the 1958 Firebird III took cues from fish, birds, planes and rockets. It had three sharp fins sticking up from the deck and four more protruding horizontally ahead of the rear wheels. Its body was a tube flattened at both ends, and two Plexiglas bubbles covered the cockpit. All three Firebirds ran, and all became Motorama showcars, but they gave virtually nothing of their styling to any General Motors passenger-car design.

Earl didn't even attempt to productionize the far-out cues from the Firebird turbine series. He consistently styled production cars that, year after year throughout most of the 1950s, led the industry, particularly with designs like the 1954 Buick Century, the '54 Oldsmobile 98, 1955 Chevrolet and the 1956 Corvette. Cadillacs consistently bested Lincoln, Imperial and Packard in sales and prestige.

With GM's 1957 models, though, Harley Earl seemed to be groping, and by 1958 he'd lost his way. Good as he'd always been, he couldn't make that transition from chromium and ornamentation and the body shapes he'd come to favor—the rounder, fatter forms—and go on to the sharper creases, the more angular, pointed shapes, the thinner, more delicate roofs, the flatter hoods and decks that characterized the 1960s. Lots of designers get stuck in an era, and at this point Earl was one of them.

GM's 1958 models were the last that were molded strictly by Earl's intuitive sense. And they sold poorly, which wasn't entirely Earl's fault: The recession that year didn't help. But GM's 1958 designs, including the relatively mainstream Chevrolet and Pontiac, looked like parodies of Earl's previous industry-leading designs.

The 1959s, which represented a total break with Earl's philosophy of "rounder, fatter, chromier," resulted from a subtle but very definite insurrection on the part of GM's studio chiefs. Bill Mitchell, Chuck Jordan, Dave Holls and a number of other young GM designers had managed to sneak a peek at Virgil Exner's fresh, new 1957 Chrysler products. This took place before Chrysler's 1957s were released, at a time when Earl proposed yet another round of fat, doughy 1959 GM designs.

Exner's 1957 two-door hardtops, particularly the Plymouth, had delicate, shallow roofs, low, clean beltlines, lots of glass, nicely proportioned fins and a great lack of ornamentation, all of which shocked GM's designers. They immediately recognized a major threat to GM's styling leadership, and they realized Earl's chromed locomotives were headed totally in the wrong direction. So the design chiefs went back to their studios and, while Earl was away in Europe, developed the lower, slimmer, more sharply defined shapes that ended up becoming GM's 1959 models (see pages 178-80).

Alfred P. Sloan Jr., the man who'd built General Motors and who'd been Harley Earl's patron and friend for 31 years, retired in 1956. Two years later, GM's mandatory retirement age of 65 meant it was time for Earl to leave, too. As a going-away gift, GM designed and built one final Motorama-like roadster for Harley and Sue Earl so that they could drive off into the Florida sunset together. Which they did. And that opened an entirely new design chapter at General Motors, the one directed by William L. Mitchell. The Mitchell chronicles begin on page 172. ◆

Harley Earl (left) and his longtime mentor and friend, Alfred P. Sloan Jr., at Sloan's retirement in 1956.

CHAPTER 8

EDSEL'S PLAYTHING

Delve into the history of the Lincoln Motor Co. and you bump smack into Cadillac. The same men who started and ran Cadillac formed Lincoln. Cadillac itself evolved from a company named for Henry Ford. Here's how it all happened.

Around the turn of the century, Henry Ford involved himself in two fragile little automotive ventures in Detroit. The first was under-capitalized and died aborning. But in 1902, the second one, called the Henry Ford Co. and subsidized by a group of rich Detroiters, teetered just on the brink. Ford's investors finally got tired of watching Henry tinker with his racing cars and decided he wasn't spending enough time developing a salable automobile, so they gave him the boot.

With Ford barely out the door, these investors called in a master machinist named Henry Martyn Leland and asked him to give them an appraisal of the Henry Ford Co.'s assets. They had in mind selling the plant and machine tools. Leland, though, came back with another thought. He suggested they go ahead and build a car, essentially the same two-cylinder car Ford wasn't spending enough time on, but using a one-cylinder engine developed by Leland. Leland demonstrated his engine, the investors liked it and renamed the company Cadillac. In 1903, the Cadillac Motor Car Co. began building and selling cars. And that's how Ford begat Cadillac.

The story of how Cadillac begat Lincoln: In 1904, Henry M. Leland became president of Cadillac, a position he held for 13 years. His son, Wilfred, joined him and soon became Cadillac's vice president and general manager. With help from Charles F. Kettering, the man behind the first successful self-starter, and engine engineer Frank Johnson, the Lelands made Cadillac a hugely successful motorcar.

In early 1917, when the United States entered World War I, the Lelands had a falling out with their boss, William C. Durant, president of General Motors. GM owned Cadillac and Durant controlled GM. The tiff had to do with building aircraft engines for the war effort. The Lelands wanted to build them and Durant didn't. So both Lelands quit. On the sheer strength of their reputation, they immediately raised several million dollars, built a huge, modern manufacturing plant and ended up producing 6500 Liberty V-12 aircraft engines before the war ended.

Unfortunately, it ended too soon, and the Lelands found themselves chin-deep in debt. On the plus side, they still had 6000 trained and willing workers, a spanking-new factory and a superb engineering staff, including Frank Johnson. Johnson laid out a state-of-the-art V-8 engine, around which the Lelands created a car. Henry Leland had voted for Abraham Lincoln in 1864 and, to honor the Great Emancipator, Leland named his new car Lincoln.

Even before the first Lincoln automobile rolled out of the factory in September 1920, 1000 buyers had put down cash deposits. Most orders came from people who'd read the headlines about Henry and Wilfred Leland and their battle with Durant over the Liberty engines. The public now recognized father and son not only for their patriotism but for what they'd done with Cadillac and the high standards they brought to everything they touched.

Lincoln's success seemed assured until customers got an actual look at the car. No one doubted that the first Model L Lincolns (L for Leland) would shine mechanically, but it suddenly became clear that the new Lincoln lacked style—not only lacked it but looked downright homely. Bodies stood tall and upright as barns.

To make things worse, the Lelands picked totally the wrong year to launch a car, because 1920 brought with it a deep postwar recession. Money stopped moving. And for good measure, the federal government mistakenly slapped the Lelands with a bill for $4 million in back taxes. They didn't really owe that, but it took a while to get the tax mixup straightened out. Meanwhile, the Lelands again made the press, causing Lincoln buyers to renege on contracts and the banks to stop lending more money. So instead of selling a projected 6000 cars in 14 months, the Lelands sold

When Henry Ford bought the Lincoln Motor Car Co. in 1922, people said he did it to provide his son, Edsel, with a "plaything." However, Edsel saw Lincoln as much more than that. He used Lincoln as a platform to launch a styling department at Ford. Henry didn't care how his cars looked, but Edsel did, and he eventually built up a design activity as good as--and often better than -- any in the world.

only about 3500—not enough to keep the company afloat.

Re-enter Henry Ford. Henry had gotten his life together, managed to crank up a going car company and, in Oct. 1908, launched the Model T. His Ford Motor Co. was now riding the crest of the T's storybook success, and Ford himself had become one of the richest men on earth. His company stood out, for the moment at least, as the largest, most technically innovative, canny, attuned and progressive of world automakers.

Henry Ford had known the Lelands for 20 years, and everyone in Detroit recognized that Lincoln was headed for oblivion. At first, Henry Ford couldn't have cared less. It probably gave him a little tingle to see the Lelands in trouble, especially since they'd built some of their earlier success on the designs and machine tools of Ford's failed 1903 car. But sentiments of another sort prevailed. Ford's wife, Clara, and his only son, Edsel, lobbied to have the elder Ford buy Lincoln. Which Ford did on Feb. 4, 1922, when the court ordered the Lincoln Motor Co. to be sold at a receiver's sale. Through an attorney, Ford offered $8 million in cash plus another $4 million to pay off creditors. And to give you some idea of the value of money back then, a brand-new Model T cost $319.

To commemorate the Lincoln buyout, the Fords had pictures taken of the signing-over ceremony. The best known photo, taken in Henry Leland's office amid portraits of Honest Abe, tells more than several thousand words. It shows an elated Edsel Ford on the left, with a gloomy Wilfred Leland seated next to him. Edsel looks extremely pleased, and it's reasonable to assume that he feels that way because his father has, in effect, just bought Lincoln for him. Wilfred, meanwhile, looks like he's lost his best friend, perhaps because he realizes that he and his father aren't going to get along with the Fords. Henry Ford had told them earlier that morning, "You run it [Lincoln] for me." But which half of that sentence Ford considered important no one yet knew.

Both young men's expressions turned out to be prophetic. The Ford-Leland liaison lasted barely four months. The two Henrys were too much alike. Both had impossibly high standards, both were unbending, fiercely competitive and independent, wholly determined to do things their own way.

Edsel Ford, like many teenagers of his generation, hopped up a Model T and equipped it with a special speedster body. He also kept scrapbooks of body styles that interested him, especially custom designs on big European chassis.

Henry Ford, never especially sensitive, soon let his manufacturing people knock down walls inside the Lincoln plant, including those of the Lelands' private offices. Ford's lieutenants countermanded the Lelands' work orders and generally made life miserable for Lincoln employees. Ford production manager Pete Martin fired a Lincoln gate keeper for having his hands in his pockets. Cast-Iron Charlie Sorensen, Ford's manufacturing guru, kicked a stool out from under a man in the Lincoln plant, ordering him to stand up. The man, however, worked for Detroit Edison, not Lincoln. When the fellow got to his feet, he took a swing at Sorensen but unfortunately missed.

This campaign of harassment had Henry Ford's blessing and might have again been his way of "getting back" for whatever long-simmering slights he felt. It was Wilfred who finally blew up and wrote the elder Ford a rambling, angry memo. Ford answered by summarily having Wilfred thrown out of the Lincoln plant. When Wilfred left, so did his father. Feelings between the Lelands and the Fords never softened.

At that point, Edsel Ford pretty much took over the running of Lincoln. Henry had made him president of Ford Motor Co. on Dec. 30, 1918, a title that carried no real authority or duties. But as Henry focused on engineering and business policy and general social pronouncements, Edsel turned his attention to what he liked best: styling.

As a teenager, Edsel loved to draw automobiles. He hung car pictures on his bedroom walls and kept scrapbooks showing all the latest, fanciest European salon models. Henry gave Edsel his first car for Edsel's 10th birthday: a bright-red 1903 Model A runabout. According to Edsel biographer Henry Dominguez, Edsel used to drive his 1903 Model A to elementary school. Four years later, he became the owner of a 1906 Ford Model N runabout, and he drove that until he got a new Model T which, like many young blades of that day, he hot rodded. Then, at age 19, he bought himself a huge and very chic French Renault. And when Edsel turned 21, Henry gave him $1 million in gold, so the elder Ford couldn't be accused of being ungenerous toward his son, at least not at that time.

Henry and Edsel had a complex and ever-changing relationship. Soon after Edsel's death in 1943, Agnes E. Meyer, who'd interviewed him recently for *The Washington Post,* wrote, "...the public paid little attention to the immature son of a sensational father. It was the kind of life that is best calculated to make any human being very unhappy or very conventional. It certainly left its mark on Edsel Ford, for a more banal exterior than his can scarcely be imagined, until you took a second look. Then the formal patterns of his mask, his dress, his behavior disappeared, and you became aware of a mind as incisive as his vision was clear. Like all people who see too deeply into the artificialities of life, his humor had

a tinge of bitterness, but it was modified when his sympathies became involved."

It's far too easy to draw Henry as the harsh, domineering father and Edsel as the obedient, misunderstood son. The two men undoubtedly loved and respected one another, and over time they worked out a division of labor which, roughly, amounted to Edsel taking charge of styling, sales, advertising, purchasing and finance, and Henry controlling engineering, manufacturing, labor relations and everything else. But even that's too simple, because Edsel later took a passionate interest in expanding the company's car lines beyond the traditional low-cost Ford. It was Edsel, not Henry, who championed the 1936 Lincoln Zephyr, the 1939 Mercury, the 1940 Lincoln Continental and most of Ford's aircraft ventures.

According to Ford historian David L. Lewis, a bequest of Edsel's company stock made the Ford Foundation the largest philanthropy in the world. As art patrons, Edsel and Eleanor Ford gave generous amounts of time and money to their own community and the world. The best-known of Edsel's commissions was to Diego Rivera, the Mexican muralist whose work covers the walls of the Detroit Institute of Arts central courtyard. These big, bold murals show the Ford Motor Co. clanking out cars in the early 1930s, but laced with Rivera's freely admitted Marxist overtones. For years, any number of outraged Detroiters wanted to paint over the Rivera murals—something Nelson Rockefeller actually did to Rivera's work inside Rockefeller Center. But Edsel held out, and today the Rivera murals rank as one of Detroit's greatest art treasures.

Styling was not a topic Henry Ford considered important. He paid either very little or no attention to it. And yet the Model T's body design underwent periodic styling revisions throughout its 18-year life. How much the younger Ford influenced all those changes we can only guess, but according to Henry Dominguez, the first Model T body that Edsel helped design was the 1911 "torpedo" runabout. Compared with its 1910 counterpart, Edsel's torpedo looked faster and more refined than the standard Ford runabout. More important, Edsel showed—even at that early stage—that a handsome body could be built just as easily and economically as one that was strictly functional.

Among the Model T's later refinements: The 1915 sedan and coupelet marked the switch from flat fenders to a more curved form, and for 1917 Ford boasted a "new look." Henry Ford referred to that year's styling changes as "streamlined." The 1917 T had crowned fenders, a different radiator shell and hood, plus bright caps for the radiator and hubs. In 1923, Model T bodies stood lower, and Ford began the process of getting the wood out. How much Edsel influenced these changes isn't clear.

Ford's Lincoln acquisition ceremony in Feb. 1922 saw Edsel (seated left) looking pleased and the Lelands (right) downcast. What Edsel inherited was a stylistically deprived but mechanically excellent automobile. The photo above shows one of Lincoln's more handsome 1922 bodies, the victoria coupe.

We do know, though, that Edsel had a major hand in restyling the 1926-27 Model T, an experience that served as practice for the 1928 Model A. He lowered the roofline of the 1926-27 T's closed body styles, softened the fender curvatures, specified a nickel radiator shell and finally added colors. The Model T had been available only in black since 1914. For 1926, Ford offered Channel green, Windsor maroon, Fawn grey and Gunmetal blue. As we'll see, there's no question that Edsel had a great deal to do with the 1928 Model A's styling plus the design of all subsequent Ford automobiles and trucks up until the second World War.

But the marque Edsel took the greatest interest in and transformed from ugly duckling into swan was Lincoln. He probably knew at the moment of purchase that

he was up to the job of rescuing a mechanically excellent but otherwise unattractive luxury automobile. Edsel brought to that task his interests in the fine arts, architecture, interior and furniture design. In time, he became a good photographer, and he trusted himself on points of style. He had confidence in his own aesthetic judgments, and his father came to have faith in them, too; more faith in Edsel's styling sense than in most of his other ideas. Edsel, conceded Henry, had taste. That's the word that everyone who writes about Edsel Ford uses. And Edsel did feel at ease talking about art and line, form, color and texture—all topics that went far over Henry's head.

Edsel Ford was not a car designer, and he often said as much. He had the ability to draw and paint pictures, but he rarely, if

ever, put pencil to paper inside a styling studio. Yet like Harley Earl, he had an intuitive, very strong sense of what looked right in and on an automobile. He recognized and appreciated good car design, had a keen eye for proportion and the appropriateness of detail, and he could explain what he liked and why.

Those, though, were nearly the only character traits that Edsel Ford and Harley had in common. Unlike Earl, Edsel was short and slight. He dressed conservatively. He was not athletic. And the cars designed under Edsel's supervision were much less flamboyant than Earl's. However, Edsel did have the same emotional feel for automobiles and auto design that Earl did.

People said Henry Ford bought Lincoln as a plaything for Edsel. Edsel, though, didn't at all view Lincoln that way. He took Lincoln very seriously. Edsel's goal—almost an obsession—was to make Lincoln nothing less than America's most respected and prestigious luxury motorcar. He realized it wouldn't be easy, especially against such established rivals as Packard, Pierce-Arrow, Locomobile, Peerless and Cadillac. Lincoln was very much the new car on the block.

Since the Ford Motor Co. lacked any semblance of a styling department—didn't have so much as a delineator when Henry

Who said the Model T never changed? Compare these coupes. (From left to right) The 1911 model still shows considerable carriage heritage. By 1920, the T had taken on a rounded, painted radiator shell and electric lamps. It also stood considerably lower. And in 1925, Ford's style changes included a nickel grille shell and a simplified greenhouse.

Edsel worked with a number of established coachbuilders and became very involved with each Lincoln's styling. Fleetwood built the 1924 sedan (left), while Brunn designed and the factory fabricated bodies for the 1926 "Police Flyer" 7-passenger touring car (center). Locke provided the design and coachwork for Lincoln's handsome 1926 roadster.

Derham equipped the 1928 Linoln sport sedan (left) with a canvas trunk cover and canework insets in the belt molding. Packard-like disc wheels were standard. Considerably more dashing was Dietrich's 1929 Lincoln convertible sedan, whose roll-up windows were supplemented by glass drop-in center pillars. Only 38 of this model were sold.

Ford bought Lincoln—Edsel initially availed himself of the design services of the independent coachbuilders. Some, like Brunn and Judkins, came to Edsel hat in hand. Other contacts resulted from meetings at the salons: bumping into LeBaron's Ray Dietrich, for instance. In the end, five coachbuilders did most of Lincoln's early design work and provided an excellent line of catalogue customs that were shown and sold by Ford/Lincoln dealers. (The five were Brunn, Judkins, LeBaron, Willoughby and Dietrich. Edsel, in fact, had played a key role in bringing Ray Dietrich to Murray; see Chapter Five.)

During 1923-26, Lincoln produced fewer cars per year than Ford built in two shifts. Lincoln did fabricate its own production bodies, but due to the relatively small volume, even those were virtually handmade and certainly hand-finished. More Lincoln bodies were supplied by such mid-sized manufacturers as Towson, American Body Co., Anderson and Lang than were made by Lincoln in-house.

Production-bodied Lincolns often took their styling directly from coachbuilt samples. When Edsel liked a certain design or a design detail and wanted to adapt it to production, he made it a practice to pay the coachbuilder for rights. Most other automakers simply "borrowed" what they wanted, without compensation or credit.

Edsel and Henry Crecelius, Lincoln's chief body engineer, would normally spend hours poring over the drawings and body drafts submitted by Lincoln's supplier coachbuilders. It was expected for Edsel and Crecelius to make changes, both large and small, and without Edsel's specific approval, a coachbuilder dared not start work on an order of catalogue-custom bodies.

These custom bodies, usually 25 to 100 per run, would be shipped to the Detroit Lincoln plant by rail. They nearly always arrived "in the white" and were immediately shuttled to a special section of the plant where they were painted and trimmed. A staff of craftsmen, numbering several hundred and under the direction of Henry Crecelius and two or three of his aides, did nothing but finish and mount series-custom Lincoln bodies. This was in addition to the planning and construction of production bodies. Crecelius had several draftsmen and detailers on his staff but no one who could remotely be called a stylist.

Edsel wrote long, detailed letters to Lincoln's coachbuilders, copies of which survive in the Henry Ford Museum's research center. These letters show how deeply Edsel cared about the subtlest nuances of design and body engineering—from trim stitching to metal finishing. He also had an impressive range of technical knowledge, some of it probably learned from Henry Crecelius. Crecelius had previously been chief body engineer for Brewster.

Soon after Ford's purchase of Lincoln and for the next 20 years, Briggs and Murray built many of Lincoln's factory bodies. By 1927, both body manufacturers had professional designers on their staffs: Ralph Roberts at Briggs and Amos

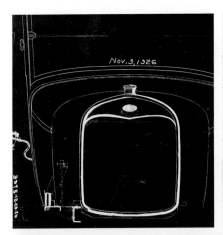

Edsel Ford played a major role in styling the 1928 Model A Ford. The actual design work took place at Briggs, with Amos Northup marginally involved and Cadillac's Joe Thompson on leave to do some of the clay and wood modeling. Edsel borrowed the Model A's widow's peak grille shape, fender contours and general body lines from the Lincoln. The 1928 A presented an infinitely more up-to-date look than the 1927 T. Since the Model A cowl incorporated the fuel tank, and since the instrument panel had to be symmetrical side to side for right-hand drive, there was little Edsel could do to style the dashboard. That aspect of the car didn't match the exterior.

Northup at Murray. These two men generated a steady flow of styling proposals to their companies' customers, particularly to Chrysler and Ford.

Henry Ford, after years of holding out, finally bowed to the inevitable and, in 1926, agreed to replace his beloved Model T with a new car. He referred to the developing replacement as the "Model A" because, he said, this was going to be such a radical departure—such a different automobile—that he needed to start a whole new alphabet. (For the record, there had been a previous Model A Ford in 1903.) So after trying unsuccessfully to develop an X-8 engine and an automatic transmission in the mid 1920s, Henry eventually engineered the conventional but extremely rugged and simple Model A that appeared in late 1927 as a 1928 model.

Edsel, who'd been advocating replacing the T for several years, had given considerable thought to the new car's styling. He now suggested making the Model A look like a smaller version of the Lincoln. Henry obviously approved the idea, because the 1928-29 Model A did end up looking like a baby Lincoln.

The Model A's actual styling, according to Joseph D. Thompson, took place inside the old C.R. Wilson plant in Detroit. This plant now belonged to Murray Corp. of America, and Murray's chief stylist, Amos Northup, apparently took some part in the design. Exactly how involved Northup became isn't known, but he did ask Joe Thompson to come over from Cadillac to help make a full-sized, clay-over-wood model of the Model A, and that's why we have Thompson's account of the design. Cadillac gave Thompson a leave of absence but didn't ask why or where he was going.

When Thompson got to C.R. Wilson's, the Model A's Lincoln look had already been decided. Edsel Ford directed the design and Northup worked somewhere in the background. Ford's longtime, very capable body engineer, Joseph (Shit-a-Metal Joe) Galamb, made sure the Model A stayed on spec, particularly in terms of roof height. Henry wanted a fairly tall roof and Edsel didn't. (Galamb, in his Hungarian accent, pronounced the word *sheet-metal* "shit-a-metal," thus the nickname.)

The 1928-29 Model A design turned out wonderfully well. It was suitably different from the Model T, although T styling also had its flashes of form-follows-function brilliance. But the Model A showed an almost feminine delicacy in its form, an overall lightness of touch and line. It was quite sophisticated in such detailing as its stamped beltline and cowl moldings, the "widow's-peak" radiator shell, the spidery wire wheels, the bumper harmonies and the general proportions of all its many body styles. The Model A's interior, though, didn't match. It lacked the charm of the exterior: too austere and too much a holdover from the Model T.

In 1931, Henry Crecelius hired a young man named Eugene T. (Bob) Gregorie, and that really marked the first time Ford had an in-house designer. Gregorie came from a well-to-do Long Island family. He'd attended private schools but never graduated. As a teenager, since he loved boats, he went to work for a firm in New Jersey that built yachts, and he learned drafting and ship-hull design there.

Gregorie's father had owned a number of high-quality European motorcars—Mercedes, Delage, Amilcar—and, as a result, Bob decided that as much as he enjoyed boats and marine architecture, what he really wanted to do was to design luxury cars. So in 1928, he applied at Brewster and was hired. He worked there for a year or so as a designer and draftsman.

In the autumn of 1929, Gregorie became restless, so he left Brewster and decided to try for a styling job in Detroit. But he did not go to Detroit directly. He first stopped in Syracuse at the Franklin plant. Franklin wasn't hiring, but Kent Haven, the man who interviewed Bob, happened to mention that Ray Dietrich, the coachbuilder, had just dropped off some body drafts for custom Franklins. Gregorie walked back to the Syracuse train station and, at the ticket counter, heard the man ahead of him say, "Reservation for Ray Dietrich, please." Gregorie naturally introduced himself, and the two men rode together in the parlor car to Dietrich's next customer, Pierce-Arrow in Buffalo, New York. "Ray pulled out a gin flask from his hip pocket and ordered orange

Briggs also became heavily involved in the 1932 Ford's design. Early scale models showed a shovel-nosed grille, like the 1932 Packard Light Eight's, plus fender-mounted lamps. The production 1932 Ford ended up pleasingly traditional.

juice and proceeded to get feeling quite nice and friendly," recalled Gregorie in his Ford Archives oral reminiscences. This was still during Prohibition. Dietrich offered Gregorie a drink, but Bob told him he was under age. Dietrich did suggest that Gregorie stay at the Lewis Hotel on Woodward Avenue in Detroit, because the streetcar went directly from the hotel to the General Motors Building.

With no design work at Pierce either, Gregorie took the steamer from Buffalo to Detroit and arrived there on the morning of his 21st birthday, Oct. 12, 1929, a Saturday. Next Monday he went straight to Howard O'Leary's office at GM Art & Colour. O'Leary looked at Gregorie's portfolio and hired him on the spot. Gregorie worked alongside other green young designers, doing sketches of hubcaps and hood ornaments but was soon let go again in GM's typical revolving-door policy of that period. But Gregorie quickly landed another job in Detroit, designing yachts again, and then got in touch with Henry Crecelius at Lincoln. Both were Brewster alumni, although Crecelius had left Brewster long before Gregorie got there.

Crecelius didn't have anything for Gregorie immediately but, in early Jan. 1931, a job opened up. One of Gregorie's first assignments at Lincoln, oddly enough, was to come up with design sketches for the small British Ford, the 1932 Model Y. Gregorie was apparently the only person at Ford Motor Co. at that time who could actually conceive and draw the exterior of a car. Gregorie's sketches were submitted to Edsel Ford, who accepted them and sent them on to the Ford plant in Dagenham, England. The 1932 Model Y appeared a year later very much as Gregorie had designed it.

In the course of conversation, Edsel and Gregorie found that they had a number of interests in common, among them art, boats, cars and car design. Gregorie also had the type of personality Edsel liked: congenial, outgoing, good-humored and yet, as Joe Galamb

described him, "...a very smart, cocky young fellow...[who] wouldn't take anything from anybody." In other words, Gregorie could hold his own in verbal shootouts with Henry Ford's cronies, and that was one of his abilities that Edsel liked. In addition, Gregorie had (and still has, of course) a charming way of telling stories and making conversation. Despite the difference in their ages (Edsel was 38 in 1931; Gregorie only 23) both men developed a deep and lasting respect for one another.

Edsel might, at one time, have had Ray Dietrich in mind for the job he ultimately offered Gregorie, that of Ford's design director. While Edsel knew Dietrich well—perhaps a little too well; they were neighbors for a time—it's possible that Edsel came to view Dietrich as a bit too slick, too much a playboy, too given to high-jinx and drink to put up with comfortably. So in choosing Gregorie over Dietrich, it became a matter of greater compatibility.

Between 1931 and 1935, Gregorie occupied an office at one end of the Ford engineering laboratory and officially worked under Henry Crecelius. He later described watching the Lincoln chassis engineers design the "face" of new models during that period—the radiator shell, hood and front fenders. "I remember that the development of the 1933 K-Model front end was handled by Frank Johnson and his crew," said Gregorie in a 1994 interview. "The way they did it was interesting. They'd just set up a couple of sawhorses, nail up a sort of hood, put on some slats and model up a fender. Then they'd hang a grille and the fender on this buck, and they'd shove a real wheel and tire under it. Strangely, it turned out very nicely. But I mentioned to Edsel Ford one day, I said, 'You know, it's like going to a tailor and having him do just one leg of the pants, without the other leg.' I think that amused him."

Throughout the 1930s, Henry Ford allowed Edsel more and more freedom with styling decisions, not just for the Lincoln but also for the Ford car. And it's a good thing he did, because

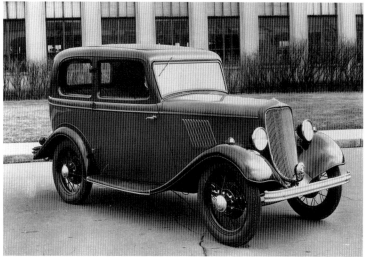

Bob Gregorie's first assignment at Ford was to do the small 1932 British Model Y (left). Clare Kramer blew up the Model Y and transformed it into the 1933 American Ford, a design many collectors consider one of Ford's finest.

Edsel now recognized that the Ford Motor Co. had to compete with the aggressive and very calculated styling steamroller that General Motors was putting on the road. Edsel must have been aware of Harley Earl's growing status within General Motors, the growth of GM Art & Colour itself, and he also had to know about the smaller styling staffs at Chrysler and the independents. After considerable discussion, Edsel was able to talk his father into making yearly styling changes and facelifts. Edsel argued basically that if Ford ignored styling or fell behind, the results could be disastrous.

Edsel still relied heavily on the design services of Briggs and Murray. Unlike the 1928 Model A, the 1932 Ford appears to have been done largely at and by Briggs, under Ralph Roberts. Early clay models had a slightly shovel-nosed grille shell, like the 1932 Packard Light Eight, but this gave way in production to a vertical grille profile. After Ford's bodies for 1932 were all sketched out, Gregorie designed a special little cycle-fendered boattail speedster for Edsel, which Crecelius' craftsmen built on the 1932 Ford V-8 chassis.

For the 1933-34 Ford, Edsel asked Clare Kramer, a body draftsman, to scale up Gregorie's 1932 British Ford Model Y. Kramer took the Model Y styling cues and simply reproportioned them to look good on a 112-inch wheelbase. It's always easier to scale up than to scale down, especially since a small, short car has to have basically the same headroom and ground clearance as a large one. Gregorie had nothing to do with the Americanized version of his design, but when he saw an early prototype of the 1933 American Ford, he immediately recognized where the styling had come from. The 1933-34 Ford

became a great sales success, and Edsel Ford seemed pleased with the design, as was Gregorie.

Briggs again stepped in to help style the 1935 Ford and its 1936 facelift. The 1935 model was done by Phil Wright at Briggs; Holden (Bob) Koto did the 1936 grille, hood and fender changes, also at Briggs.

In the winter of 1934-35, Gregorie designed an open, four-place sport phaeton version of the 1934 Ford. This car, although no one realized it at the time, became the spiritual ancestor of Edsel's 1939 Lincoln Continental. Gregorie's 1934 sportster, handbuilt this time by craftsmen in Ford's Trimotor aircraft plant, grew out of informal conversations between Gregorie and Edsel Ford. For a time they talked about having John Inskip of Brewster manufacture this phaeton in small quantities. Gregorie developed a special suspension system that lowered the frame nearly six inches. He also extended the wheelbase 10 inches. The phaeton's aluminum front fenders were made up of Ford airplane fenders. The car had no heater, no windows and no sidecurtains.

So in early 1935, in the dead of winter, Gregorie drove this windchill of a phaeton from Dearborn to New York and showed it to Inskip. Inskip expressed interest but wanted Ford to finance the

The Classic Lincolns

In 1931, the Lincoln Model L gave way to the Model K, and the K ushered in that spectacular succession of huge classic Lincolns that today's collectors prize as the pinnacle of automotive elegance and excellence. The classic K-Model Lincolns managed to survive from

1932 Lincoln KB Brunn Doublentry had doors that opened at either end.

1931 through 1939, living out the entire Depression in opulent fashion, but at a tremendous price to the company.

Throughout the Thirties, the upper crust of American cars waged war with each other in a cylinder race. If eight cylinders were good, 12 and 16 had to be better. Cadillac opened 1930 with a V-16, followed by Marmon's V-16 for 1931. Packard had built a Twin Six during 1916-23 but launched a totally new V-12 in 1932, to be joined in 12-cylinder power by Auburn, Franklin, Pierce-Arrow and Lincoln. Lincoln, in fact, built three different V-12s during the Thirties, two in the K series and one for the Lincoln Zephyr.

The Depression brought luxury-car sales almost to a halt. As a result, marques like Duesenberg, Pierce-Arrow, Peerless, Stutz and Marmon went out of business. If Lincoln and Cadillac hadn't had such rich parent companies, they too would probably have disappeared. As financially draining as this period was, the early Depression produced some of the most magnificent, luxurious and opulent cars of all time.

The first Model K Lincolns, introduced in Jan. 1931, still used the Model L's fork-and-blade V-8 but now with twin-barrel downdraft carburetion and various internal tweaks that raised horsepower from 90 to 120. Then in 1932 came the fabulous Model KB, the greatest of all Wagnerian classic Lincolns, with a monstrous 448-cubic-inch V-12 engine delivering

Brunn constructed 1940 Zephyr towncar for Mrs. Henry Ford.

150 horsepower. The Cadillac V-16 had only four more cubic inches of displacement but much more complexity. The KB, with its unique fork-and-blade 65-degree V-12, stayed on the scene for only two seasons, 1932-33, before Henry and Edsel Ford decided that the low sales volume didn't justify the expense. In all, only 2210 KB Lincolns were built, most with custom coachwork.

In addition to the 145-inch-wheelbase KB, Lincoln also offered the smaller, less expensive Model KA on a 136-inch span. The 1933 KA received a V-12 engine, but it wasn't the same as the KB's. Instead of the KB's 65-degree vee angle, the KA's was 67 degrees. This engine had side-by-side rods and, instead of displacing 448 cubic inches, the KA V-12 displaced 382. All of which meant that Lincoln was putting a lot of effort and money into essentially two different low-volume luxury motorcars.

Factory-bodied 1934 sport phaeton's curved windows lowered into doors.

And, as the Depression wore on, the market drove Lincoln prices down, not up as would be normal to compensate for lower production.

Even so, only the wealthiest of car purchasers could afford any classic Lincoln. As enticement, dealers let customers choose from dozens of catalogue-custom body styles. Buyers pored over colorful coachbuilder brochures that showed custom bodies from Judkins, Willoughby, Brunn, Rollston, Murphy, LeBaron, Dietrich and Waterhouse.

For 1934, Lincoln settled on a single engine: a version of the KA V-12 displacing 414 cubic inches but again developing 150 horses. There was no more KA or KB, just the Model K after 1933, and Lincoln wouldn't offer a V-8 again until 1949. From 1934 through '39, Edsel Ford kept the huge, granitic Model K alive, and the few cars that Lincoln managed to sell usually came with custom bodies by the few remaining coachbuilders. Miss E.R. Sears, the Chicago mail-order heiress, had the bullet headlights on her 1935 Brunn convertible sedan chrome plated for added exclusivity, but she needn't have bothered. Model K's weren't so popular that she'd ever see another car like hers.

Two of the final and most famous Model K's were the King George phaeton and the Sunshine Special, both built in 1939. The royal phaeton was especially built for a summer visit to the U.S. and Canada by Britain's King George VI and Queen Elizabeth. It served only as a parade car.

As did the Sunshine Special, which was built at the request of President Franklin Delano Roosevelt. FDR initially had Packards and Pierce-Arrows as cars of state, but to show himself a man of the people, he himself drove first a Model A Ford phaeton and then a 1936 Ford Deluxe convertible sedan equipped with hand controls. In 1939, partly to help heal a rift with Henry Ford, whose factories he needed for the war effort, FDR asked the Secret Service to put a Lincoln in the White

Brunn also built 1939 Sunshine Special.

House garage. Lincolns have been in presidential service ever since.

The Sunshine Special started as a 1939 Model K with a Brunn phaeton body. Leased to the federal government for $1 a year, a 1942-style front end was grafted on during the war. To protect the president, armor and bulletproof glass were added, along with step plates and wider runningboards for Secret Service bodyguards. The Sunshine Special was huge in every way: 160-inch wheelbase, 21.5 feet long, 9300 pounds. It remained in service for 11 years, leading parades in such farflung places as Malta, Yalta and Casablanca. At the bitter end of the Model K's run in 1939, Edsel Ford remarked that Lincoln hadn't stopped building luxury cars; the public simply stopped buying them. ◆

1935 KB phaeton was commissioned by W.H. Annenberg of Chicago.

LeBaron (Briggs) supplied 20 of these 1936 Lincoln rumbleseat roadsters.

Edsel tried to get Brewster's John Inskip to produce this 1934 phaeton but wouldn't underwrite venture.

project. Edsel didn't care for that idea and instead offered the chassis and suspension design to Jensen Motors in England. Jensen built a series of Ford-based sportsters from 1935 through 1939. Clark Gable owned a Jensen Ford for a time. Edsel, by the way, gave the original 1934 phaeton to Gregorie, who eventually sold it for $500.

Edsel Ford certainly concerned himself with the styling of early Depression Ford cars and trucks, but the division that gave him sleepless nights was Lincoln. As the domestic economy worsened, Ford sales slipped, but Lincoln's dropped like a rock. Lincoln production went from a precarious 3515 cars in 1930 to a grim 2150 in 1934.

Throughout the 1930s, Edsel did everything possible to keep the Lincoln competitive and appealing. Development and manufacturing costs of Lincoln's new V-12s, the chassis updates and grille/fender ensembles must have been phenomenal, especially considering the return. Henry, though, remained generous and didn't begrudge Edsel the working capital. Then, when Lincoln sales didn't rebound—in fact, got worse—Edsel took the losses to heart.

He realized as early as 1932 that the only way to save Lincoln would be to create a medium-priced model that Ford dealers could sell in volume. That model eventually ended up being the 1936 Lincoln Zephyr, and if it hadn't been for the Zephyr, there'd prob-

ably be no Lincoln today.

The Zephyr began as the longtime dream of John Tjaarda. Tjaarda had been hired by Briggs along with a personal friend of Edsel's named Howard Bonbright. Bonbright arrived earlier than Tjaarda, but Briggs hired both men in response to complaints from Galamb and Sorensen, who were claiming that Briggs paid too much attention to Chrysler, particularly the Airflow's body development, and not enough to Ford. Bonbright became Briggs' ambassador to Edsel Ford, and Tjaarda's job was to come up with new designs that might appeal to Ford Motor Co.

Tjaarda's hobbyhorse and longtime dream had been a car he called the Sterkenburg (sometimes spelled *Sterkenberg*). This was a mid-engined sedan that he'd conceived around 1926 at Locke and refined in 1928 at General Motors. Tjaarda was more than a dreamer, though: He showed great talent as an engineer, was quite a good stylist and had a background in aerodynamics.

John J. Tjaarda was born in the Sterkenburg region of Holland on Feb. 4, 1897. He served as a WW-I pilot for the Royal Dutch Air Force and also studied aerodynamics in England. He came to the U.S. in 1923, worked as a design engineer for the coachbuilder Locke in New York and, in 1928, took a job at GM Art & Colour under Harley Earl.

In its purest form, Tjaarda's Sterkenburg had a mid-mounted, watercooled V-8, all-independent suspension and a unitized, frameless body—much like the radical Czech Tatra of 1934. Tjaarda made scores of sketches and models of the Sterkenburg in different guises, refining its styling again and again until he'd gotten it, he thought, just right.

When Tjaarda went to Briggs in 1932 as chief production design engineer, he made it a point to show Edsel Ford the Sterkenburg's advanced and novel ideas. Edsel seemed suitably impressed, and Tjaarda soon managed to have Briggs and Ford co-sponsor the construction of mockups and three running, mid-engined proto-

  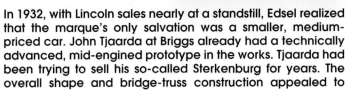  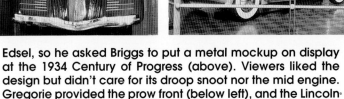

In 1932, with Lincoln sales nearly at a standstill, Edsel realized that the marque's only salvation was a smaller, medium-priced car. John Tjaarda at Briggs already had a technically advanced, mid-engined prototype in the works. Tjaarda had been trying to sell his so-called Sterkenburg for years. The overall shape and bridge-truss construction appealed to

Edsel, so he asked Briggs to put a metal mockup on display at the 1934 Century of Progress (above). Viewers liked the design but didn't care for its droop snoot nor the mid engine. Gregorie provided the prow front (below left), and the Lincoln Zephyr arrived as a 1936 model (below). It enjoyed much healthier sales than the Airflow and essentially saved Lincoln.

 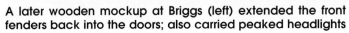 

A later wooden mockup at Briggs (left) extended the front fenders back into the doors; also carried peaked headlights

and a canted prow grille. The character line of Tjaarda's mid-engined model remained and continued into production.

types. The running cars were powered by special aluminum versions of the Ford V-8.

Tjaarda's car interested Edsel for a number of reasons, the main one being that the Sterkenburg might serve as the basis for a new, smaller Lincoln. Edsel recognized that, from engineering and styling standpoints, Tjaarda's car was way out in left field. But since the mid-priced Lincoln had to start with a clean sheet anyway, why not make it as modern as possible? Edsel might have been experiencing some of his father's mechanical adventurism, figuring that here was another of those great ideas that again would need an entirely new model alphabet.

When Briggs showed the mid-engined Tjaarda prototype at the 1934 Century of Progress in Chicago, Ford pollsters were circulating through the crowd, soliciting comments. They found that most people didn't like the idea of placing the engine behind the rear seat and that the sloping nose looked too much like the 1934 Chrysler Airflow's "waterfall" grille.

By now, Edsel had noted the Airflow's styling mistakes and vowed not to repeat them. But he'd also heard about the car Packard was coming out with for 1935, the One Twenty, and that bothered him. Rumor had it that the 120's styling was conservative but recognizably Packard. No one would mistake it for anything else.

The Zephyr, therefore, presented a styling dilemma. It couldn't look as odd as the Airflow, yet it also couldn't be overly conservative and capitalize on the big Lincoln's design cues. For one thing, there simply weren't that many Lincoln cues to build on; certainly nothing with Packard's strengths. So Edsel and Gregorie decided to take a styling middleground. They made the Zephyr look modern and "streamlined" but avoided the odd shapes and decorative touches of the Airflow.

Edsel liked Tjaarda's idea of all-steel, bridge-truss body/chassis construction. He also liked the fundamental lines of Tjaarda's prototype. What needed immediate attention were engine placement and the sloping grille. "So he asked me whether I could design a more appropriate front end," recalled Bob Gregorie in a recent telephone interview. "One morning, we both went over to Briggs, and I sketched up—with a soft pencil on the back of a blueprint—what we referred to as a 'pointy' front end. Edsel Ford liked things pointy. He didn't like bluff, brutal-looking front ends. Within an hour or so, I'd sketched up this front end, and it pleased him." The predilection of both designers for things pointy might have come from their appreciation of ship design.

You can still see the early Zephyr's VW Beetle-like droop snoot in the character line behind Gregorie's prow grille. The production 1936-37 Zephyr also showed some remarkable and then-futuristic touches: fender-mounted, faired-in headlights; an alligator hood; a smooth teardrop bustle; the lack of fussy ornamentation; and a striking art moderne interior. The 1936 instrument panel was fairly conventional, but the 1937 re-do took a leap into the future. It had a vertical floor-to-dash center console with a big speedometer at the top, gauges surrounding the speedo and a clock beneath it. Ads for the 1937 model said that the console and gauges came from an airplane cockpit. The driver and front-seat passenger each had a glovebox and an ashtray, and the resulting symmetry—as on the Model A and later Fords—made it easy to change the Zephyr from left- to right-hand drive. Chrome pipe frames reinforced the front bench seat, and parallel stitching gave the interior its art moderne refinement.

The Zephyr meant a huge investment for both Ford and Briggs and represented a tremendous gamble for Edsel personally, yet it remained the only chance Lincoln had of surviving the Depression. Henry okayed the Zephyr's development costs and left its styling to Edsel. The car's engineering, on the other hand,

Engines to the Rear, Please

The Society of Automotive Engineers talked a lot about rear-engined cars in 1932-36. The motoring press, too, was full of the pros and cons of mid- and rear-engined passenger sedans. John Tjaarda wasn't the only person building prototypes. Overseas, Dubonnet, Burney, Porsche and Ledwinka put running cars on the road. Andre Dubonnet, the French aperitif millionaire and suspension inventor, brought his highly advanced mid-engined car to the U.S. in 1936 and demonstrated it to several major American automakers.

Throughout the 1930s, Chrysler, GM and Ford were all secretly building and testing mid- and rear-engined cars. Placing the engine aft seemed to hold an aerodynamic advantage: the blunt end of the teardrop could precede a tapering tail rather than vice-versa. Around 1930, Chrysler put an engine in the rear of an Airflow-like prototype. Chrysler quickly became convinced that, due to the rear weight bias and horrific handling, full-sized cars with heavy, water-cooled, cast-iron-block engines in the rear were definitely not for the masses.

Then, too, the rear-engine configuration really went against automotive fashion at that time. The public firmly believed in the long hood as a measure of horsepower. The longer the hood, the more powerful the engine, as in racing cars. To the American public of the late 1920s and early '30s, a stubby hood looked weak and awkward. Chrysler discovered that with the Airflow, and Edsel Ford noticed it when the droop-snooted Tjaarda/Briggs prototype went on display in 1934 at the Century of Progress. ◆

Rear engine placement enjoyed a vogue among stylists and engineers throughout the 1930s. At top is a GM blackboard sketch, and above is the engine compartment of Tjaarda's Briggs mockup for the 1934 Century of Progress.

was extremely conventional. Frank Johnson, at Henry Ford's suggestion, simply scaled up the Ford chassis and engine to fit the Zephyr's larger dimensions. Suspension used Ford's usual transverse springs and solid axles. The Zephyr's 110-bhp V-12 engine was essentially the Ford V-8 with four cylinders added. The one major difference between the 1936 Zephyr and the 1936 Ford was the Zephyr's bridge-truss unibody, worked out by Tjaarda and Briggs. Briggs tooled the body and absorbed that expense. The Chrysler Airflow used similar construction (see page 155), but the Zephyr did it with much more grace. Zephyr prices for 1936 started at $1275, approximately twice as much as a new Ford V-8.

The Zephyr's basic development was fairly complete by the end of 1934 and, just after New Year's, Edsel decided to take a little time off. He needed a rest. He packed up his wife, Eleanor, and their four children and went down to their winter home in Hobe Sound, Florida. Then around mid January 1935 and for timing reasons known only to Edsel Ford, he placed a phone call to Bob Gregorie in Dearborn. Long-distance connections at that time took half an hour to complete, and when Gregorie came on the line, Edsel asked him if he'd like to set up a design department that could serve both Lincoln and Ford. Gregorie said he'd be delighted. So at last, Ford, too, had a design department—nearly eight years after General Motors and seven after Chrysler.

Before that phone call, Gregorie had technically been a member of Ford Motor Co.'s engineering staff. His bosses were Henry Crecelius at Lincoln and Larry Sheldrick at Ford. And although Edsel was also Gregorie's boss and surely his patron and mentor, many of the styling ideas the two of them suggested got shot down by Sorensen and his production people. Edsel and Gregorie faced much the same problem Harley Earl had to deal with at Fisher Body. The body and production engineers simply wanted to be left alone. Styling ideas cost time and money.

Before Edsel phoned Gregorie from Florida, though, he must have talked to his father—and through his father to Sorensen—asking them not to undermine Ford's fledgling design section.

Sorensen, who'd been almost hostile to styling ideas in the past, suddenly became, said Gregorie, "gentle as a lamb." Sorensen helped with the physical expansion of Gregorie's area in the engineering laboratory and, unlike at Chrysler, styling soon became separate and distinct from engineering, yet the two staffs worked in harmony.

Gregorie noted that, "The setting up of a styling department at Ford coincided with Mr. Edsel Ford's overseeing the development of the Lincoln Zephyr." The Zephyr emerged as what New York's Museum of Modern Art later called "the first successfully designed streamlined car in America." That might have been a slight hyperbole, but the public did accept the Zephyr's "streamlining" after largely rejecting the Airflow's. The Zephyr wasn't an instant bestseller, but it did turn Lincoln around. Sales of the big

Eugene T. (Bob) Gregorie, under Edsel Ford, directed FoMoCo design from 1935 through World War II.

luxury Lincolns, however, continued downward. Lincoln's catalogue customs and the factory-bodied K-Models never recovered.

Bob Gregorie wasted no time setting up Ford's new design center, and it immediately became quite active and busy. "We acquired our head modeler, Dick Beneicke, from Briggs," recalled Gregorie, "but we got most of our other early people from within the company. Then gradually we started hiring some from outside.

In 1939, when this photo of design area was taken, Ford's styling staff was 1/9th the size of GM's, yet Gregorie and his people sometimes leapfrogged Harley Earl with cars like the low-grilled 1938 Lincoln Zephyr and the 1940 Continental.

It was probably a year before we had a staff of a dozen or so. We had Ed Martin; he was our coordinator between design and engineering. And we brought several men up from the Ford pattern shop and got them into clay modeling. They were very adept at that and understood body shapes." Except for Gregorie, the department still had no real designers, though.

Gregorie introduced the styling bridge to Ford, a device he used while doing ship-hull design. Automotive styling bridges were being used by Gordon Buehrig at Cord and possibly by a few bodymakers and coachbuilders. As full-sized clay models became common in the design industry, the earliest way to transfer shapes from clay to the wooden die-model masters was to make cardboard or Masonite templates. Templates, though, were time-consuming and difficult to cut accurately, so the styling bridge soon swept the industry. By taking vertical and horizontal "points" with the movable bridge, body surfaces could be logged on graph paper and also mathematically described in a table of "offsets," just as in ship-hull design. Ford's use of styling bridges preceded GM's and Chrysler's.

Since Ford now had its own styling staff, the company didn't need Briggs' or Murray's design proposals anymore. As a result, those departments within the body suppliers slowly atrophied, although Packard and Hudson continued to use them to some extent.

Styling Bridges

Gordon Buehrig was among first designers to use a styling bridge (left). He constructed this one at ACD in 1934 to take points off a rear-engined scale model. (Right) Technicians check wooden 1955 Dodge die model with templates before making steel roof dies.

Like so many design innovations, styling bridges started with shipbuilders. Gordon Buehrig used one in 1934 when he made a scale model of a rear-engined Auburn. Buehrig undoubtedly wasn't the first car designer to use a styling bridge, but his is the earliest automotive application we know about. Willys P. Wagner, working under Bob Gregorie at Ford in the 1930s, developed a series of aluminum, full-sized modeling bridges that were used to do the 1938 Ford lines. Ford built its own bridges at the Rouge plant.

The classic styling bridge consists of a big upside-down U that rides over a clay model on parallel rails. On Buehrig's bridge, dowels poked through the U and registered distances to the model itself. The main purpose was to record accurate surface measurements. The Ford bridge that Bill Wagner designed could take points at 1/10-inch intervals on any of the three-dimensional axes. It thereby became possible to make a table of "offsets": numbers that recorded exactly where the surface stood relative to a zero point and the fore/aft positioning of the bridge.

Early styling bridges served a number of functions. They were useful, as mentioned, to take measurements for drawings and to locate key engineering hardpoints (engines, axles, etc.) on clay models. They also made it possible to accurately reproduce one side of a model on the other side. They helped locate and space the templates used to transfer surface contours to die models. And they were occasionally used to drag sweeps along over the model surface.

In the mid 1940s, Fred Norton began to make "inspection angles" for use by engineering and tooling people in model and pattern shops. An inspection angle looks like an upside-down L that sticks out from a vertical column and can move up and down. The column moves fore and aft on tracks on a surface plate. The Norton Equipment Corp. made precision angles to check prototypes for surface accuracy, but they weren't intended as styling aids. GM modelers soon found, though, that to form a bridge, all they needed were two Norton inspection angles set on opposite sides of a model, connected with a crossbar. Norton angles were fairly inexpensive, reasonably accurate, easy to use and lightweight, built mostly of magnesium. Large angles came with wheels so they could be tipped and rolled out of the way to give a clear view of the model. But they did take two people to operate as a bridge.

In 1953, a company called Progressive Tool & Industries Co. supplied 12 new styling bridges to Ford. The bridge uprights had wheels that traveled in vee-shaped tracks attached to the sides of a surface plate below floor level. The Progressive crossbar and side scale holders allowed infinite movement. It was so easy to use that one person could now take points (measurements) quickly and accurately.

In 1963, an Italian engineer developed the so-called "coordinate measuring machine," or CMM. The CMM measured and recorded surfaces electronically. The aircraft industry started using CMMs in 1967, and Ford bought one soon afterward. The Ford CMM mounted a gantry (crossbar) on high rails supported on multiple pillars along either side of the model. The gantry contained an interchangeable probe or milling head that moved up, down and sideways. The head scanned a styling model and/or milled lines or surface into the clay. By recording the surface digitally, the data could be transmitted via wire or satellite to another CMM, which could then mill an identical surface on another model in any scale anywhere in the world. CMMs came and still come in a variety of sizes and are now used throughout the auto, aviation and aerospace industries.

Also in 1967, the German company, Schiess AG, supplied a refined type of

Ford ordered 12 "new type" bridges from Progressive in 1953. Each could be operated by one person.

The 1937 Ford became a design by Gregorie, borrowing conspicuously from the 1936 Lincoln Zephyr, especially its prow front end. The original 1937 Ford designs featured pod-mounted headlights that stuck out from the grille. Bill Wagner fought for fender-mounted headlamps and ultimately prevailed. So Ford got in-fender lamps three years before General Motors.

The 1938 Ford, the 1939 Mercury and all subsequent Ford products through the 1948 model year were done by Gregorie's small but growing Design Department. Gregorie referred to his area specifically as the Ford Design Department. (When George Walker took over, he renamed it the Ford Styling Office. After Walker retired, his successor, Gene Bordinat, called it the Ford Design Office.) John Najjar arrived in Gregorie's design department in the autumn of 1937 and recalled that there were four designers there at that time. Willys P. Wagner, who'd trained as an architect, did all the Ford bumpers, tail lamps, door handles, and hardware. Wagner also loved trucks and later designed most of Ford's trucks. John H. Walter designed all of Ford's instrument panels and steering wheels, while Bruno Kolt's specialties were grilles and sheetmetal surface development. The fourth designer, Walter Kruke, was a serious musician and bandleader, but he came to Ford with an interest in fabrics and ended up doing car interiors: trim, color, seats, upholstery and door panels.

Najjar also mentioned that Gregorie had a well-rounded design support group in 1937. Ed Martin did 1/10-scale drawings, charts and write-ups. Jim Lynch oversaw the wood and sheetmetal fabrication shop. Dick Beneicke directed the clay-modeling staff, and Burt Pugh handled plaster castings.

Najjar himself had been drawing cars since childhood and attended classes at the Henry Ford Training School as an apprentice machinist. One day, the elder Ford saw Najjar's sketches and sent him to work in engineering and eventually to talk to Bob Gregorie. Gregorie offered Najjar a job and, in time, he too became a designer. Soon after Najjar arrived, Gregorie similarly took some additional young apprentices under his wing, including Robert M. (Bob) Thomas, Eugene (Bud) Adams, Frank Francis, Emmett O'Rear and Benny Barbera.

"Bill Wagner had good ideas, but he couldn't illustrate them very well," commented Gregorie, "so we added Ross Cousins in 1938. What we wanted was a man who could take the ideas and put them into presentable form; who had the knack of drawing people and perspective as well as cars. Ross was very good at that. Then we got Martin Regitko [from Willoughby]. I set him up as our development draftsman. And Charlie Waterhouse came in from Waterhouse, the coachbuilder. This was 1938-39." Regitko did the department's full-sized body drafts and also acted as liaison with Ford engineering. He was a disciple of Edgard DeSmet (see page 132) and had taken DeSmet's course in planography.

Ross Cousins, who was 22 when he arrived at Ford in '38, mentioned in a recent interview that, "...I look back now and realize that we were all flying pretty much by the seat of our pants. Back then, car design was a cut-and-try thing, based on the T-square and sweeps." Cousins' personal mentors were designers Bill Wagner and Bruno Kolt, and Cousins observed that, "Guys like Wagner and Kolt were basically architects. They'd been trained in terms of scale and proportion, and I learned quite a lot from them. Bruno Kolt had a great sense of detail and knew how to make things work so they could be produced. Wagner was a little more philo-

bridge to Ford's design center in Cologne. This used an electric motor to move the bridge or the crossbar on recirculating roller bearings and hardened steel ways. The longitudinal axis used digital readouts.

Another related and handy piece of equipment was the "Portage layout machine." This was a lightweight device originally conceived for inspection and surface-recording duty (like the Norton and CMMs). It consisted of an upright aluminum column attached to a cast-iron base. It

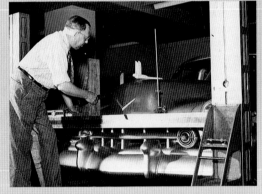

General Motors began using Norton angles fairly late; 1948 photo shows a modeler working on 1950-51 Cadillac.

looked like a cross-T, with a single horizontal arm traveling up and down and in and out over the model. GM began using manual Portage layout machines in the 1960s but later converted them to electronic scanners. In the early 1970s, Chrysler and GM used a version with all axes driven by electric stepper motors, controlled by computer. The purpose was to scan a clay model, take points electronically with a non-contact probe and record the surface that way.

More recent machines, again developed for inspection duty, are the CMMs from Tarus Products Corp. The Tarus "clay mill dual configuration machine" has heavy-duty columns with separate carriers and cross-T arms that travel like the Portage machines. Columns mount on either side of the surface plate and run fore and aft. Modelers again place two machines on opposite sides of a model to form a full bridge.

Tarus also makes a portable "five-axis" scanning and clay-milling machine that uses air pads so it can be moved around the studio. (There aren't really five axes, but that's what it's called.) Air pads lift the equipment a few thousandths of an inch so one person can push it from place to place. This Tarus clamps to existing studio rails or surface plates, is self-leveling and all controls travel with the machine. Offsets are registered automatically.

According to master modeler Fred Hoadley, the most advanced styling bridge to date was introduced by Al Lamerson in 1985. The Lamerson bridge is lightweight but very stiff and precise. It comes either with mechanical control plus electronic scanning or with full CMM scanning and milling capability.

Hoadley points out that in many instances, the car companies helped engineer these styling bridges. He also notes the differences between the two most commonly used model measuring systems. True styling bridges serve specifically for modelmaking inside the studios. They're easy to use and can quickly be moved away from the model to make it fully visible. The second type, CMM inspection equipment adapted to modeling, is cumbersome and gets in the way of viewing. CMMs are usually found in a room outside the design studios. Neither system can work accurately without stable surface plates, armatures, fixtures and positioning systems. (*Information from Frederick E. Hoadley's book,* Automobile Design Techniques, The Men, The Methods and the Materials, ©1996, *used with permission.*) ◆

Latest bridges like this DEA have scanner and clay-milling head built in, can send digital information anywhere in the world.

sophical, and between them they kept me on my toes."

Cousins also attributed the Ford look of that era as coming from the Lincoln Zephyr. "We kept borrowing from it, and that was quite evident when I came in 1938. The new Mercury was based on that same Zephyr form, as was the Ford and the rehashes of the Zephyr itself. The Continental was also basically a chopped Zephyr, so they all belonged to one big family, all with a very strong identity."

During the 1939 World's Fair in New York, Ford started a talent search to find new young designers. They held interviews inside the old Brewster factory at the foot of the Queensboro Bridge. Tucker Madawick, fresh out of Pratt, joined as a result of those interviews. Ford now had a core of able and gifted designers. "I believe it was Bob Gregorie who really gave me the confidence that this was a great opportunity," said Madawick in his Ford Archives oral reminiscence. "He had a warm personality. [The first time I met him, he was wearing] this beautiful glen plaid suit and buckskin suede shoes. Then that spring he would wear seersucker. This man was totally different. He had an air. He had something to sell, and you could feel it....

"He spent a lot of time on the water, and he would ask a certain group of us...three or four of us who would go down to the yard where he kept his boat, and he'd take us out...Duncan McRae,

Eddie Martin and myself." One day a diesel engine arrived at Ford for Bob Gregorie's boat, and he asked his designers to help install it. "She was a beautiful, beautiful ketch," recalled Madawick, "a 40-footer with two masts and a black hull." Together, Gregorie and this inner circle of young designers slipped the heavy engine into the hull and bolted it down.

When asked whether Ford was influenced by what GM was doing at that time, Gregorie answered, "No, we weren't. And I think that was one of the reasons we were able to develop a certain purity in our design. We never wanted to copy anything that was already in existence. I never had to go to Mr. Ford and say, 'Isn't this nice?' Matter of fact, I never heard Mr. Ford make a suggestion based on any other car. He'd never refer to the front end or any design feature of any other car. We...tried to create everything from our own imagination, keep it original. We agreed on that principle. That's why those Fords from the 1930s and '40s had such purity.

"I should mention, too, that Edsel Ford didn't care for groups. He didn't want to discuss design with half a dozen other people. He was very proud of his own judgment. He wanted to handle things personally and quietly. He made up his mind, and that was the last word. For me it was an ideal way to work. There were never any jealousies, no politics, no conflicts, no committee meetings. He just didn't care for that. I never heard him raise his voice."

Mr. DeSmet's Planography

Before electronic scanners and software came into common use to record and "sweeten" body surfaces, many autobody designers and draftsmen did the job by hand, working with a system called "planography." Planography was developed by Edgard Camiele DeSmet. Born in 1890, he apprenticed with Van den Plas in his native Belgium and came to this country in 1915. He worked in turn for Handley-Knight, Locomobile, Dodge, Briggs, Hudson and Willys-Overland.

DeSmet never explained planography in simple terms, perhaps because it wasn't simple. It was based on surface cross sections and flow lines. DeSmet described planography as a non-mathematical system for recording—on a blackboard or on paper—a non-geometric surface as developed by a stylist or clay modeler. But beyond just describing the surface, planography sweetened it so it flowed without a ripple. And that's what made it important.

In the late teens and early 1920s, as his colleagues began to notice the quality of DeSmet's two-dimensional interpretations of three-dimensional surfaces, they asked him to show them how to use planography. His reputation spread by word of mouth and, in 1922, while working at Dodge, DeSmet began to teach planography classes in his home. Each student paid $100. And because planography was difficult to explain and cost money to learn, DeSmet kept the details secret and swore his students to do the same. He never made the details public, never wrote a book and was vague in articles published by various engineering societies and trade magazines.

The results of planography, though, were obvious. By applying DeSmet's principles, a student was able to smooth a body surface and make it free of the dips and high spots that so often crept in with the use of templates and other non-electronic methods of recording surface. DeSmet used to point out that even a subtle .003-inch dip could destroy a highlight or the visual flow of a glossy body surface.

Planography evolved as the shapes of automobile bodies became more complicated. DeSmet upgraded his system in 1933 while working at Hudson and offered free refresher courses to all his graduates. Tuition soon rose to $250, and by the mid 1930s some car companies advertised specifically for DeSmet graduates. DeSmet went to Willys-Overland in 1936 and, while working there, began holding classes at the YMCA in Toledo (and later at the Detroit Y). About 100 men applied each year, of whom 60 were accepted. Courses by that time consisted of 24 two-hour sessions.

When accurate, full-sized clay models became common, planography lost favor, and modern electronic point-to-point recording systems made the process less important. Edgard DeSmet left Willys in 1956 but continued to teach until 1959. That year he turned his school over to his chief instructor, George Dolengowski. DeSmet passed away in 1969, by which time his alumni assocation numbered some 1100 members. The course is still offered today, and about 30 students take it each year. The present instructor, George Petsch, notes that the surface program in the CGS Design/Drafting software used by General Motors, the so-called Gordon Surface Operator, is based on DeSmet principles. ◆

After the original Lincoln Zephyr, the next important design detail—one that turned out to be extremely influential throughout the industry—was Bob Gregorie's 1938 facelift. The '38 Zephyr grille had an immediate and momentous effect on the entire styling establishment due to the fact that it pioneered the *horizontal*, as opposed to the predominantly vertical, radiator grille. After Gregorie's low 1938 Zephyr grille, every car manufacturer in America would shift from basically upright grille shapes to horizontal ones, early examples being the 1939 Buick, the 1940 Hudson and especially the 1941 Cadillac.

Paradoxically, the 1938 Zephyr's grille came in response to a mechanical problem; it was never conceived as the aesthetic trendsetter it quickly became. The problem had to do with the original Zephyr's tendency to overheat in very hot weather. The cooling fan on the Zephyr V-12 was mounted low on the front of the crankshaft, and with an upright radiator, it drew air through just a small portion of the core. "Out in Arizona and Texas," said Gregorie in his Ford reminiscences, "we were getting overheating complaints, and old Frank Johnson would come to me about twice a week and say, 'Bob, can't we do something about this to get more air through the radiator...?'"

Walking back to his office from lunch one day, Gregorie took note of a Zephyr chassis standing outside the engineering lab and was struck by its tall, skinny radiator and the inefficient placement of the fan. He measured the radiator core and found that it would easily fit sideways between the frame rails. He immediately had one of his people cobble up a horizontal core ahead of the engine and a low, horizontal opening for the grille. When Edsel Ford came in that afternoon, they ran the engine under full

The 1938 Lincoln Zephyr's low, horizontal grille created panic at GM A&C.

The new-for-1939 Mercury looked like a 1939 Ford on steroids.

The 1940 Ford became one more in a parade of Gregorie/Edsel styling hits.

load to see if they could make it overheat and found they couldn't. The crosswise radiator cooled beautifully.

Gregorie and his staff then got to work designing the low, catwhisker 1938 grille, still with a slight prow vee in it. Edsel agreed that the 1938 version looked infinitely better than the 1936 original, and that's how the 1938 Zephyr's horizontal grille came about.

From the beginnings of autodom, car design had moved steadily toward more horizontality, but until the 1938 Zephyr appeared, the fronts of American production automobiles stood basically upright. So the '38 Zephyr became a very important car. The case can be made that Gordon Buehrig's 1936 Cord 810 preceded the 1938 Zephyr as an earlier example of a horizontal grille, but most auto designers agree that the Cord didn't influence mainstream auto design much at that time. The 810 stood on a pedestal. Stylists admired it and loved to redo it in sketch and model form, but very little of its influence showed up in production until much later, in cars like the 1966 Oldsmobile Toronado and 1978 Dodge Mirada. There's also the opinion that the 810 Cord fostered the "no-grille" school of design (e.g. 1941 Chrysler Thunderbolt and 1963 Studebaker Avanti) rather than the horizontal school.

However, as noted in Chapter 7, when Harley Earl, who was in Europe in late 1937, saw a photo of Gregorie's low 1938 Zephyr grille, it gave him quite a jolt. Earl had resisted low grilles and catwalk cooling, but now, following Gregorie's lead, he quickly went to horizontal grilles for all GM cars. Not only that but Earl also overruled Bill Knudsen's "no-fender-mounted headlights" edict and, by 1940, all GM cars had those as well. The move from vertical to horizontal in American car design had begun.

(It's noteworthy that European stylists didn't take to the horizontal grille idea until the 1950s, and some, like Mercedes, Rolls-Royce and Bentley, resist it even today. In this country, LaSalle and Packard had an identity problem in switching from their thin, tall grilles to something lower and more fashionable. Designer/author Jeff Godshall points out that GM didn't have to come up with a solution for the LaSalle, because they discontinued the nameplate after 1940. Packard, on the other hand, waged a losing battle against verticality until 1951, when designer John Reinhart finally managed to broaden and flatten Packard's traditional ox-yoke grille. The occasional vertical grilles that popped up in the 1950s, like Dick Teague's 1956 Packard Predictor and Roy Brown's 1958 Edsel, didn't meet with much public approval.)

Throughout the late 1930s, Edsel strove to give the Ford Motor Co. a fuller product line that would match General Motors' and Chrysler's market range; in Alfred Sloan's words, "a car for every purse and purpose." The Lincoln Zephyr provided a model in the Buick Century/Chrysler Royal price range, but even in 1938 Ford had nothing to challenge the Pontiac Eight, Oldsmobile and DeSoto. So Edsel encouraged his father to let him create what at first came to be called the "Ford Mercury," later produced as the 1939 Mercury. The Mercury would fit into the price gap between the Ford and the Zephyr.

The 1939 Mercury owed its success totally to styling, and it looked basically like an overfed 1939 Ford. Both cars took their styling cues from the '38 Zephyr. The family resemblance was extreme but calculated. Briggs supplied the Mercury's bodies, and the 1939 Mercury sedan-coupe had an elegant roof treatment plus elements borrowed from the 1938 Cadillac 60-Special: two-piece doors and arched windows with thin chrome surrounds.

By 1939-40, Gregorie had built his staff up to about 50 people, including secretaries, shop workers, sweepers, etc. Considering its size, especially compared with GM Styling's 450 or so, the sheer volume of work that Gregorie and Edsel turned out was amazing. They created all the yearly styling changes and all body styles for the standard and deluxe Ford cars, the Mercury, the Lincoln, Ford trucks, Ford tractors and buses, all interiors and some dealer accessories. To produce so much consistently good work gives testament to Gregorie's and Edsel's abilities as both designers and administrators.

Ford styling reached a high in 1939-40. The outstanding car of those years, without question, was the Lincoln Continental. This design became the jewel in Edsel Ford's crown. The Continental's artistry stands as a lasting monument to his and Bob Gregorie's talent.

Bob Gregorie affirmed in numerous conversations that the Continental idea went back to that 1934 Ford phaeton built in the Trimotor plant. "After that, Edsel Ford and I would occasionally talk about making a special little sports car," recalled Gregorie. They initially thought about basing it on the Ford chassis, but they ran into the problem of disrupting the plant routine. Sorensen was very much against anything that might interfere with any of Ford's production lines. Next, Edsel and Gregorie talked about making the sportster a Mercury, but that involved the same disruptions.

"Then one day in November 1938, Mr. Edsel Ford and I had another conversation, just to pass the time," continued Gregorie. "We again talked about some car we might build in the future. And then it occurred to me...I figured, Well, we've got the Zephyr, with a 12-cylinder engine, and we've got one whole bay empty in the Lincoln plant. This was the bay along Livernois Avenue where the Lincoln craftsmen used to finish up the K-Model custom bodies as they came in. Also we had a nucleus of very fine body people at Lincoln—a couple of hundred, really—left over from the K, who could do beautiful custom painting and trim work. By this time, of course, the big Lincolns were almost gone; no one was ordering them anymore.

"So one day after lunch, I sketched up a profile of this car that later became the Continental. I did the whole thing in about an hour. I put a sheet of vellum over a 1/10-scale side-view blueprint drawing in the Zephyr sales handbook and sketched in the Continental with a yellow crayon pencil. That original sketch showed the extended, lowered hood, the convertible top and the little squared-off trunk with the spare tire on the back. In the actual car, we lengthened the Zephyr hood about seven inches, stretched the front fender and added to the bottom of it. We moved the passenger compartment back, sectioned the whole body three or four inches and shortened the trunk.

The jewel in Edsel Ford's crown had to be the original Lincoln Continental, conceived in 1939 and built initially as his personal car. Edsel soon put Lincoln craftsmen to work handmaking the 404-car "production" run for 1940. Job One was a sectioned Zephyr convertible with stretched hood, cowl and fenders, abbreviated trunk and hallmark bustle spare tire. Early Continentals contained lots of lead, because Henry didn't authorize body dies until 1941.

"Well, he [Edsel] came into my office after lunch, looked at the sketch and smiled, and he said, 'Don't change a line on it! How soon can we build it?'

"This was in November 1938, and he wanted the car for his holiday down in Florida in March, so that gave us about three months. We went to work, and Eugene (Bud) Adams made a little 1/10-scale clay model, which was about 20 inches long; painted it up in Mr. Ford's favorite gunmetal grey. The model had wide whitewalls and nice little chrome bumpers on it. It took us four or five days to finish. Edsel came in, looked at the model and said to us, 'Let's not change a thing! I wouldn't change a line on it.'"

Ross Cousins remembered the day Gregorie presented the 1/10-scale model to Edsel. Cousins had made two airbrush renderings of the proposed Continental. One was a four-door sedan version with an airplane in the background. The other was a coupe in a European seaside setting. The model and renderings formed a tableau. "Edsel came in," recalled Cousins, "and we were all standing there. It was one of the few times I saw him burst out in a smile. He was a reserved man, not emotional, but he sure did smile that day."

Gregorie resumed his narrative by saying, "We never did make

a full-sized clay. After the 1/10-scale clay model, I just turned the offsets over to Martin Regitko, my head draftsman, and he made a quick paper draft. The draft went right over to the Lincoln plant, and they hammered the car out by hand; didn't have any hammer forms or anything; just did it all by eye.

"Anyway, the long and short of it...we finished the car and shipped it down to Florida. After Edsel had driven it around Palm Beach for about two weeks, he called me up and said, 'Bob, I can sell a thousand of these things! You better get over to the Lincoln plant and talk with Robbie [the superintendent] and see what we can do about a limited-production version; set up some Artz presses and whatnot.'

"And he said, 'Meantime, you'd better start a second car right away,' handbuilt to work out the mechanical details like the column shifter, which was just going into production that year. I went over and told Robbie, 'The boss wants a second one of these,' and Robbie said, 'Oh God, not that again!'

"At that point, I talked to Mr. Ford about the advantages of building the car as a Lincoln. For one thing, we could get more money for it that way. Also, we had the chassis, the frame, suspension system, engine, steering gear and all the mechanical parts.

We weren't interfering with any Ford production. We had all the components and the workmen right there in the Lincoln plant, so it was a natural. It just fell together."

It was fortunate, too, that the Continental arrived at precisely the time when Edsel was shutting down the Lincoln Model K operation. Not only was the timing good, but the Continental came at that moment when Lincoln needed a new line leader—something spectacular and special to capture the public's attention and get buyers into Lincoln showrooms.

In 1940, the price of a new Continental was $2840. There weren't any real body dies at first, so the full run of 1940 cars—350 cabriolets (convertibles) and 54 coupes—were all handmade by the same craftsmen who'd finished and trimmed the K-Model Lincolns. The Continental coupe, by the way, was introduced six months after the cabriolet and cost $100 less. The coupe was literally a hardtop convertible, its steel roof welded to the cabriolet body. For 1941, with the Continental now a fixture in the Lincoln line, Henry Ford released the money for body dies, and the later cars had much less lead filler.

The Continental's name came about in an equally relaxed way. Gregorie and Edsel often got together to critique pictures of the latest European designs. Edsel referred to these as "continental" cars. The Continental had what Edsel considered continental styling, so the name stuck.

Continental bodies, along with the Zephyr, were all new for 1940, and 1942 marked the first major facelift, with squared fenders and a massive over/under double grille. The war suspended all U.S. auto production, and Edsel passed away on May 26, 1943. He'd had surgery for ulcers, was diagnosed soon afterward as having stomach cancer but also fell victim to undulant fever caused by unpasteurized milk. (Many sources say this milk came from "the Ford dairy herd," implying that Henry Ford indirectly caused Edsel's death. However, Edsel also kept cows at his Haven Hill retreat outside Detroit, and he drank raw milk from that herd, too.) The cancer spread and soon proved fatal.

Without Edsel to champion it, production of the first-generation Continental ended after 1948. Sales volume remained low, and it never had made money. Even so, Hollywood movie studios favored Continentals and kept fleets on hand for guests and stars. Among those who personally owned and drove Continentals were Clark Gable, Ronald Reagan, Mickey Rooney and Rita Hayworth.

In 1951, the Museum of Modern Art chose to show a 1941 Lincoln Continental as one of eight cars that represented excellence in automotive design (see sidebar, page 247). And in 1959, 100 of the world's leading designers, architects and teachers of design were surveyed by the Illinois Institute of Technology ranked the Continental sixth among the 100 best-designed commercial products of all time.

Pearl Harbor and then Edsel's death transformed everything at Ford. Gregorie's staff was cut to 25 people. Like GM, Ford's remaining stylists designed camouflage, did some work on military trucks and also modeled aircraft turrets for the bombers Ford built at Willow Run. Gregorie sandwiched work on postwar cars between his wartime assignments.

The postwar automobile designs that Gregorie's staff produced during the war show lines and shapes that stylists felt universally would be popular after the war: envelope bodies with basically heavy, doughy fenders, roofs and hoods—the "inverted bathtub" school so common at that time.

With Edsel gone and the elder Henry Ford now too senile to effectively run the company, Edsel's 25-year-old son, Henry Ford

Edsel served his father well as the company's setter of taste and fashion standards. Henry soon came to respect Edsel's styling decisions.

II, received an emergency discharge from the Navy in Aug. 1943. According to Bob Gregorie, "...he came in the back door of my office, and he said, 'Father [Edsel Ford] told me everything starts here.' And we had quite a discussion. We drove over to the Lincoln plant, and I told him there were some problems over there getting things going. We talked to Robbie over there, but after that he [Henry Ford II] never showed much interest in designing a car; I mean it was difficult to....

"I couldn't assume full responsibility for this thing, and there was no one left...to back me up as far as okaying this, okaying that, which his father had always done. I thought [Henry II would] more or less take up where his father left off, but he wasn't [interested]. He acted bored with it [styling]."

In that first conversation with Henry II, Gregorie became disappointedly aware that he'd lost his patron. The younger Ford expressed no particular interest in styling and, even if he'd wanted to take on Edsel's previous role, there was so much confusion and unfinished business within the company that Henry II would not have had time.

By mid 1943, the elder Henry Ford, aged 80, was wrestling the demons of senility. With Edsel gone, he seemed to be in favor of letting his security chief, Harry Bennett, take charge of Ford Motor Co. Bennett began manipulating Henry Ford to purge potential rivals, among them Sorensen and Sheldrick. During these 1943 goings-on, Gregorie's department came under engineering, a move instigated by Joe Galamb. Gregorie protested and, in Sept. 1943, found himself out of a job.

To replace Gregorie, Galamb brought over Tom Hibbard, who'd been doing war work in Ford's Rouge plant. This was the same Tom Hibbard who'd co-founded LeBaron, worked with Darrin in Paris and for Harley Earl during the early and late 1930s. Gregorie, meanwhile, opened a private industrial design firm in Detroit.

Six months later, in Apr. 1944, Henry Ford II phoned Gregorie and asked him to come back. Henry II offered Gregorie his old job but at a better salary. What about Galamb, asked Gregorie. Henry II immediately phoned Galamb and fired him. Gregorie was shocked. What about Tom Hibbard, he asked more quietly. Hibbard, said Henry II, had agreed to become Gregorie's assistant.

With some trepidation, Gregorie accepted and promptly set about facelifting what had been the 1942 Ford, Mercury and Lincoln, transforming them into what became the 1946

Backstops and Patrons

Any accomplished head of a corporate design department owes at least part of his success to a patron—someone high up in the company. At Ford, Bob Gregorie's patron had always been Edsel Ford. After Edsel died, Gregorie couldn't forge a similar relationship with Henry II nor with Ernie Breech or any other patron at Ford Motor Co. Gregorie thus never regained the status he'd enjoyed under Edsel.

Ernie Breech favored George Walker and later backed the incoming ex-GM designers, John Oswald, George Snyder and Gene Bordinat. Walker eventually won Henry II's support but never William Clay Ford's. Henry II and Bill Ford both favored Gene Bordinat and Don Kopka in their turns. Ford's most recent design vice president, Jack Telnack, won the support of William O. (Bill) Bourke and Donald E. Petersen while working at Ford of Australia and Britain. Petersen later became Ford's chairman.

At General Motors, Harley Earl enjoyed the patronage of board chairman Alfred P. Sloan Jr. Sloan actively backed Earl on any number of occasions, and Sloan's protectorship held one of the keys to Earl's great success as a designer.

Ironically, Earl's successor, William L. Mitchell, had no patron in GM's highest ranks. He and General Motors chairman John F. Gordon hated each other. Mitchell thus had to rely on GM's divisional general managers for patronage. Edward N. Cole of Chevrolet was as high-up a backstop as Mitchell ever got, but Mitchell was also friendly with John Beltz of Oldsmobile and Pete Estes at Pontiac. After Mitchell retired, Irvin W. Rybicki's patron was GM president Howard Kehrl, and Rybicki's successor, Charles M. Jordan, had Roger Smith and then Robert Stempel and Lloyd Reuss on GM's 14th floor.

At Chrysler during the 1930s, Ray Dietrich nominally enjoyed Walter P. Chrysler's backing at first, but not enough of it, because Dietrich couldn't break through the stone walls of engineering. Virgil M. Exner's patrons at Chrysler in the 1950s and '60s were presidents K.T. Keller and Tex Colbert. Elwood Engel, who followed Exner, was a personal friend of Chrysler chairman George Love and also enjoyed the patronage of president Lynn Townsend. Richard G. Macadam's links to the top were weaker than Engel's. Don DeLaRossa's backer was the man who brought him to Chrysler: Lee Iacocca. Tom Gale, Chrysler's current design v.p., likewise enjoyed Iacocca's support and presently (1996) has the backing of Chrysler president Bob Lutz. It's an interesting political phenomenon, the patronage system. No design executive can succeed long without a strong and dedicated patron. ◆

Here's what Gregorie envisioned as the full-sized postwar Ford. Tooling had already begun, and when Ernie Breech digested this car's size and weight, he proclaimed that it might make a good Mercury but never a feasible Ford.

models. He also resumed work on two all-new postwar Fords, a small Light Car on a 98-inch wheelbase that Ford's marketing manager, Jack Davis, thought the company ought to have--since General Motors was known to be developing a small postwar car --and the standard Ford on a 114-inch wheelbase.

The war ended, yet Ford's tribulations continued. In Sept. 1945, Eleanor Ford, Edsel's widow, joined forces with Clara, Henry's wife. The two women gave the senile senior Ford an ultimatum: Either fire Harry Bennett and make Henry II president or she (Eleanor) would sell her 41.6% of the family stock. Henry, darkly able to comprehend, didn't want strangers taking over Ford, so he gave Bennett the sack and elevated the 28-year-old Henry II to the presidency. Henry II now found himself in the unenviable position of trying to shore up a company that was losing as much as $10 million a month.

Realizing he couldn't save Ford alone, HF-II hired the best business talent money could buy. Immediately after the war, the so-called "Whiz Kids" wired Henry II and offered themselves as a package deal. The Whiz Kids were 10 bright young ex-Air Force officers, all of whom held advanced degrees in economics and business management. They were Robert McNamara, Charles (Tex) Thornton, Ben D. Mills, Arjay Miller, George Moore, W.R. Anderson, C.E. Bosworth, J.E. Lundy, Francis C. Reith and James O. Wright.

Ford next lured former GM vice president Ernest R. Breech away from Bendix Aviation in June 1946 and empowered him to do whatever he had to do to save the company. Breech was a pep-

Initially conceived at Studebaker, the 1949 Ford ended up saving the company. After Walker submitted "his" design, Gregorie's modelers made a wooden armature (top left), then did their own full-sized clay to Youngren's specs (top center). Walker's group made a rival clay, first with a plain grille and then with Joe Oros' spinner. Elwood Engel set the tail lamps horizontal, and that became the 1949 Ford. Company also toyed with a fastback. The 1949 line proved very popular and set the Ford body format for a decade.

pery little man with a mustache and great presence, and he simply took charge. He essentially ran Ford until Henry II became mature and confident enough to make major decisions himself.

After stopping the flow of red ink, Breech convinced Henry II that Ford Motor Co. should rebuild itself along GM lines. With HF-II's okay, Breech hired Harold T. Youngren, former chief engineer of Oldsmobile and at that time chief engineer with Borg-Warner Corp. Youngren took the same title at Ford and quickly put together a staff of 120 additional engineers, many of them from GM.

Like every other U.S. automaker, Ford yearned to get a new, restyled postwar car on the road as quickly as possible. Since the company had no formal product plan, Gregorie's Light Car and the rebodied, full-sized Ford were both being tooled and well along toward becoming 1949 production models by the time Breech arrived. When Breech heard that two postwar cars were already in tooling, he decided that, first chance he got, he'd go down to Gregorie's area in the engineering building and see what they looked like. So when Youngren arrived, they walked down to Ford Styling together to check out the full-sized clays and body drafts of the new 114-inch-wheelbase Ford.

One look was all they needed. They called in Henry II, and then Breech told Gregorie, "It's too big!" Youngren did a few quick calculations and concluded that there was no way Gregorie's 114-inch Ford could compete with any conceivable Chevrolet or Plymouth. Gregorie's car would be far too heavy and thus too expensive to be sold in that price range.

"They got all panicky," recalled Gregorie in his reminiscences, "and they got one of those little Studebakers out there—the double-ended [1947] Studebaker. 'Now that's the size car we want.'"

Unlike Henry II, Breech did take a keen interest in styling; "Too damn much at times," said designer Robin Jones. In looking around Gregorie's department and talking to his people, Breech noticed that the staff was made up largely of men whose heyday had been the golden age of classic coachbuilding: Tom Hibbard, Hermann Brunn, Charlie Waterhouse, John Dobben, Martin Regitko and, when you came right down to it, Gregorie himself. Could designers, managers and modelers of that era really design cars for the 1950s? Breech thought not and, perhaps even more to the point, he didn't like Gregorie's direct access to Henry II. Breech wanted more control of styling than that.

The immediate problem, though, was the Light Car and

Gregorie's 114-inch Ford. Since both were partially tooled and the company already had money tied up in them, Breech, Youngren and HF-II decided that the Gregorie Ford should become the 1949 Mercury. Gregorie's proposal for the 1949 Mercury, which had not yet gone into tooling, would become the 1949 Lincoln Cosmopolitan. The Cosmopolitan would compete with Cadillac, Packard and Chrysler Imperial, but there would also be a smaller 1949 Lincoln, one based on the 1949 Mercury (previously Ford) body shell. This smaller Lincoln would sell in the Buick/Chrysler price range.

Theoretically, then, Breech had cleverly turned the tooling crisis around. Ford would now have a model for every purse and purpose, just like GM and Chrysler. And the future Mercury would have a visual link with the Lincoln rather than being a pumped-up Ford as in the past. (GM's postwar small car never materialized and, with that threat gone, Ford shipped the tooling for the Light Car to France, where it became the postwar Ford Vedette V-8-60.)

But the question also remained: What to do about developing a viable 1949 Ford? Where was that design going to come from? As Breech drove home that night, he prayed for divine guidance. Next morning, according to Ford historians Allan Nevins and Frank Hill, he received the answer: "Start afresh!" At that morning's policy committee meeting in Dearborn, Breech announced, "I have a vision. We start from scratch. We spend no time or money phonying up the old Ford, because this organization will be judged...on the next car it produces, and it had better be a new one. So we'll have a crash program, as if in wartime."

The crash program included bringing in Breech's golfing buddy, industrial designer George W. Walker. Breech and Walker had met years earlier on opposite sides of a plan to develop an airport along Eight-Mile Road north of Detroit. Walker favored the airport, Breech didn't. But Walker, an inveterate joiner, bumped into Breech again later at the Grosse Pointe Country Club. They played golf together and formed a friendship.

Soon after deciding to start afresh, Breech phoned Walker and invited him to become a consultant not just to Ford Motor Co. but specifically to Bob Gregorie. Gregorie, said Breech, needed help. He also told Walker that if he took this job, he (Walker) would soon find himself $5 million richer.

No one had talked to Gregorie about all this and by the time Gregorie heard of Walker's imminent arrival, it was too late to say anything. Gregorie mentioned afterward that, "...the last thing in

Walker's group submitted these models as possible 1949 Lincoln (left) and Continental, but Gregorie's designs were already tooled, so those became the 1949 Mercury, Lincoln and Cosmo.

the world I needed was an outside consultant," and the two designers, predictably, did not get along. Besides, the assignment wasn't really for Walker's group to *help* Gregorie. It amounted, as everyone knew from the beginning, to a contest: Walker versus Gregorie to design a clean-sheet 1949 Ford.

The ground rules were these: Ford's chief engineer, Harold Youngren, would draw up "the package," including weight, seating dimensions, etc. The specifications were all very straightforward except for one. A milk can had to fit upright inside the trunk. Based on Youngren's package, Walker and Gregorie would produce sketches and clay models suggesting a lighter, tighter, less bulky 1949 Ford; something more along the lines of the 1947 Studebaker. Ford's product committee, consisting of Henry Ford II, his brother Benson, Ernie Breech, Youngren and a few others, would choose among these designs. Then, as a final step, Walker and Gregorie would each work up full-sized clays, and the product committee would choose again. The winner would be either Walker's model or Gregorie's or an amalgam of the two.

The design that won Round One came indirectly from, of all places, Studebaker. A designer named Dick Caleal, who'd worked for Raymond Loewy on Loewy's Studebaker account in South Bend, had just been let go. Bob Bourke, his boss, had not wanted to fire Caleal, but Loewy ordered him to trim the staff. Bourke felt bad about letting Dick go but had no choice. Caleal went to Detroit and interviewed with George Walker. Walker told him he'd give Caleal a job if he could come up with a design for the 1949 Ford.

Caleal said he'd do it and went home to Mishawaka, near South Bend. He dropped in on his old Loewy buddies at Studebaker, all abuzz with the prospect of working for Walker, and his Studebaker friends got excited along with him. Caleal then asked Bob Bourke whether some of the Loewy people could help him make a quarter-scale car model, because he had only three weeks to report back to Walker. Bourke saw no problem. The guys could help Caleal in the evening.

"Could I," Caleal then asked Bourke, "borrow some clay? I'll pay you back." Sure, said Bourke. "How about a quarter-scale modeling buck?" Bourke gave him a buck and then asked where Dick planned to do the work. On my kitchen table, Caleal answered. And what will you use to heat the clay? The kitchen oven. Bourke felt sympathy for Caleal and okayed lending him the supplies.

Over the course of the next few weeks, designers and modelers from Loewy's Studebaker studio came over to Caleal's house in Mishawaka and went to work. Everyone liked Caleal and they wanted him to succeed with Walker. Joe Thompson, the ex-Cadillac modeler who'd helped Edsel Ford with the 1928 Model A, kicked off the modeling on the first evening. Bob Bourke dropped by to make styling suggestions, and Bob Koto (formerly with Briggs) also did some design and model development. Additional sculpting was done by John Lutz, also previously with General Motors, and John A. Bird, who later became GM's director of sculpting. Bird felt Bob Koto did most of the actual design work, although Bourke conceived the front end.

The 1949 Ford model, then, evolved as a group project, a team effort, and how much actually ended up being Caleal's creation remains controversial. Opinions vary widely. Caleal justifiably took credit, though, for getting the design assignment and seeing

it through. Caleal made no secret that the model was being done for Walker, but he didn't mention the make of car it was intended to become. Loewy's sculptors placed four little squares on the hood where the letters of the nameplate would go. "We thought it was going to be for Nash," said modeler John Bird. "We never dreamed Ford would go outside for design help."

Caleal carefully loaded the quarter-scale model into a borrowed car and drove to Walker's office in Detroit. When he showed Walker the model, Walker was reportedly stunned. "Perfect," he said. Caleal then drove back to Mishawaka and had Koto help him make a final plaster cast of the model. The plaster version was painted blue and mounted on blue velvet. Caleal's model, along with drawings and scale clays by Joe Oros, Elwood Engel and Bob Gregorie's people, went on display in Walker's offices for the Ford product committee to vote on. Needless to say, Caleal's model won.

The competition now progressed to Round Two, which meant that both styling groups—Walker's and Gregorie's—would make full-sized clays conforming to Youngren's package. Walker's group based their clay largely on the Caleal quarter-scale model, and Gregorie's staff used the same package but pursued a theme of their own. The idea was to base the final vote on aesthetics alone.

Since Walker didn't have enough space in his office to do a full-sized clay, Ford lent him an area inside the Dearborn engineering labs. Gregorie's designers were now locked into their studio complex at one end of that same building, with a guard posted at the door. At the other end were Oros, Engel, Caleal and their own modeling team, all behind similarly locked and guarded doors. Theoretically, neither group would be allowed to see the other's work. As it happened, though, one night Youngren did let Gregorie walk through the Walker studio, although Oros and Engel never got a similar opportunity. Oros mentioned this to Walker but felt that it didn't matter, because Gregorie didn't have time to change his model anyway.

As it turned out, the Caleal model served just as the basis for the larger iteration, because in going from quarter to full size, the Walker group had to make a fair number of changes. First, they raised the Caleal model's roof to conform to package for better entry and seating. Second, the cowl height needed to be changed to accommodate the engine. Third, the trunk needed more height for the milk can. And finally, the beltline had to be changed for manufacturing reasons. (Fred Hoadley, the Ford master modeler, stresses that anytime a styling model goes from a smaller scale to full size, the modeler has to make aesthetic adjustments. The reason a model needs to be adjusted is this: When a person views a scale model, he's nearly always looking down from above, so he sees the car from an abnormal angle. Looking down tends to make the model appear lower and more stretched out. So when exactly those same dimensions and proportions are blown up to full size in clay, the resulting model looks too tall and too short. A good modeler recognizes this and compensates to preserve the designer's aesthetic intent, and that's one reason a good modeler is so important to the design process.)

When both Walker's and Gregorie's models were judged, the Walker model won again. But approval called for a number of additional detail changes. The 1949 Ford grille, which apparently had a spinner in the Caleal model, went to a straight horizontal center bar during the scaling up process. This was reworked by Joe Oros and ended up with a round central spinner. Oros did this spinner on a full-sized buck off the main model, and one of Ford's engineers at first thought the spinner would block airflow to the radiator. Oros had a mockup built and tested it in a windtunnel, showing there was no problem with engine cooling.

Oros and Engel collaborated on the 1949 Ford's instrument panel, whose theme repeated the grille spinner with a single dial ahead of the driver and wide, vee-tipped raised sections stretching out horizontally. One of the subtlest and cleverest touches of the interior, though, was Gil Spear's small depiction—under clear plastic on the inside door molding beneath the front windows—of a futuristic car. Only the deluxe Fords had this, and it captured the spirit of Ford's entirely modern, youthful design and undoubtedly helped sell some cars.

Elwood Engel modified the rear of the Walker full-sized clay by turning the originally vertical tail lamps 90° and then adding gentle windsplits that faded forward into the rear fender. At this stage of the full-sized clay, the elder Fords, Henry and Clara, were given a tour of the Walker studio, and Oros, who was present, got the feeling that Henry liked the design. There's an oft-repeated story about Henry or Clara yanking the door handle off the clay model, but Oros said this took place with an entirely different car, not the 1949 Ford.

With the Walker model nearly finished, word came down from Ernie Breech that Walker's consultancy contract had been fulfilled and his services would no longer be needed. The parting was oddly amicable, especially considering that George Walker hadn't gotten anywhere near the $5 million Breech had mentioned initially. However, Breech assured Walker that there would be more Ford design work in the future.

Soon after Walker's crew left, chief engineer Harold Youngren, who'd already brought a number of GM engineers to Ford, likewise started hiring former General Motors designers. Breech placed Gregorie under Youngren and at the same time authorized Youngren to start hiring outside designers to add to Gregorie's staff. It was all part of Breech's plan to remake Ford in GM's image.

This latest assault on Gregorie's authority, the new constraints of working under Ford engineering—along with a painful divorce—got to be too much. Recognizing Gregorie's frustration, HF-II doubled his salary in an effort to keep him on, but on Dec. 15, 1946, Gregorie went to Henry II's office and quietly resigned. "I think I'd be an obstacle in the path of this changeover arrangement," Gregorie told HF-II, "and if it's all right with you, why, we'll part good company." He again recommended that Tom

Hibbard take his place, and Hibbard did take over as director of Ford styling for a short time, starting on Jan. 1, 1947.

The first outside designers Youngren hired were Gene Bordinat and Don DeLaRossa from GM. Soon afterward, John Oswald arrived. Oswald had previously been with Oldsmobile, and Youngren now made him the head of Ford's restructured design department under engineering. At that point, Hibbard resigned.

John Oswald's strength lay in body engineering, but he was also an able designer whose experience went back to the Duesenberg J and the L-29 Cord. In Apr. 1947, Oswald recruited George Snyder to become his assistant. Snyder began his career at Brewster, then went to GM and became studio chief at Oldsmobile. There he'd done the 1937, 1939 and 1946-48 Olds front ends, among others. Snyder was a crackerjack designer, but moody and given to drink. Harley Earl fired him after the war, wouldn't take him back, and Snyder was pleased when Oswald offered him a job at Ford.

Other designers brought in from GM included Bob Maguire, Dave Ash, Gil Spear, Rollin Taylor, Frank Hershey and Bob Weiland—all very good men. Two first-rate modelers, Charles and Leonard Stobar, came over, too, Leonard as head modeler in the Ford studio and Charlie to take charge of overall modeling and shop operations.

Gene Bordinat mentioned in his reminiscences that the GM newcomers, under Oswald and Snyder, finished up the few remaining details of the 1949 Ford, logged the surface measurements and released the body for production.

Just as the Zephyr had saved Lincoln, the 1949 Ford saved the entire company. That first-generation postwar Ford and the 1949 Mercury/Lincoln were obviously cut from very different bolts. The 1949 Ford, while not revolutionary in the overall scheme of auto design, ended up being aesthetically agreeable and highly successful commercially. And it brought back some of the clean, unfussy styling of the pre-1941 Ford products.

The 1949's most eye-catching detail was Joe Oros' spinner grille, which lent some interest to a pleasant but otherwise neutral form. The spinner put life and character into the front end and provided a focus. It also gave the car instant identity. The 1949 Ford's first point of importance was that it saved the company and, second, that it set the direction and theme for all three nameplates for years to come. Ford reworked the spinner and used variations through 1954.

Walker's group was now gone, Gregorie and Hibbard likewise, and Oswald was trying to meld the new with old members of Ford's design team. There was no purge, and among those who stayed on from the Gregorie era were Bill Wagner, Hermann Brunn, Charlie Waterhouse, Ted Hobbs (who'd come over from GM earlier), John Najjar, Fred Hoadley, Dick Beneicke, Bruno

Gregorie added interest to the 1949 Mercury bodyside with the "kickdown" crease on the door (above). Smaller 1949 Lincoln shared Mercury body shell, while the Cosmopolitan used a similar-looking but totally different body. Lincoln's recessed headlights were originally supposed to be hidden. When that became too expensive, Gregorie chromed the tunnels and gave the tail lamps a similar treatment. Cosmopolitan fastback was offered only in 1949.

George W. Walker
THE CELLINI OF CHROME

When *Time* magazine did a cover story on Ford design vice president George Walker in Nov. 1957, they called him "The Cellini of Chrome." Walker loved the sound and sparkle of that title. It compared him with the great 16th-century Italian sculptor and silversmith. But the *Time* editors also had in mind Cellini the famous sexual acrobat, another area in which Walker excelled.

If Bordinat and others can be believed, Walker boasted of bedding his high-school English teacher, and his trysts on the $30,000, inch-deep, black lambswool carpet of his private office at Ford were legendary, especially after the installers had to keep coming back to cut out soiled spots and replace them with plugs of fresh carpet.

George William Walker was born on May 22, 1897 in Chicago. His mother was an Oklahoman and part Cherokee, a fact in which Walker took great pride. His father, a conductor for the Erie Railroad, kept moving the family as his routes changed. As a result, George's schooling suffered. But he grew up big and husky and, at 15, became a semi-pro football player. He later played professionally with Jim Thorpe for the Cleveland Panthers. His main source of income to age 27 was football.

After many broken fingers and a flattened nose (later fixed), Walker decided to take advantage of an artistic bent. He attended the Cleveland School of Art and also attended the Otis Art Institute. After graduating, Walker opened an illustration studio in Cleveland and began doing artwork for bodymaker Baker-Raulang as well as for ad agencies, a paint company and Dura Corp., manufacturers of automotive door hardware.

Walker's business success, both at this early stage of his career and later, rested on his extremely upbeat and jovial personality. He was outgoing and vital and had great powers of persuasion. People just plainly tended to like him. He also carefully crafted a long string of social and business connections by becoming a member of dozens of clubs and fraternal organizations. He prided himself on being a 32nd-degree Mason and belonging to country clubs all over America. As president of Detroit's elite Recess Club (1939-49) high atop of the Fisher Building, Walker controlled who could join and who couldn't, and when a friend of someone like Harley Earl or Harlow Curtice applied, it gave Walker another of his many bargaining chips.

Walker lucked out in the timing of his career, because American business was just growing style conscious in the late 1920s and early '30. He came in on the coattails of industrial design's founding fathers, people like Raymond Loewy, Walter Dorwin Teague, Norman Bel Geddes and Henry Dreyfuss. After opening an office near GM headquarters in Detroit's New Center Building, Walker decided he needed to put his name before the Detroit business community, so he hired a publicist. His publicist did such a good job that Walker found himself famous even in Europe.

Not that he wasn't a skillful and moti-

vated designer, but his real strengths lay along commercio-political lines. And he also had a knack for hiring the right people. He soon built a sizable clientele, including Burroughs office machines, Admiral radios, International Harvester, Packard and Nash-Kelvinator. To service his automotive accounts, he took on former Chrysler designer Don Mortrude, who did the 1939 Nash (see page 197). Through Mortrude, Walker claimed to have had a hand in designing the 1941 Packard Clipper, but if so, his role was minimal (see page 225).

One automotive account Walker kept trying to get was Ford. He'd sold the senior Henry Ford some Dura door handles in the early 1930s by showing his samples on black velvet while his rivals laid theirs on the bare table. Joe Galamb told Walker that "Mr. Ford doesn't like unfunctional things," but Walker paid no attention, and his velvet background apparently sold Dura to Ford. Then in 1935, Walker put together an elaborate, expensive portfolio of futuristic car designs to show to Henry Ford, not realiz-

ing that Edsel made most of the styling decisions. When Henry opened the huge portfolio, the binding broke and all the pages dropped out. Without a word, Henry got up and left. Walker didn't try to woo Mr. Ford again after that.

George Walker would find himself in various minor moral and legal scrapes throughout his career, but somehow he always squeaked through. Once, when a grand jury investigated him for non-payment of taxes, his attorney literally pleaded him "dumb," saying a designer of Walker's stature couldn't be bothered with anything so mundane as taxes. Walker, sitting tanned and impressively dressed, told in his reminiscences of smiling at the women on the jury and the effect that had on them. Needless to say, he got off.

For many years, Walker owned a third interest in a Detroit company called Trim Trends. Trim Trends supplied stamped brightwork to nearly all U.S. automakers. After Walker got the 1949 Ford contract, he made sure that Trim Trends supplied all of Ford's stamped brightwork. And for many years afterward, Trim Trends kept getting Ford Motor Co. orders. Walker, of course, encouraged his designers to specify stampings rather than cast trim.

The Walker styling touch extended not only to his clients' products but also to himself. He proudly maintained a huge and elegant wardrobe and racks of expensive shoes. His office, his cars and his dogs were all black and white. According to Time, he once had Saks Fifth Avenue make him four "cocktail suits": the male equivalent of cocktail dresses. These featured white fabric trimmed in different colors of braiding. He decided at the last minute not to wear his cocktail suits in public, lest he be considered "eccentric." *Time* also mentioned that Walker wore so much Fabrege cologne ."..that it lingers on long after he leaves the room."

Walker, who'd initially worked for Ford on a consultancy basis, finally became the corporation's first styling vice president on May 2, 1955. As politically savvy as Walker was, he didn't get along at all well with William Clay (Bill) Ford, the one Ford family member who cared as much about styling as his father, Edsel, had. Walker referred to Bill Ford as "the fuckin' kid" behind his back and, of course, that came back to haunt him.

George Walker left Ford in 1961. He retired to Gulfstream, Florida and, at age 80, was elected town mayor. He later became Gulfstream's police commissioner and also served as a director of the Palm Beach County Hospital District and two Florida banks. Around 1980, still spry and sprightly, Walker built himself an elaborate home on a golf course in Tucson, where he passed away on Jan. 19, 1993. He was 96 years old. ◆

Kolt, Martin Regitko and George Martin.

As Gene Bordinat described it, Ford styling was pretty chaotic and disorganized during that year when Walker wasn't around. Oswald was trying to blend the two remaining staffs, which was not easy, and morale remained low. Oswald did, however, manage to organize specific studios: Ford, Mercury, Lincoln, advanced design, special projects, etc.

Bordinat recalled working on a major restyle for the 1950 Ford, but nothing came of it. Fortunately, the 1950 Ford products didn't need much actual redesign. All three car lines remained carry-overs from 1949. Ford did introduce the Crestliner for 1950, with its vinyl-coated fabric roof and classic sidesweep. The Crestliner came in weak response to GM's hardtops. Padded roofs were also available on the 1950 Mercury Monterey, Lincoln Lido and Lincoln Capri.

In Aug. 1948, George Snyder was named Oswald's assistant, and Gordon Buehrig, the Duesenberg/Cord/GM designer, joined Ford in 1949 as an advanced designer and body engineer. It was about this time that Charlie Waterhouse became Ford's styling-engineering liaison—a position of considerable power—and Gene Bordinat acted as Waterhouse's assistant. George Snyder, meanwhile, had angered so many people in Dearborn that he was sent over to England, where he soon died of cancer.

In early 1948, Breech had decided that Ford design still wasn't headed in the right direction, so he again phoned George Walker. He asked Walker and his group to return on a consulting basis. Walker said he would, but only if he were given full charge of Ford design and could put his own people in high places. Breech agreed.

George W. Walker Associates had a number of good auto designers, not just Oros and Engel but also Ted Ornas and Kurt Witke, who handled the International Harvester account. Oros and Engel, though, were the men who ended up representing Walker within Ford.

Oros and Engel met initially in 1939 at the Harley Earl design school (Bordinat was one or two rotations ahead of them). Both later served as interns at GM Styling. Oros, in fact, worked under Bill Mitchell in the Cadillac studio. Just after Pearl Harbor, Oros was let go by Styling, but Mitchell got him a job the next day as

a Cadillac body draftsman. Engel joined the military, and the two men kept in touch via V-Mail.

After the war, Oros, who'd graduated from Cleveland East Technical High School and Cleveland Institute of Art, both of which were also Walker's alma maters, took a job with Walker and suggested hiring Engel. Walker did. Oros tended Walker's Nash account as well as Baker-Raulang and others. Engel initially had no automotive accounts but had also worked on the Ford consultancy contract when Caleal brought in his quarter-scale model.

At the time of Walker's second consultancy at Ford, Dick Caleal still worked for him. Walker later put Caleal on Ford's payroll but, seeing he wasn't a strong designer, got Caleal a job at Chrysler in 1949.

It seems odd that Oros and Engel were so close, because they had totally different personalities and ethical standards. Oros had a certain nerdiness about him. He was a driven workaholic, totally dedicated, painfully sincere, rather slow and almost humorless. "Unpleasant to work with," said designer Robin Jones. "I didn't like working under Joe Oros at all. Not many people did, but he got the job done. And although I didn't like working under him, meeting him socially or on the street, you couldn't know a nicer guy."

Many designers who worked under Oros later came to have great respect for him. George Shumaker, who helped design the 1965 Mustang (see page 258), recalled, "Joe Oros was a straight arrow, a non-nonsense type...but if you worked hard and didn't screw around, he rewarded you for what you did." Virgil Exner Jr. added, "Joe was very demanding and a hard man to convince, but once he had confidence in you, he was great to work for and really went to bat for you."

Engel was an Oros opposite: outgoing, funloving, casual, happy-go-lucky. He liked to pitch pennies in the studios with the clay modelers. People tended to like him. And when Engel met Margurite Imboden at Walker's and asked her to marry him, who should they choose as Elwood's best man but Joe Oros? Oros and Engel made an unlikely pair, but they were great friends and worked together in harmony at Ford.

Joe Oros came from a humble Detroit background. He showed an early aptitude for art, did extremely well in school and received

Quite daring for its day, the 1952 Mercury combined bumper with grille, had tunneled headlamps and a non-functioning hood scoop. Bob Weiland originated the design in Gene Bordinat's Lincoln-Mercury studio. The 1952 Lincoln (bottom right) shared inner body stampings with Mercury, and all three FoMoCo lines ended up with a strong family resemblance from that year through 1955.

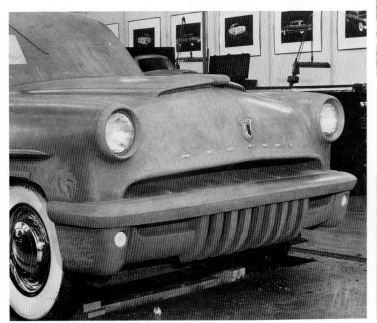

a number of scholarships, including a 1939 Agnes Gund stipend to study design in Sweden. He came back to the U.S. just as Germany was marching into Poland, and that's when he enrolled in the Harley Earl school. A year later he was working for Bill Mitchell, and in 1941 he married his college sweetheart, Betty Thatcher. Betty was then a designer at Hudson (see page 192).

Gene Bordinat described Oros as one of those very straight arrows you could leave alone in a roomful of $100 bills and never worry about recounting them. Engel, on the other hand, had a reputation for a much looser moral outlook, and Bordinat also wrote him off as not terribly bright. Needless to say, Bordinat never cared for Walker and wasn't especially fond of Oros or Engel either, although he and Oros worked together for decades.

During the year between Walker's two Ford consultancy contracts—late 1946 to late 1947—George Snyder, who had a history of drinking problems, was let go by John Oswald. Snyder couldn't find another job and remained out of work for several months, so Oswald, feeling responsible, hired him back and made him director of styling. That didn't work out, so Oswald sent Snyder over to Ford of Europe as chief designer, a move which aggravated Snyder's drinking and didn't improve Oswald's standing in Dearborn. As a result, Oswald was let go, and that now made Charlie Waterhouse Ford's in-house design manager. Gene Bordinat, meanwhile, had become head of the Lincoln/Mercury studio, while Frank Hershey was named chief designer of Ford cars and trucks.

When the Walker group came back to Ford in late 1947, George Walker made Joe Oros his man in charge of Ford car and truck design. Elwood Engel had the same responsibility for Lincoln and Mercury. The two men collaborated with and advised Hershey and Bordinat, but their responsibilities were not rigidly defined. If a disagreement came up about a design or a design detail, Oros and Engel had the authority to create new clay models in competition with the studios. This didn't happen often, but as Oros said in a 1994 telephone interview, "That [could develop] into a tug of war, a contest; there was no other way." He added that competition was good, because it gave Ford management a choice of design ideas.

However, Gil Spear, who arrived at Ford in 1947, said that in those days, when Oros worked on a model that competed with the studios, they usually shared the same clay modelers. The modelers worked after hours for Oros and often picked up the best ideas from the studios, which Oros then sweetened and presented to Walker and management. Spear felt this gave Oros an unfair advantage—one that the studios resented. Spear mentioned, too, that Walker was known by the studio people as "the big smiler," and Oros and Engel were called "the gold dust twins."

Walker spent a lot of time on the Ford account at first—at the beginning of his second coming—but by 1952 or so, he showed up less and less often and relied increasingly on Oros and Engel to handle the daily doings. They kept Walker informed, and the dual-authority arrangement—for better or worse—tended not to be confrontational. Morale was getting better but still wasn't good.

The first cars produced during Walker's second consultancy were the company's 1952 models. That year's Mercury, conceived largely by Bob Weiland in the Mercury exterior studio under Bordinat, was by far the most radical and revolutionary of the

three 1952 marques, basically because its front bumper and grille formed one impressive monolith. Headlights were "tunneled," a much less striking touch than the grille, but very noticeable all the same. Frenched headlights came from the Barris Kalifornia Kustom school, and all three 1952-55 FoMoCo marques had highly recognizable, basically rectangular profiles, based on the softly squared lines of the 1949-51 Ford. Richard H. Stout, who arrived at Ford as the 1952 models were being finished, noted that the company's styling was rigidly dictated by engineering, first by Youngren and then even more by Earle S. MacPherson. "MacPherson did so much locating of body points like door entrance heights, windshield angle, center-pillar location, roof/deck intersections, etc., that all styling could do was connect the dots. That's what made Ford cars look so square at that time. It became a major reason Ford styling wanted to get out from under engineering, which finally happened when Walker became v.p. in May 1955."

In time, FoMoCo designers also borrowed ideas from GM, like the wraparound windshield and various faux hood and fender scoops. Colin Neale reported that the 1955 Ford wasn't originally designed to have a wraparound windshield, but when word reached Dearborn that the 1955 Chevrolet would have one, Ford launched a last-minute program. "It was very costly for Ford," noted Neale, "and not a strong design statement."

Studio organization tended to change throughout this period, and the department participated in a physical move when Ford finished a new engineering/styling complex in 1953. It was about this time that Alex Tremulis took charge of advanced design, an area where young stylists apprenticed before going to other studios. Gil Spear, who'd headed the advanced studio before Tremulis, now became head of a special projects studio, and Wes Dahlberg was given international design.

George Walker also established what came to be known and sometimes

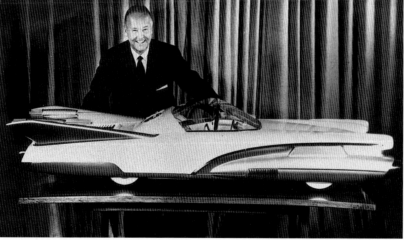

George Walker ran a loose ship at Ford and worked comfortably within the company's policy of decision by committee.

dreaded as "show days." These were weekly presentations made by the studios to top Ford management. The general practice continues even today with only minor change. In the mid 1950s, according to Gil Spear, "Friday was Ford show day, and Wednesday was show day for Lincoln-Mercury. Depending on the importance of the project, each presentation would be attended by Henry Ford II and all the top corporate and divisional people. Matter of fact, there were usually two parts to show day. In the morning we'd show off the new stuff, and then after lunch we'd show what had been modified from the previous week.

"There was a lot of pressure from some of these shows. We worked overtime almost steadily, especially on Tuesday or Thursday nights. We were often still modifying things while they were hauling models out of the studio and taking them out to the display area. Some people used to refer to this as design by committee, which it was, but those weekly shows did make us get things done."

Ford's system of making styling decisions differed considerably from that at General Motors. GM had what was called a "key man" system. That meant that each divisional general manager cast the deciding vote on a design. In other words, if Buick's

Frank Hershey and his staff applied chop-and-section techniques to 1955 Ford to bring in the classic 2-seater Thunderbird. Oros added the hashmarks and door/fender character line. Although the Corvette beat the T-Bird to market, the Thunderbird outsold the Vette by a ratio of 24:1. The removable hardtop was optional.

Harlow Curtice favored one grille over another, he would say so, and the grille he liked would be the one used. We're over-simplifying here, because Curtice and GM's other general managers did listen to members of their own and other staffs, but "key men" did ultimately make GM's key decisions.

Styling decisions at Ford, on the other hand, were made by committee. The composition of Ford's decisionmaking committees changed over the years, but in 1954, for example, a corporate product-planning committee was empowered to make final styling decisions. Meanwhile, each of Ford's car divisions (Ford, Mercury, Lincoln) had (and has) a general manager. Under the general manager was a divisional product planning committee. Styling ideas went up and down the line from divisional studios through divisional product planners to the corporate product planners to the company's top executives. Individual studios often had to tone down or broaden presentations so that they would please the various committee members, which was probably one reason Ford's designs lacked the sharpness and individuality that GM's had.

Ford's styling themes in the 1950s weren't derivative, but the company didn't lead or inspire the industry either. And yet, despite the committee system, Ford did manage to produce some highly successful cars (from an aesthetic standpoint) during the 1950s and '60s. The 1955 Thunderbird was one, as was the 1956

Lincoln line, the 1956 Continental Mark II and the 1961 Continental. There were also some notable lapses, like the 1958-60 Edsel, 1957 Mercury, 1958 Ford and the 1958-60 Lincolns.

The two-seater Thunderbird was done in Frank Hershey's studio by Hershey, David Ash, Damon Woods, Bill Boyer and Bob Maguire. Again considerable disagreement surrounds the exact authorship of that design, but according to Frank Hershey, "Early...around 1952, a friend of mine called up from GM. He said, 'Can I come over tonight? I want to show you something.' So he came over, and he showed me a picture of the [1953] Corvette. Boy! I hit the ceiling! I said, 'My God, that's fantastic!' And I said, 'Are they serious about building a sports car like that?' And he said, 'Oh, yeah, they're putting it in production.' I said, 'Oh Jeez, we can't be left out of this.'

"So I went to work the next day and told all my guys what was happening, and I said, 'Look, we're going to make our own sports car,' and...I got hold of Charlie Waterhouse, and I told him what we were going to do, and he said, 'Yeah, go ahead.'

"The next day, I went out and bought a new Jaguar XK-120 and brought it out into the [Ford styling] courtyard. We took dimensions off of it, and we used the same wheelbase, same seating position, same steering-wheel angle and all that, because the Jaguar was so perfect. So the Jaguar was the basis of our interior.

Lincoln took a huge leap in size for 1956, especially in terms of rear overhang, yet the car looked fantastic. Its designers favored matching interior and exterior colors, mostly in pastels of fuscia, lavender, pink and aqua against complementary off-whites. Restrained brightwork plus great emphasis on horizontal lines made the Lincoln look even longer than it was.

Ford Dreamcars and Nightmares

Dreamcar fever grew rampant in the early 1950s, and Ford responded to GM's Motorama showcars by designing a dreamcar fleet of its own. Ford's first was the X-100, also called the Continental 195X, released in 1952. Joe Oros conceived the X-100's futuristic exterior while John Najjar worked on the interior. The

1953 Ford XL-500.

rocket-like X-100 rear treatment set the theme for the 1961 Thunderbird's low deck-lid and bumper/tail lamps.

Next came the 1953 Ford XL-500, with

Frank Hershey points out a gadget.

its glass greenhouse and basket-handle B-pillar. The XL-500 predicted the Plexiglas roof section of the 1954 Ford Sunliner and Mercury Sun Valley. And the 1954 Mercury XM-800 prophesied the general shape of the 1956 Lincoln hardtop coupe: hooded headlights, low front-fender cutouts and a delicate roof.

The 1954 Ford FX Atmos looked almost like a throwback to GM's wartime scale

1961 Ford Gyron 2-wheeler.

models. It had an all-glass roof, huge fins, pointy bumper bullets and wheel cutouts so low that the front tires barely turned. The four-place cockpit contained a radar screen, its purpose unexplained.

William M. (Bill) Schmidt had major responsibility for designing the 1955 Lincoln Futura. Schmidt's Futura later gained noteriety as television's Batmobile. The Futura, which was designed after the

1955 Ford Mystere.

1956 production Lincoln, took the 1956 Lincoln's styling cues to an almost cartoonish extreme. The 1955 Ford Mystere, with its rear-mounted gas turbine engine, simply

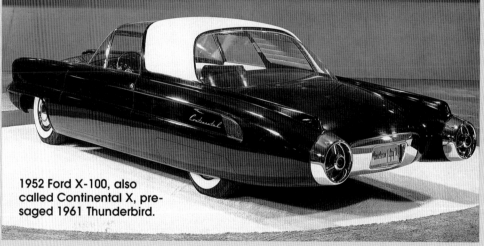

1952 Ford X-100, also called Continental X, presaged 1961 Thunderbird.

looked amateurish. And from the Mystere until the mid 1960s, Ford dreamcars suffered severe credibility problems. Their extreme nature made them not so much futuristic as unreal and unbelieveable.

The 1961 Ford Gyron, conceived by Alex Tremulis (who'd done the 1940 Briggs/Chrysler Thunderbolt), serves as an example of the dreamcar gone completely awry. The Gyron was a long two-wheeler, triangular in plan view, that supposedly used a huge gyroscope to keep itself upright. The public simply didn't accept the

Gyron as a glimpse of the future. Nor the six-wheeled 1962 Ford Seattle-ite XXI.

One of the fundamental purposes of dreamcars was (and remains) to show the type of styling that each auto company believed people would want, or at least would accept, in the future. Ford, under George Walker, often went overboard, beyond reason and credibility. Early

1955 Lincoln Futura.

Chrysler's dreamcars, conceived mostly by Virgil Exner, tended to be too Italianate for American tastes. Exner was exercising his own personal tastes and admiration for

Italian designs, and the average U.S. car buyer wasn't that sophisticated.

Which left Harley Earl as, once again, the guiding apostle of dreamcars. GM's Motorama vehicles probably showed more realistically what could and would work in the marketplace of the future. Earl also had more of a knack for pushing the viewer's emotional buttons. So in the industry as a whole, GM's dreamcars ran ahead of the others, with Ford, Chrysler and the independents trying to keep up or doing cars that often seemed inappropriate. ◆

And then we started doing the Thunderbird.

"We roughed the car out. I had Bill Boyer make the drawings, and he worked with my other two guys [Ash and Woods]. Bill did not contribute anything, but he did what he was told to do." So the two-seater Thunderbird began to take shape before there was any official authorization for it.

According to George Walker's account in *Time* magazine, Henry Ford II became interested in a sports car while the two were

touring the 1953 Paris show. HF-II, admiring the Jaguars, Ferraris and other sports cars on display, asked Walker, "Why can't we do a car like that?" Walker, knowing through Oros that Hershey was already working on one, placed a call to Dearborn. When he and HF-II got back, Walker showed Henry II the T-Bird clay. The Thunderbird arrived on the market in Sept. 1954, 15 months after the 1953 Corvette.

Hershey's staff created the Thunderbird essentially by applying chop-and-section methods to the full-sized 1955 Ford. They took inspiration from the Kalifornia Kustomizers. Oros, who spent a good deal of time in Hershey's studio, said that he didn't do a competing model (as Hershey claimed) but did contribute the 1955 Thunderbird's horizontal character line along the fenders and also the false louvers ahead of the door, where that line ends. Oros pointed out that the headlight bezels, tail lamps and the main instrument cluster were taken directly from the full-sized Ford.

The two-place Bird was never designed to be a true, all-out sports car. Rather it became what the press called a "personal car." Whatever definition goes with that term, the two-place Thunderbird immediately became a much more popular two-seater than the Corvette. The 1955 Thunderbird outsold the 1955 Vette by a ratio of 24:1. (In fairness, the 1955 Thunderbird enjoyed a much longer selling season than the Vette, but even adjusted for time, T-Bird sales led by a huge margin.)

And now another battle loomed, this time in the luxury segment. All Detroit cars had grown larger in the early 1950s, yet Lincolns had remained consistently shorter and narrower than Cadillacs, Imperials and Packards. This was especially noticeable during 1952-55, when Lincoln's target had been the Olds 98 rather than Cadillac. For 1956, though, Lincoln management decided to compete with Cadillac and Imperial (Packard was no longer much of a threat) and figured the way to do it was to make the Lincoln *bigger*. So for 1956, the largest of the large would be Lincoln.

The '56 Lincolns grew longer, lower, wider, heavier, more powerful and more colorful. Yet despite their striking size, the 1956 models had a great cleanliness of line and a harmony of detail that made them very appealing and handsome. Tim Howley called the 1956 models "the First Ladies of Lincoln," citing their tiara-like wraparound windshields, jewel emblems and color choices. Two-tone paint schemes ranged from white and coral to combinations including amethyst, lavender, turquoise and wisteria.

To familiarize the public with the 1956 Lincoln's size and styling themes, Bill Schmidt designed the $250,000 Lincoln Futura showcar. He did the Futura *after* the production cars had been styled, but Ford showed it before they appeared and made it look like the 1956 Lincolns had been derived from the Futura rather than the other way around.

Good-looking as they were, and despite the fact that Lincoln doubled its sales that year, the standard '56 Lincolns were upstaged by the arrival of the Continental Mark II. The public had been teased and primed for the Mark II for years, and when the car finally did arrive in October 1955, the Continental stole the thunder from that season's redone 1956 standard Lincoln line.

Not that the second-generation Continental came together easily. It began in early 1952, when Ford set up a Special Projects Div. and earmarked $1 million toward the design of an encore to the original Continental. Projections mentioned an $8000 target price and, after heated arguments, the company decided not to expect the car to show a profit, ever. Its purpose was to establish Lincoln as the best and best-looking quality car in America. Details never became clear, but Ernie Breech apparently later insisted that the Continental had to show a profit after all since Ford Motor Co. would soon go public. Henry Ford II got caught in the middle—between his brother, William Clay Ford, and Breech. There were times when the Continental program faced cancellation, and this on-again, off-again uncertainty probably became one factor that led W.C. Ford to begin drinking.

William Clay Ford took charge of the Continental project and set a deadline of Dec. 1952 to come up with a suitable "picture." He gathered five designers—John Reinhart, Charles Phaneuf, Fred Beamish, Ray Smith and Bob Thomas—plus several engineers and moved them into the old Henry Ford Trade School gymnasium. The Continental group soon came to be known as the "Trade School Boys" or, alternately, the "Country Club Set." Bill Ford, 26 at that time, wanted the security and independence of being totally away from the company's styling and engineering quarters.

John Reinhart, who'd been design head of Packard, became the Continental's chief designer. Harley Copp had charge of the Continental's engineering (he later did the Ford Falcon), and Gordon Buehrig was the project's body engineer. Buehrig and Reinhart had worked together years earlier in Auburn, Indiana and again on Loewy's Studebaker account in South Bend in the late 1930s (see page 206).

Around Christmas 1952, right on schedule, the Trade School Boys held the grand unveiling. The "picture" stood behind velvet drapes on an easel in the old gym. As the curtains parted, a somber and expectant committee of high Ford officials said not a word. Finally, HF-II told his brother, "I wouldn't give you a dime for that car!"

After doing the Lincoln Futura, Bill Schmidt's early sketch for the 1956 Continental Mark II (below) looked downright tame. After an initial false start, Ford opened the Mark II design to competition. Five teams were invited to compete. All had to adhere to strict rules, and each earned $10,000 whether chosen or not. In the end, John Reinhart's home team emerged the winner.

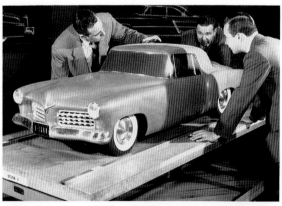

The 1956 Continental Mark II was Bill (William Clay) Ford's baby. He's shown here in 1953 discussing early development with two modelers. By Mar. 1954, Bill had a metal prototype up and running (top right). Except for different wheelcovers and the removal of exhaust gills from the front fenders, prototype looked very much like the production version above.

Crushed, William Clay Ford decided to start over. This time, though, rather than having just his own group develop a design, he decided to stage a competition. He asked his staff to suggest names of outside stylists, and the groups invited were: George Walker Assoc., consultant to Ford Motor Co.; Grisinger & Miller, independent designers, previously with Chrysler and Kaiser-Frazer; Vince Gardner, formerly with Cord and Loewy; and Henry

II's brother-in-law, Walter Buhl Ford, who later merged with Harley Earl Assoc.

The Continental project now became a five-way contest. The four outside teams would receive $10,000 each for their Mark II designs, chosen or not. To keep everything fair and consistent, each team had to deliver side-, plan- and end-view drawings plus 3/4-front and 3/4-rear perspective sketches. Rules stipulated that

The Kustom King

Just before and especially just after World War II, an automotive artform called "customizing" (or sometimes *kustomizing* with a "k") took root in Southern California. Car magazines, notably the Petersen group—*Hot Rod, Motor Trend, Rod & Custom, Car Craft*—regularly published photo features and how-to articles about Kalifornia kustoms, and the kraze soon spread across the kountry. (Okay, enough kays, but we'll continue to use the word "kustom" to differentiate the postwar California type from coachbuilt custom bodies of the 1920s and '30s.)

In time, although there's argument on this point, kustomizing came to have some influence on Detroit. The disagreement stems from the fact that Detroit was simultaneously being bombarded by a lot of other influences: postwar British sports cars, Italian car design, American hot rods, jet aircraft, etc. So kustoms were only one part of that mosaic. Evidence of the impact of kustoms, though, can be seen in such items as the tunneled headlamps on the 1952 Mercury, the dechroming of the 1954 Pontiac Parisienne Motorama showcar and the entire 1955 Thunderbird, which was

essentially a shortened, lowered, sectioned, two-place version of a full-sized 1955 Ford convertible.

The early and undisputed leaders of the kustom movement were George and Sam Barris. George Barris, in particular, became heralded as the King of the Kustomizers, partly because he had a gift for promotion

The Barris Brothers finished what Harley Earl had set out to do: make cars look longer and lower. The Barrises, though, did it literally. This is Sam's 1949 Merc in classic form: restrained use of chrome, great linear simplicity, yet the car's identity remains intact.

and enjoyed a symbiotic relationship with the L.A.-based national car magazines.

George was born in Chicago, grew up in Sacramento and, in 1944, aged 19, drove his kustomized 1936 Ford to Los Angeles and took a job in a bodyshop. Here he soon started kustomizing cars for friends and customers. He opened his own shop the following year in south Los Angeles. In 1950, Barris moved his by-now-considerable operation to the southern Los Angeles suburb of Lynwood.

His older brother Sam had joined George after the war and became the shop's star metal shaper. George's expertise lay in painting, and he was soon spraying wild lacquer over Sam's handiwork, including (later) kandy-apple metalflakes. In the words of designer Harry B. Bradley, who looms large in kustomizing circles, "George was really the genius behind the Barris success. He was the painter, the visionary, the promoter and a tireless innovator. Sam was enormously important, too. He never chopped a top incorrectly. Together, they had an excel-

all artwork had to be the same size, same matting, use the same supplied perspective grids and be of the same color. No sketches could be signed or identified. Judges—five executives from Lincoln—could cast only one vote each and had to pass through the final display area separately so they couldn't talk, nod or read each other's body language.

The final judging took place in Apr. 1953, and the design that ended up winning this competition came from Bill Ford's own Special Projects group: Reinhart, Buehrig, Copp, Phaneuf, Beamish, Smith et al. (Designer W.E. [Bill] Robinson, who was with Briggs at that time, mentioned that the Reinhart Mark II body side originated with Jack Kenitz, also at Briggs. Kenitz had proposed it to Packard. When Packard designer Fred Beamish went to Ford, he took the design with him.) At first Bill Ford didn't want a hood ornament, but he later changed his mind, and designer Robert M. (Bob) Thomas added the final touch by drawing up the Continental "compass."

Ford promptly built a $25 million plant to produce the Continental Mark II, and it went on sale in Oct. 1955. Lincoln decreed that each car had to be flawless, and anyone in the plant who noticed a mistake and didn't report it faced instant dismissal. Bodies were finished in handrubbed lacquer. Leather came from Scotland because the Scots didn't have barbed-wire fences, so their cows tended to be less scarred. The Scottish hides, though, had to be dyed in Dearborn, because U.S. dyes didn't fade. The Mark II's chrome had twice the rust resistance of standard plating. And each Mark II was shipped to the dealer under a fleece-lined plastic wrap.

This was a time when car marketers began to worship styling, not just at Ford but throughout the industry. Polls showed over and over that American car buyers were basing their choices more on styling than any other factor. As a result, management got uncharacteristically generous with its design budgets. *Time* magazine reported in 1957 that Ford spent $400 million on 1956 styling changes, then another $610 million for '57, "...to produce George

---

lent eye for design. Sam's 1949 Mercury is considered...the first postwar Mercury that established the etiquette for that look."

The Barris Brothers initially specialized in restyling conventional Detroit automobiles. They applied their signatures mostly to older Fords and Mercurys but occasionally also turned out kustomized Buicks and other makes. In the beginning, the Barrises and their peers tended to simplify the appearance of production cars by removing

Jesse Lopez's 1940 Barris Ford and Nick Matranga's 1940 Merc inspired imitators all around the country.

chrome and emblems, lowering the chassis, lowering ("chopping") the roof, sometimes lowering the actual section height of the body ("sectioning"), simplifying grilles, molding in ("frenching") lamps, extending fenders and filling body seams. As designers, their overall theme was to create a simpler, better proportioned, more organic look, at the same time making each car distinctive and individual.

As the kustomizing gospel spread across the country, every car-struck kid became a stylist of sorts. Future professional designers like GM's Chuck Jordan and Dave Holls made pilgrimages to the Barris shop, talked to the masters and cruised the streets of Hollywood to study kustoms first-hand. Jack Telnack, at age 16, personally channeled his 1941 Mercury—a car that was rediscovered and given to him on the occasion of his 25th anniversary

with Ford.

The notoriety and success of the Barrises convinced other kustomizers and bodyshop owners to go professional, the best known being Joe Bailon, Bill Cushenbery, Valley Customs, the Alexander Brothers, Gene Winfield and Ed (Big Daddy) Roth. Between them, this extended family of kustomizers produced a number of wildly innovative cars.

The impact of Kalifornia kustoms became most strongly felt when Detroit's young designers—those like Jordan, Holls, Shinoda, Teague and Telnack who joined GM, Ford, Chrysler, Packard and AMC in the 1950s—reached senior positions and started advocating designs that showed the hallmarks of kustoms: less chrome, lower proportions, stretched fenders, simpler grilles and so forth

The Kalifornia kustomizers had always been counter-culture, going upstream against the styling trends of Detroit. By the time kustomizing reached its peak in the late 1950s, most backyard kustomizers—including Barris—did another 180° turn and, instead of simplifying and uncluttering, began to create complicated, heavily ornamented body shapes. These often left the original car unrecognizable, and some were very bizarre.

The kustom kraze—like American styling in general—seemed to sleep

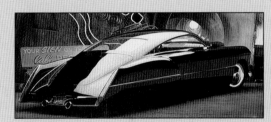

Billy F. Gibbons' CadZZilla, designed by GM's Larry Erickson, built by Coddington and based on a 1949 Cadillac fastback, has evoked an earlier, simpler Barris-style kustom.

through the 1970s and early '80s, but it awoke again in the mid 1980s as the result of now-affluent adults who could finally afford the kustoms and hot rods they'd wanted as teenagers. This group usually didn't build its own cars but left their meticulous construction to professionals. Some, like Boyd Coddington, worked with professional auto designers, as in the case of the radical CadZZilla and Joe Hrudka's 1957

Chevrolet CheZoom. On the east coast, Ken (Posie) Fenical did similar work in Hummelstown, Pennsylvania, and in the midwest, Doug Thompson created kustoms in Raytown, Missouri.

This latter round of one-offs often took inspiration from classic hot rods and kustoms of the nostalgic past. The more sophisticated modern kustoms again proved of interest to professional car designers, many of whom made pilgrimages to major gatherings of street rods and kustoms at meccas like the Oakland Roadster Show, St. Ignace on Michigan's upper peninsula and Good Guys meets.

Today (1996), Coddington, Posie and Thompson continue to build six-figure cars for demanding clients. Barris, who in 1961 moved his dream factory to North Hollywood, designed and fabricated scores of cars for TV and the movies; also one-offs for individual movie stars. Today's actual influence of kustoms on Detroit designers is hard to quantify, but kustoms seem to remain one of many inspirations. ◆

By the mid 1950s, kustomizers were adding to rather than subtracting from. This had once been a 1957 Chevrolet.

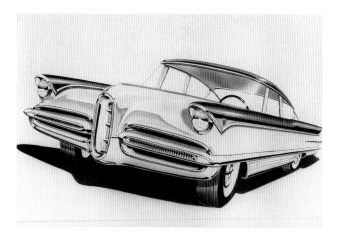

Roy Brown, who kicked off his career in the 1930s in Bill Mitchell's Cadillac studio, accomplished what he was asked to do with the 1958 Edsel: make it instantly recogniz-

able. The public, however, did not take to a modern rendition of vertical grille (left). Ford Div. enjoyed much greater success with its 1957 Fairlane 500 (above) and Galaxy.

Walker's ideas of beauty." By way of comparison, General Motors budgeted $730 to make 1958 styling changes and Chrysler set aside $150 million (Chrysler had done a total and extremely expensive revamp for 1957, but no cost figures were available).

Gene Bordinat, who in 1961 replaced Walker as Ford's design vice president, expressed company largesse this way: "...the designer, who had always reached for the moon hoping to get just halfway there [was now hearing from management], 'Okay, go ahead and take the damn moon!' That's when [the designers'] own immaturity and lack of practice in accepting responsibility showed up, and that led to some of the cartoons that were put into steel. The public bought them, but they were hardly tasteful: Triple-tone paint jobs with anodized aluminum in gold and silver really are not the epitome of good taste. There are words for it: gorp, schlock...." Bordinat commented that every car Ford Motor Co. produced in 1958 had enough gingerbread on it for five cars.

The 1958 Edsel had been market-researched into a mish-mash of styling requirements. Also, instead of giving the Edsel its own platform, Ford forced the car's body engineers and designers to

build on Ford and Mercury chassis and inner body shells. Thus, far from being unique, the Edsel couldn't become anything more than a recooked Ford/Mercury. The car's primary focal point, its horsecollar grille, went against all convention, yet the 1958 Edsel did just what Ford's product planners wanted: Kids could identify it a block away. And the kids then usually made off-color jokes about the grille. So the 1958 Edsel flopped, in part, for the same reason as the 1929 Pregnant Buick: People didn't want to be seen driving a national joke. Other reasons included the 1958 recession, a shrinking of the mid-range auto market and build-quality problems.

As for the massive, slab-sided 1958-60 Lincolns, these cars again overwhelmed their luxury rivals in terms of sheer size and bulk. They were destined to become—and remain to this day—the largest unit-bodied automobiles ever mass-produced anywhere. But Ford soon discovered that bigger was not necessarily more salable, and for 1961, Lincoln product planners decided to downsize.

The theme for the smaller, smarter 1961 Lincoln came initially

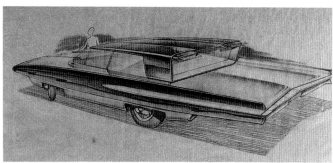

John Reinhart, who succeeded stylistically with the 1956 Continental Mark II, submitted concept sketches (top right) for the monstrously large 1958 Lincoln line, which Ford man-

agement accepted. By this time, Detroit was caught up in the "more-" and "bigger-is-better" syndrome. GM wasn't the only company pushing the "bizarre" envelope at this point.

Unit-bodied 1958 Lincoln (above) came out with many of the excesses it picked up from its rejected antecedants. Its unitized cousin, the 4-place 1958 Thunderbird (center), had a much more lasting influence than the 1955-57 2-seater. Although less loved today, 4-seater opened up a new market. The 1961 T-Bird (right) shared 1961 Continental's theme.

The 1961 Continental originated in Elwood Engel's stiletto studio with the model seen here. According to modeler Fred Hoadley, Engel picked up the idea for the wire-framed fender peaks and beltline from Wes Dahlberg's German Ford Taunus 17M. Ford president Robert McNamara, who wanted a smaller Lincoln, asked Engel to stretch his T-Bird clay into a 4-door, and it soon evolved into the highly successful '61 Continental.

from Germany. In June 1958, Elwood Engel toured the German Ford studio in Cologne where Wes Dahlberg was developing a new Taunus 17M. Fred Hoadley, Dahlberg's head clay modeler, recalled later that Engel took a keen interest in the 17M, particularly its fender and hood contours. These looked like the designer had taken wire frames, formed the stiff outlines of the fenders, covered the wire with light canvas and then had gently blown compressed air up into the canvas from underneath. The hood and fenders flared out ever so slightly, but there was a hard edge where the "wires" would have been. Engel was very taken with that design idea.

When Engel got back to Dearborn, Walker talked to him about doing a new Thunderbird in what was then called Ford's "stiletto studio." The stiletto studio was down in the basement of the design building. Engel, who up to that time had been more of a roving studio manager, poking here and critiquing there, was given complete charge of the stiletto studio. The name was dreamed up by Colin Neale, and it had a double meaning. First, the studio was shaped like a stiletto: long and so narrow that only half a full-sized clay could be built in it. A mirror had to be placed

along one wall to represent the other half. The second meaning had to do with the purpose of the stiletto studio. Walker still wanted Engel to prod and challenge Ford's other studios, so the stiletto studio's intent was to provide rival designs. "It was a stiletto in the sense that every time Ford or Mercury or Lincoln designed a car," recalled Neale, "we would do one, too, just to probe the stiletto into their sensitive areas." John Najjar became the executive in charge of the stiletto studio under Engel, and working with them were Colin Neale, John Orf and Bob Thomas.

Elwood Engel oversaw the creation of this Thunderbird, and the first thing he brought to it was the wire-and-canvas concept he had seen in Wes Dahlberg's studio.

Neale tackled the rear end of the clay model, John Orf produced the electric-razor front end, while Bob Thomas did a lot of the side sculpting. "I laid out the side view on the blackboard," said Thomas, "and developed the body section with the peaked fender top. Elwood made that into a chrome molding, which was a great touch!"

George Walker took an interest in the evolving Thunderbird model, as did Robert S. McNamara, the Whiz Kid who later became Ford president and then JFK's secretary of defense. McNamara felt that the 1958-60 Lincoln's size had gotten way out of hand, and he was looking for a smaller format. When he saw Engel's T-Bird clay, he asked that two more doors be added so

Engel did himself proud with the 1961 Continental design. Without it, he probably wouldn't have landed the Chrysler vice presidency.

he could view it as a smaller Lincoln. Engel, with the help of Najjar and the rest of the team, transformed their two-door Thunderbird model into the four-door '61 Lincoln sedan.

Neale again had responsibility for the Lincoln's rear aspect, and that's when it came to him to make the main body section look like a large, flattened tube. "I was very interested in the idea of the back of a car not looking like a solid form but looking extremely light and absolutely like a squashed tube," he said later. This was similar in concept to the 1961 Taunus 17M. Neale inserted a fine, eggcrate grille texture into the rear face of the decklid and surrounded it with a roll—like the squeezed-out overhang that would result from the squashing process—and John Orf repeated the rear grille texture in the front.

The tube of the main body section was flanked by Engel's clean, unadorned, chrome-outlined envelope fenders. The bright edging served, in effect, as the fenders' "wire frames." The two-door Thunderbird model hadn't used a kickup for the rear fender, but the designers added one to the four-door Lincoln. The 1961 Lincoln's hood and fender cheeks puffed out slightly per the Dahlberg Taunus example. And the greenhouse, one of the earliest with curved side glass, stood inboard of the fender highlines and had so much tumblehome that it almost seemed to be falling in on itself.

Jeff Godshall, the Chrysler designer and historian, makes an interesting point here. "The forward wheel opening," he reflects, "is cut so high into the fender that the front overhang seems ready to 'break off' visually. The Lincoln designers...caused a sort of 'balancing rock' scenario via an appearance that is almost not right. The visual tension this creates, like a balanced rock, endlessly fascinates me."

The downsized, beautifully conceived 1961 Lincoln became one of the division's most successful and enduring designs. Boldest body type in the line was the four-door convertible sedan. Although the Lincoln's convertible top was nylon, a steel retractable hardtop had been considered and would have borrowed its technology from the 1957-59 Ford fliptop. A coupe was added to the line for 1966. The last four-door convertible was built in 1967, and the body shell endured through 1969. All Lincolns during those years were called Continentals.

George Walker turned 65 in 1961, and 65 meant mandatory retirement. This naturally raised the question of Walker's successor: Who would become the next vice president of Ford's styling office? Industry observers felt that the choice boiled down to Walker's two longtime aides, Joe Oros and Elwood Engel. Walker himself favored Engel, but Engel got caught double-billing Ford for a business trip to England. And at nearly the same time, Ford reluctantly rejected Oros as not being dynamic enough.

So in May 1961, they named Gene Bordinat the company's new design vice president (see page 251). Walker, when he heard the news, immediately arranged a lunch with Chrysler president Lynn Townsend and talked Townsend into hiring Engel as Chrysler's design vice president (page 170). Thus Bordinat and Engel became rivals of another sort; grist for future design battles. ◆

CHAPTER 9

EARLY CHRYSLER STYLING

On June 6, 1925, Walter Percy Chrysler became the last person ever to start a successful, enduring American car company. Hundreds had tried before, and scores have tried since, but only Chrysler managed to pull it off. In five short years, Chrysler built himself a company whose range of makes and models covered the auto market from top to bottom. His Chrysler Imperial, Chrysler, Dodge, DeSoto and Plymouth weren't just good value; he'd put them together like chessmen to play off GM's Cadillac, Buick, Oldsmobile, Oakland/Pontiac and Chevrolet. And it's no wonder Chrysler was trying to out-GM General Motors, because that's where he got his training.

Walter Chrysler slipped into the car business sideways. He'd been a railroader most of his young life. One day in 1908, he hopped off a Pullman in Chicago and decided to have a look at the auto show. There he fell madly in love with a new Locomobile. "I saw this Locomobile touring car; it was painted ivory white and the cushions and trim were red. The top was khaki, supported on wood bows. Straps ran...to anchorages on either side of the hood. On the running board there was a handsome tool box that my fingers itched to open.... I spent four days hanging around the show, held by that automobile as by a siren's song." Thus he confessed in his 1937 autobiography, *Life of an American Workman.*

Chrysler had always been romantically inclined toward all things mechanical, even as a child. He'd worked his way up from roundhouse sweeper through apprentice machinist to a job with the Chicago & Great Western Railroad that made him supervisor of 10,000 machinists. Chrysler's annual salary in 1908 was $4200. The Locomobile cost $5000, which put it totally out of an American workman's reach. Or so you might think.

Chrysler wanted that Locomobile not for transportation but to study how an automobile worked, how it was put together and the manufacturing techniques. He could have chosen another make, something cheaper, but he'd fallen in love with the Locomobile. So he buttonholed every friend he could find, and he finally got Bill Causey, a fellow railway superintendent, to co-sign a note.

The Locomobile arrived in Oelwein, Iowa, where Chrysler then lived, chained to the bed of a railway flatcar. Walt hadn't bothered to learn how to drive, so he had the car towed home by a team of horses. He parked the Loco in a barn behind his modest house and proceeded to take it completely apart. He laid everything out on newspapers on the floor, studied every nut and bolt and finally, satisfied that he understood its innermost workings, put the Locomobile back together. Wonder of wonders, it ran!

For three months, Walt left the reassembled car in the barn. He couldn't work up the nerve to try to drive it. He and his wife, Della, would go out and sit behind the wheel, and sometimes Walt would fire up the engine and listen to it purr. Finally, he decided to take the plunge. Word spread through Oelwein, and a small crowd gathered. The monstrous touring car, wrote Chrysler, bucked, shot forward, lurched through a ditch and finally came to

rest in a neighbor's garden. Horses pulled the Loco back out, and Chrysler took off again. This time he barely missed a stray cow, but he managed four miles of country road and finally came home in one piece, dripping with sweat.

Chrysler managed a locomotive factory at that time, and by 1912, his career had progressed to the point where he was earning $12,000 a year. And that's when, through a friend, Buick president Charles Nash offered him a job as works manager. Chrysler had not lost his enthusiasm for automobiles, and despite the fact that Buick would pay him only $6000 a year—half his current salary—he grabbed it anyway.

Since he was coming into Buick without preconceived notions, Chrysler could see what was slowing Buick's production processes. Many of the workmen, and especially the foremen, cut their teeth in the carriage industry. Standard practice dictated, as one example, varnishing each chassis frame, a process that took weeks. Chrysler reasoned that since no one saw the frame anyway, why make it a work of art? Item by item, he put common-sense solutions to production problems, made use of assembly lines, cut painting time and soon increased Buick's output from 45 cars a day to 550. Buick jumped from 26,666 cars produced in 1913 to 124,834 in 1916.

Buick had long been General Motors' prime moneymaker, and Chrysler made it even more profitable, but he'd never gotten a raise. He was still earning $6000 a year. So he walked into Charlie Nash's office one day and told Nash that he wanted more money. Nash looked up from a pile of paperwork and asked, "How much?" Chrysler paused and answered, "$25,000 a year." Nash, who Chrysler said was so tight that he still had the change from the first nickel he'd ever earned, reluctantly agreed and then went back to his papers. As Chrysler left Nash's office, he turned and said to Nash, "And next year I want $50,000!" Which he also got.

In 1916, W.C. Durant was back running GM, and Charlie Nash had left to work a deal to take over Packard. With Nash gone, Durant told Chrysler he'd give him $500,000 a year plus GM stock if he'd take the presidency of Buick. Meanwhile, Charlie Nash wanted Walt Chrysler to join him in the Packard takeover. Chrysler showed some interest in Nash's offer but finally passed, and it was well that he did, because the Packard transaction didn't go through.

At that time, the Fisher Brothers were supplying Buick and other GM makes with most of their autobodies. Chrysler could see that it made more sense for GM to build its own bodies, so he suggested to Durant that GM buy Fisher Body and cut out the middleman. After a lot of back and forth, GM did buy 60% of Fisher in 1919.

Durant soon made Chrysler GM's manufacturing vice president, and that's when things started to fall apart. Chrysler felt that Durant wouldn't let him do his job; kept meddling. That happened in a big way not twice but three times. On the third, Chrysler stormed into Durant's office and quit. Alfred P. Sloan Jr., in the office across the hall, remembered Chrysler slamming Durant's door on the way out. That bang, said Sloan later, opened the door on the Chrysler Corp.

By the time Walter Chrysler stormed out of General Motors, he'd accumulated $10 million in GM stock. Chrysler was 44 years old, rich beyond his wildest dreams and, at that point, he decided to simply retire. He'd worked hard all his life and wanted time with his family. But after a year at home, he was ready to go back to work. As luck would have it, a New York banker pulled Chrysler out of retirement and thrust him into the role of doctor of ailing motorcar companies. Chrysler put Willys-Overland back on its feet and then did the same for Maxwell-Chalmers. His salary in both cases was $1 million a year.

From 1912 through 1918, Willys-Overland had been America's second-bestselling nameplate, led only by Ford. But the 1920-21 recession left W-O over-expanded and $50 million in debt when Chrysler stepped in. His reorganization brought W-O back to profitability. He took on Maxwell-Chalmers before he finished the Willys-Overland job and managed to bring that company back

1924 Chrysler included two powerful styling identifiers: winged radiator cap and blue ribbon emblem (previous page). Here Carl Breer (left) congratulates Walter P. Chrysler.

from a $26 million debt to profitability also. Maxwell became, essentially, the foundation for Chrysler Corp.

What's important here, though, without going into all the intricate machinations of the Willys-Overland and Maxwell-Chalmers rescues, is that in the process Walter Chrysler met and worked with the engineering trio of Zeder, Skelton and Breer (ZSB). The three engineers had met at Studebaker and later went out on their own. Chrysler called them the Three Musketeers. In the early 1920s, ZSB had built up a staff of about 15, and theirs was one of the sharpest automobile engineering consulting firms in the industry. At that time, ZSB was developing several cars simultaneously, among them new models for Willys-Overland, Maxwell and now for Walter Chrysler himself.

But one of the cars they had on the drawingboard—the best and most modern—was intended to become the Zeder, named for senior partner Fred Zeder. Zeder prototypes evolved into Chrysler prototypes, and Walter Chrysler—still retained by Maxwell-Chalmers—launched a car under his own name in 1924 and began distributing it through Maxwell dealers. Next year, he reorganized Maxwell as the Chrysler Corp.

Walter Chrysler was another of those intuitive automotive geniuses who knew exactly what the public wanted, probably because he himself would want such a car. The 1924 Chrysler came with four-wheel hydraulic brakes and a high-compression engine, two features that were cutting-edge at the time. But just as important as the engineering, the 1924 Chrysler *looked* good. It

stood slightly lower than its competitors—something we can't see today but a very noticeable difference to buyers of that period. Its lowness gave the car a certain restrained raciness, but what helped put the design across—a classic lesson in the importance of detailing—was a series of brilliantly conceived stylistic jewelry: the rolled, rounded radiator shell, the winged Viking radiator cap and the Chrysler emblem.

The curvaceous, nickel-plated radiator shell gave the car a solid, substantial, durable look and made a wonderful base for the Viking-helmet hood ornament. What child or kid-at-heart, seeing that cap with its outstretched wings, could help dreaming about Norsemen adventuring through the New World? The Viking cap became a cleverly chosen symbol, selected not because Walter Chrysler had Scandinavian ancestors (his family came from Germany; the name was originally Greisler) but simply because the helmet evoked romantic notions.

And the Chrysler seal just below the Viking cap...the early company logo...made it look as if someone had handed the car a blue ribbon at a county fair. The emblem implied that a wise, respected judging panel, folks who knew quality and value, had somehow carefully looked the car over and awarded it first prize.

All three of those initial Chrysler styling devices came as the result of marketing genius; whose we don't know, but there's no doubt that they helped make the car the instant success it became. The 1924 Chrysler's overall styling was probably done, or at least overseen, by body engineer Oliver H. Clark, but there's no record of whether he also dreamed up the details. Probably not. You can be sure, though, that Walter Chrysler had to okay everything about the car, and the ornamentation obviously pleased him.

Fisher supplied most of Chrysler's bodies through 1926, the year when Fisher sold the remaining 40% of its stock to General Motors. And even after 1926, Fisher continued to build some bodies for a few non-GM automakers, including Chrysler. But as GM began more and more to discourage outside business, Chrysler switched to Briggs, Murray and Budd as the company's principal body suppliers.

Walter Chrysler's first move toward expanding his product line came in 1926 with the introduction of the Chrysler Imperial 80. The "80" referred to 80 miles an hour, the Imperial's guaranteed top speed. And while the Imperial 80 looked basically like a stretched Chrysler (which it was), its front-end styling took on a distinctive fluted hood and scalloped grille shell that, supposedly, Chrysler had appropriated from the British Vauxhall. The horizontal hood flutes remained a Chrysler Imperial hallmark until 1931.

The standard Chrysler 70 was selling for $1595 in 1926, roughly the same as a Buick, while the Imperial 80 sold for $2500, $500 less than a Cadillac. Chrysler quickly contracted with three coachbuilders to supply catalogue custom bodies for the Chrysler Imperial: Locke, Dietrich and LeBaron. Locke concentrated on open body styles, and John Tjaarda, assisted by W.E. Miller at Locke, designed a series of beautiful Imperial roadsters and phaetons. The standout was the 1927 Locke Touralette, a two-door, close-coupled, four-passenger phaeton. This used painted-on canework that wrapped from the doors all the way around the back of the body. It also had a bright molding that extended the chrome-lined hood flutes back along the beltline and around the rear sill.

Then in 1928, Chrysler Corp. added three more nameplates: Plymouth, Dodge and DeSoto. Plymouth and DeSoto had been gestating for several years, but Dodge came along fairly unexpectedly. Dillon, Read & Co., the New York banking firm, bought Dodge from the founders' widows in 1925 and had been trying to sell it to Walter Chrysler since 1926. Chrysler, though, never felt the price was right. Finally, on July 31, 1928, Clarence Dillon offered Dodge to Chrysler for no cash and $170 million in Chrysler Corp. stock, and Chrysler accepted. Dodge brought with it some excellent manufacturing plants, a solid, extensive dealer network and a fine reputation.

Imperial 80 (above) topped Chrysler's 1927 line, took model designation from its top speed, 80 mph. John Tjaarda at Locke designed 1927 Imperial Touralette (below), with its canework and built-in trunk.

The name *DeSoto* meanwhile, went back to the 16th-century Spanish seeker of Florida's fountain of youth. Explorers looked like good name sources in the late 1920s, *Cadillac* and *LaSalle* being two others that had already succeeded. (Early Chrysler ads had a line at the bottom that instructed people to pronounce the company and car name *Cry-sler*. Seems some people were including the "Ch" sound.)

Now, in 1928, with the Chrysler Imperial 80 headlining the Chrysler Corp. marquee, Plymouth at the low end, and Dodge, DeSoto and Chrysler centered against Pontiac, Olds and Buick, Walter P. found himself with a full house of nameplates. Walter Chrysler had rapidly and efficiently built himself an empire that, by 1929, was manufacturing 375,000 cars a year. It's true that that number didn't yet hold a candle to Ford and GM, but Walter P. Chrysler had both those giants in his sights.

Chrysler Corp. set up an embryonic styling section called Art & Colour (another borrowing from General Motors) in July 1928, the same month Plymouth came into being. Chrysler's Art & Colour staff, though, unlike GM's, remained strictly under the thumb of engineering. And at Chrysler, engineering ruled. The ZSB group—Zeder, Skelton and Breer—controlled the technological side of the company, including body design.

Even so, an early member of that original staff, Tom Martin, when asked whether Walter P. Chrysler took an interest in styling in those early days, answered, "Oh, definitely. It was kind of a hobby with him, I think. He liked to see the sketches we drew. He'd come around to my board—used to put his arm on my shoulder and say, 'Well, what do you have here, son?' Everyone was 'son' to him. Of course, we were a lot younger than he was.

"But he was always very friendly and very much interested. He'd discuss the thing with you. And they'd have meetings right there in our studio—Mr. Chrysler, [chief body engineer Oliver H.] Clark, [engineers] Fred Zeder, Carl Breer, Owen Skelton; they'd discuss what they were going to do next year and what they'd seen that day. It was interesting and quite a nice thing for us, because we got it first-hand that way; it wasn't somebody else's opinion."

The man who directed Chrysler A&C at first was Herbert V. Henderson, an interior decorator with an artistic flair who'd done

Walter Chrysler hadn't really counted on Dodge coming his way, so he'd already planned the Plymouth and DeSoto. The Plymouth bowed on June 8, 1928, 24 days before the Dodge purchase, and DeSoto arrived on Aug. 4, four days after the Dodge acquisition. Plymouth competed in the Chevrolet price range, just above Ford. And while it was too late to abort the DeSoto, that particular line now didn't make much economic sense. DeSoto managed to set first-year sales records, but it *did* overlap Dodge in price, so Chrysler soon lowered Dodge prices and raised them on the DeSoto to position DeSoto between Dodge and Chrysler.

Like the 1924 Chrysler, the Plymouth and DeSoto again carried some beautifully conceived marketing imagery. First and foremost, both names were good. "Plymouth" supposedly came from that great American farm institution, Plymouth hay-binder twine. Walter Chrysler strongly felt that "Plymouth," as in "Plymouth Rock" and the Mayflower, said America. The Mayflower image gave rise to the sailing ships that became first radiator emblems and then stood out as hood ornaments on all Plymouths through 1954.

1930 Chrysler 77's thin "ribbon" grille was intended to make hood look longer, but buyers felt it cheapened the car. Nor was 2-tone paint scheme popular. Hood louvers picked up wing theme of Viking helmet hood ornament.

1931 Chrysler Imperial adopted prow grille inspired by Cord L-29, with gazelle leaping from Viking cap. Cleanly styled dual-cowl phaeton above had veed windshield, dual cowl vents, wheelcovers over wire wheels and canvas-covered trunk. Imperial spanned a 145-inch wheelbase.

Walter P. Chrysler's son owned and proudly drove this 1932 Imperial 8 roadster with LeBaron body. Valanced front fenders contained storage compartments, and chrome trim strips formed extensions of the freestanding runningboards.

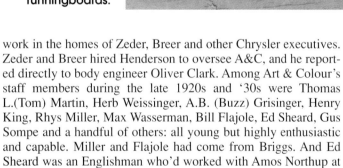

work in the homes of Zeder, Breer and other Chrysler executives. Zeder and Breer hired Henderson to oversee A&C, and he reported directly to body engineer Oliver Clark. Among Art & Colour's staff members during the late 1920s and '30s were Thomas L.(Tom) Martin, Herb Weissinger, A.B. (Buzz) Grisinger, Henry King, Rhys Miller, Max Wasserman, Bill Flajole, Ed Sheard, Gus Sompe and a handful of others: all young but highly enthusiastic and capable. Miller and Flajole had come from Briggs. And Ed Sheard was an Englishman who'd worked with Amos Northup at Murray.

For 1929-31, the Chrysler Imperial, along with Chrysler's four other lines, used what were called "ribbon" radiator grille shells. These looked like narrow chrome ribbons taped to the leading edge of the hood. The idea was to make the hood look longer by making the grille shallower, but in actuality ribbon grilles made the entire front ensemble look weaker, cheaper and less substantial. The public didn't like ribbon grilles, and yet they became something of a corporate identity symbol during those two to three years.

Herb Weissinger, one of the charter members of Chrysler's Art & Colour section and barely 21 when he arrived, greatly admired the front end of Al Leamy's 1929 Cord L-29 (see page 235). He carefully copied the veed L-29 grille for the 1931 Chrysler and Chrysler Imperial. Henderson liked the dynamism of Weissinger's renderings and, like Weissinger, was an admirer of Leamy's work. So for 1931, out went the ribbon grille (except for DeSoto) along with the Chrysler Imperial's Vauxhall hood flutes.

The Chrysler and Imperial were totally re-engineered and restyled for 1931. On the engineering side, both marques got long, straight-eight engines. These new engines lent justification for the longer 1931 hoods. That became the year, too, when Chrysler asked Budd to develop all-steel bodies for 1931 Chrysler and Imperial sedans and limousines. At the same time, Chrysler engineering worked with Ralph Roberts at LeBaron on styling both new cars, a happy collaboration that resulted in lower bodies, lower and even longer hoods, veed and gracefully raked windshields, plus the wonderful clamshell fender lines so characteristic of those years.

The 1931-33 Chrysler Imperials, in particular, had some of the most inspired custom and factory bodies available during the classic era. Ralph Roberts managed to sell Chrysler on a program of LeBaron catalogue customs on the Imperial chassis. Briggs Mfg. Co. also supplied most of Chrysler Corp.'s production bodies for Plymouth, Dodge, DeSoto and Chrysler—then and for two decades afterward.

Chrysler Corp.'s ribbon grille had come and gone, and while it hadn't succeeded visually, the idea—to lengthen the hood—was sound. So with the same thought in mind, the 1932 Chrysler Imperial took another hood-lengthening approach. Its designers that year decided to borrow from the 1930 Jordan Speedway Ace sedan and run the rear edge of the hood back nearly to the front-door cut. In other words, the hood overlapped most of the cowl and formed one unbroken mass from the grille shell to the windshield. This eliminated the vertical cowl line, so often highlighted by bright trim, and gave a tremendous boost to the overall horizontality of the body. It was a clever, inexpensive way to make a

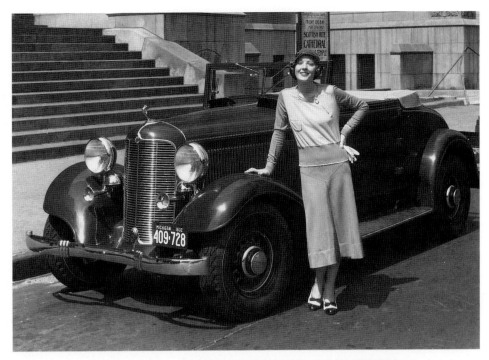

Rounded grille shape of Harry Miller's front-drive race cars inspired Chrysler stylists to put similar grille on 1932 DeSoto.

car look longer and more unified. By 1934, most U.S. automakers were using similar hoods that overlapped the cowl. Jordan came up with the idea, but Chrysler popularized it in production.

DeSoto kept the ribbon grille one year longer than its running mates, but for 1932, DeSoto received a striking front-end design that took inspiration from the wraparound grille of Miller racing cars. Miller racers provided Detroit with a steady flow of styling ideas, and DeSoto's was one of the most successful.

These styling upgrades, though, seemed (and were) minor compared with Chrysler's much more serious effort to bring a truly aerodynamic car to market. The story of the 1934 Airflow's development has been told many times, so we're going to touch on just the highlights here. Early experiments included running rear-engined test mules. These carried large, heavy Chrysler engines behind the back seat and were soon abandoned due to quirky handling.

ZSB then designed some front-engined prototypes and engineered them from the interior out. The Airflow, for example, became one of the first American production cars with three-abreast front seating—perhaps the first. The bench seats had chrome pipe framework, an idea borrowed from art moderne tube-frame furniture. And ZSB specifically positioned the rear bench well ahead of the rear axle. Nearly all cars of that day placed the back seat directly *over* the axle, and that caused two problems. First, it gave rear-seat passengers a very jouncy ride; second, it made the rear roof higher than it needed to be. By cradling both benches inside the wheelbase, ZSB were able to bring the overall height of the Airflow down without sacrificing headroom.

Another way they lowered the Airflow's body was to tilt the rear of the engine and transmission slightly downward. This dropped the driveshaft, making the floor and central tunnel several inches lower. And the relatively thin frame side-rail sections also dropped the step-over height. Zeder, Skelton and Breer weren't interested, though, in a low silhouette for the sake of styling. They wanted a low center of gravity so the Airflow would corner and handle better at speed. Filmed demonstrations, distributed free to moviehouses throughout the country in 1934, showed Airflows slewing around corners, running over ramps that lifted two wheels and yet, as the announcer said, "It's impossible to tip a Chrysler Airflow."

The Airflow also introduced what came to be called the "boulevard ride." This involved lengthening the front and rear springs (especially the front) so road oscillations excited a lower frequency in the suspension system, and the car essentially "walked" over bumps and potholes rather than leaped and bounded. Other cars

adopted longer springs soon after the Airflow introduced them.

The Three Musketeers tried hard to maximize everything about the Airflow, and body design was only one of many interrelated factors. They worked with Budd to develop the all-steel "bridge-truss" body/frame construction. This represented a radical departure from normal practice, because the typical car of that day had a separate, heavy steel chassis frame; then, bolted on top stood the body structure, usually framed in wood. In that format, the body added almost no rigidity. The Airflow, on the other hand, ran structural cage members up, over, around and throughout the body and then simply panelled the ribwork with steel sheets. The result was a stronger, lighter, lower, more rattle-resistant car.

As for the body shape, ZSB wanted very much to follow aircraft principles and make the Airflow as aerodynamic as possible. They recognized that an automobile couldn't be as streamlined as an airplane, given its necessarily more boxy configuration. But by conducting extensive windtunnel tests on wooden scale models (some of the tests set up and administered by flight pioneer Orville Wright), they were able to keep wind resistance and wind roar to a minimum.

Rather than let Chrysler Art & Colour make significant contributions to the design of the Airflow's exterior (the staff as well as Briggs did take a hand on the interior), ZSB insisted on doing most of the styling themselves. Carl Breer and Oliver Clark became heavily involved and so, presumably, did some of the body engineers from Budd. Ralph Roberts maintained that John Tjaarda and Briggs played no role in the Airflow's body engineering.

Chrysler A&C apparently was called on to add to the 1934 Airflow's details, and some were quite good: the multi-tiered bumpers and rear fender skirts with a repeat of the Viking-wing hood ornament. But the Airflow's front end had no grace at all. In fact, the 1934 model's built-in headlights gave both the DeSoto and Chrysler Airflows a sad-eyed look, and the waterfall grilles seemed almost an afterthought. Realizing this, Chrysler changed the Airflow grille twice during the 1934 model year, first from an expensive thin-bar style to a coarser texture, then to the peaked 1935 grille at the end of that first season.

What the Airflow did do for the corporation—and it rarely gets credit—was to spell out the importance of body-panel inter-changeability and elongation. Chrysler had started a body-sharing program with Plymouth and DeSoto in 1929 and now began to pioneer the commonality of specific panels and components. Chrysler worked closely with Budd in this regard. For example, in 1934 the DeSoto Airflow body became basic. The Chrysler

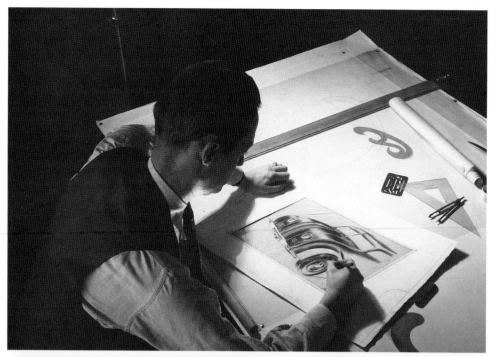

Chrysler engineering supervised the company's tiny Art & Colour staff, which initially did mostly ornamentation and trim. Tom Martin (left) sketched alternate Airflow fronts, while Buzz Grisinger (on right in photo below left) demonstrated clay wind-tunnel models to chief engineer Fred Zeder and body engineer Oliver Clark (behind Zeder). Selected clay models were cast in plaster and placed into a small windtunnel (bottom) that Orville Wright helped set up. Phantom drawing (top) illustrates Airflow's bridge-truss framing. The Airflow actually used a fairly conventional main frame. It had channel-section side rails and kickups at each end. Hoop sections and some body panels were welded to main frame. Budd helped develop this type of construction.

year ever, 1933, with a penetration of 25.8%. That meant ample cash reserves. And Chrysler also sold lots of non-Airflow models during the Airflow years (1934-37), so the company pulled through without ever being in financial peril.

Styling of the 1934 Plymouths and Dodges, meanwhile, copied the 1931-32 Chrysler format. The 1934 Dodge had Chrysler's cowl-overlapping hood, and both nameplates made use of low windshields and high beltlines. Coupes and open two-door models had short cabs and tall rear decks that gave them a fast, sporty appearance.

The Airflow hurt Chrysler's styling reputation and tended for decades to make the

Airflow added seven inches in the dash-to-front-axle area, the Chrysler Imperial Airflow on the 128-inch wheelbase added five inches to the rear quarters, and the Custom Imperials had nine-inch elongations in the front and rear doors. Coupe doors were also nine inches longer than those in sedans.

Budd supplied the three main body sections for all 1934 Airflow bodies. One stamping, consisting of the rear roof, rear deck panel and bumper pan, was common to all Airflow sedans. Rear side panels were likewise interchangeable, and on long-wheelbase Chrysler Imperials, Budd simply flash-welded a section into the standard cage. Sedan doors became interchangeable with some fairly minor die changes, meaning that with wheel cuts the left rear door became the right front and vice versa. Airflow coupe doors were identical to all four doors on the Chrysler Custom Imperial sedan (which, by the way, pioneered the use of the one-piece curved windshield). All Airflow body styles used the same basic floor

and roof stampings, differences again being in lengths and demanding a welded-in insert.

In the end, the Airflow turned out to be a roaring technological success and a howling commercial failure. Airflows were offered in Chrysler Imperial, Chrysler and DeSoto forms and, for 1934, the company produced a grand total of 25,179 Airflows. Fortunately, Chrysler Corp. had just gone through its best market-share

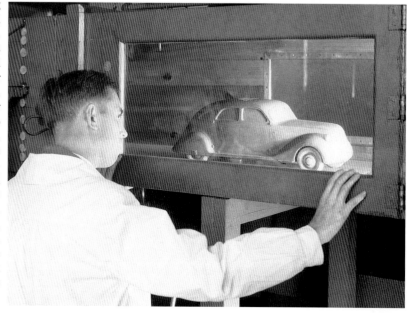

1934 Chrysler and DeSoto Airflows placed back passengers (top left) ahead of rear axle for better ride and lower roof. Chromed seat frames, inspired by art moderne furniture, added strength. Airflow's "waterfall" grille, shared by Union Pacific locomotive, tended to visually shorten and raise hood. Grille was redesigned twice in 1934; this is the original.

company conservative in all matters having to do with design. But at the same time, the Airflow added to Chrysler Corp.'s engineering prestige, because even people who hated the Airflow's styling had to admire the company's moxie for championing such a radical program during those very uncertain years of the Depression.

We've already described Walter Chrysler hiring Ray Dietrich in 1932 and Dietrich becoming head of Chrysler's Art & Colour section (page 54). In 1934, after it became clear that the Airflows' appearance was mainly responsible for its sluggish sales, Dietrich was given the assignment of making the 1935-37 Airflows more attractive. He began making sketches, but none of his early facelifts seemed appropriate. (Concurrently, Chrysler gave independent industrial designer Norman Bel Geddes a similar commission. Bel Geddes suggested a heavier, less expensive 1934 grille, which Chrysler accepted, but little else came of Bel Geddes' efforts.)

Meanwhile, Ralph Roberts at Briggs asked Phil Wright to design what became the 1935 Airstream series. Buzz Grisinger recalled seeing a beautiful book that Wright made. This book showed scale illustrations and was given by Briggs to Chrysler engineering vice president Carl Breer. Breer admired the designs and then passed the book along to Ray Dietrich in Art & Colour. The book showed Airstream proposals for the Chrysler Imperial, Chrysler and DeSoto, all of which looked thoroughly modern. Wright's Airstreams were "streamlined" in the artistic sense, with no pretense at genuine aerodynamics. Chrysler Corp. accepted the Wright/Briggs

proposals virtually without change. Airstreams went into production for 1935 and enjoyed healthy sales from the beginning.

After Phil Wright's Airstream illustrations arrived at Chrysler, Dietrich was asked to adapt their front ends to the 1935 and later Airflows. Airflows thus took on some of the Airstreams' identity, with more conventional, more vertical, more veed grilles. However, the company now advertised the Airstreams more and the Airflows less, and Airflow production stopped after 1937.

Chrysler styling in the mid to late 1930s kept up with the competition but never led. The 1936 Chrysler Airstream, for example, looked very much like that year's Buick, complete with fencing-mask grille. Rhys Miller, who arrived at Chrysler in 1935, said that while the exterior room contained some very progressive designers, management "...didn't want to do anything unless they had seen it done before by somebody else, and it had been successful." For years, then, Chrysler followed GM's lead. Briggs, meanwhile, continued to make design proposals to Chrysler for all five product lines, and Chrysler routinely accepted either Briggs' entire package or, more often, bits and pieces.

Chrysler's Art & Colour staff remained at half a dozen or so designers throughout the 1930s. They were situated on the sixth floor of the Highland Park engineering building and were divided not into studios but into two rooms, one working on exteriors and the other on interiors. The engineering building had a long hall running down the middle, and on one side was

exterior design, with interiors on the other. Herb Weissinger was the lead designer in the exterior studio, with Henry King taking that role in interiors and color.

Designer Gil Spear recalled that, "...in the prewar Chrysler exterior studio we occupied 15 to 18 3x5-foot Hamilton adjustable drafting tables crowded together in a small room. Flat filing cabinets ran along the door wall, with windows on the opposite wall. A series of corkboards covered the three non-window walls above waist level. And no one could enter this room unless an elderly guard sitting outside buzzed the locked door.

"The corkboards were completely covered with tacked-up Mi-Teintes renderings—so many that we designers had to agree among ourselves to allot the space equally. We put up our latest renderings and couldn't take down anyone else's to make more room. Designers could not enter the separate clay-modeling room unless they were invited, which was rare."

Chrysler's clay-modeling room, which was also the body drafting and layout department, was at the far south end of the hall, while the engineering showroom where design proposals and full-sized wooden mockups (not full-sized clay models) were presented to Chrysler engineers and management, was at the north end. The body layout department didn't have styling bridges for full-sized clay models until well after the war. Instead, modelers used simple L-shaped gantries, usually made of wood, that stood up from the individual modeling platforms.

According to Buzz Grisinger, Chrysler's clay modelers at that time were mostly former woodworkers. He also mentioned with some regret that union rules forbade

(Left) Kitten adorns catwalk of 1935 Chrysler Airstream. Designed by Phil Wright at Briggs, the Airstream kept Chrysler Corp. profitable despite Airflow losses. Dodge and DeSoto likewise used Airstream styling for 1935. The year before, however, the company's non-Airflow lines stayed with traditional styling, here exemplified by the 1934 Dodge coupe (below).

designers from taking part in the sculpting of full-sized clays. For that reason, Chrysler stylists designed mostly in sketch form, occasionally making scale clay models in the exterior design room. Henry King's interior studio across the hall was allowed to make full-sized clay models of instrument panels and seating bucks and had its own non-union modeler, Jim Shorey. And Briggs had the facilities to make full-sized clays: ovens, bridges, bucks, etc. Unlike Chrysler, Briggs' modelers weren't unionized.

Briggs continued to work with Chrysler body engineering to make production sheetmetal more and more interchangeable. By the late 1930s, commonality extended to cowls, roofs, doors, decklids, runningboards and fenders. Briggs kept coming up with stamping restrikes that would transform, say, a Dodge front fender into one with a slightly different shape or different character lines so it blended with the larger proportions of the same-year Chrysler or DeSoto.

That technique was especially evident for 1939, when most corporate front ends used the same basic stamping dies for the grille/catwalk/front-fender ensemble. The 1939 noses used the same draw dies but used restrikes along with grille and trim differences to distinguish the various nameplates.

By 1939, Chrysler's in-house styling staff, still nominally under Dietrich, had grown to roughly 25 members. Designers now included Buzz Grisinger, Herb Weissinger, Rhys Miller, Tom Bannister, Ed Sheard, Tom Martin, Charles (Chat) Bills, Gus Sompe, Gil Spear, John Hauser and Max Wasserman. Bob Cadwallader was the liaison between Art & Colour and Chrysler engineering. There were also four modelers and half a dozen draftsmen, so by that time Chrysler A&C was doing much more of the company's design work, and Briggs was contributing virtually nothing.

And yet the in-house styling staff acted merely as an idea facto-

Gil Spear Talks about Chrysler A&C in 1940

As a young designer, Gil Spear always preferred to put foregrounds and backgrounds into his design sketches, something Chrysler didn't encourage; in fact, did not allow. "I would never let Bob [Cadwallader] see those," said Spear in his Ford Archives oral reminiscences, "because he would feel I was wasting time.... Well, I was doing backgrounds: putting aircraft behind cars, putting pretty girls in front of them.

"One day...Fred Zeder was going to come into the studio: a very dignified man, an executive engineer...white haired, a bit portly.... Now the assistant head of the studio was Herb Weissinger...a very kindly fellow.... Herb came around and wanted me to put these illustrations up, and I absolutely refused. I didn't want to be fired. But he had his way and put them up, and finally the big man came in.

"Well, one of these renderings [with a background] was in a prominent place right near the door. It had a girl between the

viewer and the car, and she was stretching in a yawn, and you could see through her clothing somewhat...and [the sketch] had another girl leaning over...putting something in the trunk. There were also distracting aircraft and other images in the picture, including a second rear view of the same design.... We weren't supposed to waste time on things like that.

"When Zeder came in, he walked about 10 feet into the studio and stopped. He took off his glasses and got out another pair and put them on and proceeded to study this drawing...[and] then he left. In the meantime I'm thinking I'm going to get fired."

Spear wasn't fired, and Zeder chose the front end from that particular sketch—the wraparound grille—to go onto the

1942 Chrysler. More importantly, Cadwallader realized that he didn't have to control the designers' artwork so rigidly, and some of the barriers between styling and engineering began to come down. Meanwhile, Chrysler's managers and engineers began encouraging Spear to draw more cars with girls and airplanes, and they then "borrowed" these to decorate their offices. ◆

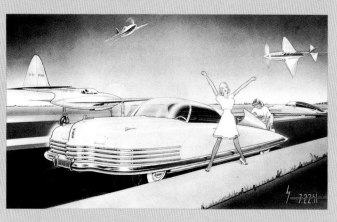

ry for engineering. Art & Colour had no patron, no one to champion a specific design or design direction; nobody to "sell" ideas to management or marketing. Styling remained under the control of body engineering, meaning that Chrysler's engineers had final say on the appearance of everything that went into production.

According to Rhys Miller, "Engineering...looked upon styling as a necessary evil. They knew they had to have us, but they didn't like us. And if we wanted...something that was advantageous to style, they'd [usually] say, 'Oh, you can't do it. It just isn't feasible....' For example, we had to stay with the butterfly-type [side-opening] hood for a long time, because there were overhead structures on the assembly line that would interfere with open alligator hoods on cars coming down the line. It was things like that...."

The 1940 Chrysler and Chrysler Imperial were the company's first models to adopt horizontal grilles. By 1942, the grilles wrapped completely around the fronts of both cars, and chrome trim repeated the grille theme on the rear fenders. The fenders themselves became modified suitcases.

The most intriguing body style of the immediate prewar era had to be the 1941 Chrysler Town & Country fastback sedan. Buzz Grisinger sketched the original design around 1938, and Oliver Clark's body engineers adapted it to existing sheetmetal. The Town & Country combined the dark-and-light woodwork of a station wagon—white ash ribbing and mahogany paneling—but used Chrysler's seven-passenger sedan roof plus the cowl, fenders and windshield from the Chrysler Windsor.

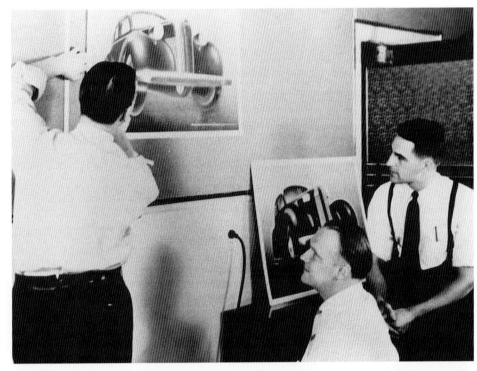

Walter Chrysler hired Ray Dietrich (center) to manage Art & Colour section, but Dietrich proved relatively ineffectual, especially since engineering dominated. That's Herb Weissinger standing and Buzz Grisinger seated. Photo dates from 1935.

The wooden decklid had the same shape as a conventional trunk but was split down the middle, vertically, and the two small doors hinged from the sides.

After Ray Dietrich left Chrysler in 1940, Robert Cadwallader took over as chief exterior designer. According to Gil Spear, Cadwallader was no designer, but he wanted very much to please the engineering people. In his efforts to please, Cadwallader strictly controlled what he wanted the engineers and Chrysler's upper management to see. He was also the only person in design who had access to the body development room, where full-sized clays were done. All 1942-48 Chrysler lines were done under Cadwallader, including the 1942 DeSoto, with its hidden headlights, and the 1942 Chrysler, for which Spear did the wraparound grille.

During the war, there were usually only four designers left in Chrysler's styling

Chrysler Corp. used one basic front-end die for all 1939 lines (below left), with restrikes giving individuality to each nameplate. Hayes 1939 coupes had 2-piece doors as on 1938

Cadillac 60-S (center). Stylists considered making a similar sedan for 1941 (below right). Designers could work in scale, but union modelers had to do full-sized clays (bottom).

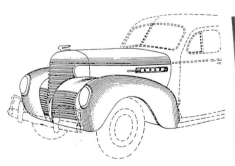

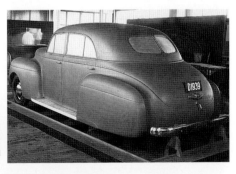

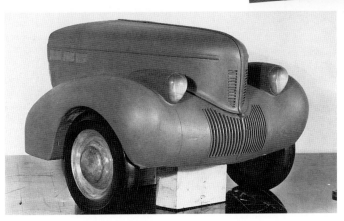

Inspired by Gil Spear's sketch, Chrysler adopted a clean wraparound grille for 1942 (left). Wood-bodied 1941 Town & Country sedan below had a 2-door decklid that opened outward from the center. It used white ash framing and mahogany panels, came in 6- and 9-passenger forms.

room: Cadwallader, Rhys Miller, Ed Sheard and Herb Weissinger. Buzz Grisinger would return occasionally from his work on the Manhattan Project. Between war work, which consisted mostly of camouflage development and illustrations for technical military manuals, Chrysler's stylists managed to propose a number of postwar designs, many in the form of scale clay models. Like similar designs from Ford, GM and the independents, Chrysler's wartime body shapes tended to be rounded fastback sedans with through fenders. These might have taken some inspiration from Alex Tremulis' Briggs/LeBaron Thunderbolt. Chrysler's renditions were generally less radical than GM's; had no fins, no spinners, no scoops and no glassed-in greenhouses. Surviving photos show several wartime Chrysler clays with thin, sharply defined windows and full wraparound body moldings that ran from the fender-mounted headlamps around the flush sides to become horizontal bezels for slit-like tail lights.

The corporation's facelifted 1946-48 models were probably more changed than they needed to be. The postwar Chrysler Crown Imperial, Chrysler, DeSoto and Dodge used new sheetmetal that blended the front fenders into the doors like the Packard Clipper. The 1946 Imperial, Chrysler and Dodge grilles took inspiration from the 1941 Cadillac's bold, bright eggcrate pattern, and thanks to a ravenous demand for new postwar cars, Chrysler Corp. managed to end 1946 with a near-record 25.7% share of the U.S. automobile market.

During the war, Bob Cadwallader had some run-ins with Oliver Clark, his boss in Chrysler body engineering. Cadwallader left Chrysler in 1944 to go first to GM and then, in Nov. 1946, to Kaiser-Frazer. Herb Weissinger also left, he and Buzz Grisinger joining Cadwallader at Kaiser-Frazer in 1947 (see page 243). That meant that Chrysler had lost its design management and most of its best stylists.

Those remaining at Chrysler Art & Colour—Tom Martin, Tom Bannister, Ed Sheard and a few others—were put under the direction of Henry King, who now had charge of both exterior and interior design. And it was under King that Chrysler

Corp.'s 1949 models were styled. Grisinger remembered doing the 1949 Chrysler instrument panel before leaving for Kaiser-Frazer, and he also recalled that Ed Sheard did most of the 1949 grilles. "They had that furniture look," said Grisinger, "and Ed was a furniture designer way back when."

Chrysler's boxy, tall, uninspired postwar body styles have been attributed to the iron will of K.T. Keller. Keller took over as company president after Walter Chrysler became board chairman in July 1935. From then until he himself assumed the chairmanship on Nov. 3, 1950, Keller ran all aspects of Chrysler personally. (In 1950, Keller also accepted a federal appointment to head the U.S. guided missile development program.) And he held some strong convictions, favoring,

among other things, chair-high seats. But he also favored a high roof, because Keller wanted to be able to wear a hat inside a car and not have it knocked off when he got out. "We don't build cars you can piss over; we build 'em to sit in," he would say. It wasn't that Keller didn't understand the commercial value of styling. He was very much atuned to the market and genuinely a "car guy," but like most Chrysler managers, he valued engineering above design.

Keller had the good sense, though, not to trust his judgement entirely and, in the late summer of 1949, he hired Virgil Max Exner. Exner had been Pontiac's studio chief under Harley Earl from 1936 through 1938. He left GM in '38 to go with Raymond Loewy as chief designer on the Studebaker account, working first in New York and then in South Bend, Indiana. It was Exner who, under Loewy, oversaw development of the trendsetting 1947 "double-ender" Studebaker.

Then in early 1949, Exner had had a messy falling-out with Loewy (see page 207), after which he went on Studebaker's payroll. At Studebaker, Exner's patron had been Roy Cole, the company's chief engineer, but the bad news was that Cole was about to retire. Before he left, though, Cole made sure Exner found another job. Exner almost got hired by John Oswald at Ford, but that fell through when Walker came back. So Cole called Keller, and Keller

1942 DeSoto (above) had hidden headlights and hallmark vertical grille bars. After WW-II, using one basic 1946-48 body in different sizes, Chrysler faired front fenders into doors, built seven hardtops on Town & Country convertible base (below).

Virgil M. Exner

Virgil M. was born in Ann Arbor, Michigan on Sept. 24, 1909. He was adopted by the Exner family in Buchanan, Michigan soon afterward and, as a youngster, learned woodworking and shop skills from his grandfather, a head machinist at Clark Equipment Co. in Buchanan.

In 1926, Exner enrolled at Notre Dame, some 15 miles south in South Bend, Indiana, where he studied art and design. His teachers found he had considerable artistic talent and encouraged him to pursue art as a profession. He did well at Notre Dame but, after 2 1/2 years, left when his money ran out.

Exner had an abiding interest in cars. He and some of his friends from school would take the train to the Chicago Salon to see the latest styles and, for his own amusement, he often made designs of cars that interested him. His son, Virgil M. Exner Jr., still has sketches that Ex did showing a modified Duesenberg Model A and a Kissel roadster. Exner was also an avid car-racing fan. When he was 16, he talked his father into taking him to his first Indy 500, and he never lost his enthusiasm for race cars.

After Notre Dame, Exner, then 19, interviewed for a job in South Bend with a firm called Advertising Artists. Not only did he get the job but, three years later, he married the secretary who'd interviewed him, Mildred Marie Eschleman.

In 1928, when Exner got there, Advertising Artists was producing brochures and catalogues for Studebaker. Exner began by painting picture backgrounds, but when his boss noticed how good he was, he gave Exner the task of illustrating Studebaker cars and trucks. Exner soon became a very adept, versatile commercial artist, excellent at quick sketches and particularly good with transparent watercolors. He also developed a knack for sculpting clay, all of which later helped him as a car designer.

In 1934, Exner heard that GM was looking for designers, so he drove to Detroit, interviewed with Howard O'Leary and got hired into the Pontiac studio under Frank Hershey. Exner's quality of artwork set him apart even from those highly skilled artists at General Motors. His drawings had a style and a personality that made them instantly identifiable. When Hershey went over to Opel in 1937, Exner took his place as head of Pontiac design.

The year before, in 1936, Raymond Loewy had landed the Studebaker account and launched a talent search to service it. He did a little discrete corporate raiding and hired first Clare Hodgman at Sears-Roebuck, then Paul Zimmerman and Virgil Exner at GM. Earl pleaded with Exner to stay, because the two men got along so well, but Loewy's salary offer and the lure of New York were too strong. Exner, his wife and their young son moved to Long Island and lived there until mid 1941, when Studebaker insisted on having Loewy stylists on the premises in South Bend. This was like a homecoming for the Exners, who rented a small house on the Paul G. Hoffman estate. Hoffman was Studebaker's president.

At Studebaker, with Loewy's blessing, Exner built up a lively,

talented and compatible design staff that eventually included Bob Bourke; Gordon Buehrig, John Reinhart and Vince Gardner (all ex-ACD); Bob Koto (ex-Briggs); Jack Aldrich, modelers Frank Ahlroth, Joe Thompson and John Lutz (all ex-GM). They were known collectively as the "Loewy Gang," but Loewy rarely showed up in South Bend, having spread himself thin worldwide. Exner reported basically to Roy E. Cole, Studebaker's chief engineer.

During the development of the 1947 Studebaker, Exner became frustrated with Loewy's long absences plus the fact that Loewy gave Gordon Buehrig equal rank within their design group. Buehrig and Exner remained good friends, but Exner now felt that his allegiance was more to Studebaker than to Loewy and, with Roy Cole's encouragement, he and modeler Frank Ahlroth began to make a rival clay model of the 1947 Studebaker in Ex's basement at home (see page 207). When Loewy found out, he accused Exner of insubordination and fired him. Studebaker, meanwhile, chose Exner's clay over Loewy's, and Cole put Exner on the Studebaker payroll the next day.

Cole, though, was nearing the end of his career, and he knew that Exner didn't stand a chance at Studebaker without his patronage. Thus, in early 1949, Cole began to search for a new job for Exner. One of Cole's first calls was to John Oswald, who'd just gone to Ford from Oldsmobile. Oswald very much wanted Exner and offered him a handsome welcoming salary. It all looked set: The Exners began to search for a house in Detroit and had almost signed the papers when Oswald called to say that Ford had taken on George Walker's firm and no longer needed Exner. Roy Cole then phoned K.T. Keller at Chrysler, and Keller willingly hired Exner in the late summer of 1949—at a considerably lower salary than Oswald had offered. In time, Exner became Chrysler's design director, brought Chrysler's design department into modern times, built up a staff of 300 and, in 1957 was named Chrysler's first vice president of design.

All was going extremely well when Exner suffered a severe heart attack in 1956. Chrysler brought in William M.Schmidt, formerly Studebaker-Packard's styling vice president, as a temporary replacement. Exner returned to work a year later but in Nov. 1961, Chrysler president Lynn Townsend brought in Elwood Engel as corporate styling vice president. Exner took an early retirement and opened his own private industrial design firm with his son but remained with Chrysler as a consultant until 1964. During that time, Townsend assigned Exner the task of developing a Jeep-like vehicle for Chrysler.

In his own firm, Exner generated artwork for an article that appeared in *Esquire*. The *Esquire* drawings led to the design of the classic Stutz Blackhawk, the Duesenberg II and the Mercer Cobra. The Exners consulted with toymaker Renwall, who made scale plastic model kits of these cars. The Exner firm also did some automotive designs for U.S. Steel, Dow Chemical and Ghia in Italy. The Ghia contract called for one design per month, and from those sketches came the Ghia 2100S, the Ghia Selene II, the Renault Floride (Caravelle in the U.S.) and the VW 1500 series. Virgil Max Exner passed away two days before Christmas in 1973. ◆

Metal Dodge mockup from 1947 (above) set the pattern for all Chrysler lines from 1949 through 1954. During this period, Chrysler prided itself on engineering rather than styling. Company president K.T. Keller favored chair-high seats and cars he could wear a hat in. As a result, the roofs of Chrysler products stood relatively tall. Applied rear fenders followed the GM/Studebaker convention. And while Chrysler had pioneered the modern hardtop "convertible," the company put it into production two years after GM.

became Exner's first patron at Chrysler.

By 1950, as the demand for new cars began to taper off, Keller found Chrysler's market share falling. Wall Street blamed the corporation's poor sales on styling. Only buyers who wore hats, sat on tall chairs and liked mud fences bought Chrysler products. The rest of America went for jazzier cars, and there were now plenty to choose from.

Something needed to be done in a hurry, especially since Keller wanted to borrow several hundred million dollars from Wall Street to pay for Chrysler's 1951 hemi V-8, development of its new power steering, continued research into a fully automatic transmission (Chrysler wouldn't have one until 1955) and the retooling of its 1953 car lines. Wall Street had to be convinced, though, that the company could hold its own against GM and Ford in future styling wars, because as of 1949, it really didn't look that way.

So Keller hired Exner as director of advanced styling and set him up in a small advanced studio separate from what was then known as Chrysler Styling—formerly Art & Colour. Exner called his advanced studio "solitary confinement," but for now, Keller

York's financial community. He wanted to prove physically that Chrysler could design more than bloodless production cars. Ex promptly hired two young designers, Cliff Voss and Mauri Baldwin, plus Harry Peterson, a clay modeler. The Chrysler Imperial parade phaetons were quickly designed, and Chrysler built them in its own prototype shops. The side sculpting of the phaetons predicted the lines of the 1955 Imperial, Chrysler and DeSoto. All went well with these big cars, the only problem being their cost: $83,000 each. That's the figure cited by both Cliff Voss and Exner's son, Virgil Jr., who himself later became a designer at Ford.

About the time the parade phaetons were finished, K.T. Keller arranged with two Italian coachbuilders—Carrozzeria Ghia and Pinin Farina—to make up sample bodies for Chrysler so that Exner could evaluate their workmanship. Both coachbuilders received chassis through Chrysler's overseas branch, and both fabricated sample bodies on them. Keller didn't care what the designs looked like, but he wanted Exner to compare Ghia's and Pinin Farina's craftsmanship and standards of quality.

Among Virgil Exner's first projects at Chrysler was the design of three 1952 Crown Imperial parade phaetons. These fore-shadowed the side treatment of Exner's 1955 designs. The

phaetons saw use in New York, Detroit and Los Angeles. Curved glass was used for both windshields. Rear cowl housed a clock and two ashtrays. Each car could carry eight passengers, and all three were subsequently updated in the style of 1956 Imperials.

didn't want him involved with production design. Indeed, he told Exner, "I want you to design the most beautiful cars you can," and gave him three specific mandates: 1) design a futuristic Chrysler Imperial dual-cowl parade phaeton, 2) design a series of knock-out dreamcars, and 3) generate advanced styling ideas that Chrysler can use in future production.

Of the Chrysler Imperial parade phaeton, three would be built: one for New York ticker-tape parades, one to ferry movie stars and dignitaries around Los Angeles and a third for similar service in Detroit and Chicago. These and the dreamcars had an immediate purpose. Keller needed them and their high visibility to wow New

Several things about Ghia and Pinin Farina appealed to Exner. First, he greatly admired Italian car design in general. Immediately after WW-II, the Italians took the international lead in styling. Postwar Germany and England were trapped in time and kept repeating body styles from the mid 1930s. The Italians, though, made amazing advances both before and after the war and kept turning out beautifully fresh, clean, simple, almost naked autobodies. Alongside them, American cars looked overstuffed and overdressed.

Just as wondrous, the Italians still had the postwar remnants of a coachbuilding industry. Coachbuilding had never gone away in

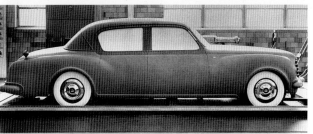

Exner and Ghia's Luigi Segre discuss Chrysler K-310, Ex's first showcar and his answer to Harley Earl's GM Motorama fare. Exner attempted to blend Italian with American design.

Italy, because a coterie of wealthy Europeans continued to want custom-bodied automobiles, particularly sport coupes and roadsters. So those small, sometimes wartorn shops in Turin and Milan reopened after VE Day and could now make anything out of sheetmetal that anyone might want. Italy still had the best craftsmen and, some say, the best designers in the world.

Not only did Italy's cottage-industry coachbuilders produce first-rate carbodies but they worked for peanuts, and that again appealed to Exner and Keller. Both Ghia and Pinin Farina were eager to do complete showcars for between $10,000 and $20,000 each, this as compared with the $83,000 Chrysler "paid" for its parade phaetons and the $125,000 quoted for building the K-310

in Chrysler's own shops. Exner also recognized in Ghia's and Farina's craftsmanship that the Italians set a vastly higher standard than we demanded in this country. Ultimately, Exner found Ghia's quality a little better than Farina's, so he signed a contract with Luigi Segre of Ghia to fabricate a series of handmade Chrysler show- and dreamcars for Chrysler. These would be built in Italy on American chassis and shipped to this country as they were finished.

Exner's first showcar was the 1951 Chrysler K-310 sport coupe, the "K" standing for Keller and "310" being the horsepower of the modified Chrysler hemi V-8. Like GM's LeSabre, the K-310's styling had far more impact than most of Chrysler's subsequent

Ghia built several Imperial limousines with K-310 grille (top left). Chrysler d'Elegance of 1953 (top center) godfathered VW Karmann-Ghia. The 1953 DeSoto Adventurer I (top right) became Exner's personal car and one of his favorites. Clean

and simple, the 1954 Dodge Firearrow (above left) was typical Exner. Both grille bars swept entirely around the body, which was twice as wide as its cowl height. Unitized 1955 Chrysler Falcon became smallest of Exner/Ghia roadsters.

showcars, because those that followed immediately were variations on the K-310 theme. All showed, though, what Exner valued in car design.

These were not copies of anything Italian, yet they had a lot of that flavor: clean side sculpturing, very little ornamentation in most instances, fully rounded wheel openings totally filled with huge knock-off wire wheels and fat wide-whitewall tires, lots of glass, no panel seams, thin pillars and very light, delicate roofs. In those aspects, the K-310 and several of its successors could have passed for Italian. What made them unmistakably American, though, was their size and the treatments of their fronts and rears.

The K-310 front had a bold, beak-like vertical grille and coved, inboard headlights. A continental spare cover was stamped into the decklid, and the rear fenders carried "gunsight" tail lights. These lamps stood up like chromed microphones from the tops of the fenders, and Exner justified them by saying they made the car easier to park, because you could see where the rear fenders ended (more or less).

The K-310 plus its brothers and sisters—the 1952 Chrysler C-200 convertible and Chrysler Special coupe, the 1953 GS-1, DeSoto Adventurer I (Exner's favorite) and the VW Karmann-Ghia-inspiring 1953 d'Elegance—apparently did help Keller and Colbert raise the money they needed, and the designs certainly got plenty of ink for Chrysler's growing styling department. So there's no question that they paid their way and, of course, so did Exner himself.

Soon after the K-310, Ex and his staff were asked to design a four-door version of the coupe for possible production. They did, and it was mocked up full size in wood and displayed in engineering's sixth-floor showroom. Cliff Voss remembered it being maroon and black and very chic. But when asked whether a K-310 sedan—those lines—should serve as a future Chrysler, Voss and Exner felt not. It was, like the Airflow, too different for the American public to accept.

By this time—1950—Chrysler Styling was divided into six separate studios: Plymouth under Henry King, Dodge under Herb Weissinger, DeSoto under Tom Bannister and Chrysler under Tom Martin. There was also Exner's advanced group and a separate

Ghia at Work

Cliff Voss was one of Exner's young designers helping on the K-310 and other early Chrysler showcars. He describes the coachbuilding process that Ghia used in those days.

"If you watched those people put cars together, you couldn't believe it," said Voss in a 1992 interview. "They'd just bang them together by eyeball. Everything was eyeballed.... The first car, the K-310, was sent over as a 3/8-scale plaster model, but even as carefully as we packed it, it broke up. By the time they [Ghia] got it, it was in bits and pieces. But we did have 3/8-scale drawings, so Ghia took those and blew them up to full size. Now when you take 3/8 and blow it up full size, you get some monumental differences. So when they translated the design into a full-sized wooden model, it needed approval. And modification. So Ex went over on the K-310 and several of the other cars, and I would go over on some of them.

"When you'd go over there, they'd have a full-sized wooden model. It wasn't solid; just 10-inch sections, but full size. The o u t e r surfaces...you could run your hand over them and it was like a mirror. But there was still bark hanging down on the

inside! The thing was, they'd do them so *fast!* You could ask for a change. Maybe you'd change the whole front end. And they'd have it done in a couple of hours. It was just unbelieveable.

"They had this open courtyard, and here's what really impressed me. You hear about the *old* masters; master craftsmen. Well, these were 16-18-year-old kids! In the center of this open courtyard, inside this atrium with [a quadrangle of] old plant [buildings] around it—really old—it had been a carriagebuilder's plant...so in the center was this brick cobblestone courtyard where they used to [bring] the horses from the stable. Anyway, that's where they'd have the wooden model, sitting there.

"All around it, maybe 30 feet away,

were a bunch of wooden tree stumps. The tops of these tree stumps had been shaved to different curvatures. Some were round, some spherical, hemispheres, flat, slightly domed, peaked; all different shapes. These

kids would take 10x10-inch squares of aluminum and their hammers, and they'd eyeball...they would *look* at the wooden model and then start to hammer [the metal over the tree stumps]. They'd walk over, put the piece of metal [over the wooden full-sized model], and it fit! I mean the fit was phenomenal.

"Then they'd have these other young kids who'd come over and weld this virgin metal to virgin metal. So the roof might be 30 different squares all welded together. You'd look at it and it would look terrible because of all these burn marks. But when it cooled, you could run your hand over it: It was like a mirror. These guys were geniuses.

"And if it didn't look right, if you wanted to change it, they'd just cut that piece out and do another one. You know, *boom,* like that. And the trimmers were just as good. It was just incredible craftsmanship. And a lot of fun to watch." ◆

1957 Chrysler Dart showcar offers insight into Ghia's construction methods. First, Ghia made wooden forms, complete with openable decklid, doors and hood. Craftsmen then beat out small sheetmetal panels to fit precisely over these contours. Panels were finally welded together and the seams leaded.

industrial design department that did trucks and special projects. Each automotive studio worked on both exteriors and interiors, and modeling was done in separate rooms adjacent to each studio.

Clay modelers at Chrysler were unionized, so their tasks were clearly defined. Chrysler stylists were also unionized for many years, but one of them, Harold Pilkey, hired an attorney around 1951 and proceeded to get designers out of the union. Before that, stylists had been allowed to make 3/8-scale models but were limited on full-sized models to scribing lines and showing section. They were not allowed to do any full-sized surface development. That remained the province of Chrysler engineering, which controlled the modelers.

In 1953, Chrysler bought Briggs Mfg. Co. and, with that purchase, finally gained the plant capacity to manufacture all of its own bodies. (Chrysler continued to supply Packard with bodies until Packard had a chance to buy part of Briggs and become self sufficient.)

Lester Lum (Tex) Colbert was a former Texas cotton buyer who'd put himself through Harvard law school. Working in New York in 1933, he met and impressed Walter Chrysler and K.T. Keller. In 1935, Keller made Colbert vice president of Dodge Div., and from there, his career with Chrysler spiralled upward. Henry Ford II wanted to hire Colbert in 1948, but Colbert stayed put, knowing he would probably be heir to the Chrysler presidency. When he took over from Keller in Nov. 1950, Colbert began to champion styling, and it was with his patronage that Exner came into corporate prominence.

Chrysler Styling had finished all production car and truck designs through the 1952 model year, and Exner's small, separate staff had relatively little to do even with the 1953-54 models. Still under Henry King, all Chrysler products—particularly the 1953 Plymouth and Dodge—were downsized slightly that year in response to marketing surveys. Plymouth and Dodge became an average of 670 pounds lighter for 1953. More important, they were visibly smaller than Ford, Chevrolet, Pontiac and other traditional rivals.

Chrysler's downsizing didn't help. Combined, Plymouth and Dodge lost roughly one percentage point of market share for '53 and then another 5.66 points for 1954. Chrysler Corp. as a whole posted its worst sales year in 1954 since 1931. Whereas from 1936 through 1950 Chrysler had stayed ahead of Ford in market share,

On the strength of surveys that asked *Does your neighbor want a smaller car?* Chrysler downsized the 1953 Plymouth and Dodge. Neighbors might have wanted smaller cars, but the buyers themselves wanted bigger ones, and the 1953-54 Plymouths lost market share to Ford and Chevrolet.

in 1951 it lost its #2 status to Ford and, after that, the sales gap kept widening. By 1954, GM held nearly 51% of the market, Ford 31% and now 13% for Chrysler. This was Chrysler's second crisis, the first being the Airflow, and something had to be done in a hurry.

Profits rebounded in 1955 with Exner's first production designs. The tremendous expense of retooling all four car lines was offset by success of 1955 Plymouth, Dodge (top), DeSoto (center) and Chrysler. Chrysler 300 (above) took its model designation from horsepower rating of its hemi V-8.

In late 1952, according to Virgil Exner Jr., K.T. Keller came to his father and invited him to critique what Henry King's production studios had cooking for 1955. Exner Sr. told Keller "they won't do," whereupon Keller replied, "All right then, how about you doing the '55s?" When Exner said he'd like to try, Keller gave him 18 months to redo the entire corporate lineup.

At that point, Tex Colbert elevated Virgil Exner to corporate director of styling and told him to do whatever was needed to bring Chrysler back from the edge. When Exner took over as director, there were all of 17 people in what was soon renamed Chrysler Styling. It's fair to say that, over the next three years, Exner brought Styling out of a state that hadn't changed since the late 1930s. He and King now worked together, building up the staff and equipping the studios so that Chrysler's design operation finally began to equal GM's and Ford's.

Work began on Chrysler Corp.'s 1955 models even as Exner and Henry King were hiring more designers. They put out the word and then made their selections carefully. Among those who had joined Chrysler by that time were Don Kopka, Bill Brownlie and Homer La Gassey. In Apr. 1956, Exner's staff numbered 280 people, including modelers.

Engineer Harry E. Chesebrough, meanwhile, was assigned to set up Chrysler's first formal product-planning staff. Product planning worked closely with styling, and Chesebrough also put together a group that took rival cars apart and, piece by piece, analyzed the manufacturing techniques and costs of other auto companies. This led to cost controls plus a renewed program of body component interchangeability.

For the 1955 lines, Henry King became styling director of Plymouth, Dodge and special bodies. Under him were studio managers Harold Pilkey of Plymouth and Homer La Gassey of Dodge. Tom Bannister was now chief stylist of DeSoto, Chrysler and accessories, and he directed studio managers Dick Baird (DeSoto) and Fred Reynolds (Chrysler). Cliff Voss was named chief stylist of the Imperial and advanced studios, with Bill Brownlie managing the Imperial studio. Bob Bingman had charge of interiors (Walt Wengren, manager), custom cars and special products, while Dick Caleal managed truck design. James Charipar became the engineer in charge of advanced projects, and S.L. Terry headed styling engineering, including preliminary design. Exner himself kept a small advanced design studio and continued to work closely with Voss.

Even in his showcar days, Exner insisted on autonomy and particularly on being allowed to follow through with his own designs. His solitary-confinement studio took him out of engineering's gravitational field, and now that he had charge of production-car design, he began campaigning to loosen engineering's and the union's grip on styling. No longer would Chrysler engineers have control over the development of full-sized clay models. Clays would henceforth be done by studio designers, although still not inside the studios proper. But each studio now had access to an air-conditioned "clay room," complete with modeling platforms, clay ovens, etc. Before 1956, the studios themselves were still without air conditioning, but the clay rooms had to be cooled so the models wouldn't sag in Detroit's summer heat. With strong backing from Colbert, Chrysler styling was finally approaching par with other service staffs: marketing, advertising, sales, etc.

The first production cars to come out under Exner's styling direction were the radical (for Chrysler) and highly successful 1955 models. The corporation sold more vehicles in 1955 than in

any year to that time: 1.6 million, nearly twice as many as in 1954 (884,000). The company gained four percentage points of market share and made lots of money, much of which balanced out that year's extensive, expensive restyling and tooling costs.

The 1955 Plymouths and Dodges had grown larger again. All five car lines (Imperial was now a separate marque) became more youthful and appealing. Ads called Exner's 1955 effort the "*Forward* Look," and while all five nameplates kept a family resemblance, each division had strong individual identity and lots of visual character. Dodge and DeSoto, for example, introduced three-tone paint schemes, and upmarket Plymouths, DeSotos and Chryslers had bold, contrasting bodyside inserts called "color sweeps." Color became an important part of the *Forward* Look. Chrysler offered 56 solid hues, 173 two-tone combinations and several three-tones. The three-tones usually included an off-white, onyx black plus one striking color like fuscia, bright yellow or lavender.

Model years 1955-56 brought such impressive sales gains, most of them obviously tied to styling, that Chrysler finally overcame the conservatism brought on by the Airflow. No one at any management level could now ignore the importance of design. Exner had made huge strides in convincing Chrysler's divisional managers that his activity should no longer remain engineering's stepchild. The success of his 1955-56 models boosted Exner's prestige and credibility to such an extent that Colbert handed him considerably more budget than styling had ever enjoyed before.

Riding high, Exner decided to go for another total restyling program for 1957. The '55s had been longer, lower, wider, more colorful and more in the mainstream, but Exner now pushed to make the '57s the recognized style *leaders* of the industry. To meet that goal, he first had to convince engineering to help him drop the average height of all 1957 Chrysler Corp. hardtop coupes a full five inches. Five inches might not sound like much, but body engineers will tell you it can't be done; surely not on the scale Exner had in mind. He wanted to lower sedans and wagons, too, although not necessarily a full five inches.

He was asking the impossible. Even if this had been 1915, when the typical car stood 80 inches tall, a five-inch drop would still have been tough to put across. But this was 1954-55, when cars were already about as low as anyone could make them. Studebaker had come out with the 56-inch-high Loewy coupes for 1953, and those had driven the body engineers nuts. Yet here came

Exner aimed extremely low with early 1957 Chrysler prototype (above). Engineering forced him to raise body sections somewhat, but he still managed to lower the entire 1957 range a full five inches.

1957 Plymouth

1957 Chrysler 300-C

Exner's low, clean, light-roofed 1957 coupes gave GM designers a jolt when they spied early examples through the plant fence on Detroit's Mound Road.

1957 DeSoto

Exner asking for a line of hardtop coupes with an overall height of 54 inches? Chrysler engineers, who'd at last been ordered to cooperate with styling, said that making coupes in five car lines a mere 54 inches tall absolutely, *absolutely* couldn't be done.

But Exner persisted, and Chrysler engineers came through with space-saving torsion-bar front suspension systems, 14-inch wheels, drop-over carburetor aircleaners, thin pre-formed headliners and a number of other tricks which, together, did take five inches out of the height of the average 1957 Chrysler Corp. hardtop. The 1957 Plymouth Fury hardtop coupe indeed stood 54 inches tall.

The 1957 cars themselves looked sensational. They had a basic wedge shape, an almost dart-like appearance, with large, clean fins, delicate pillars and gently curving, thin-section, light-looking roofs, especially on the hardtops. Body sides weren't slabby but rather showed some cross-sectional sculpting. And the 1957 Imperial became one of the first production cars ever to use both a compound-curved windshield along with curved side glass.

A handful of GM designers, seeing pre-release 1957 Chrysler cars in a holding pen behind the plant on Mound Road, were thoroughly shaken by how low and gorgeous the '57 hardtops looked. Among the GM spies were design director Bill Mitchell and stu-

Color Me Colorful

"Form speaks to the intellect, color to the emotions," wrote Jules Andrade, a designer for Chandler-Cleveland Motors in 1926. He also talked about warm and cold colors. Andrade felt that warms—reds, yellows and oranges—made automotive surfaces look larger. They also suggested life and cheerfulness. Cold colors, he said—blues, blacks and icy whites—expressed tranquility.

Color has always been an important part of auto design, but in the early days of motoring, light, bright colors weren't practical. They dried more slowly and chalked and faded more quickly than dark ones. Besides, the public back then seemed to prefer darker, more muted tones. Henry Ford offered deep red, grey and dark green on his first Model T's, then only dark green until 1912, then dark blue before switching to black only in 1914. Henry gave the customer no color choice until 1925, when he added red and burnt orange.

After the rainbow of Duco nitrocellulose lacquers came on the market in 1925 (Pontiac alone offered "true blue" in 1924), auto buyers went wild for color. In describing the 1926 New York coachbuilders' salon, the trade magazine *Automotive Industries* proclaimed, "Visually, color dominates everything else in the show." Even Ford grudgingly offered Duco colors a year later.

It wasn't long before auto companies hired color experts. The study and use of color resulted in GM and Chrysler calling their styling departments "Art & Colour," the British spelling seeming more sophisticated at the time. Harley Earl's secretary, Miss Ramshaw, said she and Howard O'Leary used to choose colors at GM in the beginning, but in 1928 Earl hired Capt. H. Ledyard Towle as A&C's resident color expert. "Cap" Towle had been with Duco in the 1920s. He left GM in late 1930 to become art director of Chevrolet's ad agency, Campbell-Ewald Co. Earl replaced him with Chester Hill, who died suddenly of pneumonia, after which Steve McDaniel took over trim and color.

Packard gave similar status to interior designer and "colorist" Herbert T. Strong.

Strong staged "color salons" as part of Packard's 1934 new-model presentation at the Hotel Roosevelt in New York. "Over 80% of the sensations reaching the brain," said Strong, "have to do with color." Colorists helped set and react to early color trends. Howard Ketchum, the New York industrial designer, began his career as a colorist. He chose colors for the Pan American China Clippers in 1934 and avoided browns and yellows, saying they made people airsick.

Theories on automobile exterior colors abounded. Dark colors were deemed "heavy" and light ones were "less weighty." George J. Mercer wrote in 1926 that light, showy colors look best in the country while darker tones were more at home in the city. "Color is not to be used to create;" he wrote in *Autobody*, "its office is to emphasize." In 1927, coachbuilder Ray Dietrich postulated that somber colors were appropriate for times of economic depression while contrasting, extreme colors expressed a spirit of prosperity.

In 1928, Lincoln ran a series of dazzling ads with the theme "taken from nature." These keyed car colors to pictures of bright birds and butterflies. That same year, Fisher and Fleetwood based automobile colors on art masterpieces—the *Mona Lisa*, Gainsborough's *Blue Boy*, etc. In 1938, Pontiac began charting paint-color preferences by state, trying to discover a pattern. The only conclusion the researchers reached was that tastes changed quickly.

In 1946-47, according to GM's Steve McDaniel, General Motors began to standardize colors throughout the corporation. Before that, each division had its own palette, and many hues were virtually the same. George Moon contended that standardized colors didn't arrive fully until 1959 and at that point it saved GM millions.

Color trends have always tended to run in cycles. In the 1950s, pastels and pale colors became popular along with two- and three-tone combinations. In the early 1980s, reds took a jump in popularity, partly because paint suppliers developed pigments and stabilizers that made reds look richer and wear longer. The popularity of reds required pigments many times more

expensive than, say, whites. Reds cost the automakers more, yet there's never been an additional charge for red on new cars.

Today, predicting color preferences amounts to big business. Several respected color services exist, all with experts who meet regularly in different parts of the world. Their job is to predict future color preferences, but at the same time they *influence* trends, so theirs are often self-fulfilling prophesies.

The Big Three automakers all subscribe—for a few thousand dollars a year—to color services like The Color Council, Color Box, ESP/Ellen Sideri Partnership Inc., Here & There, Pat Tunsky and Promostyl. Most of these services are based in New York, and their main customers are ready-to-wear clothing manufacturers. Each issues short- and long-range forecasts predicting which hues will become popular. Their short-term pronouncements are of particular interest to the garment industry. Views two to three years into the future can affect not just auto designers but also makers of electric appliances, tiles, home furnishings, sporting goods, etc.

Paint suppliers also play a role in bringing color trends to the auto industry: DuPont, BASF, Sherwin-Williams, Martin-Senour, etc. And for automotive interiors, June Roche of Milliken, who represents the textile industry, stages a color-trend show for all Detroit automakers each spring.

Modern-day color trends usually start with services agreeing that a specific color—say teal—will become popular. They pass this information along to their constituents, who take the prediction to heart and begin promoting teal in fashion magazines, on TV shows, in movies, all of which serves as subconscious conditioning. People notice that national trendsetters are starting to wear teal, then their friends show up in teal, and finally they do the same. Teal now constitutes a full-fledged trend. Auto designers watch the acceptance of teal, and if it seems to have staying power, the color soon begins to show up on cars. By this time the public wants teal and eagerly buys teal-colored automobiles. Meanwhile, the color services are busy analyzing the next hue to introduce to the world. ◆

dio chiefs Chuck Jordan, Irv Rybicki and Dave Holls. They realized that if GM brought out the fat, overchromed designs Harley Earl had in mind for 1959, Chrysler would wipe the floor with all of them. So while Earl was in Europe, Mitchell and the studio people staged a quiet rebellion that

be just the way Exner wanted it, but his suit would be ready for the cleaner.

Management wanted both skills—designer plus manager—in one individual. When they found out that Exner didn't like to administer, they urged him to name a styling administrator, someone who could

Chrysler styling. One remained loyal to Exner but the other aligned itself with Schmidt. Exner would wheel through the studios and direct the various works in progress, then Bill Schmidt would follow—sometimes an hour later, sometimes after a day or more—and countermand

Auto design went a little nuts in the late 1950s, not just at Chrysler but throughout the American industry. Exner's staff briefly considered outrageous fins and a tacked-on continental kit for the 1957 300-C but leveler heads prevailed. The fins, in slightly more subdued form, did appear on the '57 Plymouth. This was a time when design managers encouraged bizarre explorations. Any stylists would couldn't provide these wild concepts risked being replaced.

totally changed General Motors' styling direction for 1959 (see page 178).

Chrysler's 1957 models again set record sales and gave Exner's styling credibility another tremendous boost. The company built 1.2 million cars that year and posted $119 million in earnings, a figure not topped until 1963. But the effort and responsibilities had taken their toll on Exner. Almost overnight, his hair turned from prematurely grey to silver. He'd been a heavy smoker all his life, drank coffee by

relieve the pressure. In Oct. 1954, Exner chose Carl Reynolds. Reynolds had worked with Exner at Pontiac in the 1930s. Later, as an independent industrial designer, Carl had styled most of Powel Crosley's minicars. Reynolds, though, didn't work out, so Exner replaced him with William M. Schmidt. Schmidt, previously Studebaker-Packard's design vice president, now held the title executive stylist at Chrysler.

In July 1956, during Chrysler's 1957

Exner. The studio managers found themselves in the middle, not knowing which chief to follow.

While Exner had still been recuperating at home, Schmidt elevated some of "his" people to key positions within the studios. Dick Teague, for example, became chief stylist of Chrysler and DeSoto. This didn't sit well with the old guard, and the two factions grew more and more resentful.

In 1957, to show his support for Exner and perhaps in an attempt to resolve the

If you compare these Chrysler full-sized clays from 1956-57 with their counterparts at General Motors (page 178), you'll find them surprisingly similar. And they're too close to be coincidental; it's obvious that industrial spies were having a field day. The 1959 Olds-like model at left was badged Chrysler, as was the Pontiac-like clay above right. Buick fins and Pontiac tail lights (center) graced a study for the 1960 DeSoto. Even the roofs were similar to GM's (or vice versa).

the pot and put in a brutal workday.

Virgil M. Exner had always been much more a designer than an administrator--*a designer's designer,* they called him. He loved to design and disliked spending time on paperwork. He had a perfectionist streak and felt compelled to do a lot of things himself that he probably should have left to his studio people. Designer Bill Robinson, who arrived at Chrysler from Briggs in 1953, told of Exner often coming into the clay room dressed in his usual expensive silk suit, sitting down on a modeling platform and sculpting a wheel opening or some other part. By the time he'd finished, said Robinson, the model would

model changeover and soon after Schmidt arrived, Exner—at age 47—suffered a massive heart attack. He had open-heart surgery, nearly didn't survive and then started a slow, lengthy recovery. Colbert didn't know whether Exner would ever be his old self, so he put Schmidt in charge of all studios on an interim basis.

Bill Brownlie, manager of the Imperial studio at that time, remembered Exner coming through the studios in a wheelchair a few months after his heart attack. "He oversaw what was going on in the studios, trying to be as much in control as his doctors allowed under those conditions." But this was a time, according to Brownlie, when two factions began to form within

Schmidt/Exner standoff, Colbert named Exner vice president of styling—the first time in company history that anyone had held that office. But Exner still wasn't well, and the title didn't deter Schmidt. The situation became so critical, especially in the high-volume studios where Plymouths and Dodges were being designed, that it all finally exploded. At a heated executive meeting, Chrysler management relieved Bill Schmidt of his duties as Exner's second in command. Chrysler announced that, in the best interests of the company, Schmidt would henceforth serve as a styling consultant.

This time, though, Schmidt didn't become a consultant in name only, as so

Toward the end of his Chrysler tenure, Exner made the mistake of basing high-end cars' styling themes on those introduced by economy cars. His 1961-62 Chrysler proposal (above) borrows visibly from 1960 Valiant (right).

often happens when a company eases someone out. Harry Chesebrough, by then Chrysler's executive engineer in charge of product planning (and soon to become general manager of Plymouth), had arranged a six-month, $250,000 consultancy contract with Bill Schmidt's private industrial design firm. The contract called for Schmidt to create alternatives to Exner's in-house designs. In addition, Chesebrough commissioned Schmidt's firm to draw up ideas for a future body interchangeability program.

As he left, Bill Schmidt asked for a number of Chrysler designers, modelers and technical people to be let go so that he could immediately hire them—what later became known as "fire-and-hire" day. Schmidt had made a list, and the designers on it had no choice. Among those who went over to Bill Schmidt Associates were Chrysler designers Homer La Gassey and Dick Teague, modeler Tom Beaubien and body engineer Fred Adickes. Schmidt put together a group of 17-18 people and moved into a newly built 9000-square-foot facility on Harper Avenue in Grosse Pointe Woods. This became Schmidt's design and engineering area. He also converted a former supermarket on the next corner south, in which he made his full-sized clay models and fiberglass prototypes. Chrysler supplied the body armatures, interior bucks, modeling clay and ovens.

Schmidt split his design force into two teams. La Gassey became Schmidt's Plymouth/Dodge styling chief, and Dick Teague did the same for DeSoto/Chrysler. Each team generated one full-sized clay sedan model, and the engineering group, under Fred Adickes, worked on body-component interchangeability.

Ironically, the Schmidt group had everything finished, including some extras like interior seating bucks and scale drawings for different, non-assigned body styles, in three months, not the six the contract allotted. Schmidt then set up a showing for Chrysler Corp. managers. Among those attending were Chesebrough, several divisional general managers and sales people plus Exner and his studio chiefs. According to Homer La Gassey, Exner pooh-poohed Schmidt's designs and very

little ever came of them, although Exner did borrow a few of Schmidt's ideas. On the engineering side, Fred Adickes claimed that Schmidt's work on body-panel interchangeability helped save Chrysler some $25 million on its 1962 body program.

Schmidt's contract wasn't renewed after that first six months, but he was apparently invited to several meetings in New York to talk with Chrysler directors about becoming Exner's replacement. Bill's wife very much wanted Schmidt to take the job, but Chrysler required him to give up his private design firm, something Bill didn't want to do. So negotiations broke off. Meanwhile, La Gassey, Teague and most of the others realized they wouldn't be welcome back at Chrysler, so they found jobs elsewhere. This was when Dick Teague went to American Motors. Fred Adickes took a job with Mattel toys and developed Hot Wheels. Homer La Gassey became an executive designer at Ford.

And now we have to weave in a few loose ends. In 1960, Tex Colbert became Chrysler's board chairman. His hand-picked successor was executive vice president William C. Newberg. Newberg took over as president in Apr. 1960 but lasted only two months and two days before he was done in by a conflict-of-interest scandal. The scandal focused on his investments in Chrysler's major suppliers. After firing Newberg, Colbert returned to decisionmaking until Dec. 1960, when he named Lynn A. Townsend administrative vice president. Townsend assumed day-to-day control of the company and continued in that capacity after the Chrysler board approved him as president in July 1961.

(According to rumor, the federal government had been investigating Chrysler and wanted blood. Colbert supposedly assured Newberg that "...if you'll take the hit, Chrysler will make it up to you later," implying some sort of payoff. Newberg took the hit all right, but Chrysler merely fired him and apparently never came through otherwise. Later, when Newberg ran into Colbert in a country-club locker room, they argued and Newberg knocked down his former colleague with a well-publicized punch in the nose.)

During his brief tenure as Chrysler pres-

ident, Newberg managed to muddy the corporate waters by claiming he'd overheard then-Chevrolet general manager Ed Cole talk about downsizing the 1962 Impala. This bit of eavesdropping took place at a Detroit garden party. What Cole probably said was that for 1962, Chevrolet planned to introduce a smaller car: the compact Chevy II. Newberg didn't understand that Chevrolet's full-sized lines wouldn't be affected.

In a panic, Newberg rushed back to Chrysler, and before his ouster, pushed through a crash program to downsize the 1962 Plymouth and Dodge. To meet his proposed deadline, Exner's designers had no choice but to work around the clock. They did this in two shifts—a day shift and a night shift, with half-hour overlaps to pass along design information.

The downsizing program had the effect of throwing out much of what Exner had hoped to give his 1962 models: competitive size and good proportions, large expanses of curved side glass and wraparound bumpers. Those plans went by the board. Instead, engineers shortened wheelbases, bodies became narrower, side glass remained flat, and the cars looked like, as Exner put it, "plucked chickens."

Despite styling that Exner didn't care for, Chrysler Corp.'s profits soared from $11 million in 1961 to $65 million in '62, due mostly to the sale of '63 models. These were not bad times. But Lynn Townsend, who'd come to Chrysler via the corporation's accounting firm, wasn't happy with Exner's styling direction. Exner, he felt, seemed intent on using the styling cues he'd developed for the 1960 Valiant—the company's least expensive car—on some of the company's upmarket models.

The 1960 Valiant put into production some of the themes from Exner's Ghia showcars: the long hood, the short sloping rear deck with debossed spare tire, the classic grille shape, ridged fenders, the speedboat cowl and squared-off greenhouse. These themes now showed up on 1962 Dodges, 1962 Plymouths and 1963 Chryslers and took a direction very different from accepted design practice. A styling trend or innovation usually trickles down from a top car line to less expensive models, but Exner was going the opposite direction. Even the 1963 Imperial had fender wings that were first seen on the Valiant. Townsend observed this and began to talk about a different image for Chrysler. He had a point, although the company's cars continued to sell well.

Over at Ford, meanwhile, George Walker had retired and the man he'd chosen to be his successor, Elwood Engel, had been passed over. That hurt Walker, and it was then that he realized that Exner was vulnerable at Chrysler. All the changes of command, the lingering bitterness between Exner and Bill Schmidt, Townsend's unhappiness with the 1962-63 Valiant lookalikes: Walker picked up all those cards. He knew the timing was right, and he had someone to take Exner's place.

Walker now either arranged a luncheon with Lynn Townsend at the Detroit Athletic Club or ran into him there; at any rate, they started talking. Salesman Walker urged financial man Townsend to consider Engel as a replacement for Exner. Townsend sat there listening and pondered the big picture. He felt Chrysler needed some styling changes. He had no particular loyalty to Exner, and no one could rely on Exner's health. So Townsend hired Elwood Engel as his new vice president of styling. Engel arrived in Nov. 1961, and that's when Townsend announced that Exner would stay on as a "consultant."

Imperial studio manager Bill Brownlie happened to overhear Walker when he visited Engel at Chrysler one day soon after Engel's arrival. "I know this for a fact, because I heard Mr. Walker say the words.... It was Nov. 1961 [and] Walker wasn't speaking directly to me. There were a couple of others...standing with us. I've forgotten who they were, but he [Walker] said that he decid-

Elwood P. Engel

Engel's Chrysler turbine car reprised his 1961 T-Bird/Continental theme.

ed, because one of his boys was not put in charge of the Ford design office, that he was making it his...what's the word I'm looking for...his vendetta to make sure to prove that Ford had made an error, and he would put one of his boys, Oros or Engel, in the highest position within a Big Three design office....

"Walker was a very influential person," continued Brownlie. "He knew all of Detroit's elite, had that charisma, and he could say, 'Hey, this is what you'd better do.' Of course, Chrysler was ripe. So a combination of events allowed it to happen. And after Elwood walked into the door, I never saw Exner there. He left very quietly. He still had an office at Chrysler, but I'm sure his heart wasn't in it. Every day he came in must have been torture. I know Exner was tremendously hurt, and I'm sure it didn't help his health at all. But Elwood came in and brought a different light to the whole thing."

Brownlie got along well with Engel, as did most other designers at Chrysler. Engel had a much looser, more relaxed management style than Exner. Engel left the styling process and even the generation of styling ideas much more to the individual studios.

According to Carl Cameron, a designer who arrived at Chrysler in 1962 and became good friends with Engel: "You have a couple of kinds of managers. One likes the other person to do it exactly the way he'd do it himself, and that was Exner. Then you have the other, like Elwood, who can look at a design and support it, and although it might not turn out exactly the way he'd have done it, he recognizes that it's a good job."

Cameron also commented on Engel's personality. "Elwood never made people feel uncomfortable. You didn't have to snap to attention or worry about what you were doing when he walked into a room. It wasn't that he didn't care; he just didn't make everybody feel like they were being watched."

Colin Neale, who'd worked with Engel on the 1961 Lincoln, didn't quite agree. "He had an informal demeanor," said Neale, "but he could be very menacing and unpleasant."

Brownlie, who later became a major contender to succeed Engel, added that, "...Elwood had, in my opinion, this uncanny ability to be commercial. There's a big difference between designing and being commercial. So he would do some things that would rock us as designers. He would do crazy things: put a molding here and stick a badge there, do this to the fender and that to the rear. 'There, that's it!' He'd walk out of the studio, feeling he had really made the design contribution that was going to make the car succeed. And I honestly believe he had that ability."

Brownlie agreed that Exner had controlled designs much more rigidly than Engel. "It was almost like Elwood was saying, 'I don't have time to be in this studio.' He wanted to go out and play and be a big shot, and the stories about that go on and on. He'd walk into a studio quickly, and if things were going well, you wouldn't see him again for days. If things *weren't* going well, he'd...be in there absolutely raising hell." Several designers mentioned that Engel would kick or pound a clay model with his fist to dramatize his displeasure. "He could be very flamboyant in that regard," noted Brownlie, "something he must have learned from George Walker.

"Anyway, he and I got along wonderfully. I respected his capabilities and really tried to protect some of his weaknesses. Chrysler's upper management also recognized his weaknesses and then started to slowly control him. And he had many weaknesses, as did Exner. But I had a tremendous respect for both men for completely different reasons. Exner had more of an appreciation for how cars were built, and I think he was more sophisticated when it came to that side of the business. Elwood was more showbiz, Barnum and Bailey, Hollywood, flashing lights, bells, whistles, razzle dazzle. But he also had, as I said, a sensitivity for being more commercial, and I'm not sure he appreciated that himself. He loved good design, and when good design was going, he did not interfere, and I can say, my relationship from 1961 when he came in to 1974, when he retired, was nothing but the best. I had a lot of respect for the man."

But not everyone did. In Bill Robinson's words, "I couldn't communicate with Elwood.... His language was part of it, kind of crude and coarse. I had lost some respect for him, because he had such a high position, and he could have exerted his power and influence, but he'd get bored, for instance, during meetings. Many of the meetings would be conducted right in front of the designers. We worked right in the clay room, so when they'd make presentations, we'd be sitting right there.

"Well, we'd see these important decisions being made, and he'd

Engel turned out some great-looking cars toward the *end* of his career, among them these 1968 Dodge Chargers and 1970 Challenger (right).

go off and talk with some girl or throw a clay ball at something. He'd lost his opportunity to champion the design. In the beginning he was very, very forceful, because design had been pushed around at Chrysler. So when he came over [from Ford], he commanded a great deal of respect, and he got things done for design. I have to give him credit for that, because up to then, engineering was king, even under Exner."

Thunderbirds, although he didn't use that name.

"I think one of the cars that really exemplifies what [Engel] expected to see would be the 1965 Plymouth Fury. He liked those kinds of cars versus what Exner had been doing. I established a pretty good rapport with [Engel]. I could talk to him because he was, really, a common man. He was a Russian farmer. You could joke and cajole with him. He'd walk out of the room, and you could get done what needed to be done."

Designer Darin Yazejian recalled an approval meeting with top Dodge management when someone criticized the roof treatment of a proposed 1969 Polara hardtop. This particular roof had rear-extending sail panels that thrust out behind the glass, like the '68 Charger's. When the person questioned the Polara sail panels, Engel walked up to the full-sized clay, tore off the panels with his bare hands, grabbed a knife and smoothed over his finger marks. Management immediately approved the more rounded roof and backlight, and that's how the 1969 Polara went into production. So Engel did have some flair and presence.

As for his design philosophy, Carl Cameron pointed out that, "Elwood liked to fill out all the corners of the box," so he took Exner's 1960 Plymouth Valiant, for example, with its sloping rear deck and fender line and, for 1963, squared

Like the '61 Continental, Engel returned to an almost austere simplicity with designs like this big 1972 Imperial LeBaron hardtop.

Elwood Engel did not leave a vast array of memorable designs at Chrysler. He's remembered as the man who removed the tailfins from Chrysler products, although they were nearly all gone by the time he arrived. One of his first projects was to style the 1963 Chrysler turbine cars, and for those he pretty much recycled the design of the stiletto-studio 1961 Thunderbird/Lincoln in coupe form. Designer Dave Cummins recalled that, "Engel established the turbine car as the kind of design that he favored and wanted to see happen in the studios. He made quite a presentation when the first fiberglass [model] came in; grouped everybody together and said—and I'm paraphrasing now: Forget Exner, forget tailfins, forget the *Forward* Look and all that, and we're going to have

up the rear area and brought down the rear wheel opening. Engel's production cars tended mostly to be squarish and stiff until he got to the 1968 Dodge Charger, done by Richard Sias under Bill Brownlie. The Charger had a great, muscular look and went accordingly. Engel's 1970 Dodge Challenger and the 1970 Plymouth Barracuda, done by John E. Herlitz under Dick Macadam, were also quite handsome, and some of the 1970 full-sized Chrysler Corp. cars had a clean, impressive look.

Elwood Engel retired from Chrysler in 1973 but stayed on as a consultant until June 1974, at which time Richard G. Macadam was elevated to the vice presidency. Engel died of cancer on June 24, 1986. ◆

CHAPTER 10

THE MITCHELL YEARS

On a wintry Detroit Monday morning, Dec. 1, 1958, William L. Mitchell walked into Harley Earl's former office at the General Motors Technical Center and sat down at Earl's huge desk. This was the rounded, wooden, "die-model" desk designed especially for Earl. Mitchell could see right away that he didn't fit. Earl was a much taller man, so the desktop stood too high. That's when Mitchell realized, graphically, the size of the shoes he'd have to fill.

Mitchell idolized Earl. One of Mitchell's tenets, and he repeated this like a mantra, was: "I'll never let him down," meaning Earl. It's pretty much agreed today that no man could have filled Earl's shoes better. Mitchell turned out to be as strong a design vice president in his era as Earl had been in his.

People who worked for and with Bill Mitchell either liked him or hated him. There weren't many on the fence. He was tough and dictatorial, a bigot, a womanizer; he often drank too much, had a foul mouth, and yet he had this wonderful sense of humor and a light touch that Earl simply couldn't match. He made people laugh just as easily as he could hurt their feelings. As Strother MacMinn put it, "...[Mitchell] would leave you rolling on the floor laughing, aching, and you'd wish he'd stop. And then you'd wish he wouldn't. He'd just tear you up completely...."

Bill Mitchell could defuse a tense situation with humor. According to GM Design Staff activities manager Tom Christiansen, who worked under both Earl and Mitchell, "Harley Earl, when he'd blow up at someone, would storm out of the studio, red in the face, and everybody just sat there shattered and trembling. Bill, on the other hand, would come in and blow up in the same way—probably a little more violently—but on his way out he'd usually turn and make some funny remark, a one-liner. Everybody would laugh, and he'd laugh. That was his way of smoothing it over. He had that ability. As a result, I think he commanded the respect of those designers more than Earl did."

Most of his people remember Mitchell as authoritarian and tough. He had to be tough, because he was much more on his own than Earl had ever been. In the early years of his vice presidency, Mitchell didn't have anyone like Sloan to back him up. Division managers at that time were all older than Mitchell, and seniority intimidated him. Later, when Ed Cole and Pete Estes and Bunkie Knudsen took over the divisions, Mitchell felt more comfortable. But he always had to remain courageous in defending his art, and that often meant fighting toe to toe with some of GM's general managers and the engineering establishment. Cadillac chief engineer Bob Templin remembered a knock-down, four-hour shouting match with Mitchell regarding the styling of the 1976 Cadillac Seville.

Mitchell was a tremendously driven person, confident of his talent and arrogantly imperious. "Yessir...I'm a dictator," Mitchell once told Paul Lienert, a reporter for *Automotive News.* "Goddam right I'm a dictator. If I don't have opinions, I shouldn't have my job.... Frank Lloyd Wright didn't ring doorbells asking what kinds of houses people wanted.... How the hell could you explain a martini to anybody? I don't like engineers or salespeople or any-

body...I don't give a shit what they say. I don't go up and talk about transmissions to them."

Due to his dictatorial nature and his defiance of what GM considered due process, Mitchell made lots of enemies, especially in high places. He would often anger someone on impulse with a thoughtless remark. Or if he didn't get his way, he'd throw one of his famous temper tantrums. But more often he'd make an enemy with an intentional insult. Mitchell referred to engineers as "no-no boys," and when someone disagreed with him on a point of style, he'd take a verbal punch at him. "Yeah," he once told Buick gen-

eral manager George Elges, "but just look at that suit you're wearing. I've got better-looking linoleum on my kitchen floor!"

Homer LaGassey mentioned that Mitchell never failed to eyeball his designers and the division people from head to toe, checking out their fashion. He knew fabrics, and he'd sometimes walk up and unceremoniously finger someone's lapel, just to satisfy his curiosity. If the suit didn't meet his standards, Mitchell would say to the wearer, "Where did you park your truck?" He sometimes actually sent people home to change if he didn't approve of the clothes or color matches they were wearing.

Mitchell's womanizing and some of his more notorious escapades have entered the folklore of auto design. "He certainly loved women," said Charles M. (Chuck) Jordan, his longtime second in command, and Mitchell himself liked to say, "If God made anything better than a woman, He kept it for Himself." According to someone who was there, he once hired seven women for a noontime romp and afterward found he didn't have enough cash to pay them. So he sent one of his minions to the bank with a $1000 personal check and then handed out $100 bills.

One of Mitchell's former secretaries remarked that if sexual-harrassment suits had been in vogue during the time she worked for him, she could have filed a hundred of them. Mitchell's first marriage ended in a bitter divorce, and relations with one of his two daughters became seriously strained, especially since Mitchell remarried the day after his divorce.

His bigotry was perhaps typical of the era. "Minorities had a difficult time under Bill," observed designer Stan Wilen. "If you were Black or Latino or Asian, he'd put an adjective in front of a reference that would make conversation a little awkward. I qualify as a minority, so I hear those things. Sometimes when he did not like the design of a front end, he'd say it looked like a grouper. But if someone was in the room who was Jewish, like me or Jerry Hirschberg [later vice president of Nissan Design International in California], Bill would use the word 'jewfish' instead of grouper. Maybe he was just teasing, but maybe he wasn't.

"Or he'd be up in the executive dining room, and there'd be all of his men around him. We'd be eating lunch, and Bill—with no alcohol, because it wasn't allowed there—would start telling stories. And Juanita, the waitress, would be serving a salad or something, and he would come up with some of the most outrageous sexual comments. Even the guys around him would curdle. But Juanita would look straight ahead...and pretend she didn't hear any of it. I mention this to demonstrate a dimension of cruelty in his humor."

Jerry Hirschberg had another explanation: "Mitchell was never an introspective man. He was all reflex and intuition, and it was clear to me that there was little intent in many of his statements and actions. I heard the jewfish comments but also found myself being moved up the management ladder as swiftly as anyone. The words Jew, Jap, Wop and Nigger tumbled out of him, but his passion for beautiful cars and the talents needed to make them prevailed. Being Jewish never seemed to hurt my career at GM Design Staff, although it occasionally did hurt!

"Mitchell's contradictory nature," continued Hirschberg, "reflected the turmoil and pain around him—and the levels of energy and even inspiration that prevailed. I remember his legendary motivation sessions and speeches in the styling dome, where he'd rally his forces with the most outrageous sports analogies and war metaphors. It was 'us against them,' and we were the good guys, but we always needed to 'give them more hell.' We all winced and joked, but Mitchell consistently managed to inspire us. Ultimately his passion and respect for talent showed through, and we were moved to perform for him."

Chuck Jordan likewise maintained that Mitchell didn't intentionally hurt people; he was just thoughtless. And Corvette designer Larry Shinoda, who's Japanese-American, said he never noticed any racial malice in Mitchell, "...none at all." Shinoda often accompanied Mitchell on racing junkets and the two became quite close until Shinoda left to go to Ford. Strother MacMinn further pointed out that Art Ross, who was Jewish, not only worked closely with Mitchell on cars like the 1941 Cadillac but was also his friend and faithful drinking companion.

In fairness to Mitchell and to balance the portrait, Jordan and others who knew him well called attention to his "teddy-bear" side. Mitchell showed great generosity to those who helped him early in his career. For example, he gave one of his older modelers—a man no longer able work a full day—an unused office in the truck studio where he could sleep. Or when one of his top

designers developed muscular dystrophy, Mitchell refused to let him go, encouraging him to hold his pencils inside a rubber ball so he could continue to sketch. Those acts were as typical of Mitchell as his sudden cloudbursts. Unlike Earl, Mitchell rarely fired anyone, and he often came to Tom Christiansen and asked how he could make it up to someone in the studio that he'd just crucified. He did feel remorse and compassion. Christiansen said, too, that Mitchell never held a grudge.

It's hard to present a dispassionate portrait of Mitchell, but it's clear that he could be a loose cannon in an organization that valued orderliness. He was also so good at what he did that everyone tended to turn a blind eye to his faults. People excused his volatility and his darker side when they recognized the extent of his genius. By any measure, Mitchell ranked as one of the world's great auto designers, admired not only by his peers in this country but throughout the international design community.

Bill Mitchell had that same intuitive instinct for the American public's taste in automobiles that Earl did, but there are those who maintain that he was a better designer than Earl. Mitchell, according to advocates and critics alike, gave life to some of the handsomest automobiles General Motors ever built. Case in point: His entire 1965 line of full-sized cars. Each one of them still shows remarkable grace and beauty.

And the '65s were not done in easy times. The studios were past deadline for that year's coupes, and Mitchell needed GM president John F. (Jack) Gordon's immediate decision on which version to develop for production: a notchback or a modified fastback. Gordon arrived at Design Staff, looked at both clay models, had no appreciation for anything he was seeing and said, "Aw, Bill, it doesn't matter. They both look about the same, don't they?" Mitchell nearly choked. "The same! *The same?* That's like saying Chicago and Paris look the same because they both have rivers running through them!" The modified fastback ultimately got the nod.

His '65s stand out as the shining stars of his career, although he mightn't agree. He had his own favorites: the 1963 Buick Riviera, 1960 Corvair, 1963 Pontiac Grand Prix, 1963 Corvette Sting Ray, 1966 Riviera, 1966 Oldsmobile Toronado, 1967 Cadillac Eldorado, 1970 Chevrolet Monte Carlo, 1970 1/2 Camaro and Firebird, 1976 Cadillac Seville, 1977 Chevrolet Caprice, 1980 Cadillac Seville plus his showcars and personal customs.

In commanding the largest army of automobile stylists in the world, Mitchell carried over quite a few traits he'd learned from Harley Earl. He had Earl's flair down pat: the flamboyance, showmanship, confidence and pugnacity. Yet Mitchell differed in his fundamental design philosophy. His disagreement wasn't so much with Earl's credo of "lower, longer, wider," but Mitchell's idea of good design focused more on the overall shape of the car: the underlying form. Earl spent time on form, too, but he frosted it with a lot of chrome and ornamentation. Mitchell's cars hit the eye as a piece, one homogeneous whole, whereas Earl's moved the viewer's eye from a dominant focal point to secondary lines and

Mitchell Up a Tree

GM interior designer George A. Moon and his family lived next door to Bill and Jane Mitchell in Birmingham, Michigan during the 1950s and '60s. "One night Bill came to our house for a party," recalled Moon. "He drank a lot and then simply disappeared. Next morning, my mother woke up, opened the back door to let the dog out and heard this plaintive cry from atop this huge elm tree in our backyard. 'Elsie, Elsie, get me down; help!' said the voice.

"There, some 50 feet up, straddling a branch was Bill Mitchell. He was terrified. In his inebriated state the evening before, he'd somehow managed to climb the tree, too drunk to care about the danger. Then in the light of dawn, with a return to sobriety, his 50-foot perch must have seemed to him like it was 1000 feet up!

"My mother phoned the police, who got a fire truck with a long ladder to drive over to the house. A fireman went up and hauled Bill out of the tree, and my mother—who was godmother to Bill's daughter Wendy—never let Bill forget that moment."

Moon also cited another time when, "...Bill got drunk in New York, along with [Oldsmobile studio chief] Art Ross, and they stole a horse-drawn cab from Central Park. They tried to drive it into the lobby of the Ritz-Carlton hotel, but the horse got stuck in the door." ◆

patches—from a grille, say, or the entire front end to details like speed streaks or fins and then, finally, to the overall shape of the body. Form was Earl's canvas, and he pasted over it like a collage. With Mitchell, form was the entire picture.

Soon after Mitchell took over from Earl, he realigned his staff and put what he called his "young Turks" in charge of GM's five exterior design studios. All were 30-ish. Chuck Jordan remained chief of the Cadillac studio, Dave Holls had Buick, Stan Wilen Oldsmobile, Irv Rybicki Chevrolet and Jack Humbert Pontiac.

The man he made his first design director, before Jordan, was Ed Glowacke. Glowacke is remembered as a remarkable person and very unlike Mitchell: understated, not loudmouthed, not a braggard, a self-taught designer of great ability, admired and liked by absolutely everyone, Earl and Mitchell in particular.

Ed Glowacke grew up in Detroit, went to Cass Tech High School, couldn't afford college and joined GM Styling just before World War II. Harley Earl recognized Glowacke's talent immediately and put him into a special studio where he helped Earl devel-

op his (Earl's) masterpiece, the 1950 Motorama LeSabre. In Sept. 1948, Earl made Glowacke head of the Chevrolet studio. Ed did the 1953 Chevy. And in April 1951, Glowacke took over the Cadillac studio.

Mitchell had been Glowacke's mentor, tutored him on design and style, and Glowacke admired Mitchell even more than he admired Earl. Mitchell and Glowacke thought the world of each other and respected the other's judgements. Glowacke was meticulous in his designs, meticulous in his artwork, meticulous in his dress. He was an accomplished race-car driver, which Mitchell admired; a fine pilot; owned a white Siata roadster, a Beechcraft Bonanza, a German Schweitzer glider and an iceboat that he'd sail on Lake St. Clair at 110 mph. He was an amateur musician, played a mean piano and organ all by ear but never learned to read a note of music. Glowacke was full of life, fun to be with, a wonderful complement to Mitchell himself. Mitchell not only made Glowacke his director of design—his second in command—but let it be known that Ed was his heir apparent. He might not have

Mitchell's Wheels

Bill Mitchell had something like 55 personal cars built during his 18 years as GM Design Staff vice president—an average of three cars a year. (By way of contrast, Harley Earl commissioned only two special cars for his own use: the 1938 Y-Job and the 1950 LeSabre.) These were usually customized versions of new production models, often lowered, sometimes shortened (the Corvair Spyder), occasionally with special engines, chopped tops and stretched fenders.

One of Mitchell's first personal vehicles was a 1956 Corvette SR-2, a racing model converted to street use. Mitchell had his SR-2 painted red and wore a red driving suit and helmet when he took it out.

In 1958, he paid $500 for the chassis of the abandoned Corvette SS mule (XP-87) that Fangio and Moss had tested at Sebring. Mitchell then announced a contest to design a new body for this car, reportedly basing the theme on a Ghia showcar he'd seen in Turin in 1957. Junior designers Peter Brock and Charles F. (Chuck) Pohlmann in Bob McLean's special studio won the contest. Pohlmann put Mitchell's ideas into a little 8 x 10 pencil sketch, and he and Brock developed coupe and roadster versions. At that point, the project moved to the so-called "hammer room," a secret area downstairs in Design Staff where GM's top execs never went. The reason for secrecy was the AMA racing ban and the fact that Mitchell was building this car without corporate approval. Pohlmann was joined in the hammer room by Corvette designer Larry Shinoda, who oversaw construction of the roadster body and mated it to the XP-87 mule chassis.

The resulting roadster didn't look like any other sports car in the world. The Sting Ray's fiberglass body had a sharp break line running all the way around the perime-

ter and fender peaks over all four wheels, an open cockpit, a faired-in headrest, tiny single windshield and a sharp nose on the low hood. Mitchell later transferred the lines of the racing Sting Ray to the production 1963 Corvette.

Mitchell campaigned his Sting Ray privately in SCCA road races throughout the 1959-60 season, often flying to weekend race sites in GM's company planes. The car wasn't called a Corvette then, and GM

Mitchell and his SR-2 Corvette

had nothing to do with it. Dick Thompson, the Chicago dentist, became Mitchell's principal driver, with John Fitch and Anatole (Tony) Lapine as backups (Lapine later became Porsche's chief stylist). The Sting Ray suffered from brake and other prob-

lems and didn't do well in the 1959 season, but in 1960 it won the national SCCA C-Modified class championship.

The Sting Ray was initially painted red, then refinished in metallic silver when it took on a new set of lighter body skins between seasons. In 1961, Mitchell retired the Sting Ray, converted it for street use and took it to the Chicago auto show as a Corvette "idea car." Many of GM's concept cars and restyled production cars were initially announced as show vehicles before Mitchell took them for his own use.

Mitchell would sometimes drive three and four restyled cars interchangeably. From roughly 1963 through 1971, his favorite make was Pontiac but his favorite car was the Riviera, and he had several redone with chop-and-stretch treatments. He called his Rivs "Silver Arrows," one from each generation, each painted silver.

Bill traditionally preferred cars with large, powerful engines, like his 1971 Pegasus, a restyled Firebird with a Ferrari V-12, or the blue 1973 Camaro with a Chevrolet seven-liter Can Am racing engine. Four of his restyled personal cars, in fact, carried big Can Am V-8s.

He was also in the habit of buying the latest imported sports- and showcars and billing them to GM engineering. He would use these cars both as stylistic adrenaline

Mitchell and his Sting Ray race car

said it in so many words, but everyone knew Glowacke was next in line for GM's design vice presidency when Mitchell reached 65 in 1977.

Then one day in early 1962, during a routine medical exam, Ed Glowacke was diagnosed with leukemia. He told no one, and by the time anyone knew, he was in the hospital. Mitchell visited him there, returned to the Cadillac studio and confided, "Ed is never coming back." He never did. He passed away in June 1962, a death that deeply shocked and saddened everyone who'd known him, particularly the young Turks. He had mentored them all. In 1965, Mitchell named Chuck Jordan his design director.

Mitchell, like Earl, made it a point to lead the industry. He intentionally created trends and set fashion. This push for leadership remained a conscious effort on Mitchell's part, not that every other design vice president wasn't trying to do the same thing. One way he stayed ahead was to pit studio against studio. All his studio chiefs and all their designers actively competed to please Mitchell. As a result, Mitchell evolved a management style very different from Earl's. Earl staged contests early in his career; Mitchell made the daily routine a contest in which designers competed endlessly.

He kept designers on their toes by letting them know that the studio next door was ahead of them. This was a very tricky thing to do and required some subtlety. With too heavy a hand, Mitchell's strategy could backfire: discourage or intimidate those he was trying to egg on. But he had that ability to convince one studio that it was being passed by another in terms of aesthetics and at the same time not damage any egos. Just the opposite: He somehow inspired and built up people's *desire* to compete, spurred them on to try harder, to do new things. If Mitchell had a magic, that was a good part of it. "Bill could mobilize his staff to tremendous heights of creativity," said Harry B. Bradley, who worked under Mitchell in the 1960s and later became a design instructor at Art Center in California.

One way the studios kept score and gauged how they rated in

1968 Manta Ray

Biker Bill

and as his own personal wheels. Engineering wasn't pleased to get the invoices, but his power within the corporation was such that no one ever questioned these purchases. As for the cars themselves: Mitchell arranged with Alejandro De Tomaso to get a Mangusta with a Chevrolet (instead of a Ford) V-8. He bought the second E-Type Jaguar roadster imported into the U.S., the first Porsche 904 and a number of show vehicles at various European auto exhibitions. No one else at GM ever did anything similar.

Around 1972, Mitchell took up motorcycling. He owned a great number of cycles and usually had them radically redesigned and engineered, often to match one of GM's showcars. For example, he owned a Honda CB500 with custom fiberglass bodywork and firefrost kandy-apple red paint that matched the 1974 Firebird Banshee showcar. When riding his Honda, Mitchell wore red leathers, red boots and a red helmet. In the mid-1970s, his bike collection consisted mostly of Hondas but also included Ducati, Norton, Moto Guzzi, Yamaha, Laverda and Harley-Davidson. It was one of the largest and most exotic private collections of restyled prototype motorcycles ever assembled.

Mitchell would often suit up in an outfit

1963 Silver Arrow I

whose color perfectly matched the motorcycle or car he was driving. He usually asked chief interior designer George Moon to have these suits custom made. Moon would select leather or fabric in the correct hue, then arrange with Gwinn's in Birmingham, Michigan for the actual tailoring. Mitchell borrowed the idea of a vehicular wardrobe from McClure Halley, a New York businessman and customer of Zumbach's garage in Manhattan where all the wealthy auto enthusiasts hung out and had their cars serviced. Halley often wore color-coordinated motoring outfits.

Mitchell was not a good motorcycle rider and often had minor accidents. Once, wearing a metallic silver lame suit and helmet, he and his motorcycle got pinned by an electric gate at the GM Technical Center in full view of the Oldsmobile studio. ◆

Mitchell's eyes was by watching his favorite parking space in the executive garage. Mitchell had four reserved stalls, and the car he liked best always stood in Stall #1. He usually drove restyled or special versions of GM's production cars, and when one of Mitchell's studio chiefs pulled into the garage in the morning, the first thing he'd do would be to glance over at Mitchell's #1 parking space. If the designer's make of car was parking there, he knew it was a homerun for the home team. Mitchell drove Riviera-, Camaro- and Corvette-based customs more often than other GM makes, although he liked Firebirds, too. He rarely drove Oldsmobiles, because he got mad at the Olds guys a lot and that was his way of getting back at them.

Corporate life got easier for Mitchell after 1967. That was the year Ed Cole became GM president—followed in 1974 by another Mitchell supporter, Elliott M. (Pete) Estes. Before that, when he wasn't getting his way, Mitchell had to fight, and that became one more opportunity to make enemies. His nemesis for years was Jack Gordon, who preceded Cole in the GM presidency. Gordon and Mitchell never got along; in fact, Mitchell used to tell about Gordon coming into his office around Christmas 1958 and saying to him in effect, "You might have gotten this job, but I'm not sure you're right for it. I wouldn't have picked you, and you're going to have to prove yourself to me."

After that, it seemed Mitchell intentionally taunted Gordon just for the fun of it. In 1959, Mitchell's private race car, the Sting Ray, represented (among many other things) a slap at GM's proclaimed but rarely observed racing ban. After Mitchell started campaigning the Sting Ray, Gordon realized he couldn't stop him, but he ordered Mitchell never to bring the car on GM property, even though it had been engineered, styled and fabricated there.

Chuck Jordan added, "Mitchell,

Mitchell's love of motion showed in the thundering Bentley sketch of his ARCA logo.

God love him, didn't give a damn what anybody thought. He told me about the time his immediate boss, [GM car and truck group vice president] Howard Kehrl, came into his office and started chewing him out about something. Mitchell said to him, 'I don't have any respect for you, and I don't ever want you to tell me what to do....' He wouldn't put up with anything."

Mitchell had a saying: "Never get in bed with a general manager. They change so fast that the next morning you'll wake up with somebody else." His point was that all GM designers, including Mitchell himself, worked first and foremost for Design Staff, second for the car divisions and third, perhaps, for a general manager. Many general managers couldn't accept the low status Mitchell assigned to them. Two who didn't get along with Mitchell at all were Buick general manager Ed Rollert and Pontiac/Chevrolet general manager John DeLorean.

DeLorean, even in his early days as chief engineer of Pontiac, had his own ideas about car design, and he'd tell Mitchell in no uncertain terms just what he wanted. When DeLorean was named Pontiac's general manager, he became even more explicit and insistent. Mitchell didn't mind general managers asking questions and making occasional suggestions, but he usually showed them finished designs and expected them to approve. When general managers came in and started telling him how to design, as he felt DeLorean often did, Mitchell reminded them that he was the designer and they were the general managers. He was providing them a service—a good one—and he felt they ought to let him do his job.

When DeLorean became Pontiac's general manager, he and Mitchell used to get into terrible fights. Mitchell would say to his aides, "Get that guy out of here," and then he'd hide and become

unfindable. Yet Mitchell consistently gave DeLorean some of GM's best designs and kept doing so even after DeLorean became Chevrolet's general manager.

Bill Mitchell's unpredictability increased after he'd had a few too many drinks at lunch. This didn't happen often, but his chief designers learned that if Mitchell came into a studio a bit wobbly, he could be hard to handle. He was volatile cold sober, but a martini lunch left him testy and sometimes downright mean. His chief designers knew from experience that, under those circumstances, if Mitchell stayed in the studio longer than about 20 minutes, he'd likely find fault with whatever they were working on, no matter how much he'd liked it before. Heads of studios became vulnerable at those times, especially since Mitchell had a habit of ordering not just changes but total re-do's. "Bill would sometimes blow up and throw out a whole car," observed Orval Selders, a technical stylist in the Olds studio during the late 1950s and early '60s.

So on those occasions especially, the chiefs wanted to get Mitchell out and on his way as quickly as possible. The routine was to give him the standard tour of the studio, keep him moving and then, as Mitchell talked, the chief designer would be inching toward the door, drawing Mitchell with him. This worked until the next time, when everyone had to go through the dance again. So Mitchell's visits sometimes met with a certain dread. And a number of young designers were plainly afraid of Mitchell, just as they'd been of Earl.

Stan Wilen summed Mitchell up by saying: "He was volatile, but he could be full of fun and very friendly. He could also be very threatening and intimidating. He was a showman, a salesman, an actor and a lot of other things, but he was a very confident corporate person.... As a designer, he...knew what he wanted. And when you watched him make a presentation, you saw characteristics that any salesman would envy.

"Remember, Bill became vice president at a time when everything was right for a man of his talent. Here was a guy who knew where he was going when the rest of the corporation's executives were a little unsure. They'd just been through the Eisenhower recession, and they said, 'Oh, good, we've got a leader; let's let him lead.' This was an era when the American public still felt some romance for the automobile: hot rods, musclecars, drive-in movies. It was a good era for Bill, but if Bill came into the vice presidency today, it might not be as good."

William Leroy Mitchell was born on July 2, 1912 in Cleveland. While he was still in his infancy, the family moved to Greenville, Pennsylvania where his father, Guy Mitchell, became the local Buick dealer. Guy Mitchell would bring home Mercers and Auburns and other trade-ins, and it was not long before young Bill fell madly in love with cars. He started drawing them in grade school.

When he reached his early teens, Bill's mother and father divorced. Hazel Mitchell moved to New York, and Bill spent his summers with her in Manhattan but lived in Greenville during the school year, sometimes with his father and at other times with his aunt.

His mother worked for the Barron Collier advertising agency in New York, and when Bill turned 15, she got him a summer job there as an office boy. On weekends he'd walk up and down Manhattan's auto row, checking out all the import- and luxury-car showrooms. At that time Park Avenue was home to some very exotic nameplates, Hispano-Suiza, Mercedes, Rolls-Royce and

Isotta-Fraschini among them. All the American luxury makes had dealers over on Broadway.

Bill also befriended the three car-crazy young sons of his boss, particularly Sam Collier, who was Mitchell's age. When the father, Barron Collier, discovered Bill's talent for drawing automobiles, he set him up as an apprentice in the agency's art department. Mitchell soon began laying out and illustrating the ads displayed on most of New York's streetcars, and he later did prospectuses for Hudson and Packard, which they never bought. His ambition at the time was to become a car illustrator.

In 1929, after Bill graduated from high school, his father sent him to Carnegie Tech to study design. "I don't want you to be a car salesman like me," he told Bill. Then in the summer of 1931, again working at the Collier agency, young Mitchell took evening courses at New York's Art Students League, studying anatomical drawing.

It was during this period that Bill Mitchell became involved with the Collier Brothers in their passionate amateur auto-racing adventures on Long Island. Now, instead of haunting auto row on weekends, Mitchell would hop into his Ford roadster and roar out to Pocantico Hills, near Tarrytown, New York, where the Collier Brothers had bulldozed a dirt track on their father's property. They called the track Sleepy Hollow Ring, after the famous Nurburgring race course in Germany. These were wealthy kids who'd gone from early go-karts to Austin- and Willys-powered racing specials, then to MGs and Bugattis and Auburn speedsters. Mitchell occasionally got behind a wheel and raced along with them, but that wasn't his forte.

More often he'd grab a pad and pencil and sketch the action. Some of his illustrations survive, and they're as fresh and dynamic and noisy as the man himself. We see scenes of roadsters going wheel to wheel, raising clouds of dust, flashing out from speed-blurred turns and careening straight off the page. It was Mitchell who conceived the charging Auburn logo for the Colliers' hobby organization, ARCA (Automobile Racing Club of America, which

later, indirectly, became Sports Car Club of America or SCCA).

One of the people attending those races was Walter B. Carey, a Detroit businessman whose company insured GM's east-coast assembly plants. Carey saw Bill's sketches hanging in the ARCA clubhouse and admired them. He asked Mitchell if he'd ever thought about designing cars. Mitchell said he had but didn't know how to go about it.

In early 1935, Carey arranged for Mitchell to send his racing sketches to Howard O'Leary at GM Art & Colour. O'Leary wrote back suggesting Mitchell put together a portfolio. Mitchell spent the summer of 1935 creating original designs and, as an added touch, he dramatized them with the illusion of speed and action, same as his racing illustrations. O'Leary and Earl liked the young man's verve and technique, and Mitchell came to work for Art & Colour on Dec. 10, 1935. He was 23 years old. Harley Earl was 42.

Their initial meeting had an element of mistaken identity. Earl had just come back from a cruise, and he was strolling through Art & Colour with a business friend. Mitchell didn't recognize either of them and thought they were visitors, but the taller man struck up a conversation. "That day he had on a blue suit and blue shoes and a blue shirt, and somebody mentioned the name *Harlierl,* like it was one word," recalled Mitchell in a 1980 interview. "Finally I said, 'Well, where is Harley Earl?' And they said, 'That was him.' I said, 'My God, I was talking to him for half an hour and never knew it...!' So that's the way I met Harley Earl."

The two men struck an immediate spark that soon turned into something like a father/son relationship. They were very similar, not only in terms of personality but also in their love of car design, clothes and motorsports. Harley Earl initially turned Mitchell over to Boss Kett, GM's research vice president who in 1936 was working on a car called the Albanita, an experimental, rear-engined, unit-bodied sedan.

Next Earl pitted Mitchell against Frank Hershey, asking both men to do a catwalk-cooled Buick. He gave Mitchell a studio in

Mitchell posed in his Cadillac studio during creation of 1939 model. He also stood alongside a full-sized rendering of the 60-Special to show scale. His designs and sketches always contained action, and he occasionally put helmeted race drivers in the cockpit. Several of his drawings from the Harley Earl Scrapbooks make use of front-wheel-drive axle banjos below the radiator. Except for the in-fender headlights, Cadillac accepted Mitchell's 1937 LaSalle design, shown at right in mockup form.

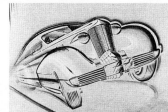

GM's 1959 models went through a period of bizarre trial and error. The studios tried especially hard to come up with alternate treatments for quad headlights. Also, it's interesting to compare tail light treatment on Buick clay (second from top) with Chrysler model on page 168. Pontiac called its heavy fins and chromed tail lamps "bunny ears" (above), and this particular fiberglass mockup exhibits a roof treatment that was seriously considered for production.

the back of the styling department together with two other designers, Art Ross and Bill Lange, plus two modelers, John Lutz and Matty Schumer. Earl declared Mitchell the winner of the Buick design competition, and Mitchell figured he was in line to become

the next head of the Buick studio—an assignment he desperately wanted, because his dad was a Buick dealer. But it happened that Earl had scheduled Clare Hodgman to take over the Cadillac studio, and when Hodgman left suddenly to go with Raymond Loewy in 1937, Earl did a very daring thing: He gave Mitchell the Cadillac studio. "It broke my heart," recalled Mitchell years later, "but it was my best move, because Cadillac was the car Earl cared most about." Cadillac at that time was GM's lead styling division.

Mitchell justified Earl's confidence and immediately made his mark with the 1938 Cadillac 60-Special. We talked about that car in Chapter Seven. At that time Mitchell still had all his hair. He was 25, thin, dressed well and cut a dashing figure, but it was his confidence and forcefulness that impressed people.

Bill had married his high-school sweetheart, Jane, and fathered two daughters. He spent World War II in the Navy, in Washington illustrating flight training manuals. (When she read this in manuscript, Mitchell's daughter, Lynne, noted, "I remember Dad showing me copies of the training manual when I was a child. He created a monkey named Iffy, who was the little mascot. Dad made up the name from the letters I.F.F., meaning Information Friend or Foe, the signal to unidentified aircraft.")

After the war, Mitchell returned to the Cadillac studio, and four years later Harley Earl tapped him to run his private industrial-design firm (see sidebar, page 112). When Mitchell came back to GM again in 1953, Earl elevated him to director of styling.

But the big question was always, "Who will replace Misterl?" Around 1947, it seems that Earl had favored Henry deS. Lauve as his successor. Lauve was more socially adept than Mitchell: more diplomatic, reserved and even-tempered. Lauve was also an excellent designer and had a major hand in doing, among other cars, the 1942 Buicks. But then Earl must have changed his mind, because Mitchell mentioned in one of his interviews that Earl had assured him of the vice presidency as early as 1953, at the same time telling Sloan and Curtice of his choice.

For a while, Mitchell shared equal rank with Jules Andrade, whose title at GM Styling was executive assistant of production body design programs. Mitchell and Andrade became Earl's right and left hands. When Earl hit a snag in the studios, he'd sometimes call for Jules and at other times for Bill. He'd listen to both and then usually do what he'd decided beforehand.

During the mid to late 1950s, Andrade lost some respect among most studio chiefs. He came from a different generation, and toward the end of Earl's tenure, Andrade got the reputation of being Earl's yes man. That's when Mitchell gained status and, during Earl's absences, Mitchell had full authority to make styling decisions of the highest order. His first real test came with the creation of GM's watershed 1959 models.

Whatever else they represented, the '59s marked the transition, the line between Earl's era and Mitchell's. Those cars and how they came to be—that story—marked the passing of the baton from one man to the other. And it's important to mention here that roughly two years before Harley Earl retired, a growing number of his younger designers started to feel he was losing his touch. Everyone except Earl agreed that GM's 1958 models turned out pretty dreadful, particularly the 1958 Buicks and Oldsmobiles. Those two cars took on the nickname "chromed elephants."

Buick's then-assistant chief designer Stan Parker remarked years later that for the 1958 Roadmaster, Earl had ordered him to put 100 pounds of chrome on the car. Parker made several sketches and showed them to Earl. "Hell, I thought I told you 100 pounds," Parker quoted Earl as saying. "That's only 80 pounds. Now put on some more!" So Parker added spears and hashmarks and shovels, most of which did end up on the 1958 Roadmaster.

In early concept studies for the 1959s, it became clear that Earl was still refrosting the old cake, rebaking the same domed hoods and vaulted roofs, Dagmar bumpers, massive grilles and doughy shapes that characterized the 1957-58 models. But as much as they wondered about Earl's competence, no one—not even

Mitchell—questioned Earl's judgement. People just didn't do that. Earl had always known the right way to go and, in the end, always came up with winners. Or mostly. Even so, some of his top studio people started mentioning that the Old Man seemed to be groping, especially after he ordered a big Motorama LeSabre nose grafted onto a clay 1959 Buick. Was that really what GM wanted for the 1960s?

And then came that cataclysmic event, the discovery of Chrysler's 1957 models. Chuck Jordan, driving down Mound Road one August noontime in 1956, happened to see the next year's Chrysler Corp. cars through a chainlink fence. The cars wouldn't be out for months, yet here they were, parked in orderly rows for the world to see. Jordan realized immediately that Exner's 1957 *Forward* Look was so far ahead of anything GM was doing for 1959 that it seemed futile to keep going in the direction Earl was headed.

"Chrysler had this big holding pen back behind the plant on Six-Mile near Mound Road," recalled Jordan, who himself retired in Dec. 1992 as GM Design Staff vice president (see page 272), "and I used to go past there because I was anxious to see next year's cars before anyone else did. Well...there through the chainlink fence, I saw all these brand-new 1957 Plymouths, and *wow,* that was really a shock! They looked so clean and lean, with that thin roof and all that glass, those nice proportions and the fins; just the opposite of what we were working on at GM at that time."

Jordan raced north to the GM Technical Center and excitedly described to Bill Mitchell and a few others what he'd seen. Together they drove back to the Chrysler plant. Mitchell was just as stunned by Exner's 1957s as Jordan had been. Word spread through the GM design studios, and that afternoon carloads of GM stylists made the trip down Mound Road to gawk through the fence.

Harley Earl was in Europe, and the quiet revolution started in his absence. With Bill Mitchell in authority and obviously anxious for change, the studios spontaneously abandoned the Earl themes and began to develop their own answers to Chrysler's 1957 cars. General Motors designers rapidly came up with the leaner, cleaner, more linear clay models that eventually turned into GM's 1959 production cars. "The designs we did at that point," said Jordan, "had a lot more flair than those big, cement-looking things we'd been working on. No one liked those earlier cars, but now we were on our way."

GM president Harlow Curtice, who routinely visited Design Staff—the Buick studio in particular—saw these new designs taking shape and liked them a lot. He showed as much enthusiasm as the studio chiefs. Then, as the revolution spread, Curtice made it a point to tell the division general managers, rounding up their support for the change in styling direction.

"But it was Mitchell who had that vision," said Jordan 25 years later. "It wasn't Harley Earl...and it wasn't Harlow Curtice. Those were tension-filled days, and you surely listened to Curtice, because he was president of the company, but he was no designer. You also listened to Harley Earl, because he was your boss, and he could kick you where it hurt.

But Mitchell was the guy who made the '59 models happen. When Harley Earl wasn't around, Mitchell was in all the studios, and he was it! You have to hand it to Curtice for support, but the real credit goes to Bill Mitchell."

The move away from the old shapes proceeded quickly. It might even have moved a little too quickly because, when Earl returned from Europe, he couldn't quite get his mind around what he was seeing. Dave Holls, a senior designer in Ed Glowacke's Cadillac

Rear-end treatments looked just as strange. At top is a Buick clay with three tailfins. Two of them went into production. Below that, Dave Holls' Cadillac studio tried big rocket-like pods flanked by tall fins. Again, the fins saw production, but with rocket-like tail lamps faired into them. The Oldsmobile's tubular beltline (center) represented a rocket set into the side of the body. Sketch by Irv Rybicki set the front-end theme of the 1959 Oldsmobile. Ned Nickles reworked this theme slightly and applied it to the 1960 Chevrolet Corvair.

studio, remembered that, "He [Earl] didn't like [the transition] at all when he got back. We all had our new designs going, either on one side of an old clay model or as a completely new model. Every studio had something new going. There was just so much concern over these [Chrysler] cars, and what we'd been doing [previously] was so old that everybody rebelled. So when Mr. Earl came back from Europe, the studios were saying, in effect, 'This is how we want to do it.'"

Ordinarily, such insubordination would have led to mass firings. But the scale of the rebellion was too big. Due to this majority opinion among his studio people and possibly because Mitchell, Curtice and most of GM's general managers were so eager for change, Earl felt overwhelmed and outvoted. Holls said that Earl walked around stunned for days, going from one studio to another, not saying a word to anyone.

Nor would he ever admit the effect those 1957 Chrysler products had on himself or his staff. Earl did say eventually, referring to Virgil Exner who, after all, learned much of his craft in Earl's Pontiac studio during the 1930s: "Maybe they've stumbled onto something." Earl specifically said "they've," not "he's." But that was as far as he'd go toward acknowledging Exner as his peer.

Pontiac studio head Paul Gillan recalled later that, "Ex owned a boat and belonged, as I did, to the Grosse Pointe Yacht Club. One weekend the club had a rendezvous up at a St. Clair river marina, and I attended with my boat. It rained, and some of us spent the afternoon in the club lounge. I talked with Ex at some length about Chrysler's *Forward* Look. He was very proud that Chrysler's design strategy had such an impact on old Harley Earl and the GM group. When he spoke of the 1957 tailfin Chryslers, you could almost sense his feeling of 'I guess I showed you guys and beat you to the draw.'"

Once Earl accepted GM's '59 themes, though, he got behind Mitchell and the other designers and mustered considerable enthusiasm. It was actually Earl who dictated the final refinements. Fisher engineers, meanwhile, also got involved and showed that it would be more economical in 1959 to scrap GM's traditional A-B-C-D body plan and go with one basic platform for all five makes. This all-serving platform would be shortened or lengthened to give different wheelbases and body lengths. In addition, all 1959 GM cars shared the cowl, the windshield and four-door-sedan front doors. Due to Curtice's influence, the Buick's front door became the standard, and all other GM cars made their doors distinctive with die inserts or appliques added onto the beltline. Dick Stout recalled that at Lincoln-Mercury, they put on a demonstration, "...where we poured milk through the hollow applique on an Olds sedan front door to demonstrate how shoddy GM body construction had become. This was met with much laughter!"

Several interesting sidelights on the 1959 body program: In their frenzy to come up with a new and different look, nothing seemed too bizarre to warrant serious consideration. In fact, any designer who couldn't produce ever-wilder ideas risked losing his job. So this turned into a brief period when the freakish prevailed, when designers set headlights in the middle of hoods, tailfins in the middle of decklids and huge jet-like exhausts in the center of rear bumpers.

Stylists at all other U.S. automakers were stretching out in similar directions. Photos from Chrysler and Ford during this period show the same sorts of hood-mounted lamps, huge tailfins (especially at Chrysler), bizarre roof treatments, rear grilles and convoluted side sculpting.

By some miracle, most of these oddities didn't make it beyond GM's styling courtyard as fiberglass mockups, but a few did survive, like Bob Cadaret's gullwing rear fenders on the 1959 Chevrolet and Buick. Mitchell dubbed them "pagoda rear ends." Or Dave Holls' spectacular, high-finned 1959 Cadillac, which the postal service recently put on a 15¢ stamp.

At least two major styling innovations became highly successful in GM's 1959 program. One was the double-nacelle grille on the 1959 Pontiac, which replaced the Silver Streak as the marque identifier and remains a Pontiac symbol even today. The second was the "flying-wing" or "cantilever" roof on the 1959 GM four-door hardtops. Credit for that design goes to a young Japanese-American GM stylist named Bud Sugano, who proposed it in early 1957. Carl Renner, under Clare MacKichan in the Chevrolet studio, was instrumental in "productionizing" the flying wing for 1959. Renner had done the fluted roof on the 1954 Motorama Corvette Nomad and the 1955 production Nomad. He now extended the flying wing not only to all five GM lines but also to the 1960 Corvair sedan.

A 1959 styling/engineering idea, Pontiac's Wide Track, came from Chuck Jordan working in Bob McLean's advanced studio. Jordan had modeled a mid-sized concept sedan whose wheels stood noticeably farther outboard than normal. Chuck felt that the wider stance gave this car—which carried no name—a more stable, substantial look. Bunkie Knudsen, Pontiac's general manager, happened along with his two top engineers, Pete Estes and John DeLorean. All three were so taken with Jordan's idea that they asked to use it on the 1959 Pontiac. Pontiac's admen promptly coined the term "Wide Track" and made the theme a highly successful selling point.

Oldsmobile's identity symbol had long been the rocket and, for 1959, Olds designers integrated the rocket directly into the new model's beltline. This was another of those strange tales that characterized the development of the '59s. Oldsmobile design chief Art Ross had a 10-foot-tall "rocket" standing near his studio door. "One day Mr. Earl walked into our studio," noted Ross's assistant, Irv Rybicki, "and he didn't like what we had going. At the entrance to the studio, though, Art Ross had positioned this rocket—the standard Oldsmobile symbol at that time.... So as Earl was leaving...he stopped and stared at this rocket. He looked over at me and said, 'Get a couple of the fellows to move that over here to the clay.' So I did, and he had them pick it up and hold it alongside the clay model. And then he said to me, 'That's what I want you to do, Irv: Create a rocket up there at the beltline.' And that's how the tubular beltline on the 1959 Olds door got started. It went through maybe 100 variations before we [got what we] finally produced, but that was the beginning of Oldsmobile's 1959 theme."

As it ended up, GM's 1959 cars not only succeeded in the marketplace but also let Harley Earl save face. He was starting to lose his touch, no doubt, and he probably should have retired two years before he did. The irony was that Virgil Exner's 1957 models pushed Mitchell to rally the troops and ultimately to re-established GM's design leadership. Without Chrysler's 1957 *Forward* Look, the fat 1958 models might have been Earl's swan song instead of the turnaround 1959s.

Another transitional Earl/Mitchell design was the 1960 Corvair. The Corvair's guiding light, Ed Cole, shared Earl's and Mitchell's respect for styling, and everyone involved was aware that the Big Three would all launch new compacts for 1960: Ford the Falcon, Plymouth the Valiant and Chevrolet the Corvair. Cole and Mitchell were determined to make the Corvair the style leader of the three.

The Corvair's extreme lowness and basic lines had their begin-

"Young Turks" played nearly as big a role in bringing about GM's new design direction as Mitchell himself. In this 1965 photo, they were (L-R): Dave Holls, Stan Wilen, Irv Rybicki, Stan Parker, Paul Gillan, Jack Humbert and Chuck Jordan.

nings in an experimental design studio run by Ned Nickles. Carl Renner was Nick's assistant, and Drew Hare did the interior. The Corvair's combination of a high wraparound beltline and the undercut just below it derived from the rear of the Biscayne Motorama showcar. Nickles adapted a downsized 1959 Olds front end to the Corvair along with Bud Sugano's flying-wing upper. That first-generation Corvair became one of the most copied cars GM ever produced. Among those who paid it the highest form of flattery were the German NSU Prinz and BMW, the British Sunbeam/Hillman Imp, Japanese Mazda 800, Italian Fiat 1300/1500, Russian Zaporozhets plus the French Simca 1000 and Renault R8.

The 1963 Riviera became one of Bill Mitchell's all-time favorite designs. The concept began when it dawned on him that GM needed a car to challenge the four-seater Thunderbird. Early concept studies in Ned Nickles' advanced studio looked like a jet plane on wheels, similar to the theme of the 1961 Thunderbird. No one, though, was happy with that direction. So after a trip to England, Mitchell came back and suggested to Nick, "Let's make it look like a Ferrari-Rolls-Royce; give it that look." Mitchell had in mind a very sporty car, the Ferrari essence, but also incorporating the razor-edged elegance

1963 Riviera became one of Mitchell's favorite designs. Crisp razor edges, inspired by Rolls-Royce, blended into the sporty overtones of a Ferrari. Again, Ned Nickles did the execution. This design was initially envisioned as a LaSalle, thus the upright "grilles" in the leading edges of both fenders, but Cadillac didn't want it and Buick did.

The GM Design Process in the 1960s

During the Bill Mitchell era, individual studio teams were relatively small and intimate. Exterior production studios consisted of two or three designers, one or two body engineers and three to four clay modelers. In the early 1960s, each exterior studio was fully responsible for an entire line of cars. The Buick studio, for example, styled not just the full-sized LeSabre/Invicta but also the compact Special, the Wildcat and the Riviera. When Motorama showcars were due, the team designed those as well. Six-day work weeks were normal, often stretching to seven, with 14-hour days common.

GM's product planners, unlike Ford's, had no input into the design or the styling process. New body shapes and facelifts were generated entirely by Mitchell and his staff. Divisional general managers and other GM executives could have their say, but it was usually Mitchell's intuitive styling sense that ruled.

The typical design began with dozens of sketches, and most studio groups recognized the two or three that had potential. With Mitchell's approval, those two or three were airbrushed full size on black paper. After Mitchell and the divisional managers chose among these, the surviving designs went immediately into clay, sometimes 3/8 scale but usually full size. And it was at this point that a skillful clay modeler could make or break a design.

Advanced studios operated in basically the same way but with half the personnel. In advanced, the making of scale models was more common, because these smaller studios didn't have the manpower to do full-sized proposals.

Mitchell didn't believe in large meetings and rarely held even small ones. Division general managers, engineers and corporate people would drop by Design Staff at will or when called in to help make crucial decisions. Once production designs received final approval, they were turned over to GM's body engineering staff for release to the divisions, Fisher Body and GM Assembly Div. (GMAD). Fisher and GMAD at that time operated GM's body plants and manufactured all of GM's automobile bodies, although front sheetmetal was sometimes supplied by the divisions.

Each year, the big push was toward the board of directors' show. Under Harley Earl, board shows were often held at the Waldorf-Astoria Hotel in New York, but under Mitchell they took place each August at the GM Proving Grounds near Milford, Michigan. Here divisional and corporate management rubbed elbows with the board, and the focus became the highly realistic, full-sized, fiberglass styling prototypes. These provided a preview of next season's cars so the board could inspect them and nod approvingly. Designs were fixed by that time, but the show had great social significance within the corporation; a celebration of GM's styling and engineering vitality. ◆

1963 Corvette was classic Mitchell. It combined rounded and peaked forms plus a little retro in the boattail and split rear window. The basic theme came from Mitchell's Sting Ray racer.

of a Rolls-Royce.

Nickles understood immediately, and one of his first sketches indeed captured the requisite Ferrari-Rolls-Royce look. Later, when Mitchell decided to sell the idea of a Thunderbird rival to Cadillac, Nickles added two upright mini grilles to the front fenders, which led Mitchell to call this car the LaSalle II. Officially, the LaSalle II carried the designation XP-715. Cadillac, though, politely declined, so Mitchell next showed the XP-715 to Chevrolet, but Chevy wasn't interested either, and Pontiac was lukewarm. However, when

favored Buick because of its more upmarket status. Buick could charge more for the car than could Oldsmobile. And now that Buick had it, the decision was made to call this new car the Buick Riviera.

The 1963 Riviera epitomized the type of design Mitchell loved. Its very distinctive form combined long, carefully peaked folds that highlighted the broad, softly sculpted surfaces of the hood, roof, decklid and body sides. Except for false airscoops on the flanks, there was very little ornamentation. The Rolls-Royce impact was easy to see. Less obvious was the Ferrari

least three Rivieras customized for his personal use. The first, called the Silver Arrow I, had a chopped top, extended front fenders, modified rear fenders and no front ventipanes.

Another pleasing and memorable Mitchell design was the 1963 Chevrolet Corvette. This car took its theme from Mitchell's Sting Ray racer. Chuck Jordan makes the point that Mitchell became deeply involved in all Corvette designs and basically conceived their shapes and detailing personally. "Don't flatter yourself, kid," Jordan quoted Mitchell as say-

1965 model year was one of Mitchell's finest, far superior to any of GM's competitors. Pontiac Bonneville (left) maximized the entertainment value of peeled-back headlamps, wide ribbed rockers, twin-nacelle grille and 8-bolt alloy wheels (not shown). Olds Delta 88 took on a cleaner version of GM's 1965 look, and even Chevrolet had the same massive grace.

Buick and Oldsmobile saw the clay model, both of those divisions wanted it and started to vie for the rights to produce the car.

In fairness, GM decided to let Olds and Buick compete for production rights. Both divisions were asked to submit marketing plans, sales targets, manufacturing costs, projected price, etc. Buick brought in its ad agency, made a sensational presentation and won hands down. GM might also have

influence. But the Riviera did have something of the sports-car flair along with its restrained formality.

The first production Buick Riviera bowed as a 1963 model and became an immediate, resounding success. (The name Riviera had been applied to 1949 and later Buick B-pillarless hardtop coupes.) Mitchell was delighted with the purity of the design and, through the years, had at

ing, "I do the Corvettes. You don't do the Corvettes."

There's some confusion about the origin of the 1963 Corvette. In 1957, Peter Brock and Charles (Chuck) Pohlmann were junior designers in Bob McLean's research studio. Brock remembered that Mitchell, just back from the Turin auto show, brought in some pictures of Tom Tjaarda's Ghia IxG dragster. (Pete Brock later designed, among other cars, the Shelby Cobra Daytona coupe. Tom Tjaarda, son of Lincoln Zephyr designer John Tjaarda, did the DeTomaso Pantera.) Mitchell told him and Pohlmann that he wanted to see the IxG character in the next-generation Corvette. The problem with that story, though, is that the Ghia IxG dragster didn't appear in Turin until 1959, so Mitchell must have brought in pictures of some other, similar showcar.

At any rate, Brock and Pohlmann developed a coupe in full-sized clay called the Q-Car. This preceded and was the basis for Bill Mitchell's Sting Ray racer. The 1963 Corvette used the same theme in every form except for the high, rounded coupe upper and just slightly softer surfaces.

"Then in early 1959," added designer Gene Garfinkle, "I was reassigned from the Buick studio to work with Mitchell and technical stylist Ed Wayne, doing the full-sized line drawings to convert the Sting Ray racer to the production configuration of the 1963 Corvette. Bill...dictated or authorized every line and detail on the car. About two months later, in the spring of 1959, Mitchell

through 1967 virtually without change.

The 1966 Oldsmobile Toronado offered Mitchell an opportunity to do a strikingly modern version of the classic 1936 Cord 810. Olds had engineered a large, front-wheel-drive coupe with torsion-bar front suspension and a low, flat floor: elements all designers perennially pray for. David R. North had drawn up a concept car in Stan Wilen's Olds studio—a full-sized airbrush rendering that came to be known as "the flame-red car." Wilen recalled that, "The thing just sang. It stood there in the room, and as people walked by it, they stopped and sat down and just studied it."

The 1966 Toronado introduced three oft-copied design elements. First and foremost was the elimination of the front ventipane, the No-Draft windwing that General Motors had introduced for 1933 with such fanfare. The 1966 Riviera also got rid of the ventipane, and most American cars soon followed suit.

The second noteworthy styling feature was the shoulderless B-pillar/rear-fender junction. Some designers dubbed this the "monocoque" look, monocoque in this case meaning "of a piece"

Buick became the lead division in styling the 1966 E-Car. Although '66 Riviera and that year's fwd Olds Toronado shared platforms, cowls, glass and inner sheetmetal, they had totally different character. Dave Holls' studio created the Riviera (above), while the Toronado (right) came from a concept sketch by Dave North. In 1967, Cadillac released its version of the E-Car, the fwd Eldorado, which again had a distinctive appearance.

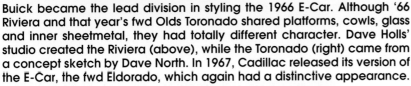

visited the Buick studio to show Hank Haga and me what he was doing to make the split-window coupe out of the roadster...." And that was the point when Larry Shinoda became involved in productionizing the coupe.

Again, the 1963 Corvette showed the use of sharp edges combined with softly rounded, billowy forms and tasteful jewelry—very different from the Corvettes designed under Harley Earl. The original '63 Corvette coupe is now fondly and universally referred to as the "split-window," due to the windsplit that runs up through the backlight. Mitchell liked the divided rear window, but the Corvette's chief engineer, Zora Arkus-Duntov, didn't. Nor did most 1963 Corvette drivers, who complained that the windsplit made them more vulnerable to speeding tickets. So the split window went away for 1964. The body style itself, though, continued

or "continuous shape." (The stylists did not have in mind the engineering definition of monocoque, which is a type of body construction that makes use of load-bearing body skins.) In the 1966 Toronado, the sail panels glided smoothly down from the roof into the fenders without a shoulder. What made this blending remarkable was the absence of any beltline break. And since the angle of the tumblehome, taken from the rear roof sail panel, continued down into the fenders and doors, the doors were thinner at the beltline and widest down at the ridge line that connected the fender lips. Again, a lot of cars have copied the monocoque look since then.

And the third intriguing design element consisted of the Toro's thick, heavy wheel lips. In side view, these looked like tunnel entrances leading into the wheel wells. The Toronado drew more attention to the fender openings than any previous car, and the idea again inspired imitators.

The front ensemble borrowed visual cues from the 1936 Cord 810: hidden headlamps, a grille with horizontal bands that floated between vertical, sharply peaked, chromed, flush-fitting front fender blades. Wilen reflected later that the 1936 Cord did influence that aspect of the Toronado design.

Concurrent with the Toronado's development was David R. Holls' work on the 1966 Buick Riviera. The 1966 Riviera and Toronado (and the 1967 Cadillac Eldorado) shared platform, inner sheetmetal, cowl, windshield, A-pillars and door glass. Buick had actually been the lead division in the design of all three cars. Holls' second-generation Riviera ended up even cleaner than the Toro. Seen in plan view, Holls used a W-shaped front end, and the

The 1968 GTO (left), with its body-color Endura grille, pioneered the soft front end. The 1970 1/2 Camaro RS (center) also had an Endura grille but took its face from the Jaguar XJ-12 sedan. One of Mitchell's less successful designs was the boattail 1971 Buick Riviera (above). Two years later, Mitchell put almost this same design on the front of the 1973 Pontiac Grand Am--same central prow but with headlights and catwalks in place of the tail lamps--and again it failed.

The 1971 Cadillac Eldorado (above) was one of GM's largest cars ever and just the sort Bill Mitchell loved. So did Cadillac buyers. Unfortunately, by 1973 big-cubic-inch cars like this came back to haunt GM. Meanwhile, Mitchell and his staff created the ultra-exotic 1973 Aero Vette, set up initially for a rotary engine and later converted to a midship Chevy V-8.

W was repeated very subtly in the rear. These were both marvelous designs, and so was the 1967 Eldorado, which was built on the same platform. Even more amazing was how *different* each car in this trio looked.

When Ed Glowacke passed away, Jordan became Mitchell's second in command. It's generally agreed among the studio chiefs that Jordan initiated and rode herd on many of the designs that went into production during the Mitchell years. Jordan would occasionally countermand Mitchell's wishes, and at those times two strong wills clashed. Jordan, though, could hold his own. He was learning the martial arts from the best in the business. Problem was, he didn't have Mitchell's sense of humor, so he often left designers and modelers angry and frustrated.

Like the 1966 Riviera/Toronado/Eldorado E-Cars, GM's 1970 F-Cars—the Firebird and Camaro—were done simultaneously and by studios that worked together on the two different cars. Henry (Hank) Haga ran the Camaro studio, while William L. (Bill) Porter was chief of the Firebird studio.

The 1970 1/2 F-Cars again took the overall sculpture of the body as their primary styling element. The upper--the basic roof design --came from a Vignale-bodied Ferrari 212 coupe and, like that lovely little car, eliminated the rear quarter window. The windshield, meanwhile, had a wide, inverted-U shape. The challenge now became to give each coupe—Camaro and Firebird—a unique character and personality. Bill Porter used Pontiac's twin-nostril Endura grille as his identity symbol, Endura referring to the body-colored, steel-backed, soft plastic nose developed by GM designer/engineer Warren Fitzgerald. The Endura bumper was first used on Pontiac's 1968 GTO.

The Camaro offered an entirely different Endura-framed open grille on its sportier RS model and took its front-end theme from the 1968 Jaguar XJ6. The basic 1970 1/2 F body stayed in production for over a decade, and it's still considered one of GM's more timeless designs.

Mitchell very much enjoyed overseeing the design of big cars like the 1971 Cadillac Eldorado, especially the convertible. This particular Cadillac, done in Wayne Kady's advanced studio, represented a short, golden moment in GM's history when cost seemed no object and styling still ruled. Mitchell now had the full backing of people like Cole and Estes, times were good and money flowed into GM Design Staff with virtually no constraints. Tom Christiansen commented that anytime an oversight committee questioned Design Staff's expenses, he could show where the money went and make a good case for styling as a sales stimulant. GM's moneymen might shake their heads, but they never trimmed Mitchell's budget, unlike Chrysler's beancounters, who constantly cut the funds available to Engel and Macadam.

Large cars like the 1971 Eldorado stood for an age that was about to end. By 1971, Cadillac had a 500-cubic-inch, 365-horsepower V-8 that delivered eight miles per gallon. Large Detroit cars with single-digit fuel mileage were common in the early 1970s. So when the first oil embargo hit in late 1973, it sent American car buyers scurrying into small, lightweight, fuel-efficient Japanese cars. That plus a flurry of new federal standards that regulated everything from bumper heights and strength to tailpipe emissions suddenly lifted the engineer into prominence, shoved money toward safety, downsizing, front-wheel drive and fuel economy and pushed the designer into a secondary role. The stylist's glory days were suddenly and unceremoniously over.

Mitchell, along with everyone else who shaped sheetmetal, had major problems with the often contradictory mandates of the new laws and requirements. Fuel-economy standards, for example, suggested smaller, lighter cars, while impact and rollover standards required heavier, bulkier pillars and bumpers. These tough times very much tested the stylists' skills and, in the opinion of many, made men out of boys. George Moon commented that this was the period when stylists became car designers.

To compound Mitchell's misery, he disliked small cars and always had. He'd often stated, "Designing a small car is like tai-

With downsized 1976 Cadillac Seville (right), Mitchell led entire industry into the "sheer look." Before settling on sheer look, Wayne Kady's studio suggested an Opel-derived Seville (top) and several stretched Novas.

loring a suit for a dwarf." But he did exactly that with the 1971 Chevrolet Vega subcompact. Again designed in Hank Haga's studio, the Vega looked like a miniaturized second-generation Camaro. Actually, the result wasn't bad. Mitchell and Haga tailored that particular dwarf nicely.

However, the Vega quickly earned a reputation for rust and durability problems. Its Ford counterpart, the Pinto, established a similar reputation for fuel-tank fires. Between them, they gave American small cars such a black eye that the Japanese, who'd been engineering, styling and producing inexpensive, high-quality subcompacts for years, had no trouble pushing domestic small cars off the sales charts, especially after the oil embargo of Oct. 1973.

Ford had downsized the Mustang for 1974, basing its new, smaller version on the Pinto platform. The timing was right, because gasoline prices had just tripled and every filling station in

the country had lines around it.

Mustang sales likewise tripled in 1974, but Detroit still viewed downsizing as dangerous business, not to be taken lightly. Billions stood at risk. But Pete Estes, who'd trained as an engineer and was now president of the largest corporation in the world, decided that General Motors should take the plunge at the deep end.

The strategy of that plunge was to introduce new downsized models in two carefully planned phases, the second building on the first. The first phase involved designing and launching the "international size" 1976 Cadillac Seville, a luxurious, smaller but more expensive model which, Estes hoped, would bring errant Mercedes and BMW buyers back to Cadillac. The 1976 Seville weighed nearly 1000 pounds less than that year's full-sized Cadillac 60-Special Brougham, stood two feet shorter, yet cost $1500 *more!* It shared GM's X-body chassis components with the mid-sized Chevrolet Nova.

Estes realized that aesthetics would play a big part in the

Visitation Rites

A visiting dignitary's tour of any car company nearly always includes a visit to the styling department. That's where the automaker previews the future, an impressive display even to those not terribly interested in cars. At General Motors, informal tours for special guests began under Harley Earl but really hit their stride during Bill Mitchell's vice presidency. We can't name all the guests who toured GM Design Staff during the Mitchell years, but here's a sampling.

King Leopold of Belgium and 25 members of his retinue, King Umberto II of Italy, the Count and Countess of Chastel, Crown Prince Abdallah Senussi of Libya, Prince Mohammed ben Abdul Aziz of Saudi

Bill Mitchell usually insisted on taking important guests through GM Design Staff personally. Here he shows what appears to be a Motorama roadster to Eleanor Roosevelt and her aide.

Arabia, Eleanor Roosevelt, Baron von Rothschild, cartoonist Walt Disney, musicians Eugene Ormandy, Sergio Franchi, Hoagey Carmichael, Stan Kenton, Pat Boone and Glenn Campbell, astronauts Alan Shepherd, John Glenn and Gordon Cooper, race drivers Lance Reventlow, Phil Hill and Stirling Moss, General Curtis LeMay, actors Walter Brennan, Florence Henderson and Lorne Green, skier Jean Claude Killey, Fiat president Giovanni Agnelli, designers Howard (Dutch) Darrin and Sergio and Pinin Farina, stuntman Evel Knievel and Linda Bird Johnson. ◆

Seville's acceptance. Irv Rybicki, the executive in charge of Olds-Buick-Cadillac exteriors, mentioned that, "Pete Estes practically lived in our place," meaning at Design Staff. He also remembered that early Seville clay models looked so much like a Nova with Cadillac end caps that, "We couldn't hide the Nova at first."

The Seville's target car was the 1973 Mercedes 280SEL, and two styling proposals from Wayne Kady's advanced Cadillac studio suggested making the Seville out of the German Opel. But the Opel idea didn't last long, especially

Downsized 1977 Chevrolet Caprice shared Seville's sheer look but didn't copy it.

after Stan Parker took over the advanced Cadillac studio and started styling a slightly longer, different Seville on the other side of the Nova-like clay model. This version had longer doors and three inches more rear-seat leg room. Ed Cole questioned the cost, since an insert would have to be welded into the Nova floorpan and the doors would have to be unique. "Well, Ed," said Rybicki, "it will carry the Cadillac name." Cole soon found the money.

Parker recalled that Bill Mitchell got back from one of his trips to England and, "...we had the car in clay, and Bill came rushing in and said, 'Goddam it, Parker, make that backlight damn near vertical. Make it look like a Rolls-Royce!' I said to myself, 'Well, maybe the guy's gone bananas,' but we tried it, and it worked."

The 1976 Seville ended up representing more than an international-sized Cadillac: It set a new styling direction; what Bill Mitchell termed the "sheer look." He was referring to the sharp-edged, unbroken surfaces that looked like they'd been sculpted with a single sweep of a huge knife: sheer in the same way a woman's leg inside a Nylon stocking looks smooth and voluptuous. Sheerness applied to the Seville's surfaces: roof, decklid, hood, sides and ends. Precipitous drops fell away into gently rolled or puffed-out, totally unadorned fender and door sections.

The sheer look came about for a number of reasons. In the process of downsizing, stylists discovered that in side view, rounded drop-offs on hoods, decks and roof lines made a short car look even shorter. Also, since boxes hold more than spheres, squarer exteriors give more interior space: more rear-seat head room and more trunk volume. Several European makes, Mercedes and Volvo among them, showed the practicality of the square body format.

So the 1976 Seville optimized space through squareness and added the sheer look as a stylistic device. Mitchell directed the Seville so it appeared formal and stiff, with the linear elegance he so much admired in the Rolls-Royce. Yet he softened the severity of the design with those mildly rolled sides, the full wheel openings, the wide-track front stance and the tire-accenting fender flares. Wayne Kady, who by then had gone into the Cadillac production studio, put the finishing touches on the 1976 Seville and released the final body design.

Cadillac's smaller, more environmentally correct Seville sold well from the beginning, and this time the public took warmly to the sheerness of its styling. The sheer look quickly became a styling trend that every Detroit automaker adopted over the course of the next 10 years. Nameplates ranging from Chrysler's K-Cars to Ford's Fairmonts adopted the sheer look and sold well as a result.

Then for 1977 came the second and considerably more daring phase of GM's downsizing program. This involved making GM's bread-and-butter cars, notably the Chevrolet Caprice and Impala, 600-800 pounds lighter, 10.6 inches shorter and 3.5 inches narrower than they'd been in 1976. Again, to give the downsized Caprice/Impala as much interior space as practical and as much stylistic appeal as possible, Mitchell had Terry Henline's advanced Chevrolet studio apply the sheer look.

Henline remembered Mitchell coming in with a photograph of a rebodied Jaguar by Italian designer Giorgio Giugiaro. The Jaguar had the sheer look that Mitchell wanted for the downsized Chevrolet. There seems to have been no direct influence from the Seville, but the 1977 Caprice/Impala did have the same design philosophy, albeit from another source. Henline's Caprice had the Seville's upright, linear, squared-off constructs and the same fully rounded wheel openings. Before it left Henline's studio, however, the 1977 Caprice/Impala took on something of a wedge look: more mass over the rear than the front.

Henline's development program lasted five or six months, after which the finished clay went into Don Lasky's production Chevrolet studio for final release. Here Lasky turned the wedge around to emphasize the front and then gave the car one final touch—a very subtly arched curve or "spline" that ran from end to end through the fender tops and beltline. This spline gave the finished car a greater illusion of length.

The public again showed its approval of the downsized Chevrolet by registering 131,165 more 1977 Caprice/Impalas than their counterparts for 1976. The same basic downsized standard Chevrolet remained in production, with one facelift in 1980, through the 1990 model year. So Chevrolet's downsizing gamble turned out to be extremely profitable, and all other GM makes soon followed. Meanwhile, the sheer look came to predominate as the automotive shape of the decade. It remained in favor until the Ford released the "aero look" with the Taurus/Sable for 1986.

Bill Mitchell's last noteworthy production car was the 1980 Cadillac Seville, the embodiment of what Mitchell referred to as the "London look." This car received mixed reviews at its launch and still provides a controversial cap to Mitchell's GM career. Some feel that he, like Earl, was losing it toward the end; that instead of being overly fond of Rubenesque forms as Earl had been, Mitchell was overly fond of razor edges and the Scott Fitzgerald classics. The 1980 Seville had all the Rolls-Royce elements: the long hood, classic standup grille, raked C-pillar and squared-off bustle. The 1980 Eldorado and Seville shared the same platform, cowl, hood and windshield, and that year's Seville was actually the Eldo coupe made over into a four-door sedan. The 1980 design concept again came out of Cadillac's advanced studio, where Wayne Kady started that theme even before he began to work on the 1976 Seville. Cadillac management had doubts about the 1980 look, but Mitchell and Pete Estes liked it, and Mitchell eventually pushed it through.

When Bill Mitchell took over from Harley Earl in late 1958, only one GM division had two car lines: Chevrolet had the Corvette. All other divisions consisted of just one car line: Pontiac, Oldsmobile, Buick and Cadillac. But by 1977 when Mitchell retired, the number of GM nameplates had grown to 33. Chevrolet alone had eight cars of different sizes, prices and purposes in 1977: Chevette, Vega, Nova, Chevelle, Monte Carlo, Chevrolet, Camaro and Corvette. Pontiac also had eight different nameplates, Oldsmobile seven, Buick six and Cadillac four. Many of these 33 nameplates came in several different body styles. Add government regulations and ever-tighter fuel-economy standards, and it's easy to see why some people might have felt Mitchell was losing it. The logistical pressures at the end of his career were so

Controversial 1980 Cadillac Seville again took inspiration from Rolls-Royce.

great that just turning out any designs at all amounted to a minor miracle.

Mitchell's final automotive styling statement at GM was the 1977 Phantom, a low, slinky two-place fastback coupe on a non-running Pontiac Grand Prix chassis. The Phantom was Mitchell's ultimate modern classic and represented, some felt, the design direction he planned for his successor. If that's what Mitchell had in mind, it was totally out of keeping with the smaller, lighter, more space-efficient shapes that GM needed at that time.

In 1977, Mitchell brought the Phantom to a big GM board show at the Milford proving grounds. He intended to present it to the

ness of the environment."

Interior designer George Moon summed up the era this way: "Bill Mitchell ruled over GM Design Staff during its most creative, most exciting years in corporate history. No matter his mood, his manner, his style—he gave the place a verve and an excitement it never had before or since. He brought out the best creative energies from all of us, and he oversaw the design of the greatest diversity of cars ever produced.

"Bill couldn't have survived in today's arena: too many rules, too many handcuffs, committees and bosses. Nor could today's corporation tolerate Mitchell's flamboyance, impertinences, ego and lifestyle. He was his own man, flawed and gifted, crude and creative. You had to love him or hate him, but no one in America could ignore him."

Mitchell retired in 1977 and opened a private industrial-design consulting firm in Rochester, Michigan. After he left GM and as he looked at the boxy cars he and his designers had put on wheels, he apparently had mixed feelings about the sheer look. "You know," he said in a 1979 interview with Corvette historian Michael B. Antonick, "years ago when you went into an auto styling department, you found sweeps...racks of them. Now they design [cars] with a T-square and a triangle."

Bill Mitchell might have had the retro look of the Phantom in mind as a styling direction for his successor to follow. His boss, Howard Kehrl, would not let him display it at the 1977 director's show.

corporation's directors as a surprise. Howard Kehrl, the victim of many a Mitchell insult, spotted the Phantom in the staging area and ordered it removed from the proving grounds forthwith. Mitchell was furious, but this was one battle he couldn't win. His clout had ebbed away; he was too near retirement and no longer had anyone at the top to back him up. In many ways, the Phantom brought back the same look that Mitchell had put into his 1935 portfolio sketches. The 1977 car had a pointy nose, crisp standup fenders, moustache-like bumpers, a catwalk filled with horizontal headlamps instead of grilles, a very long hood, flowing roof and very simple Rolls-Royce-inspired wheelcovers. He used brightwork only where he put pencil lines on his design sketch. The Phantom represented that nostalgia Mitchell felt for the classics during those waning days of his vice presidency.

But Bill Mitchell remained Bill Mitchell, and he couldn't have held his office much longer than he did. Jerry Hirschberg observed, "As the years passed, Mitchell's rather narrow biases and hardening vision limited GM styling. He was fighting old battles and withdrawing increasingly from a world that was being redefined by consumerism, Naderism and an emerging conscious-

In addition to consulting, Bill Mitchell took up painting again, a hobby he now had time for and loved. He also became happily involved with classic cars; bought, restored and modified a vintage Mercedes and took an active role in popularizing Detroit's prestigious Meadowbrook concours. In the early 1980s, Mitchell suffered heart problems and underwent bypass surgery. He closed his office in 1984 and passed away at his home in Bloomfield Hills, Michigan on Sept. 12, 1988. ◆

CHAPTER 11

THE INDEPENDENTS

All American automakers known as *independents*—names like Hudson, Packard, Studebaker, Pierce-Arrow, Cord, Auburn, Duesenberg, Marmon, Hupmobile, Nash, Franklin, Willys-Overland, Graham and Kaiser-Frazer—suffered one of two fates. They either went out of business *or they became part of Chrysler Corporation!*

Although their individual identities are long gone, the Chrysler-absorbed independents live on. Hudson and Nash, for example, merged to form American Motors Corp. (AMC) in 1954. AMC bought Kaiser-Jeep Corp. in 1970, which had previously been Kaiser-Willys out of Kaiser-Frazer, a company ancestrally linked to Graham-Paige Motors. Among Graham-Paige's antecedents were Jewett and Paige. Finally, in 1987 Chrysler purchased AMC's automotive assets from Regie Renault, technically absorbing Hudson, Nash, Kaiser-Frazer, Willys-Overland, Graham-Paige and all those other ghosts.

Heritage notwithstanding, this chapter looks at the styling activities of several major independent carmakers. We can't include them all, because thousands came and went during the first half of this century. But we hope to touch on the more significant and influential. ◆

HUDSON MOTOR CAR. CO.

In the formative years of the auto industry, one individual often designed an entire automobile, including the body. Design of the first 1910 Hudson is attributed to a skunkworks coalition of Hudson engineers Howard E. Coffin, R.B. Jackson and George Dunham. They likely had help from Hudson's early body suppliers, which at that time included Fisher, Briggs and the C.R. Wilson Co.

According to Hudson historian D.J. Kava, Hudson's body engineers used "wax," meaning a wax-based clay, to make scale and full-sized models as early as 1913. Kava also notes that in April 1914, Coffin and Hudson president Roy Chapin "...laid out the 'yacht line' body of the 1916 Hudson Model 40 on the sandy beach of Sapelo Island while Chapin was waiting to be introduced to his future wife." The Model 40's "yacht line" was a molding-less highlight that ran along the hood and continued through the cowl and into the beltline.

During the 1910s and '20s, Hudson offered a tremendous range of body styles, including some handsome, luxurious towncars. In the 1920s, the styling of most Hudson bodies was done in the company's experimental engineering shops by chief body engineer Millard Toncray. Again, though, the company's body suppliers—among them Budd, Briggs and Biddle & Smart—contributed. Hudson led for a time in the advancement of closed bodies, and both Briggs and Budd offered engineering expertise which Hudson used in the trendsetting 1922 Essex coach (see

page 29). According to Hudson engineer Stuart Baits, interviewed in 1977 by Kava, "I was a carpenter. Toncray also worked for my dad, and he was a carpenter.... He and I personally built the first Essex coach out of wood and cardboard. We designed it so there was no draw in it, only the cowl and two quarter panels that required drawing. Everything else had a warped surface: back panel and doors. The roof had wooden rails and a cloth insert top. We took it over to Briggs and asked them, 'Can you build this?' 'Oh sure,' they said. 'We can build it.'"

The company also produced a steady stream of Hudson and Essex speedsters. Then toward the mid 1920s, Hudson began commissioning coachbuilders to design series-custom bodies. Among those who produced coachbuilt Hudsons were Anderson, Pioneer and LeBaron. LeBaron, by then part of Briggs Mfg. Co., designed and built a few (a very few) Hudsons, and the Walter M. Murphy Co. in Pasadena, California was asked to submit designs that led to several production bodies made by Biddle & Smart: the 1928 Hudson landau sedan, victoria coupe and limousine, for example. And here we arrive at a bit of irony.

Walter Murphy had taken on Hudson's southern California distributorship in late 1924. Murphy made a lot more money selling Hudsons than selling coachbuilt bodies. In fact, Murphy's custom activities—founded while Murphy was a Lincoln distributor—were almost a sideline, valuable not so much in dollars and cents as to keep the Murphy name before the southern California pub-

Before 1931, when Frank Spring arrived from Murphy, Hudson's body engineers, under Millard Toncray, undertook much of the company's styling activity. They often called on their body suppliers to suggest designs as well as construction methods. The sporty, moldingless 7-passenger 1920 Hudson phaeton (above) had a raked windshield, rounded door cuts and wire wheels. Stodgier 1924 Hudson coach (above right) followed severely square format of the highly successful 1922 Essex coach. By 1927, the youthful Essex boattail speedster (right) helped propel Hudson toward third place in national car sales for 1929.

lic, particularly its movie colony and wealthier citizenry. Murphy took a lesson from Cadillac distributor Don Lee, who similarly had a coachworks as part of his business.

Murphy's brother-in-law and the general manager of his coachbuilding operation was Frank S. Spring. And it was through Murphy's dealings with the Hudson factory—periodic visits to Los Angeles and Pasadena by Hudson officials—that Frank Spring got to know some of that company's top executives.

The irony arises from the fact that Spring's experiences paralleled Harley Earl's. Both were native Californians, both directed southern California coachbuilders, both ended up going to Detroit to set up design departments for major automakers. Earl founded GM Art & Colour in 1927 and Spring joined Hudson in Sept. 1931 to start its formal design activity.

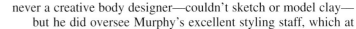

Frank Spring was born in 1893. His mother was French, and his father belonged to an established, wealthy California landowning family that at one time claimed title to most of what's now called the Silicon Valley, between San Francisco and San Jose (the Spring mansion still stands in San Francisco). As a child, Frank was small and slight, the only boy among five children. He did poorly in American schools, so when he was 12, his mother sent Frank to Paris and hired a private tutor for him. His tutor, the son of a Scottish laird, soon began taking Frank on long bicycle trips throughout Europe.

When Frank became old enough, they bought a pair of motorcycles and expanded their horizons. Spring attended the Paris Polytechnic and graduated just before World War I, taking a degree in aeronautical engineering. Young Spring joined the U.S.

Frank S. Spring

never a creative body designer—couldn't sketch or model clay—but he did oversee Murphy's excellent styling staff, which at that time included Frank Hershey, Phil Wright, George McQuerry Jr. and W.E. Miller. Spring effectively acted as Murphy's director of design, and he oversaw the creation not only of custom automobile bodies but later of special aircraft as well.

Spring, along with most other coachbuilders, regularly attended the major U.S. salons, including New York's automobile week. The salons allowed Spring to strengthen his ties with Murphy's clients, and he also socialized at these events with Hudson's Detroit executives. In Apr. 1929, William J. McAneeny became Hudson's new president, and Spring suggested to McAneeny that Murphy design and build him a rakish, cream-colored 1931 Hudson convertible sedan. This car had Woodlites and a body very much along the lines of Murphy's custom movie-colony Duesenbergs.

The educated, urbane Spring hit it off well with McAneeny, chief engineer Stuart Baits and Hudson's other executives. McAneeny, seeing GM, Chrysler, Briggs, Murray and others all with active styling departments, decided that Hudson needed one, too, so in 1930 he offered Spring a position as Hudson's "style engineer." By 1931, things weren't going well at Murphy, so Spring accepted and went to Hudson in September.

The higher-ups at Hudson viewed Frank Spring as a man of taste, a cultured, capable body designer with an added insight: He thoroughly understood how machines of all sorts worked. That knowledge impressed Hudson's engineers. And like so many of his styling and engineering compatriots, Spring admired European automobile design. Whenever a foreign dignitary visited Hudson,

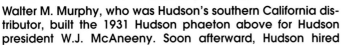

Walter M. Murphy, who was Hudson's southern California distributor, built the 1931 Hudson phaeton above for Hudson president W.J. McAneeny. Soon afterward, Hudson hired

Spring as its "style engineer." One of Spring's first projects at Hudson was to design and build himself an aluminum-bodied concept roadster on the 1932 Essex-Terraplane 8 chassis.

Signal Corps and became involved with aircraft production in Detroit. It was here that he learned to fly, and he subsequently owned a number of pleasure aircraft. He also kept up his interest in motorcycles and enjoyed driving and tinkering with fast, mostly European sports cars.

In 1919, Spring took his first job in the auto industry, but as an engineer, not as a body stylist. He initially designed engines for Paige-Detroit. Then in 1921, he laid out an entire car for the Standard Steel Car Co., including its overhead-cam Straight Eight powerplant. In 1922, he became chief engineer for the short-lived Courier Motor Co. of Sandusky, Ohio, where he helped develop the Courier's dry-sump engine, four-wheel brakes and one-shot chassis lubrication system, all ideas ahead of their time.

In 1923, Spring returned to California and joined the Walter M. Murphy Co. in Pasadena. He started with Murphy as a consulting engineer and became general manager in July 1924. Spring was

Spring acted as factory ambassador. He also encouraged the relationship between Hudson and the famous English engineer/designer/car builder Reid Railton. Railton ultimately applied his name to a series of fast, sporty, limited-production British touring cars based on Hudson mechanicals.

One of the first cars that Spring designed and built at Hudson was a low, open four-seater based on the sprightly new 1932 Essex-Terraplane. This became primarily an idea car, and Spring might also have had in mind using it for his own pleasure. The car was unusual in that it had no doors, no runningboards, no body moldings and no louvers of any sort. The aluminum bodywork extended down and covered the frame side rails, and the top of the hood stretched back all the way to the windshield.

It was obvious that Spring was trying to make the body as cleanly integrated and of-a-piece-looking as possible. Except for the Essex-Terraplane being too large, its appearance was decidedly

British. The ultimate touches of English design included leather bucket front seats and cut-down bodysides. The side cuts, in fact, were the car's most striking feature, but totally out of keeping with the rest of the design. Also, how anyone was supposed to get into the rear seat remains a mystery.

Frank Spring fit well into Hudson's hierarchy and, while he didn't let himself be dominated by engineering, he worked harmoniously with that department. He was not, however, cast in the same mold as the typical, traditional, conservative Hudson executive. Spring studied oriental philosophy, practiced yoga and slept on the floor. He and his second wife, Clara, believed in health foods and physical fitness long before those beliefs became trendy. In good weather, Spring rode to work on his BMW motorcycle or in one of his many sports cars, always impeccably dressed. During his days with Hudson, he flew a Beechcraft Staggerwing and an AT-6 and was among the first in Michigan to own an Autogiro. His colleagues indulged his gentle eccentricities and excused them as the birthright of an artist.

In early 1932, Spring had wired Frank Hershey, the very talented Murphy designer, inviting him to join Hudson. Hershey accepted, lasted about four months, then went to General Motors to design the 1933 Pontiac. After Hershey left, individual stylists passed through Hudson's revolving door, and it's never been established who actually designed most of the company's Depression-era cars. Briggs supplied some of Hudson's bodies throughout the 1930s, so it's reasonable to assume that Briggs helped generate some of Hudson's designs. Dick Stout maintained that Spring would hire stylists when needed for new models or facelifts and let them go again after they'd finished a job. Hudson historian E.L. Myerson took a different view. He said stylists usually left out of boredom when they wearied of facelifting the same body over and over and re-designing knobs, trim, etc.

Hudson's 1933-35 cars were contemporary and certainly commercial enough, but each one also had a quirkiness that somehow made it miss the mark. Spring abandoned the very plain, of-a-piece British look he'd been reaching for with his 1932 Essex-Terraplane idea car. Instead, he now seemed to be taking an array of adornments from rival carmakers, principally Buick, and putting them all together on Hudsons. Yet he did manage to stay modern and in step with the evolving "streamlined" shapes of the 1930s.

In May 1933, McAneeny became Hudson's chairman and A.E. Barit took over, first as general manager in 1934 and then as company president in 1936. Barit was conservatively old-school, a former purchasing agent, very pinchpenny and not terribly interested in new ideas. But he and Spring did get along, and Barit usually—although not always—accepted the designs Spring handed him. Design was often a team effort that involved Spring and Hudson's top engineers.

In 1934, Frank Spring hired an assistant, Arthur H. (Kib) Kibiger, a soft-spoken, thoughtful, gentlemanly sort who came to Hudson after one year with Auburn. He'd worked at Auburn under body engineer Roy Anderson as a sketch artist and draftsman. At Hudson, Kibiger now acted as Spring's detail man and his liaison between engineering and styling.

Among the first cars they worked on together were the 1936 Hudson and Terraplane. Both cars shared the same body, and both turned out to be more mainstream than Spring's earlier designs but still nothing spectacular. The 1936 Terraplane used an interesting, Dali-esque central instrument cluster that draped as though it had melted over the rounded top of the dash sill. Another entertaining touch was the translucent, orange, plastic "flying cigar" hood ornament.

The 1936 Hudson had a double grille of sorts: a slender upright center section, widening toward the top, flanked by a fine-mesh second grille that seemed like a 1935 Oldsmobile fencing mask lurking underneath. Jeff Godshall, the Chrysler designer, said it always reminded him of a grasshopper's face. But beyond the face, the greater significance of Hudson's 1936 body was that it stayed in production through 1947. Spring and Kibiger had to keep restyling the 1936 shell, using the same doors, cowl and roof until the Stepdown came out for 1948. The best of those earlier revisions had to be the 1940-42 models, although the 1939 model wasn't bad either.

Spring directed Hudson design through Kibiger. Fitz Fitzpatrick recalled that, "Spring and Kib ran a pretty tight ship, especially compared to other places I've worked. Spring insisted that we all had to be at our boards, pencil in hand, when the 8:00 a.m. whistle blew. I got fired on the spot one morning when Kib walked into the studio at 8:03 and I was still reading the

(Top to bottom) Spring got off to a good start with Hudson's 1933 Essex-Terraplane 8. That's company president Roy Chapin showing it off. By 1935, Spring was taking cues from everything in sight, especially Buick. His 1936 model had a double fencing-mask grille, and the "flying cigar" hood ornament on some models lit up at night.

newspaper. He made an example of me. I was only a day or two back from a one-week honeymoon and had $5 in my bank account. I had to go home and tell my bride of 10 days that I'd lost my job. Luckily, I started work at Packard two days later with a 30% increase in pay." Spring consulted with Kibiger and made the tough calls, but

Holden (Bob) Koto had made Hudson styling proposals while at Briggs. When he joined Spring's tiny staff, he conceived these and many other sketches. Koto preferred to work in clay but was an excellent artist as well.

Designing Women

Among the earliest known female creators of cars were Margaret E. Knight, an engineer, and her niece, Beatrice Davidson. In 1912, they brought out their short-lived K-D automobile in Brookline, Massachusetts. The K-D's touring body, constructed by coachbuilder Moore & Munger, was quite advanced and fashionable for the day. Whether Knight and Davidson actually styled the K-D isn't known, but they surely controlled the design.

The 1916-19 Biddle roadster took its rakish styling from the whims of Miriam W. Hubbard, a Philadelphia banker's daughter

Corp., makers of automotive window-lift mechanisms. Dura, said Walker, paid Helen Dryden $35,000 a year as an "interiorist." As such, she drew up proposals for Dura's clients and potential customers, much like Briggs and Murray designers made exterior proposals. Around 1935, however, Dura could no longer afford Dryden's services, so she started her own industrial design firm and did the interior of the 1936 Studebaker line.

Raymond Loewy contracted with Helen Dryden to help him design 1938-40 Studebaker interiors. She also did some of Nash's interiors for George Walker during

All were in their 20s at that time. Earl proudly called them his "Damsels of Design." GM's female designers again worked mainly on interiors and designed instrument panels, steering wheels plus trim for doors and seats. They also chose fabrics and interior colors for GM's Motorama showcars. Says former GM interior designer George Moon, "The women did interiors as gutty and with as much 'gasoline' as the men. Their 'soft' side was less feminine and more just good design than Harley Earl or anyone else expected."

After many years in Olds and Cadillac interiors, Peggy Sauer left GM for Loewy & Snaith and designed part of the 1963 Studebaker Avanti interior. Sue Vanderbilt

As women made more car-purchase decisions, automakers began to hire female designers. Woman above is working on, of all things, a Mack truck. Betty Thatcher Oros (top right) joined Hudson in 1939. At right is a female modeler at GM.

who was among Biddle's earliest customers. She asked Biddle to build her a special sport roadster that looked like it was "...going 60 mph standing still." When asked what that meant, she proceeded to specify: no runningboards, crowned cycle fenders, a veed radiator, veed headlight lenses, portholes in the hood, wire wheels and spare tires mounted behind the doors. Biddle built Miriam Hubbard her car and then put all of her ideas into the firm's production roadster.

It wasn't at all unusual for auto manufacturers to ask famous women to help design car interiors. Lady Gordon Duff, known to the fashion world as "Lucille," made the 1917 Chalmers "a sun parlor on pneumatics.... There's milady's toilette," said the ads, "a cut glass flower vase, a lounging pillow of eider down and silk and a dainty hassock." Lucile also chose Chalmers' color schemes.

In the 1930s, a few companies began hiring female designers, again primarily to work on automobile interiors. Among the best known was Helen Dryden, who initially had a contract, according to industrial designer George W. Walker, with the Dura

that same period. Chrysler, meanwhile, advertised the 1937 Royal with interior fabrics and appointments "approved" by Lady Mendl (Elsie de Wolfe). The idea was to entice female buyers by stressing the female fashion touch.

As for U.S. auto companies employing women designers full-time, Hudson was among the first—perhaps *the* first—when they hired Betty Thatcher in 1939. Thatcher designed, among other things, the 1941 Hudson instrument panel and some of the '41 model's external trim. She soon married GM designer Joe Oros, who subsequently worked for Walker and Ford Motor Co. (see page 142).

Raymond Loewy employed sisters Virginia and Nancy Spence and Audrey Moore Hodges in the early 1940s to work on his South Bend Studebaker account doing scale clay models and woodwork.

Harley Earl at General Motors began hiring female auto designers in 1943, but even in 1958, the year Earl retired, there were only seven women involved in GM car design: Sue Vanderbilt, Ruth Glennie, Marjorie Ford, Sandra Longyear, Jeanette Linder, Gere Cavanaugh and Peggy Sauer.

became chief designer of Chevrolet interiors, the first woman at GM ever to be given that title. And in Jan. 1967, Cadillac's Joan M. Klatil became one of the industry's first female *exterior* designers. Nelly Toledo, who had worked on interiors at GM, took a job with Ford in 1988 and later moved to exteriors. Her first exterior-design project was the 1998 Mercury Cougar. Ms Toledo stated recently that exterior design is a snap compared with interiors.

At the beginning of 1994, Ford employed 21 designing women (27% of Ford's total styling staff). General Motors also had 21 women involved in the design process, including eight clay modelers, and Chrysler had 15. ◆

Contemporary styling of 1940 Hudson convertible, with its low horizontal grille and flared doors covering the running-boards, hid the fact that this was still the 1936 body in very clever disguise. Spring and his staff were forced to facelift the same body from 1936 through 1947.

it was Kib who actually oversaw the day-to-day styling activities. He kept projects on track, made all the less important design decisions and managed the designers. Not that Hudson ever had many designers to manage. Strother MacMinn arrived from GM in the autumn of 1938 and, at the time, Hudson's styling staff numbered all of eight, including Spring and Kibiger. There were MacMinn, John B. Foster, John (Jack/Jake) Aldrich, Holden (Bob) Koto and

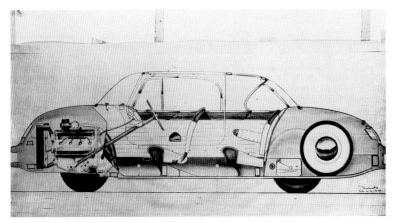

From June 1942 through Sept. 1943, Art Kibiger worked on his Program 5. This example, one of many, had a V-8 and fwd. What got carried over into 1948 was his perimeter frame.

Earl Hovey. MacMinn, Foster and Aldrich had been with GM previously; Koto had been let go by Briggs after Ford began doing its own design work. In addition, George Fullerton acted as Hudson's designer/draftsman. And that was it. A little later Ted Pietsch, Betty Thatcher, Arthur M. (Fitz) Fitzpatrick and Robert M. (Bob) Thomas arrived. Betty Thatcher might have been the first woman designer ever employed by an automobile manufacturer (see opposite page).

Spring's fairly large and luxurious office stood next to a room that contained Kibiger's desk and also served as a drafting studio. The actual design studio, where the creative peo-

Hudson's 1948 "stepdown" construction revolutionized the way all automakers built bodies. Today nearly every carmaker in the world uses a variation of this same format, with an integral perimeter frame plus floor wells front and rear. Stepdown architecture allowed Hudson to lower its cars five inches so that its seat benches were wider than the car was tall.

ple sat at drawingboards, was several offices away, next to the accounting department at the other end of Hudson's engineering building. This studio, according to Don Butler, measured about 18 x 22 feet.

And Hudson had another room on the floor below where full-sized plaster body models were made. Until late 1938, Hudson didn't do large clays but rather cast full-sized models in plaster—an extremely messy, dusty, unhealthy, hard-to-alter way to represent automobile bodies. At the end of 1938, Kibiger hired clay modeler Pete Woczena, and gradually Woczena went from sculpting details like lamps and moldings to representing an occasional full-sized Hudson in Chavant clay.

Despite most modelers' displeasure with plaster of Paris, Hudson body engineer Joseph W. Eskridge contended that, "Plaster models were very satisfactory and could be prepared far more quickly than clay. Incidentally, our use of plaster came about in an interesting way. Jim Grieg, our experimental engineer, noted that the construction of fancy movie palaces had slowed markedly with the onset of the Depression. Much of the elaborate plaster forms and ornamentation used on the interiors of these movie houses had been the work of Italian craftsmen who'd been brought over for the job. Grieg hired two of these out-of-work sculptors and had them make our first plaster models. Until 1941, we used no other material."

According to Fitz Fitzpatrick, "Spring had a rule that all the designers had to render cars using only two Prismacolor pencils on black paper: a reddish brown and a greenish blue. These were to represent the paint colors. Spring reasoned that management shouldn't be influenced by color bias in choosing a design. It wasn't a bad theory, but it was boring to us!"

As a technology enthusiast, Frank Spring eagerly embraced new ideas and was ultimately in a position to present some of them to

Hudson's decisionmakers. Hudson's final fling—the car that popularized the "stepdown" design along with the integral, welded-steel construction that all cars use today—was the 1948 Hudson. This large, low (for the time) car was probably as much a milestone as the Chrysler Airflow had been 14 years earlier. Hudson ads called the body design "stepdown" because the floor was welded to the *bottoms* of the perimeter frame, so in essence you had to step over the side rails and down onto (or into) the floor of the car. The stepdown Hudson helped pioneer what's now been universally adopted as "frame-integral" or fully unitized body construction with stepdown floor wells. (The 1936 Cord 810 used similar construction, including floorboards lower than the rocker sills and a front subframe that carried the powertrain and suspension; see page 241.)

The projected bodies for Kibiger's Program 5 were sometimes unitized, sometimes semi-unitized, always with perimeter frames that protected the passengers from side impacts. This work, which started out almost as surrealistic mind exercises, got more and more real and eventually, with help from Hudson's body engineers, led to the postwar stepdown Hudson of 1948. The one feature that never changed—the genesis of the 1948 Hudson—was the perimeter frame.

Two other men who played pivotal roles in the stepdown's creation were body engineer Carl W. Cenzer and stylist Robert F. (Bob) Andrews. Cenzer began his career in 1927 at Dodge as a chassis draftsman. He subsequently took jobs in body engineering at Graham-Paige and Willys-Overland, joining Hudson in 1929. He became head of Hudson's small experimental engineering staff in 1939 and was manager of aircraft engineering during the war.

In 1944, in his spare time, Cenzer began to apply aircraft principles to automotive body design and thus became a spokesman for, and a major contributor to, the 1948 Hudson's engineering development. His boss Millard Toncray, by then Hudson's chief engineer, wasn't hard to convince when it came to semi-unitized construction. We use the term "semi-unitized" because the Hudson body was built in two parts: a main section from the firewall back that was wholly unitized plus a forward subframe that carried the engine, transmission and front suspension. During the assembly process, Hudson welded the subframe onto the main body section. Hudson was not the first to use semi-unitized construction. Cord introduced this same type of construction in 1936.

Frank Spring's one and only re-do of the basic 1948 Hudson outer skins arrived in this sad form for 1954. It borrowed every cliche in motordom. By this time, Hudson could not compete stylistically. Nor was its venerable flathead 6 a match for the industry's ohv V-8s. Hudson was forced to merge that year with Nash to form AMC (American Motors Corp.).

The 1948 Hudson took root because Kibiger shared Spring's fascination with advanced body design. During World War II, although the government discouraged design work on postwar automobiles, all car companies kept informal programs going anyway (the unofficial ban was lifted in early 1944). Spring, Kibiger and others had time on their hands throughout the war and began to look into unconventional drivetrain and body layouts that Hudson might base a car on after hostilities ended. Hudson was busy making aircraft parts and other military equipment, so the company had no timetable, no deadline, no immediate need for a postwar car. This meant that Spring and Kibiger—so long as they were discreet—could dream up and even build whatever they wanted.

Spring, being interested in motorcycles, began with an aircooled Square Four, like the British Ariel motorcycle engine, and applied this to a small front-wheel-drive car on an 85-inch wheelbase. A steel prototype was ultimately built, although on a longer wheelbase and with a six-cylinder Hudson engine amidships.

Alongside, Kibiger went through a number of ideas and finally conceived what he called "Program 5," a series of streamlined, Dymaxion-like three- and then four-wheelers that took on a variety of possible power configurations: front engine/rear drive, front engine/front-wheel drive and front drive with a rear engine. Among the engines Kibiger envisioned was an opposed, modular type that could grow from four to six to eight cylinders by simply adding crank throws and cylinder barrels.

Cenzer, in a 1970 interview with Dick Wright of *Automotive News*, said, "We wanted unitized body construction because our particular facilities favored it and because of the economics. We also wanted a low silhouette." Dropping the floor to the bottom of the perimeter frame immediately lowered the body a good five inches. And according to Cenzer, it was relatively easy to set up Hudson's postwar assembly plants for semi-unitized body construction, mostly because the detachable front subframe made the

The tall, boxy, unpopular Hudson Jet provided the final blow to Hudson's independence. In retrospect, it's easy to say that Hudson should have spent its money on a modern V-8 rather than this ungainly compact.

Just as Chrysler contracted with Ghia to provide its show- and dreamcars, Frank Spring got together with Touring, another Italian coachbuilder, to provide 16 copies of his grand finale, the 1954 Hudson Italia. Built on the Jet platform, Italia was another less-than-successful design.

main body section short, therefore more transportable. The body, minus the front subframe, had to be physically hauled from one plant to another, usually by truck.

The stepdown Hudson's principal stylist was the young and gifted Bob Andrews. Andrews came to Hudson in 1945, right after the Japanese surrender. Also in Hudson's small design studio at that time were Bill Kirby and Dick Brudzynski. According to Andrews' colleague, Don Butler, who arrived at Hudson as a junior stylist in May 1946, much of the 1948 car's design work was finished by the time he got there. Butler, in a Crestline book he wrote about Hudson, attributes the stepdown's basic body shape to Art Kibiger, with major details like side sculpting, grille, bumpers, lamps and interior by Andrews. Andrews joined Raymond Loewy in 1949 and in 1960 became a member of the team that designed the Studebaker Avanti (see page 215). Art Kibiger left Hudson in late 1946 to become Willys-Overland's director of styling.

Spring kept a 1942 Buick fastback on hand throughout the 1948 Hudson's development and made this his benchmark car. It was from the Buick that the stepdown Hudson got its high beltline and narrow windows. Full-sized bucks and models were again done in plaster. The use of plaster rather than clay made day-to-day styling changes a real chore, but the 1948 Hudson—due in large measure to its low silhouette—became a great success and gave the company several profitable years before the new wore off.

One problem with unitized and semi-unitized construction is that it's hard to make styling changes inexpensively. Major body-panel revisions cost more than with body-on-frame construction. For that reason, Hudson stayed with the 1948 body through the 1954 model year, with only one major facelift for 1954—and not a successful one at that.

Hudson's fortunes began to wane after 1950, and the company ran into serious money problems when it introduced an expensive, ugly compact car for 1953, the Hudson Jet. Frank Spring had been asked to give the Jet the overall look and styling cues of the 1952 Ford, but with Olds 88 tail lights. He did, and the car turned out dated,

tall, narrow and graceless. Bernie Siegfried, who was working at Hudson when the first Jet arrived, remembered Spring's reaction: "I went up into Styling and saw Mr. Spring standing there with tears in his eyes, and I found out that he was kind of heartbroken....

And according to Trevor Constable, who talked with Frank Spring after the Jet debacle, the production design was one of three final styling proposals that were presented to Hudson management. Two were favored by Spring. The third satisfied the requirement that it resemble the 1952 Ford, but Spring intentionally made this design so tall, short and ugly that no one in his right mind could possibly choose it. To everyone's horror, Hudson president A.E. Barit chose the third candidate.

Soon after the Jet's debut, Spring worked with Carrozzeria Superleggera Touring, the Italian coachbuilder, to design and fabricate a short run of Jet-based sport coupes called the Hudson Italia. The Italia represented Hudson's response to other automakers' mid-1950s dreamcars and limited-production two-seaters: Corvette, Kaiser-Darrin, Nash-Healey, Thunderbird, etc. The Italia again picked up details and ornamentation from a number of sources and simply assembled them into what many considered a gorpy hodgepodge.

Spring stayed on after the 1954 Hudson-Nash merger and retired in 1955 at age 62. After he retired, he began restoring his 1936 BMW roadster. In addition, he owned the Hudson Hornet X-161 Italia sedan prototype and for everyday transport drove his gull-wing Mercedes 300-SL. He had also modified a tiny Hudson Metropolitan to give it better performance, something it sorely needed.

In July 1959, AMC executive vice president Roy Chapin asked Spring to bring his Metropolitan to Detroit to show the modifications to company engineers. On their way to that rendezvous, on Aug. 8, 1959, Frank and Clara Spring were approaching Ardmore, Oklahoma when a Ford station wagon lurched across the median and crashed head-on into them. The wagon's driver had fallen asleep at the wheel. Frank Spring died, and Clara was severely injured but managed to survive. ◆

NASH MOTORS CO.

Charles W. Nash had been president of Buick even before Walter Chrysler. Unlike Chrysler, though, and more like Henry Ford, Charlie Nash didn't care much about styling. Despite having been a student of Andrew Johnson's, he simply wasn't interested. So from 1917, when Nash started building cars under

Sakhnoffsky had overwhelmed Walhlberg. According to stylist Don Mortrude, who arrived in 1937 with George Walker as Nash's next styling consultant, "Alex Sakhnoffsky came in and tried to woo Wahlberg. Sakhnoffsky was in there making drawings for Nash long before we came into the picture. He made all

his own name, through 1951 and the last of the Airflytes, company engineers had final say on styling.

From the beginning, the Seaman Body Corp. of Milwaukee supplied Nash with all its bodies. This was an unusual arrangement, because Nash had no other body supplier and Seaman built bodies only for Nash. Seaman had been a furniture manufacturer before going into the autobody business. In 1928, Nash assembled cars in Kenosha, Racine and Milwaukee. Seaman shipped bodies to all three plants. Whether Seaman helped to style Nash bodies we don't know.

To their credit, Nash's factory body engineers managed to design cars that looked mainstream. In 1932, anticipating the industry's move toward more integrated and "streamlined" forms, Nash hired Count Alexis de Sakhnoffsky as a styling consultant. Sakhnoffsky held similar contracts with Packard and Studebaker and divided his time between all three.

Sakhnoffsky ultimately styled Nash's 1934 car lines, including the low-priced LaFayette. The 1934 Nash and LaFayette boasted grilles reminiscent of the K-Model Lincoln. They also had speed streaks pressed into all four fenders. The big, impressive, dual-ignition Eights—the senior Nashes—featured skirted rear fenders and looked ultra modern that year.

But Sakhnoffsky quickly wore out his welcome at Nash. The man in overall charge of Nash's technical and styling development was Nils Erik (Wally) Wahlberg. Finnish-born Wahlberg had studied mechanical engineering in Zurich and came to this country in 1909. His first job here was with the E.R. Thomas Co., maker of the famous Thomas Flyer. He soon moved to Packard, then to Maxwell and later to General Motors, where he became friendly with Buick president Charlie Nash. When Nash left GM in 1916 to take over Jeffery (which became Nash Motors Co. in 1917), Wahlberg went with him. Nash made Wahlberg his vice president of engineering in 1931.

Charlie Nash (above left) asked Sakhnoffsky to style 1934 Nash. Beside Mr. Nash is company president E.H. McCarty. Sakhnoffsky's loose sketches were hard for Nash body engineers to follow, so they designed the 1936-38 models themselves, including fencing-mask-grilled 1936 Nash below.

kinds of fancy drawings right there in front of Wahlberg, and Wahlberg's eyes were bugging. Alex was just giving him the old Sakhnoffsky show. And then when Nash tried to build his stuff from just perspective illustrations—pencil sketches on black paper—why they had one helluva time trying to transpose those designs into reality.

"So by the time Walker and I got there, the fellows at Nash were real gun-shy of stylists. Nash engineering fought us like crazy. But between [Nash president] George Mason and W.F. Armstrong, who was a vice president and Mason's right hand, they just railroaded us right through."

After Sakhnoffsky did the 1934 Nashes and before Mortrude arrived, Wahlberg and his body engineers took it upon themselves to style the next four model years. Some of those 1935-38 Nashes

Wahlberg's engineering staff also did the 1937-38 Nash and Lafayette (right). For the 1939 model (below), Nash hired George Walker and Don Mortrude as styling co-consultants. According to his colleague Rhys Miller, Mortrude did the vertical-grilled 1939 Nash based on designs he'd done earlier at Chrysler.

tall, narrow grille and horizontal catwalks. These were not, as sometimes reported, copied from the LaSalle. The rest of Mortrude's 1939 Nash design had elements of Ford and Dodge, again more by coincidence than conscious intent.

Count Sakhnoffsky, by the way, re-approached Nash in 1939 and proposed modifying the standard body and transforming it into a sport roadster, very much along Packard-Darrin lines. Sakhnoffsky showed Mason a prototype with cutdown doors, a low convertible top and sidecurtains—no roll-up windows. He would build copies of this car, he told Mason, if Nash would help promote and sell them. His sport roadster, Sakhnoffsky explained, would serve as Nash's answer to the heavily publicized Packard-Darrin and Edsel Ford's new Lincoln Continental. Mason okayed Sakhnoffsky's plan, but he was more interested in the publicity value than in helping Sakhnoffsky sell cars. Ultimately only 11 Sakhnoffsky roadsters were built.

Mortrude also had a hand in styling the 1941 Nash 600. That car's significance had little to do with its appearance but a great deal to do with its body construction. The Nash 600 became America's first mass-produced automobile to use a fully integrated body and frame. Today, virtually all passenger cars use frame-integral (or unitized) construction. It's true that the 1934 Chrysler Airflow and 1936 Lincoln Zephyr came close in concept to Nash's body architecture. Both used bridge-truss construction, meaning they had lightweight steel cages covered with unstressed sheet-metal skins. Even closer in concept were the 1936 Cord and 1948 Hudson, both of which used semi-unitized construction. These two cars had frame-integral rear body sections with front subframes bolted or welded at the cowl. The subframes carried the suspension and powertrain. The 1941 Nash 600, though, made the *entire* body one welded steel entity. The Nash's structural members and skins were self-supporting and inseparable. And that's the construction method used by all but a handful of passenger cars today.

Nash hired industrial designer Norman Bel Geddes in late 1940 but let him go again in 1942 after using none of his ideas. During the early part of World War II, when all car companies concentrated on wartime work, Walker and Mortrude put their Nash contract on hold. And that's when two young designers who'd been

looked amateurishly done.

In 1937, Nash Motor Co. merged with Kelvinator Corp., mostly so the 70-year-old Charlie Nash could bring in Kelvinator president George W. Mason as his successor. Mason had always had gasoline in his veins. He was a portly, energetic, cigar-chomping auto enthusiast and former motorcycle racer. He'd been Walter Chrysler's works manager in the 1920s and recognized the power of styling. Soon after Mason stepped into Charlie Nash's shoes, both George Walker and Don Mortrude visited him with styling proposals. They arrived at Nash-Kelvinator headquarters in Detroit at nearly the same time, and Mason—instead of accepting either presentation—suggested they work together. Walker, who was more interested in designing Kelvinator refrigerators than Nash automobiles, signed a consultancy contract with Mason in 1937, then hired Mortrude as his chief car stylist.

Mortrude had worked briefly for GM Art & Colour in 1934, then spent two years with Chrysler under Ray Dietrich. He opened his own industrial design office in 1937 but promptly closed it again when Walker offered him the Nash assignment. Rhys Miller, who worked with Mortrude at Chrysler, recalled in his oral reminiscences for the Henry Ford Museum: "Don did the 1939 Nash, and that car had the very narrow upright grille. It was a typical Don Mortrude design. He did the same car at Chrysler. One of the first things he did at Chrysler was that design, and just about everything he did after that looked like it. He finally sold it to Nash. But that turned out real well."

The 1939 Nash and LaFayette shared all major sheetmetal stampings. They also shared Mortrude's

Count Sakhnoffsky tried to do with Nash what Dutch Darrin had done with Packard. Nash took advantage of the publicity but didn't help Sakhnoffsky sell cars, and the entire "production" run ended after 11 cars were built.

1949 Nash Airflyte (above and right) ended up looking more like a typical wartime concept rendering than other postwar cars. Airflyte became another Wahlberg engineering/styling job although basic design seems to have come from Koto and Pietsch after they left Hudson. Wahlberg tested models in windtunnel and made aerodynamic adjustments. Tiny 1950 Nash NXI concept car (center left) was created by Bill Flajole, became 1954 Metropolitan (center right). 1950 Nash Rambler supposedly arose from designs that George Walker's firm did for 1949 Ford. Although resemblance seems weak, spinner grille and vertical tail lamps appeared on early 1949 Ford clays. All 1950-51 Ramblers were convertibles, with top riding up and down on fixed window frames.

let go by Hudson—Bob Koto and Ted Pietsch—approached Wally Wahlberg with a design presentation for the postwar Nash. They'd printed up letterhead and now hoped to replace Walker and Mortrude as Nash's design consultants. Koto's family had known Wahlberg for years. When Bob was a teenager, he'd asked Wahlberg to recommend a college. Wahlberg suggested Cornell. As a result, Koto attended Cornell for 3 1/2 years, studying engineering and architecture. He never graduated but took a job with Briggs in 1933 instead.

Now, according to Koto, he and Pietsch, fresh out of Hudson, appeared in Wahlberg's office. Pietsch had made some beautiful renderings of a fairly typical wartime design, which Koto sculpted as two 1/8-scale clay models. They tried to sell one design in particular—a rounded, highly streamlined, flush-sided, four-door fastback sedan with a tapered rear deck.

Wahlberg admired the presentation but told Koto and Pietsch he couldn't hire them due to the dormant arrangement with Walker and Mortrude. Soon after the meeting at Nash, Koto and Pietsch went to work for Raymond Loewy at Studebaker. Then in late

1948, when Koto caught sight of the first 1949 Nash Airflyte, he immediately recognized the design. It was the same one he and Pietsch tried to sell to Wahlberg. Wahlberg had added skirted front fenders and made a few detail changes, but the Airflyte's basic theme and shape were, according to Koto, identical. Designer Robert M. (Bob) Thomas said, though, that when he worked for Nash in 1950-52, he saw several old 1/4-scale plaster 1949 Nash proposals, all of which had the "inverted bathtub" lines.

Walker and Mortrude resumed their design work for Nash toward the end of the war and showed postwar models to George Mason in 1944-45. But in late 1945, when Walker got the call from Ernie Breech at Ford, it suddenly struck Walker that a contract with Ford might be a lot more lucrative than his Nash consultancy. So he asked for and got Mason's permission to abandon the Nash contract.

Before he did, though, Walker started his search for a suitable design for the 1949 Ford. And that's when Dick Caleal came along with the Mishawaka model that Bob Bourke, Bob Koto, Joe Thompson and others at Studebaker had helped create and that eventually blossomed into the 1949 Ford (see page 138).

But before he got out of his Nash contract, Walker apparently showed the Mishawaka model—or one very much like it—to George Mason. George S. May, in *The Automobile Industry,* wrote that, "In summer 1948 Mason previewed the new 1949-model-year Ford...[and] in anger he cried, 'Walker has given the goddam Nash design to Ford.' Walker admitted that the new slab-sided Ford was a close copy of the prototype Walker had developed for Nash. But Nash had done nothing with the prototype after the war. 'Hell,' Walker declared later, 'I figured Nash wasn't going to use the design. It was a good one, so I had it modified a little and it became the 1949 Ford.' However," continued May, "Walker's

(Above) Pinin Farina Nash prototype from 1955 was *not* the one
he submitted as his original 1952
proposal. This car repeated the
theme of his Nash-Healey design
in sedan form. (Above right) Ed
Anderson's staff developed this
clay, but Nash management
didn't like it nor Farina's. The
actual 1952 Nash (right) ended
up taking its basic styling cues
from Flajole's NXI: the oval grille,
pleats on the tops of the doors,
windshield angle and shape,
hood and headlight treatment.
One of the few items brought
over from the Farina proposal
was the dogleg C-pillar.

prototype was used extensively in 1950 when Nash introduced the first compact car, the Rambler."

So that became one more layer of intrigue that now surrounds the development of the 1949 Ford. The 1950 Rambler's design was a far cry from the Ford, although it did have the vertical tail lamps and a small spinner, both of which supposedly appeared on Caleal's Mishawaka model.

George Mason now realized that Nash needed to update and organize its styling activity, and toward that end he did two things. First, he worked out a design agreement with Batista (Pinin) Farina, the Italian designer and coachbuilder. Second, he hired Edmund E. (Ed) Anderson, who previously had been a studio chief for Oldsmobile and Chevrolet.

The Pinin Farina connection began when several Farina designs caught Mason's fancy at the Paris auto show in Oct. 1949. Alfa, Lancia and Cisitalia all displayed wonderful Farina bodies that year. When Mason got back to the U.S., he asked his aide and successor, George Romney, to go over to Turin and see if he could talk Farina into submitting ideas for the 1952 Nash passenger car and the Nash-Healey sports car. Farina said he'd be delighted. Not only would he provide designs but he would submit running, full-sized, metal prototypes. Each prototype would cost Nash $25,000 to $30,000. Romney and Farina shook hands, and that became as formal as the contract ever got.

In Feb. 1950, with a few preliminary sketches tucked under his arm, Farina and his son-in-law, Renzo Carli, visited Nash on a tour of the Detroit area. On the day Farina and Carli left the U.S., Ed Anderson arrived as Nash's director of styling. The three designers—Farina, Carli and Anderson—met briefly in George Romney's office that afternoon, ostensibly so both design teams could be given package dimensions for the 1952 Nash lines. The idea, according to Romney, was to have Farina and Anderson

cooperate on the 1952 Nash design.

Ed Anderson had worked at General Motors from 1934 until 1947, where he headed up the Oldsmobile studio just before the war and became Chevrolet studio chief after he came back from the military in 1945.

Anderson fell into the Nash job because George Mason had a passion for fly fishing, and so did Anderson's parents. Mason owned property on the Au Sable River in northern Michigan and, over the years, he kept bumping into Anderson's parents on fishing trips.

After Ed Anderson left GM in 1947, he did some design work for a plastics company that wanted to do business with Nash-Kelvinator. Mason had heard about Anderson's GM experience from Ed's parents, and when Mason found out that Ed was indirectly involved with a firm that was wooing Nash-Kelvinator, he invited Anderson up to his office for a visit. The conversation turned to fly fishing, and the two men had such a good time talking that after half an hour or so, Mason asked Anderson if he'd like to become Nash's styling director. Without hesitating, Anderson said yes.

Strother MacMinn, who'd worked under Anderson in the prewar Oldsmobile studio, always felt that Ed was a better manager than a designer. MacMinn recalled in his Henry Ford Museum oral reminiscences that: "...many administrators, when they realize their creative powers are a little shaky, will work their way into the [managerial] hierarchy as quickly as possible.... They can tell people what to do. Ed was okay at that." However, Bill Reddig, who came to Nash from Ford in May 1950 to be Anderson's assistant, considered him both a good administrator and a good designer. "He was like a surgeon with a clay knife," noted Reddig.

When Anderson arrived at Nash in late 1949, the company's styling routine was to make 1/4-scale clay models, then full-sized drawings, and finally—sometimes—the shop staff would fabri-

Farina did design 1952-54 Nash-Healey (above), and Anderson transferred that grille theme, with the headlights set inside the oval, into Nash's production 1955 models. Continental kits were optional even on low-priced Statesman (below).

cate full-sized plaster models to show to management. In the case of the 1949 Nash, body engineering went directly from a 1/4-scale model to the actual car, which might explain some of the bloated and too-tall proportions of that design.

When he came to Nash, Anderson switched to 3/8-scale clays as quickly as he could, then had designs rendered as full-sized drawings and finally went to full-sized clay models. "This made it a heckuva lot easier for management to see exactly what a car was going to look like," commented Reddig.

Anderson and his small styling staff—only about five people at that time—developed a full-sized plaster proposal for the 1952 Nash and, soon after they finished, the Farina metal prototype arrived. Bill Reddig recalled that the Farina design, "...looked like a pumped-up little girl whose dress no longer fit. It looked bulbous."

Bob Thomas, in his book *Confessions of an Automobile Stylist,* revised edition, mentioned that Farina took some of his cues from the NXI mini concept car that Nash was promoting at the time, "[The Farina prototype] was awful," wrote Thomas. "From the windshield forward, the hood broke downward and took the front fenders with it. The deck from the backlight to the rear did the same thing. The car was in three parts: diving front and rear ends attached to a straight-through body.... It was so bad that we put a cover over it and stored it in a corner of the styling studio."

No photos exist of the Farina prototype, but the NXI Thomas referred to was a subcompact that Bill Flajole, the independent Detroit designer, had been working on for Mason since 1945. Flajole's NXI eventually turned into the 1954 Nash Metropolitan, but its basic lines—the squareness, setting the hood lower than the front fenders, the embossed tuck-and-roll inserts on the door uppers—those were ideas that George Mason liked and that Farina borrowed for his prototype. Flajole, in turn, borrowed some of his NXI ideas like the dropped hood from Rhys Miller, who proposed a similar design to Chrysler when both designers

worked there together.

Nash management didn't care for either proposal—not Farina's and not Anderson's. Meade Moore, who worked under Wahlberg didn't like Ed Anderson and insisted that Nash go with the Farina design. Since Farina and Carli were due to revisit the U.S., Mason had the Farina prototype trucked over to Bill Flajole's office for an informal meeting that weekend. In attendance were Mason, Romney, Meade Moore, body engineer Ted Ulrich and designers Anderson, Reddig and Flajole. The outcome of this meeting—mostly at Moore's behest—was a recommendation that Anderson's staff re-do the Farina design.

Anderson had no choice but to refine the Farina theme. Thomas recalled, "How do you save that thing? I was given the job. Every line and surface on that design model was changed. The whole car had to be straightened up. My finished drawing went to body engineering and that was the way the 1952 Nash was designed...almost unbelievable but true. Meade Moore got his way, and now Nash could advertise the car as being designed by Pinin Farina. Ed Anderson was fit to be tied." Farina, Carli and Farina's young son, Sergio, came back to Detroit one more time to check progress and, during that visit, gave their approval to the Anderson re-do.

According to Anderson, just before the 1952 Nash came out, he ran into George Romney in the hallway. Romney put his arm around Anderson's shoulder and said, "Ed, I know you and your staff did most of the styling of the 1952 Nash, but the ad agency and our sales department feel it might be good publicity to give Farina credit. What do you think?" Anderson replied, "George, I'm a corporation man as much as you are. If Farina's name will sell one more car, then I'm all for it." The ads gave Farina full credit, and Anderson didn't mention it again until he was interviewed in 1978 during his retirement in Mexico.

As early as 1948, George Mason had tried to work out a merger between Nash, Hudson, Packard and Studebaker. But the timing was wrong: all postwar cars were selling well, so the incentive wasn't there. Mason knew, though, that all independent U.S. automakers would be in trouble once production caught up with demand, and that happened in 1950. By 1953, all four independents were headed downhill.

So Mason made his pitch again. This time Hudson was interested but Packard and Studebaker still weren't. On May 1, 1954, Nash and Hudson merged to form American Motors Corp. (AMC), Nash becoming the dominant partner due to its healthier financial situation. Six months later, George Mason died and George W. Romney took over as AMC president.

During the first few years of AMC, Nash and Hudson still sold cars under their own names. However, in 1955 AMC scuttled the seven-year-old Hudson stepdown body shell and began marketing facelifted, rebadged Nashes as Hudsons. In more recent times these cars have become known as "Hashes." Richard Arbib, creator of the Packard Pan American and former manager of Harley Earl Associates, was called in by Meade Moore to do some of the early Hash facelifts—to make them look as little like Nashes as possible. Arbib's role in AMC design, however, was minor.

After the merger, Frank Spring closed down the Hudson styling section and retired in 1955. The AMC design operation arose, then, from the Nash side, with Ed Anderson named director of styling. The uphill battle to keep AMC solvent would bring, naturally enough, a multitude of changes. ◆

AMERICAN MOTORS CORP.

American Motors kept the Nash and Hudson names alive through 1957, although both car lines were now built only on Nash platforms. Soon after the Hudson/Nash merger, AMC's styling director, Edmund E. Anderson, hired additional designers and modelers to keep up with the increased workload. He then set up not two but four studios. Each studio had a chief designer, an assistant chief plus one or two junior designers and one or two modelers.

The main studio, called simply the "body studio," was overseen by Anderson and his assistant, Bill Reddig. This studio concentrated on developing and engineering the core Nash/Hudson body.

AMC concentrated on 1956 Rambler and dropped Hashes after 1957. Despite conflicting elements, this design somehow came out looking amazingly coherent.

Hudson shared Nash body shell from 1955 through '57, came to be called "Hash."

Then there was a Nash studio, headed by Jack Garnier, and a Hudson studio under Ken Samples. In the fourth studio, Don Stumpf had charge of interiors. The Hudson and Nash production studios took the core body and individualized it by designing specific front, rear and side treatments so that each nameplate had its own look. For 1955-56, Nash picked up the inboard headlights that Pinin Farina had set into the grille of the 1952 Nash-Healey sports car. This grille design, along with the semi-skirted front fenders, identified Nashes. Hudson, meanwhile, used normal wheel cuts and conventional fender-mounted headlamps.

After AMC president George Mason arranged the marriage of Hudson and Nash, he still entertained hopes of someday bringing

much as offering the public a series of sensible, economical, compact cars when Detroit was marketing ever-larger and ever-thirstier dinosaurs.

It became clear that AMC would never become a foursome when Packard bought Studebaker on Oct. 1, 1954. George Mason died a week later, and George Romney decided to leave full-sized cars to other manufacturers and base AMC's future on the compact Rambler. Ed Anderson designed a mid-sized Rambler for

1958 Rambler American (above) became the car that put AMC into third spot for 1960, behind Chevy and Ford. Anderson's last and one of his cleanest AMC designs was 1963 Classic (left). AMC revolutionized body engineering with its "uniside" construction. One stamping (below) replaced what had previously been 52 separate pieces welded together. The 1964 Rambler American, designed under Dick Teague, used uniside stampings identical to Rambler Classic and Ambassador.

Packard and Studebaker into AMC. Toward that eventuality, Mason saw Nash as the foursome's entry-level division. Packard would be AMC's luxury carmaker, with Studebaker rivaling Pontiac and Hudson taking on Olds and Buick. But instead of positioning Nash against Ford and Chevrolet directly, Mason saw future auto buyers wanting smaller, more economical cars. He had the courage to show the Nash NXI showcar (which became the 1954 Metropolitan) as early as 1950, and he launched the 1950 Rambler compact 10 years before the Big Three introduced cars of a similar size.

Mason and his successor, George Romney, both felt that AMC had a counter-culture image, so why not capitalize on it? This wasn't niche marketing so

1956, and as the re-re-*re*-facelifted larger Nashes and Hudsons faded out after 1957, AMC named all its cars "Rambler" and reissued the 1953-55 Rambler as the 1958 Rambler American.

Romney's timing was spot-on. In 1958, the U.S. economy went into recession. As a result, the Big Three's car sales plummeted but AMC's rose. People wanted smaller, thriftier cars, and AMC had them. For 1959, the Rambler became this country's fourth bestselling nameplate, behind Ford, Chevrolet and Plymouth. By 1960, Rambler had miraculously taken Plymouth out of *third* place! Indeed, Volkswagen and Rambler had come up from nowhere and became two of the great success stories of the late 1950s. But AMC's luck couldn't last, because the Big Three introduced their own compacts for 1960. George Lawson styled the frowning 1961 Rambler American line, and the American's styling now paled against the compacts introduced in 1960-61 by Ford, Mercury, Plymouth, Dodge, Chevrolet, Pontiac, Buick and Oldsmobile (Falcon, Comet, Valiant, Dart, Corvair, Tempest,

Special and F-85 respectively). The compact field was becoming saturated.

Meanwhile, Dick Teague had come to American Motors from Chrysler in 1959 (see below), and his first assignment, according to designer James W. (Jim) Alexander, was to re-do the front sheetmetal on the 1961 Ambassador. Ed Anderson, who retired in Dec. 1961, had just finished his last design for AMC: the highly pleasing 1963 Rambler Classic and Ambassador. Anderson left, supposedly, over a disagreement with George Romney. Romney intended to retain Walter Hoving, chairman of the Tiffany jewelry emporium in Manhattan. Romney wanted AMC cars to have what he called the "Tiffany touch." Hoving, though, wouldn't lend just his name but insisted on actively participating in AMC design. His ideal car, again according to Jim Alexander, was "the 1959 Cadillac without fins but on Rambler American proportions." Anderson wasn't having any of this, so he departed.

Teague then replaced Anderson as AMC styling director and

Dick Teague, Designer on a Shoestring

Richard A. Teague was born in Los Angeles the day after Christmas in 1923 and became a child movie actor. Dick's stage name was Dixie Duval. His mother found him jobs in four movies that Dick always stressed were not *Our Gang* comedies. They were similar one-reelers by a producer named Stan De Lay.

When he was six, his mother was driving Dick to work one morning when she collided with another car. The collision left her an invalid. Dick lost one eye, several teeth and suffered a broken jaw. That ended his movie career. His father was killed a year later in another auto accident.

Dick developed an early interest in hot rods and went to school with Ed Iskenderian and other early Southern California speed merchants. His first car was a powder-blue 1932 Ford three-window coupe with 16-inch wire wheels and a chromed instrument panel. He was 16 and paid $125 for the car in Beverly Hills. He later owned several other Ford hot rods, including a four-port Riley Model A and a V-8-engined Model A, both of which he ran at Muroc, the dry lake northeast of Los Angeles.

Teague always drew cars as a kid. Because of his eye, he couldn't get into the military, so in 1942, aged 19, he took a job as an illustrator with Northrop Aircraft. Teague loved airplanes as much as cars, and at Northrop he worked under Paul Browne, a former GM auto designer who'd been in Bill Mitchell's studio during the 1938 Cadillac 60-Special's creation. "Both Browne and I were drawing cars when we should have been drawing aircraft," confessed Teague many years later. Browne encouraged Dick to get into auto design and recommended he attend Art Center, which Teague did during the war.

After the war, Dick worked briefly for Henry Kaiser in Oakland, designing a small, pre-Henry J economy car. He also did magazine illustrations, including an early cover for *Road & Track*. One day a friend phoned him to say that GM was interviewing for stylists at the Biltmore Hotel in Los Angeles. The interviewer turned out to be Frank Hershey. Hershey was also a friend of Paul Browne's, so with those connections, Teague got the job. He started at GM on Mar. 15, 1948.

"All of us neophytes" recalled Teague,

"were put into Hershey's experimental studio over at 'Planet 8,' which we called boot camp. GM had two sections. Hershey got all the greenest kids, and then if we stayed, we graduated to Ed Anderson's area. Ed had a more advanced experimental studio." Like all entering designers, Teague worked on details: lamps, trim, hood ornaments, that sort of thing.

Teague remained a designer in advanced Cadillac and then left GM in early 1951. He married, returned to California and worked briefly for Rhodes Lewis on weapons designs, doing illustra-

tions of tanks, rocket launchers, etc. Later that year, Frank Hershey phoned Teague from Packard, told him John Reinhart had left and that if Teague wanted the chief stylist's job he could have it. Dick missed cars and accepted. In early 1952, Hershey went to Ford and Teague moved up to become Packard's styling director under Ed Macauley. That's when Teague hired Richard G. Macadam, who later became Chrysler's design vice president (see page 286).

By 1956 Packard was terminal, so Teague went to Chrysler along with Bill Schmidt. Before Virgil Exner came back from his heart attack, Schmidt made Teague chief stylist of the Chrysler studio. But then when Schmidt lost a power struggle with Exner (see page 169), Teague left Chrysler and soon took a job in Sept. 1959 at American Motors Corp., under his old GM boot-camp mentor, Ed Anderson. "It's funny," commented Teague, "how you go around in a circle. A friend of mine says that if you stay in styling long enough, you'll eventually be working for your mother-in-law."

Anderson left AMC in late 1961, and Teague took over as the corporation's styling director. He was named design vice president on Feb. 6, 1964 and remained with AMC for 24 years—until his retirement in 1983.

Dick Teague had a long and very passionate love affair with classic and antique cars. He habitually haunted swapmeets and did nearly all his own restoration work, often laboring long into the night to unwind from the stresses of his AMC routine. He amassed a wonderful, mixed-bag collection of cars, which he loved to drive and occasionally showed at *concours d'elegance*. Few designers could match Teague's genuine devotion to automobiles and his broad knowledge of automotive history. He passed away in California in May 1991. ◆

AMC's 1965 Marlin grew out of Tarpon showcar. Tarpon, however, had been built on a Rambler base while Marlin used Classic platform, rendering it too big and bulky looking.

Teague's 1968-68 Cavalier concept car (top) proposed using same stampings for all four doors and fenders, hood, decklid. Teague shortened Javelin to make AMX 2-seater above.

oversaw the design of the all-new 1964 Rambler American. He did this car in a three-way competition with independent designers Brooks Stevens and William M. Schmidt. The fact that Teague's design won helped secure his position.

The 1964 Rambler American and the 1963 Classic/Ambassador pioneered what came to be called "uniside" construction. This meant that a single stamping formed the door surrounds. In the old method, 52 separate stampings were welded together, so uniside construction was much more efficient. For even greater economies of scale, identical unisides were used for the 1963 Classic/Ambassador and the 1964 American, that being a given in the design contest.

This sharing of major body parts showed AMC's tight tooling budget, a handicap that continually plagued Teague and his staff. Teague was forever, in Jerry Palmer's words, "putting a new

Another redesign was the 1968 AMX, a two-place, shortened version of the Javelin ponycar. The 1970 Gremlin was a Hornet with its tail lopped off (and redone as the AMC Spirit fastback for 1979). The Hornet, subsequently rebadged the Concord and ultimately the AMC Eagle, was another clean Teague design: unspectacular but very tasteful. The Gremlin, on the other hand, banked on "cute" for its appeal, as did the Pacer (and more recently, the Chrysler Neon). But whatever Teague touched, he had to think it through toward later moves, like a chess player, and consider how he might reshape or repackage it for bonus mileage. And to do that, he worked very closely with AMC's product planning group. He was one styling vice president who got along well with the product planners and marketers of that era.

In 1970, AMC bought Kaiser-Jeep Corp., thereby becoming one of the world's leading manufacturers of four-wheel-drive vehicles. The Jeep purchase turned into one of those remarkable niche-

AMC became adept at making two or three entirely different cars out of one, the import-fighting Gremlin (above) being a

case in point. It shared everything except floorpan length with the AMC Hornet, shown here as the Sportabout wagon.

dress on the old girl." The *Wall Street Journal* said that, "...Teague's specialty is styling on a shoestring."

Some of Teague's shoestring re-do's included the 1965 Rambler Marlin, a sad car that transformed the Rambler Classic into a pudgy fastback coupe. The Tarpon showcar that inspired the Marlin was built on the Rambler American chassis, but in production, AMC's sales and marketing people insisted that the Marlin use the larger Classic as its base, and that supposedly spoiled the Tarpon design. AMC designers referred to the Marlin as the "Carp."

market deals that paid off for AMC. Just after the Jeep acquisition took place, though, a national business magazine called it "Chapin's Folly," referring to AMC chairman Roy D. Chapin Jr.

"To his credit, Dick Teague could see the future design possibilities [of Jeep vehicles]," wrote Chapin in a 1994 letter to the authors. "Dick was a staunch supporter of the deal. We subsequently did some clinics where would-be buyers of four-wheel-drive vehicles were shown a number of styling alternatives to the Kaiser Jeep Wagoneer station wagon.

"There were four in all: one by an Italian design firm, one by an

Teague put so much glass in the 1976 Pacer's greenhouse that the side windows didn't roll all the way down into the doors. Car sold well in its first year, thanks partly to pitchman Ed McMahon.

independent U.S. designer, one by Dick's people and the fourth was simply the old Jeep Wagoneer from about 1965. To our considerable surprise, the clinics produced a strong preference for the old Kaiser version! This apparent reluctance to accept major design changes resulted in Dick keeping the flat glass, heavy wheel cuts, etc., but very deftly refining the Wagoneer design to give it broader appeal, especially to buyers not interested in all-wheel drive.

"The success and growing popularity of go-anywhere vehicles made the Jeep acquisition, I feel, one of AMC's wiser moves. I only wish Dick could have been around to see it."

Bad times were usually good for AMC, the next fateful windfall coming in the form of the two major Middle East oil crises. Again AMC lucked out by being in the right place with small, economical cars. In mid 1975, AMC introduced the roly-poly Pacer. Teague said the Pacer came from a "grubby doodle—a four-wheel football that was half glass, with a rollbar in the mid-

Only eight copies of the mid-engined AMX/3 were built, and Teague owned two of them.

dle." Flying with AMC's then-president Gerald C. Meyers, Dick sketched the Pacer concept on an airline barf bag. Meyers liked it and gave it the go-ahead. The AMC Pacer was far to the left of mainstream, very unlike any other small car. It was wide, glassy, totally original, bold but also heavy and expensive to manufacture. People either loved or hated the look. The Pacer sold extremely well in its first year, but after AMC raised its price to the level of GM's bestselling Olds Cutlass, sales tapered off and never came back.

Dick Teague's tiny staff, which at its peak numbered around 50, did remarkable things not only with AMC's production cars but

with a series of rational, interesting showcars. The original AMX made its debut in Detroit in Jan. 1966 as a styling exercise. It was handmade in metal on a 1965 Rambler American chassis. The AMX showcar's design was by Chuck Mashigan and Eric Kugler under Teague's direction. This AMX had a "ramble seat" in the trunk and a backlight that flipped up like a tonneau windscreen. The AMX showcar preceded the AMC's 1968 Javelin ponycar which, with 12 inches chopped out of the floorpan and quarter panels reshaped to look like the Vignale job, became the 1968 1/2 production AMX two-seater. Later that year Teague introduced four additional showcars, one called the Cavalier that used four interchangeable doors and interchangeable hood and decklid. The interchangeability highlighted the sorts of economies AMC was hoping to produce.

The 1967 AMX III showcar was a handsome station wagon with cues anticipating the Javelin. Teague and his people designed the 1970 AMX/3, a mid-engined exoticar that would have competed with the De Tomaso Pantera that Lincoln-Mercury began importing in 1970. Giorgio Giugiaro's Ital Design did one design proposal for the AMX/3, and Teague's staff submitted another. Teague's version won. The AMX/3 chassis was engineered by Giotto Bizzarini, maker of Italian exoticars, and used an AMC V-8. Subsequent AMC showcars included the 1972 Gremlin Voyageur, with a

slide-out pickup box; the 1973 Hornet GT hatchback; and the 1974 Gremlin G/II, from which the 1979 Spirit fastback took shape.

Dick Teague also oversaw the perennial updates of AMC's range of Jeep products. In 1977, he suggested the Concept Jeep II as a modernized revival of the original WW-II Willys Jeep. Teague's staff became involved with Americanizing Renault's product line after the French carmaker started investing heavily in American Motors in 1979. Teague retired in 1983, and Chrysler Corp. bought AMC/Jeep in 1987. Subsequent Jeep styling developments were done by Chrysler designers. ◆

STUDEBAKER CORPORATION

After World War II, Studebaker became America's bestselling independent automaker. From the late 1940s through 1957, Studebaker proudly marched a distant fourth behind the giant Big Three: GM, Chrysler and Ford.

Studebaker's landmark postwar cars reached dealer showrooms in May 1946, two months before Kaiser and Frazer rolled out their first cars. The sudden, unexpected unveiling of Studebaker's all-

eling throughout the war? These Studebakers didn't look like that. And they had flush sides but used applied rear fenders. Why? Was this an aesthetic consideration or something functional, something to do with manufacturing or economics?

The Big Three and several independents rushed out and bought early 1947 Studebakers, took them apart, studied their construction and compared the Champion and Commander series with

Loewy assembled quite a styling team in South Bend after WW-II. In studio at right, that's a balding Gordon Buehrig modeling in foreground. Behind him stand Loewy and Exner. Bob Bourke is just left of center in tie. Everyone was working on 1945 models ultimately displayed on tables above. Model that came closest to 1947 Champion is at right rear. Exner and Loewy soon had a bad falling out, and Studebaker engineering gave Exner the correct package dimensions while Loewy got false ones. Directors went with Exner's design.

new designs had more impact and stirred more emotion than any production car since the 1934 Chrysler/DeSoto Airflow. Here was a glimpse of the future, but this time most people liked it. Studebaker had caught America off guard and shocked the public with this audaciously styled automobile. And then, almost as if to break the tension, radio comedians began to make jokes about the car. Was it coming or going? How could an owner tell the hood from the decklid? Why not put headlights on both ends and have three gears in reverse?

But what impressed people when the car appeared was the huge leap in styling. Here was a car with not just flush front fenders and six more inches of usable seat width, but in plan view the body's center section looked like an airplane fuselage. The hood tapered toward the front and the decklid came to a blunt point at the rear. On the 1947 five-passenger coupe, the curved rear glass wrapped halfway around the greenhouse, again like the cockpit of an airplane. This was more curved glass than anyone had ever seen in a production automobile. The tapered fuselage also had its origins in aircraft design.

The nation's automakers were likewise caught off guard, not only because Studebaker managed to get a restyled postwar car out faster than they could but because its design raised some interesting questions. What happened to the rounded, doughy, bubble-domed, streamlined shapes stylists had been sketching and mod-

their own postwar designs. Engineers, stylists and marketers were particularly intrigued with the lightweight Champion. Its size, weight and its eye appeal had a tremendous impact on the entire auto industry. Ford for 1949 went along with Studebaker's squared-off body format. GM used applied rear fenders to help give its 1948-49 models some of Studebaker's crouching, takeoff stance. And Chrysler combined both ideas in all its 1949 lines.

Industrial designer Raymond Loewy got full credit for styling the 1947 Studebaker. The company extolled him in ads and brochures; in fact, Studebaker gave Loewy credit for designing most of its cars and trucks from 1938 through 1956 and the Avanti for 1963. Loewy and Studebaker were very much linked in the minds of most Americans—much more than any other designer and car name. In the late 1940s and early '50s, Studebaker publicity made Loewy a household word. His picture appeared on the

1948 Studebakers

1949 Commander

Loewy signed sketch at top right, but it was probably a community effort by his staff. Cars Studebaker introduced for 1947 (1948 models shown above) startled the industry with their use of glass, their light weight and squarish format. Both Champion (left) and Commander (above) offered 5-passenger coupes with aircraft-inspired wraparound backlights.

cover of *Time* in 1949. To the average citizen, Loewy's fame rested not so much on the thousands of other products his firm shaped and packaged—from Bulova watches to Pennsylvania Railroad locomotives—but much more on his designs for Studebaker. Studebaker put Loewy in the public consciousness.

And while we don't want to take away from his tremendous contribution to Studebaker's fortunes, the 1947 Studebaker was a Loewy design very indirectly. It started out as a mix of ideas by designers Robert E. (Bob) Bourke and Virgil M. (Ex) Exner. Exner had been Pontiac's studio chief in the late 1930s (see sidebar, page 161) under Harley Earl. Loewy hired Exner away from GM in 1938, set him up in his New York office and soon made him styling director of his Studebaker and International Harvester design accounts. At first, Exner worked in Manhattan. Then in 1941, at Studebaker's insistence, he moved to the company's headquarters in South Bend, Indiana. Exner had gone to college in South Bend and worked there as an advertising illustrator, so he knew the small city like a native; knew the people and got along with them.

Loewy, on the other hand, was an outsider. He was generally viewed as a foreigner. He dressed fancy, talked funny and wore cologne. To Studebaker's engineers and particularly to its engineering vice president, Roy E. Cole, Loewy belonged in New York or Paris, whereas Virgil Exner...now there was a person you could talk to. Ex was a car guy. All Loewy could do was wave his hands and cost the company a lot of money—money which, incidentally, came out of Cole's engineering budget.

Cole resented Loewy partly because he believed Loewy was milking the company. Studebaker paid Loewy's retainer based on the number of hours his people worked. Loewy's contract guaranteed Studebaker a set number of hours of design time. Anything beyond that meant extra payment. Being privy to Loewy's contractual arrangement, Cole now reasoned that the longer Loewy dragged his feet on the 1947 Studebaker project, the more money he stood to make.

In addition, board chairman Paul G. Hoffman, who'd hired Loewy and signed his contract, gave Loewy standing authority to double any out-of-pocket costs when submitting his expense

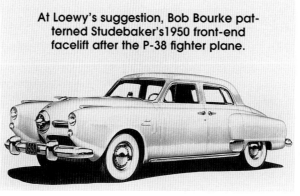

At Loewy's suggestion, Bob Bourke patterned Studebaker's 1950 front-end facelift after the P-38 fighter plane.

accounts. Cole felt that Loewy was abusing both privileges: stretching his design assignments to collect overtime and allowing his designers to run up big, reimbursable tabs at places like the South Bend Country Club so he could recoup their expenses with a 100% markup.

This was not a situation conducive to warm feelings between Loewy and Cole. And because Cole and Exner worked together and couldn't help talking about Loewy, the situation led to bad feelings between Exner and Loewy as well. From 1941 on, the two men became less and less trusting of one another, mostly because Exner had a better working relationship with Cole than he'd ever had with Loewy. Loewy quite reasonably began to doubt Exner's loyalty.

So in 1942, Loewy hired Gordon Buehrig. Buehrig had been chief stylist for Auburn-Cord-Duesenberg (see page 233) and brought with him a distinguished design portfolio. Among the cars he'd designed were dozens of custom Duesenbergs, the 1935 Auburn line, including the speedster, and the 1936 Cord 810. Loewy now hired Buehrig and installed him above Exner; making Buehrig Exner's boss. Oddly enough, Exner and Buehrig got along fine. Harsh words never passed between them. Loewy soon reappraised the situation and made Exner *Buehrig's* boss. Still no reaction. So Loewy finally gave them equal status. If Loewy was trying to cause a rift or create competition, he failed. Buehrig and Exner remained close friends, both personally and professionally, for the rest of their lives.

Exner had very much admired Loewy when he first went to work for him in New York. As time passed, though, he began to resent Loewy for a number of reasons. One had to do with Loewy taking credit for sketches, clay models and designs he didn't do himself. Loewy would routinely sign the sketches his designers created. Actually, Loewy had good reason to do this. When he presented design sketches to management, he wanted his designers' work to look consistent, as though one person had done everything. To get that consistency, he would sometimes have his designers—under Bob Bourke—do their drawings in assembly-line fashion. Ted Pietsch, for example, had a good eye for perspective, so Pietsch would set up the basic 3/4-front outline for 10-20 drawings intended to show, say, different grilles. Four or five designers would then sketch in various grilles. At the end of the line, Bob Andrews, an expert with opaque watercolors, would finish all these drawings. Finally, when Loewy showed up in South Bend, he would sign them. They now appeared to have been completed by one person in a single style. And being the boss, Loewy did have the right to sign anything he wanted. It even made economic sense for him to do so, because credit for a design enhanced Loewy's reputation. And yet the bad feeling that developed because Loewy refused to give or share credit became one of several sticking points that eventually led to a traumatic rift between Loewy and Exner.

Preliminary designs for the 1947 Studebaker started in 1942 and became serious in 1943-44. At the beginning of the war, Loewy had 10-12 people working for him in South Bend, but soon after Pearl Harbor only three remained: Exner, designer Bob Bourke and clay modeler Frank Ahlroth. Bourke was a Studebaker employee assigned to aircraft engine designs, and Loewy had gotten Exner and Ahlroth deferments so they could also do military design work.

According to Exner's son, Virgil Jr., Loewy was juggling so many consultancy contracts during and just after the war—spread himself so thin—that months would pass when Loewy didn't show up in South Bend at all. Loewy's three-man Studebaker design team wasn't empowered to make major decisions, and the delays irked not just Exner but especially Roy Cole, who was anxious to get a restyled car into dealer showrooms as soon after the war as possible.

Loewy began hiring more people, starting in late 1942. That's when Ex hired modeler John Bird, John Reinhart, Bob Koto and a number of others. This larger Loewy styling group began turning out impressive numbers of sketches and 1/4-scale concept clays. But Loewy still showed up so rarely and his styling direction tended to be so vague that Cole and some of his people lost patience. Cole became more and more convinced that Loewy was stretching out the job for financial gain.

Cole and Exner discussed these problems, and it wasn't long before Roy Cole decided that Studebaker might be better off without Loewy. Exner was, after all, quite capable of handling Studebaker styling himself. So in 1944, Cole told Exner—perhaps at Exner's suggestion—to design a postwar car on his own, without the Loewy group, in secret. Exner already had a small studio in his basement at home. In fact, Bourke had occasionally come to Ex's house during the war so they could work on car designs together. That's how the 1947 Studebaker got started initially.

But after Cole told Exner to do a model in secret, Ex set up drafting tables in one of his bedrooms and, in confidence, asked modeler Frank Ahlroth to come over evenings and on weekends to help him create this new car. A full-sized version of the "Cole model" would eventually compete with rival models being prepared by Loewy's official styling team under Gordon Buehrig. Both models would be shown at a meeting of the Studebaker board of directors, and the board would decide which design should be rushed into production.

Buehrig recalled in his book *Rolling Sculpture* that Exner would show up in the Loewy studio around 11 o'clock every morning and tell Buehrig he'd been over in Cole's office, about two blocks away. In reality, Exner had been sleeping late because of the hours he and Ahlroth were putting in on the Cole model. Buehrig said he never suspected a thing. Exner, of course, knew he was undermining Buehrig and the entire Loewy operation but, according to Virgil Jr., he felt a greater allegiance to Cole and Studebaker than to Loewy.

The Exner model had its roots in work he and Bourke had done together early in the war, so the shapes of the Cole model and the Buehrig models weren't all that different. However, Cole had intentionally given Buehrig the wrong package dimensions and Exner the correct ones. Exner finished his 1/4-scale clay and, with Cole's approval, shipped it to the Edward G. Budd Co. in Philadelphia to be done as a wooden mockup, full size. Budd supplied Studebaker with body dies and panels and routinely built wooden mockups for clients as a courtesy.

When Budd had nearly finished Exner's wooden mockup, Cole called Buehrig into his office and laid out the whole story. He told Buehrig that he'd given him the wrong package dimensions and that the models he and Bourke were working on for Loewy were too big. According to Buehrig, "[Cole] also explained he was going to get rid of Loewy. He asked me to accompany Exner to Philadelphia to inspect the finished [wooden] design model and to

Giving Credit Where Due

Although he rarely designed anything literally, Raymond Loewy claimed credit for every successful design he ever sold. This included all Studebakers from 1938 through 1956 plus thousands of non-automotive products ranging from toasters to ocean liners.

Loewy had no choice; he had to take credit personally for all those designs. It became a commercial necessity; a vital part of doing business. Each time he received credit for designing a product, he added to his reputation, especially if that product sold well. Ultimately, his name and fame became his most valuable assets.

It's sometimes hard for an observer to decide who should get the actual credit for designing a particular car. Is it the person who dreamed up the original styling concept? Or the sketch artist who made that concept palatable to corporate decision-makers? Or the clay modeler who translated the cheated sketch into some form of reality? Or the studio chief who shepherded the design through a gauntlet of nay-saying engineers? Or the executive in overall charge of the entire design operation—the vice president or styling consultant—whose job was on the line throughout this entire process?

The answer is simple. Ultimately, full credit has to go to the person in overall charge because, theoretically at least, it's his judgement that counts. If the design succeeds, he's a hero. If it fails, he's out of a job. He's the person responsible. And that's the stark, total answer.

All Harley Earl, Bill Mitchell, Edsel Ford, Bob Gregorie, George Walker, Gene Bordinat, Elwood Engel, Ed Macauley, Frank Spring, Virgil Exner, Dick Teague or Raymond Loewy ever had to sell was their judgement. They also had to have the competence to move a design from an image in someone's mind into dealer showrooms. Each man had to be judged on those two abilities and nothing more. It didn't mean any of them ever had to lift a pencil or a clay knife. A few of them could—Mitchell and Exner being two of the best—but they didn't have to.

When we say, for example, that "Bill Mitchell designed the 1963 Buick Riviera," we don't mean he sat down, took out pencil and paper and drew a picture of what the 1963 Riviera would ultimately look like. Even Ned Nickles had help on the Riviera from various designers and modelers in his studio. Virtually no car gets designed by one person; they're all amalgams. In the Riviera's case, Mitchell directed the design, suggested changes, approved or disapproved the evolving nuances and details, then sold the design to (in this case) Buick. The word "handwaving" is usually used pejoratively, but to handwave convincingly and successfully takes great skill. Far fewer designers can handwave than draw or sculpt.

So when Raymond Loewy signed sketches and took credit for cars that Virgil Exner created at Studebaker, he did so because he had to. He had no choice. Taking credit was one of the most important acts of Loewy's career. ◆

turn in my expense account to him. This was the first time I was aware of Roy Cole's dirty trick."

In effect, Cole was inviting Buehrig to join him and Exner in ousting Loewy. But Buehrig decided to remain loyal to Loewy and at the same time decided not to tell him about the subterfuge. Buehrig's team, which had based its competing full-sized clay on Cole's too-large package dimensions, now had to quickly rework its model for the directors' show. To get the full-sized model ready in time, Buehrig's group cut the clay lengthwise and crosswise, took out two-inch sections, then narrowed and shortened it to bring it into spec. Not only did the Buehrig team's design proportions suffer but the last-minute changes made the clay look butchered. In the end, Exner's sleeker wooden model got the directors' nod and became the basis for Studebaker's postwar car.

Loewy, who was present at the board show, exploded when he found out about the Cole/Exner plot. He fired Exner two days later. Cole, though, immediately put Exner on Studebaker's payroll, an act intended to make Loewy angry enough to tear up his Studebaker consultancy contract. Loewy didn't do that, though. Instead, he vented his anger at Buehrig for not telling him about the intrigue. Within two weeks of firing Exner, Buehrig was out, too. (Buehrig soon directed the construction by Derham of the Tasco, his sports car, and then took a job with Ford.)

Bob Koto modeled the 1947 Studebaker five-passenger coupe (called *Starlight* in 1949) from a sketch originally done by Exner. The 1947 Champion grille was the work of Vince Gardner, while the Commander grille was Exner's.

In 1946, Loewy made Bourke his chief stylist at Studebaker, whereupon Cole forced Bourke and his crew out of the engineering building. They went first into a former gymnasium on Studebaker property and then moved again to quarters on the unair-conditioned second floor of Sherman, Schaus & Freeman, a Studebaker dealership a few blocks from the plant.

"They tried to make it tough for Bob," recalled designer Tucker Madawick. "Believe it or not, we had to wheel our full-sized clay bucks through the streets of South Bend to show them to Studebaker management. We covered the model with canvas and prayed the clay wouldn't fracture through the buck." Cole and Exner were trying to demoralize Loewy. But if anything, the move made Bourke and his team hang tough. Loewy did ask Bourke to cut his staff by 10%, and that's when Bourke let Dick Caleal go. Caleal went to George Walker for a job, which led directly into the design of the 1949 Ford (see page 138).

Exner took over the luxurious former Loewy studio inside Studebaker's engineering building and worked there on a major facelift for the 1950 model. Exner's 1950 designs competed with Bourke's, and this time it was the Loewy crew that won out. Raymond Loewy had urged Bourke to think in terms of aircraft, specifically mentioning the P-38. But instead of focusing on the P-38's tail section as Harley Earl's people had done in designing the 1948 Cadillac's fins, Loewy took cues from the front end. He specifically wanted Bourke to do a hub-like spinner grille flanked by two forward-thrusting fenders. Bourke's original concept wrapped this in a tight-fitting chrome bumper, but due to production costs, the bumper had to become more conventional. Loewy's personal 1950 Studebaker had a propeller on the spinner that turned in the breeze, and several aftermarket manufacturers soon made similar propellers available.

Exner stayed at Studebaker until Roy Cole retired. He then left in 1949 to go with Chrysler (see page 162).

Despite these corporate tremors, there's no doubt that Loewy did for Studebaker what very few others could have done. He gave the venerable South Bend automaker consistently salable styling and occasionally made Studebaker an industry design leader.

Loewy was not an auto designer, although he sometimes would grab a clay knife and make a few ceremonial swipes at some innocent model. Rather, Raymond Loewy was the archetypal front man, the consummate handwaver, the salesman *par excellence*. He could sell a design idea to other salesmen, and he knew which ideas would sell to the public. His batting average was so good

that he became, in the course of his career, the world's most famous industrial designer; an international icon. Loewy not only developed the ability, after years of trying, to sell his services to hundreds of companies worldwide, but he also had an unfailing ability to recognize talent. And he could organize and manage the teams of designers who did the actual work.

Loewy pioneered and tirelessly promoted industrial design. In the process, he also promoted himself. His fame built on itself, layer upon layer, because each successful design confirmed his golden touch and brought a greater demand for it. Loewy became much better known than most of the company presidents he served and, in time, his carefully groomed image made Loewy not just famous but amazingly rich.

Raymond Fernand Loewy was born Nov. 5, 1893 in Paris, the youngest of three sons. His father was an Austrian-born French journalist, and his mother liked to remind her boys that, "It's better to be envied than pitied." One Loewy son became a surgeon, another a banker and Raymond showed a lively interest in motorcars, airplanes and locomotives. He sketched them endlessly in school.

Young Raymond entered Paris University as a precocious 12-year-old and majored in electrical engineering. Three years later, in 1908, he designed a balsa-wood, rubberband-powered model airplane that won the J. Gordon Bennett prize when it flew farther than any other in the competition. Loewy patented his airplane design, manufactured kits and sold them in France and England.

In 1910, he enrolled at the Ecole de Laneau hoping to study for an advanced degree in engineering, but World War I intervened. Loewy enlisted in the French army corps of engineers as a private and came out in 1918 a captain. He later enjoyed telling that his first military uniform looked so baggy that he couldn't stand to wear it. He took it to a tailor who made it fit like a fine suit. Loewy also did up his muddy trench with Paris wallpaper and artwork.

In the early part of the war, Loewy's job was to lay telegraph cable. Night after night, he ran wire from lonely French outposts as far as possible into German-held territory so that French operatives and advancing troops could send messages to Allied positions. He usually had to slither along on his belly dragging a great spool of wire behind him. During one of these missions, he was gassed and burned. Loewy received the Croix de Guerre with four citations plus an Inter-Allied medal. Toward the end of the war he installed radios in aircraft and also acted as a liaison officer to the U.S. Expeditionary Forces. This last assignment helped him polish his English.

He finished college after the war and, in 1919, with $40 in his pocket and only his blue officer's uniform to wear in public, he boarded a ship bound for America. His brother Georges, an M.D. and medical researcher in New York, underwrote his passage. On the way over, someone asked Loewy for a charitable donation, but since he had no money he drew a portrait of a young woman on board and auctioned it off. To Loewy's surprise, the sketch brought $150. The buyer was Sir Harry Armstrong, the British consul in New York. Sir Harry was so taken with Loewy's talent and charm that he introduced him to Conde Nast, publisher of *Vogue* and *Vanity Fair*. Loewy, then, began his American career as a fashion illustrator. Between magazine assignments he designed displays for Macy's and Saks Fifth Avenue and costumes for the Ziegfeld Follies.

Industrial design had recently emerged as a recognized business when Loewy hung out his shingle in 1927. Two years later he met Sigmund Gestetner, maker of a popular duplicating machine. Gestetner's old-fashioned duplicator hadn't changed much in three decades. Loewy offered to create a clay model of a new Gestetner machine. Mr. Gestetner agreed, liked it, paid Loewy $2000 and continued to sell the Loewy version through 1947.

Loewy once remarked that his early career consisted of "25% inspiration and 75% transportation," meaning he was forever dragging portfolios and samples through subway and train stations. He became a design consultant to Westinghouse in 1929 and

Loewy's first major automotive account was Hupmobile. He designed the sophisticated "H" hood ornament and grille, and the 1932 cycle-fendered Hupp's styling (below) was taken directly from a customized 1930 Hupmobile he had built for himself. The 1934 Aerodynamic Hupp (bottom) looked almost as radical as Chrysler's Airflows. Loewy arranged to be paid for the design as a percentage of all Aerodynamics sold after the first 10,000. Hupp sold fewer than 10,000, and Loewy never received a dime for his work on this car.

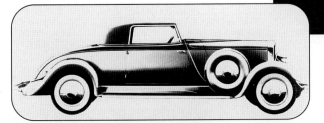

Hupmobile in 1930. To persuade Hupmobile's reluctant management to use his services, he had a custom Hupp convertible sedan built at his own expense. The bodywork cost him between $18,000 and $20,000 in 1930, or as much as a coachbuilt Duesenberg. Loewy entered it in several French *concours d'elegance*, taking first prizes at Le Touquet, Trouville and Dieppe in 1931 and a grand prize for "aerodynamic design" at Cannes in 1932. Seeing this car in metal and the success it had in Europe, Hupp management based its cycle-fendered 1932 models on Loewy's design and in turn won styling prizes at Paris, Monte Carlo, Nice, Cannes and Le Touquet. Loewy's production cycle-fendered Hupp had crisp, sporty, distinctly European overtones but, due to the Depression, not a lot of sales success.

Even so, Hupmobile allowed Loewy to design its 1934 Aerodynamic series. These were quite advanced for the day, with fender-mounted headlamps and a wrapped three-piece windshield. Loewy didn't charge Hupp for his design work on the Aerodynamic, but the company agreed to pay him a commission for every car after the first 10,000 were sold. Unfortunately Hupmobile never sold anywhere near that number, although the Aerodynamic remained in production into early 1936.

And yet one commission led to another and in 1934 Loewy redesigned the Coldspot refrigerator for Sears, Roebuck & Co. Actually it was Clare Hodgman, a young, former GM car designer hired by Loewy, who did the redesigning to Loewy's instructions. Hodgman amputated the vintage Coldspot's Queen Anne legs, hid the compressor and coils under a metal skirt, placed the door handle in a scooped round niche and suggested using rust-proof aluminum shelves. Coldspot sales skyrocketed.

By the mid 1930s, Depression-weary marketers recognized that style boosted sales. They now wanted streamlining or cleanlining or the streamlined moderne applied to everything from typewriters to toasters. One of Loewy's major accounts was Studebaker, starting in 1936. He wooed and was hired by Paul Hoffman.

Helen Dryden, the automotive interior designer, had consulted for Studebaker even earlier and would continue to work with Loewy until 1940. Loewy's influence showed up in the 1938 Studebakers, whose Commander series looked very much like the 1938 Oldsmobile. The 1938 Studebaker President and State Commander had beehive headlamps, rather like the 1936-37 Lincoln Zephyr.

Studebaker relied for many years on Budd to help make wooden mockups, die models, steel body dies and to supply sheet-metal stampings. Budd, in turn, took pride in quick turnarounds. As a result, Studebaker got used to going from body drafts into production faster than bigger auto companies. And that became one reason Studebaker managers and engineers, Roy Cole in particular, wanted stylists on the premises rather than back east in Loewy's New York office. So starting in late 1938, Exner began spending one week a month in South Bend, commuting to and from New York by train. Exner also visited Loewy's International Harvester account in Ft. Wayne, Indiana during those trips. The rest of Loewy's Studebaker design team stayed and worked in Manhattan. Exner's week-long visits still weren't enough for Cole, so in 1941 Loewy sent Exner to South Bend full-time, naming him chief stylist on the Studebaker account. Exner soon began building a separate staff in South Bend.

Clare Hodgman, the Coldspot designer, remained in New York, where he had styled the 1939 Studebaker Champion before Exner came to Loewy. The Champion was a project near and dear to Roy Cole, because Cole had spent several years working on a light car that Studebaker could bring out in the Ford/Chevy/Plymouth price range. The first Champion of 1939 became that car.

When Loewy began his Studebaker consultancy in 1936, he and Cole seemed very much in agreement. They saw eye to eye on the need for a smaller, lighter, less expensive car. After reviewing Cole's original 1939 Champion package, Loewy stated in an interview, "Studebaker engineers gave us the chassis and some parameters, primarily involving reduced weight. There were no problems as I was dealing with intelligent people who understood that weight was the enemy. In fact, I had 30 or 40 big posters printed up saying *Weight is the Enemy,* and we hung these on the [New York studio] walls and even put some of them on the floor, covered with clear acetate."

Clare Hodgman, in a 1976 interview, added, "Design work on the 1939 Champion—all preliminary sketches, drawings, 1/4-scale models, etc.—was done in the Loewy studios in New York. After approval, full-sized clays and metal prototypes were built in South Bend. I was influenced by some European cars of that period...."

When Exner got to South Bend, he and Loewy carefully built up one of the best design teams in the business. Exner recruited Bob Bourke from Sears in 1940. During the war, Bob Koto came over from Briggs and Hudson; John Reinhart from Budd and Packard; Jack Aldrich and Ed Hermann from GM; Gordon Buehrig and Vince Gardner from Auburn-Cord-Duesenberg and Budd. Modelers included Joe Thompson and John Lutz from GM, Frank Ahlroth, John Bird, Larry and Stan Brom plus the mother/daughter team of Virginia and Nancy Spence. After the war, Albrecht Goertz joined Loewy (Goertz later did the BMW 507 and Datsun 240Z), as did John Cuccio and Tucker Madawick, who later went to Ford.

Clare Hodgman designed the lightweight 1939 Champion (above), while Virgil Exner did 1941 Commander, giving it a version of GM's C body. Ex added the contrasting belt stripe and interesting rear fender. Studebaker's Skyway series had curved windshields.

Exner himself designed the 1940-42 senior Studebakers. Having left GM in 1938, he was intimately aware of GM's 1940 "torpedo" C-body and now incorporated the essence of that style into his 1941 President and Commander Skyway Land Cruiser series. These cars had the simple beltline of the GM C-body, the five-window roof and the tapered decklid. But Exner went GM several better by adding one-piece curved windshields to the two-door sedan; also skirted rear fenders and a low, sleek catwalk grille. That next year, the 1942 President grille by Bob Bourke showed a touch of Cadillac.

Loewy kept taking on new clients and hiring new designers so that by 1953 his staff numbered 200 and his firm had 125 accounts. Gross income topped $3 million a year. Raymond Loewy Associates (RLA) incorporated in 1945 and occupied the penthouse and top floor of 580 Fifth Avenue in Manhattan. RLA also had branch offices in London, Paris, Sao Paolo, Los Angeles, Chicago and South Bend.

RLA clients ranged from Pepsodent to the Pennsylvania Railroad. Loewy had a sliding scale for billing specific jobs, depending on how difficult each one was. He said that making a farm tractor more attractive was easy, so he couldn't charge much for that, but if he had to redesign a sewing needle, it would cost a fortune. His rates in 1949 for the design of a single item ranged from $500 to $200,000. After the war, Studebaker supposedly began paying Loewy $1 million a year on a 10-year contract. "It is a poor designer," Loewy told *Life,* "who cannot save his clients more than the fee they pay him." Loewy often researched his customers' old designs personally, riding long distances, for example, on old Greyhound buses before starting his design of a double decker.

Loewy himself was often mistaken for the debonair movie idol, Ronald Colman. He stood 5-10, held his weight to 165 pounds with careful dieting, fencing, boxing and hiking, wore a medium mustache and, according to *Life,* changed clothes "at least three times a day." Typical Loewy business attire consisted in 1949 of a double-breasted, sky-grey suit, silvered tie and salmon-pink shirt. Loewy spoke in muted, French-accented tones (some felt he could enrich his accent at will) and presented different personalities in

different situations.

One on one, he tended to be almost timid, yet he was always thoughtful, charming and outgoing. His conversation had an entertaining quality, and he could hold forth on a wide range of topics, art and design being only two of them. In business meetings or speeches, Loewy could hold a group spellbound by sheer force of personality. He rarely showed anger and had a very definite streak of kindness. But his inscrutability, said *Time,* "shames a Monte Carlo croupier."

At age 56, "Lucky Ramon" shed his wife of 14 years on friendly terms and married Viola Erickson, a former model exactly half his age. The Loewys maintained six homes: apartments in New York and Paris, houses in Palm Springs and Mexico, a red-tiled villa overlooking the Cote d'Azur at Saint-Tropez and a 16th-century chateau near Paris. His California home had an indoor/outdoor swimming pool that entered the living room under a glass wall. When a guest accidentally fell into the pool one afternoon, Loewy jumped in after him, fully clothed, not to rescue him but merely to neutralize any embarrassment.

Almost everyone ever employed by Loewy—Exner and Buehrig excluded—liked him and enjoyed working for him. Many designers from Loewy's Studebaker days said spontaneously in interviews that he was the best boss they'd ever had. Loewy made it a point to ask his designers, "What do you think?" He certainly wasn't dictatorial, but people eagerly did what he asked. Bob Koto said he "loved working for Loewy."

Robert F. (Bob) Andrews, who was instrumental in designing the 1948 Hudson and worked for Loewy on a number of different occasions, remembered him as a good motivator. "The best compliment I can give Mr. Loewy," said Andrews in a 1985 interview, "was that he was such a fine director that when you worked on a project for him, it was the most important project in the world.... I felt just great about it and did some of my best work for him."

Bob Bourke called Loewy a "good editor" and admired his abilities as a graphic designer. "He could swing a script right in front of your eyes," noted Bourke, "but he couldn't draw automobiles; not at all. He was just ridiculous as far as cars were concerned, and he knew it."

Loewy's right-hand man in the New York office—RLA's man-

To compete with Hudson's inexpensive 1922 Essex closed coach, 1925 Studebaker offered fixed, pillarless hardtops on its touring cars (left) and roadsters. These body styles were called Duplex. Sidecurtains rolled down from inside. The 1931 Four Seasons convertible (above) had fender-mounted parking lamps, folding windshield and golfbag doors.

ager of transportation, packaging and product design—was A. Baker (Barney) Barnhart. Barney Barnhart often stood in for Loewy at meetings in South Bend or attended with him when there were big decisions to be made. Barnhart had previously worked at GM and had a good sense for auto design.

For Studebaker board shows and important meetings, Loewy and Barnhart would arrive together in South Bend, often on the overnight train from New York. Loewy preferred the train to flying. Looking dapper and refreshed, Loewy would stop by Bob Bourke's office before a big meeting and tell Bob to listen for tough questions. If Loewy couldn't answer, he would drop his chin and stare at the floor. This signaled that he wanted Bourke to answer for him. And if the questions got too tough, or if Loewy wanted to escape from a meeting, he and Barnhart had another signal. At that point, Barnhart would leave the room and phone New York. The New York office would call back and tell Loewy that an "emergency" needed his immediate attention, and Loewy would excuse himself. Everyone knew the ploy but no one questioned it.

Once, before one of the shows for the 1950 Studebaker, Loewy and Barnhart were walking around the styling area with several engineers and stylists. Loewy was taking stock and asking questions. When he came to a full-sized clay model of the 1950 Commander, he noticed that there wasn't yet a hood ornament on it. He also spotted several prototype ornaments on a table nearby. He picked one up and set it on the hood. But in this instance, he put it on backwards. None of the stylists said a word, although a few glanced at each other. When the production car came out, it had the same hood ornament on it but pointing the right way.

Prior to Loewy's arrival, Studebaker styling was done mostly by body engineers, and the results were fairly ordinary. In the 1910s, J.G. Heaslet, vice president of engineering and production, developed the "Heaslet top," a half roof with long landau bars. The Heaslet top was designed to shade the rear compartment of a seven-passenger touring car. The famous "Three Musketeers" engineering team of Zeder, Skelton and Breer worked under Heaslet and might have had some influence on body design.

In 1916, J.H. Bourgon arrived from Brewster to head up Studebaker's short-lived custom body department. Bourgon probably did some of Studebaker's production designs as well and eventually became Studebaker's chief body engineer. Not much has been recorded, though, about those early days.

In 1913, Studebaker became one of the few carmakers able to fabricate all of its own production bodies. The company stayed relatively self-sufficient until the mid 1930s, when the Edward G. Budd Co. started making Studebaker's body dies and supplying some of its sheetmetal stampings. The Budd arrangement lasted until 1966, when Studebaker stopped making cars.

In 1925, the company tried to match Essex with an inexpensive closed body called the "Duplex" phaeton. The Studebaker Duplex amounted to a factory-built, non-removable California top on a conventional touring-car body. The result was a pillarless hardtop with sidecurtains that rolled up above the windows.

Studebaker brought in Ray Dietrich as a styling consultant around 1925. Dietrich styled the company's 1927 small car, the Erskine, named for company president Albert R. Erskine. Studebaker hoped to sell the Erskine automobile both in the U.S. and abroad, so Dietrich gave it his European touch. A raised, pennant-shaped hood panel started at the radiator peak and widened as it ran back to the windshield, then lapped down along the door sills to form very thin belt moldings. The hood pennant, moldings, fenders, rockers and roof were all painted in one color and the body in another. Stylish as it was, the Erskine didn't sell very well.

Studebaker never established a radiator shape or identity symbol, certainly nothing like the Packard hexagon or Pierce's fender-mounted headlamps. The only way a six-year-old could recognize a Studebaker was to look for the cloisonne radiator emblem: a spoked wheel with the name Studebaker angled across it.

Albert Erskine decided in the early 1920s to expand Studebaker into a full-spectrum auto company. Like General Motors, Durant Motors and later Chrysler Corp., Erskine wanted to offer a car for every price and use. He initially tried to buy Maxwell but was outbid by the banking group that hired Walter Chrysler. In the late 1920s, with the Erskine as Studebaker's low-priced offering and a line of Studebaker Sixes and Eights above that, Albert Erskine went looking for a luxury nameplate. The ailing Pierce-Arrow Motor Car Co. came up for sale, so in 1928 Studebaker bought it for $9.5 million.

The Studebaker/Pierce-Arrow marriage lasted five years. It ended in 1933, by which time the Depression left both companies financially drained. Studebaker went into receivership on Mar. 18, 1933, then sold Pierce to a group of New York investors for $1 million, and on July 1 Albert Erskine committed suicide.

One of the few good things to come out of the Studebaker/Pierce-Arrow marriage was a growing awareness by both partners that styling helped sell cars. In an effort to give Pierce and Studebaker a shared look, Studebaker—very much in the driver's seat—began to dictate Pierce styling. By 1932, both nameplates offered two bodies in common: a roadster and a five-passenger victoria coupe (called a brougham). In other respects, too, the big, early-'30s Studebaker Presidents looked like Pierces and vice-versa.

During the late 1920s or early '30s, J.H. Bourgon left, and Studebaker's tiny styling department came under the direction of James R. (Jimmy) Hughes. Hughes was an Englishman who'd worked for Rolls-Royce and Daimler in England, then for the Lelands' Lincoln venture in the early 1920s, after which he'd joined Studebaker. He was a peppery little man with a short fuse, but he knew body engineering and had an eye for line and proportion. Under Hughes were Paul Auman, superintendent of Studebaker's experimental body department, and craftsmen Julius Hezler, George Nemeth and Frank Horvath, all of whom later worked for Raymond Loewy.

Also in the early 1930s, Studebaker brought in Herb Newport as a resident stylist and put Count Alexis de Sakhnoffsky on retainer to consult on body design. Newport had worked with Gordon Buehrig at Duesenberg (see page 238), and Sakhnoffsky—art

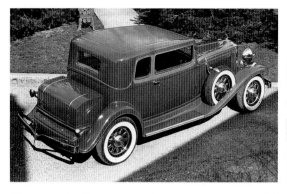

Because both companies were now wedded together, Studebaker shared St. Regis brougham body (above) with Pierce-Arrow for 1932. More dramatically, Phil Wright's 1933

Pierce Silver Arrow showcar inspired Studebaker to offer the 1934-35 Land Cruiser fastback. All sheetmetal ahead of the front doors was the same as on conventional Studebakers.

director for the Hayes Body Co.—concurrently consulted for Packard and Nash. Again, no records exist of what designs or ideas Newport and Sakhnoffsky contributed to Studebaker designs of that era.

Pierce-Arrow and Studebaker styling found its highest expression, though, in a 1/8-scale model that designer Phil Wright showed to Pierce sales manager Roy Faulkner in 1932. We go into greater detail in the Pierce-Arrow section (page 229), but briefly: Wright left Walter M. Murphy in California and had gone to Auburn-Cord-Duesenberg in Indiana, where he'd designed a gorgeous pontoon-fendered L-29 Cord speedster for Faulkner, who was then Cord's sales manager. Soon afterward, Wright took a job with GM Art & Colour. Wright, along with John Tjaarda and a number of other designers, participated in one of Harley Earl's perennial styling competitions. For this one, Earl asked each team to style a "car of the future." As so often happened at that time, three months after he started at GM, Wright found himself out on the street again. John Tjaarda left during the same purge.

So Phil Wright contacted Roy Faulkner and showed him his GM contest model. Faulkner was trying everything he could think of to attract customers to Pierce, and in his desperation no expense seemed too great. To stay competitive with other doomed luxury carmakers—Duesenberg, Marmon, Peerless, etc.—Pierce developed a V-12 engine. The 12-cylinder Pierce set speed and endurance records, went through a major restyling program and launched a monumental ad campaign.

In keeping with all this bravura, Faulkner decided to make a showcar out of Wright's design and approved the construction of five very advanced and futuristic 1933 Pierce Silver Arrow fastback sedans. These were built in Studebaker's experimental shops for Pierce and became major sensations at the New York Auto Show and the Century of Progress in Chicago.

What's important here is the fact that the 1933 Pierce Silver Arrow inspired production fastback sedans from both Pierce and Studebaker. Pierce brought out a weaker version of the Silver Arrow for 1934, and Studebaker also launched a spinoff, the 1934 Land Cruiser. Of the two, the Land Cruiser design turned out to be more modern and interesting. It made use of a four-window backlight, had skirted pontoon rear fenders and a tapered trunk that extended out behind them, like GM's 1940 torpedo C-body. The 1934-35 Land Cruiser fastbacks were identical to those years' normal sedans from the B-pillar forward; only the rear doors, rear roof and deck area were different.

Neither the 1934 Silver Arrow nor the 1934 Land Cruiser had the original showcars' through fenders, though, nor the hidden runningboards, hidden sidemounts or the stunning proportions. Studebaker's 1935 models also had a LaSalle-like, thin, steeply raked grille and very simple horizontal hood louvers like the 1934 Pontiac. As an aside, the 1936-37 Studebaker coupes used a narrow, veed backlight reminiscent of the original Silver Arrow.

The 1953 Studebaker coupe, which turned out to be one of the landmark American designs of that decade, originated as a

showcar. It came from Loewy's South Bend studio, with Bob Bourke's group finally back from exile on the second floor of the Sherman, Schaus & Freeman dealership.

Studebaker management—notably Harold Vance, who was now chairman and president—sent word to Loewy in the early spring of 1951 to design an attention-getting, four-place coupe that the company could show to the press and public in the same way that GM, Ford and Chrysler were doing. Loewy passed the assignment along to Bourke, gave him free rein to make preliminary designs and then left for Europe.

Loewy had some 40 people working in South Bend at that time, 10 of them designers. The studio was already behind schedule doing production cars and trucks, but Bourke put four designers on the showcar project and also made sketches and scale models himself. Proposals soon went from 1/4-scale models to full-sized clays. Bourke wrote later in *Automobile Quarterly* that his workload was so heavy that 14-hour days and seven-day weeks were common; that he and his people sometimes put in three continuous days at a time with no sleep at all.

Harold Vance took an unusual interest in the show coupe's development and would drop by regularly in the evening to check progress. Bourke felt that Vance showed an inordinate fascination with this project. Vance had never come through Bourke's area before without Loewy himself being there. At one point, Vance started telling Bourke to "watch the costs," and that gave Bourke another jolt. He asked himself, "Why?" The request didn't make sense since the coupe would never see production. It was strictly for show. Wasn't it?

As the full-sized clay developed, Bourke worked on the driver's side along with modelers John Lutz and John Bird while Bob Koto did a competing design on the passenger's side, aided by modelers Hugh Bush and Don Hein. When Loewy came back from Europe, he reviewed both sides and chose Bourke's for further development.

As Bourke came to work one morning soon afterward, a security guard happened to mention that the night before Harold Vance had come through with some of Studebaker's board members. Vance had shown them the coupe. A few days later, Vance and several board members came through again and, at that point, the word was out. The coupe would indeed go into production. It arrived for 1953 looking much more graceful, low and elegant than most of that year's showcars. From that year onward, it's been known as the "Loewy coupe."

Bourke gave credit for the Loewy coupe's 56.5-inch overall height to engineer Eugene Hardig. Hardig not only managed to keep the cowl extremely low but reworked the carburetor and air-cleaner to get enough hood clearance. The down-thrusting headlights and nose plus the canted tail lamps, said Bourke, were inspired by the Lockheed Constellation airliner. The greenhouse faired up from the cowl into the windshield and then swept down again from the wraparound backlight onto a low, gently rounded rear deck. The trailing edge of the decklid cascaded down into the bumper in an almost unbroken flow. His original intent with the

Bob Bourke's masterpiece, and certainly one of Loewy's, too, had to be the 1953 Starliner hardtop (above). This coupe's low silhouette, beautiful shape and restrained use of ornamentation shocked the industry. The "Loewy coupe," as it's been called ever since, later appeared in many forms, among them the 1956 Golden Hawk (right), a facelift by Bourke, and the 1962 GT Hawk by Brooks Stevens.

tail-light housings and bumper was to make them one single piece, all shaped as continuations of the body sheetmetal. This would have made the tail lamp bezels part of the bumper—a proposition too costly for Studebaker to accept. The tail-lamp bezels eventually became separate chrome-plated diecastings.

It wasn't just the Loewy coupe's shape, proportions and clean lines that made it such a delight to the eye. The wheelcovers were of equal artistry: simple, conical, silver discs with a three-inch anodized gold dimple in the middle and short, tri-star arms radiating out from the dimple. Mercedes forced Studebaker to drop the tri-star motif after 1953. The rear fenders—and only the rear fenders—had very subtle stainless trim along their top edges, this to hide a seam. The grille consisted of twin nostrils filled with simple horizontal chrome bars. Emblems that distinguished V-8 from six-cylinder models stood on the hood, decklid and just behind the doors. Everything was understated but, at the same time, very powerful.

Vance and others wanted the 1953 Studebaker sedans designed along the same theme as the coupe. But the coupe simply didn't translate into a graceful sedan. The 1953 Studebaker sedan stood taller and came out looking angular and dumpy. It totally lacked the coupe's subtlety. Those two basic shells—the 120.5-inch-wheelbase coupe/Land Cruiser and a shorter, 116.5-inch sedan/wagon—served Studebaker, sometimes with minor and sometimes with major facelifts, until the bitter end in 1966.

Soon after Packard bought Studebaker in 1954, James J. Nance and his new regime brought in their own stylists. It was rumored that Studebaker-Packard had to pay Loewy $1 million to buy out his consultancy contract. Nance hired William M. Schmidt as vice president of Studebaker-Packard styling, and Schmidt named Duncan McRae to the post of chief stylist for Studebaker in South Bend and Richard A. Teague as head of Packard's design department in Detroit.

All 1955 Studebakers were still facelifted by Loewy's South Bend group under Bob Bourke. The 1955s got a big, chrome-dipped front end because someone high up in Studebaker's sales department believed Buick's success was due in part to its dazzling chrome grille and wanted the 1955s to match it in sparkle. For 1956, Bourke transformed the coupe into that year's much more pleasing Hawk series, with a front-end ensemble consisting of a nearly upright, diecast grille, a tall hood and tiny fender-mounted parking lamps reminiscent of the classic era. Independent designer Brooks Stevens restyled the coupe one

more time for 1962. That year's Gran Turismo Hawks had a squared, Thunderbird-inspired roof, no fins and updated detailing.

According to Dick Stout—and also Don MacDonald writing in *True* magazine—the 1956 Studebaker sedans were designed by Vince Gardner in a warehouse in Mt. Clemens, Michigan. Gardner's proposal in clay over a steel sedan bodyshell was trucked to Loewy's studio in Studebaker's Chippewa plant, where a big meeting took place. "Nance and other Packard brass in one group," recalled Stout, "Loewy's people in another, Packard product planners (including me) huddle in another area. Lots of growling, speaking, glaring, etc., etc. Finally the Loewy group did a minor grille change, and then on into production!"

Studebaker-Packard was in deep financial trouble, and things only got worse. Nance resigned along with Hoffman and Vance, whereupon longtime Studebaker engineer Harold Churchill became president. Churchill was a fine engineer and a good businessman; he knew the industry and essentially saw S-P through that critical 1956-59 period.

One of the first things Churchill did was to order a crash program to redesign and redirect Studebaker's 1953-derived sedans and wagons. He wanted more compact, more affordable bread-and-butter cars, and the job of styling them fell to Duncan McRae, assisted by Virgil Exner Jr. and Bill Bonner. McRae, Exner and Bonner, in 10 short months, transformed the 1953 sedan platform into the 1959 Studebaker Lark series. The Lark became tremendously successful during its first year, earning the company a

$28.5 million profit. By 1960, though, the Big Three all came out with Lark-sized compacts, and that essentially sealed Studebaker's fate. The Lark went through a number of facelifts, the most technically interesting being the 1963 Wagonaire, whose rear roof section pushed forward to carry young trees and other bulky, upright objects. Brooks Stevens designed the Wagonaire's sliding roof, basing it on a similar job he'd done for Olin Aluminum—the Scimitar wagon displayed at the Geneva auto show in 1959.

In Feb. 1961, the Studebaker-Packard board released Churchill and named a new Studebaker president: Sherwood Egbert. Egbert came from McCulloch Motors in California, makers of chainsaws and superchargers. He was 41 years old, charismatic, full of energy, an avid pilot and auto enthusiast.

Early in Egbert's presidency, Randy Faurot, a member of Duncan McRae's staff, unveiled a design presentation for the 1962 Studebaker. Faurot's full-sized mockups were made of fiberglass, and due to the South Bend summer heat and poor lamination, the fiberglass models had warped and buckled. It was difficult for Egbert to "read" what Faurot had in mind.

So Egbert phoned Raymond Loewy and asked him to fly out to South Bend and give his opinion of Faurot's fiberglass models. Studebaker had already spent $3-$4 million on them and didn't want to simply abandon them. Loewy came out to South Bend, bringing along John W. Ebstein from his New York office. Loewy

Studebaker design consultant Brooks Stevens also suggested the sliding rear roof on the 1963 Wagonaire. His idea was to allow the hauling of young trees and other upright cargo.

and Ebstein looked at Faurot's warped fiberglass mockups and told Egbert to forget them. Warped or not, they'd never sell.

Egbert and Loewy went to dinner that evening, and Egbert said that he felt what the company really needed was a more sophisticated sport coupe than the Hawk, something modern in imagery to bring in younger buyers—a halo car to draw people into Studebaker showrooms.

Studebaker dealers had started selling Mercedes-Benz cars in mid 1957, because Mercedes didn't want to set up a totally new distributor network. The arrangement called for Studebaker to distribute Mercedes in exchange for the rights to Mercedes-Benz's technical patents. As it turned out, the only patent Studebaker used was a door latch on the Avanti, but Mercedes inherited some Studebaker dealers after 1966.

In 1961, Egbert reasoned that a stylish coupe would fit nicely between the plebeian Studebaker and the aristocratic Mercedes. Loewy, who'd already styled and built half a dozen personal luxury coupes for his own use, assured Egbert that he could design just such a car for Studebaker. They discussed terms, Egbert okayed a contract and everything seemed set. The only problem was the deadline. Loewy's finished designs would have to be in South Bend in 40 days!

Loewy immediately flew to his home in Palm Springs and phoned his longtime friend and assistant, John Ebstein in New

York, asking Ebstein to join him. Ebstein, born in northern Germany in 1912, had studied architecture in Stuttgart and fled Hitler on his motorcycle in 1933. He went first to Paris and then to Prague, where he finished his degree. When the Nazis marched into Czechoslovakia, Ebstein fled again, this time to the U.S. and got a job in 1938 with Loewy as a photographer and airbrush artist. When Loewy made presentations to the Pennsylvania Railroad, Ebstein would photograph an existing locomotive and then airbrush one side of the picture to show how Loewy would redesign it. Ebstein had remarkable talents in any number of areas and soon became one of Loewy's top aides.

"When I got there [to Palm Springs]," said Ebstein, "Mr. Loewy told me he had just hired a young student out of the Art Center by the name of Tom Kellogg. He was very impressed with Kellogg. And he asked me who else to get. I suggested Bob Andrews, who'd been in and out of the Loewy organization so many times before. We all got together in Palm Springs, and Loewy leased a house there. We didn't want to do the work in his private home."

Actually Kellogg, then 27, had graduated from Art Center five years earlier and was working for a boat-design firm in Newport Beach, California. He'd slept late one Saturday morning when the phone rang. It was Raymond Loewy asking whether Kellogg might be interested in helping design a sports car for Studebaker. In his haze, Kellogg thought someone was putting him on and hung up. Loewy called him back and finally convinced Kellogg the call was genuine.

Loewy had been given Kellogg's name along with four other candidates by George Jergenson, head of Art Center's transportation design department. Loewy now asked Kellogg to drive out to Palm Springs that same day. When Kellogg rang Loewy's doorbell, all nervous and knowing he wouldn't get the job, Loewy answered and invited him in. Loewy immediately apologized, because he'd forgotten that he'd agreed to judge a local concours, and he had to leave immediately to do that. Did Kellogg want to come? Tom tagged along and watched Loewy throughout the judging.

After they returned to Loewy's home, Loewy talked with Kellogg at some length, admired his portfolio, liked him personally and couldn't help noticing a nervous eagerness. Kellogg said in a recent interview that he'd idolized Loewy for years and that that day seemed to unfold like a dream. He still knew, though, that he wouldn't get the job, and he was absolutely sure after Loewy showed him to the door. As Kellogg walked slowly down the driveway toward his car, he heard the door reopen behind him, and Loewy called his name. "Could you come back to Palm Springs on Monday morning?" asked Loewy. "We're on a very tight deadline."

That Monday, Mar. 20, two weeks before Easter, 1961, Loewy, Kellogg, Ebstein and Andrews went to the leased house on the outskirts of Palm Springs. Once inside, Kellogg noticed that Loewy had taped a picture of a 1961 Lincoln Continental to one wall. Loewy said he liked the Continental's thin-bladed fenders. He also had a picture of an E-Type Jaguar plus a rough sketch—done by Loewy himself—that in plan view showed an idealized, pinched, wasp-waisted "Coke-bottle" body shape. "And this is what we went by," said John Ebstein. "We sat and drew. Bob Andrews started a little clay model, and Tom Kellogg made beautiful sketches...."

Loewy had also posted rough drawings of the hard points of the proposed Studebaker sports car. Kellogg requested that Loewy add photos of some of his recent personal cars: his customized Jaguar, BMW and Lancia. "Then Loewy explained about Egbert," recalled Kellogg, "what kind of person he was: a California guy, real aggressive, young, with lots of energy, a pilot." Andrews had met Egbert earlier and the two had talked about airplanes. Egbert, said Loewy, liked the Jaguar and wanted, as Kellogg put it, "...something kind of California-ish; tail up in the air." Loewy told them to imagine the car on posh Palmdale Boulevard in Palm Springs.

Bob Andrews, who was also an avid aviator, said he imagined

Loewy's other automotive masterpiece was the 1963 Avanti, Studebaker's answer to the Corvette. Some inspiration for the body shape came from Loewy's Lancia coupe (below). Design team in Palm Springs consisted of (L-R) John Ebstein, Loewy, Bob Andrews and Tom Kellogg, shown here with the first model delivered to South Bend.

the typical Avanti owner to be a young airline pilot who appreciated performance and style. Loewy made Ebstein, in effect, his studio chief, his design interpreter, and Ebstein watched and guided the two designers when Loewy wasn't there. Loewy dropped by regularly, however, and did a lot of the directing himself.

"I sat next to the fireplace," Kellogg remembered, "at this little, tiny, ridiculous desk. Bob [Andrews] was working on the counter near the sink. He had a bunch of chunky little clay bits, and John [Ebstein] just kind of oversaw us. So Bob came up with some sketches and I came up with some sketches, and John encouraged us. But each one of us was trying to pull in a different direction at first. Bob had a preconception and wanted to make the car a two-seater. I had a preconception and wanted to make it a four-seater. And Loewy had his preconceptions, too. So we had to put it all together. I was pushing more in the direction of his BMW coupe. Something about the roundness of the rear I liked. Bob had kind of a more downward-sloping rear end, like the 1953 Studebaker and more Ferrari, more traditional."

After two weeks of intensive work and very little sleep, Easter arrived, and Loewy gave the two designers a three-day break. He flew to South Bend with the two concept models, showed them to Egbert, and Egbert approved the four-passenger theme.

After Loewy's 3-man crew made the 40-day deadline, French coachbuilder Pichon et Parat constructed two running metal prototypes (above left) with one door on one side and two on the other. Proportions and detailing weren't right and, after Avanti coupe finally came out (above), Kellogg was asked to do a 4-door clay based on coupe.

Brooks Stevens designs for Studebaker assumed the company could live past 1966. These prototypes, built by Sibona & Basano in Italy on Lark chassis, still exist. Futuristic coupe at left had a light bar beneath fluted leading edge of hood.

Meanwhile, Easter vacation brought an invasion of pretty, bikini-clad high-school and college coeds into Palm Springs, "...and since we'd have to go downtown to eat, we'd see these girls," said Kellogg, "and we'd come back to our boards in rather a stimulated state. I'm sure the sensuality of the car was intensified by our trips to downtown Palm Springs during that Easter week."

Most of their early designs had conventional grilles, but Loewy urged Andrews and Kellogg to eliminate the grille altogether and add a chin scoop—like the Citroen's—beneath the thin, clean front bumper. The final model and sketches took another two weeks to finish, and by the time they went back to South Bend with Loewy, the design looked very much like the Avanti finally came out: high haunch, Coke-bottle waist with a horizontal bone, thin-bladed front fenders slightly taller than the hood, no grille, an off-center speed ramp running up the hood, the roof and door borrowed from Loewy's BMW/Lancia design, the round rear likewise, and wheelcovers derived from the 1953 Studebaker but with a starfish pattern over a brushed inner cap. It was all of a piece, totally non-derivative.

The full-sized clay was made in South Bend under Loewy and Bob Doehler's direction. Andrews later said he was heartened to hear that the Avanti's first customer was an airline pilot. Soon after the Avanti came out, plagued as it was with production problems, Egbert commissioned Loewy to design an entire line of 1964 Studebakers around the Avanti theme. This time, Andrews and Kellogg worked in Loewy's New York office. Together, they designed an Avanti four-door sedan, a convertible and a station wagon. Loewy then sent Ebstein and Andrews to Paris, where they finished up the designs.

Ebstein later oversaw the construction of two metal-bodied, running Avanti sedan prototypes. These were fabricated by the French coachbuilder Pichon et Parat. Pichon et Parat had earlier made the body for Loewy's personal BMW coupe. Both prototypes—a fastback and a notchback—had two doors on one side and one door on the other. They were shipped to South Bend and driven on Studebaker's test track, but Egbert felt that neither proposal looked quite right, so Loewy brought Kellogg to South Bend and had him develop several full-sized Avanti clay models of the other body styles. This ultimately led to an unmounted fiberglass Avanti sedan body, again with two doors on one side and one on the other. The two metal-bodied prototypes ended up stored in the former Avanti plant in Youngstown, Ohio. No one seems to know the fate of the fiberglass body. Studebaker was in no financial condition to take advantage of any of these Avanti design proposals.

According to Studebaker historian Fred Fox, Egbert commissioned Milwaukee industrial designer Brooks Stevens to facelift the 1962-64 Larks. An independent industrial design firm, Marcks, Hazelquist and Powers of Dearborn, Michigan, did the 1966 Lark. Stevens, meanwhile, styled and built three 1964-67 Studebaker prototypes based on the Lark. Stevens had these cars—a coupe, a sedan and a wagon—handcrafted from steel by Carrozzeria Sibona & Basano in Italy, and they all still survive, housed at Stevens' private museum in Mequon, Wisconsin (see page 248). Both Stevens' and Loewy's ideas came to naught when Studebaker sales collapsed in 1963.

In 1963, Sherwood Egbert resigned due to poor health. Studebaker shut its South Bend plant that December and produced cars only at its Hamilton, Ontario assembly facility. Passenger-car production ended there in 1966, but rights to the Avanti passed through a number of private companies which produced various versions of the car in limited numbers from 1966 through 1991. Sherwood Egbert died of cancer on July 31, 1969, aged 49. ◆

PACKARD MOTOR CAR CO.

For most of its life, Packard cashed in on two wonderful, long-standing identity symbols: the ox-yoke radiator shell and the red hexagon on the hubcaps. The ox-yoke radiator arrived with Packard's Model L in 1904. Engineer/race driver Charles Schmidt copied the radiator conformation from the French Mors, a car-maker he worked and raced for before joining Packard.

The Packard hex began with the 1906 Model S. Owners needed a big Allen wrench to twist the hubcaps on and off. From 1906 to 1912, the sunken hexes in the hubcaps were painted black. In 1913, for reasons unknown, Packard switched to red paint. And in 1940, when the company "improved" the red-hex hubcap by superimposing the word "Packard" over it in script, so many owners protested that Packard backed down. Both identity symbols—the ox-yoke grille and the hex—stayed intact to Packard's very end.

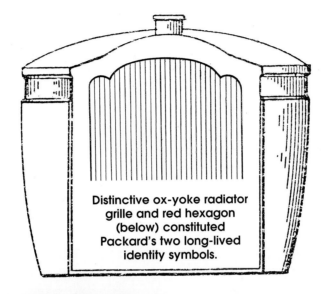

Distinctive ox-yoke radiator grille and red hexagon (below) constituted Packard's two long-lived identity symbols.

As with most automakers, early factory bodies were designed mostly by company engineers with the help of body suppliers. Vincent D. Kaptur Sr., who arrived at Packard in autumn 1916, stated in a 1980 interview: "All the designing was done by the engineering department. They elected a bodyman, who was really supposed to have done that kind of work [styling]."

Packard established a design format around 1910 that left no question about the car's identity. The radiator shape and hex, along with a decidedly massive, substantial look (as opposed to the Ford Model T's light, spindly look), became instantly recognizable. Clever advertising, developed by Ralph Estep, capitalized on those strengths, and soon any child could tell a Packard from several blocks away. The company slogan, "Ask the man who owns one," reinforced Packard's status, and this became one of the few U.S. makes whose early prestige and mystique rivaled the big imports.

Within its styling format, Packard offered a staggering number of different body styles; perhaps as many as 100 just before WW-I. Even as late as 1931, Packard listed 81 individual body choices in its dealer information booklet. Some of these designs weren't built, but Packard did offer them.

Vince Kaptur, who later became a body engineer at General Motors, reported that Packard was already using scale clay models in 1916. The modelers were actually woodworkers who'd been shown how to develop body surfaces. Scale clay models often served the function of demonstrating and "selling" body-engineering proposals to management.

Although Packard, like Ford, tried hard to keep all manufacturing in-house, the making of car bodies was mostly done outside. Both before and after World War I, many of Packard's "factory" bodies were built by independent suppliers, among them

C.R. Wilson, Briggs, Towson, Pullman, Buffalo and Anderson. Soon after the Great War, coachbuilders started offering custom bodies on the Packard chassis, and since Packard could sell an unbodied car for 80% of the price of a finished one, it didn't mind doing so. (All bare chassis traditionally consisted of frame, axles, running gear, radiator with shell, hood, cowl, fenders, running-boards and lamps.) Brewster and Fleetwood built quite a few early custom Packards, followed in the 1920s by Judkins, Holbrook and LeBaron.

Col. Jesse Vincent, Packard's engineering vice president since 1915, took a profound interest in styling, as did his first chief engineer, O.E. Hunt. In May 1917, Packard named Archer L. Knapp chief draftsman of the "body art department." His title alone implied that "art" played a role in bodymaking. Knapp's area, probably physically within experimental engineering, was where Packard's factory bodies were laid out and transformed from two dimensions into scale clay models, then full-sized clay over wood-slat armatures and ultimately into wood-and-metal prototypes. Knapp, as head of Packard's body art department, reported to L. Clayton (Clayt) Hill, who later became an executive with Murray.

In 1925, Knapp was given a new title: body engineer. According to author C.A. Leslie Jr., writing in *Packard, a History of the Motor Car and the Company,* Packard had no creative stylists during those years and often copied the ideas of various coachbuilders, adapting their designs to mass production. It's not known whether Packard, like Edsel Ford, paid the coachbuilders for these ideas.

Ray Dietrich had come to Detroit in 1925, had set up Dietrich Inc. as part of the Murray Corp. of America (see page 52) and subsequently impressed Packard president Alvan Macauley by building and selling a number of very handsome coachbuilt Packards. Macauley was not a man easily moved, but he sized up young

1908 Packard runabout used flexible isenglass curtains for windshield.

Today, 1921-22 Packard enclosed-drive limousine (left) seems no less upright than early Lincolns. By 1927, Packard 8 (below) ads pushed new nitrocellulose lacquer colors.

Dietrich and decided, in late 1925, to offer him a consultancy. Dietrich, who held or would soon hold similar consultancies with Lincoln, Studebaker, Franklin and Dodge, accepted and became Packard's official "body critic."

Beyond just critiquing bodies, though, Dietrich actually became one of Packard's outside stylists from roughly 1926 through part of 1931. The way he designed bodies during that period was to first create and produce them as coachbuilt customs. After that, he allowed Packard's body engineers to take whatever styling ideas they wanted and adapt them for production. By 1926, Packard was building most of its own factory bodies, with only two styles supplied by an outsider, in this case Briggs.

When Ray Dietrich left LeBaron in 1925 to set up Dietrich Inc., he initially hoped that master illustrator Roland Stickney would come with him to Detroit. Stickney, though, refused to leave New York, so Dietrich offered the job to a younger but equally gifted former LeBaron illustrator named Werner Gubitz. Gubitz would go on to become perhaps the greatest of all Packard designers, but he's rarely been credited as such. For now he accepted Dietrich's offer and moved to Detroit.

Gubitz stayed with Dietrich Inc. for just a short while. It's likely that in working with Dietrich, Gubitz helped design at least a few coachbuilt Packards, although we have no real record. In any case, Gubitz soon left Dietrich and moved briefly to Cleveland before returning to Detroit in 1927 to take a job with Packard.

Packard still didn't have an actual styling section, but Gubitz was brought in as an illustrator by Vince Kaptur, who by that time held the title "chief body designer." When Kaptur left for General Motors in Aug. 1928, Packard engineering handed Gubitz more design responsibility for its factory bodies. During this period, then, Gubitz and Dietrich worked together, Dietrich designing and producing coachbuilt customs and Gubitz incorporating ideas from those cars into production.

The Packard 645 DeLuxe Eight of 1929 was styled largely by Dietrich, and Gubitz used Dietrich themes for a number of different factory bodies; for example, all closed cars through the Ninth series (1932), individual coachbuilt bodies through the Tenth (1933) and open styles through the Eleventh series (1934). In

addition, LeBaron (now part of Briggs) took inspiration from the 645 for its Tenth- and Eleventh-series towncars. So Packard capitalized on Dietrich's styling help in many ways.

Another use made of the Packard 645-series design involved adding slightly non-standard trim and minor styling touches, applying a body tag that said either "Dietrich Inc." or "Custom Made by Packard" and marketing those cars at a premium. The emblems and modifications allowed Packard to charge $2000 or more above the price of a standard production 645. Leslie called these cars "pseudo customs" and wrote, "Thus, by the use of a professional stylist, hanging on a few accessories and adding a 'custom' body plate, Packard was able to get twice as much for the 645 as it could for the 633, and fifty percent above the price of a 640. That was a very nice markup."

Sheetmetal stampings and wooden framing for bodies that Packard merchandised with "Dietrich Inc." tags were supplied mostly by Packard to Murray, not the other way around. Packard often sent fully assembled bodies-in-white to Murray or Dietrich Inc., whose craftsmen then painted and trimmed them, mounted the bodies on chassis and made all the final panel adjustments.

By the Seventh series (1930), Dietrich's coachbuilt cars laid down the styles for all factory bodies as well as those that carried the "Custom Made by Packard" emblem. The Seventh series, specifically the 1930 Model 745, also introduced the Packard hood spear to factory-built production cars. The famous spear, which came to be as recognized a Packard symbol as the red hex and grille shape, originated on Hibbard & Darrin coachbuilt customs. H&D allowed Packard to use the spear, and the company applied it to all 1932 and later models (see page 48). Packard added a sporty 734 speedster and simply took production bodies off the assembly line and turned them over to what now was, in effect, the company's own custom body department. There they were upgraded so they could wear the "Custom Made by Packard" label. In-house fabrication of the factory's custom bodies came under Packard engineering, not manufacturing, and everything—the stamping of sheetmetal as well as the framing of wood—all ended up in one Packard building, not at Murray nor at Dietrich Inc.

Meanwhile at Murray in late 1929, economics and politics con-

Americans viewed 1930 Packard towncar (below) in a league with Springfield Rolls-Royce and the big imports. The 1931 roadster at right was the last to use a flat grille.

spired to make life difficult for Ray Dietrich. After Briggs and Murray held their secret talks aimed at a merger, Edsel Ford put Clarence Avery into Murray's presidency (see page 30), and Avery promptly named Clayt Hill as vice president and general manager of Dietrich Inc. Neither Avery nor Hill had much liking for Ray Dietrich, and by 1931 they'd maneuvered him out of the company.

But not before Dietrich had a chance to style the classic coach-built Packards of the early Depression. One such car—a custom that showed Dietrich's intentions for future production Packards—was the 845-series 1931 sport sedan made specifically for Alvan Macauley. This was a close-coupled four-door with a victoria-like bustle. It had no window reveals, no visor, a low, raked windshield and chromed Woodlites: classically elegant but in no way stodgy. Again, Packard carried cues from this car over into its Tenth and Eleventh series.

With the Eighth series came the Depression, and Packard dropped all independent coachbuilders from its catalogue—all but

Werner Gubitz

Werner Hans August Gubitz was born in Hamburg, Germany on July 29, 1899. In 1905, he and his parents came to this country, and his father took a job with the Venus Pencil Co. in Jersey City, New Jersey.

As a teenager, Gubitz loved automobiles and showed great flair as a graphic artist. In 1919, he approached Fleetwood's Ernst Schebera in New York and asked for a job. Schebera hired Gubitz as a delineator. According to Gubitz's longtime friend, designer and design historian W. Everett Miller, young Gubitz soon moved to LeBaron Carrossiers, where he worked for Ray Dietrich and Tom Hibbard. He left LeBaron in 1922 to join J. Frank deCausse. DeCausse had just lost his Locomobile account, hadn't yet picked up Franklin and was designing custom bodies for east-coast coachbuilders on the same basis as LeBaron. Gubitz also entered MIT, class of 1924, but didn't graduate.

When Murray Corp. of America set up Dietrich Inc. in 1925, Ray Dietrich asked Gubitz to join him in Detroit as an illustrator/designer. Gubitz stayed with Dietrich for a short time, then moved to Cleveland to work first for Peerless and then for the Ohio Body & Blower Co. Among Ohio Body's customers were Moon, Jordan and Gardner.

Cleveland automakers weren't doing at all well, so Gubitz left the design business to open a restaurant. He and his wife, Lillian, poured not only their hearts but their life savings into the venture, all to no avail. Everett Miller recalled Gubitz telling him that the only thing he and Lillian saved from the restaurant was a glass juice squeezer.

So it was with considerable relief that, in 1927, Werner Gubitz found a job back in Detroit, first with Dietrich and then with Packard. Packard had no real styling department at that time, but his new boss, Vincent D. Kaptur Sr., asked Gubitz to make scale side-view renderings of all of Packard's production bodies. Gubitz used that very tight, wonderfully detailed style that Roland Stickney had brought to LeBaron.

At Packard, Gubitz shared a large office with two engineers, this on the fourth floor of the company's headquarters on East Grand Boulevard. According to Miller, Gubitz often worked far into the night, long after everyone else had gone home. He made these meticulous sketches, some of them in 3/4 scale but most smaller than that.

And he soon developed a way of creating perhaps six to eight sketches at once by drawing in one component at a time. He would first outline the body in pencil, then start painting in the details in groups: all the tires at one sitting, then all the brightwork, followed perhaps by brilliant renderings of textured convertible canvas tops and highlighted sheetmetal. He would do the reflections and shadows together, too. Undercarriages were done in muted colors, and then he would turn his attention to doing perfect lettering on the hubcaps and

representing every nut and bolt exactly where it was in real life. His drawings would all be finished together, as a set.

Kaptur left for General Motors in Aug. 1928, and from that time on Gubitz gradually took on more actual design responsibility. He transposed some of Ray Dietrich's custom design ideas into Packard's production bodies and, after Dietrich left Murray, Werner Gubitz effectively became Packard's chief stylist, although he didn't have that title. He at first shared some of his stylistic duties with airbrush artist F.W. Walker. Young W.E. Miller arrived at Packard as a designer in Feb. 1929. Miller commented that for some time after he got there, he and Gubitz were Packard's sole in-house stylists. Gubitz now reported to chief body engineer Archer Knapp and would style all the production bodies. Miller designed "custom" Packard bodies for the company's captive coachbuilding department under sales manager Horace Potter.

In 1932, Packard announced the establishment of a formal styling section, and company president Alvan Macauley named his son, Edward, to head it. Ed Macauley began hiring a few additional designers, among them Count Alexis de Sakhnoffsky, Howard F. Yeager, Harold J. Gottlieb and Lynn Mosher. Mosher had previous experience with Derham and Gottlieb with Fleetwood.

Ed Macauley was more a design manager than a designer, and Gubitz did most of Packard's actual styling throughout the classic period. Gubitz gave Packard not only the unmistakable grace of its 1930s designs but also the all-important styling continuity it enjoyed during those years. All factory-bodied senior Packards—particularly the large, classic, closed body styles—had an elegance and an awe-inspiring, cathedral-like aura that no other automaker began to match. Cadillac and Lincoln formal sedans and limousines seemed amateurish alongside Gubitz's wonderfully understated Packard Super Eights and V-12s.

Throughout his life, Werner Gubitz was quiet and almost shy. He stood about five-seven, had a medium build, was liked by everyone who worked with him, and it's not known why he left Packard at so early an age. He was only 48 when he retired.

Everett Miller and his wife remained close personal friends of the Gubitzes throughout their lives. When Gubitz left Packard, the Millers talked Werner and Lillian into coming to California. Werner Gubitz had long been a camera buff, an excellent movie and still photographer, and he also enjoyed carpentry, cabinetmaking and modelbuilding. When the Gubitzes moved to Palm Desert in 1947, Werner designed a number of houses for their property and modeled them all in scale. Local architects and homebuilders heard about his skill and asked Gubitz to make house models for them, too. He eventually constructed an entire miniature city in his home, complete with houses, factories, stores, streetcars, railroads and an oil refinery. Werner Gubitz passed away on Sept. 27, 1971. ◆

Dietrich Inc. Dietrich Inc. was now Packard's house label. Other coachbuilders like LeBaron, Holbrook, Locke, Rollston, Judkins, Derham, Waterhouse and Murphy continued to offer custom Packard bodies but without factory backing or promotion in company catalogues. And why this sudden change of policy? Because the Depression slowed Packard sales to such an extent that the company wanted coachbuilding profits for itself. Packard also needed the volume to keep its recently created custom facilities going.

And then came 1932, the year Packard introduced not one but two important new car lines: the ultra luxurious V-12 at the top of the prestige market and the very sporty and, unfortunately, underpriced Light Eight at the bottom. Packard's

Packard launched a new V-12 for 1932. Golfer Gene Sarazen took the keys to his impressive Model 906 Dietrich dual-cowl phaeton from no less than Alvan Macauley (above). Clark Gable also seemed justifiably pleased with his 1932 coupe roadster. And how about that little '32 Ford V-8 cabriolet in the background?

outlay for tooling and manufacturing facilities had to be enormous that year.

The 1932 senior Packards looked more massive and handsome than ever and marked what many collectors now consider the epitome of Packard styling. The Ninth series V-12 brought with it the veed radiator shell, veed ox-yoke headlamps and massive barrel-like bumper ends. The bumper ends contained spring-loaded weights suspended in oil. The weights oscillated up and down to counter road vibrations.

And the 1932 Packard Light Eight, or 900, became the company's attempt to compete with Buick—not that Buick was doing that well either. The basic idea was good. Packard did need a less expensive model, because the Depression had put the sale of its senior lines into freefall. Yet the Light Eight, despite its successful engineering and styling, ran into three problems.

First, it cost too much to produce: roughly the same as the higher priced Standard Eight. Second, most Light Eight body types looked a tad too sporty and youthful to appeal to the typically mature Packard buyer. The 900's grille was unmistakably Packard, but it was wider than usual and had a forward scoop at the bottom: "shovel-nose" some people called it. Packard later polled dealers and found that many customers objected to the Light Eight's shovel nose. A few Light Eight body styles were

downright rakish—the roadster, for one, and a handsome coupe-sedan. These might have been all right as coachbuilt customs for owners who wanted to stand out from the crowd, but they were a little too flip for conservative Packard buyers. And third, owners of senior models felt the Light Eight's low price compromised the Packard name and image.

So the year 1932, despite all of Packard's investment and planning, saw only 9010 cars go out the door, and the automaker lost money on every one. Of that total, the majority were Light Eights: 6622. Cadillac and Lincoln, by the way, were in similar straits, and Pierce-Arrow would soon go out of the automobile business altogether. For 1933, Packard put its traditional shuttered vee grille on the Light Eight and rebadged it the "Standard Eight."

In January of 1932, Alvan Macauley named his son, Edward, to manage Packard's newly created styling section. Ed Macauley was not a designer, had no art training, couldn't sketch or model clay and, if he hadn't been Alvan's son, would never have gotten the job. Ed, who was 30 when he became Packard's director of styling, kept that title until his retirement in 1955.

Ray Dietrich had been forced out of Murray in 1931, so Packard would henceforth rely on Ed Macauley, Werner Gubitz, W.E. Miller and an always-small staff of in-house designers plus outside consultants to style future models. Why Alvan Macauley did not hire Ray Dietrich poses a question. He did offer the job to

In addition to the V-12, Packard introduced the Light Eight in 1932 to entice more Depression buyers. The Light Eight failed, however, because it cost a lot to build and perhaps looked too sporty for Packard traditionalists.

"Car of the Dome" sport sedan (above) became Packard's featured model at the 1933 Century of Progress. Rear-mount-

ed spare left fenders clear to emphasize hood length. Sakhnoffsky sketched 1933-34 LeBaron phaeton above.

Count Alexis de Sakhnoffsky in 1930, but at that time Sakhnoffsky was committed to the Hayes Body Co. However, one month after Ed Macauley became Packard's styling director, Sakhnoffsky did come in as a freelance "consulting art director." Sakhnoffsky simultaneously held similar assignments with Studebaker and Hayes. He spent three days a week at Packard and received $800 a month in return. It was during this period that W.E. Miller showed Sakhnoffsky the magic of colored wax pencil on Canson or Mi-Teintes paper.

Macauley, despite what's been said and written about him, was not an inept or ineffectual styling administrator. Packard might have done better, but it surely could have done worse. When Sakhnoffsky arrived, Macauley assigned him the task of coordinating and modernizing the designs of

Fender valances and chromed wire wheels grace 1934 Packard V-12 sport phaeton. Bumper ends contained suspended weights inside hydraulic cylinders to damp vibrations.

Packard's senior models. The count's consultancy lasted about a year, during which time Packard added front-fender valances and developed an extended hood and hidden cowl much like those of the 1930 Jordan Speedway and 1932 Chrysler Imperial.

leagues in the auto-design business, Ed Macauley commissioned three specials for his own personal use. The first was a boattail speedster, the second started as a Darrin-like 1941 One Eighty convertible, and the third was a 1951 Packard club sedan redone as a long-deck, two-place coupe. The first two became rolling expressions of Macauley's ever-changing tastes in style and did influence production design to some extent, just as Harley Earl's Y-Job affected Buick and GM cars. Macauley's 1951 coupe, though, left no mark at all.

Ed Macauley bought his speedster in 1932 and began to restyle it immediately. The car was a used 1930 Packard 734 boattail, the retired factory test vehicle in which Col. Jesse Vincent once raced and beat a flying golf ball. Young Macauley simply started adding and changing things, hot-rod fashion. He replaced the original eight-cylinder engine with a new Packard V-12, adapted a later cowl, added a veed windshield and veed radiator shell. He installed a tachometer, vacuum gauge and aircraft altimeter. Then in 1933, he put on extend-

Factory-bodied 1934 Packard sport coupe looked remarkably like the 1934 Mercedes Autobahn Kurier. This Packard debuted at the New York Salon, the Mercedes at the Berlin Motor Show

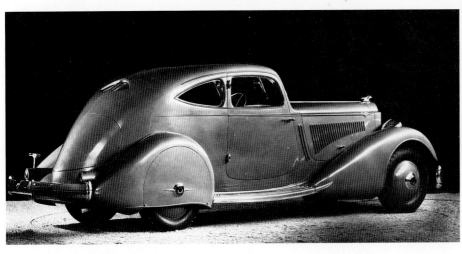

ed pontoon rear fenders and skirts along with full wheelcovers. Later he added pontoon front fenders and horizontal hood louvers. Generally, he just kept upgrading his speedster until it became quite a Detroit conversation piece. The actual modifications weren't done at Packard or even at Briggs but by the Prince Bros. bodyshop on Larned Ave. in Detroit.

One of the most memorable Packards to be done during Sakhnoffsky's consultancy was the so-called "Car of the Dome." This was a lovely five-window sedan, labeled a Dietrich custom, that Packard exhibited as the highest expression of automotive art and luxury under the dome in the 1933 Century of Progress travel and transportation building. Who actually styled the Car of the Dome isn't known; possibly Dietrich before he left Murray; possibly Sakhnoffsky.

Over the course of his styling career and like so many of his col-

The Macauley speedster did affect production design to some degree. Its rear pontoon fenders, for example, presaged those on Packard's 1935 Twelfth series cars. The front fender shapes saw production with the 1935 Packard One Twenty and the Sixteenth and Seventeenth series. The Macauley instrument panel also showed up in production on the Tenth series.

Ed Macauley's second personalized car also had some effect on production styling. "The Phantom," as he called it, began life as a

Ed Macauley's 1932 Packard speedster became a test bed for styling ideas. He was constantly updating it (inset). Several of his innovations turned up in production, like his gauge panel and pontoon fenders.

1941 factory-built Packard-Darrin. Macauley restyled the car with help from designer John Reinhart. Hess & Eisenhardt, the hearse manufacturer, did the actual modifications. Macauley had Hess & Eisenhardt replace the factory soft top with a deauville metal half roof and asked Reinhart to design a clear Plexiglas section over the front seat. Macauley changed the tint of this insert several times in an effort to soften the greenhouse effect.

In 1942, Macauley and Reinhart restyled the Phantom's tall 1941 Packard grille and hood, and Briggs fabricated what came to be known as the low "mouth-harp" grille and bullnose hood. Macauley eventually adapted this front-end theme to the 1948 Packard but in a more refined form. At one point Macauley had a V-12 installed in his Phantom. People around the plant called the Phantom the "Dog Car" and the "Brown Bomber," brown or golden tan being the colors Macauley preferred.

Packard's second attempt to produce a less expensive car, the 1935 One Twenty series, was considerably more successful than the 1932 Light Eight; so successful, in fact, that it kept Packard alive through the rest of the Depression. The One Twenty's styling was contemporary, restrained and very *Packard* but nothing remarkable; not in a league with Lincoln's savior, the Zephyr, nor Cadillac's LaSalle.

Much more remarkable was the styling continuity and the consistency that Werner Gubitz, under Ed Macauley, brought to all senior Packards during the mid to late 1930s. It's generally agreed today that Gubitz's sedans and limousines—those big, usually hulking body styles—showed much more grace and design sophistication than the chauffeured Cadillacs and Model K Lincolns of

Edward Macauley

Edward Rector Macauley was born on Aug. 29, 1902 in Dayton, Ohio, the youngest of three children. The Macauleys moved to Detroit when Ed was a young boy, and he attended the Detroit Country Day School and Lawrenceville Academy, a prep school. At Lawrenceville he tapped into the headmaster's electrical outlet so he could clandestinely listen to his radio. The headmaster was not amused, and Macauley was asked not to come back. He didn't graduate and never went to college.

His best friend was a flier in the Naval reserve, and Ed Macauley developed an early interest in aviation. On Sundays, when his parents thought he was in Sunday school, Ed would go down to the naval base on Grosse Isle, where his friend taught him how to fly. He was under age and never got a pilot's license, nor did he ever own a plane, but his lifelong fascination with aviation stayed with him.

Macauley also built his own motorcycle as a teenager, one that his father, Packard president Alvan Macauley, delighted in telling about. When Ed started the engine for the first time and let out the clutch, the motorcycle shot backwards through the garage wall. His father always chuckled when he told the story.

Ed's wild side made his father a little uneasy. Alvan Macauley was pleased with his son's mechanical aptitude and inventiveness but didn't know how to channel all that enthusiasm for airplanes, speedboats, fast cars and jazz. Ed played a hot jazz saxophone in a local four-man band. After

Ed was asked to leave Lawrenceville, Alvan wondered whether his son had the discipline to ever be a Packard executive.

Alvan Macauley would have been a hard act for any son to follow, and the old man probably realized that. He resolved, therefore, to have Ed learn all aspects of

the auto business. So in 1922—which was also the year Ed got married for the first time—Alvan Macauley put his youngest son to work as a car salesman at a Packard factory outlet on Grand Blvd. Ed took the streetcar to work because his father didn't want him to become elitist and also insisted that his son earn and save up the cash to

buy himself a new automobile.

Even before Ed Macauley became Packard's styling director in 1932, he'd gotten a reputation as a playboy. His eldest daughter, Estelle Macauley Ritter, feels that people probably got that notion because her father never really grew up; always had a bit of Peter Pan in him. He divorced in 1930, drove fast, flashy custom speedsters and convertibles, loved to hunt and fish and generally enjoyed himself during a time when the rest of the nation was wrestling with the Great Depression. Ed Macauley remarried in 1935.

His daughter remembers her father's wonderful sense of humor, his booming laugh and the fact that he knew everyone at the plant by name. He felt as comfortable talking to Packard's line workers as he did in meetings with company executives. The former Packard designers we interviewed and others who knew him all agreed that Ed Macauley was a warm, affable man. And while he didn't bring great depth or conviction to his work as Packard's styling director, Ed Macauley did take the job seriously and gave it his best.

He retired from Packard in 1955, aged 53, after James J. Nance set up a pension system that encouraged the old guard to leave. Macauley soon became fascinated with the prospect of importing the Volkswagen, but he died before he got the chance. Edward Macauley had been a heavy smoker all his life, had shoveled snow that afternoon, went to the yacht club, loaded up his plate with a buffet dinner, sat down and died. He was 56. Most of Packard's longtime workers and all of Detroit's automotive society attended the funeral. ◆

the same era. Packard kept its status by supporting its Super Eights and Twelves as the undisputed leaders of luxurious motoring, while the cash-cow One Twenty held off the economic wolves. In the eyes of America, Packard remained the mayor's car, the banker's car, the automobile that junior executives aspired to and dowagers owned until they died. Cadillac hadn't yet upstaged Packard and wouldn't until after World War II.

As war loomed, Packard management made a decision to abandon the upper luxury market and to concentrate on models with broader appeal. In 1937, Packard introduced a six-cylinder series whose prices began at $1075, less than the cost of a Nash Ambassador. For 1938, Packard dropped the Six to $888.

With equal significance, Packard discontinued its big, expensive, 12-cylinder senior lines after 1939 and replaced them with the narrow-grilled 1940 One Sixty and One Eighty Super Eights. The bodies of these now-top-of-the-line cars looked like larger versions of the One Twenty. Grilles and catwalks appeared to be identical. The identity crisis gave rise to the following one-sentence parable: *Coming home one afternoon, the estate owner met his off-duty gardener headed out the driveway, and they were both driving new Packards!*

Not only had Packard lost status by dropping its big, distinctive senior series but, in terms of styling, the company no longer had anything that adequately matched the contemporary Lincoln Zephyr and Cadillac 60-Special. Packard sales plummeted in recessive 1938, the year Cadillac introduced the 60-S and Zephyr put on its low, modern radiator grille. And the entire industry was soon aware that Cadillac would launch yet another styling blockbuster for 1941.

So in late 1938, Packard management called for a crash program to develop a totally new line—one that could compete in every way with the 1940-41 Lincoln Zephyr, 1941 Cadillac Series 61 and the 1941 Buick Roadmaster. Why was Buick on this list? Because Packard felt that the Zephyr/Roadmaster/Cadillac 61 price range—$1400 to $1500—offered greater sales potential than anything loftier. So as the target car for what would soon become the 1941 Packard Clipper, the company chose the Buick Roadmaster.

Packard felt so pushed to get the Clipper into production, recalled clay modeler Arthur E. (Bud) Hall, that "...we worked five weeks straight, night and day, making one model a week. We really had to rush it." Hall had been hired in 1938 by Werner Gubitz to fill in for designer/modeler Howard Yeager, who was hospitalized suddenly. Hall had previously been with GM, and since Packard had no styling bridge and its clay-modeling operation was pretty unsophisticated, Hall's first task was to build a large steel modeling table. "We could do two front ends on this table at the same time, one person working on one and someone else on the other, both in 1/8 scale. Or we could do one single model in 1/4 scale. We'd go from that to full size, and then engineering would come in and take off templates. Of course, we made umpteen different models."

As of 1938, Packard's entire styling staff consisted of Gubitz, stylist Ed Nowacky, modeler Hall and Howard Yeager, who soon

1935 One Twenty accomplished what the Light Eight could not: It pulled Packard through the Depression. One Twenty's styling unashamedly traded on senior Packards' prestige.

returned from the hospital. They were joined in 1939 by designers John Reinhart and Phil Wright and, in 1940, by William M. (Bill) Reithard and Fitz Fitzpatrick. Fitzpatrick would later team with Van Kaufman to do illustrations for a wonderful series of maga-

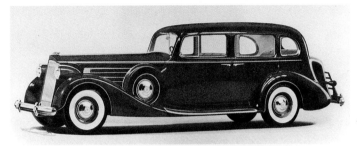

Werner Gubitz, meanwhile, maintained traditional grace and sophistication of Packard's senior lines. The 1937 and '38 bodies were essentially identical but didn't look it.

zine ads for Nash, Buick and especially for Pontiac during the 1960s.

According to Bud Hall, who stayed with Packard throughout the 1941 Clipper's styling development—and according also to Bill Reithard—primary credit for the Clipper goes to Howard Yeager. Macauley served as styling administrator and Gubitz contributed, but Yeager put the design together—stopped the blended front fender in mid door and adapted the GM-like five-window sedan and fastback coupe configurations.

There were, however, several factors that complicated and still do complicate giving Yeager full credit for the design. It's not that

By 1939-40, it became difficult to tell the junior from senior Packards because both used the same stamping dies for

front-end sheetmetal. That's the least expensive 1940 Packard 6 at left and a costly One Eighty towncar above.

Dutch Darrin, back from France, began building a line of sporty Packard convertibles in California, the first one delivered in 1937 to actor Dick Powell. He built car at left on 1940 One Eighty chassis for drummer Gene Krupa. Darrin then became involved in providing Packard directly with cut-down convertibles; also produced handsome sedan at top.

simple, mostly because Packard brought in a number of outside consultants. To give the company the broadest possible choice of styling ideas, and in view of Ed Macauley's tiny department, Packard management asked for help not only from the design staff of Briggs Mfg. Co., which was s.o.p. at that time, but also enlisted three independent designers: William Flajole, George W. Walker and Howard A. (Dutch) Darrin. Walker turned over his Packard duties to Don Mortrude, who simultaneously worked on Walker's Nash account.

It's pretty much agreed that neither Flajole nor Mortrude contributed much to the Clipper design. Mortrude might have added a detail or two to the instrument panel. But it's Dutch Darrin's role

distinctive European look, and Dutch later designed and built some beautiful, sectioned, five-window sedans. Art Fitzpatrick, who later went to Hudson and then Packard, helped Darrin design these sedans and convertible sedans. "The objective," said Fitzpatrick, "was to produce a Darrin Packard four-door consistent with the Darrin look. My inspiration and direction, other than the famous Darrin arm waving, was the existing convertible coupe and some of Dutch's cars from the early 1930s; in particular a Hispano-Suiza and a 1935 Rolls towncar."

Darrin lucked out with the timing of his Packard-Darrins, because they provided a quick, tidy answer to Lincoln's important new image car, the 1940 Continental. That year, Darrin persuaded Packard's new president, Max Gilman, to play up his special cars in company ads and sales literature. Darrin now had the attention of the company's three most important decisionmakers: Gilman, Alvan Macauley (who'd by then been elected board chairman) and engineering

Phantom version

Ed Macauley chose a 1941 Packard Darrin as his second styling testbed and personal car. He had it modified with a deauville roof (left), later added "mouth-harp" horizontal grille, quad lights and different front fenders. This ensemble led to 1948 Packard theme.

that's become controversial, and the controversy stems from his well-known propensity to take credit for everything he touched. In this case, Darrin might have bragged too much about his role in the Clipper, causing a backlash. He tended to oversell. He took responsibility for the Clipper in a 1946 SAE paper and repeated it to anyone who'd listen. His insistence became almost a joke. The irony is that he probably did lay down the car's basic theme, and here's how that came to pass.

In 1937, soon after Darrin returned to the U.S. from his coachbuilding venture with Fernandez in Paris (see page 51), he began to produce and sell the sporty Packard-Darrin. The first 13 Packard-Darrins were made from One Twenty business coupes. Darrin transformed them into convertibles by cutting off the roofs. He then cut down the doors by adding the characteristic "Darrin dip." All Packard-Darrins had a

Brown Bomber version

Packard's styling studio occupied a tiny space inside the engineering building. In 1939, Packard suddenly realized it would have to come up with something stylistically new to compete with 1941 Cadillac. During crash program, unidentified designer sketched proposals (left) while modeler Bud Adams (left above) helped sculpt scale 1941 Clipper.

vice president, Jesse Vincent. All were suitably impressed with Darrin.

So in late 1938 or early 1939, after Ed Macauley's group had struggled and failed to come up with an acceptable design for the 1941 Clipper—and likewise Briggs, Flajole and Mortrude—Max Gilman wired Dutch Darrin at his shop in Hollywood. Gilman asked Darrin whether he could come up with a concept design within 10 days and offered him $10,000 to do it, whether the design was usable or not. Naturally Darrin said he'd try. Gilman also stipulated that Darrin submit his design in the form of a 1/4-scale clay model. He imposed the impossible deadline so that Ed Macauley could pick up the model during a quick trip to California. On his return, Ed would bring the model back to Detroit for review.

Darrin miraculously managed to finish the scale clay on time, Macauley duly picked it up and delivered it not to his own styling department but to the Briggs showroom. It was here that Packard and other Briggs clients put proposals on display for executives to visit and appraise. Briggs had a modern, well-lit, locked showroom with a stage and two turntables, whereas Packard had nothing like it.

Photos, drawings, models and other evidence of the Clipper's design evolution are long gone. If photographs were ever taken of the Darrin Clipper model, they've been lost. From remembrances of people who saw it, designer Alex Tremulis probably described the Darrin model best. Tremulis was working for Briggs at the time and wrote in a 1971 letter to Darrin that the model came as a "shocker." He instantly recognized the characteristic Darrin-dip beltline, the lack of runningboards, the blind quarters and the notchback trunk. These looked very much like Darrin's sectioned Packard custom sedans.

More important, Tremulis noted that Darrin's model had what became the Clipper's most important styling feature, the blended front fenders that flowed back into (and in this case through) the doors. The flowed fender wasn't a new styling idea. John Tjaarda's 1933-34 Briggs Lincoln Zephyr prototype had fenders that faded into the front doors. Amos Northup's original design patents for the 1938 Sharknose Graham likewise showed blended fenders. So Darrin's 1/4-scale model

probably did set the theme for the 1941 Clipper, but judging from Tremulis's description and later reconstructions based on eyewitness accounts, Darrin's model looked very different from the final production car. And here's where Howard Yeager applied his talent. He didn't use the Darrin dip but specified a more conventional horizontal beltline. He also stopped the blended fender midway into the front door instead of running it all the way back to an applied rear fender as Darrin had done. Yeager covered normal runningboards with flares at the bottoms of the doors, and his roof and body shapes were different, too, taking inspiration from GM's 1940 "torpedo" C-body.

After he'd submitted his model, Darrin went to Detroit and tried to help Gubitz, Yeager and the others finish the intermedi-

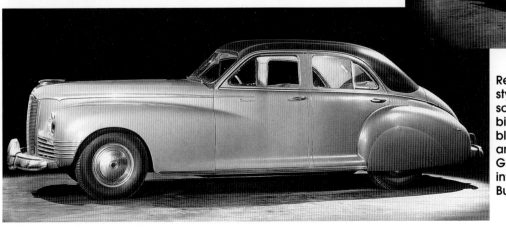

Resulting 1941 Clipper incorporated styling inputs from several different sources. Its designers skillfully combined vertical with horizontal grille, blended front fenders into doors and borrowed rear elements from GM's 1940 C-body. Clipper was intended to compete more with Buick than Cadillac.

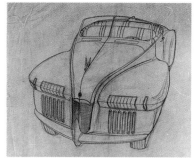

Before he left to join Gordon Buehrig at Budd in 1942, John Reinhart tried to modernize the postwar Packard (sketches at left). Meanwhile, Briggs put together some plaster scale models with the mouth-harp grille (right), starting in1940.

To develop 1948 "pregnant" Packard, Briggs used an actual 1941 Clipper as a clay armature. Roof, cowl and inner sheet-metal remained carryover, but '48 did look different.

ate and final clay models. Hall and Reithard remembered him as pleasant and likable but essentially a salesman and handwaver, friendly but bothersome, someone who got in the way. So at that stage, with no more input from Darrin, the Clipper ended up—as

has been said many times—as a well-done committee effort. Hall and Reithard maintained that the pieces were ultimately put together by Yeager, counseled by Gubitz and overseen by Edward Macauley. All these men undoubtedly influenced the shape to some extent. But the ultimate 1941 Clipper design had to suit not

only those stylists but Gilman, Vincent, Alvan Macauley and probably many more.

Unfortunately, the Clipper led too short a life. It arrived as a 1941 model and enjoyed some success that year, but production stopped on Feb. 9, 1942 when all carmakers turned to the war effort. Packard resumed building the Clipper in late 1945 but ended the run in mid 1947 when the company's "new" body style arrived.

Packard, knowing that Cadillac would introduce an all-new body for 1948, needed and wanted to match it. This styling race led to the 1948 "pregnant Packard," a hugely compromised design that was built, quite literally, on top of the Clipper.

In 1942, Packard had gotten a new president, George T. Christopher. Christopher was a farmer and former GM manufacturing man who kept pennies in a big glass jar. He showed no interest in spending money on styling, and by 1946 Ed Macauley's area—instead of expanding to meet the challenges of GM, Ford and Chrysler—took cuts in staff and space. There was not room in Packard's postwar styling area to make a full-sized clay model, so the '48 body was designed and modeled over at Briggs on Mack Avenue in Detroit. Briggs built all Packard bodies from the 1941 Clipper through mid 1954 and continued to offer its customers styling services at no charge. John Tjaarda and

John Reinhart fathered '51 Packard (top), which finally expressed ox yoke grille in horizontal form. Engineers forced Reinhart to raise beltline to cut down on costly window glass.

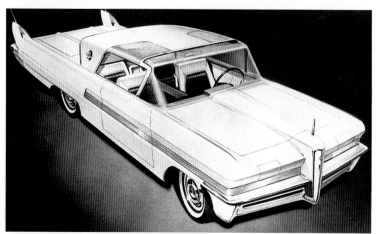

Richard Arbib designed 1953 Packard Pan American (left below) at Henney, while Dick Teague conceived fiberglass 1954 Panther (top) and 1955-56 Packard Predictor (above).

Ralph Roberts had left Briggs, and Al Prance took over the body-maker's small but still excellent styling staff. Briggs designers included Walt Wengren, formerly with Murphy in California; Cliff Voss and Bill Brownlie, both of whom would soon go to Chrysler; W.E. (Bill) Robinson, later with Kaiser-Frazer and Ford; Jack Kenitz and Fred Beamish, who likewise had Ford in their futures; Ted Pietsch, later with Studebaker and Chrysler; plus Russ Coupland, Paul Colbrooke, Steven Boran, Jim Sarlow, Rollin Taylor and apprentice Robin Jones. Briggs also had a clay model-er.named Walt Bracher. It was Bracher who did virtually all the modeling on the 1948 Packard, using an actual 1946 Clipper as his armature and applying clay over that car's sheetmetal.

Ed Macauley's staff at the beginning of the 1948 car's development consisted of two men: Gubitz and Yeager. As mentioned, Macauley had updated his Phantom in 1942 with John Reinhart's "mouth-harp" grille. The Phantom's front fenders at that time still ended ahead of the doors. Reinhart spent the war years working

for Raymond Loewy at Studebaker and didn't return to Packard until 1947, just after Gubitz retired. Reinhart came back too late to influence the 1948 Packard.

So here was a car done essentially by Macauley, Gubitz and Briggs designers. All agreed that the Clipper didn't look modern enough and that its tall, thin grille was now an anachronism. To give the 1948 Packard a more modern appearance, Macauley wanted the low grille and bullnose hood from his Phantom set into the Briggs clay, although in modified form. The '48 clay also used a very soft, stepped beltline. The upper belt continued the hood, and the lower one connected the through fenders.

The resulting 1948 Pregnant Packard followed the postwar "inverted bathtub" idiom and looked acceptably up to date for its time. Ed Macauley was happy, because he'd gotten bits of his Phantom into production. George Christopher was ecstatic, because an all-new body would have been much more expensive. And yet the 1948 Packard, even though it kept all of the Clipper's underbody, inner sheetmetal, roof and decklid, was anything but a retooling bargain. According to Packard historian William S. Snyder, who researched company records, Packard spent nearly twice as much tooling its 1948 models as Hudson did that same year on a truly new body. "Maybe Packard had become too accustomed to government work," said Snyder. But to the public, the Pregnant Packard really did look new. Yet it also kept the company's styling heritage and continuity.

Packard outsold Cadillac in 1948 by 32,000 cars (although by now most Packards were in Buick's price range). Production rose to 104,593 for calendar 1949, then plunged to 42,640 for 1950. The seller's market was over. Chief engineer William H. Graves threatened to quit if Packard's 1951 restyling weren't total. This time, he said, Packard couldn't get away with just a facelift. The 1951 body really had to be all-new.

The acknowledged father of the 1951 Packard was John Reinhart. Reinhart entered auto design in 1936 at General Motors, where he worked on the 1938 Cadillac 60-Special interior under Bill Mitchell (see page 103). He left GM shortly afterward and joined Gordon Buehrig's private design organization for a time, doing gauge faces and instrument panels for King Seeley Corp. Buehrig's firm didn't have enough business, though, so when Reinhart got an offer from Gubitz in 1939 to help with the 1941 Packard Clipper, he eagerly accepted.

Reinhart left Packard in 1942 to join Budd, where Buehrig had set up a design department before the war. Buehrig wasn't with Budd anymore, and Reinhart held the title "production illustrator" until 1943, when he joined Raymond Loewy's Studebaker team in South Bend, Indiana. At war's end, Loewy sent Reinhart and Bob Koto to England to handle his Rootes Group account, and the two of them styled the postwar Sunbeam, Hillman and Humber. Then in 1947, when Werner Gubitz retired, Ed Macauley contacted Reinhart, offered him Gubitz's old job and asked him to design an all-new 1951 Packard.

Reinhart immediately went to work and gladly accepted help from Briggs modelers and the Briggs design staff. Ed Macauley's authority, which had never been great, dimmed after his father retired in 1948, so he wasn't of much help to Reinhart. Alvan Macauley had played the role of his son's patron and backstop whether the two of them realized it or not.

Clipper styling studies for 1956 looked 1955 Lincoln-esque. Later, Ernie Breech at Ford agreed to let Packard use 1956 Lincoln body dies but reneged at the last moment.

In doing the 1951 Packard, one of Reinhart's challenges was to come up with a fully horizontal grille that still included the Packard ox yoke. He and his two designers, Charlie Phaneuf and Robin Jones, tried several styles, but they all looked like a double grille: a "fireplace" opening below, topped with a chrome "mantelpiece" or brow that carried the yoke shape. Finally Jones, previously with Briggs and Ford, came up with an integrated, wraparound grille whose massive upper bar incorporated the yoke. This was modified and accepted. It turned out to be the biggest grille diecasting produced to that time. Jones also suggested the hard-edged scallops on the hood.

Reinhart said later that he wasn't happy with the 1951 Packard, but he quickly added that he was never happy with any of his production designs. What bothered him about the '51 was what he called the "high-pockets" look. Packard's engineers had brought in a new 1949 Olds 88 and asked Reinhart to go with the same roof and cowl heights.

Reinhart did, but now the engineers felt his model showed too much glass area. Glass is heavier than sheet steel and costs more, so to cut production expenses, they ordered Reinhart to raise the 1951 Packard's beltline for a lower window height. Reinhart balked, arguing that the car would look a lot better if he could drop the roof instead. But the engineers wouldn't budge, so Reinhart gave in and always regretted it. The bottom-heavy side section and especially the massive rear fenders always bothered him aesthetically. On the other hand, he liked the fact that the front fenders and hood lay in the same plane—unlike the big, tall power-dome hoods that Harley Earl favored at that time.

In 1952, Packard management hired Frank Hershey as Ed Macauley's new assistant, effectively putting Hershey above Reinhart. In Reinhart's mind, this made Hershey next in line for Macauley's job. Since he'd previously seen himself as Macauley's successor, Reinhart quit. He phoned his friend William Clay Ford and left for Ford Motor Co. just before Hershey arrived. Reinhart's styling group at Ford, which included Gordon Buehrig as body engineer, soon won the design competition that led to the 1956 Lincoln Continental Mark II (see page 145).

A young designer named Richard A. (Dick) Teague had worked for Hershey at GM, and Hershey now brought him over to Packard (see sidebar, page 202). Meanwhile, Richard Arbib, who'd just been let go by Harley Earl Associates, landed a freelance job with the Henney Motor Co. Henney built ambulances and hearses on Packard chassis and wanted to expand its business.

Duncan McRae got caught in the middle of a number of conficting management design requirements and couldn't help coming up with the ill-begotten 1958 Packard Hawk. McRae was a much better designer than this indicates.

So Arbib designed a sporty show version of a 1951 Packard convertible for Henney. He sectioned and lowered the Packard body, took off most of the ornamentation—spears and lettering—made a new grille, added chromed wire wheels and a hood scoop, and named the car the Packard *Pan American.* The Pan American looked terrific. It didn't bring Henney more body business, but it did lead Dick Teague to create the 1953 Packard Caribbean convertible. The Caribbean served as Packard's answer to the 1953 Buick Skylark, Cadillac Eldorado and Olds 98 Fiesta. Caribbeans were made out of standard Packard convertibles by a company that supplied wooden station-wagon bodies to General Motors, Mitchell-Bentley Co. in Ionia, Michigan.

After Hershey left Packard in early 1953 to go with Ford, Dick Teague became Packard's chief stylist. He oversaw Packard's extensive 1955 facelift, with its cathedral tail lamps and all-new sheetmetal. But the '55 line had to be based on Reinhart's 1951 car. Packard couldn't raise and surely didn't have enough money for another all-new design.

Throughout Teague's 3 1/2 years as Packard's design director, the company regularly availed itself of outside help. Bill Robinson, who was still with Briggs in 1953, recounted some of the details. "When Packard would start a new design program at that time, Briggs wasn't the only company that would do competitive designs. Sundberg & Ferrar, Richard Arbib and [independent designer] Bob Bingman also contributed on a consultancy basis. And usually we at Briggs got to see all the presentations, because we had the only decent showroom. So this gave the Briggs designers a chance to check out what the competition was up to.

"Most of it was pretty bad," continued Robinson, "except for Sundberg & Ferrar. They did some beautiful things. At first I couldn't understand how a product-design outfit could do such a thing, because product designers don't have that special touch that you need for automobiles. Usually product designers, when they do an automobile...it just doesn't have the right feeling. But Sundberg & Ferrar's presentations were outstanding. In fact, the 1955 Packard Caribbean convertible was practically dead right off the Sundberg & Ferrar presentation.

"Years later I found out that the reason they did such a good job was because they hired three modelers and three designers from GM to handle that account. So they had professionals. I'd say Sundberg & Ferrar's were the best of all the designs presented— better than ours and better than Packard's." (When Robinson read the foregoing in draft form, he added this sad footnote, "When Chrysler bought Briggs in 1953, we were told to destroy all of our Packard work. I can remember the drawings being piled in the middle of the floor; a ton of them. We saved some but not too many. There were also old drawings from the era of Ralph Roberts, John Tjaarda, Alex Tremulis, etc. Bill Brownlie saved a lot of those, and Dick Teague did, too.")

It was under Teague that Packard's more notable showcars were conceived: the Balboa, the Panther, the Request and the futuristic Predictor. By the time the Request and Predictor came out, Packard had bought Studebaker, and James Nance had hired William M. Schmidt as Studebaker-Packard's styling vice president. Teague now headed Packard design, and Duncan McRae oversaw Studebaker. The last real Packard appeared for 1956; after that they were rebadged Studebakers.

In the mid 1950s, Nance asked both GM and Ford to sell bodies to Studebaker-Packard. GM refused outright, but Ford—perhaps because Nance and Ford's Ernie Breech were good friends—entertained the notion. Ford discussed the possibility of making its 1956 Lincoln body shell available to S-P for redoing as the 1957 Packard. The idea was for Ford to sell the core Lincoln body to Studebaker-Packard, who would then add its own, distinctive front and rear ends and identity symbols.

Teague and his designers produced renderings and clay models that transformed the 1956 Lincoln body into a Predictor-themed 1957 Packard. According to Dick Stout, who was there at the time, "Our proposed 1957 Packard with the 1956 Lincoln body was much more impressive than the 1956-57 Lincoln. Packard's dash-to-front-axle distance was 24 inches, whereas Lincoln's was something like 18 inches, resulting in about a 132-inch wheelbase [for Packard]: very elegant. I think our styling department did 3/4-front views with no dimensional detail." After a few months' negotiations, though, Ford nixed the plan and that was that.

Teague designed the Studebaker-based 1957 Packard line, in which he preserved elements of his 1955-56 models. Duncan McRae did all four body styles of the 1958 Packard, including the wide-mouthed Packard Hawk. That design, which his colleagues agree was not up to McRae's standards, was dictated by a management group who wanted an ever-lower, more sloping hood and wider grille. When it became obvious that Studebaker-Packard was terminal, Teague and Schmidt both left for Chrysler. As Maurice Hendry once wrote in *Automobile Quarterly,* "Packard expired in fact in 1956, in fancy in 1958, and in name in 1962." ◆

Pierce -Arrow Motor Car Co.

Even before Pierce-Arrow added the "-Arrow" to its name in 1909, two men guided the company's styling. One was James R. Way, a crusty, reclusive bachelor who'd trained with Brewster before Brewster even started making automobile bodies. Mr. Way became Pierce-Arrow's longtime chief body engineer and was totally dedicated to his work. Except for his cat and housekeeper, though, Jim Way rarely spoke to anyone, yet he had an undeniable gift for designing and engineering cast-aluminum car bodies. As a result, Pierce used cast-aluminum coachwork into mid 1920.

The other important figure in Pierce-Arrow's early styling history was young Herbert M. Dawley. Dawley was Way's opposite: cheerful, outgoing, good with people. He held a degree in mechanical engineering and was an accomplished sketch artist.

The 26-year-old Dawley came to Pierce-Arrow (P-A) almost by accident. P-A had staged a body-design competition in 1906, which Dawley entered and lost. But the contest brought him to the attention of Col. Charles Clifton, who was company treasurer at that time and would later become president and chairman of the board. In 1907, Clifton hired Dawley without really knowing what to do with him. Herb Dawley initially had no job title, no office and no formal duties. Col. Clifton told him to simply walk around the plant and familiarize himself with Pierce-Arrow's operation.

In those days, P-A ranked as one of the "Three P's," the nation's preeminent luxury motorcar manufacturers, the other two being Packard and Peerless. Pierce prided itself on the quality of its cars and the quality of its customers. Most people who bought Pierce-Arrows were wealthy, established, conservative easterners. Pierce, with its factory and headquarters in Buffalo, New York, was far removed from the sooty business of industrial Detroit. As a result, Pierce went about doing things its own way, and the Pierce way was obviously correct, because in some years an entire run of cars was spoken for before the season began.

When Dawley arrived, Pierce was producing a few thousand cars a year. Dawley soon met and began helping buyers tailor their cars to their individual tastes: choosing body styles, interior fabrics, color schemes, accessories, that sort of thing. And in the course of his

duties, Dawley developed what he referred to as his "electric chair." This was an adjustable seating buck. He would seat a client on the buck and then, by a series of adjustable dowels and pegs, would raise or lower the cushions and angles until everything fit and felt comfortable. Dawley would have these seat settings built into the customer's particular car. It was all part of P-A's personalized customer service.

Dawley also developed a system of clear acetate silhouettes of P-A bodies. He could slip samples of different-colored paper behind these "windows" to show what various paint schemes would look like. In time, as Dawley worked with and recognized what Pierce buyers wanted, he became more and more involved with interior and exterior styling.

Styling, though, like body engineering, was officially Jim Way's area. So Way and Dawley at times clashed in some classic styling/engineering debates. Way tended to be conservative, Dawley less so, and Col. Clifton often had to mediate. One of Dawley's ideas that Way did accept was the use of styling clay to speed the making of scale and full-sized models. We don't know when P-A began to use clay, but Jim Way personally enjoyed sculpting it, and clay replaced—at least to some extent—the expensive, time-consuming, full-sized wooden body mockups his staff had made earlier.

It was Dawley, too, who conceived Pierce's fender-mounted headlamps. This must have been in 1911, because the first such lamps went into production in July 1913. Dawley felt that normal headlamps were mounted too near the ground and therefore didn't give enough down-the-road illumination. He said in an interview with New Zealand auto historian Maurice Hendry that ideally, light should shine on the road from directly above. But that being impossible, the next best thing was to place the source up high. Atop the fenders seemed like the best place. Dawley presented his idea to Col. Clifton, who approved making a set of experimental fender lamps. To keep Jim Way from interfering, Dawley had the first set built off-site. These were simple metal fairings with round lamps that bolted to the crowns of standard P-A fenders. One night, Dawley demonstrated his lights to a group of factory engineers and executives, including Way. Most of them pooh-poohed the idea.

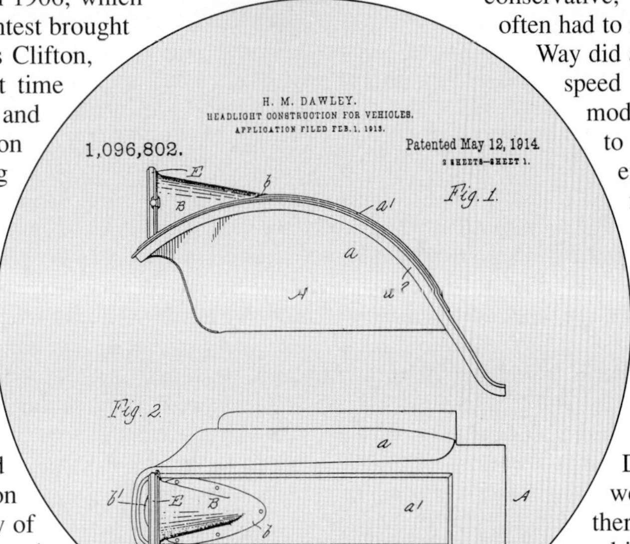

H. M. DAWLEY.
HEADLIGHT CONSTRUCTION FOR VEHICLES.
APPLICATION FILED FEB. 1, 1913.

1,096,802.
Patented May 12, 1914.
2 SHEETS—SHEET 1.

Fig. 1.
Fig. 2.

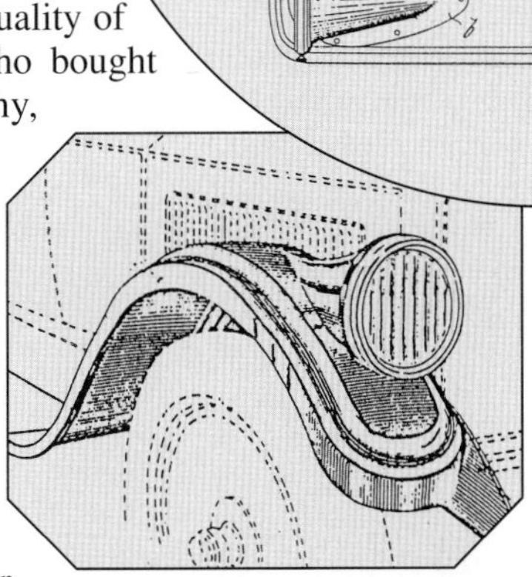

Herb Dawley came up with fender-mounted lamps around 1911 (center). Applied lights were optional at first, but so many people ordered them that they became Pierce-Arrow's hallmark, yet P-A didn't make them standard until 1932. At top is a 1924 ad, above are 1926 and 1929 fender versions.

Fender-mounted lamps truly held no lighting advantage; were, in fact, easily knocked askew in a minor accident and were harder to replace or readjust.

Clifton decided, however, to offer fender lamps as an option. Since they said *Pierce-Arrow* so unmistakably and since Pierce cars were so highly prized as status symbols, more customers soon ordered their cars with fender-mounted headlights than otherwise. These lamps served as Pierce-Arrow's primary recognition symbol for

During both these initial stages, Pierce-Arrow assembled its bodies from diecast aluminum sections. Each section was formed in varying thicknesses that ranged from about 1/8 to 1/3 inch. Wall thickness depended on whether the area was load-bearing or subject to shearing. Judging where strains would occur amounted to an art, because the science of stress analysis hadn't yet come into being.

To make the sand forms into which foundrymen poured the molten aluminum,

of highest stress. Wood also served as tacking strips for roof inserts, convertible tops and upholstery. Each body received a final sanding in preparation for painting. And since the multi-coat varnishes used in those days weren't very flexible, the goal was to make bodies totally rigid to prevent cracks in the finish.

The practice of diecasting bodies stopped soon after a new management group took over Pierce-Arrow in 1918-19. Pierce had not been able to stay competitive, and

Pierce-Arrow began making cast-aluminum bodies as early as 1904. The 1911 touring-car body (left) represented end of Pierce's first stage of body casting, with separate cowl and front doors not shown. By 1912, Pierce's casting technology

had improved. Large sections were riveted together, and the castings were so precise that seams were all but invisible. Pierce used light ash framing to aid rigidity, but the wood wasn't nearly so heavy as in conventional composite bodies.

the rest of the marque's life. In 1932, fender-mounted lamps became standard P-A equipment, although conventional headlights remained available through the end of production.

Roger Sherman, writing in *The Arrow*, the magazine of the Pierce-Arrow Society, feels that the company went through five important stages of body development. The first two stages involved the making of diecast aluminum bodies. Sherman sees an "early" diecast stage, 1904-11, and a "mature" diecast stage, 1912-20.

craftsmen first had to carve and shape very precise, often curved wooden patterns. When each aluminum casting came out of the mold, it was carefully inspected for flaws, then weighed to find any internal voids and finally filed and sanded. Ornamental body moldings were cast in, not applied, and individual sections were designed to overlap. Adjoining sections were riveted together. Seams in these P-A bodies were so tight and so beautifully matched that they became almost invisible.

After assembly, the aluminum body shell went into the woodshop, where minimal ash bracing was used against those points

some of the former owners sold their interests to the Wall Street banking firm of J. & W. Seligman & Co. Seligman put civil engineer George W. Goethals in charge of operations. Goethals' company had recently finished building the Panama Canal, and since P-A wasn't doing well, Goethals immediately cleaned house. One of his

To prevent rivals from using fender-mounted headlamps, Pierce patented every conceivable design. These patent drawings date from 1929-33.

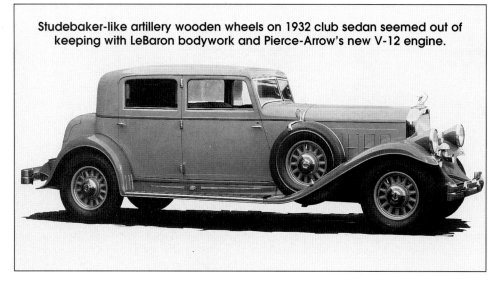

Studebaker-like artillery wooden wheels on 1932 club sedan seemed out of keeping with LeBaron bodywork and Pierce-Arrow's new V-12 engine.

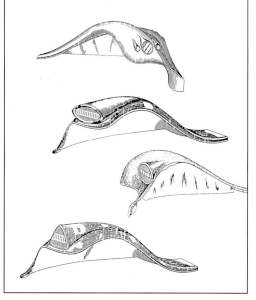

It seems likely--but it's never been shown--that Phil Wright took some inspiration for 1933 Pierce-Arrow Silver Arrow's through front fenders from German 1932 Maybach Zeppelin (inset). Studebaker body engineer Jimmy Hughes added multiple belt moldings and tiny backlight, insisted that 4-door be built on Pierce's shorter, 139-inch wheelbase. Sidemounted spare tires stood hidden inside both front fenders. Five Silver Arrows were built and sold for $10,000 each.

goals was to reduce the number of body styles from 60 to 10 and to make them more consistent, with interchangeable parts and more conventional construction.

Amos Northup had joined Pierce's truck division in 1918, the year after Dawley left. P-A had built some 5000 trucks for the military during the Great War, and trucks were the then-successful part of the company's operation. With Dawley gone, Northup worked not only on trucks but also helped select color and trim combinations for passenger cars. And now as Goethals began his push to consolidate body styles, he hired French-born designer Leon Rubay as a styling consultant (see page 72). Rubay, probably working with Northup (they later did a number of projects together), styled Pierce-Arrow's 1921 line. In keeping with tradition, these designs remained on the conservative side.

Production 1934-35 Pierce Silver Arrow reverted to standard fender and runningboard format, lacked grace of Wright's much more modern Century of Progress showcar.

Rubay's revised P-A bodies, along with George Goethals' efforts to modernize the company, ushered in Sherman's third stage of body development, 1921-27, during which—instead of using aluminum castings—P-A bodies were skinned with handformed sheet aluminum over structural wooden frameworks. These more conventional composite bodies were easier and less expensive to fabricate. James R. Way was still manager of Pierce's body plant, so it's likely that he also had some say in the styling of these new composite bodies.

According to Roger Sherman: "The structural integrity of these bodies was furnished by a framework of white ash, assembled to near-metalworking standards. Their joints were laminated for strength. The body panels were butt-welded 2S6 gray, half-hard aluminum plate, hand-hammered after cooling to increase strength, hardness and smoothness for paint. Cast aluminum was still used for window frames and moldings, plus wheel housings on closed cars. Closed models were also fitted with roof vents.

"Pierce's junior line—the Series 80, which sold for the price of a mere Cadillac—was introduced in the summer of 1924. Mr. Way followed the pattern of the larger models when he laid out the body lines of these cars. Both Series 80 and 36 had a minimum of body curves for ease of manufacture.... More curves marked the bodies on Mr. Way's last designs for the Series 81 of 1928."

Although Pierce still produced large, impressive, luxurious cars, and while the country's best coachbuilders offered a selection of custom bodies, P-A was no longer the industry leader it had once been. Its styling certainly didn't set any standards. Nor were Pierce's six-cylinder engines as impressive as the Cadillac V-8 or Packard's V-12. For a time, Pierce ads contained picture inserts that showed 10-year-old cars with their famous owners, implying how Pierce's conservative styling policy and reluctance to change still made these older cars fashionable. But as a result of intense competition in the luxury-car field, Pierce-Arrow again found itself in deep financial trouble.

The marriage with Studebaker in 1928 seemed a way out, and it might have been if the Depression hadn't intervened. The Studebaker merger led to Stage Four, 1929-33, in Pierce's body evolution. This saw the use of sheet steel over wooden framework—the same composite construction used by nearly the entire industry. It was Studebaker's way of blending Pierce into its own operation. Many P-A bodies were built by Studebaker in South Bend. They were probably also designed in consultation with Studebaker. And although we don't know the names of any factory designers, Ray Dietrich of Dietrich Inc. served as a Studebaker styling consultant during this period and visited the Pierce plant in Buffalo fairly often. His missions also had to do with his coachbuilding activities for the Murray Corp. of America.

As we mentioned in our Studebaker section, P-A and Studebaker made a concerted effort to develop a family resemblance. Bodies and particularly body moldings became similar. The partners even shared two specific body styles. Pierce-Arrows of 1932 were beautifully styled, as lovely and pure as any of its classic peers, and some of the coachbuilt bodies were stunning. The company's new 1932 V-12, which must have been tremendously expensive to bring to market that year, topped the line. Ab Jenkins, the famed "Mormon Meteor," set dozens of international speed records at the Utah Bonneville salt flats with 1932-34 V-12 P-A roadsters. In one run, he topped 127 mph for 24 hours.

Pierce-Arrow still looked good in 1936, but the company realized too late that it would need a smaller car like the Lincoln Zephyr or Packard One Twenty to survive. P-A filed for bankruptcy in 1938.

But Pierce-Arrow sales kept slipping, and in Oct. 1932 Studebaker hired former Auburn sales manager Roy Faulkner to become P-A's vice president of sales. It was Faulkner who commissioned Philip O. Wright's wonderful Silver Arrow for P-A's 1933 New York auto show and Century of Progress exhibits. We talked about that briefly in our Studebaker section, but here's how this very important, influential design came into being.

After Phil Wright showed Faulkner his sketches and the model he'd done for Harley Earl at GM, Faulkner authorized the construction of five running Silver Arrow prototypes. The work didn't fit in at the Pierce-Arrow body plant in Buffalo, so Faulkner arranged to have the cars built in Studebaker's experimental shops in South Bend.

Wright, who had worked with Walter M. Murphy in California and had put in untold hours with one of the country's finest coachbuilders, now wanted to take an active part in the construction of "his" cars. So he went to South Bend and immediately came face to face with Studebaker's chief body engineer, James R. (Jimmy) Hughes. Hughes, the entrenched, authoritarian, drill-sergeant Englishman, wasn't anxious to be told how to design or build cars by a 25-year-old stylist from California. And thus began a contentious but mercifully short confrontation. Incredibly, it took Hughes' staff only 13 1/2 weeks to build all five Silver Arrows, and they finished the first one in a mere eight weeks!

Phil Wright originally had in mind putting the Silver Arrow on Pierce's longest 147-inch wheelbase. Hughes insisted on using the 139-inch span, and he won that argument by simply ordering up the shorter chassis. Wright had no power at Studebaker, and Faulkner couldn't help him.

Wright's original scale model apparently showed a *two-door* fastback sedan with four separate pontoon fenders. This evolved into a through-fendered two-door and finally into a through-fendered four-door fastback. Hughes filed two design patents in April and November 1932 showing both two-door styles. (Patents don't necessarily name the true author of a design. Patent applications are usually made in the name of the head of a department or company rather than crediting a designer who's lower on the corporate ladder. So it's possible that design patents issued to Hughes show bodies and refinements created by Wright or others.)

In the process of going with the shorter wheelbase and switching from two to four doors, the Silver Arrow gained six inches in height. This bothered Wright, but again, what could he do? Hughes likewise dictated the Silver Arrow's grille design to make it conform to production Pierce-Arrows. And he added more definition to the multiplicity of belt moldings—or perhaps more moldings; this isn't clear. Hughes did dictate, but all these of details conformed to Wright's original design and actually complemented it. The smaller, veed rear window was also Hughes' idea, and a less successful one. He supposedly insisted on it to minimize headlight glare from following cars. Wright originally wanted a larger, more wrapped backlight.

Warren W. Fitzgerald, writing in *Car Life* magazine in 1968, felt that Wright's primary contributions were confined to the overall theme and shape of the car and the through front fenders. Fitzgerald was one of the few people who actually interviewed Wright about the Silver Arrow. Most of the details of his excellent article came from Wright's testimony, and for Wright to give Hughes that much credit speaks volumes about his credibility. Wright was by that time retired and living in Long Beach, California. He passed away in 1982.

Back in South Bend 50 years earlier, Studebaker craftsmen hand-hammered the Silver Arrows' steel bodies over what Fitzgerald described as "cast-iron" forms. These cars' interiors were again beautifully done, with a very unusual instrument panel floating in a veed dashboard whose lower edges receded forward.

The Silver Arrows had foot-thick doors, burled walnut garnish moldings and ornate inner door trim. The fact that the body was channeled over the frame...the resulting lack of runningboards and the high frame sills...made entry and exit difficult for people of short stature or in skirts or high heels. But such styling nuances as hidden door hinges, the through fenders, recessed door handles and tapered trunk were harbingers of production design decades ahead.

Today, it's hard to conceive the impact the Silver Arrow had at its 1933 introduction. This tremendous visual jolt especially affected people in the auto industry. Here came one of those remarkable, radical shapes that, in the blink of an eye, changed the way designers saw the automobile. And what's important: The Silver Arrow exemplified *good* futuristic design—"good" as opposed to what the contemporary press began calling "Zepps." The Zepps included Buckminster Fuller's Dymaxion and the Stout Scarab—cars too far out and Buck Rogers-ish to be taken seriously. The name "Zepp," incidentally, might have come from the German 1932 Maybach Zeppelin, a car that had even more of an envelope body shape than the Silver Arrow. The Maybach Zeppelin no doubt influenced Wright and Hughes to some extent, but its surfaces and detailing were less sophisticated than the Silver Arrow's.

Despite the Herculean tasks of designing and building those five Silver Arrows in so short a time, Pierce-Arrow's fortunes continued to plummet. The fifth and final stage of Roger Sherman's body evolution began with the Silver Arrow and ended with the company's bankruptcy on May 13, 1938. By 1935, Pierce-Arrow management recognized, as had Lincoln and Packard, that its only salvation would be a smaller, less expensive line. In an attempt to float that line, Pierce made some nipped-in-the-bud arrangements with Reo and Graham-Paige to share Budd-built bodies. The end came, though, before those arrangements crystallized. ◆

AUBURN-CORD-DUESENBERG

No man ever produced cars more consistently beautiful than Errett Lobban (E.L.) Cord. His legacy includes the Auburns, Cords and Duesenbergs that now rank as the great masterpieces of classic American automobiles. Designer Gordon Buehrig borrowed the Museum of Modern Art term "rolling sculpture" and applied it to E.L.'s productions. With few exceptions, Auburns, Cords and Duesenbergs still draw crowds at *concours d'elegance*. While all of E.L.'s automotive ventures ultimately failed, the designs themselves succeeded so well that most have become extraordinarily valuable as automotive *objets d'art*.

Cord's transportation empire, which ranged from Auburn, Cord and Duesenberg automobiles (ACD) to Checker and Yellow cabs, Stinson aircraft, Century Airlines, American Airways, New York Shipbuilding Corp. and much, much, *much* more, sprang up overnight, grew huge and then collapsed almost as quickly. Interesting parallels exist between E.L. Cord and Walter Chrysler. Both rescued ailing car companies and both quickly built them into vast, booming enterprises. After that, though, two subtle differences in vision led Walter Chrysler to succeed and E.L. Cord to fail as car manufacturers. First, Walter Chrysler always put engineering first, not that he didn't appreciate styling also. Cord, on the other hand, valued styling above engineering, but again, he certainly had an appreciation for mechanical innovation and excellence. But second and more important, Chrysler targeted the low end of the automotive market while Cord entertained the middle and high end. When the Depression came, economics favored Chrysler Corp. and frowned on ACD. (We should mention that the designation ACD didn't exist when E.L. Cord manufactured Auburns, Cords and Duesenbergs. It has become a common designation since then. We use it here for convenience.)

E.L. Cord grew up in California. He attended Los Angeles Polytechnic High School but dropped out after the middle of the 10th grade, aged 15, and started selling used cars. His father died two years later.

The first car E.L. owned was a Model T Ford "cutdown." Cutdowns were the early equivalent of hot rods. E.L. had bought a well used T, stripped off the body and mounted a speedster body on the Ford chassis. When a customer offered to buy E.L.'s cutdown for $500 more than he had in it, E.L. happily sold the car.

Young Cord had discovered a market for cutdowns and, over the next few years, he fabricated and sold 20 or so, each at a profit of around $500. E.L. worked as a mechanic at the J&B Auto Co. in downtown Los Angeles and used space there to build his cutdowns after hours and on weekends. Sometimes he would install a kit speedster body—one of many available at that time—and at others he'd make his own from scratch. No two of E.L.'s speedsters were alike.

The speedster business soon got E.L. involved in racing, especially after he discovered that a winning car brought $200-300 more than one that just went fast.

E.L. married Helen Frische in 1914 and became a father a year

later. After venturing into and out of a number of unsuccessful businesses, the Cord family moved to Phoenix, where E.L. took a job selling Paige automobiles. In 1916, his dealership sponsored him in a 273-mile Arizona road race, which he won. But things weren't going well in Phoenix, and after several more family moves and dead-end jobs, E.L. got word that Chicago was the place to go.

He soon found work there with a man named Jack Quinlan, the Chicago distributor of Moon automobiles. Quinlan offered E.L. a 25% stake in his business if E.L. would help him set up Moon agencies throughout the midwest. E.L. could pay Quinlan out of future commissions. E.L. accepted, worked very hard, did a first-rate job and was soon rewarded with a Moon distributorship of his own. His territory included Iowa, Wisconsin and Minnesota. It was here, as a Moon distributor, that E.L. had his first dealings with bankers. His education in high finance had begun.

But what E.L. Cord really wanted was to build a car of his own. This desire might have come from the days when he built Model T cutdowns. Cord designed a sport sedan and paid an artist $50 to make a styling sketch of it. The drawing showed a basically conventional car, but with some interesting stylistic touches: cycle fenders, step plates instead of runningboards, a clear-vision windshield and the most eye-catching feature of all: a two-tone paint scheme that swept a contrasting color back from the radiator cap, widening along the top of the hood like the wake of a boat, spreading side to side to join the belt moldings and then running along the doors and around the back of the body. This drawing showed not only Cord's early interest in styling but his intuitive sense of the salable. It represented one of his first attempts at automotive art direction.

Errett Lobban Cord

Moon automobiles must have appealed to E.L., too, because they had a grille shape much like the British Rolls-Royce's and looked, in some body styles, like miniaturized Silver Ghosts.

The most important Moon that E.L. sold went to an investment banker named Ralph A. Bard. Bard, through his financial connections, served on the board of the Auburn Automobile Co. in Indiana. Auburn was still reeling from the recession of 1920 and, as the two men talked about cars and Auburn in particular, E.L. convinced Bard that he could make the company thrive if he, Bard, and his co-directors would give E.L. control of Auburn. Cord offered his services for an annual salary of $10,000 plus stock options and 25% of any profits—a mere fraction of the $1 million a year Walter Chrysler received to rescue Maxwell.

The Auburn directors balked at the 25% profit clause but reluctantly agreed. They had little choice, because 300-700 assembled Auburns stood unsold and aging on the factory's backlot. E.L. ordered the cars painted in bright, multiple colors, splashed on some nickel plate, mounted a national ad campaign, wholesaled a number of the cars "as-is" to an organization in New York, sold the better ones at retail and generated enough immediate cash to stave off bankruptcy.

E.L.'s next move was to convince the Auburn board to let him put his dreamcar into production—the car he'd paid the artist $50

Auburn sales took off after E.L. Cord restyled the 1925 Auburn (left). This particular roadster doesn't show the hood pennant, but it did have optional balloon tires. The '26 touring car (right) displays Auburn's hallmark hood pennant, which sweeps into belt molding and then loops around back of the body.

to sketch. The board reluctantly agreed again, and Cord's design became Auburn's 1925 line. The 1925 Auburn stood eight inches lower than the '24 models and now led rather than followed fashion. To the board's amazement, sales of the restyled Auburn took off. Gross income reached nearly $8 million that year, then $10 million in 1926, nearly $15 million in 1927 and a whopping $37.5 million for 1929. E.L. Cord had pulled off a miracle. He, along with Walter Chrysler, were heralded in the press as the *wunderkinder* of the auto industry.

E.L. had all the personal attributes it took to put together an automotive empire: salesmanship and a great feel for the market, ambition, charm and now also the confidence of the financial community. He had an eye for automotive style and trends, but he also put great stock in a car's performance and the publicity value of speed and endurance. He introduced the Auburn speedster in Jan. 1928, and factory race driver Wade Morton launched a speed campaign that netted a 104.347-mph international AAA flying-mile record. Morton later set a 24-hour endurance record in another 1928 Auburn speedster, all of which brightened the marque's already high-flying reputation. Although other automakers offered similar speedsters—Stutz, Packard and Hudson among them—Auburn became and remained *the* boattail with an *affordable* image for speed (ACD didn't used the word *boattail*, however).

Also in 1928, E.L. commissioned a showcar called the Auburn Cabin Speedster. The racy, tapered aluminum body took on the elements of a small private airplane: steeply raked, veed windshield, tight cabin, cycle fenders and no runningboards. The cockpit contained wicker bucket seats, an altimeter and a compass. The Cabin Speedster very much cashed in on Lindbergh's transatlantic flight, which was still a topic of national conversation in 1929. The Auburn Cabin Speedster generated great publicity and became one of several sensations at the 1929 New York auto show. People immediately identified it as an Auburn by its characteristic prow-wake hood moldings and two-tone color scheme. After New York, the Cabin Speedster toured the show circuit. At

the end of that tour, it was caught in the fire that swept through the Los Angeles tent display in Mar. 1929, and the car ended up as a puddle of aluminum. Although the factory initially offered to sell duplicates, no other Cabin Speedster was ever made by Auburn, although two replicas have been built in recent times.

Nineteen twenty-nine marked E.L. Cord's automotive coming-out party. That was the year he formed the Cord Corp., capitalized at $125 million, and made it the catch-all for his by-then-considerable personal fortune. Auburn stock had risen from $31.75 a share in the mid 1920s to as high as $514 in 1929 on the strength of Auburn's 15-fold increase in sales.

E.L., meanwhile, had bought Duesenberg in 1926 with the goal of making it his uppermost car division, and he chose the 1929 model year to introduce the ultra-luxurious Duesenberg J. The lavish Model J beat the 16-cylinder Marmon and Cadillac to market and delivered more advertised horsepower than any American production engine until 1955. As an automobile, the Model J was physically larger than its rivals, generally more costly and offered a range of impressive and often flamboyant custom bodies. More about those in a moment. Additionally, the year 1929 marked the first coming of the front-wheel-drive (fwd) Cord L-29.

What this meant in broader terms: E.L. had put together—all within five busy years—a car company that now covered the mid and upper reaches of the price spectrum. Auburn stood as his volume seller and competed roughly with Buick, Studebaker, Graham-Paige, Peerless and Elcar. The Cord L-29's price rivals included factory-bodied Packards, Pierces, Lincolns, Cadillacs, Stutzes and the Chrysler Imperial. And the Duesenberg J aspired simply to be this country's premier luxury motorcar: the American equivalent of the most expensive and prestigious European marques—e.g. Rolls-Royce and Hispano-Suiza—but offering better performance.

In viewing ACD as a classic-era styling force, we have to talk first about the Cord automobile, because that's where E.L.'s fledgling styling department got its start. Cord was the only nameplate that E.L. started from scratch. The Cord meant a good deal to him, both emotionally and financially. In the end, he introduced Cords not once but twice: in 1929 and again in 1936.

The L-29 had its roots in Harry Miller's front-drive race cars. In the mid to late 1920s, the fwd concept got a tremendous boost when Harry Miller's fwd creations began to set the pace at the Indy 500; in fact, at tracks all around the country. Not only were these

Auburn set a number of speed and endurance records in 1928. One member of that record-setting fleet was Auburn's rakish speedster.

cars fast, but they *looked* so good. By not needing a conventional driveshaft, Miller's fwd racers could be built so low to the ground that the cowl stood at thigh height instead of chest height. The main purpose of fwd in race cars was to lower the center of gravity to give better roadholding. A secondary benefit was to reduce frontal area for less drag and better aerodynamics. Miller's very low cars had up to a third less frontal area than its rear-drive rivals.

The idea of bringing Miller race-car technology, and especially that seductively low profile, into passenger-car production intrigued everyone in the auto industry. But E.L. Cord was one of

the few who capitalized on it. E.L., with his combined interest in racing and his sixth sense for predicting sales trends, reasoned that a shoulder-high fwd passenger car—at a time when most sedans stood taller than any adult could peer over—built along race-car lines, would not only look fantastic but could be promoted from the vantage points of handling, roadholding, safety and traction.

So the first thing E.L. did was to buy patent rights to Harry Miller's fwd racing transaxle: the part that did away with the driveshaft. This was in 1927. He also hired Harry Miller as a consultant. Another consultant was race driver Leon Duray. Duray became a good friend of Cord's and, as such, told E.L. that the Miller transaxle might be all right for racing but it wouldn't do at all in a passenger car. (Actually, the Miller transaxle was marginal even for racing, because the thin, highly stressed gears lacked durability. The gears couldn't be speed-shifted, were expensive to machine and needed more attention than the average car owner would ever give a transmission.) Duray did recommend, however, another fwd setup from a racing car, one developed by Harry Miller's colleague, C.W. Van Ranst. The Van Ranst transaxle, due to the location of the gearset, was much stronger than Miller's and could be shifted up or down without worrying about overloading or breaking the gears.

E.L. hired Van Ranst to be the L-29's overall project manager and asked him to keep costs down by using as many off-the-shelf parts as possible. So for the powertrain, Van Ranst chose a Lycoming in-line Eight engine (Cord now owned Lycoming), a conventional three-speed transmission, and a Columbia differential (Cord also owned the Columbia Axle Co.), which stood upside down ahead of the transmission. In other words, the entire power unit was a compacted version of a standard rear-drive layout, but turned around backward at the front of the frame and driving the front wheels.

Compact as it was, the powertrain was still quite long. And while the length of the in-line Eight plus transmission and differential would prove detrimental to traction and handling, it was seen by E.L.—in fact by everyone at that time—as a tremendous

E.L. Cord took advantage of Lindymania by introducing the 1929 Auburn Cabin Speedster showcar. Its tapered rear body and airfoil hood graphic made it look like a small, wingless airplane. Interior was outfitted like a cockpit, with wicker seats and altimeter.

styling advantage. It forced the stylist to work with an unusually long hood, and long hoods were all the rage, just as streamlining, tailfins and cab-forward would become later.

Over the next five months, Van Ranst struggled to build the first L-29 prototype in Harry Miller's race-car shop in Los Angeles. Miller's top engineering draftsman, Leo Goossen, engineered the L-29's front axle, brakes and suspension system. Van Ranst and Goossen finished the first L-29 prototype at the end of 1927, at which time E.L. Cord flew out to L.A. to test drive it. On the prototype's maiden voyage, with E.L. at the wheel, Van Ranst beside him and Goossen and Duray in the back seat, they headed out onto back roads of the Santa Monica coastal range.

This first car used single Cardan joints at the outer ends of the halfshafts, and while E.L. loved the way the prototype rode and handled, the steering wheel showed some horrific rhythmic jerking when the front wheels were crimped to full lock under power. Cord thought maybe the driving public wouldn't notice, but the other three men felt that no buyer of a luxury car would ever put up with that sort of misbehavior. So Van Ranst replaced the single Cardans with compact double joints of his own design, and that solved it.

Another problem that showed up early was a tendency for the prototype sedan's doors to fly open on washboard roads. The ladder-type frame wasn't rigid enough. The Auburn engineers added a hefty central X-member (possibly a first) to the frame, and that cured that.

While the L-29 prototype had been engineered and built in Los Angeles, production development took place in Indianapolis, still under Van Ranst. And here's where designer Alan H. Leamy and Auburn's chief body engineer, John Oswald, came together. There's still some confusion about who actually styled the L-29's

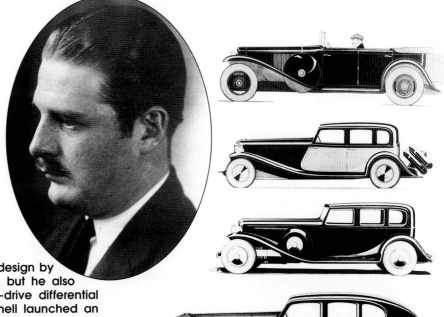

Alan H. Leamy not only maximized Cord L-29's design by emphasizing the low silhouette and long hood, but he also topped it off by drawing attention to the front-drive differential beneath the radiator. His body-colored grille shell launched an industry trend. Leamy's sketches at far right depict not only a Cord phaeton but also Auburns and Duesenbergs.

Front-wheel drive got a big boost with the success and sleek looks of Harry Miller's fwd race cars. That's E.L.'s friend, Leon Duray (left), in the 1929 Packard Cable Special. Cord introduced L-29 (below) and Duesenberg J that same year.

Phil Wright designed breathtaking La Grande L-29 speedster (center) for Auburn president Roy Faulkner, the same person who later went to Pierce-Arrow and commissioned Silver Arrow. Frank Hershey designed and Walter Murphy built low, elegant towncar above for actor John Barrymore.

then 26, and immediately made him the corporation's chief and only stylist. It must be remembered, though, that Cord himself was always vitally involved with style, and it was he who directed and approved Leamy's and Oswald's work.

Despite the confusion about who designed the L-29's basic body, Leamy generally gets credit for conceiving the veed grille with its body-colored outer shell, the differential cover, emblems, the dynamic split bumpers and the beautifully arched clamshell fenders that made this car so influential. The basic grille idea later appeared on the 1931 Chrysler and the Reo Royale, among many others.

Leamy initially tried to hide the fwd differential with an unadorned panel covering the L-29's front frame horns, but E.L. said no. He wanted to call attention to the fwd differential. So Leamy repeated the puffed-out shape of the differential cover below the radiator, emphasized it with a chrome oval and covered the mandatory crank hole with a cloisonne Cord coat of arms. These details added tremendous interest to the front end, and so did the lovely clamshell front fenders—the way they hugged the

body, some saying Leamy did the entire design and others crediting Oswald with all but the grille and details. Oswald, by the way, later went on to General Motors as Oldsmobile's chief body engineer, then headed up Ford's styling staff briefly after World War II (see page 139).

Alan Leamy was again one of those gifted intuitive designers who spent his short life with hardly any personal or peer recognition. He'd had polio as a child and walked with a noticeable limp. Thus frustrated at an early age, Leamy began to sketch cars. As a young adult, he took a correspondence course in architecture and later designed tract houses. He also tried selling real estate, but what he liked best was to draw cars. He filled the shelves of his bedroom with sketchbooks of car designs.

Leamy got his break through a family friend, the chief engineer of Marmon in Indianapolis. Leamy worked for Marmon as a body designer for about a year, but he didn't do much there and finally became impatient. When he heard that E.L. Cord was planning to bring out a radical fwd passenger car, he wrote to E.L., who passed his letter and sample sketches along to Van Ranst.

Van Ranst met with Leamy at the Indianapolis Duesenberg plant, studied his portfolio and was so impressed that he set up a meeting with Cord himself. E.L. was similarly taken with Leamy,

Ruxton: The Other Front Driver

Many automakers experimented with front-wheel drive in the late 1920s and early '30s, including Packard, Chrysler and Checker. But only two actually brought cars to market. The second, hot on the heels of the Cord L-29, was the Ruxton. Developed by engineer William J. Muller, the Ruxton had the same low silhouette and long hood as the L-29. The Budd Co. and Baker-Raulang built Ruxton's bodies, and stage-set designer Josef Urban conceived an unusual paint scheme using horizontal bands of color. Financier Archie Andrews couldn't keep Ruxton production going, and the public wasn't willing to take a chance on so new and unproven a concept as front-wheel drive. Those factors plus the commercial climate of the Depression put an end to both Ruxton and the Cord L-29. ◆

tires and then swept majestically back into the runningboards.

The L-29 made its debut in Aug. 1929 amid great acclaim by the public and press. People flocked to Cord showrooms to oooh and aaah the daringly low design. The L-29 was also one of the great hits of the European *concours* circuit, winning 39 prizes for beauty, style and innovation. Among early L-29 owner-enthusiasts were architect Frank Lloyd Wright and film stars Dolores del Rio, John Barrymore and Ronald Colman.

The L-29, however, picked exactly the wrong tick of the clock. The stock-market crashed within three months of the car's introduction, and after that very few buyers had the courage to take a chance of the L-29's technology and newness, no matter how good the car looked. Rumors began to circulate, too, about the L-29's excessive front-tire wear (true). And its poor uphill traction (true). And its axle joints failing (also true). But the real kicker had to do with the L-29's performance. It looked fast, but a Model A Ford could take it from a stop light.

The L-29 Cord offered four factory body styles, and a number of coachbuilders put custom bodies on the low, slinky chassis, among them Walter M. Murphy, LeBaron, Derham and Weymann. In his capacity as art director for the Hayes Body Co., Count Alexis de Sakhnoffsky created a marvelous one-off coupe that won first prize at the 1930 Monte Carlo *concours d'elegance*. (Herbert Snow, Auburn's engineering v.p., hired Sakhnoffsky in Aug. 1931 as a styling consultant, but there's no record that Sakhnoffsky contributed to ACD production designs.) Another glorious L-29 was the La Grande speedster designed by Phil

sold to a Duesenberg customer, but he might then see an identical body on a Lincoln chassis. The coachbuilt Lincoln cost half as much as the Duesenberg, yet here were two new cars with the same-style body. Feeling his own personal exclusivity compromised and much of his money wasted, the Duesenberg customer might threaten to cancel his order.

So Ames decided to offer Duesenberg buyers bodies that were exclusively theirs. And that became the main reason he hired Buehrig: to design coachwork specifically for Duesenberg clientele. But Ames had very stringent requirements for a body designer. He wanted more than just a stylist; he wanted someone experienced in making body drafts as well. And that was one of Buehrig's strengths. He had the ability to draw accurate body drafts in scale and full size.

Ames needed someone versed in both disciplines for two reasons. First, he recognized that when a stylist simply handed a coachbuilder a side-view rendering of a car and asked for the body to be built from that, the finished product was usually full of the little touches that characterized that particular coachbuilder. Every bodymaker had his own "signature." So even though Derham, say, or Murphy or LeBaron worked from the same sketch, each coachbuilder would turn out bodies with idiosyncratic differences. Anyone familiar with them could tell which coachbuilder had made each body simply by these subtleties. Ames didn't want that, so when Duesenberg submitted Buehrig's factory body sketches to a coachbuilder, he sent along detailed body drafts. That way, no matter who fabricated it, every body came out the same.

The second reason Ames wanted someone who could generate body drafts had to do with competitive bidding. Duesenberg made

Fred Duesenberg took a spin at Indianapolis Motor Speedway in a supercharged 1932 SJ, a 320-bhp La Grande dual-cowl phaeton. The Duesenberg chassis alone cost $9500 and, with coachwork, could easily top $18,000--this at a time when you could buy a Ford V-8 sedan for $590.

Wright and commissioned by Auburn president Roy Faulkner.

As delightful as it was to look at, the L-29 ultimately led too short a life. Between Aug. 1929 and the end of the line in 1932, Cord managed to sell only 4429 L-29s in the U.S. By way of contrast, Packard sold roughly 55,000 cars during the same period, Cadillac 35,300 and Pierce 14,000. And even those luxury carmakers were or would soon be in financial trouble.

Word got out that Harold T. Ames, Duesenberg's vice president, was looking for a body designer. No one knows how many people applied for the job or whether Al Leamy was in the running, but in June 1929 Ames interviewed Gordon Buehrig and soon hired him. The prestige of Duesenberg made this one of the plum jobs of the industry, and here was Buehrig, all of 25, chief designer.

For the next three years, Duesenberg's styling department consisted of Buehrig and Buehrig alone. Ames' reason for hiring him was simple. All Duesenberg bodies were custom made by coachbuilders. Which led to a problem that soon came to Ames' attention, namely that bodies designed by coachbuilders often appeared not only on Model J's but also on other carmakers' chassis. For example, a Brunn-designed convertible victoria might get

it a practice to send drafts out to different coachbuilders and invited them to submit bids. With all the construction details and materials laid out in draft form, there could be no question about what Ames expected. During the J's first two years, when demand for Duesenbergs still remained fairly high, every established coachbuilder in the country submitted designs and sketches to be included in company catalogues.

Earlier, in June 1928, several months before the Model J's debut at the 1929 New York Salon, Duesenberg had sent chassis drawings to eight prominent coachbuilders, inviting them to submit design proposals. This became something of a competition. The bodies chosen by Ames to be shown at the New York Salon were the famous LeBaron sweep-panel phaeton and a towncar by Holbrook. LeBaron's Roland Stickney traditionally gets credit for designing the sweep-panel body and, in a way, the sweep amounted to an elaboration of the Auburn's prow-wake molding and its similar contrasting color scheme. The Duesenberg J's "face"—its grille, headlamps and lip-shaped front bumper—along with the clamshell front fenders, are sometimes attributed to E.L. Cord and sometimes to Alan Leamy. According to author/historian Fred Roe, Ames said in 1976 that he and E.L. Cord initially laid out the design for the Duesenberg J's front ensemble on Cord's kitchen table in Auburn, Indiana. Roe feels that this indeed took place, but the J's lip bumpers and curved hood louvers weren't part of the original face. "I think their sketches were given to Leamy, and he did the styling details," said Roe. "There were two or three prototype bumpers submitted before the lip style was settled on. The original layouts given to the coachbuilders showed grouped horizontal louvers somewhat like the Stutz's." There are Model J fender and grille drawings by Leamy okayed by Fred Duesenberg on 8/20/28.

Gordon Miller Buehrig had already packed in an amazing amount of design and coachbuilding experience before Ames hired him. He'd started his career five years earlier as an apprentice with the Gotfredson Body Co. in Detroit. Here he did whatever came up, from woodworking to drafting. In 1926, he went to New York and landed a drafting job with LeBaron. When Briggs bought LeBaron, Buehrig returned to Detroit and worked for Packard briefly; then joined Harley Earl's growing Art & Colour section in 1928 and finally went to Duesenberg the next summer.

Gordon Buehrig at Duesenberg.

At Duesenberg, Buehrig—answering mostly to Ames and occasionally to E.L. Cord—developed a styling shortcut that saved hours of tedious work. He virtually eliminated the need to do repetitive wheel and chassis sketches. Duesenbergs came in two wheelbase lengths: 142.5 and 153.5 inches. Gordon carefully drew these two chassis in 1/16 scale, complete with factory fenders, lamps, radiator, hood, cowl, runningboards, etc. He used India ink, and in these drawings he added just the faintest touch of perspective. He established perspective by moving the foreground wheels apart one scale inch and the background wheels together one scale inch.

Duesenbird" hood ornaments were handmade from two pieces of flat brass soldered together, then ribbed and plated.

He then had these originals photostatted and could thereafter concentrate on doing just the body in side view.

Exactly how many different body designs Buehrig created for Duesenberg over the next three years even he couldn't estimate. In his book, *Rolling Sculpture*, he did say that about half the Duesenberg bodies that appeared in metal were to his designs. The other half came from a number of different coachbuilders. But in addition to the Buehrig designs that were actually produced, he conceived many more that remained in sketch and draft form.

Buehrig also designed the "Duesenbird," the Model J's wonderfully simple, bird-like hood ornament. He mentions in his book that the over-riding concern was to engineer the hood ornament so it needed no tooling. Hand labor was cheap at Duesenberg, but tooling cost money. So Buehrig designed the Duesenbird so the outline could be handsawed from two pieces of flat brass. The two halves were then brazed together and the ribbing milled in, again by hand, after which the ornament was plated and polished.

In 1930, Buehrig hired Phil Derham of the Philadelphia coachbuilding family to be his body engineer. And in 1932, designer Herb Newport also joined Duesenberg. Buehrig and Newport worked together briefly, but in 1933 Buehrig returned to GM Art & Colour for most of that year. Newport might have designed a few body styles for Duesenberg, but not many, because very few Duesenbergs were built after 1933. In fact, estimates put the total number of Models J and SJ at 480 by the marque's demise in 1937.

About the time Buehrig returned to GM Art & Colour, Harley Earl staged yet another of his blue-sky design competitions. The prize: a paid trip to the Century of Progress in Chicago. Earl named five teams, the leaders being Buehrig, Tom Hibbard, Jules Agramonte, Jack Morgan and Frank Hershey. Just before the contest, Earl delivered a lecture about the aesthetic importance of the front end of a car and how designers ought always to emphasize the face.

Buehrig stood up and took issue with Earl. He argued that it was the body shape, not the face, that represented the most important aspect of a design. Buehrig said later that he was naive to argue with Earl, especially on this particular point. But having come from Duesenberg, where the face always remained the same and the body design determined the personality of a car, that's how he felt.

In any case, the contest began, and Earl laid out the assignment: to design a futuristic four-door sedan and display it as a 1/4-scale clay model. The judges would be Earl, some of the Fisher Brothers and several GM executives.

Buehrig wanted to show Earl how stylistically insignificant the front of a car could be, so he conceived a coffin-nosed, pontoon-fendered, fastback sedan with hidden headlights and without any semblance of a conventional grille. He intentionally made the face as featureless as he could. His design did have a few horizontal louvers low on the prow, but the cooling system consisted of two small outside radiators set between the fenders and the sides of the tapering hood.

In his book, *Rolling Sculpture*, Buehrig also tells a second story. He says the over-riding idea behind his contest model's grille-less front and the side-mounted radiators was to keep the inside of the engine compartment clean. Buehrig had owned a custom-bodied Model A Ford that he dearly loved, and one of his great joys was to keep it spotless. He spent hours wiping the engine compartment, which took in dirt and dust through the radiator. It was in an effort to eliminate this frontal dust sieve, he wrote in *Rolling Sculpture*, that he came up with the theme for his contest model. In later interviews, however, Buehrig soft-pedaled the clean-engine idea. This might have been a secondary reason for the coffin-nose design, but more important was his wanting to show Harley Earl that a car could look good even without a face and that grille design—particularly vertical grille design—wouldn't be so important in the future.

After all five teams had finished their models, Harley Earl first held a straw vote among his designers. Excluding their own, which contest model did they like best? In this round, Buehrig's model received the most votes. However, in the official judging by Earl, the Fishers et al, Jack Morgan's team won the trip to Chicago, and Buehrig's design finished dead last.

Late in 1933, while Buehrig was still with GM, he and Harold Ames discussed the possibility of designing a "small

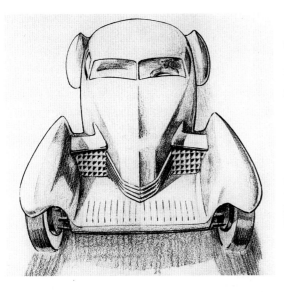

Gordon Buehrig's 1933 GM contest sketches provided basis for "Baby Duesenberg," which became Cord 810.

Duesenberg." Senior Duesenbergs weren't weathering the Depression at all, and Ames saw a normal-sized companion car as Duesenberg's only salvation: same idea as the Lincoln Zephyr and Packard One Twenty.

Encouraged by Ames, Buehrig left GM, returned to Duesenberg and, in effect, presented his contest model as the baby Duesie. Ames liked it and gave his approval for the A.H. Walker Co. to build a running metal prototype on an Auburn chassis. This prototype, finished in April 1934, had most the characteristics of what later became the 1936 Cord 810. The differences included veed B-pillars, the positioning of the hidden headlamps plus small dual radiators under the short airfoil struts that linked the fenders and hood. The A.H. Walker Co. prototype's greenhouse had seven instead of five windows, the door shapes were totally different and the more numerous louvers did not extend back along the hood.

A l Leamy had designed Auburn's 1934 bodies and left soon afterward for a job with General Motors—sort of a job swap with Buehrig. Leamy's '34 Auburns weren't bad, but they surely didn't have the sparkle of their predecessors, and sales were terrible. The sales situation, though, had less to do with styling than with production delays caused by the changeover to all-steel bodies.

As sales fell, E.L. Cord made Harold Ames a vice president of Auburn in addition to his duties as Duesenberg's president. The idea was for Ames to bring Auburn out of its doldrums, so Ames

immediately put the small Duesenberg on hold and tapped Buehrig again to give Auburn a major facelift for the 1935 model year. The entire 1935 Auburn retooling budget, according to both Ames and Buehrig, was less than $50,000.

Buehrig totally redesigned the 1935 Auburn's face, meaning everything from the cowl forward: grille, headlamps and hood. He also took the hallmark prow-wake moldings off the hood and removed a debossed sweep from the front fender valances. Everything else remained the same as for 1934. The 1935 Auburn looked much more modern and impressive and was introduced in Sept. 1934, but despite the success of the facelift, sales stayed flat.

Since the redone Auburn would be old hat by the time of the 1935 auto shows, and since Auburn needed something new and spectacular to publicize the 1935 line, Harold Ames came up with the idea of re-introducing the Auburn speedster. Leamy had restyled the speedster for 1931, but sales got so slow that Auburn discontinued it in 1933. There were, in fact, 70-80 speedster bodies sitting unsold in the Union City body plant. Ames now suggested that Buehrig modernize the speedster by redoing the existing bodies in the facelifted theme of the 1935 Auburns.

Buehrig had a sample body brought over from storage and found that it didn't really fit the 1935 frame. The cowl was too narrow, and the rear kickup didn't match. Even so, he lopped off the rear of the speedster body behind the top well, replaced the missing section with a wooden armature and clayed up a new,

Buehrig and his tiny staff, consisting of modeler/designers Vince Gardner, Dale Cosper, Bill Robinson plus draftsman Bart Cotter, worked mostly in three dimensions on scale models. Cotter then translated the models into full-sized drafts. Scale model of Cord-like 2-door at left was probably done later, after Buehrig had joined Budd's styling staff.

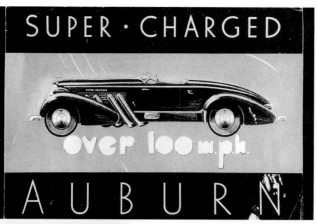

to introduce each next year's models in October so that autoworkers could spend more time on the job throughout the winter and spend more money shopping during the holidays. September and October new-car announcements continue even today.) Then, to raise the speedster's performance image, the company had Ab Jenkins re-establish Auburn as the nation's fastest production car. Chrysler's Airflow had broken a series of AAA stock-car records previously held by Auburn, and Jenkins recaptured those in a 1935 speedster. Auburn subsequent-ly advertised that Jenkins tested every speedster personally and attached a little dashboard plaque, signed by Jenkins, stating that the car had been driven at 100+ mph. In addition, Auburn's adver-tising agency commissioned Alexis de Sakhnoffsky to create art-work for a series of magazine ads. These again reinforced Auburn's guarantee of 100 mph. So although only 180-200 1935-36 Auburn speedsters were actually built, their promotional effect was tremendous, especially among car and racing enthusiasts.

more vertical "stern." He based the dropping slope of the stern and the leaping rear pontoon fenders on a Duesenberg Weymann speedster he'd designed in 1933.

Buehrig kept the previous speedster's windshield and doors, but he cut the front out of the cowl and totally reshaped its forward wall. Buehrig shortened the cowl for the 1935 speedster, length-ened the hood and reshaped both so the top of the 1935-36 hood formed a broad vee that paralleled the windshield. This allowed the hood sides to stretch back nearer the doors.

Since the 1931-33 speedster's body was narrower than the 1935 Auburn frame, Buehrig covered the side rails with sheetmetal cladding. He left off runningboards and designed pontoon fenders that were unique to the speedster. Chrome wheel discs covered the wire wheels, and stainless-steel flexpipes came out of the left side of the hood. These pipes stood as a visible reminder that the 1935-36 Auburn speedster came equipped with a supercharger. Final detailing included repeats of the winged goddess hood ornament applied behind the doors, chrome stone guards at the leading edges of the rear fenders and chrome step plates beneath the for-ward halves of the doors.

With Auburn's labor pool skilled and plen-tiful, a directive went out not to order new tooling. So the speedster's front fenders were made up of seven small pieces handwelded together and its bodies were formed mostly by hand. Individual sheetmetal sections were lap-welded together and then leaded smooth. The pressed-in beltline moldings on the 1931-33 bodies had to be hammered flat, after which new, applied moldings were added. Auburn craftsmen hastily built four super-charged speedsters for the New York auto show and then settled down to fabricating "production" speedsters in batches of 10 and 20. Ames knew too well that speedster cus-tomers could be fickle.

The New York show jobs did create the intended sensation. (Incidentally, the 1935 auto show was the last one to focus on Jan. 1 as the intro date for new models. For 1936, President Roosevelt asked the auto industry

During the months that Buehrig had been working on the 1935 Auburns, Duesenberg dropped the "baby" project. That divi-sion had all but shut its doors. But Harold Ames now had another thought. Why not turn the baby Duesenberg into another front-wheel-drive Cord automobile for 1936? E.L. Cord, who had gone to England to avoid embarrassing inquiries into company finances and supposed kidnap threats against his children, first saw proto-types when he returned to the U.S. in mid March of 1935.

Lycoming had developed a slick little V-8 that seemed ideal for a fwd car. Auburn engineers now turned their attention to design-ing a four-speed transaxle with a Bendix preselector gearshift. The Cord body would be semi-unitized, with a stepdown floor and front subframe—12 years before Hudson used the same plan. Ames authorized Buehrig to hire a small staff of designers, mod-elers and body engineers and asked him to transform the baby Duesenberg into the 1936 Cord 810. Buehrig did this work on Auburn property. He hired Vince Gardner and Dale Cosper as his designers and Dick Robinson as a modeler. They worked mostly in clay, that being the medium Buehrig now preferred. He rigged up a small styling bridge—one of the first in the auto industry—

Although the Packard 120 paced the 1936 Indy 500, Cord contributed cars for race officials. Every 810-812 Cord body was virtually handbuilt from small stampings.

and set to work making his former GM contest model suitable for production as the 1936 Cord.

The miracle Buehrig wrought wasn't just the creation of a magnificent motorcar—one of the most influential and treasured designs in autodom—but the fact that he did it under such tight time and money constraints. Again, tooling costs had to be kept to a minimum. So he ended up using essentially the same bumper front and rear—a design that the supplier, the Buckeye Bumper Co., had tooled earlier for Cadillac. The steering wheel was a very plain off-the-shelf type that Buehrig tricked up with a horn ring so it looked thoroughly modern. Window-crank handles were a type used before, but Buehrig disguised them with large, flat, disc-shaped knobs.

On the Cord 810 sedan, all four doors shared a common outer skin; the rear doors simply had cutouts to clear the fenders. Bodies required much more handwork than those built by mainstream car companies. GM could stamp an entire Turret Top from a single steel sheet, but the Cord 810 roof consisted of seven separate sections welded together and leaded. Cord couldn't afford electric motors for the retractable headlights, so Ames authorized handcranks at either end of the instrument panel. The beautiful, machine-turned dashboard insert used pre-existing gauges with new faces. The Cord 810's impact at its first showing in Nov. 1935 was seismic. It created a sensation and very much upstaged that other contender for the national autoshow spotlight, the 1936 Lincoln Zephyr. The Zephyr was certainly interesting and influential, but nothing like the Cord.

Aside from its lowness, which seemed sensational enough, here stood a car without a conventional grille. No one had ever seen anything like it. Every other automobile still had a grille that essentially framed the radiator: upright, prominent, one of the constants in motorcar design. The Cord grille, if it could even be called that, emphasized the horizontal. This shattered every precedent of accepted car design. Stylists immediately began doodling variants, putting more horizontality into their sketches and models. We begin to see the results as early as the long, horizontal hood louvers of the 1937 Studebaker and the 1938 Cadillac 60-Special.

The Cord 810's very simple, molding-less beltline likewise exerted an influence. It showed up on Bill Mitchell's Cadillac 60-Special and carried through into Bob Gregorie's first Lincoln Continental. Many of the 810's more subtle details, like the fuel filler door and hidden headlamps, were soon copied by other carmakers. The Cord won lots of design awards, including being named one of the eight best automobile designs of all time in 1951

by the New York Museum of Modern Art (see page 247).

The 1936-37 Cord allowed E.L. to exit the auto industry in one final blaze of glory. He'd once again created a car that became entirely successful aesthetically, yet it failed heroically in the marketplace. The enormity of the company's financial losses had to be staggering. Here was a car totally engineered, styled and tooled from the ground up, yet fewer than 3000 Cord 810s and 812s were ever sold (812 designated the 1937 version, available that year with an optional supercharger). Auburn and Duesenberg closed shop in 1937, after which Cord sold all leftover 810 body panels and hammer forms to Hupmobile, who used them to build the short-lived 1940 Hupmobile Skylark, styled by John Tjaarda at Briggs, and the Graham Hollywood.

Despite the fall of ACD, E.L. Cord remained an extremely wealthy man thanks to wartime contracts, real-estate holdings and other business interests. But he never again applied his talents to automobiles. He did, however, in the late 1950s, buy the remains of a disassembled General Motors' Motorama showcar, the Oldsmobile F-88, and had it shipped to a warehouse in Reno, Nevada. E.L. never did anything with the F-88, and it's not known what he had in mind for it. We should mention, too, that Cord Corp. at one time owned two bodymaking operations: Central Body Co. in Connersville, Indiana and Limousine Body in Kalamazoo, Michigan. ACD also made use of the Union City Body Co. in Union City, Indiana. Union City fabricated bodies that Duesenberg then finished, trimmed and sold under the name La Grande (see page 62).

Before Auburn expired, Central Body began making steel kitchen cabinets for Montgomery-Ward, the income from which partially financed the creation of the Cord 810. During World War II, Central Body—renamed Auburn Central and then re-renamed American Central—produced Jeep bodies for Willys-Overland and Ford plus wings and fuselage sections for warplanes.

E.L. Cord lived and worked in Reno until the end of his life, becoming a state senator in 1956. He passed away at age 79 in 1974. Harold Ames spent his final years in Rancho Mirage, California. Alan Leamy died of blood poisoning in 1935, aged 33. Gordon Buehrig was replaced at ACD by Alex Tremulis. After leaving ACD, Buehrig worked at Budd, then became one of Raymond Loewy's chief Studebaker designers and joined Ford in 1949, where he had a major hand in creating the 1956 Continental Mark II (see page 145). Buehrig retired in 1965 and passed away in early 1990. The automotive heritage these men created together, however, lives on. ◆

KAISER-FRAZER CORP.

Of all the new automakers who entered stage left after World War II, only Kaiser-Frazer (K-F) stayed for a second bow. All the rest played walk-on parts: Tucker, Davis, Playboy, Keller, King Midget, Del Mar, Hoppenstand and dozens more. And like so many other independents, K-F eventually devolved into Chrysler Corp.

K-F had its roots in Graham-Paige, which stopped making cars before the war but then got rich producing armaments. Joseph W. Frazer, who'd previously been sales v.p. of Chrysler and president of Willys-Overland, bought a controlling interest in Graham-Paige and wanted to get back into the car business. In shopping

Kaiser-Frazer called in Dutch Darrin to style the 1947 Frazer (below) and Kaiser (right). Darrin's original designs called for his characteristic beltline dip on rear doors, but it got lost in the rush toward production.

around for money, Frazer traveled to California and found a kindred spirit in Henry J. Kaiser. Kaiser also wanted to build a postwar car. He'd made his early fortunes in highway and dam construction and then went into aluminum, concrete and wartime shipbuilding.

To prevent plant closures and layoffs after the war, Kaiser—from 1942 to VJ Day—dabbled in the development of a lightweight, inexpensive postwar car. So when Joe Frazer talked with Henry Kaiser about money and especially about Kaiser's ties with the Bank of America, the two men decided to pool their resources and launch what they hoped would become the first all-new American automobile to hit the postwar market.

Kaiser's wartime car designers included Dick Teague and Bob Robillard, both of whom worked for E.H. Daniels Inc., the Los Angeles industrial design firm. Teague later joined GM, then Packard and Chrysler and eventually became design vice presi-

dent for AMC. Robillard became K-F's director of advanced styling. The concepts Henry Kaiser favored included front-wheel drive, torsion-bar front suspension and fiberglass as a body material. Teague and Robillard came up with several unlikely fiberglass prototypes ranging from a tiny cyclecar-like two-seater to an envelope-bodied, four-place, fastback two-door sedan.

In early 1945, even before Kaiser-Frazer incorporated, Joe Frazer hired two distinctly different sorts of designers: Howard A. (Dutch) Darrin and William B. (Bill) Stout. Darrin was the former Paris coachbuilder, designer of the Packard-Darrin and a contributor to the 1941 Packard Clipper. Stout's career included development of the 1914 Imp cyclecar and his own mid-Depression line of minivan-like Stout Scarabs. Stout also designed a number of aircraft, among them the Ford Tri-motor. Darrin's immediate assignment was to design a car that could be quickly put into production. Stout, meanwhile, went to work on far-out future K-F designs.

By mid 1945, Darrin had come up with a sedan, and K-F licensed this design and agreed to pay him 75¢ for every car built. Darrin also kept the rights to the design and, intending to go into the car business himself, he built a fiberglass convertible on the same theme, doing the fabrication in his Los Angeles shop. Darrin then used this convertible to interest the Wall Street firm of Lehman Brothers to help put his convertible into production. He made arrangements with the Hayes Mfg. Co. in Grand Rapids, Michigan to produce his convertible, and the Lehman Brothers envisioned distributing it through major department stores like

Darrin used the same K-F envelope body format on his fiberglass-bodied convertible. He tried to launch this car under his own name. Like so many postwar hopefuls, Darrin couldn't get financial backing. That's Dutch behind the wheel (left).

Immediately after the war, huge Willow Run plant hummed and K-F easily sold all the cars it could produce. Once the bloom came off the seller's market in 1950, however, the company had to struggle to stay competitive.

Macy's and J.L. Hudson. As manufacturing costs rose, though, Lehman Brothers pulled out.

Like Darrin's fiberglass convertible, the proposed 1947 K-F sedan used a full envelope body, was rounded at both ends and had a small, low grille. It wore no jewelry but did have the distinctive "Darrin-dip" beltline on the rear doors.

For reasons that in hindsight don't make much sense, a "me-first" race developed at war's end—a competition to bring out America's first all-new postwar car. K-F, having no prewar models to facelift and sell, had more reason than most automakers to win that race. But in the process of readying Darrin's design for production, K-F rushed the body engineering process and compressed schedules that ordinarily took nine months into three. One of the shortcuts K-F's body engineers took was to eliminate Darrin's dipped beltline. As metal prototypes were built, Darrin watched the dip vanish and saw additional styling changes being made in the name of expediency, none of which he liked.

When the 1947 Kaiser and Frazer came out, each car carried the tag line *Darrin Styled* in chrome script on the decklid. Darrin insisted that this script be removed. The company pointed out that it wasn't possible, because all Kaiser and Frazer decklids were pre-drilled to accept the chrome tag. It wasn't until mid 1948 that K-F released decklids without the *Darrin Styled* logo.

K-F had an agreement with Darrin that gave him "permission"

to submit new design ideas at any time. The company also signed consultancy contracts with industrial designers Brooks Stevens and E.H. Daniels Inc. The Stevens and Daniels firms submitted facelift proposals for the 1948 Kaisers and Frazers, but those early postwar cars were selling so well that no major body changes appeared until the 1949 model.

Bill Stout left K-F in Sept. 1946, and Joe Frazer realized that Kaiser-Frazer needed a resident design staff for future products. So in Nov. 1946, he hired Bob Cadwallader, the former Chrysler design manager, to be the corporation's chief stylist and to set up a styling department.

Cadwallader's first hiree was Cliff Voss, fresh from John Tjaarda's private design firm. Next he offered his "retired" buddy from Chrysler, Herb Weissinger, a job. And in 1947, he enticed another Chrysler designer, A.B. (Buzz) Grisinger, to come over by paying him twice his former salary. K-F usually did pay designers more than other car companies to compensate them for the 80+-mile daily commute between Detroit and K-F's huge Willow Run plant in Ypsilanti, Michigan.

Although all K-F designers worked together in one big room, Cadwallader now set up three separate studios: Kaiser with chief stylist John Chika, Frazer with Herb Weissinger as chief, and Buzz Grisinger handling advanced design. John Chika had fled Czechoslovakia before the war, became a stage-set designer and illustrator, later landed a job in GM's Pontiac studio, then went on to Chrysler, and Cadwallader brought him over from there. Chika left K-F after a few months, and Buzz Grisinger took over the Kaiser studio.

Damon Woods, soon to join Frank Hershey's team that gave Ford its first two-seater Thunderbird, was among the four members of Grisinger's studio. Weissinger's included Cliff Voss, later a studio chief for Chrysler Corp.; Duncan McRae, subsequently with Ford and Studebaker-Packard; and Charlie Phaneuf, who had a major hand in styling the 1965 Ford Mustang (see page 254). Later additions to K-F's design staff included Alex Tremulis, fresh from Tucker, and Bob Robillard, who took Grisinger's place as head of K-F advanced design in 1952. Carleton Spencer had charge of K-F interiors, completing a most gifted group of stylists.

Their immediate job: Facelift the 1949 Kaiser and Frazer. After that, create the Kaiser Traveler and Vagabond utility sedans, with their fold-down rear seat, hatch-like decklid and wooden cargo floor. Then convert sedans into the first postwar production four-door convertibles. And finally, present designs for a totally rebodied 1951 Kaiser.

As with so many successful designs, some controversy sur-

1951 Frazer (above left) recycled K-F's 1947 roof, door and cowl stampings and merely added new fenders, grille and bumpers. It was so masterful a redesign that virtually no one suspected the old body lurked under new clothes. The 1951 Kaiser, however, did receive a totally new body that again became mostly the product of Darrin's talents (above). This time he got his Darrin dip on the rear fender, along with the "widow's peak" windshield and a bright rubstrip along the rockers. Despite highly successful styling, Kaiser-Frazer never had the financial resources needed to survive.

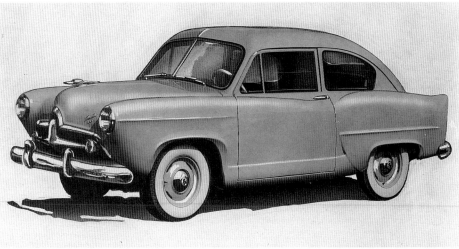

Kaiser spent a lot of money developing 1951 Henry J (right) for a market soon to be overcrowded by the Nash Rambler, Hudson Jet and Aero Willys. 1952 facelift clay (below) had no fins, but Edgar Kaiser insisted on keeping them.

rounds the authorship of the 1951 Kaiser. Three teams worked on the car: Brooks Stevens, Dutch Darrin and Kaiser's in-house styling group. The home team's initial clay model looked like a stretched version of the 1947-50 Kaiser, and Brooks Stevens' rendition, designed by his assistant Jim Floria, also continued that general theme: the upside-down bathtub format.

Darrin almost missed his chance to contribute to the 1951 Kaiser and would have if Joe Frazer hadn't come to see him at his home in Palm Springs. When Darrin learned from Frazer that K-F's resident designers had a serious but uninspiring 1951 Kaiser clay model in progress, he immediately showed Frazer some of his own recent sketches. Frazer liked them and invited Darrin to come to Willow Run and compete with Weissinger, Grisinger and Stevens.

When Darrin arrived, the resident designers initially gave him full cooperation. According to Richard M. Langworth's book, *The Last Onslaught on Detroit*, Darrin didn't yet know it, but the home team wasn't all that worried about Darrin's chances. So they lent him Duncan McRae as an assistant plus five clay modelers and supplied him with a full-sized clay armature and a blackboard.

It wasn't long, though, before Darrin and McRae had enough form in their model to make the K-F designers realize that maybe

they'd better get worried. Darrin said he and McRae needed to put in lots of overtime to catch up, but the in-house team wanted to prevent them from working at night. The K-F group also felt that Darrin was borrowing their ideas and incorporating them into his own clay. There's no doubt that tensions existed, but the rivalry apparently did what it was supposed to do: make the competing teams improve on the best features of each others' designs.

When management came in to review the final full-sized clay models, Darrin claimed that the K-F designers intentionally stood in front of his model to hide it from Henry and Edgar Kaiser. To get the Kaisers' attention, so said Darrin, he unbuckled his belt and dropped his pants. Buzz Grisinger, who was there at the time, remembers no such thing, but Darrin liked to repeat the story. At any rate, Darrin did get their attention and launched into an animated presentation. His 1951 Kaiser model—so clean and lean, very low, with a simple grille and a beautifully understated presence—actually sold itself and would have even without the histrionics.

The '51 Kaiser went into production with just a few changes, the most obvious involving the rear roof section. The final roof stood higher and looked thicker than Darrin would have liked. But the 1951 Kaiser did come out with all the Darrin touches: the beltline

Dutch (inset) designed the Kaiser-Darrin on his own in California, figuring K-F would need a competitor to the Corvette and Thunderbird. This was totally lost on Henry J. Kaiser, but his young wife liked the design and encouraged K-F to built it. Fewer than 500 were sold.

dip beneath the rear window, the "widow's peak" windshield and backlight, the generous use of side glass, thin roof pillars, the dogleg C-pillar (more extreme than BMW's) and the side rub strips that looked like they continued the bumpers all the way around the car. Darrin held a design patent on those rub strips.

Herb Weissinger was responsible for the major facelift that distinguished the 1951 Frazer. Because K-F still had a lot of leftover 1950 bodies, the company decided to sell them in the form of an entirely different-looking Frazer. The '51 Frazer shared no body stampings with the 1951 Kaiser; instead Weissinger came up with all-new front and rear sheetmetal that simply bolted onto the previous center section. This masked the old body so well that hardly anyone suspected the 1951 Frazer as being any less changed than the '51 Kaiser.

In contrast to the stylistically successful 1951 Kaiser and Frazer, the 1951 Henry J compact ended up as something of an embarrassment to the K-F design staff. But the Henry J resulted from a strange set of circumstances.

In 1948, a Detroit supplier named American Metal Products Inc. approached the K-F engineering staff with an appealing proposition. AMP already had all the tools and dies to make inner sheetmetal stampings for a small, economical car. Was K-F interested in producing such an automobile, because if so, AMP would donate the tooling, especially since the small Kaiser-Frazer car would showcase AMP's capabilities.

There was only one little hitch: The AMP car had no sheetmetal dies for the *outer* skins. Tooling existed only for the "bones." K-F would have to style the outer body based on existing inner sheetmetal and then make the appropriate stamping dies.

K-F management took AMP up on its offer and then decided that the new car had to come out in Feb. 1950 as a 1951 model. That left very little time to style the outer skins, especially since the K-F design staff was still busy working on the 1951 Kaiser and Frazer. "When we were given the [Henry J] job," recalled Buzz Grisinger, "there was no time for sketches or anything. We just got on it. Herb [Weissinger]

Frazer production ended after 1951, and the last American-built Kaiser looked like this for 1954. Buzz Grisinger borrowed the grille and headlamp shapes from the Buick XP-300 Motorama showcar. After 1955, body tooling went to Argentina, and the car continued there through 1962.

worked on the front end of the clay, I worked on the side and Darrin worked on the back end. We cooperated with Dutch to that extent." Edgar Kaiser insisted on tailfins, so Darrin tacked them on.

Also, Dutch Darrin had initially wanted to scale down his 1951 Kaiser design so it would fit the AMP inner sheetmetal, but K-F engineers said it couldn't be done. They maintained that the proportions of the AMP skeleton and any scaled-down Kaiser skins would be too different. Darrin claimed he later built such a prototype in California at his own expense, using 1951 Kaiser sheetmetal over Henry J inner body panels. There's reason to doubt that these inner panels were truly from a Henry J, however. Darrin showed his handiwork to Kaiser, but by that time it was all academic. In the end, the production Henry J ended up being a camel-by-committee job consisting of Darrin's dipped beltline and widow's-peak backlight; thrusting front fenders, grille and hood ornament by Weissinger; a main body section by Grisinger; the C-

pillar dogleg lifted from the big Kaiser plus Edgar Kaiser's mandatory tailfins.

Soon after the Henry J's debut, Dutch Darrin, back in Hollywood, started developing a two-place sports car: a fiberglass roadster. This roadster made use of the Darrin dip behind *sliding* doors that moved on rollers into the front fenders. Darrin held a patent on this feature, too. The advantage of sliding doors, said Darrin, was that they wouldn't snag curbs or bang against parked cars.

In Aug. 1952, Darrin invited Henry Kaiser to an unveiling of the roadster in his shop. Kaiser brought along his young second wife and some members of his staff. When Darrin, in his typically dramatic fashion, took the wraps off his roadster, Henry Kaiser became very agitated. How could Darrin build such a car without authorization? Darrin explained that he built it on his own time and at his own expense. And why, said Mr. Kaiser, would Darrin expect Kaiser-Frazer to suddenly go into the sports-car business? Darrin tried to explain that Chevrolet and Ford were supposedly working on two-seater sportsters, Nash already had one, and this roadster would provide K-F with a response to those cars.

Henry Kaiser still wasn't convinced until his wife spoke up and purred that this was the most beautiful car she'd ever seen, and why *shouldn't* Kaiser-Frazer go into the sports-car business? At that point, Henry calmed down, and it wasn't long before Darrin won him over.

This roadster again had all the Darrin hallmarks: the requisite beltline dip, the widow's-peak windshield, virtually no external ornamentation, a demure kiss-mouth grille and full wheel openings. It looked very of-a-piece. The Kaiser-Darrin, as it came to be named, went into production in late 1953 with two important changes: higher fenders and headlights to meet state requirements, and the elimination of a reverse curve at the bottoms of the rear fenders. Even so, the production roadster looked mighty good.

The Kaiser-Darrin arrived at a time when Kaiser-Frazer was in sad financial shape, and setting up production facilities for the roadster didn't help. Only 435 were ever built and sold by the factory, nowhere near enough to recoup expenses. Dutch Darrin bought 50 or so leftover Kaiser-Darrins that were parked at Willow Run, had them shipped to California, reconditioned those that needed it, installed Cadillac V-8s in a few and sold them all, the last one in 1957.

Buzz Grisinger facelifted the 1954 Kaiser's front end, borrowing cues from GM's XP-300 Motorama showcar. The idea was to give the Kaiser a Buick look. While the '54 facelift succeeded in that regard, Kaiser-Frazer did not. Kaiser bought Willys-Overland in 1953, sold the big Willow Run plant to General Motors that same year and consolidated operations in Toledo, Ohio. Kaiser-Willys stopped building passenger cars in the U.S. after 1955. Production of the Kaiser Manhattan/Carabella continued in Argentina, however, through 1962, and variants of the Willys Aero and Jeep station wagon were built in Brazil through 1972. In this country, Kaiser-Willys concentrated on Jeep and Jeep-like vehicles for civilian, government and military use. ◆

WILLYS-OVERLAND CO.

How quickly we forget those who finish second. Ford's Model T consistently led the American auto sales race, but did you know that from 1912 through 1918, Willys-Overland (W-O) just as consistently kept coming in second? Chevrolet passed W-O in 1919, after which Willys-Overland ran fourth through sixth throughout the 1920s. The Great Depression helped drop W-O to 11th in 1934. From then on, the company plunged to dead last and stayed in the basement through 1941.

The point is that W-O did finish second through most of the 1910s and did win some glory in the 1920s. John North Willys built his empire in much the same way as W.C. Durant, buying and creating a roster of nameplates. His bestsellers were the low-end Overland and the medium-priced Willys-Knight. The Overland gave rise to the Whippet in 1926, which successfully challenged Ford and Chevrolet and managed third place in 1928.

Some of the cars that Willys-Overland produced in its salad days were quite handsome and advanced. The 1917 Overland Country Club roadster had a panel that hid the fuel tank. You opened its "trunk" by tilting the rear seat forward. Most Willys-Knights had attractive lines, too, and by 1927 the marque's recognition symbols

included the "jousting knight" hood ornament, shield-shaped headlamps and a Buick-like grille (which Buick borrowed from Packard). The entire Willys-Knight package showed the touch of a dedicated stylist, but who that stylist was we can't say.

Amos Northup went to Willys-Overland from Murray Corp. of America in Mar. 1928 and was soon joined by Jules Andrade, formerly of Fleetwood (see page 60). Once there, Northup designed the stunning 1930 Willys-Knight 66B plaidside roadster. He also restyled the entire line of Whippets, after which he left again

(Left) 1917 Willys-Overland Country Club 4-place roadster had a rear storage compartment accessible through back seat. (Below) Amos Northup tried to minimize visual distraction of door cuts with his 1930 Willys-Knight plaidside roadster.

to rejoin Murray. Yet since Murray built most Willys-Overland bodies, Northup kept a hand in styling them.

Among the 1930s cars that we know Northup designed were the 1933 Willys

Northup also designed the 1933 Willys 77 and 99 (the stillborn 99 is shown above) plus sharknosed 1937 Willys at right. W-O sales quintupled in 1937.

77, Willys 99 and the rebodied 1937 line (there might have been others). The compact Willys 77 and 99 took their grille cues from another Northup design, the 1932 Graham Blue Streak. But there the similarity ended. The 77/99's hood sloped downward toward the radiator—very unusual for that day—while the fender-mounted headlamps seemed to point skyward. The Willys 77, despite its lower-than-Ford pricetag, didn't find many customers, and even fewer of the six-cylinder Willys 99s were built.

In designing the next generation 1937 Willys, Northup adopted a front end similar to the Sharknose Graham's, which he also had a major hand in designing. Again, despite the '37 Willys' low initial price, the public wasn't swayed. Willys-Overland had a little better luck with the 1941-42 Americar, a facelifted version of Northup's 1937 design.

W-O's fortunes improved greatly with the outbreak of World War II. The company became one of three contractors chosen by the government to build wartime Jeeps. Despite ads and claims, Willys did not "invent" the Jeep and certainly didn't design the body. The Jeep body was drawn up by an anonymous member of the U.S. Army Quartermaster's Corps who had no inkling that his simple sketch would end up as one of the great vehicle designs of all time.

A tiny automaker named American Bantam in Butler, Pennsylvania was producing an equally tiny car just before the war. American Bantam, along with Willys-Overland and two other auto manufacturers, had been wooing the Army Quartermasters Corps (QMC), hoping to land a contract to engineer and build a small scout car for the military. When Hitler invaded France and the British evacuated Dunkirk, the QMC suddenly felt a sense of urgency to develop what became the Jeep—the small scout car in question. Dreaming up some impossible specifications and a five-day deadline, the QMC asked the four interested auto manufacturers to submit detailed plans and cost esti-

Willys-Overland delivered Quad pilot model (above) to Army in Nov. 1940, months behind American Bantam, yet Willys and Ford got major Jeep contracts. W-O built Jeeps and 1941 Willys Americars on same assembly lines (right).

mates. Only American Bantam met the deadline with anything resembling a buildable Jeep.

According to engineer Charles O. Probst, whose father, Karl Probst, created the initial Jeep plans for American Bantam, "The Quartermaster Corps came to Butler in late June, 1940 and...tested the American Bantam roadster and piled sandbags on the frame, tested carrying capacity and checked ramp and departure angles. But then someone in the Quartermaster Corps actually drew the outline of what the Jeep was going to look like. Whoever it was specified the doorless sides, the two front seats and single rear seat, the square back, the very shallow body stampings...and the shallowness was important.

"The Quartermasters did not, though, design the grille or the fenders. Those were left to the individual manufacturers, which is why the American Bantam Jeep came out with rounded fenders and a rounded front end while Ford and Willys eventually had flat fronts and more angular fenders."

After becoming the QMC's only successful bidder on the Jeep project, American Bantam had to build 70 pilot models and deliver the first one for testing at Camp Holabird, Maryland within 49 days. Karl Probst personally drove the first prototype from Butler to Camp Holabird and made the deadline with half an hour to spare! After thoroughly testing the American Bantam Jeep prototype, the military called for certain mechanical refinements. And due to American Bantam's tiny production facilities, the QMC awarded "backup" manufacturing contracts to Willys-Overland and Ford. Willys did engineer the Jeep's four-cylinder engine, using the same powerplant that originated in the 1926 Whippet.

American Bantam eventually built 2643 Jeeps, most of which were shipped to Russia. Willys-Overland and Ford together produced nearly 600,000 wartime Jeeps, and in W-O's case, the windfall saved the company.

With Jeep money pouring in, Willys-Overland began planning a postwar car. To style this car, W-O's engineering vice president, Delmar G. (Barney) Roos hired Brooks Stevens, the Milwaukee-based industrial designer (see next page). Stevens began submitting proposals to Roos as early as 1942.

At the same time, John Tjaarda, the father of the 1936 Lincoln Zephyr (page 127), approached W-O board chairman Ward Canaday and suggested that the Willys Jeep become the basis for what he envisioned as a postwar "world car." Tjaarda pointed out that since the Jeep and Jeep parts were already stockpiled all over the globe, why not sell civilian and military versions worldwide after the war? Canaday considered Tjaarda's idea but then put it on hold.

Meanwhile, Stevens designed and Roos built two running prototypes of a small, postwar passenger car codenamed "6/66." The 6/66 used the four-cylinder Jeep engine and other Jeep components and sported quite a contemporary body, but that project was also sidelined when W-O changed presidents. Joe Frazer left and

The Jeep at MOMA

In 1951, New York's Museum of Modern Art (MOMA) staged an exhibit called "Eight Automobiles." This show in the museum's courtyard had its beginnings in a symposium held on Apr. 12, 1950 at which the museum's director of architecture and design, Philip Johnson, asked seven people to join him in talking about and evaluating automobile design. The seven were GM engineering v.p. James M. Crawford; Wilder Hobson, a car enthusiast and former editor of *Fortune*; Geoffrey Smith, editor of the British magazine *Autocar*; D. Cameron Peck, auto enthusiast and president of both the Sports Car Club of America and the Antique Automobile Club of America; Elliot Noyes, architect, designer and former

director of MOMA's industrial design department; Howard A. (Dutch) Darrin, a Kaiser-Frazer design consultant; and Raymond Loewy, industrial designer. These seven formed the informal jury that Philip Johnson

used to select his eight examples of what he called "hollow, rolling sculpture" (thus the name of Gordon Buehrig's book). The eight cars he chose for the 1951 show ranged from a 1931 Mercedes-Benz SS 4-place roadster—the epitome of sporty, shiny elegance—to the simple U.S. military Jeep. Rounding out the selection were the 1937 Cord 812, the 1941 Lincoln Continental, 1949 MG-TC, 1939 Bentley, 1949 Cisitalia coupe by Pinin Farina, and 1939 Talbot-Lago. Johnson's selections have all stood the test of time extremely well, and there's no question today that the Jeep—the most unlikely of the eight cars—holds its own stylistically against the rest. ◆

Brooks Stevens designed 6/66 (far left) as a possible postwar Willys, and while W-O built and tested prototypes, the car never got off the ground. Stevens was no more successful in his attempt to get Willys to produce his "Victory" model, essentially a rebodied military Jeep.

Charles Sorensen, previously of Ford, came in. Sorensen, along with Canaday and Roos, decided that the company's future lay with the Jeep and that a small passenger car, which would probably cost more than a Ford or Chevrolet, wouldn't sell. Another reason for abandoning the 6/66 had to do with a company employ-

ee getting killed when one of the prototypes was hit by a train during testing.

So when the war ended, W-O simply continued Jeep production and made postwar Jeeps available to civilians. But this very basic, spartan, three-passenger vehicle wasn't really suitable for normal

Brooks Stevens: The Seer Who Made Milwaukee Famous

Brooks Stevens contracted polio as a child and, from age seven to nine—1918-20—wasn't allowed out of bed. His father, William C. Stevens, a mechanical engineer and vice president of design and development for the Cutler-Hammer Co. in Milwaukee, gave his son pencil and paper to help pass the time. As young Brooks lay propped up on pillows, he drew pictures, mostly of cars.

His father had developed a pre-selector gearshift during World War I, and as Brooks' health improved, his father took him on visits to major and minor automakers to demonstrate the device. The elder Mr. Stevens did convince such car companies as Premier, Apperson and Gardner to use his pre-selector and, as a by-product of those wonderful trips with his father, Brooks became thoroughly taken with automobiles.

He enrolled at Cornell in 1929 to study architecture. He put much more detail into the cars in his architectural drawings than into the buildings. When he graduated in 1933, he returned to Milwaukee, where his father suggested he open an industrial design studio. Cutler-Hammer became one of his first clients. Brooks redesigned the company logo and styled some of their hardware.

Like Raymond Loewy, Walter Dorwin Teague and Henry Dreyfuss, Brooks Stevens grew with the profession of industrial design. It was he who put the teardrop fuel tank and fenders on the 1936 Allis-Chalmers tractor. Stevens also created the first clothes dryer with a glass window (for Hamilton Mfg. Co.) and designed fleets of specialized trucks for Milwaukee's breweries.

More than anything else, though, he wanted to get into car design. In 1942, he presented a paper to the Society of Automotive Engineers entitled "The Practical Postwar Car." The paper contained a number of his styling drawings and got picked up in *Popular Mechanics,* where it caught the eye of Barney Roos, v.p. of

engineering for Willys-Overland. Roos phoned Stevens and asked him to come to his office in Toledo on a certain day, but he didn't say what time. Stevens arrived at eight that morning, and at four Roos finally got around to seeing him. "I almost lost my mind sitting in that lobby," Stevens recalled in a 1974 interview, "and finally I was ushered into an office that's 20 feet wide and 75 feet long, with Barney sitting at the far end. I walked that full distance and just wilted. But I lived through it and must have impressed Roos, because Willys retained me. We began immediately with postwar designs."

The results were the ill-fated postwar

Willys 6/66 sedan and the highly successful 1946 Jeep station wagon, 1946 Jeep truck line and the 1948 Jeepster. Stevens landed a similar consultancy with Kaiser-Frazer in 1948 and kept that contract long after Willys moved to Brazil. His firm restyled the Brazilian Aero Willys and the Willys Rural wagon several times between 1955 and 1974.

Stevens also designed or helped design, among others: the 1951 Alfa Romeo 1900 Sprint series, his own 1951 Excalibur J and SJ racing cars, Robert McCulloch's

1952 Paxton experimental mid-engined steam car, the 1954 Gaylord, three 1956 Scimitar showcars for Olin Aluminum, the 1957-59 Willys Jeep cab-over truck line and other commercial Jeep vehicles, the 1962 Willys Jeep Gladiator truck plus a number of Brazilian Willys Jeep trucks and wagons. In addition, he styled the classic Harley-Davidson 1950 motorcycles and Cushman scooters.

In 1960, Stevens styled the 1962 Studebaker Hawk, applying a new, squarer roof and different sheetmetal to what was essentially the 1953 Loewy coupe. He also penned the 1963 Jeep Wagoneer and gave it a number of facelifts throughout its long and happy life. Brooks Stevens and two of his sons launched the Excalibur SS retro phaeton in 1963 and by 1988 had built 3600 of them. The prototype Excalibur SS was originally intended to be a Studebaker showcar, but when Studebaker adopted the slogan "The Common Sense Car," its public-relations people withdrew the Excalibur from the New York show, so Stevens displayed it as a private entry.

Stevens also designed the 1963 Studebaker Lark Wagonaire, then had Carrozzeria Sibona & Basano in Italy build three marvelous steel prototypes as proposals for the 1964-67 Lark line. He aided Budd in conceiving the 1968 Volkswagen 411 series and at the same time worked with American Motors on the 1969-70 Ambassador, Hornet, Gremlin, AMX and Javelin Landau. In 1979, he proposed the compact Jeep XJ-100 Wagoneer, which went into production in 1984 as the Jeep Cherokee. Stevens subsequently worked with Chrysler on the entire Jeep line.

Brooks had always been a car collector, and in 1954 he opened a private auto museum in Mequon, Wisconsin. Among the jewels on display were or are: the Sakhnoffsky 1930 Cord L-29 Paris and Monte Carlo Salon coupe, Walter Dorwin Teague's 1933 Marmon V-12 prototype, Roscoe Hoffman's 1935 experimental rear-

Stevens did succeed with his designs for postwar Willys Jeep derivatives. His popular all-metal 1948 Jeep station wagon (above) used Di-Noc to simulate wood siding. Stevens' 1950

Jeepster, a true roadster with sidecurtains, came out with doors and a few more amenities than this early sketch indicates. It did manage to retain original Jeep's sporting flavor.

engined X-8 prototype built for the Fisher Brothers, the ex-Caracciola 1928 Mercedes phaeton, the ex-King Alfonso 1925 Rolls phaeton, the 1933 Studebaker Indy race car driven by Tony Gulotta, a 1934 Miller Indy car, the ex-Von Neumann 1939 Jaguar SS-100 plus an assortment of similarly pedigreed wonders.

Stevens prided himself on being the man who coined the phrase "planned obsolescence." The concept predated his use of the term in a 1953 speech before the Milwaukee Advertising Managers Club. "I never expected 'planned obsolescence' to be publicized and misinterpreted as 'planned waste,'" Stevens said later. But simply giving the concept a name brought a shower of brickbats. Vance Packard's *The Waste Makers* had a field day with the idea. Stevens explained that he meant, "In modern United States living, planned obsolescence stems from our desire to own something a little newer and a little better a little sooner than is necessary. Our whole economy...is based upon this constant improvement, this constant change. It is the force that keeps production, employment and public purchasing power at a maximum."

Brooks Stevens, who was born in 1911, continued to design products in semi-retirement, at the same time teaching college courses in industrial design. He gave spirited, articulate interviews right up to the day of his passing on Jan. 4, 1995, all brimming with his experiences of more than half a century. ◆

(Clockwise from upper left) Brooks Stevens loved racing. Together with his sons, he fielded a team of Willys-powered Excalibur J roadsters. The showcar they originally built for Studebaker became their Excalibur SS, of which they built 3600 between 1963 and '88. Stevens redesigned several Willys vehicles for manufacture in South America--an Aero and Rural wagon shown here. And Olin Aluminum commissioned him to design three 1956 Scimitars along neo-classic lines.

1952 Aero Willys became Phil Wright's last production design. It began as an exercise in *Road & Track* magazine. Like Hudson and Kaiser-Frazer, W-O had a hard time selling a compact, partly because the Aero Willys was $200 more expensive than a full-sized 1952 Ford, Plymouth or Chevrolet.

transportation needs, so in 1944 Sorensen and Roos commissioned Brooks Stevens to design a number of Jeep derivatives, the first of which became the all-steel Jeep station wagon. The W-O Jeep wagon made its debut in 1946. It borrowed the Jeep's face and engine but used an entirely different frame and body.

One of the requirements of the Jeep wagon's body was that draw depth be kept to six inches. Stevens held the roof's draw to just under that and the body draw to 2.5 inches. The Willys-Overland wagon met with great success and stayed in production for many years: a handy, unpretentious family and commercial vehicle for all seasons. (By the way, the Jeep's and Willys wagon's offspring are still very much with us today in the form of Chrysler-built Jeep Wranglers, Cherokees and Grand Cherokees.)

At the same time Stevens conceived the Willys wagon, he also proposed another sporty Jeep derivative—a phaeton—to be called *Jeepster.* Jeepster production began in the spring of 1948 and ended after 1951. By that time, Willys-Overland had decided to go ahead with a more serious, much more ambitious project: the compact Aero Willys series.

Proposals for the 1952 Aero Willys had long been suggested to Ward Canaday by Packard's former chief engineer, Clyde Paton. Paton had been indirectly involved in Ford's postwar small car—the one that ended up as the French Ford Vedette (see page 137). The Vedette project left Paton a firm believer in light, compact cars, and after he left Ford he patented some of his own ideas. The artist who drew Paton's patent illustrations was Philip O. Wright, the former Murphy/Auburn/GM designer who'd styled the 1933 Pierce-Arrow Silver Arrow (see page 188 and 231). Wright was working for Briggs at the time.

Paton had been trying since 1948 to sell his small-car ideas to Canaday and Roos at Willys-Overland. And then in May 1950, *Road & Track* magazine published an article called "A Present Day Model A." The author and illustrator was Philip O. Wright, but the piece was probably written with Paton's help. Ward Canaday read the *Road & Track* article, either at Paton's request or otherwise, and soon afterward phoned Paton. He asked Paton to begin engineering what he then called the "Willys Wing," later renamed the "Aero Willys." Canaday also asked Paton to bring Phil Wright in as the project's stylist.

Between July and October 1950, Wright whipped up a full-sized clay of the Aero sedan, following the general theme he'd sketched in the *Road & Track* article. With time so short, Wright didn't wait for formal approvals and began to release some of the inner body panels for tooling. The body was to be built by Murray Corp. of America, because W-O had no deep-draw stamping presses and couldn't handle unitized construction. So while mahogany die models were being hand finished at Murray, Wright was still ironing out some of the surface details on the Aero clay model.

Clyde Paton felt confident that Wright's design would be accepted, but when Canaday and the Willys board met in Oct. 1950 to

formally pass judgement, they turned the design down. Production was scheduled to begin in less than a year, and here was Wright with a semi-released body and Murray with woodcarvers already working on mahogany die models when suddenly everything screeched to a halt.

There was nothing for Wright to do but get back to work. He called in an old friend, a clay modeler and sometime wrestler named Bill Mitchell (*not* William L. Mitchell, the GM design vice president) plus another modeler named Caesar Testaguzza. Together, these three had exactly one week—seven days and seven nights—to pull together another full-sized clay model. Mitchell had an industrywide reputation for being fast, and W-O was paying him $1000 a day to be just that. Wright, Mitchell and Testaguzza brought in cots and worked in shifts. This all took place at the Murray plant in Detroit where, ironically, the Hudson Jet was simultaneously being developed in an adjoining room. The bodies for both cars were eventually built alongside one another on Murray assembly lines.

Fortunately, Wright's rejected design merely needed cleaning up. Its first iteration had a massive, complicated grille that the directors didn't like. It also lacked tailfins, that magic ingredient of so many designs from the early 1950s. Fortunately Wright soft-pedaled the fins, and while Mitchell worked up six different variants in clay, the fins chosen were blessedly tasteful. So was the entire car. The grille also became simplicity itself, with a single, horizontal chrome bar bearing a large "W." Mitchell carved two "W's" out of wood, wrapped them in foil, placed one on the clay's grille and the other on the decklid. These and a high rubstrip were the Aero's only ornamentation.

The unadorned nature of the Aero Willys might have been one of its failings. The other was surely its price, because the least expensive Aero sold for $1731, roughly $200 more than the cheapest 1952 Ford, Chevrolet, Plymouth or Studebaker. So the Aero Willys became anything but a runaway bestseller. To complicate matters, Henry Kaiser bought out Willys-Overland in 1953, forming the Willys Motor Corp., which now had two compacts of similar size and price: the Aero Willys and the Henry J, neither of which was going anywhere. The Henry J passed on in 1954 but the Aero Willys continued in this country through 1955, after which the body dies were shipped to Brazil. Brazilian variants of the Aero sedan and the Jeep Wagoneer continued to sell in South America through 1972. Brooks Stevens updated both vehicles' styling a number of times, and Buzz Grisinger worked on them also. (In 1963, Willys Motors Corp. became Kaiser Jeep Corp., which merged with American Motors in 1970. Chrysler Corp. bought AMC in 1987.)

In this country, Willys Motors/Kaiser Jeep concentrated on Jeep derivatives, and Brooks Stevens carried out several restylings of the Jeep station-wagon line here, too. He created the initial designs for the Jeep Wagoneer, Grand Wagoneer and the downsized Cherokee wagons for 1980. ◆

CHAPTER 12

FORD GOES FROM BOXY TO AERO

There's a wonderful story about how Gene Bordinat followed George Walker into Ford's design vice presidency. Seems Eleanor Ford, Edsel's widow, had the final say. She didn't like Walker, partly because he called her son, Bill, "the fucking kid," and she'd met Elwood Engel and didn't much like him either. Nor did Joe Oros seem right for the job.

Bill Ford mentioned to his mother that he favored Gene Bordinat. Eleanor Ford didn't know Bordinat, but somehow she heard that he and his wife would be shopping at a local J.L. Hudson department store one Saturday morning. She had her chauffeur drive her out there in her 1961 Lincoln four-door convertible sedan. Then she put the top down and waited in the parking lot.

When the chauffeur, who knew the Bordinats by sight, saw Gene and his wife come out of the store, he went over, introduced himself and asked them to come meet Eleanor Ford. So a very informal interview took place in the open Continental, and apparently the Bordinats passed muster.

Gene Bordinat moved into George Walker's office on June 1, 1961, inheriting not only his lambswool carpet and the black-and-white furniture but also Walker's bulky corporate title: vice president and director, styling office, Ford Motor Co. Bordinat held that position for 19 1/2 years, making him the longest-serving design vice president in U.S. automotive history. (Harley Earl became a GM vice president in Sept. 1940 and retired in Dec. 1958, so while Earl's *career* was longer, his vice presidency was about 15 months shorter than Bordinat's. And Bill Mitchell's was 10 months shorter than Earl's.) Bordinat skated through good times and bad, served five FoMoCo presidents, weathered two international oil crises and had the very difficult task of helping tailor Ford cars and trucks to fit an ever-growing body of government fuel-economy, emissions, bumper and safety mandates.

Within the company, Bordinat's principal patrons were Bill (William Clay) Ford, who'd initially suggested him for the job, and board chairman Henry Ford II. The strength of Bordinat's Ford family ties made some of his subordinates a little nervous, because when the unavoidable tugs of war took place between styling and upper management, his studio chiefs worried—and rightly—that Bordinat mightn't plead their case quite so vigorously as otherwise. The fact that Bordinat was very much a team player—in ways that Bill Mitchell, for instance, would never have dreamed of becoming—ultimately made FoMoCo designs more commercial and neutral than GM's.

In Bordinat's time, Ford rarely led the industry in styling. Leadership didn't mean that much to Bordinat; it wasn't his obsession the way it was with Earl and Mitchell. Bordinat cast himself more as a designer/businessman and tended to measure success in unit sales rather than styling impact. When *Automotive News* reporter Paul Lienert asked Bordinat in 1978 what his favorite car designs were, Bordinat answered, "You must remember that my pride in various cars is a function of a good 10-day sales report. Beauty is whether or not [the car] is a moneymaker, because beauty is a thing that the public judges.... Now you asked me if there are cars out there that I'm rather prideful of, and I'd say yes. For example, I'd say the present Pinto. Remember, [the Ford Pinto subcompact] is nine years old. Also remember that we've sold over 2.5 million of them, and there aren't too many people who can touch that."

Bordinat's Pinto answer might make some auto designers snicker, but he was being bluntly honest. Success in the commercial design business, Bordinat would say, *has* to be tallied in terms of sales. Yet Bordinat's management style, by which he tried to blend his own function into all other corporate activities—product planning, engineering, market research, finance, sales, advertising, etc.—was very unlike the rough, autocratic rule of men like Earl and Mitchell, designers who made decisions pretty much unilater-

Young designers traditionally apprenticed in advanced studios. Gene Bordinat had charge of Ford's advanced activity in 1952, when this photo was taken. Modelers worked on 3/8-scale clay, and full-sized airbrush rendering graced wall.

ally and who said, in effect, "Like it or not, this is what we're going to build." Bordinat wasn't like that. You could even say that he pioneered the way design centers operate today: through teamwork and cooperation.

The penalty—or at least the result—of Bordinat's management style was a blander overall product and fewer of what Chuck Jordan would call "home-run cars." The one important, incontestable home run that Bordinat delivered was the 1965 Mustang. All other cars styled during his vice presidency, if they were three-baggers at all, weren't up to GM's standards under Bill Mitchell—at least not in most peer opinions.

Soon after he took office, Bordinat changed some of the ways Ford went about designing its cars. He expanded his staffs and doubled the size of their workspace, adding two huge wings to the design center. He brought the advanced studios and fabricating shops out of the basement, then abandoned 3/8-scale clays and had all models done full size so that management could "read" them better.

Then around 1964, he started scheduling weekly styling shows for Ford management, a routine that's basically unchanged today. The primary show was and is called "Part One." Part One shows are get-togethers held every Friday for top corporate and divisional managers. Among other things, Part One shows give the production studios a weekly deadline to meet. That sometimes causes a scramble as Friday approaches, but it's the routine that's existed since early in Bordinat's vice presidency.

Bordinat later set up an additional program of weekly approval shows first thing every Monday morning. The purpose here was and is to get everyone together to plan out the rest of the week. Advanced studios weren't held to these rigid schedules but did and still do hold shows whenever it seems appropriate. Part One shows take place in the design center showroom or courtyard, not in the studios, whereas advanced shows usually were and are held in the studios.

Gene Bordinat Jr. grew up in the Detroit suburb of Pleasant Ridge, Michigan. The Pleasant Ridge of the 1930s, all four by eight blocks of it, was one of those tiny neighborhoods where everyone knew everyone and sometimes too well.

It happened that George W. Walker also lived in Pleasant Ridge and that Bordinat, one generation younger than Walker, went to high school with Walker's son and daughter. Walker occasionally drove the kids, including Bordinat, to Lincoln High School in Ferndale in his Marmon convertible sedan. On some of those trips Bordinat couldn't help noticing the illustrations lying on the Marmon's back seat. The George Walker of that time was on his way to becoming one of Detroit's most successful industrial designers.

It was in the back seat of Walker's Marmon that the teenaged Bordinat got his first glimpse of the design world. And Bordinat couldn't help being impressed. Walker, the former football pro, dressed elegantly, drove a beautiful car and had this mysterious ability to create products and packages from nothing more than a few squiggles on paper. Walker must have seemed a much more exotic being than Bordinat's own father, a very solid citizen who'd been a plant engineer with Willys-Overland in Toledo and who, in 1936, took a job with Chrysler in Detroit.

The younger Bordinat was born on Feb. 10, 1920 and, at an early age, discovered a talent for sketching. "Gene was always a quick sketch," commented his brother Philip Bordinat in a 1994 interview. "He could always sit down and draw things. I envied him tremendously, because I couldn't do that. And if you lived in Detroit as we did, you were surrounded by cars. Everyone worked either for a car company or for one of the suppliers. As kids, we were keen on cars and knew every model. That part was

there...cars were part of our consciousness."

Gene Bordinat skipped a year in high school, graduated at 17 and enrolled at the University of Michigan, majoring in art. In 1938, while still at the university, he heard about Harley Earl's school for automobile stylists, and it suddenly dawned on him what he really wanted to become. He immediately applied.

Bordinat was one of 33 students accepted that quarter, and among his schoolmates were Joe Oros and Elwood Engel (as well as Irv Rybicki, Homer LaGassey and Richard Arbib). Bordinat took additional evening courses in anatomical drawing at Cranbrook Academy in Bloomfield Hills. After graduating from Harley Earl's school, Bordinat entered GM Styling in 1939 as a $1800-a-year junior stylist in one of GM's advanced studios. Here he caught Harley Earl's attention by designing a new front end for the 1941 LaSalle, a car Earl favored but that GM dropped after 1940, so Bordinat's design had no chance of production. Earl did, however, reward him with a $25-a-month raise and moved him into the Chevrolet studio, where Bordinat played a minor role in facelifting the 1942 Chevy.

Bordinat spent the early part of World War II helping set up a tank production line in GM's Fisher Body plant in Flint. He then joined the Army Air Corps and waited out the rest of the war in what he termed "an uneventful military career." He returned to GM Styling in 1946, at a time when trained, experienced auto stylists found themselves in big demand. There weren't enough to go around. So Bordinat, along with the rest of his GM colleagues, watched with fascination as Ford, Kaiser-Frazer, Loewy, Briggs and other firms tried to outbid each other for their talents.

Ford Motor Co. aggressively courted GM designers (including Harley Earl) by promising high salaries and bright futures. Among the first to leave GM Styling for Ford were Oldsmobile stylist/engineer John Oswald and George Snyder. Oswald worked at Auburn as a body engineer before going to GM. Snyder had been in overall charge of Chevrolet, Pontiac and Oldsmobile studios just after the war.

After Snyder joined Ford, Bordinat ran into him one evening in the summer of 1947 and, according to Bordinat, "George said, 'Hey, you're missing out on a great opportunity [at Ford].' He told me to get my samples together and come on over, and I did and, of course, for me that was a quantum leap. I'd had a taste of supervision—not in styling but in the manufacturing end [at Fisher Body]—and to go back to the board seemed to test my patience a little bit, so I was more than pleased to come over in a supervisory capacity...and...the money was pretty good, too." Bordinat made the switch in Aug. 1947 and was put in charge of Ford's advanced styling activity.

Ford styling seethed with politics in those days, one of the principal actors being George Walker, the man who'd chauffeured Bordinat to high school in his Marmon. Walker brought Elwood Engel and Joe Oros into Ford with him and parked them in fairly high managerial positions. They became Walker's eyes, ears and hands in Dearborn even before Walker got his Ford vice presidency in May 1955. At that time, Bordinat was just another young Ford stylist on the way up, but he might have had an edge over those who hadn't known Walker in Pleasant Ridge.

By 1954, Bordinat became manager of the Lincoln-Mercury styling department. Under him were William M. Schmidt, chief stylist of the Lincoln studio, and Don DeLaRossa, chief stylist in the Mercury studio; also John Najjar, head of Lincoln-Mercury's body analysis and advanced styling section, and Hermann C. Brunn, head of L-M trim and color.

Bordinat was bright and driven and politically aware, having learned not only at Harley Earl's knee but by knowing and watching Walker. When Walker invited Bordinat to join him as a

Gene Bordinat Jr.

  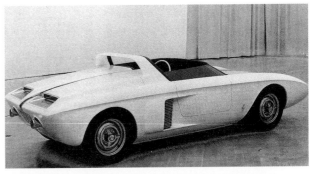

Ford's 1962 Mustang 2-seater shared only its name with the 1965 production car. Two running prototypes were built, each using a fwd German Taunus V-4 in the rear (same idea as Pontiac's 1984 Fiero). Troutman & Barnes built the aluminum bodies. Ford product planners deemed this Mustang too sports-car-like for the masses, and they were probably right.

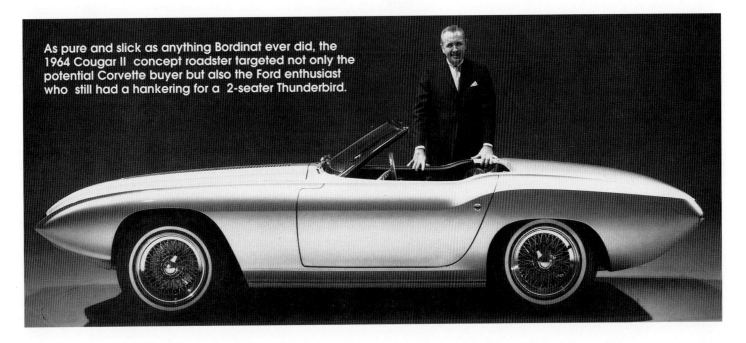

As pure and slick as anything Bordinat ever did, the 1964 Cougar II concept roadster targeted not only the potential Corvette buyer but also the Ford enthusiast who still had a hankering for a 2-seater Thunderbird.

Mason—an organization Walker was proud to belong to but one that Bordinat saw as polarizing Protestant and Catholic factions within Ford's styling staff—he politely declined.

Walker split Lincoln and Mercury into separate studios and made Najjar chief designer for Lincoln and Bordinat head of the Mercury studio. Walker gave Bordinat first choice, and Bordinat chose Mercury because he felt it had more variety and advancement possibilities. A little later, Oros became head of Ford car and truck styling and Walker put Engel in charge of Lincoln-Mercury plus advanced design. Concurrently, Engel became Walker's roving design critic with considerable clout throughout the department.

In 1961, toward the end of Walker's five-year stint as a Ford v.p., Elwood Engel, whom Walker had chosen to be his successor, managed to self-destruct [see page 150], whereupon Walker told Joe Oros that he (Oros) would succeed him (Walker) as v.p. Bill Ford, however, hated Walker and made it known that he'd have none of Walker's people in the vice presidency, and that's when he suggested Bordinat to his mother, Eleanor Ford. (As an aside, after Walker retired from Ford, not only did he maneuver Elwood Engel into the design vice presidency of Chrysler but he also lobbied George Romney, president of American Motors Corp., to hire Joe Oros as a replacement for Ed Anderson. There were industry rumors that Anderson wasn't happy with Romney's bid to bring in Walter Hoving from Tiffany (see page 202). Oros attended a dinner meeting with AMC management but then decided to stay at Ford, where he worked amicably with Bordinat for the rest of his career.)

For many years now, MBA candidates have studied the 1965 Ford Mustang not so much as a car but as a marketing case history. The Mustang, in contrast with the Edsel, shows one very right way to merchandise anything big and important, be it a car, a suburban subdivision or a politician. Ford Motor Co. made almost no mistakes with the Mustang. In fact, the Mustang's rightness helped erase memories of the $250 million Edsel fiasco.

In 1968, three and a half years after the first Mustang came out, Ford published a resource paper written specifically for college business and economics majors. Its purpose: to show the world that correct decisions, correct design and proper timing have their roots in a balanced mix of careful market strategy and gut hunches. The man who supplied the hunches, or who at least gets major credit for the Mustang hunch, was Lido Anthony (Lee) Iacocca. Iacocca made the Mustang and very much vice-versa.

Lee Iacocca's father came to America from Italy at age 12 and earned a lot of money by renting out Model T and A Fords. The family's car-rental and real-estate holdings totalled more than $1 million before the Depression, and the Depression didn't appreciably diminish that fortune. *Time* magazine, in a cover story at the Mustang's introduction, said, "Lee Iacocca never wavered from early youth in his desire to go into the auto business—with Ford. For him, it was something like wanting to join the priesthood."

Iacocca breezed through high school, then Lehigh University, took a master's degree from Princeton in mechanical engineering on scholarship (!) and finished an 18-month Ford marketing program in nine months. Ford offered him a job as a transmission engineer, but Lee favored sales and moved to an outpost in Pennsylvania. He did so well there that by 1956, Ford Div. general manager Robert S. McNamara took notice and borrowed a sales idea that Iacocca invented: his "$56 a month for a 1956 Ford" plan. It worked so well nationally that McNamara later credited Iacocca with selling 72,000 additional cars that year.

From there, Iacocca's Ford career went straight up. He kept a series of "little black books" and wrote in one of them that he intended to become a Ford v.p. by age 35. Iacocca's black books were talked about all over Dearborn, especially after he passed out blank copies and asked members of his staff to jot down their goals for the next few years. Every three months, he collected the books and graded the authors' performance against their goals.

To Iacocca's disappointment, his own 35th birthday came and went without a vice presidency. He thought about leaving Ford, but a year later Henry II called him into his office and asked him if he'd like to replace McNamara as vice president and general manager of Ford Div. Iacocca, of course, said yes, and as it happened, McNamara soon became John F. Kennedy's secretary of defense.

The Mustang, so goes the legend, sprang from one of those journal entries in Iacocca's little black book. His sales intuition told him that there must be a market out there looking for a car. Customers were still asking Ford to *please* revive the two-seater Thunderbird. Meanwhile, Chevrolet had struck gold with its sporty, bucket-seated, highly affordable Corvair Monza. The Monza accounted for 76% of Corvair sales soon after its Mar. 1961 intro. Imported sports cars, too, like the MG, Jaguar, Triumph and Austin-Healey, were selling 80,000 cars a year despite fairly steep prices.

Iacocca figured that if the looks and personality of a sports car could be packaged in an inexpensive automobile for the mass market, people would buy it. The concept was a little hazy at first; the car had no name and even Lee didn't know whether it ought to be a two-seater or a four-seater, front- or mid-engined, steel or fiberglass. All that came later, but Ford insiders give considerable credit for the original Mustang idea to division product planning manager Donald N. Frey, saying Frey saw the market months before Iacocca did. Frey configured the car as a four-seater and suggested basing it on the economical Ford Falcon. Iacocca latched onto Frey's concept, refined it and

Lido Anthony Iacocca

pushed it through corporate finance and management.

Even before he could tackle the Mustang, though, Iacocca knew that his first job was to rescue Ford passenger cars from the conservative stamp McNamara had put on them. McNamara's first Ford, the 1957 model, was good-looking and had done extremely well. Ford, in fact, outsold Chevrolet that year, much to McNamara's delight. The 1958 four-place Thunderbird was another McNamara winner, as was the 1960 Falcon, but he hit some bumps in the road, too, notably the frumpy 1958 Ford. Due to the recession and the Edsel, 1958 was not a pleasant year for Ford, and McNamara's reaction was to cut back; retrench. He managed to keep Ford Div. profitable that way, but the gain was short-term. As *Time* pointed out, most Ford cars under McNamara's leadership were "...like McNamara himself: rimless glasses and hair parted in the middle."

Iacocca arrived at Ford Div. too late to do much about the 1961-62 lines, but he jazzed up the 1963 1/2 models by dropping the first V-8 into the Falcon, adding fastbacks to Ford's full-sized and intermediate coupes and plunging Ford headlong into serious racing. After Lee talked Henry II into re-entering NASCAR, Ford dominated all the big southern ovals. Ford also soon won Sebring, won Indy and won twice at Le Mans (1966-67). The imagemakers coined the term "Total Performance" and made it part of Iacocca's drive to give Ford Div. more youth appeal.

Iacocca now took up the question of the Mustang—not yet called that—at the first meeting of the "Fairlane Group," an eight-member committee that included Don Frey, Frey's young assistant Hal Sperlich plus representatives from Ford's PR, advertising, marketing and racing areas. The Fairlane Group took its name from the Fairlane Inn Motel on Michigan Avenue in Dearborn where it met, the idea being to get off Ford property and brain-

Ford's entire design staff struggled to develop a 4-place Mustang that Iacocca would like and Henry II would approve. A deadline loomed when a plant would have to be committed. At that point 11 different full-sized clays took part in a courtyard "bakeoff." Photos show some candidates, including winning white model created by Oros/Phaneuf team.

storm in relative tranquility. The Fairlane Group agreed that the sporty-car idea might merit further exploration and tentatively called it "Project T-5."

Iacocca, working mostly with corporate chief stylist Bob Maguire and his executive designer, Don DeLaRossa, in one of Ford's advanced studios, put forth a number of T-5 proposals, none of which impressed Henry Ford II. These efforts continued for nearly eight months, but Henry Ford II had been so shaken by the Edsel that he wouldn't commit. HF-II also felt that the Corvair Monza market, even with imported sports cars tossed in, wasn't big enough to bother with.

Mustang's tremendous success set all auto-makers scrambling.

Iacocca, though, stuck to his mission. Through Frey, he asked Hal Sperlich to do some heavy market research aimed at showing economic and demographic reasons to bring out the T-5. Sperlich, a very sharp go-getter with lots of marketing savvy, recognized that the purpose of his research was to either prove or destroy Frey's and Iacocca's hunches. He further realized that only if Iacocca could show that the T-5 would sell in big numbers would Henry II go for the idea.

Sperlich, after weeks of surveys and studies, concluded that, yes, there was a good-sized market out there. But HF-II still wasn't convinced. The Edsel had left him so gun-shy that it shook his faith in market research as well. As a last resort, Iacocca decided that the only way to convince HF-II would be to show him something so impressive that he couldn't resist. At that point he asked Bordinat to launch a fleet of proposals, a group of totally new T-5s and, as a result, Buzz Grisinger's Lincoln-Mercury studio submitted one, the Ford production studio did another and advanced came up with three more. By this time the T-5 was being referred to as the "special Falcon."

The styling hierarchy under design v.p. Bordinat at that time consisted of: 1) design directors, 2) design executives, 3) studio managers and 4) senior designers, in that order down the ladder. Under each senior designer were several studio stylists—usually two or three per team.

Also as background, all Ford Div. styling was done by four basic groups: 1) the Ford production studio, which did the final designing and release work on full-sized Fords, Fairlanes and Falcons; 2) the production Thunderbird studio; 3) the production Ford truck studio; and 4) the Ford pre-production studio. The pre-production studio had the task of feeding advanced designs to the other Ford groups.

Physically, the Ford/Fairlane/Falcon/T-Bird studios occupied "bays" inside one huge room of the Ford design center off Oakwood Boulevard in Dearborn. The full-sized Ford studio area and the Fairlane/Falcon group shared one bay with an open door between them. The Ford truck studio was in a separate bay at one end of the same building. Ford's pre-production studio was located in a smaller room across the hall from the main area. And it was

in this smaller pre-production studio that the eventual Mustang got its start.

At the time of the Mustang's development, Joe Oros was the director of all Ford studios, so he had overall charge and reported directly to Bordinat. David L. Ash was Oros' executive stylist in charge of all Ford car exterior studios. Gale L. Halderman was manager of the Ford production studio. Director of all corporate advanced studios was Bob Maguire, and Don DeLaRossa acted as his executive, with Charles H. (Charlie) Phaneuf as manager of the Ford pre-production studio. To complete the roster, Buzz Grisinger was director of Lincoln-Mercury production design; Damon Woods was director of corporate interiors; John Najjar had charge of Ford car and truck interiors; with John B. Foster manager of Thunderbird and Mustang interiors.

Charlie Phaneuf's pre-production studio was an idea shop where advanced designs got done without interference from engineers, financial people and others. George Schumaker, who worked as a designer under Phaneuf, called this pre-production studio "Joe Oros' sandbox and the perfect place to start a new project." In a written report of the Mustang's initial development, Schumaker went on to say, "Late in the first week of Aug. 1962, our Ford pre-production studio was asked to participate in a final shoot-out to come up with a sporty car—one that HF-II would approve of. Charlie Phaneuf, along with the five of us in his studio—Marty Kalman, Rod Lloyd, Frank Ruff, John Starr and me—got called into Charlie's office one Friday morning by Dave Ash, and Dave told us that we had 11 days to come up with a clay model of a sporty, youth-oriented, four-passenger car derived from Falcon components. This car would be referred to in the studio as 'the special Falcon.'"

(Ford, by the way, did build and publicize an experimental two-place roadster in 1962 called *Mustang*. This used a V-4 powertrain from the front-drive German Ford Taunus but moved it to the rear so the car became mid-engined and rear-drive. That first Mustang, styled by John Najjar and Jim Sipple under Bob Maguire and Damon Woods and engineered under v.p. Herb Misch, was never seriously considered for production due to its limited sales potential. Hardcore sports-car buffs would have bought it, but the mid-engined Mustang didn't have the broad appeal of the ultimate 1965 production Mustang.)

The 11-day deadline came about because, if the T-5 or "special Falcon" *were* to be built at all, it would have to be produced in one certain plant. The plant manager had to have a yea or nay commitment. He explained that if the T-5 *weren't* going to be built, he'd reassign that plant for other uses. Iacocca, anxious to have the T-5 produced, ordered Bordinat and Oros to whip up a T-5 proposal HF-II could approve.

Joe Oros was attending a management seminar on the day Ash huddled in Phaneuf's office, but when Oros returned nearly a week later, he didn't like the work that had been done in his absence. That first day after lunch, he called a meeting of his full staff in the styling showroom and asked each person to describe what he thought the "special Falcon" ought to be and look like.

John J. (Jack) Telnack Jr., at that time a young stylist in the Ford studio, recalled, "Joe sat us down, and we did a brainstorming session. It was probably the most significant meeting I ever heard Joe Oros handle. It was a real design-y type meeting, the kind you always learned how to do in school but don't put into practice too much, especially back in those days. But we...developed an image strategy for the car and carried it out that way. It was a textbook sort of beginning for the program."

In Oros' words: "We talked about the sporty car not being too masculine, too macho. It had to appeal to women as well as to men. We agreed that it had to be sporty and personal, that young people would enjoy driving it, a car that would look like fun."

Schumaker added: "Joe hung two large sheets of sketching vellum on the wall behind my drawingboard and wrote a *do* list on one sheet and a *don't* list on the other. Everyone contributed and commented and added to both lists. These sheets stayed on the wall of our studio until the model was finished, and during the next few days Joe came in and crossed off each item, one by one."

Gale Halderman made some sketches at home; he hadn't had time to do them at work because of the deadline of the 1965 big Ford. Oros liked one of Halderman's sketches and handed it to Charlie Phaneuf in the Ford pre-production studio. Phaneuf com-

The Styling Labyrinth

It used to be, long ago, that one person could literally style and lay out a car body by himself. He could then turn his body drafts over to a handful of skilled craftsmen and watch his ideas take shape in wood and metal. That's how most automobile bodies were designed and built in the early days of the motorcar. With coachbuilders, this process survived into the late 1930s. The typical body designer of that era usually had a good technical background and was often as much a body engineer as a stylist.

Between that time and this, autobody design has evolved into a tremendously complicated process that's rarely done by fewer than dozens of people working together as a team. Today, the process demands Napoleonic managerial skills, a high degree of logistical organization and an array of sophisticated, expensive electronic machinery.

Each corporate styling department has its own way of doing things, and the design process changes constantly, but it might be helpful to understand the essential design procedures as they used to take place in a typical auto company. As our core example, we'll focus on Ford Motor Co. around the mid 1960s, because Ford was fairly representative of the industry at that time and reflects in many ways what's still practiced today.

Ford had what all car companies now have and rely on to an ever-greater extent: a product-planning department. Ford described its approach to auto design as a "three-legged stool." The three legs were product planning, engineering and styling, not necessarily in that order.

Product planners made recommendations to management, who decided whether to offer a new car or change an old one. If new or changed, what audience and pocketbook should the car appeal to? What features should it have? And in a very general way, what should the body look like?

At that point, company engineers would draw up "the package," the parameters of the proposed car. These might take the form of an engineering drawing, but the emphasis here would not be on style. Package elements would include seating and pedal positions, trunk space, powertrain location, dash-to-front-axle dimensions and other particulars known as "hard points." The resulting specifications would determine wheelbase, length, height, width, weight plus the engine power and gearing required for good performance and fuel economy. Concurrently, based on these data, cost analysts would begin estimating production expenses. And it would be at this point that styling was handed the package.

Ford styling in the mid 1960s had roughly 1000 staff members. Of these, approximately 170 were designers, 290 were clay modelers, 60 were administrators, 340 were studio engineers, and 140 were fabricators and skilled artisans working in the wood, metal, plaster, fiberglass, paint and trim shops. In addition, there were secretaries and support people in administration: purchasers, timing coordinators, personnel, etc.

At that time, most FoMoCo designers worked in huge, high-ceiling, tall-windowed rooms. Each room was divided into "bays," with each bay devoted to one specific project or car line. In other words, Thunderbird designers occupied one bay of the Ford production studio, and those designing the Ford Galaxie worked in a neighboring bay. Each group usually consisted of four or five stylists, eight to 10 modelers and two or three body engineers. And each bay would contain several such groups.

Overall studios were broken into six different types:

•**Advanced studios** turned out dream-cars and "Buck Rogers" designs envisioned for four to eight years in the future. Advanced was also a catch-all that submitted production designs for Ford International, Ford of Canada, tractors, trucks, etc.

•**Ford pre-production studios** created preliminary studies and designs "to package" for management approval. They worked on Falcon, Ford, Mustang and Thunderbird.

•**Ford production studios** readied approved designs for production.

•**Lincoln-Mercury production studios** readied L-M designs for production. These studios worked on Mercury, Comet, Cougar and Lincoln. There was no L-M pre-production studio.

•**Interior studios** served all other studios in designing and preparing seats, instrument panels, trim; determining sightlines, ergonomics; also in the selection of fabrics, colors, door hardware, mirrors, etc. Ford estimated that its interior studios designed approximately 2600 different items each year.

•**Industrial design studio** did graphics and designs for Philco, tractors, other Ford subsidiaries plus architectural studies and models.

The actual design process usually began, then as now, with pencil sketches: hundreds of them. Designers in advanced studios didn't have to adhere to specific packages and could let their imaginations run wild. Young designers usually apprenticed in advanced studios so the corporation could glean their freshest ideas before production reality set in.

The styling vice president or one of his top aides might take themes or ideas from an advanced studio into a pre-production or production studio to illustrate the direction a design should take. That's not to say that the production or pre-production studios weren't simultaneously generating hundreds of idea and theme sketches of their own. All were constantly turning out drawings, and it was up to the design manager to choose the most appropriate one or several for the project at hand. Any number of different preliminary sketches might have lent ideas to a single production design, and at that point the manager's job was to amalgamate them into a harmonious whole. It's always easier to spot a production car whose contributing sketches weren't well integrated than one whose were.

Once idea sketches were chosen, the next step was to make full-sized tape drawings or airbrush renderings of the design in dead-on side view, front view and rear view. This preceded the making of clay models, which were usually based on these non-perspective drawings. Changes were still easy to make at this stage and often were. And sometimes the designer became the modeler, some designers preferring to work in three dimensions rather than two.

Meanwhile, the interior studios would

bined Halderman's ideas with the silhouette of the 1956 Continental Mark II, a car Phaneuf had also worked on. Phaneuf scaled the whole thing down to fit the Falcon platform. He kept the Mark II's hop-up on the rear fender, the long hood, the short deck, the general shape of the greenhouse, but he put more rake in the windshield.

George Schumaker didn't recall the Halderman sketch, and he emphatically credited Phaneuf with the major design elements, including the high, above-bumper grille. "The front end was a problem," recalled Schumaker. "I remember Charlie wanting a high mouth, but he had to convince Oros, who was from the wider-is-better school of sedan design. I remember a heated meeting between them in Charlie's office. Charlie finally came out holding a rough sketch of the front end he wanted, and he told me, 'Here, put this in clay.' I led the modelers on the front end, and we used oval headlights from a German Ford Taunus, the nerf-blade front bumper per Joe's *do* list, and tunneled parking lamps in the bumper pan."

Oros didn't remember the grille discussion with Phaneuf and said the group had agreed beforehand that, "...the front end had to have a Ferrari-like mouth with a dominant center diecast motif similar in strength to the Maserati trident." All four design teams

start designing seating and instrument-panel bucks, usually in full-sized clay. Seating and i.p. bucks often also included details fabricated from Styrofoam, wood and paper. The aim was to make the interior match or complement the exterior. In the 1970s, Monsanto introduced a product called Fome-Cor—a material that sandwiched Styrofoam between sheets of heavy white paper. Fome-Cor was widely used in interior styling bucks.

To make full-sized clay models, clay was applied over huge wood-slat armatures that had real wheels and tires spaced to specification. Armatures for full-sized clays were and still are sometimes made of large blocks of urethane foam. (The latest armatures use modular aluminum frames that can be adjusted for different car sizes. These are covered with blocks of rigid foam before clay is applied.) Little by little, a full-sized "car" began to emerge. Changes in the clay surface were fairly easy to make, and when the design began to approach its final form, with approval imminent, the model could be skinned with a thin, paintable plastic film called Di-Noc that could be stretched over the clay. Brightwork was surfaced in a special soft aluminum foil smoothed over the clay surface. Or it might also be molded from fiberglass and vacuum plated. Or cast in low-melting-point alloys that buffed up like chromium. Headlights and trim details were often real.

One side note about the clay modeler's skill. A scale clay model, say in 3/8 or 1/4 size, cannot be a literal, miniaturized version of the real thing. The modeler has to cheat some of the proportions, because the viewer sees the small model from an abnormal height and angle. A good modeler takes this into account when he creates his scale model. He likewise can't simply blow up his 3/8- or 1/4-scale model to full size, because again it wouldn't look right. The parts he cheated in miniature would look strange at 100%. For those reasons, Ford went to full-sized models (except for windtunnel testing) in the early 1960s.

Concurrent with the sculpting of the full-sized clay, "blackboard men" kept changing

the full-sized views of the design on huge upright boards. These boards were painted black in the early days, and the body outline—with all cut lines, windows, moldings and details—was carefully drawn in chalk. Every dimension had to be dead accurate, and it took great skill to do these drawings correctly. Later, colored pencil or airbrush on dark paper replaced blackboards. Later still, thin colored tapes on vellum replaced the pencil lines. Tape drawings were easier to repair or change as the design progressed.

When Ford management approved the finished full-sized clay model, points were taken and templates were made from it. Afterward, a more permanent fiberglass model was cast from the clay—first as a series of female plaster molds and then as a huge male fiberglass replica. The fiberglass model became the most realistic rendition of the design—an accurate, three-dimensional picture—until actual metal stampings became available.

After approval of the full-sized clay, the making of tools and sheetmetal stamping dies could begin. This first involved the

Fiberglass 1961 styling mockups in Ford's viewing area gave executives one last chance to make minor styling changes.

cutting of cardboard or wooden templates and using these templates to create surface drawings on paper. The drawings were then transferred onto huge, white-painted aluminum sheets, using a gold stylus to make the lines. The aluminum sheets didn't shrink or distort the way paper might. These drawings now served as drafting masters for the exterior surface and structural sheetmetal components.

From the aluminum master drafts, high-

ly skilled craftsmen would make mahogany master models ("impregs"), one for each major approved surface panel. Die models were later duplicated from these mahogany masters by huge Kellering machines. Kellering machines used "feelers" moving over the master surfaces to guide grinders and cutters that ultimately milled exact duplicates in specially hardened steel. These steel dies were then used to stamp the body sheetmetal.

A certain amount of "springback" inevitably takes place when the stamping press releases the pressed steel part, especially in large panels like hoods, fenders and decklids. So there are usually two mahogany die models made, one for styling-surface approval and a second, oversized or undersized master developed by experienced body engineers to stamp the actual steel sheets. When the body engineer misjudges the springback, as he occasionally does, you'll see doors or hoods that curve inward ever so slightly at their edges.

Several addenda to bring the narrative up to date. Early body prototypes through the 1930s were often made entirely of wood rather than clay or plaster. These wooden mockups were done full size, had glass windows, opening doors, real wheels and tires, were fully trimmed and upholstered inside and looked very much like the real thing. General Motors used wooden body prototypes through World War II, after which GM switched to full-sized plaster casts for a short time and then went to fiberglass full-sized body representations in the early 1950s. Soon afterward, the entire industry began making fiberglass body prototypes.

In recent years, much of the earlier handwork has been taken over by machines. Electronic scanners and point takers ensure dimensional accuracy. Computers now make repeated geometric patterns much easier to design; e.g. the spokes of a wheel or the texture of a grille. Autocad computer programs make it possible to mill three-dimensional objects out of clay, metal, plastic or virtually any other material after they've been rendered numerically (see sidebar, page 268). ◆

knew roughly what the others were doing, because the bays were open and discussions took place constantly. Oros made the point that the Mustang wasn't the product of any specific designer or studio. It was definitely, he felt, a group effort. Oros also said that, to meet the deadline, he asked all designers who could to stay until 9:00 p.m. He also asked modelers to work in three eight-hour shifts at one point. This was the only way the proposals could be completed on time.

Boxy 1965 Ford marked a 180° turnaround from the finny, rounded shapes of the 1950s. Ford body engineering dictated its styling, and the car became surprisingly successful.

Oros, according to Schumaker, personally did the body sculpturing on the driver's side of the model and added a functional airscoop ahead of the rear fender to feed cool air to the rear brakes. "Since I was directing the modelers on the front, and the driver's side was already committed but with nothing on the passenger's side, I just kept on going around the car and down the passenger's side. Needless to say, it didn't turn out all that great, but no big loss."

The driver's side, though, did look good; in fact, better than good. It looked great. Oros had the model Di-Nocked white, so it stood out from the others, and Phaneuf added red brake drums peeking out from behind Dayton chromed wire wheels. This Phaneuf/Oros model, along with six others, was taken out into the design courtyard on Aug. 16, and Iacocca picked it as the hands-down winner. Gale Halderman observed, "Lee [Iacocca] was so convinced we had a design that he asked the cars to be left there [in the courtyard]. He went back to world headquarters and brought Mr. Ford over later that same day. It was confusing at the time, because Lee wanted to review the car with everyone present: sales, marketing, finance, etc., so that they would all...support the program."

Everyone favored the white car, specifying the Oros side treatment that eventually went into production. And with that, Oros placed the design into Gale Halderman's Ford production studio. Charlie Phaneuf said later that Halderman and his crew, plus a swarm of engineers, did 90% of the work from that point on, meaning the job of "feasing out" or preparing the car for manufacture.

The production Mustang won a number of design awards and received much praise for coming to market "as styled." But no car goes into production "as styled," and Gale Halderman remarked in a recent interview that Ford engineering drew up a list of 78 items that needed to be changed on the "special

Falcon" clay to make the Mustang less expensive and easier to manufacture. When Halderman showed the 78 changes to Oros and asked how to handle them, Oros replied dryly, "One by one." And early in the productionizing process, Iacocca, who was just as concerned with the changes as Halderman, addressed the engineers and made a threatening speech about leaving the Mustang as much "as styled" as humanly possible.

But changes there were, like moving the delicate bumpers out slightly for more clearance. And combining the tail lamps in bezels instead of making all six separate. Oros' chromed airscoop on the Mustang's rear fender was initially designed to push air over the brakes, but ducting and other hardware would have cost $5 per car, so the scoop ended up being decorative. And the body character line that led back into the scoop—slightly curved in Oros' initial version—was straightened to make the stamping process simpler.

Henry Ford II, being a tall man, sat in the Mustang seating buck and asked that the roof over the rear seat be raised 3/4 inch. "This we were happy to accommodate," said Oros. Halderman also shortened the trunk an inch and lengthened the hood by the same amount. These few examples illustrate the normal give-and-take between styling and body engineering, and none of the changes, obviously, affected the Mustang's aesthetics to any great extent.

The finished car bowed on Apr. 16, 1964 in a blizzard of national press teasers and Ford-orchestrated publicity. Both *Time* and *Newsweek* ran Iacocca and the Mustang on their covers that week. The car's base price, $2368, was even lower than the $2500 target the Fairlane Committee had set. By the end of the Mustang's first full year of production, Ford sold 418,812 copies, beating even the record-breaking Falcon's inaugural season. The company earned $1.1 billion in two years on the Mustang alone, and Iacocca found himself a marketing hero.

Stylistically, the Mustang looked fresh and sporty, but more than that, it had the requisite *personality*. That was the key. You saw the car sitting there and knew it had to be fun to drive: the stuff sports cars are made of. And the Mustang formula—appearance combined with character at an affordable price—moved American automobile design in a new direction. The Mustang popularized the long-hood/short-deck look and inspired a fleet of "pony-car" imitators, both here and abroad: the Mercury Cougar,

Ford's ultimate Mustang muscle concept car, 1967 Mach I (top), took cues like quick-fill gas cap from the company's

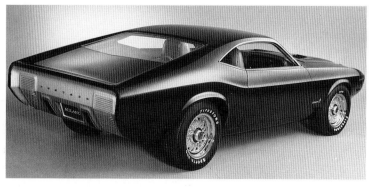

LeMans wins, while the 1969 Techna (left) highlighted innovation and the 1970 Milano stressed elegant simplicity.

Chevrolet Camaro, Pontiac Firebird, Dodge Challenger, Plymouth Barracuda, AMC Javelin, the European Ford Capri and the Japanese Toyota Celica.

The long-hood/short-deck theme wasn't new—it traced back through the 1963 Buick Riviera, through the 1940 Lincoln Continental and into the classic era, where long hoods symbolized powerful multi-cylinder engines. The Mustang picked up that message and then added a crouched, ready-to-pounce stance to the rear quarter. The buying public responded to that look, and it became the fashion not just for ponycars but also in personal luxury coupes like the Lincoln Mark series, the Thunderbird, GM's Toronado/Eldorado/ Riviera, Chevrolet's Monte Carlo and Pontiac's Grand Prix.

The Mustang, while very much Iacocca's baby, was—let's face it—a car designed by committee. Committees have a way of producing camels, but not always. The Mustang was not a camel. It became a committee car because that was the way Ford operated. It was a system that affected Gene Bordinat and his entire staff, but it was one he worked within comfortably. Bordinat, unlike Mitchell, was not a radical. He wasn't a risk taker. Bordinat used to say that when potential customers walked into a Ford showroom, he wanted them to see old friends...cars they were already familiar with. Nothing too new; no surprises; no visual jolts. Wavemaking wasn't in Bordinat's nature.

Perhaps for that reason, only the 1965 Mustang comes forward as a truly influential, widely copied design done during Bordinat's vice presidency. Most of his other cars—Fords, Mercurys and Lincolns of all shapes and sizes—were workmanlike, well-wrought, commercial designs, and a few did show some flair, like the 1964 Thunderbird and the 1969 Continental Mark III. But even those weren't daring, and none set trends. Bordinat traveled a committee-guided middle of the road, producing basically derivative cars; no great highs, no great lows, but no big mistakes either, unlike Bill Mitchell, whose gaffes were expensive the few times he made them (the 1971 boattail Riviera comes to mind). So Bordinat's overall track record wasn't bad, just lackluster.

Bordinat was so much a team player that engineering and manufacturing could and at times did dictate what had to be designed. Take, for example, the 1965 line of full-sized Fords. These were preceded by fairly soft and rounded cars from 1961 through 1964. The 1965 models, though, ended up boxy and square; all crisp, sharply bent corners. Why? Joe Oros felt it was an aesthetic decision, and others believed the design came in answer to the 1963 Pontiac, but as Gale Halderman tells it, "On the previous cars—

those with round headlamp bezels—the stamping process was such that the plant would spiral the sheetmetal, then tack-weld it, and finally put that piece into the die to get the areas where the round headlamp went. But then for some reason—either cost or ease of manufacture—the stamping people said they weren't going to do that anymore. They didn't want to go through that spiraling process.

"So we decided the only way we were going to get the inside down as deep as we wanted was to basically fold the outside front-fender line. The fender of the 1965 Ford was a #1 sweep, with just one fold at the edge. And this, in turn, dictated the theme of the car. It started the stacked headlights and square lamp bezel arrangement. The crisp front fender dictated not only the sharp beltline but also the rear fender, the squared-off roof shape and the rest of it."

The 1965 Ford, then, was styled basically to accommodate the tool-and-die people and the stamping plants. Yet because of, or despite, their very square configuration, Ford's 1965 full-sized cars sold very well. The industry, though, had little respect for what Ford was doing. GM stylists called the 1965 Fords "the box the 1963-64 Pontiacs came in." And Jeff Godshall, the Chrysler designer, noted that Ford at that time had an industry reputation for shaving manufacturing costs. This handicapped their designers. "It would never have happened at GM," said Godshall, "where Fisher Body took great pride in working out hard-to-make parts, like the 1971 Riviera rear bumper, the crisp, multi-piece Cadillac bumpers and the deep-draw Cadillac wheelcovers."

This isn't to say Ford designers couldn't do excellent work, and for evidence we need only look at some of the showcars produced during that era. One of the finest was the 1963-64 Cobra/Cougar II coupe and roadster. Another was the original mid-engined Mustang. Also noteworthy: the 1967 Mustang Mach I show coupe, the 1969 Techna and the 1970 Mustang Milano. Any one of them would have done Bordinat proud had they gone into production.

And there were some striking production designs, too. The 1969 Continental Mark III, done in Buzz Grisinger's Lincoln-Mercury studio, broke tradition by resurrecting the classic upright grille. And where did that grille come from? In his book *Ford*, Robert Lacey reported that Lee Iacocca was in a hotel in Canada one night and couldn't get to sleep. Iacocca had a "vision," according to Lacey, picked up the telephone and called Bordinat. "Put me a Rolls-Royce grille on the front of a Thunderbird," Iacocca told a half-asleep Bordinat, and the next morning Bordinat relayed the message to Grisinger.

The Rolls grille didn't go on a

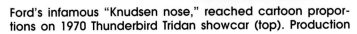

Ford's infamous "Knudsen nose," reached cartoon proportions on 1970 Thunderbird Tridan showcar (top). Production versions of Knudsen nose on Mercury Montego (left) and Thunderbird led government to mandate 5-mph bumpers.

Lincoln-Mercury studios, under Buzz Grisinger, led the movement toward architectural front ends. The 1969 Mercury Marquis (top left) had a wide, textured central porch flanked by upright columns at each end. Lincoln's 1969 Mark III

added the neo-classic grille, which made that front end look like a Greco-Roman temple. Tom Land captured the classic spirit in his 1970 Mark III dual-cowl phaeton (left), and by 1979, the Continental's grille was unabashedly Rolls-Royce.

Thunderbird, though; it went on the Mark III. And the first version wasn't a direct copy of the Rolls-Royce grille—not yet—but by 1973-74 and the Mark IV, the resemblance was clear. This was also the time when Mercedes sales started to take off in this country, and that lent another boost to the retro-grille theme. Lincoln's Mark series gave General Motors and Chrysler the courage to copy classic grille shapes, which Cadillac started doing with the 1979 Eldorado and 1980 Seville.

Another theme Grisinger's studio introduced was the architectural front end. Starting around 1969, the big Mercurys and Lincolns used a frontal motif that had the look of a classical Greek or Roman temple. This built on the Mark III look, but the front end cap was styled more like a building facade, with upright pillars on both sides and a wide, textured porch in the center. These Lincoln and Mercury faces had no eyes; the headlamps were hidden. The cars themselves were quite wide, giving the front aspect a massive, solid appearance. Chrysler picked up the theme for the 1976 New Yorker and gave it to several others of its full-sized cars.

Gene Bordinat didn't enjoy the second half of his vice presidency nearly so much as the first. Long as it was, his term of office might have gone on another five years if there hadn't been so many political and economic lightning storms.

In late 1967, when it seemed obvious to most Detroit watchers that Lee Iacocca would become the next company president, Henry Ford II installed Semon E. (Bunkie) Knudsen in that office instead. The reason seems to be that HF-II was expecting Lyndon Johnson to make him an ambassador, preferably to the Court of St. James. In preparation, HF-II hired Knudsen, believing him better qualified to run Ford Motor Co. than the younger Iacocca. Naturally, Iacocca wasn't pleased, but there wasn't much he could do except quit, and that didn't make a lot of sense.

Knudsen, former head of Pontiac and Chevrolet, had led a relatively sheltered life at GM. His father, William S. (Big Bill) Knudsen, came from Ford initially but spent most of his career with GM, part of it as president, so Bunkie didn't exactly have to fight his way to the top. But he was extremely capable nonetheless.

Knudsen didn't like Ford's styling direction. "Bordinat was head of styling for Ford," he said in a 1994 interview, "and I did not believe that Bordinat was the type of individual that ought to be in that kind of a job. Bordinat had some problems, as you know, along with Don DeLaRossa." Knudsen was alluding to both men's drinking habits; they enjoyed long martini lunches at the Dearborn Inn and would sometimes come back drunk to afternoon meetings.

Seeking to change Ford's styling direction, Knudsen brought in Larry Shinoda, the Corvette designer and a much more daring stylist than Bordinat. Knudsen said later that the reason he brought Shinoda to Ford was to oversee the design of a sports car, one to replace the not-yet-released but already problem-plagued De Tomaso Pantera. Shinoda and Bordinat were opposites. Shinoda was direct and brusque, Bordinat tactful and politically correct. The two rubbed sparks immediately, a situation not helped when, shortly after his arrival in Dearborn, Shinoda announced to the press that he intended to become Ford's next vice president of design. Shinoda's aspirations had no real basis, though, according to Knudsen.

In the words of Virgil Exner Jr., who worked in Ford styling at that time, "There was certainly a lot of friction...and a lot less formality to our shows as Knudsen and Shinoda were picking out stuff directly from the studios. A great deal of polarization took place between the Bordinat/Iacocca and Knudsen/Shinoda camps." Shinoda also offered unsolicited styling and policy advice to Bordinat, but whenever Bordinat would tell Shinoda, in effect, to shut up, Larry would go to Knudsen for backing, and he usually got it. Knudsen's job also entailed telling Ford people how to run their business and, in the process, Knudsen drove a lot of top Ford people toward Iacocca's side.

At one point, Bunkie drew up a list of candidates to "back up" Bordinat; that is, to dilute Bordinat's authority and to eventually replace him. Shinoda's name, though, was not on that list. The one person Knudsen interviewed as a serious candidate was Charles M. Jordan, then head of GM Opel design in Germany. Knudsen initially contacted Jordan from London and then interviewed him at greater length in Dearborn. While they were having lunch at Ford headquarters, Iacocca came in and joined the conversation.

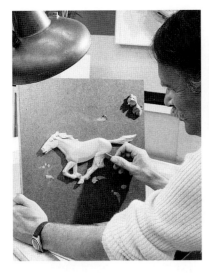  

By 1973, ponycars weren't selling well, partly because the Mustang had grown too large. So for 1974, Ford decided to downsize and built the 1974 Mustang II on the Pinto platform-- a successful move as it turned out. Sculptor Charles Keresztes refined the grille pony (left).

Jordan was tempted by Knudsen's offer but, before deciding, discussed it with his boss and mentor, Bill Mitchell. Mitchell, in Jordan's words, told him to "do what you have to do," and he added that Mitchell made him "absolutely no promises." The "no promises" clause takes on significance because Jordan later became Mitchell's choice to succeed him as GM design v.p. but was passed over in favor of Irv Rybicki (see page 272).

Jordan decided to stay with General Motors and sent word to Knudsen. Knudsen then asked Shinoda to recommend someone in-house to take over the day-to-day running of corporate production design—the Bordinat "backup" position he had in mind—and Shinoda suggested Donald F. (Don) Kopka. Shinoda had met Don through Kopka's mother-in-law, who happened to be Shinoda's neighbor. Knudsen promptly named Kopka director of Ford North American design, which left Bordinat more an international administrator than in charge of U.S. cars. Iacocca again didn't like that choice, because it meant that Kopka now became Bordinat's heir apparent, a role Iacocca had in mind for Don DeLaRossa.

Kopka recalled that, "It wasn't a very comfortable position, frankly, because I knew Lee wasn't happy about it. He didn't know me very well, and I had a tough year; real tough. I was doing what I thought was right, and he [Iacocca] didn't agree with me half the time."

The power struggle between Knudsen and Iacocca came to a head when Iacocca told HF-II that if he didn't get rid of Knudsen, he (Iacocca) would quit and take a number of Ford vice presidents with him. Iacocca had an offer, according to Kopka, from ChrisCraft, the boat manufacturer. Henry II thought about Iacocca's ultimatum and decided he couldn't risk losing his key people, so he let Knudsen go.

Shinoda, in hindsight, said that Knudsen had two strikes against him from the start. First, he didn't bring over enough GM people to reinforce his position at Ford. Second, "Bunkie never had to fight in the alley, whereas Iacocca was great at street fighting."

Henry Ford II fired Bunkie on Sept. 12, 1969, 18 months after Knudsen arrived. HF-II explained simply that, "...things didn't work out." Shinoda was in Europe at the time, but when he returned 10 days later, Bordinat sent him packing. The tale circulated that Bordinat celebrated Shinoda's leaving by painting a Japanese flag on a large sheet of paper, hoisting it on a makeshift pole in one of the Ford studios, then lowering and stomping it into the floor. Robert Lacey repeated the story in his book, *Ford: The Men and the Machine*. Ford's Tom Land later told what really happened: "A wild, crazy, wonderful designer named Harvey Wynn made a meatball on a piece of Fome-Cor, attached it to a 12-foot aluminum spline and raised it up over the partition from our studio into Larry's studio. Harvey jerked it up and down and then let it fall to the floor with a clang." Lacey's story that Bordinat and DeLaRossa toasted Shinoda's and Knudsen's departures with champagne does seem to be true.

But Henry II, who felt blackmailed by Iacocca, didn't immediately make him president. Instead, he installed a troika at the top, Iacocca ending up as head of Ford's North American operations.

Finally, on Dec. 10, 1970, Ford did name Lee Iacocca company president, but with some reluctance, because by then Henry II and Iacocca had started to bicker. Iacocca was calling the company chairman a "dumb, spoiled bastard," and HF-II was returning the compliment by referring to Iacocca as "that goddam wop."

Several months before he became company president, Iacocca arranged for Ford to buy a controlling interest in Ghia, the Italian design house and coachbuilder that earlier had fashioned so many of Virgil Exner's idea cars for Chrysler. Ford initially bought 80% of Ghia from the American Rowan Controller Co. in 1970 and the remaining 20% from Alejandro De Tomaso in 1972. Not coincidentally, De Tomaso and his wife, Isabelle, were friends of Iacocca's, and Isabelle's family owned American Rowan Controller Co. Also, it was through the De Tomaso connection that Lincoln-Mercury imported the Tom Tjaarda-designed, Ford-powered, mid-engined Pantera exoticar from 1970 through 1974. Joe Oros, who was Ford of Europe's design v.p. at the time, transferred Filipo Sapino from Ford's pre-production/advanced studio in Turin to Ghia and made him Ghia's chief designer. Sapino brought along Tom Tjaarda as his assistant.

Ghia came to be known around Ford as "Lee's playpen," and it lost money for at least the first year. Iacocca put Don DeLaRossa in charge of Ghia, and Don ran it from the U.S. He visited Italy periodically but didn't move there. Within a few years, thanks to Ford's financial people, Ghia began turning a profit. It's remained a Ford holding ever since and has become a valuable international asset, one that's contributed mightily to Ford design around the world.

Bordinat and his staff coped remarkably well with the bad industry karma of the 1970s. Ford introduced the downsized Mustang for 1974—a Pinto in a Mustang suit—just in time for the first oil embargo, and while ponycar traditionalists rolled their eyes, the miniaturized Mustang sold well: 386,000 were produced that first year alone. The car marked a gutsy decision—one of the first important downsizings in the industry. Ford, however, didn't follow through immediately by downsizing its other car lines, mostly because the company was starting to hit serious financial headwinds.

This was a time when a lot of the company's resources got siphoned off to meet federally mandated standards for CAFE (Corporate Average Fuel Economy), emissions, safety and body damageability. Yet with cash flowing into those four new engineering areas, Bordinat said he never felt strapped the way Dick Macadam did at Chrysler (see page 288). Quite the opposite, apparently, because in a 1984 interview with David Crippen of the Henry Ford Museum, Bordinat said, "The corporation never, ever shorted me on money...never, *ever*! I mean when there were purges and things of that nature, or we'd go into a recession, why then we'd all have to carry our fair load....

"As a matter of fact, at one time Henry Ford II was in a state of shock...because it was getting kind of easy for me to make these pitches, and I'd gone through the whole thing. When it was all

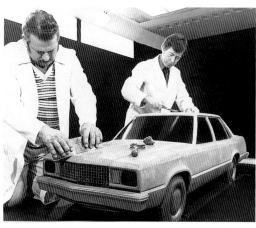

Ford tried adding post-release aerodynamic tweaks to the 1978 Fairmont and actually did improve its coefficient of drag (Cd) slightly with a front airdam and faired-in mirrors. Last-minute changes were done using a smoke wand. Modelers worked with a 3/8-scale clay model inside Ford's windtunnel. Angular 1979 Continental Mark V (below) showed no attempt at aero.

over, Ed Lundy [Ford's finance v.p.] said, 'Now Gene, are you absolutely certain that you have all the money you need?' And I said, 'Yes, Ed, I think we do.' In the meantime, Henry Ford was just about knocked out. He was just laughing uproariously. It was the first time in his life that he'd ever heard Ed trying to give away more money.... But that was the sort of attitude they had, and I guess we didn't spend it too badly or they wouldn't have offered it.

"And in addition to that," he continued, "it developed that we had fantastic flexibility. About 40% of our budget—which got up around $32-38 million at various times—was earmarked for advanced design. Well, in order to establish that budget, you had to give [the financial staff] a list of projects.... It wasn't just *carte blanche*. But I had the flexibility of changing those projects to suit the need, which is another way of saying to suit myself. And I think this has been somewhat unheard of in the business."

Henry Ford II, in an interview with historian David L. Lewis, had this to say in retrospect about Bordinat: "Gene provided good, yeoman service. He had some outstanding successes and some

outstanding flops. If I had anything critical to say about Gene, it would be that—rather than doing what he thought was the right thing—he was more apt to listen to somebody else who would go over to see him. He'd try to do something that someone else might think was right, rather than what he and his group thought might be the right thing for the company. In certain cases, that was too bad, because we didn't have available to us the approach that his group might think was best." HF-II added that he felt Bordinat was unduly influenced by Lee Iacocca.

Ford, like General Motors and Chrysler, did a lot of badge engineering throughout the 1970s and early 1980s. The last significant generation of cars styled under Bordinat were those on the 1978 "Fox" platform. This again became one of those very versatile root stocks that quickly gave rise to the Ford Fairmont, Granada, Mustang, LTD and Thunderbird; the Mercury Zephyr, Capri, Marquis; and the 1983 Mark and Lincoln Continental sedan. The 1978 Fairmont took some of its external and interior styling cues from the Mercedes-Benz and again became one of Ford's record bestsellers.

Even so, the 1970s was not a wine-and-roses decade for any U.S. carmaker. Energy prices skyrocketed, the Japanese quickly rose up to dominate world car markets, Chrysler was going down for the third time, and Henry Ford II felt that Lee Iacocca was now after *his* job. So in Oct. 1978, he kicked Lee out. By the time Iacocca left, despite the success of the Fairmont, Ford was losing more than $1 billion a year, and the 1980s looked even bleaker.

It was in that context that Gene Bordinat began thinking about early retirement. He was only 60, but the strain of the job, combined with heart problems and a deteriorating relationship with Harold A. (Red) Poling, president of Ford of Europe, convinced both him and the company that it might be a good time to leave. The clincher came when, immediately after a grueling trip to Italy, Bordinat collapsed at a company meeting in downtown Detroit.

So on Dec. 1, 1980, Gene Bordinat retired. Ford kept him on full salary until he reached 65. In his retirement, he began writing a book, the working title of which was *My Days in the Court of Henry II*. It's never been published. Bordinat suffered a major heart attack and passed away in 1987.

Before Iacocca departed Ford, he had in mind making Don DeLaRossa Bordinat's successor. The vice presidency, though, now passed to Don Kopka. And soon after Iacocca connected with Chrysler, he brought in DeLaRossa to replace Dick Macadam as styling vice president (see page 289).

Whereas Bordinat earned his medals putting Ford styling on a business basis, Kopka made his reputation as the corporate champion of automotive aerodynamics. He became interested in "aero" around 1976, when a design engineer named Jim Chabot convinced him that the easiest and least

Form Follows Function at Ford

Ford's then-design vice president Don Kopka made the point in 1984 that a portion of the form-follows-function equation is fashion. "One function of a car is to please the owner," said Kopka. "It's less important in economy cars than luxury cars, but...a lot of well-to-do women buy new Lincolns every year just as they buy new frocks from Dior; simply because they want to be seen in 'the latest.' They insist on it. They won't drive last year's model, but they need a reason [to buy a new car], and that reason becomes the facelift or change in features or new colors.

"So that's the environment we work in here in the United States. Fashion still plays a role. From the mid 1970s to the mid 1980s, the trend toward more efficient cars tended for a while to put fashion aside. But by doing that it also created a new fashion: the fashion of the efficient-looking automobile. We're seeing a backlash right now, because a lot of people who bought small, economical cars thought they were doing the right thing, being patriotic, being smart and getting in on a new fashion. After driving those cars for a while, though, they found they couldn't cram the family into them, didn't like the spartan interiors, the ride, wanted the extras they'd enjoyed in their big, older cars, and they said, What the heck, I'm going back to an American car I like. So here we are, full circle." ◆

expensive way to meet CAFE was by reshaping the American automobile. Chabot held dual doctorates in psychology and fluid dynamics, and he spread the aero word with the zeal of a missionary, not just to Kopka and Ford designers but throughout the corporation.

According to master modeler Fred Hoadley, Ford began serious aerodynamic work in Germany, starting around 1958. The 1961 German Ford Taunus was developed with the aid of windtunnel testing. Ford of Germany conceived a system of making scale clay models complete with replicated undercarriages, so the windtunnel tests were very accurate. Also, one chassis could be used to compare several clay body shapes. Hoadley introduced this system to Ford's U.S. designers and engineers in the mid-1970s, and it displaced a previous system here that used wooden scale models.

"Up to this point," said Kopka in 1984, "the engine engineers had most of the onus for meeting CAFE. It was almost all on their backs, and they didn't know how they were going to do it. They were under the gun. Then the light went on, and they began to realize that they could get some help...almost for free by just reshaping the exterior of the car, and...they embraced that idea...."

Ford cars of that era were boxy and angular, but some of the

Donald F. Kopka

means cost Ford about $200 million. The traditional (and expensive) ways to boost CAFE were by downsizing, through engine refinements like turbochargers and overhead cams, lightweight materials like aluminum and plastics and via new technology. So the early aero changes that resulted in Ford's 1.5-mpg improvement saved the company roughly $3 billion.

Kopka pointed out that the aero changes weren't entirely free, however. They cost in the neighborhood of $10-12 million to implement. He added that in 1982, the government published a report that compared the Big Three in terms of CAFE improvements over the preceding five years. Ford's corporate figure was up 13% versus 6% to 7% for GM and Chrysler. Kopka attributes Ford's record largely to aero.

Don Kopka grew up in—of all places—Pleasant Ridge, Michigan, that same tiny community where George Walker and Gene Bordinat lived. He was six years behind Bordinat in school, knew the Bordinat family, and his future wife lived across the street from the Walkers.

Kopka always sketched cars, even in grade school. He said he used to go down on Woodward Avenue, which sliced Pleasant Ridge in two, and watched for the concept cars that inevitably

Probe I

Probe III

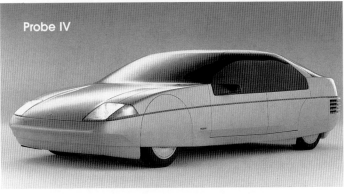

Probe IV

Probe V

Championing true aerodynamics, Don Kopka and Ghia designed Ford's Probe series to get management and the public used to more fluid shapes. The 1979 Probe I was still fairly angular but brought the Cd down to .25 vs. .40 as typi-

cal. Probe III predicted Ford's European styling in 1981. Probe IV had pivoting front fender skirts, and the 1984 Probe V used flexible "membrane" skirts that bowed outward when the front wheels turned. Probe V boasted a Cd of .137.

early aerodynamic tweaks did help fuel economy. The tweaks included adding airdams under the front bumper, rounding off edges and corners and eliminating projections. Kopka estimated that, over the next four or five years, Ford's early aero effort raised fuel mileage by roughly 1.5 mpg. To put that in perspective, internal audits showed that every 0.1-mpg improvement by traditional

rolled by, among them the Chrysler Thunderbolt and Newport, Harley Earl's Y-Job and Ed Macauley's Packard Phantom. Don served in the Navy during WW-II, majored in mechanical engineering at Western Michigan University and, in his senior year, switched to Wayne State University, where he ended up taking his degree in industrial design. He went to work for Chrysler in 1950

Continental Concept 90 (right) bowed in Feb. 1982, held a crystal ball up to the '83 Thunderbird (far right). Mid-sized 1984 Tempo (below) picked up on Ford's European styling touches, especially in the greenhouse pillars. All this aero seemed radical at the time of these cars' introduction.

and was put into a one-year program to learn clay modeling.

Virgil Exner had just been hired to do advanced designs, and Henry King was Chrysler's styling director. As a modeler, Kopka worked on some of Exner's Ghia showcars, including the first DeSoto Adventurer. In 1951, Kopka transferred into the Plymouth studio under King, did a few renderings that caught the eye of Tom Bannister, who brought Don into his DeSoto studio. Kopka later worked with Herb Weissinger in the Dodge studio and then became head of the DeSoto studio just before Chrysler dropped that marque.

Cliff Voss went over to Ford for a short time in 1963-64 and told Kopka that HF-II, "...isn't happy with what's going on around here. They're getting all vanilla, and they want some chocolate and strawberry." So in 1964, Kopka joined Ford. He worked under Joe Oros in the studio that facelifted the 1967 Mustang, Falcon and Fairlane. The 1967 Mustang, with its rounder side sections, was one of the first designs Kopka had a major hand in. Tom Land, who'd also just gotten to Ford, likewise worked on the 1967 Mustang.

Soon afterward, Bunkie Knudsen made Kopka corporate director of Ford North American design, a job Don kept even after Knudsen left. At first, neither Bordinat nor Iacocca was happy with Kopka's appointment, but it wasn't long before Bordinat and Kopka got along fine, partly because Bordinat had felt that Iacocca was pushing DeLaRossa a bit too hard.

The Bordinat-Kopka coalition essentially went along with the prevailing automotive styling trends of the 1970s and produced square, boxy cars, very much in keeping with GM's sheer look. Bordinat, meanwhile, had his eye on a young designer named Jack Telnack, in whom he recognized some promise. When Bordinat sensed a need for a Ford styling presence in Australia, he and Bob Maguire tapped Telnack to go down and set up shop in Ford's Geelong factory, near Melbourne.

Gil Spear, who now headed one of Ford's advanced design studios, decided to take his 1966 winter vacation scuba diving on Australia's Great Barrier Reef. When Bordinat heard about this, he said to Spear, "Jack Telnack's down there all by himself, and boy, he certainly needs some encouragement." According to Spear: "...I went down there, and Jack had a problem. They had given him an old drafting room in the back of the [Ford Geelong] factory...and the only way he could show anything to his executives was to have it dragged outside and display it on the gravel in a little parking lot at the back of the building. It had some cyclone fence around it. On the other side of the cyclone fence—on two sides at least—there were a bunch of quonset huts...[and] there'd

be these kids—tough urchins; they'd be climbing up the cyclone fence and hurling insults at the designer out there or the executives...."

Telnack recalled that, "I brought a couple of modelers down from the U.S., but we hired some young guys right out of the Ford Trade School. They still had a Ford Trade School in Australia at the time. These were apprentices, and we brought them in, and they turned out to be pretty good. The guys are still in the business. One runs a clay-modeling school in Japan right now, and the other's in Europe."

William O. (Bill) Bourke, brother of Loewy/Studebaker designer Bob Bourke (see page 206), was head of Ford's Australian operation at that time and therefore Telnack's boss. Telnack stayed in Australia for four years, then came back to the U.S. for three and was assigned in 1973—again under Bourke—to become head of Ford's European design operation in England. He was soon made a vice president there.

Ford International was doing beautifully at that time, as opposed to Ford of North America, which was losing up to $1.5 billion a year in the late 1970s and early '80s. Ford's U.S. market share went from 28% in 1978 to 15% in 1981.

Ford International was headed by Philip Caldwell and Ford of Europe by Donald E. Petersen. Due to their overseas success, in contrast with Lee Iacocca's poor showing in the U.S., *plus* Henry Ford II's fear that if he (HF-II) were to die suddenly—and his health wasn't good—Iacocca might become chairman, HF-II named Caldwell vice chairman and handed him the job, in effect, of saving the company. Financial writers said that Ford was in even worse shape than Chrysler at that time, and rescuing the company took even greater skill and fiscal ruthlessness—firings, cutbacks, plant closings, etc.—than Iacocca's subsequent salvation of Chrysler. Caldwell and Petersen did save the company, and by 1986-87, they'd made it more profitable than GM, the first time in 62 years that this had happened.

Phil Caldwell had brought Jack Telnack back from Europe in 1976 and made him director of North American car design in Sept. 1978, giving him the same position Kopka had held in relation to Bordinat. In other words, Telnack was now in charge of designing production cars for the U.S. market. He technically reported to Kopka, but Kopka's job now became more administrative. Don oversaw, among other things, Ford's advanced and international design operations.

Henry Ford II had always taken a special interest in the corporation's international affairs, and to keep up with HF-II's thought processes, Bordinat elevated Ford design to an international level. Bordinat also made it a point to learn the intricacies of international finance, and he tutored himself through keen observation of the latest overseas designs and fashion trends. The acquisition of Ghia in 1970 turned out to be serendipidous in that regard, because while some of Ford's European design outposts tended to be jealous of Ghia at first, Bordinat and Kopka made it clear that Ghia was a service organization for the entire company. All Ford design centers, including those overseas, were invited to use Ghia to help design production vehicles and especially to build showcars.

Telnack, who remained head of design for Ford of Europe from

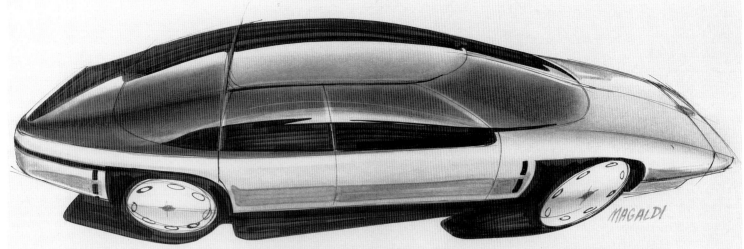

Ford and Ghia struggled together to design what would become the 1986 Taurus. Concept sketches, like this sedan done in 1981, gave way to the reality refinements below and took many attempts to get right.

June 1973 to Mar. 1976, now brought an added European insight to his U.S. jobs. He understood design on both sides of the Atlantic, and he recognized that Europe (and Japan) had already fought many of the battles that American designers were still struggling through: downsizing, front-wheel drive, fuel efficiency and aerodynamics. He and Kopka very much agreed on the importance of aero, and together they instituted an informal program to "educate" their own management and the public to accept the more radical look of genuinely aerodynamic cars.

According to Kopka: "I had developed a system aimed at not frightening management; getting them used to designs that we felt were coming. My theory was to show them, in stages, where we thought cars were headed. We'd do concept vehicles and tell them why we were going that way. We would also introduce them to other types of industrial design, product design, aircraft, again to help them see where things were moving."

Things were moving in the direction of the 1986 Ford Taurus, and Kopka continued, "Cars like the Taurus, for instance: We'd shown them sketches and clays like that two or three years ahead of time to get them comfortable. And that's how we could sell them such a radical idea. At that time Phil Caldwell was chairman, and we dreaded Phil. He was a numbers cruncher, a bean counter, and he never had much of anything to do with design. When I had truck design one time, I worked with Phil, and I liked him; he was easy to work with.

"Anyway, I was so pleased after one of our first indoctrination sessions. When we showed him some advanced stuff, we thought maybe we'd scare hell out of Phil, but as we were leaving the showroom Phil says, 'That's good, Don. Do you think we're reaching enough?' And I thought to myself, 'God, I could kiss this guy.' Anyway, that concept was very, very successful, because when we came along later with things like the Taurus,

Taurus owed much of its look to the German Merkur Scorpio (right). That's Ford's European chairman Bob Lutz beside the Scorpio and U.S. executive v.p. Lou Ross next to the 1986 Taurus.

Jack Telnack

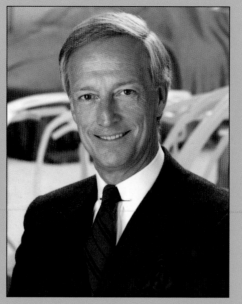

In 1987, *Fortune* magazine named Jack Telnack one of the year's 50 most fascinating people in American business. While Telnack grew up in Dearborn, he now lives on Grosse Ile, a narrow island south of Detroit in the Detroit River. The river connects Lake Erie with Lake St. Clair, and the reason he lives there is because Jack loves boating. During those rare moments when he wasn't working, he used to board his 41-foot sloop, *Mirage,* and sailed into another world. When he injured his neck, Telnack's doctor made him give up sailing, but he now captains a 58-foot Hatteras Sport Cruiser, again called *Mirage,* with twin 8V 70TI Detroit diesels.

At one point in his Ford career, Telnack moonlighted as a hull designer for a powerboat manufacturer. That experience gave him an appreciation of fluid dynamics. Today, Telnack's work consists almost entirely of captaining Ford's huge design juggernaut into the 21st century. With the company continuing to go simultaneously more electronic and more international, it leaves him with relatively little time to devote to the specifics of design. He delegates much of that responsibility to his highly qualified subordinates.   ◆

Ghia Barchetta (top) created a sensation at the 1983 Geneva show and might have aced out the Mazda Miata. When it reached production as the Australian-built 1989 Mercury Capri, however, its charm was gone and sales proved disappointing.

---

they said, 'Yeah, yeah, that's what we saw.' Whereas if you sprang something like that on them [suddenly], we would have died. That's kind of what that position was for, and to make the final recommendation on it. It was kind of scary when I think about it, because we're talking about a $3 billion expenditure, and I had to go on record as saying, 'That's the way we ought to go on that.'

"A real interesting sidelight: After we baked it in," continued Kopka, "we had a big management meeting at Boca Raton, and it was still 18 months before the Taurus was to come out. Henry Ford II got up and gave his major speech to the worldwide management group and said, in effect, that we'd gone too far with the Taurus. We'd made a mistake. And I'll be damned if Bill Ford, who was my boss—I worked for Bill—didn't echo him and say we'd reached too far and we'd made a mistake with that car. We left the meeting, and everybody said, 'Well, where are you going to work next year?' And I answered, 'It's too late to worry about now. We're stuck with it.' There was a lot of uneasiness with that car.

"I'll tell you one of the few people who *was* comfortable was Phil Caldwell, which was amazing—an Ohio farmboy who came up through the financial ranks. But the two Fords, I think, were trying to get us back in line. They wanted to rein us in a bit; pull us back. They felt we'd gotten a little too wild." The Taurus was wild, sure enough, and a 90° turn away from the old Bordinat

comfort zone. No more vinyl roofs, no more opera windows or stand-up grilles. Ford bet the farm on the Taurus, but Ford's spokespeople said, especially during the elaborate Taurus/Sable press preview in Hollywood in January of 1985, that their clinics and market studies showed the gamble to be minimal. Even so, there were no real-world benchmarks to show that the Taurus would be the runaway bestseller that Caldwell hoped for. Caldwell—and Telnack, who had ultimate responsibility for the Taurus design—staked everything on this car, including $3 billion of Ford's money.

The 1986 Taurus was, without overstatement, the single most important American production design of the 1980s. It gave Ford a decisive styling lead over all other U.S. automakers; it also gave designers at other car companies the courage to incorporate the aero look; and it marked the end of the sheer look and square cars. The Taurus was reluctantly but soon copied by General Motors and became Chrysler's acknowledged inspiration for its "cab-forward" LH cars. (Even in the mid 1990s, though, there were conservative, well-to-do car buyers who didn't like the aero look; who preferred the earlier, squarer shapes. Several luxury carmakers held onto their previous styles: the Lincoln Town Car, Cadillac deVille and Mercedes, for example.)

The design manager behind the Taurus was Jack Telnack. Born in Henry Ford Hospital on Apr. 1, 1937, raised in Dearborn,

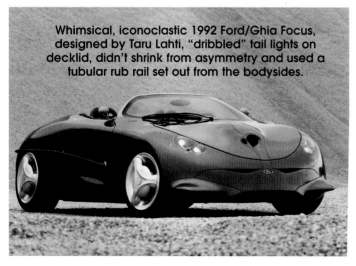

Whimsical, iconoclastic 1992 Ford/Ghia Focus, designed by Taru Lahti, "dribbled" tail lights on decklid, didn't shrink from asymmetry and used a tubular rub rail set out from the bodysides.

1994 Mach III concept roadster blended the overall shape of the Focus with the classic retro identifiers of Mustang's 1965 ancestor: the scooped-out sides and the pony emblem inside the high grille.

Thirty years later, Telnack wisely brought back all those design elements that made the 1965 Mustang so fresh and original and packaged them in modern garb (above). In enthusiasts' minds, the 1995 Mustang totally wiped out any memory of the Pinto-based 1974 Mustang II. The 1995 mid-sized Ford Contour (above) didn't fare so well, however. Based on the European Ford Mondeo, it couldn't sustain the sales volume of the Tempo it replaced.

he and some of his car-struck school chums used to climb atop the serpentine wall across from Greenfield Village and watch pre-production 1949-51 Fords, Mercurys and Lincolns circle the Ford test track. These were the designs Bob Gregorie and George Walker turned out after World War II.

Jack grew up loving cars, and as a teenager he owned a lowered, chopped and channeled 1941 Mercury convertible. He knew from an early age that he wanted to be a Ford designer, so he drove out to Los Angeles and studied auto design at Art Center College. When he graduated in 1958, Buzz Grisinger, head of the Lincoln-Mercury studio, interviewed and hired Jack. Joe Oros put him in a Ford pre-production studio and then into Ford's production areas.

Telnack's first big break came in 1966 when Bordinat sent him to Australia. Bordinat's orders to Telnack were, "Go down there and do something; just don't make my telephone ring." Previous Australian Fords had been styled in Dearborn. Telnack regularly sent back graphic reports, and his progress soon became obvious in the cars he styled for the Australian market. These, of necessity, were redone U.S. Falcons whose body dies had been willed to Geelong. The Australian assignment proved to Bordinat, Kopka and others at Ford that Telnack could adapt to and thrive under adverse conditions, and that became one of the reasons they packed him off to Ford of Europe in 1973 and made him an overseas vice president.

Telnack believed that Dearborn began to show a glimmer of aero with the 1979 Mustang. The Mustang's slantback front end took some inspiration, he felt, from the British Ford Cortina, which had a similar tilt to its grille. After Jack returned to the U.S. in 1976 as director of Ford international design, special vehicles

and advanced concepts, he joined Kopka's campaign to condition management and the public to the aero look. Kopka and Dave Reese introduced the Continental Concept 90 showcar in Jan. 1982 and Ford released the very similar-looking production Thunderbird for 1983.

The '83 T-Bird was fairly revolutionary for its time, especially since the previous Thunderbird showed a severe Fairmont boxiness. The 1983 Bird, while still on the '82 Fox platform, had a rounded, swept-back grille, curved bodysides, round wheel arches and very discreet ornamentation. The entire car was considerably rounder than its contemporaries, with a faster 60° windshield. Ford began to promote the term "aero look" and followed the '83 T-Bird with its boldly aerodynamic 1984 Tempo/Topaz compacts and the 1984 Continental Mark VII. These again were transitional models aimed at familiarizing the public with Ford's new direction.

Kopka's advanced designers, meanwhile, began working on five highly aerodynamic and efficient concept cars called the Probe series. The Ghia-built Probe I two-seater bowed in 1979, and the series ended with the 1984 Probe V, a radical four-place sedan whose coefficient of drag (Cd) was down to .137: the range of military fighter planes. The 1986 Taurus, by way of comparison, came to market with a quite respectable Cd of .32.

The Taurus had its roots in Europe, where Robert A. (Bob) Lutz—who was then Ford of Europe's chairman—saw the need for more rounded cars. Henry Ford II fought Lutz at first, but it was Lutz who pushed through the revival of the blue Ford oval and the shape that became the Taurus. "The guy initially responsible for [the Taurus] design was Ray Evert," noted Kopka. "He

continued on page 270

The Electronic Studio

Ford design managers talk about studios where holograms hover in midair and stylists sketch body surfaces entirely with a laser brush. That future seems well on its way.

Today you'll find three major electronic design tools in the typical styling studio: the scanner, the clay milling machine and the computer. Let's look at how each one works and then we'll talk about how all three fit together into an integrated system.

The scanner, technically called a "coordinate measuring machine" (CMM), uses a probe to scan and digitize a clay model or any other three-dimensional surface. Most CMMs have a tactile probe at the end of a long, articulated arm that physically touches the surface; others use laser beams.

A technician moves the probe up and down along the surface of, let's say, a full-sized clay model. As the probe moves, it registers "points." These points are like the old system of offsets that shipbuilders and autobody

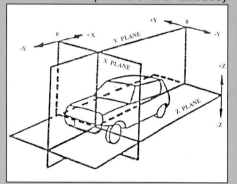

draftsmen used in the early days of the motorcar (see pages 10-11). Each point is recorded digitally as a number. The number gives the point's location relative to a central "zero point." The zero point is an imaginary dot that forms the locating reference of an XYZ coordinate system. (Zero points are arbitrarily assigned. General Motors sets the zero point somewhat ahead of the clay model, the distance depending on the overall length of the car. Ford and Chrysler put the zero point in the middle of the front-axle centerline.) Together, the digitized points form a mathematical "wire-frame" model of the entire car body. This wire-frame model, viewed on a computer screen, looks like a car made of hog wire: grids of thin, interconnected lines.

Historically, the electronic scanner (or "point taker") was first used in the mid 1960s not as a design tool but as a drafting aid. The idea was to automate the drafting process. Early scanners often recorded data on punched paper tape or magnetic reels. The data were then fed into a computer and used to drive the stylus of an automatic drafting machine. Computer-aided drafting eliminated tedius handwork,

saved time and increased accuracy.

It didn't take long to figure out that the stored scan data could also be used to *drive* a clay-milling machine. The clay-milling machine was (and is) a device that again has a long, articulated arm, but this time the arm contains a milling head. The

Electronic scanner on one side of clay model reads surface and tells clay-milling machine on the other side how to make a mirror copy.

head can mill (or "skive") the clay surface down to a configuration dictated by the math model in the computer. The clay-milling machine (also known as a CNC or "computer numerical control" machine) comes in handy to reproduce, say, the scanned half of a clay model on the other side. In other words, the job of creating a symmetrical clay model suddenly became much faster and easier. Nor did you have to make cumbersome templates by hand.

At first—and we're talking now about the mid 1970s—milling machines usually made "section cuts;" that is, grooves spaced fairly far apart. These still needed a lot of hand smoothing. More recently, due to denser wire-frame models, surface points and tool-head overlaps come closer together, which results in finer cuts that need less handfinishing.

Meanwhile, computer hardware and software became more sophisticated and computer disks replaced the older methods using punched and magnetic tape for data storage. Electronic information could now be accessed through computer networks so that design, engineering, manufacturing, etc., had it instantly available.

The next step was to develop computer programs that made it possible to work with the wire-frame data and generate actual surfaces. That wasn't simple, and it took a while to come up with good surface programs people could actually use. Early programming attempts sprang up from the database and were very user-*un*friendly. In the words of then-Pontiac designer Ron Hill, who helped pioneer GM's switch to computer-aided design (CAD) in the 1970s, "It was like using a pencil tied to two strings, working around four corners and looking through mirrors."

But by the mid 1980s, three major independent software firms had come up with surface-generating programs that design technicians *could* use. One was Alias Research in Toronto. Another was a French company named Dassault Systemes SA, which provided a program called CATIA (for "computergraphics aided three-dimensional interactive applications"). The third was Evans & Sutherland in Utah, who developed CDRS (for "conceptual design & rendering system").

American automakers soon began using all three. Chrysler and Saturn favored CATIA and CDRS, Ford liked CDRS and GM leaned toward Alias and CGS, its own body-surface program. GM had developed two in-house programs, one called "Cadence" and the other named CGS (for "corporate graphics system"). More recently, GM's EDS Corp. introduced software called Unigraphics Hybrid Modeler that combines CAD with CAE (computer-aided engineering) and CAM (computer-aided manu-

facturing). As an aside, the major design colleges—Art Center and CCS—adopted Alias equipment and made "sketching in the tube" part of their curricula.

One of the earliest serious uses of CAD was to create repeat patterns, like wheels and grille textures. To make a six-spoke wheel, say, the stylist/technician had only to design one 60° slice and the computer would repeat it "around the clock" for the full 360°. Or if the designer wanted a certain eggcrate pattern, he could create just a small sample and ask the computer to repeat and expand it to fill a grille outline. Within that outline, the size of the eggcrate texture could be changed or even set on end.

The beauty of the computer, though, was more than skin deep. Once the math model sat in the database, either from scanning a clay or by manipulating the data on the screen, a designer/technician could develop surfaces and then have a new clay model milled. The resulting three-dimensional (3D) clay model made it possible to "prove out" the design—make sure the surfaces looked right.

Electronic design also offered other benefits. For example, once the math model went into the corporate database and all the various staffs had access to it, engineers could theoretically study a car's aerodynamics and crashworthiness. The manufacturing people could judge stamping feasibility. The finance staff could start making cost estimates. As the surface design got closer to release, body engineers could start to design inner sheetmetal and structural parts. And so forth.

Beyond that, body engineers could preload "the package" into the database so that things like seats, axles and dimensions were all properly placed and adhered to. Ramp angles, wheel jounce, trunk and door hinges, deck heights, powertrain placement—all the "hard points" could be loaded in. Then, for instance, if a designer came up with a door that hit a normal curb when it swung open, he'd get a signal telling him: Door interference. Likewise if the hood stood too low, the designer might see—on his video screen—the engine poking up through the hood.

Another advantage of CAD was that designers in other parts of the world could take part in a centralized design project. By sending digitized information around the globe via satellite and electronic links, such technology gave Ford's German studio the opportunity to design the European Mondeo version of Ford's CDW27 world car at the same time as the North American studio was tailoring the Ford Contour and Mercury Mystique for the U.S. market.

Clay models could (and can) likewise be scanned in the U.S. and then an exact duplicate milled halfway around the world via satellite or wire links. With these hookups, the entire planet becomes one big design studio. Information can immediately be shared with worldwide product planning, engineering, manufacturing, purchasing and all other company disciplines. Everyone becomes immediately aware of what everyone else is up to. Lead times grow shorter and information becomes more accurate.

Chrysler's Jeff Godshall has pointed out that another important use of CAD is the "appearance verification model" or AVM. AVMs are "hard copy" checks of computer-generated surfaces. For instance, an AVM of an interior would include the instrument panel, console, doors, pillars, etc., each piece milled separately from Styrofoam or some other rigid material and assembled for revision or approval. The AVM shows how every component mates and fits with adjacent pieces, both dimensionally and in appearance. If things don't go together or don't look right, they're redigitized in the computer and re-milled as another AVM. After the bugs are worked out and everyone approves the final AVM, the surfaces can be released digitally for production.

Designing "in the tube," both in 2 and 3 dimensions, can save time, but lots of designers prefer pencil and paper.

AVMs of exterior surfaces can also concentrate on smaller "slabs" so you don't have to re-do the entire clay model. In fact, it's much more common to re-do a small section than an entire model. However, one advantage of milling a clay as a whole is that you can see the total design all at

Ford's 1995 GT-90 concept coupe was designed largely in the tube.

once. In the past, a studio might finish a front end before starting the rear, and that sometimes led to odd-looking mismatches.

Most designers still don't feel at ease with computers. And all the foregoing does not mean that the average car designer can sit down at a video terminal and create a releasable surface. Surface data still need to be manipulated and "sweetened" by a trained technician, same as most designers need modelers to create 3D clay models. It is possible, however, for nearly any car designer to "sketch" on a computer. This is entirely different than creating surface or math models. It involves another program entirely, one commonly called "2D electronic paint." It's much like paint programs for home personal computers that children use. Most professional paint programs let the designer "sketch" his ideas electronically. The results look amazingly good, but they are 2D. The paint program allows the designer to alter specific body sections, change colors, reposition light sources for different reflections, shading and shadows. Borrowing from computer animation, the 2D sketch program allows

"walkarounds" that rotate the car on the screen around any axis. And the electronic sketches themselves have a glossy, hard quality, so that when they're printed out on color printers, they look like photographs.

Despite the ease of using 2D paint programs, many designers still prefer pencil and paper. But 2D programs are becoming evermore user friendly. Taking that technology one step further, Nipon Steel and Alias have both recently come out with programs that bridge the gap between 2D and 3D. These begin to move toward converting 2D images into releasable 3D surface data. They still take some handwork, but it's a simpler transition than before.

Meanwhile Ford's Tom Scott talks about using numerical surface data to create life-sized holograms and virtual-reality images. Clark Lincoln of the GM NAO Design Center adds that GM Research has been experimenting with virtual reality to visualize and evaluate design concepts before any hard models take shape. He stresses that this is strictly experimental so far, but the possibility of replacing $300,000-$500,000 full-sized clay models with holograms and/or virtual reality continues to spur research.

Dr.-Ing. Karl H. Grote of California State University at Long Beach, a design engineer who works with holography and rapid prototyping, believes that holograms will soon be used but that they won't supplant 3D clay models in the near future. "Engineers want to actually touch and feel a model," he says. Management, too, needs to see and touch solid surfaces.

Dr. Grote mentions the evolving technology of rapid prototyping (RP) and "solid freeform manufacturing" (SFM) as better candidates to replace clay models in the future. Several types of RP machines have been or are currently being developed. One system, called "stereolithography," uses an ultraviolet laser beam to harden a liquid photopolymer, layer by layer. Another, "laminated object manufacturing," uses a laser to cut sheets of paper, which are then stacked one atop another and glued together. A third, "selected laser sintering," solidifies various materials from powder. "Fused deposition modeling" processes a thermoplastic material in a kind of gluing operation. "Light sculpting" or "solid ground curing" works like a 3D copy machine to make a prototype. All these alternatives can produce intricate, realistic-looking and sometimes functional 3D objects, although nothing the size of a car body has ever been attempted. Scale models for windtunnel testing, though, have been made by these methods. ◆

Designers of the 1996 Lincoln Sentinel (above), with controversial "new edge" styling, took some of their inspiration from Elwood Engel's 1961 Continental. Ford presented the Indigo (Indy-Go) concept roadster as a race car for the street. Its 6.0-liter V-12 produced 435 horsepower. Tiny headlights mounted in rearview mirrors. Ford Adrenalin (below left) blended sedan seating into a 4-door pickup. And Mercury's mini sport utility vehicle, the RFD-615, aimed to cash in on that market trend.

had been Ford's chief designer in Germany, where he'd done the Ford Sierra. Ray came back from Europe and started the Taurus, but it looked kind of bloated at first—fat and round. Then they put Fritz Mayhew in there to work with Ray, and between them and Jack and some Ghia influence, they gradually honed it down.

"There were two prototypes of the Taurus built that had conventional grilles. We at Ford Design didn't want a grille, and fortunately management had the guts to go without one. Don [Donald E.] Petersen endorsed the no-grille look. Petersen was another incredible influence on this whole project. You've probably heard the story, but he was in the showroom with Jack and me one time...this was during the Fairmont days...and he said, 'Are you guys really satisfied with what we're doing?' We still had the boxy crap, and we said, 'No, we don't like it at all.' And he said, 'Well, why don't we do what *you* want to do?' He had a marvelous influence. Of course, he'd worked with us before. He and I had offices adjacent to each other. He was our administrative director when I had North American design; Don was head of our engineering and administrative side of it. So he knew us and knew design really well, and I think he developed a degree of respect for the way we worked...a lot of trust, and he was a big help."

The acknowledged "father" of the Taurus was Lewis C. (Lew) Veraldi, who at that time was product director of Ford's North American operations. Veraldi conceived "Team Taurus," an idea that borrowed heavily from the Japanese way of designing and building cars. Today all U.S. automakers develop some of their

new cars with platform teams, but Veraldi institutionalized the concept in this country when he set out to develop the Taurus in 1981.

The team approach, instead of following the traditional, one-step-at-a-time process in which product planners hand a package idea to designers, who then shape it and pass it along to engineers, who make everything fit and work and then hand prototypes over to the manufacturing people, Team Taurus got everyone involved from the beginning. Team Taurus consisted of high- and low-ranking members from all the necessary walks of corporate life. They discussed concept, strategy, quality, set targets, etc., and then worked together from start to finish. They still had to get management approval along the way, but teamwork helped smooth and speed the process. (For more detail on the platform team concept, see Chapter 14).

In addition to the Probe series, Kopka also advanced a number of concept cars for the European and American show circuits. The Ghia-built Ford Barchetta debuted in Geneva in 1983 and made such a tremendous splash that it gave rise to what Tom Land called a "fan club." The Barchetta club, headquartered in West Germany, at one time boasted 10,000 loyal members. Encouraged by this grass-roots enthusiasm, Ford announced several times that the company intended to produce a Fiesta-based Barchetta. In the end, though, Dearborn turned the project over to Ford of Australia. Ital Design totally redesigned the car and Ford of

Another controversy surrounded the appearance of the 1996 Ford Taurus. The multi-oval facial expression, the car's seemingly smaller overall size (it was 5 inches longer than in '95), plus the car's higher price slowed early sales. Even those who liked the bold statement of the '96 model agreed that it wasn't likely to exert the influence of the original 1986 Taurus.

Australia eventually produced the two-seater convertible that Lincoln-Mercury sold in this country as the 1991 Capri—a very disappointing design. Ford's Japanese partner, meanwhile, designed a two-seater much more like the Barchetta in spirit, the MX-5 Miata, and watched its sales skyrocket.

Another wild and wonderful Ghia concept car was the asymmetrical Ford Focus of 1992, conceived by Taru Lahti. This car bristled with animal shapes and unusual ideas like rub strips set out an inch from the body skins. The Focus was truly a designer's delight.

Don Kopka retired as Ford's design v.p. on June 1, 1987, and Jack Telnack has held that position since then. Telnack's overseas experience stood him in extremely good stead, because as Ford Motor Co. has globalized—and it's the most aggressive of the Big Three in that regard—so has the company's design operation.

By 1995, Telnack ran the most internationally synchonized and sophisticated of all America's design staffs. Ford's styling activities remain based in Dearborn, but Telnack's electronic links and the global network he and his people set up gave him by far the industry's strongest, most immediate control over Ford's worldwide design activities. Neither GM nor Chrysler had so extensive a system in the mid 1990s. *Automotive News* called Ford's approach "the global studio."

Jack Telnack announced in Aug. 1993 that six of Ford's seven design studios around the world would henceforth report to him directly. The six were in Cologne, Germany; Turin, Italy (Ghia); Dunton, England; Hiroshima, Japan; and Ford's U.S. west coast studio in Valencia, California. The only design group not in direct contact with Dearborn was the one in Melbourne, Australia, and that studio—Telnack's alma mater from the 1960s—would report to him via Hiroshima.

Why was and is this design globalization so important to Ford? Because in the mid 1990s, for economic and efficiency reasons, Ford decided to reduce the number of car platforms it produced worldwide. So with fewer platforms serving more markets, the process of coordinating styling and engineering with a global electronic network began making it possible to tailor specific designs for each country.

Take Ford's $6 billion 1995 global car, the CDW-27. Called Mondeo in Europe, it's currently sold in the U.S. as the Ford Contour and Mercury Mystique. The Contour and Mystique were tailored specifically for the American market. Britishers, however, preferred the CDW-27 styled and outfitted a little differently, and the Germans liked still other styling variations in their version of the CDW-27.

Those individual tweaks were introduced and refined by the electronic cable and satellite links between Dunton, Cologne and Dearborn (see sidebar, page 268). Ford's design chief in Cologne could develop his version of the CDW-27, for example, and then send a signal that started a clay-milling machine in Dearborn. The Dearborn machine worked quietly, and presently Telnack and Ford's executives could see the digitized German CDW-27 clay model standing there full size. If they wanted to change something, they could suggest revisions in the computerized surface model and send them back electronically to Cologne. Dearborn and Cologne designers could then discuss the subtleties by telephone. The design process became truly global, just as Ford's markets are now global.

Telnack's great contribution to American auto design was not just the Taurus, important as that car was: It was this electronification and globalization of corporate automobile design. Electronic globalization makes it possible not only to change a basic design for each national market but renders the process relatively easy. Also saved are months of styling and engineering time. Ford announced in 1994 that it wanted to streamline all its developmental processes so a car can go from concept to showroom in less than three years and facelifts can be done in a matter of months. Those sorts of time schedules, impossible in 1990, have a good chance of becoming common by the year 2000. ◆

CHAPTER 13

GENERAL MOTORS CHANGES BIGTIME

The odds definitely favored Jordan. He was Bill Mitchell's handpicked successor, just as Mitchell had been Harley Earl's. When Mitchell retired in July 1977, Charles M. (Chuck) Jordan looked like a shoo-in. Jordan was one of Mitchell's two top aides, the other being Irvin W. (Irv) Rybicki. Few people expected Irv to become GM's next design vice president.

"By every rational standard," said Stan Wilen, whose title at that time was assistant executive designer for Chevrolet and Pontiac, "if you asked anyone in the building who was going to replace Bill Mitchell, Chuck or Irv, I think everybody—*everybody*—would have said Chuck. He was clearly the better designer, had better taste and more energy, led men better, commanded more respect and worked harder than any single individual in the organization. He wasn't pompous but he was aggressive; a natural leader. You'd say, 'Hey, this isn't even a contest.'

"But just below the surface, Jordan had this tremendous temper, and he ultimately became the victim of that temper. Sometimes it went totally beyond his control, but there were other times when he could have controlled it but let it go anyway. His temper made him a lot of enemies over the years, particularly Howard Kehrl. Kehrl didn't like Jordan, and he hated Mitchell. Chuck could be arrogant and sometimes downright brutal. I had to separate him once from a union shop foreman who'd come in and stopped all work in the studio. They were actually going to duke it out. Jordan wasn't usually physical, but sometimes his temper got the best of him."

George Moon recalled that, when both he and Jordan were at Opel, Jordan blew up at a German body engineer, Karl Bettmann, in a meeting. "The conversation heated up over some point, Jordan went into a rage, grabbed Bettmann by the lapels and

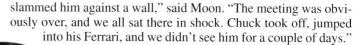

Irvin W. Rybicki

slammed him against a wall," said Moon. "The meeting was obviously over, and we all sat there in shock. Chuck took off, jumped into his Ferrari, and we didn't see him for a couple of days." Jordan's wife, Sally, phoned Moon later and asked if he knew where Chuck had gone. He duly came back and apologized, but the damage was done. Moon felt that Jordan had all the qualities of a good design leader, but his temper offset his talents.

Jordan once told off Howard Kehrl when Kehrl was still an assistant chief engineer. Then Kehrl's career took off: chief engineer of Oldsmobile and then general manager. Rybicki was Oldsmobile's studio chief, and he and Kehrl got along great. Both were soft-spoken and much less aggressive than Jordan. After his Olds assignment, GM made Kehrl an executive vice president and Jordan's immediate boss.

So like Mitchell, Jordan made too many enemies who eventually ended up in high places. Chuck had a way of alienating the division general managers by intentionally embarrassing them in front of their staff. Mitchell had done the same thing. "But even so," added Wilen, "I think that right up to the last minute, everybody thought Jordan was going to get it [the vice presidency]. We'd all forgotten the pains of the past. And Rybicki was the only other choice. The two of them were of equal rank, and if you had asked me, I would have said, 'Sure, Irv's in the running, but he doesn't stand much of a chance.'"

It was late on a Friday afternoon in June 1977 and GM's selection committee had already come to a decision on the company's next design vice president. That day, two general managers stopped Irv Rybicki in the hall. George R. Elges from Buick shook him by the hand, and Robert D. Lund from Chevrolet smiled and asked him how he felt. Irv said he felt fine. "I'd never seen them that friendly before," said Rybicki in a 1991 interview.

Next evening, Saturday, Rybicki's phone rang at home. It was Edward C. Kennard, general manager of Cadillac. "I just want to congratulate you," said Kennard. Rybicki didn't know what Kennard was talking about, and the two quickly hung up in mutual embarrassment. It wasn't until Monday that Howard Kehrl phoned Rybicki from New York and told him he'd been elected GM's next vice president of design. Rybicki was flabbergasted.

After Kehrl's call, Irv was asked to come to Bill Mitchell's office. "I went up," said Rybicki, "and...Bill was sitting at his desk— Earl's big desk—and he stood up, and he was *pale*. Bill was always red in the face, that was his normal color, but you know, this time

General Motors' advanced chief designer Allen C. Young worked on one of many Eldorado/Corvette sport coupe proposals. Young was also instrumental in several production Corvette designs.

he was white as chalk. I said, 'Are you feeling all right?' He said, 'Yeah, I'm fine, fine. Congratulations.' And he had this frown on his face, and his hand felt like a wet fish. I thought, 'Oh boy, this guy's dying, because he was definitely for Jordan, no question about it.'"

Mitchell then asked Rybicki whether he thought he could get along with Jordan, and Irv replied, "It's anybody's guess." Rybicki then left Mitchell's office and was walking to the Cadillac studio when he ran into Jordan in the hall. "Charlie had a scowl on his face," recalled Rybicki. "I don't know what he was thinking, but he said, 'What's going on, Irv?'" Jordan had just been called to Mitchell's office but hadn't yet heard the news. Mitchell summoned Rybicki to his office a second time, "So I walk back, and he and Charlie are standing there...and they're both white as sheets. Bill had already told Charlie that I got the job. I can't remember Bill's exact words, but he said something like, 'Well, Chuck, Irv's got the job, and I just hope you two guys can work together. Why don't you shake hands on it?' So I stuck out my hand, and Jordan's hand was the same as Mitchell's, like a wet fish."

By now it was a little before lunchtime. Mitchell called a two-minute meeting of his studio chiefs and announced Rybicki's appointment, after which Jordan stormed out of the building, jumped in his car, squealed out of the Design Staff executive garage and fishtailed through the 90° corners on the way out to Mound Road.

By the time of Mitchell's departure, Howard H. Kehrl occupied a seat on GM's board of directors and had authority over design, engineering, research, product planning, patents and manufacturing. GM board chairman Thomas A. Murphy was another person who'd had no love for Mitchell. Mitchell's pyrotechnical tantrums, his drinking and carousing made him too loose a cannon. If a Ralph Nader or the press had ever wanted to focus a righteous eye on Mitchell, they could have caused the corporation some serious embarrassment. Mitchell was too wild, too independent, too autocratic for comfort. And so was Jordan, whom everyone saw as Mitchell's understudy.

All this played to Irv Rybicki's advantage. It wasn't hard for Kehrl to convince Murphy to favor Rybicki over Jordan, and between them they rallied the support of the division general managers. The only holdout might have been GM president E.M. (Pete) Estes, a rousing leader himself who could identify with Mitchell's and Jordan's damn-the-torpedos style.

Soon after Rybicki's appointment, Tom Murphy called him in and told him, according to design engineering executive Kenneth A. (Ken) Pickering, "...in no uncertain terms that the Mitchell era of self-aggrandizement, the non-accountability to downtown and Mitchell's blatant disregard for what the divisions wanted...all that was over. Henceforth, Design Staff would be run like a business; would be responsive to the realities of what

1982 Camaro was born under Irv Rybicki's direction in Jerry Palmer's Chevy 2 studio.

the divisions needed and wanted." Rybicki told Murphy he was in total agreement and, with that, the future direction of General Motors design was set.

At first, the majority of GM's studio staff was pleased that Irv got the job. Everyone liked Irv, and having him in the vice president's office assured them of a certain tranquility; peaceful working conditions that they hadn't known under Earl and Mitchell. People saw Irv as a gentleman. He was also consumately fair. He could distance himself from personalities, and it didn't matter whether he liked someone or not—he judged performance on merit, held no grudges and made just decisions. So Rybicki enjoyed a honeymoon period that lasted several months and perhaps even as long as a year.

Meanwhile Jordan, who at one time had been Rybicki's immediate boss, and whose world collapsed when GM passed him over, was recovering as best he could from his tremendous disappointment. He felt, and rightly so, that the system had betrayed him. Jordan would never admit that, and in recent conversations he denied that anyone at GM—Mitchell in particular—had ever made him any promises. Yet it's unlikely that Mitchell wouldn't have discussed with Jordan his plans for succession, especially after Jordan's interview with Bunkie Knudsen at Ford in 1969 (see page 260).

The chasm between Jordan and Rybicki grew to Grand Canyon proportions very early on and kept growing right up to Rybicki's retirement. By the time Jordan finally did get the vice presidency—and this didn't happen until 1986—the two men were as different as right and left, and their enmity stretched back through years of hard feeling.

If he'd had his druthers, Irv Rybicki would have ended up not as a car designer but as a baseball player. He was born in Detroit on Sept. 16, 1921, one of three children. His father held a middle-management position with a Detroit interurban railway. In recent interviews, Irv stressed that both his parents were very gentle peo-

Chuck Jordan (left) got passed over as GM design vice president and became Rybicki's restless second in command. Here Jordan goes over Fiero GTP concept drawings with Pontiac studio head John Schinella.

One of Rybicki's more notable styling achievements, long-lived 1984 Corvette again originated in Jerry Palmer's studio (above). Early studies included both front- and mid-engined concepts. Palmer (right) positions glass for Corvette's T-top.

ple. They never yelled at him, and he remembered being spanked only once as a child, after he'd stolen 26¢ from his father. "I'll never forget it," he said, "because I could see the hurt in my dad's eyes."

As a teenager, Irv became passionately involved with sports. In high school, he joined the track, tennis, golf, swimming and baseball teams. His greatest love was and still is baseball. At one time, he played on three teams in three different leagues three times a week every spring, summer and fall. He was too small to go professional, but he continued to play baseball for fun for eight years after he married. His wife finally asked him to stop and pay some attention to the family, so he did.

Rybicki's interest in cars grew out of an early passion for airplanes. At 12 or 13, he dreamed of being a pilot. When Irv was 17, his uncle bought a new, black, 1938 Cadillac 60-Special. Irv was working in his uncle's grocery store at that time, and when his uncle pulled up in the Cadillac, Irv and his cousin, Scotty, ran out and jumped into the front seat. "I looked around," recalled Irv, "and I thought to myself, 'Holy Christ, is this a beautiful car!' And I thought, 'If somebody can make a car look this good, maybe I can do it even better.' It inspired me. So I started sketching cars, and from that day on I never stopped. I forgot about airplanes entirely."

That same year, Rybicki had put together an informal portfolio, which his dad—unbeknownst to Irv—showed to Jules Andrade at GM Art & Colour. Andrade interviewed Irv but told him immediately that they weren't hiring. It was 1938, the year of recession in the Depression, and Art & Colour was laying people off. But Andrade did put Irv on a list for future consideration. Irv continued to work in his uncle's grocery, kept playing baseball and filled notebooks with car designs.

In 1942, he was drafted, shipped to Ft. Benning, Georgia and soon became a sergeant in the tank corps. On cannon maneuvers in Tennessee one blistering May afternoon, Irv was standing on a tank above the hot engine compartment when he started to feel woozy. He told a corporal to take over and sat down in the shade behind the tank. The last thing he remembered was the corporal bringing his arm down to signal the firing of a cannon.

When he woke up, he was in a hospital. He saw doctors talking but couldn't hear them. Irv stayed in the hospital for three months, after which some of his hearing returned. He received a medical discharge in 1943 and went home. "It was a disaster for me," he recounted. "I had one helluva time living with that."

He began studying art at the Meinsinger School in Detroit, where he learned perspective and airbrushing. He also took a job at the GM Proving Grounds in Milford, Michigan. An engineer there noticed his futuristic car drawings pinned to the office walls and suggested that Irv think about the Harley Earl school. He enrolled in 1946.

Of the 15 students who started the class that year, only he and Carl Renner finished. After graduation, Rybicki went into Bill

Mitchell's Cadillac studio, where he remained for five years. He then spent five years in Art Ross' Oldsmobile studio, five years with Paul Gillan's Pontiac design group, and finally back to Oldsmobile, where he took over as chief designer in May 1957.

One of his proudest accomplishments during that period was the creation of the 1959 Olds front end (see page 179). He and his good friend, Jack N. Humbert, designed it together, each working independently at home. The design took shape over the telephone. Rybicki said that he and Humbert "talked" the front end onto paper. Harley Earl was so taken with the Olds frontal theme that he asked Ned Nickles to adapt it to the 1960 Corvair.

In July 1959, Bill Mitchell made Chuck Jordan his second in command. Jordan headed the Cadillac studio—had since August 1958—and Mitchell kept him in that position but also made him his director of design. When GM began adding more platforms and nameplates in the early 1960s—the Chevy II, Buick Special, Olds F-85, Pontiac Tempest, Chevelle, Riviera, etc.—it became obvious that Jordan needed help, so Mitchell named Rybicki as his assistant. Irv kept his job as chief designer for Olds but, in addition, became Chuck's principal aide. Whether Jordan had any say in Mitchell's choosing Irv isn't known. But at that point, Rybicki reported to Jordan.

Throughout this career, Jordan basically followed in the footsteps of Earl and Mitchell. Jordan had the greatest respect for both men and considered them the best in the business. Chuck loved cars, always had, had an instinctive feel for design and was a good rallier of troops. He could be charming and witty but, like Mitchell, he tended to be unpredictable and foul tempered. Unlike Mitchell, he didn't have a humorous side to soothe or smooth over the hurts. Some of the studio chiefs came to fear Jordan, and after his hair turned prematurely silver, many people called him "the chrome cobra" behind his back. His office was known as "the cobra den."

When asked how Jordan and Rybicki worked together, one veteran designer said, "They didn't." Thinking back, Rybicki confided that he couldn't remember a time when he and Jordan had ever exchanged a civil word. The cataclysmic split came after Stan Wilen had taken over the Olds studio. Wilen and his staff were working on a new full-sized Oldsmobile when Jordan and Rybicki came in together. This was during the time when Rybicki was still Jordan's assistant. For some reason, Jordan began ranting at Stan in front of his staff. According to Rybicki, "He just cut the guy up...I have never heard anything like that in my life."

After Jordan and Rybicki left the studio and were walking down the hall, Irv tried to explain to Chuck that he really couldn't do that sort of thing.

"Do what?" asked Jordan.

"Make someone look bad in front of his people," replied Rybicki. It undermined the studio chief's authority and made everyone feel terrible. If he had to come down on someone, do it

Although Pontiac originally wanted the 1984 Fiero to be a full-blown sports car, they sold it to GM management as a secretary's commuter car. Fiero's colored plastic body panels bolted directly to pressed-steel space frame.

privately, said Rybicki, in a closed office. Jordan told Rybicki to go to hell and marched on alone. That incident became the first major rift between them, and things never got better.

Irv Rybicki's nine years as vice president coincided with the darkest, bleakest period in GM design history. These were not happy days for anyone in the auto industry, and the blame certainly wasn't Irv's alone. This was an era of tremendous change at General Motors. To mention just a few: GMAD (the General Motors Assembly Div.) was supplanting Fisher Body bit by bit, an ongoing change since 1961. Many of Fisher Body's engineers retired, and those from GMAD who replaced them were relatively young and inexperienced. This lack of experience had a profound effect on design. Programs that previously would have sailed through got delayed and, in some instances, styling subtleties that Design Staff wanted simply couldn't be accommodated by GMAD. Toward the end of Rybicki's vice presidency, this problem got so bad that GM went to outside companies for engineering expertise (on the Pontiac Fiero, for example).

Another big change: Project centers took on the job of creating new platforms, taking authority away from the divisions. GM project centers preceded what we now call platform teams—big groups from various disciplines working together simultaneously on one car or set of cars. With project centers, the divisions relinquished control but inevitably got blamed when things went wrong in the field. Also, with project centers, styling became more or less cosmetic. Divisional identities blurred when management mandated that differently badged cars on the same platform would use identical outer sheetmetal. So while the theory was good, project centers—at least in that early form—didn't work out in the long run.

This was the period, too, of the infamous 1984 GM reorganization, when corporate chairman Roger B. Smith broke the car divisions into two unwieldy working units: Chevrolet-Pontiac-Canada (CPC) and Buick-Oldsmobile-Cadillac (BOC). Those units have since been dissolved, but they existed throughout the Rybicki/Jordan era and caused many a migraine.

Quality was another problem, one that Roger Smith tried to fix with expensive high-tech robotics and sheetmetal interchangeability. The robots went haywire and the interchangeable sheetmetal led to GM's public embarrassment with "lookalike" cars. These things and many more—like Saturn Corp.—were all coming at him throughout Rybicki's vice presidency, and they conspired to make his job extremely difficult. Yet even with all those good excuses, there's no real doubt that Irv was the wrong person in the wrong job at precisely the wrong time.

Rybicki came into office in 1977, a year when General Motors held 46.4% of the U.S. automobile market. By 1988, the year Rybicki's last designs came out, GM's market share had dropped to 35.8%. Styling contributed to some extent, but so did a lot of other factors. The most important was probably GM's growing arrogance and a feeling that anything the company built would sell. That was perhaps true in 1977, but by 1983 it definitely was not.

General Motors management didn't yet know that America was about to turn away from traditional buying habits. Roger Smith, among others at the top, failed to recognize the gravity of the price/size/quality squeeze from Japan and Europe. They thought they could get away with things like selling "Chevmobiles": Olds 88s with Chevrolet V-8s. And diesel engines that self-destructed at 30,000 miles. And anemic, rough-running Cadillacs with V4-6-8 engines. And A-body sedans whose rear side windows were sealed shut. And cars that looked so much alike that business magazines and TV commercials poked fun at them.

The lookalike problem surfaced when *Fortune* magazine published a picture of four maroon GM A-body sedans—a Chevrolet Celebrity, a Pontiac 6000, a Buick Century and Oldsmobile Cutlass Ciera—on the cover of its Aug. 22, 1983 issue. These four cars, photographed in side view from slightly above, looked so similar that no one could tell one from the other. *Fortune's* cover blurb asked the question, "Will Success Spoil General Motors?"

Among other things, *Fortune* focused on GM's practice of "badge engineering." Badge engineering—the placement of divisional badges on essentially identical cars—had been going on at GM (and all other car companies) ever since Vince Kaptur Sr. suggested the A-B-C-D body idea to Harley Earl in the early 1930s.

One of several GM gaffes during this period involved conjuring the 1982 Cadillac Cimarron (far left) out of Chevy Cavalier and trying to sell it against BMW's 3-Series. As Ford launched Taurus for '86, the sheer look still reigned at GM, here represented by 1986 Buick Regal T-Type.

But in the late 1970s, GM got so cocky that it blatantly abused the A-B-C-D body system. GM's cost cutters began to insist that for major body programs, like the A-body, the X-, J-, etc., all five nameplates had to use common, interchangeable sheetmetal. This had to be done in the name of economies of scale. Grilles and tail lamps could be different, but not cowls, doors, hoods, decks, fenders, glass, roofs and, of course, inner panels and black metal.

Rybicki and Jordan went along with this, but they had little choice. Rybicki agreed fairly willingly, Jordan less so. Both kept their mouths shut and put different faces and rear treatments on many GM car lines. The results carried the badges of Chevrolet, Pontiac, Oldsmobile, Buick and in some cases Cadillac. The 1982 Cadillac Cimarron, for example, was a thinly disguised and fully loaded J-Car, basically identical to the Chevrolet Cavalier.

Badge engineering worked for a while. GM gained some confidence from the success of the 1979 X-Cars, which Chevrolet released as the Citation. Pontiac's version, called the Phoenix, had a slightly different grille and rear, as did the Buick Skylark and Olds Omega, but all were very obviously cut from the same cloth. Because the X-Cars sold so well, GM's finance and division leaders felt comfortable launching the downsized, X-derived 1982 A-Cars.

The American public apparently didn't much care that GM's A-Cars looked as much alike as four peas in a pod. Buyers snapped up A-Cars—the Chevrolet Celebrity, Pontiac 6000, Olds Cutlass

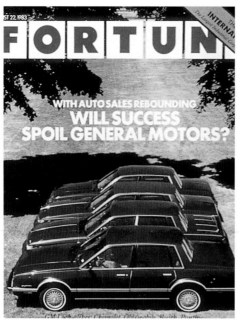

General Motors designers took *Fortune's* "lookalike" cover very much to heart. GM had become too complacent about platform and body-panel interchangeability.

Ciera and Buick Century—in record numbers and continued to do so for several years. So while badge engineering didn't slow A-Car sales, the impact of that 1983 *Fortune* cover had a profound effect on GM Design Staff. Chuck Jordan said the *Fortune* cover marked a turning point. He vowed then and there: No more lookalike cars. But such turnarounds take time, and before GM could change direction, there would be more embarrassment.

In 1985, a little more than a year after the *Fortune* article came out, Lincoln aired its famous TV commercial called "The Valet." In this, a well-dressed man and woman walk out of a fancy restaurant and hand their parking stub to the valet. "It's a Cadillac," says the man. The attendant brings back a car, and as the couple starts to get in, another man comes up and says, "Excuse me, I believe that's my Buick." A third car drives up, but it's finally identified as an Oldsmobile. Everyone's in a tizzy trying to figure out which car is which and whose. The commercial ends as another man coolly hands the attendant his ticket and says, "It's a Lincoln Town Car," and the correct sedan pulls up immediately.

Yet another lookalike insult arrived when the Radio Advertising Bureau built on GM's badge engineering and ran an ad in *Automotive News* for Nov. 14, 1983. The ad explained, "How to use radio in a lookalike era." The accompanying photo showed the same four GM A-body sedans in high side view, again indistinguishable one from the other, and the headline read: "Looks don't

To revive GM's sagging styling image, Jordan and advanced design chief Dave Holls, with the backing of chairman Roger Smith, pushed through a series of Motorama-like concept cars. The first, the mid-engined Corvette Indy (left), made its debut in 1986, quickly followed by Buick's Wildcat. These came partly in answer to Ford's Probe series.

Like Ford, GM wanted to get the public used to futuristic designs. Pontiac TranSport concept minivan (left) was shown after production version had been approved but before it came out. Like Fiero, TranSport had plastic-panelled space frame. Buick Lucerne (center) showed GM's styling direction while 5-door hatchback, the "Aero," maximized roominess.

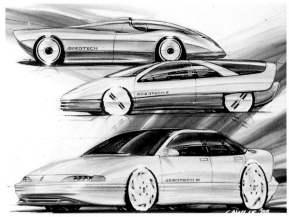

1988 Oldsmobile Aerotech (left) launched second wave of GM's far-out idea vehicles. This particular dreamcar set a number of speed and endurance records. Olds designers tried to carry Aerotech themes into passenger cars (right).

Jordan was very much aware of Earl's and Mitchell's success with showcars, and he became even more determined to reinstate GM as America's design leader after the Taurus arrived for 1986. Jordan indicated GM's future direction with one-offs like the 1988 Pontiac Banshee (left), Cadillac Voyage (center) and 1988 California Camaro.

sell cars anymore."

That line, the *Fortune* cover and the Lincoln TV spot finally put the message across to General Motors management. Everyone realized, as Jordan already had, that the company had to get away from cookie-cutter, lookalike cars—that the marque identities that Harley Earl had worked so hard to build into the public consciousness somehow had to be brought back. The Buick portholes were gone and so were Cadillac's tailfins, Pontiac's silver streak and Oldsmobile's rockets. GM's design management had carelessly thrown these symbols away and hadn't replaced them. Rybicki and Jordan now had to scramble to make GM cars distinctive and recognizable again from a block away.

Kehrl and Murphy had gotten what they wanted: a gentler, more likable, infinitely more malleable vice president than Mitchell ever was or Jordan ever would be. But the tradeoff came at a tremendous price. General Motors, during Rybicki's nine years in office, would lose not just identity but its dominance of the American industry. It would lose its half century of automotive design leadership.

GM's styling problem, which had been brought home so dramatically, consisted of several parts. One was that Rybicki had none of the fight and feistiness of an Earl or a Mitchell. Courtly, dapper, with a thin mustache and a gracious, slightly reserved manner, Irv was anything but a maker of waves. Kehrl had installed the archetypal team player: GM's version of Ford's Gene Bordinat. But Bordinat, while not a great designer, was generally conceded to be better than Rybicki and also a more forceful leader.

Irv's strength lay in administration. Kehrl wanted a good administrator, someone who could put GM Design Staff on a more businesslike footing. He got that. As a designer, Rybicki had done some nice things when he ran the Olds and Chevrolet studios, but he lacked emotion and forcefulness. He didn't have the conviction to fight for design. He was too gentle a person to do battle at all.

The corporate moneymen, the general managers, the engineering and manufacturing people too often got their way with Rybicki. While GM Design Staff was never shorted on funding, Irv could see and agree with the economic arguments for making design subservient to other disciplines, especially engineering and manufacturing and especially, too, because those staffs were working furiously on downsizing, CAFE, safety, emissions, quality, etc. Lloyd Reuss, who was Buick's general manager at the time and who later became GM president, mentioned that, "As more of our platforms converted to front-wheel drive, the engineers got more clout than the designers. Engineering led that revolution. The major emphasis was on practicality and efficiency, so the romance of design played second fiddle."

1990 Buick Bolero

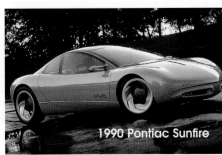
1990 Pontiac Sunfire

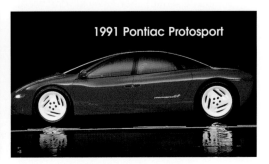
1991 Pontiac Protosport

General Motors felt that the Pininfarina name would add value to the 1990 Cadillac Allante (above). Jordan oversaw design of the 1992 Cadillac Seville sedan (left) and Eldorado coupe.

Another problem Rybicki ran into was the total confusion in sizing. Traditionally, a buyer expected more expensive cars to be bigger. In Harley Earl's day, Chevrolet produced the smallest GM cars and Cadillac made the largest. As a buyer moved up in income, he bought bigger and bigger cars.

That began to change in the 1970s under Mitchell and, by the 1980s, traditional American class and size distinctions fell apart altogether. We've already talked about Cadillac's Cimarron, a car considerably smaller than the Chevrolet Caprice.

approach than Chuck. In other words, everything done to please Jordan would have to be redone at the last minute to satisfy Rybicki. Irv was considerably to the right of Chuck in his tastes, and the studio chiefs were often caught in the middle.

And while Jordan understood what was happening, he either couldn't or didn't choose to undermine the man who was now clearly his boss. So they worked together separately and with clenched teeth, both men hating each other personally and professionally. Rybicki had little respect for Jordan's design ability, and

"I think it's too heavy. The more modern trend is to have a thinner sail panel." And then they would try to see who could outdo the other in forcing the studio to make that sail panel as slim as possible. Both would victimize the studio by pushing through their preference in sail panels or whatever other design detail came into contention although, from an engineering or aesthetic viewpoint, they had both gone beyond any practical limit.

This constant left-versus-right schizophrenia made it very hard on the studio chiefs. In addition to Rybicki's last-minute

Public did not take well to rebodied 1991 Chevrolet Caprice (below) but snapped up European-looking 1992 Pontiac Bonneville.

Cadillac loyalists couldn't accept the subcompact Cimarron. Other GM divisions also offered various sizes of cars on an alphabet soup of shared platforms, so specific nameplates didn't mean what they had in the past. Rybicki inherited that situation and couldn't style his way out of it.

Jordan was another problem. Again, for reasons that aren't entirely clear, Rybicki did choose to make Jordan his second in command. Jordan's appointment as GM design director came on Aug. 25, 1977, roughly a month after Rybicki took office. Rybicki said later that he appointed Jordan "against my better judgment" but didn't elaborate.

Jordan, then, directed the everyday work of the studios, and Rybicki concentrated on administration. However, when calls and design decisions had to be made, Irv walked into the studio, usually alone, and often advocated a more conservative

Jordan thought that Irv was a fake.

Their manner of giving directions was also entirely different. Stan Wilen observed that, "You could leave Rybicki's office and not remember a word he said, which was just as bad as leaving Jordan's office having just been brutalized. Rybicki dealt in intangibles. You never really got the straight story. Jordan would give you the story as straight as an arrow, but unfortunately it generally found its mark right in your heart."

Both men had their faults and strengths. Jordan, according to most who worked with him, had more strengths than Irv. Chuck ultimately received credit for enormous energy and total commitment. He would champion originality and creativity far more than Rybicki. But they also competed. If they came into the studio together, Rybicki would say, "What do you think of this sail panel?" Jordan would answer,

countermandates, Jordan had a habit of never being able to decide when a design was finished. He couldn't lay down the brush, as designers put it. So when Rybicki came around and declared a program done, everyone was so relieved that any desire to improve the design went out the window. The feeling was: Leave well enough alone. And that became another reason GM designs under Rybicki were so bland.

When the time came to design the Cadillac Allante, an expensive, two-passenger convertible intended to rival the sporty Mercedes SL, GM and Cadillac management felt that the name of an overseas designer might add value to the car. So they handed the assignment to Sergio Pininfarina in Italy. GM knew from the start that production volumes would be so small that it wouldn't pay to have the Allante body built in the U.S., so Pininfarina was commissioned to fabricate

One GM concept car that went into production relatively unchanged was the 1993 Chevrolet Camaro (above). Pontiac's Trans Am version of the F-Car borrowed a good number of cues from the 1988 Banshee showcar.

as well as design the bodies. In an expensive, elaborate scheme, Allante bodies were made in Italy, then airfreighted to Detroit for final assembly. Allantes did not sell well. Dealers usually discounted them heavily, and GM lost money on every one.

Some observers believed that one of GM Design Staff's early proposals for the Allante ended up becoming the Buick Reatta, but that wasn't the case at all. The Reatta came about because Buick general manager Lloyd Reuss assured GM's 14th floor that he could sell a two-place coupe. Unlike the Allante, the Reatta was designed and built in this country, but it fared no better than Cadillac's two-seater.

Under Rybicki, oddly enough, the internal chain of command at Design Staff took on a strange, ritual importance. Jordan never countermanded Irv and never tried to undermine his authority. Rybicki, meanwhile, often tended to isolate himself in his big office and rarely socialized with his staff. Why? Because to hobnob with people "lower" in the hierarchy than Jordan would have meant breaking and undermining the chain of command.

This was one of the sadder aspects of Rybicki's situation. Before he became a v.p., Irv loved to have lunch with the boys; it meant a lot to him. He looked forward to the mid-day break, and when Irv was running a studio or acting as Jordan's assistant, lunch was a time for talk and relaxation, usually over two or three martinis,

often at the Executive Inn in the company of designers Jack Humbert, Ned Nickles, Hank Haga, Stan Parker and Fidele Bianco. Rybicki was also Bill Mitchell's favorite lunchtime drinking buddy for a time.

But once Irv became v.p., those lunches stopped. His best friend and confidant was Pontiac studio head Jack Humbert. Rybicki relied heavily on Humbert both personally and professionally. Jack was to Irv what Chuck should have been: his valued right hand. They worked well together, especially since Jack had a keen sense of that very linear, architectonic style that characterized the late 1970s and early '80s. But now Irv couldn't even ask Jack to go to lunch with him—at least not very often—because that would again mean breaking the chain of command. (As an aside, he once tried to go to lunch alone with Jordan, but in his words, "It turned out to be a disaster.")

Later, Rybicki hosted luncheons in Design Staff's executive dining room for his top people, including Jordan. George Moon remembered them as being quite pleasant. "I felt that those luncheons in that very difficult and stressful period brought us all closer together," said Moon. "Whether or not that was Irv's intention, he did keep us supportive of each other."

Rybicki also began taking his secretary, Lucy Karash, and Lucy's friend from personnel out to lunch once or twice a week. Lucy reflected years later that, gregarious

and outgoing as he'd been earlier, Irv became more and more lonely and isolated as vice president. Jack Humbert's death in 1985 affected him deeply and made Rybicki even more reclusive.

Jordan, meanwhile, became more active toward the end of Rybicki's term. Chuck got along well with chairman Roger Smith, especially after Smith, during a tour of the advanced studios, asked him whether he thought GM was going far enough with its designs. Jordan said no, of course not, and showed Smith some of GM's latest concept cars. Smith, who loved futurism and technology, was delighted. As a result, Smith asked Jordan to prepare several concept designs for his (Smith's) 1987 "Teamwork & Technology" gala in New York, a display intended to impress GM's board, stockholders, Wall Streeters and ultimately the American public.

Jordan put together a mini Motorama the likes of which hadn't been seen since Mitchell's day. The Teamwork & Technology exhibit encouraged GM to go public with concept vehicles like the Corvette Indy and Oldsmobile Aerotech and, later, the Cadillac Voyage, Buick Sceptre, Pontiac Banshee III and Stinger and the Corvette Sting Ray III. This impressive flow of concept cars was intended not only to demonstrate that GM still had a vital, forward-thinking design organization, but it also helped lay the foundation for establishing distinctive identities for each GM nameplate.

Rybicki was clearly over his head as vice president. He once said to a group of his young designers, "Frankly, gentlemen, newness scares me," a line that haunted him from that day on. When asked which specific designs from his vice presidency he liked best, Rybicki answered: the 1982 Camaro and the 1984 Corvette. Both were done in Jerry P. Palmer's studio under Chuck Jordan's supervision. Irv, of course, had to approve the designs and did influence them. Other noteworthy cars styled under Rybicki were the 1984 Pontiac Fiero, the 1987 Chevrolet Corsica/Beretta and GM's futuristic APV minivans. Interestingly, the Pontiac TranSport concept van was done *after* the production APV minivans had been designed.

Charles M. Jordan

Jordan had no assurance he'd get the vice presidency even after he'd toughed out nine years under Rybicki. When he finally did move into Harley Earl's office in Oct. 1986, he realized all too clearly that he had only six years to prove himself; six years before he, too, would turn 65, GM's mandatory retirement age.

Jordan made several sweeping changes after he took office. The first was to place interior and exterior designers together in the same studios. They'd worked more or less separately in the past, usually with design management and engineering coordinating the two activities. "It's one car," Chuck reasoned, "so I put everyone to work together. The interior people really liked the recognition, because up to then they'd been considered sort of second-class citizens. Now, though, everybody was equal. We put the accent on interior design...the interior became as important as the exterior." In some instances, exterior designers worked on interiors and vice-versa.

The second major change that Jordan inaugurated was to bring strong styling identities to each division, something he'd been trying to do ever since the *Fortune* lookalike cover. He explained, "...we weren't going back to portholes and fins, but we did want to renew the focus on divisional identities in the context of international design standards." By that he meant he wanted GM cars to look just as acceptable in Europe or Japan as in the U.S. "I really believe there's an international design standard, and I think we turned out cars that could be successful and recognized, nameplate for nameplate, anywhere in the world."

Chuck Jordan was and is a complicated individual, and many people at GM tended to see just bits of him. He grew up in California in a Quaker family, and he'd been mildly religious before, but when GM passed him over for the vice presidency in 1977, he took a more devout interest in his faith.

Some of his colleagues continued to see him as volatile and unpredictable, which he certainly could be at times, but to others he was charming and generous and a pleasure to be with. He always worked hard, devoted himself in great measure to his job, yet he had time for his family. He set extremely high standards for himself and everyone around him and consciously struggled throughout his six years to win back GM's design supremacy.

Jordan remained true to his ideals and reverted basically to the Earl/Mitchell type of autocratic rule. He was hard on himself, hard

on his people, hard on the general managers, drove a hard bargain and continued to ride roughshod over anyone who didn't agree with him or gave him only 99%. As a result, he was feared and disliked by many. He had no patron to lean on, yet he himself feared no one and, above all else, he fought for the design. "His fights were never personal," said Stan Wilen. "They were all in the interest of the car, all for the division, for the corporation, all in the interest of the design."

The Ford Taurus came out the year Jordan took office, and he didn't like its styling at all. He called it a "jellybean" and said the Taurus looked like a potato, a bar of soap. But he admired Ford for breaking new ground, and the day the Taurus and Sable came out, Chuck phoned Jack Telnack and told him he appreciated what Ford was doing for General Motors. And what was that? It was showing GM's top management that styling does sell cars.

Like Rybicki, Jordan made some major staffing changes when he took office. He chose David R. Holls, who'd been assistant design chief of Cadillac and head of the Buick, Chevrolet, advanced and Opel studios, to be his design director. Reporting to Holls were Stan Wilen, who now had charge of Chevrolet, Pontiac and Saturn design; Leonard M. Casillo, with similar responsibility for Buick, Olds and Cadillac; Donald J. Schwarz, executive designer of truck and bus; and George E. Moon, head of color, trim and graphics. Jerry P. Palmer, who'd done the 1982 Camaro and 1984 Corvette, became Jordan's executive in charge of advanced design. Jordan also created a new position, executive director of engineering and design services, and installed engineer Ken Pickering to oversee fabrication and design engineering. Pickering also inherited many of Rybicki's administrative duties, which freed Jordan to spend more time in the studios.

Charles Morrell Jordan was born in 1927 and grew up near Whittier, California, a sleepy little farm community south of Los Angeles where his grandparents raised oranges. As a youngster, Chuck and his two brothers worked in the family citrus groves. Even before he'd reached his teens, Chuck learned to drive his grandfather's 12-speed Moreland truck, an experience that led to Jordan's fascination with wheeled contraptions of all sorts.

In school and at home, Chuck spent much of his time doodling trucks and cars. His mother and grandmother encouraged him and on Sundays, when the family attended church, Chuck's grandmother would bring along a pad and pencil, "to keep me quiet," because when he drew cars, he became totally absorbed. In the seventh grade, Chuck designed and built a model car in woodshop, and by the time he left high school, he'd made up his mind that he wanted to be a car designer. But he also felt that a college degree in mechanical engineering would stand him in better stead than a degree in design, so he applied to MIT and was accepted. MIT gave art courses only in architecture, so Chuck took as many as he could but also spent his summers at the Chouinard Institute of Art in Los Angeles. His thesis at MIT—very unusual even then—examined the styling of heavy-duty Mack trucks and included advanced proposals for future models.

In 1946, General Motors reinstated its Fisher Body Craftsman's Guild competition. This was a national competition in which U.S. youngsters vied for college scholarships by designing and building models of futuristic cars. Chuck built his model in the MIT machineshop over the Christmas holidays of his junior year. He

the finishing touches on the 1959 model, but his first all-new Cadillac was the less finny, crisper, more elegant '61. He also oversaw the design of the front-drive 1967 Cadillac Eldorado.

In 1967, Mitchell shipped Jordan off to Opel in Germany. At first, Jordan balked and didn't want to go. He referred to Opel as "purgatory." But Mitchell viewed Opel as a good training ground, so Jordan reluctantly packed up his family and went to Germany. He spent three years at Opel, which was the usual rotation at that time.

George Moon, who was Jordan's assistant director of design at Opel from 1968 to 1970, mentioned that

Two of Jordan's stylistic homes runs included the 1995 Oldsmobile Aurora (left) sedan and 1995 Buick Riviera personal coupe. Riviera exterior capitalized on ovals and ellipses. Both cars shared General Motors' G-body platform.

was 19 years old at the time.

His design won first prize and a $4000 scholarship—a fabulous sum in 1946. Part of the prize, too, was a four-day trip to Detroit, during which he met Harley Earl, GM research v.p. Charles F. Kettering and the presidents of MIT and Cal Tech. Chuck was also given a royal tour of GM Styling in the Argonaut Building and shook hands with all of GM's studio chiefs: Ned Nickles at Buick, Bill Mitchell at Cadillac, Chevrolet's Ed Anderson, Art Ross at Oldsmobile and Bob Lauer at Pontiac. At the end of his tour, Howard O'Leary handed Jordan his business card. "When you finish at MIT, let us know," said O'Leary. "If you want it, there's a job waiting for you here." Jordan didn't have to think twice about that offer.

In 1948, General Motors designers traditionally began by apprenticing in Styling's experimental studios. Chuck mentioned an interest in trucks, so they put him into Lu Stier's truck studio, where he created, among other things, the flush-sided concept pickup that went into production as the 1955 Chevrolet Cameo Carrier.

The Korean War interrupted Jordan's career, but he talked the military into assigning him to the art department of Patrick Air Force Base in Florida. There, in his spare time, he created a large number of sketches of concept trucks and cars and shipped them back to Lu Stier at GM Styling.

Chuck returned to Detroit in July 1953 and the next year Earl put him in charge of a new heavy-duty vehicles studio and asked him to design an articulated crawler tractor for GM's Euclid Div. Jordan, then 27, modeled this monster full size in clay. Euclid accepted not only the design but the wild chartreuse paint scheme Jordan had given it. Chartreuse, in fact, became Euclid's identifying color from then on. Chuck next designed a streamlined train for GM's Electromotive Div., the so-called Aerotrain. At that point, Bill Mitchell, who'd befriended him, took Chuck aside and gave him a piece of advice. "Hey look, kid," Mitchell told Jordan, "if you want to get anyplace around here, you've *got* to get into cars." Much as he liked working on trucks, trains and earthmoving equipment, Jordan knew Mitchell was right. He was given an advanced design studio, and the first automobile Chuck produced was the Buick Centurion dreamcar for the 1956 GM Motorama show.

In Aug. 1958, Jordan found himself chief of the Cadillac studio. "Cadillac was GM's design leader," Jordan pointed out. "I thought to myself, 'Hey, Mitchell went through Cadillac. Earl's always been concerned with Cadillac. A lot of top people came up through Cadillac,' so I figured, 'Wow, this is great!'" Jordan put

Chuck had a hard time getting along with some of the German engineers, citing the Bettmann incident as one example. Ultimately, though, Jordan settled down and gave Opel a desperately needed new look.

Ironically, Jordan later viewed his Opel exile as a very positive interlude. "Bill sent me to Germany to earn my independence," Chuck said in a 1992 interview, reflecting that Mitchell had similarly been sent to "purgatory" when he became manager of the Harley Earl Corp. "Opel turned out to be a great experience for me. By the time I was finished there, I was pretty confident. The weight of responsibility didn't bother me. It was *fun,* and we designed some exceptional Opels. We finished up the Opel GT and then did the Manta coupe, the Ascona, and the Rekord II. By the end of my duty there, we'd changed Opel's image. It was no longer a farmer's car. We made it more a sporty, sophisticated automobile. And I thought, 'Wow, if this is what it feels like to lead the orchestra, hand me the baton!' The baton, of course, passed to Rybicki before it went to Jordan.

When he finally got to the podium, Jordan called a meeting of the entire staff and talked about, "...where we were going. The people were down," he recalled, "and I surely can't blame it all on Irv. I don't know how much better I could have done. But with downsizing, we hadn't known how to get character into these cars. All of a sudden they were smaller, shorter, narrower and higher, whereas we'd been raised on longer, lower, wider: Earl's thesis. We hadn't done well. That was the state of Design Staff when I got to the vice presidency.

"So that first day, my goal was to rev up the people and give them an idea about where we were going. My priority was to rekindle the creative spirit. Second, no more lookalike cars. I said that this business used to be fun, and I wanted it to be fun again.

GM's California Concept Center, under John Schinella, developed 1992 Sting Ray III as one possible answer to the Dodge Viper. John Mack did most of the exterior design, while Jon Albert designed the interior. The running metallic purple prototype carried a 300-bhp Corvette V-8.

over the objections of his marketing people, who warned him that it clinicked poorly. Jordan put no faith in clinics and asked Burger to trust his judgement, which Burger did. After the Caprice didn't sell, GM's management put Jordan on a shorter leash and insisted that Design Staff pay more attention to clinics. Clinics have become a fixture at General Motors ever since. Some of Jordan's designs did well in clinics, others didn't. At least one car received negative clinic reviews four times, was redone four times and delayed 18 months. The division general manager simply would not go along with Jordan's intuitive recommendations.

(The clinic or "focus group" process began at GM long ago when a car division would bring 100 or so dealers into Design Staff, ask them to look at clay models and then have them rate a design in terms of sales potential. Dealers, though, brought along their own marketing biases, so now each division's product planning staff holds clinics in which ordinary citizens are asked to evaluate or compare designs. To mitigate regional preferences, the same designs are often clinicked several times in different parts of the country.)

And the 1988 W-Car (Buick Regal, Pontiac Grand Prix and Oldsmobile Cutlass Supreme) sedans were delayed, due partly to production and budget problems and partly because, in their original form, they were more rounded and more aerodynamic. They looked, some felt, too much like the Ford Taurus. The Taurus had come out during the time the W-Cars were being styled. GM had to change the design at the 11th hour, particularly the Cutlass Supreme's, to avoid being called copycat. The 1990 Chevrolet Lumina became the fourth member of the W-Car (GM-10) family and did show some Taurus influence.

But Chuck continued the good fight. In the case of the 1993 F-Car, the battle for the Camaro's rear spoiler, the Firebird's pinched waist and the F-Car's superfast windshield took months of haranguing to push through. Jordan finally went over the platform managers' heads and called a meeting of corporate managers. He orchestrated a selling job that would have done Harley Earl proud. His presentation wound up with two display models, one with a fairly upright windshield and one with the glass steeply raked. The obvious difference finally tipped it, and the corporation okayed about $50 million (in a $400+ million overall project) to put Chuck's 57° windshield on the 1993 F-Car.

Another car Jordan pushed through was the 1995 Oldsmobile Aurora. The Aurora began as a non-divisional project in one of GM's advanced studios. "We said, 'Let's design a sedan the way they'd do it at the Lockheed skunkworks—an aircraft theme,'" he noted. "We called it the 'tube car.'" When the advanced designers had finished, Chuck had a full-sized fiberglass Aurora mockup parked at the head of the Design Staff escalator. "That's a place of influence," remarked Jordan. "You pass by there so many times a day that the design either wears well or it doesn't." The design wore well, and when Oldsmobile decided it wanted a four-door Toronado, the Aurora came up as a natural. It, too, went through a rigorous clinicking process.

In fact, after that speech, little signs popped up saying, 'Are we having fun yet?' But our design goals were clear: cars that had some flair and elegance. There's nothing wrong with a beautiful car. Love starts with a look. If there's no emotional reaction, we've failed. We were dealing with emotions."

Jordan also insisted on "perfection;" his interpretation of it. His view of perfection was similar to Harley Earl's. Early in Jordan's career, for example, when he was still Cadillac's styling chief, Clarence Morgan, a studio engineer, begged to be transferred. Why? Because Jordan, in one day, had changed the height of a tailfin six times, and each time Morgan had to make a new set of templates. Morgan couldn't live with Jordan's view of perfection. But those were the minute details Chuck considered important. He'd put "perfection" on hold under Rybicki, but it returned when he took office. A design had to be "perfect" to satisfy him, an insistence that made life difficult both for him and those around him, partly because the striving never stopped.

"Perfect" to Jordan also represented an ideal as seen through the eyes of a Ferrari enthusiast. Chuck Jordan's romance with cars always put Ferrari on a pedestal. "I've had a passion for Ferraris my whole career," Jordan explained in 1986. "I had the opportunity to buy [my first] one when I was at Opel in Germany; a 1962 Lusso, and I drove it there. And then [I bought] a Daytona when I got back to the States. Then a Boxer and a Testa Rossa." Jordan also owned and drove an F40 for a time. "I made a pledge to myself," he said, "...after all those years of hard work, one of my rewards is to be able to drive the latest Ferrari."

Jordan was enough of an inspirer and salesman to push through some very exciting and beautiful GM cars. Chuck's legacy as vice president included such standouts as the Jaguar XJ6-inspired 1991 Buick Park Avenue and '92 LeSabre, the 1992 Cadillac Seville and Eldorado, 1992 Pontiac Bonneville, 1993 1/2 Camaro/Firebird, the 1994 Chevrolet S-10 Blazer and pickup, the oval-on-oval 1995 Buick Riviera, the 1995 Oldsmobile Aurora sedan and the 1996 J-Cars: Cavalier and Sunfire. The 1996 Bonneville, not yet out at this writing, promises to be another lasting design from the Jordan palette.

But he also laid a few eggs. The rebodied 1991 Chevrolet Caprice didn't sell nearly so well as the sheer Mitchell version and was viewed by some as a modernized 1948 Hudson. Robert D. Burger, Chevrolet's then-general manager, okayed the Caprice

Chuck Jordan's Home Team

All three of the Jordan children have followed in their father's footsteps; all are involved in the industrial arts. At this writing, son Mark is assistant chief designer in Mazda's California styling studio. Mark Jordan played an important role in developing the Miata roadster and the 1993 MX-6 coupe. Daughter Debra works as a freelance graphic illustrator, and the Jordans' second daughter, Melissa, is with BASF as a color specialist. ◆

design, decided to leave and took an early retirement.

When Jordan turned 65 in the late autumn of 1992, most insiders believed that the vice presidency would pass to Jerry P.

Palmer. At that time, Palmer had charge of Pontiac design as well as GM's advanced studios. Before that, he'd headed up the Chevrolet studios. Then, after Dave Holls left, Palmer functioned as Jordan's second in command.

The only other person in contention for Design Staff's top job was Wayne K. Cherry. Cherry had spent most of his career overseas, so relatively few people in this country knew him. Palmer, on the other hand, had a high profile as the longtime chief designer of Camaros and Corvettes.

Jordan officially retired on Oct. 31, 1992. On Sept. 15, word came down that Wayne Cherry would be GM's next design vice president, effective Nov. 2. "In his new assignment," said the press statement, "Mr. Cherry will oversee GM's worldwide design activities." Palmer got the #2 spot, his new title becoming executive director of design for General Motors North American Operations (NAO). And the name *GM Design Staff* was soon changed to *GM NAO Design Staff*. Changes were in the wind.

Influence of concept cars trickled down even into GM's most affordable lines, like this sporty, $12,717 Pontiac Sunfire GT coupe for 1995.

Wayne Cherry was born in Indianapolis on Sept. 3, 1937. He started drawing cars and trucks at a very tender age, and when Wayne was nine, his father, a bank teller, took him to see his first Indy 500. This was still during a time when each Indy race car was assigned its own human lap counter and timer, and for a number of years after the war, Mr. Cherry acted in that capacity. In doing so, he and Wayne were free to roam the Brickyard, and they naturally paid regular visits to Gasoline Alley and chatted with the drivers.

By age 15, Wayne had developed an intense interest in foreign cars, so just before the 1952 Indy 500, he asked his father to take him to the garage area specifically to see Alberto Ascari's Ferrari. Ascari spoke to Wayne in Italian, which Wayne didn't understand, but then he motioned him to sit in the cockpit of his car, which Wayne did understand, and he happily climbed aboard. (Forty years later, Wayne visited the basement of the Indianapolis Motor Speedway Museum and discovered Ascari's Ferrari in storage—a sight, he says, that brought back a flood of memories.)

During his teen years, Wayne Cherry worked in a neighborhood Indianapolis drugstore. Two doors away stood a repair garage whose owner raced a sprint car. Every chance he got, Wayne went over to the garage to watch the sprint car come apart and go back together between weekends. By watching, Wayne learned the basic principles of auto mechanics. It wasn't long before the garage owner began inviting the youngster along to the local races.

By now Wayne was hopelessly hooked on automobiles and particularly on auto racing. He knew he wanted to be a car designer, but he wanted to build up some hot rods before he started applying to college. So when he graduated from high school in 1955, he bought a V-8 engine out of a wrecked '55 Chevrolet and had a friend help him install it in his black 1951 Chevy convertible.

Next year he bought a used 1955 Bel Air hardtop and proceeded to modify it for D- and E-Gas class drag racing. Wayne ported and relieved the heads, installed racing pistons, a Duntov cam, twin four-barrel carburetors, electric fuel pump, Mallory ignition, racing headers, a lightened flywheel, heavy-duty clutch and 4.58:1 rear axle. The Bel Air became Wayne's daily driver, but he also raced it on weekends and consistently ran the quarter mile in the low 14-second range.

He meanwhile had been making sketches of cars and trucks, and he put together a portfolio, which he sent to just one school: Art Center College of Design in Los Angeles. Art Center accepted him in 1959, and he immediately drove his 1955 Chevy out to California. Wayne did well in all his classes and soon won a scholarship.

When he finished college in 1962, Ron Hill of GM Design Staff interviewed Wayne and offered him a job. "I'd *really* wanted to

work for GM," commented Wayne, "and it was like a dream come true." Harry Bradley, another freshman designer at GM, remembered Wayne as tall, quiet, shy and hardworking. "He showed up at Design Staff in this black 1955 Bel Air hardtop, just like Harrison Ford in *American Graffiti*," recalled Bradley. Cherry finally sold his 1955 Chevy in 1963 after buying a new Corvette roadster.

It was also during those early years at General Motors that Wayne became involved in H-Modified racing. His race car initially used a Mercury Marine outboard engine. He soon replaced this powerplant with a three-cylinder Saab that he rebuilt in the kitchen of his rented house. He put together the chassis in the basement and modified a Fiat transaxle to fit by modeling the bell-housing in clay as a casting pattern.

Like most apprentice designers, Wayne started in GM's advanced areas. He worked initially with Edward F. (Ed) Taylor, who at that time was assistant chief designer in the studio where the first Toronado was modeled. Next Wayne helped create the 1964 World's Fair "GM Shopper." He then worked with Chevrolet's assistant chief designer Leo Pruneau on projects that turned into the 1967 Camaro. Soon thereafter, Pruneau went to Vauxhall, GM's British subsidiary in Luton, England. A few months later, Pruneau asked if Wayne could join him at Vauxhall. This was in 1965. Wayne, 27, unencumbered and anxious to see European racing first-hand, jumped at the opportunity.

(Earlier, during Harley Earl's vice presidency, Vauxhall automobiles tended to look like downsized versions of GM's American cars. The Vauxhall Victor, for example, which came out as a 1957 model, had all the earmarks of a miniaturized Pontiac/Buick, complete with wraparound windshield, Dagmar bumpers and even overtones of Pontiac's silver streak. The larger 1958 Vauxhall Cresta similarly had an upper borrowed from a 1958 Chevrolet and canted fins much like the 1959 Buick's. David N. Jones, who served as Vauxhall's styling director from 1939 to 1975, carried out design suggestions from Earl and later from William L. Mitchell. It was under Mitchell, though, that Vauxhall began taking on a more British character, and Pruneau had been sent over to help do the Vauxhall HB Viva.)

Wayne thought at first that he'd be assigned to England for just a short time, but as the months turned into years, he found himself more and more comfortable at Vauxhall. Then, too, European racing proved to be everything he'd dreamed, and he also discovered that Vauxhall afforded him the opportunity to take on ever increasing design responsibilities.

Unlike the decentralized, spread-out nature of GM's farflung operations in the U.S., everything at Vauxhall occupied one site. Design, marketing, administration, engineering, vehicle development, the manufacturing and paint shops were all within walking distance. So it wasn't uncommon for a plant manager or a body engineer to frequent the design offices and suggest ways to make a part simpler or less expensive or easier to install. And Vauxhall designers likewise felt free to visit the assembly plants. An informal back-and-forth existed between all departments, a fact that gave Cherry a wider appreciation of vehicle engineering and manufacturing than he might have gotten inside a GM studio in Michigan.

Besides passenger cars, Vauxhall built a wide range of Bedford-badged commercial vehicles. Bedford vans, trucks and buses had a good reputation in England and sold well not only there but throughout Europe. Bedford also maintained distribution channels in various parts of Africa and the Arab nations.

As Bedford became increasingly more important to Luton's overall operation, Wayne got more and more involved in truck and bus design. He worked on Bedford exteriors and interiors alongside the Vauxhall car programs. He also put together the all-important annual Bedford styling presentations; important because they helped determine future budgets. Wayne's presentations are remembered even today as classics of planning and execution. Year after year, Cherry's carefully orchestrated Bedford new-model shows helped convince GM's corporate executives to give Bedford their financial and moral support.

In 1970, Wayne was named Vauxhall/Bedford's assistant styling director, a position he continued to hold under Ed Taylor after Vauxhall's longtime design director Davy Jones retired following a nasty auto accident in 1972. And when Taylor returned to the U.S. in 1975, Cherry became Vauxhall/Bedford's director of design.

Wayne K. Cherry

Meanwhile, Wayne's passion for auto racing accelerated. He followed Formula One with avid interest, attended Jim Russell's Formula Ford driving school at Snetherton and also took competition lessons from Motor Racing Stables at Silverstone and Brands Hatch, "...mostly," he said, "to get a chance to drive on those famous race tracks." Wayne became a popular, recognized figure at British competition events and showed up regularly at circuits from Monte Carlo to Nurburgring. He made friends among the European motoring press and generally thrived in his work.

At the time Cherry became design director, Vauxhall was still designing and manufacturing its own cars in England while Opel was producing a similar line in Germany. General Motors decided this arrangement didn't make much sense and that, for economies of scale, both nameplates should henceforth share common platforms. Opel enjoyed by far the better reputation for quality, so Opel was chosen to be the leading manufacturer. As a result, Vauxhalls made after 1976 were essentially rebadged and rebodied Opels. Wayne's job now consisted of giving Vauxhalls their British accents and retaining some UK identity. At the same time, Bedford accepted closer ties

with GM's North American truck and bus operations, so basically Vauxhall/Bedford became a satellite of Opel and GM Europe. (Unlike Vauxhall, Opel didn't have a longterm styling director like Davy Jones. From 1962 through 1983, Opel design had been overseen in turn by American designers Clare MacKichan, Chuck Jordan, Dave Holls, Hank Haga and Gordon Brown.)

In 1983, Irv Rybicki asked Cherry to move from Vauxhall to Opel and oversee all European car and truck design. Wayne still kept an eye on Vauxhall, but Opel now became his primary focus. Four years after he took over, at about the time his first designs came to market, Opel began to blossom. By 1987, Opel stood out as GM's profit leader, and not just in Europe but worldwide. During a period when GM North America was losing billions, GM Europe—and Opel in particular—kept producing profits. And this rise in fortune accelerated precisely during those years when Cherry headed Opel's design activity. Opel ultimately became Europe's top-selling marque.

Opel's success came about for a number of reasons, most notably due to the dynamic, team-oriented management style of John F. (Jack) Smith, Jr. and Bob Eaton. Smith ended up as GM chairman and Eaton became chairman of Chrysler Corp., so these were formidable captains of industry. But Opel styling needs some credit as well, and Wayne Cherry played an undeniably strong role in that arena. Opel won trophy cases full of European car-of-the-year and styling awards, making Wayne something of a local hero. Added Dave Holls, "What Wayne was doing over there was so good that whenever we had a GM board of directors show in this country, everybody would run over to the new Opels and ooh and aaah!" GM's U.S. designers greatly admired Cherry's work, as did those from other domestic car companies.

During his time in Europe, Cherry was instrumental in adding two new models to the Opel lineup: the sporty Calibra and Tigra. He totally reorganized Opel's studio structure and instituted massive architectural changes that doubled the size of the design area. He also added considerable staff.

Wayne stayed at Opel until 1991, when Chuck Jordan asked him to come back to the United States to take over as executive designer for Chevrolet/Geo and GM Canada. Wayne had spent 26 years in Europe, built up a terrific track record there and wasn't especially anxious to leave. Yet he saw Chevrolet as one of GM's great American institutions and in need of help. "It was a tough decision," he noted, but he did accept the challenge. Jordan said later that his motive in bringing Wayne back to the U.S. was to give GM a broader choice of leadership candidates when he retired, and Cherry, of course, was aware of that when he arrived.

These weren't good financial times for General Motors North America, and choosing a new design vice president during this period's economic and political turmoil couldn't have been easy. Rumor even had it that GM might hire Jordan's successor from the outside. When he brought Cherry over, Jordan wanted to see how Wayne acted and reacted in reference to others at Design Staff. After one year as head of the Chevrolet studios, Wayne was "like a ghost" in executive meetings, according to Jordan.

Jordan had favored Cherry's candidacy when he first brought him over but suddenly changed his mind. He then polled the divisional general managers to see where they stood in regard to Cherry versus Palmer. Most favored Palmer. Jordan launched a lobbying campaign, personally visiting GM's top executives and the NAO strategy board. He pushed Palmer's candidacy at every opportunity and, according to insiders, was generally hard on Cherry.

After that, the politics got sticky. Some people felt Jordan's endorsement of Palmer might have caused a backlash. The strategy board perhaps believed that if Palmer was "Jordan's man," he might be too much like Jordan and Mitchell. No doubt one reason Cherry got the vice presidency was his European connection with Jack Smith. Smith knew Wayne well, having been president of GM Europe throughout Opel's ascendency. At the time of the vote, Smith had just become General Motors president in this country. Another strong Cherry supporter was Chevrolet general manager Jim Perkins.

The Cherry/Palmer vote took place during that critical, unsettled period in GM's recent history when the board obviously didn't want to continue doing business as usual and Jack Smith was headed for the GM chairmanship. The world's largest corporation needed, to a certain extent, to reinvent itself, just as Chrysler had done, and GM's freshly installed top management might have felt that a man like Wayne Cherry—less volatile than Jordan and with a proven international track record—could steer the company in new directions.

When this was written, in early 1995, none of Cherry's production designs has yet come to market, so there's no legitimate way to judge his impact on the future. Some of GM's recent concept cars, however—particularly the Buick XP2000 and the Oldsmobile Antares—give indications of what the man can do. And in his very modest, quiet way, he has articulated some of his goals. "My objective is not to make a mark on the design community," he said in our 1995 interview. "My objective really is to have the design center play a value-added role in the total success of the corporate portfolio. That's where I really see my primary responsibility." ◆

No cars designed under Wayne Cherry had yet come out in this country, but he'd created some big hits in Europe, among them the Opel Calibra sport coupe.

CHAPTER 14

CHRYSLER REINVENTS ITSELF

After 13 years as design vice president, Elwood Engel retired under less than happy circumstances. Chrysler management suspected some hanky-panky and, at nearly the same time, Engel was diagnosed with prostate cancer. He flew out to Stanford for treatment, a trip that effectively marked the end of his career. Engel's design director, Richard G. Macadam, took over the running of Chrysler's styling office and, when Engel retired some months later, Macadam came into the vice presidency. The official date was June 1, 1974.

Dick Macadam was an unusual person by any standard of an unusual profession. He trained first as an engineer, then switched to the fine arts and entered car design by combining the two. During his career as an auto designer, he raced go-karts and sailboats, took up fencing, studied and danced ballet, mastered the recorder, built his own harpsichord and learned to play it, took a keen interest in French provincial furniture and eventually returned to fine art. He moved to Provincetown, Massachusetts, began painting in a very serious way, became a director of the local art league and let his hair grow down to his shoulders.

Looking back at his Chrysler years, it's easy enough to say that Macadam didn't particularly distinguish himself as design vice president. But again, his term of office was short and came at the worst possible time. He served during that terrible period when oil sheiks shook the world and the government was handing out mandates by the binderful. All U.S. car companies were in the throes of downsizing, the business climate was arctic, hyper infla-

Richard G. Macadam

tion swept the nation and aggressive competition arrived from overseas, all of which led ultimately to yet another—and the most threatening—of Chrysler Corp.'s near collapses. This time there were serious doubts whether the company would survive the early 1980s, and it was only by virtue of the K-Car, Lee Iacocca's salesmanship and $1.5 billion in federally guaranteed private loans that the company nipped through.

By the time Macadam was forced to retire from Chrysler in 1980, his budgets had been slashed to the marrow (unlike Ford and GM, whose styling money never stopped), he'd had to thin his staff, and what little morale there had been at the beginning of his term was now in tatters. As in Rybicki's situation, Macadam did not create these problems, but he did have to deal with them.

On the plus side, Macadam did fine-tune the lines of communication between himself, his staff, product planning, marketing and engineering, at least in the beginning. Toward the end, he became reclusive. Most of those who worked with him called Macadam demanding, articulate, almost clairvoyant, scrupulously fair and open minded. We tried to talk to Macadam about his Chrysler years, but he begged off, saying he wanted to forget that period of his life. When we asked him to review the manuscript for this chapter, he twice refused and finally told us in no uncertain terms to leave him alone.

Richard G. (Mac) Macadam was born May 23, 1930 in Wilmington, Delaware. He studied mechanical engineering at the University of Delaware, then suddenly switched to fine art. He attended the School of Art in Philadelphia and the Pennsylvania Academy of Fine Arts. Good-looking, personable, with training and talent that prepared him for no job in particular, he left college and began selling Kirby vacuum cleaners door to door in his native Delaware.

Discovering that not much future existed in vacuum cleaners, he decided at age 24 to become a car designer, so he wrote to Dick Teague at Packard. According to Teague, "...he enclosed a drawing that looked like Artzebachev had made it—you know, the artist who used to do those wonderfully mechanical *Time* covers: terribly detailed, in 9H lead pencil. He drew people who looked like machines and machines that looked like people. I kept that drawing for years and just sent it back recently. Mac's always been a serious guy and a good designer. He was a good designer even before he came to work for us at Packard. He had a tremendous feel. He articulates with his pencil. Good guy, but different." Teague promptly hired Macadam for Packard.

Macadam followed Teague to Chrysler in 1957 but then bolted to General Motors when the Exner/Schmidt struggle took place (see page 168). After he'd been with GM a few years, Exner asked him to come back to Chrysler and offered him a substantial increase in salary. Macadam discussed the offer with Bill Mitchell, who tried to convince him not to leave GM but couldn't match the salary. So Macadam returned to Chrysler and thrived there. Elwood Engel named him executive stylist of all Chrysler-

In the mid 1970s, when Macadam became Chrysler's design v.p., the corporation built mostly large, gas-guzzling cars like the 1975 Imperial (below left). Chrysler's fortunes sank in direct proportion to fuel prices and inflation, but even after introducing the Omni/Horizon subcompacts for 1978, Chrysler still pushed cars like the Cordoba LS (below right).

The 1981 K-Car became Lee Iacocca's primary weapon in bringing Chrysler Corp. back to profitability. Bland as it looked, the K-Car was inexpensive, fairly economical, had front-wheel drive and could accommodate six passengers in relative comfort.

Plymouth studios in 1968. In 1970, Engel put Macadam in charge of standard-sized cars, then all exteriors in 1971 and named him his director of design in 1972. As director, Macadam found himself in line for the vice presidency.

It was under Macadam's studio guidance that the 1960 Valiant compact was created; also the 1967 Barracuda and the 1968 Plymouth Road Runner series. After he became v.p., the lifesav-

the Catfish Racing Association of Michigan. CRAM still uses Macadam's bylaws today. Mac next bought a Hobie Cat and raced it in Hawaii. He and his son later campaigned a Tornado, but not in Hawaii. Antonick feels that Macadam remained an avid sailor long after he left Chrysler.

Asked about Macadam's abilities as a design manager, Herlitz responded, "Well, he was very good from a standpoint of his

Nearly everything Chrysler built after 1981 used the K-Car platform, including the bestselling 1984 minivan (left). The platform had to be considerably modified for van duty, however. Beneath its skin, the 1988 Dodge Dynasty (above) was also basically a K-Car.

ing corporate K-Cars, the first minivans, the big C-bodied cars like the 1969 Chrysler with the full-loop bumper and the '74 Imperial with the waterfall grille—those were all done under his direction.

John Herlitz, who became Chrysler's vice president of product design in Apr. 1994, had originally been hired into the Plymouth studio by Macadam 30 years earlier. In a recent interview, Herlitz recalled, "Dick was a very intense guy...very articulate in the way he described and defined design projects. He was an excellent sketch artist and used to do these very tightly rendered blue Prismacolor sketches on vellum. They were works of art in themselves.

"He was always in search of a challenge; extremely competitive. He raced go-karts competitively; go-karts were hot at the time. Then he went off to play the recorder and learned to do that extremely well. He put that away and went into fencing and even did a stint in ballet. Then he moved into sailing and was going, I believe, to try out for the Olympics...with a two-man catamaran. I think it was called a Tornado. He took that out to Hawaii and tried to qualify...but I guess it was more than he bargained for. The boat just beat him to pieces. So he backed out of that and pretty much gave up sailing. Mac typically did things by himself. He was a loner in terms of going after individual sports and individual efforts at personal excellence."

For the record, designer Milt Antonick worked under Macadam and shared his interest in sailing. Antonick points out that Macadam began his sailing career in a Catfish and soon founded

design capabilities. I learned a tremendous amount from him. If he had a problem at all, it was in his dealings with people. He tended to be confrontational. The net effect was that he was not particularly happy...while he was in the vice presidency, because he fought for everything and was very, very disturbed and frustrated when he didn't get his way."

Dave Cummins, who also worked under Macadam, remembered him this way: "He did things for styling, for Chrysler, for individual people in his own time that nobody else could have ever done. He was one of the fairest, straightest-shooting, most honest men I think I've ever known. He knew absolutely everybody in the design office: knew them all on a first-name basis, what their capabilities and weaknesses were, how many kids they had, where they lived and everything else. His weak point was that he was just a stubborn Scotsman. If you crossed him, he'd let you know it in no uncertain terms. He was a fanatic on detail. But we got along well...."

Less taken with Macadam was Colin Neale. Neale had worked on the 1961 Lincoln under Engel, then followed Engel to Chrysler and later headed Chrysler's interior design studio under Macadam. "The guy was very weird," was Neale's summary opinion. He felt that Macadam wasted great amounts of time with meetings, memos and organizational claptrap.

Another designer under both Engel and Macadam was Bill Brownlie. Brownlie reflected that Macadam suffered from, "...very difficult times, just like Irv Rybicki [at General Motors]. And it seemed as though Dick was forced into this situation. He was elated to get the title but forced into an otherwise disappointing time...and he was controlled more than given a chance to lead."

Macadam's patron was R.K. Brown, Chrysler Corp.'s vice president of sales and marketing. Brown headed Plymouth Div. when Macadam was studio chief, then became general manager of Chrysler-Plymouth and continued to guide Plymouth as the corporation's top moneymaker. Being in charge of marketing, Brown was a strong believer in product planning, and he gave that department considerable clout. So Chrysler's product planners were starting to tell Macadam what to do and how to design cars. And since engineering still held considerable sway, he did battle with that discipline, too. "Because of that, Dick worked under duress," Brownlie concluded. "The whole climate of that period was just terrible."

Don DeLaRossa

Chrysler management had accused Elwood Engel of wasting time, and Macadam inherited that reputation. He was asked to tighten work schedules and adhere to them, which essentially meant he had to do more work faster with less manpower. Engel had also given Chrysler some hairy cost overruns. Upper management handed Macadam the responsibility to control expenses and expenditures.

To get the creative job done, Macadam didn't so much lead as browbeat and confront his studio chiefs. He had a threatening way that made him hard to talk to. His principal aides were Roy Axe, an Englishman who'd designed Rootes-group cars and who was now in charge of Chrysler's large car, truck, color and trim studios. There was also E.P. Jacoby, previously with Chrysler product planning and now director of design services. And Bill Brownlie, with design responsibility for Chrysler's small cars, international and advanced studios. Macadam turned more and

bar. There'd be a phalanx of clay models lined up, all representing possible product choices. Typically, a management group would come through from each car division: the general manager along with his people from engineering, product planning, sales and marketing. They'd look around and help themselves to whatever appealed to them. "Hey, I like this fender and that roof and the wheelcover over there." It was all mix and match. Macadam and the studio chiefs might make suggestions, but their job was essentially to offer more choices.

That all changed in 1977, when ex-Ford product planner Hal Sperlich arrived at a dying Chrysler Corp., followed roughly a year later by his former boss, Lee Iacocca. Both men felt immediately that Chrysler's design office was being run by the wrong person. Macadam was obviously not the sort who could inspire designers to create the cars Iacocca and Sperlich felt Chrysler needed. They tolerated Macadam for a while and then, in Nov. 1979, Iacocca called Don DeLaRossa out of retirement. Brownlie remembered this as, "...another very, very trying situation."

DeLaRossa came aboard initially, much to Macadam's discomfort, as a design "consultant." That gave DeLaRossa unusual powers because, in that capacity, he could do pretty much anything he wanted. He also had direct access to Iacocca, which meant he could make recommendations and champion this or that specific design while Macadam still had to go through channels, many of which he had himself devised.

Macadam didn't feel at ease with Iacocca, naturally enough, but he had an even harder time with Hal Sperlich. Sperlich was used to planning the product and having styling respond. And Iacocca expected to come into a studio—as he had at Ford—and see lots of expensive fiberglass models with gorgeous finishes standing

One of DeLaRossa's most enduring styling contributions was the 1987 Chrysler LeBaron coupe and convertible. The convertible (above) remained in production through 1995. Much shorter-lived was the Maserati TC (right), which cost roughly twice as much as the LeBaron convertible but offered very little more for $33,000.

more of the daily chores over to these people and kept increasingly to himself, working out systems and strategies. He reinforced his design policies by writing memos and exercising by-the-book control. Added Brownlie: "Dick had a personality that, unfortunately, as hard as he tried to be friendly—and he certainly wanted to be friendly—he was looked upon as being very cold and almost aloof. The coldness that the troops sensed was again not conducive to being creative. And the situation did not make for good products...."

Another problem was the corporate design process itself. In those pre-Iacocca days, the styling auditorium was like a big salad

there, ready for review. But Chrysler didn't have money to build full-sized fiberglass mockups, and Macadam, who was trying to stay within budget, would caution Iacocca to concentrate on the finished end of a half-finished clay. Iacocca couldn't make those visual leaps, the result being that Macadam disappointed him time and again. Mac also happened to be going through a stormy divorce, which didn't help.

Finally, in 1980, the pressure became too great. Macadam was being squeezed out, but at age 50 he wasn't prepared for retirement. He wanted to leave with a clean resume. Iacocca was glad to see him go, and Macadam landed a job as art director with

Designed by Craig Durfee under Tom Gale, Dodge Viper created a sensation at 1989 Detroit auto show. Durfee successfully intended discontinuity ahead of door to cause doubletakes. Coupe (above) captured the flavor of Viper's Daytona Cobra heritage.

National Cash Register Corp. in Cincinnati.

DeLaRossa, meanwhile, took up the Chrysler design vice presidency in Feb. 1980 with Iacocca's blessing and patronage. Don knew what Iacocca wanted, and money suddenly became available for shiny fiberglass models. But at the same time, DeLaRossa was asked to reduce his staff by a third. The company was pruning every department and again cutting back in major and minor ways. Brutal as this was, it worked. There's no question that Lee Iacocca rescued the company in the early 1980s, even managing to pay off Chrysler's bank loan eight years early. In just a few short seasons, Chrysler stock went from $3 a share (1980) to $48 (1986), bolstered by a three-for-two split.

The K-Car, a Macadam legacy, plus another oil crunch were two important factors that helped return the company to profitability. The original K-Cars were not aesthetic triumphs by any standard but, marketed as the Dodge Aries and Plymouth Reliant, they were downsized and front-wheel drive, economical and good value. As a result, lots of people who'd been putting off purchases of all sorts bought K-Cars. And then for four solid years, 1983 through 1987, the Chrysler roller coaster clanked uphill and Iacocca became a national hero. His very from-the-hip video persona ("If you can find a better car, buy it!" and "You either lead, follow or get out of the way!") helped turn him into a bestselling author. There was even talk of drafting him to run for president of the United States in 1984 and '88.

Trouble was, Chrysler had put most of its automotive eggs in the K-Car basket. The K-Car platform turned out to be extremely versatile: Stretched, gussied up, relettered and renamed, it served as the basis for any number of passenger cars ranging from the Dodge Daytona, Lancer and Dynasty through Chrysler LeBarons, New Yorkers and even to the dachshund-like LeBaron limousine. And the man who furiously styled and restyled most of these K-Car variants was Don DeLaRossa.

Donald R. DeLaRossa was born on July 7, 1922 in Indianapolis. He went to school there and started college in Indiana but interrupted his education to go into the military. He served as a pilot in the Army Air Corps from 1942-45. Don always enjoyed flying and stayed in the Air Force reserves until 1960. He remained an active hobby pilot until recently.

As a youngster, Don lived with his uncle, the manager of an auto-insurance "club" in Detroit. His uncle wanted Don to become an insurance salesman, but Don preferred cars and spent hours drawing them. An auto engineer who dated Don's cousin happened to see his sketches and arranged for Don to interview for a design job with Ford. That job, though, didn't materialize, so Don went to GM Art & Colour and talked to Jules Andrade. In 1946, Andrade gave young DeLaRossa a trial position as a junior designer in Henry Lauve's Buick studio. "Henry was an outstanding designer and certainly a talented illustrator," said Don. "He really took what I had and helped me polish it, including introducing me to airbrush work...and gouache, which turned out to be

one of his favorite media; that and also Prismacolor pencils on black paper. I became hooked on that."

DeLaRossa got transferred into Bill Mitchell's Cadillac studio in early 1947 and worked there with Ed Glowacke. Soon afterward, George Snyder, who'd gone from GM to Ford, invited Don over to Dearborn. In Oct. 1947, Don moved and worked for Bill Schmidt in the Lincoln studio. Schmidt had his own industrial design office on the side. Through Schmidt, DeLaRossa worked on a few non-competing jobs outside Ford. (Schmidt later left Ford to become head of Packard design.)

Don moved up the Ford design ladder and became manager of the Lincoln studio in the mid-1950s. Buzz Grisinger was his counterpart at Mercury. In 1955, DeLaRossa was transferred into Ford's advanced and international design areas and spent some time in Europe. Henry Ford II and William Clay Ford wanted their company to have more in the way of a European styling presence, so they asked Don to check out the prominent overseas design houses and coachbuilders. He did but spent more time at Ghia than the rest. Luigi Segre owned and ran Ghia at that time, with Giovanni Savonucci as his chief designer. DeLaRossa, who spoke Italian, became friendly with both men. During this time, several Italian coachbuilders, including Ghia, made steel-bodied experimental cars for Ford.

DeLaRossa's work in Ford's advanced area brought him into contact with Lee Iacocca. They worked together for eight months on preliminary "Project T-5" studies for the 1965 Mustang (see page 255). Clays from DeLaRossa's studio were done in competition with other Mustang proposals, and while the Phaneuf/Oros Mustang model ultimately inspired the production design, the working relationship between DeLaRossa and Iacocca grew quite strong during this period.

After Ford bought Ghia in 1968-70, Don became its president and chairman. He administered Ghia from his office in Dearborn but made frequent trips to Turin. He held that responsibility until 1978, when Iacocca and he left Ford pretty much together. Both were unceremoniously fired. DeLaRossa was 55 at the time, and he'd long nursed a drinking problem. He retired to Florida to start a new life and had serious doubts that he'd ever work in the auto industry again.

"Anyway," recalled DeLaRossa, "Lee [Iacocca] called me. I'd gone down to Boca Raton to try to put myself together, and Lee called after I'd been there for a couple of months and wanted to know if I'd like to join him at Chrysler. I said, 'Absolutely!' So it was a real thrill for me."

The cars initially done under DeLaRossa were uncommonly common: square as breadboxes, totally derivative and with no more flair than Macadam's had been. The one notable exception was the 1987 Chrysler LeBaron sport coupe and convertible. "Lee wanted a small luxury coupe off the K-Car," noted DeLaRossa. "I worked hard on a blind-quarter coupe with a vertical opera window. That got in motion pretty much as a result of my effort and Lee's interest." These J-Cars, as they were called, represented the

Chrysler, more than any other U.S. automaker, has reached back into the past for its showcars. This 1990 Chrysler 300 concept sedan tried to recapture the flavor of Exner's 1950s Ghia cars, especially in the Italianate grille. Modern 300 also played off Chrysler's big performance cars of that same era. It even had suicide rear doors and *faux* quad lamps.

In fairness, DeLaRossa's other lasting achievement under Iacocca was the establishment of the company's west coast studio, called Chrysler Pacifica. This was an operation Iacocca very much wanted. The idea met with resistance at first. At that time, Hal Sperlich, by now Chrysler's president, and corporate engineering v.p. John D. (Jack) Withrow both wanted to keep design in Detroit. But with Iacocca's support, DeLaRossa saw to the planning and building of Chrysler Pacifica and, in 1983, also chose the staff. The operation soon started proving its value, and DeLaRossa took great pride in it. "It was only with Iacocca's backing that Chrysler Pacifica went through," he maintained.

And then one evening in 1984 at Detroit Metro airport, after flying back from California, Don stepped onto a down escalator and blacked out. He tumbled unconscious over the sawtoothed steps to the marble floor below. A bystander gave him CPR, and an ambulance rushed him to the Wayne County General Hospital. The diagnosis was pressure on the brainstem caused by spinal fluid. DeLaRossa stayed in bed for six months, during which time the day-to-day running of Chrysler's design office fell to Tom Gale.

In 1985, Lee Iacocca decided to ease DeLaRossa out of the design vice presidency and replace him with Gale. He didn't want to hurt his old friend and arranged to make the transition as gentle as possible. Basically, he posted DeLaRossa out to California as fulltime head of Chrysler Pacifica. This amounted to a soft-landing retirement for DeLaRossa, who was still two years short of his 65th birthday.

That done, Iacocca made Tom Gale corporate design vice president and named John Herlitz director of production car and truck exterior design. Gale and Herlitz were so atuned that Herlitz often said that one would finish the other's sentences. On an equal level with Herlitz were K. Neil Walling and Trevor Creed. Walling became director of advanced packaging and international design, including Chrysler Pacifica, and Creed, in a surprise move, left Ford to join Chrysler as director of car and truck interior design. After Chrysler bought AMC, Creed took on Dodge truck and Jeep as well, with both exterior and interior studios combined. Those four—all young, vital, capable men, firmly supported by top man-

first major break with the square-riggers produced under Macadam. Both versions of the J-bodied LeBaron were neatly designed and well received, but they didn't cause the styling revolution some expected. All of Chrysler's other cars done or facelifted under DeLaRossa continued to look like they'd been designed with a straightedge.

DeLaRossa's important contribution to Chrysler wasn't so much in automobile design but rather in his ability to spot and make use of talent. He recognized Thomas C. (Tom) Gale early on and made him his director of interior design in 1981. That year he also named John Herlitz director of exterior design. In 1982, DeLaRossa switched these two around. And after that, DeLaRossa, whose drinking problem kept resurfacing, stepped aside with increasing regularity to let Gale and Herlitz make styling presentations for him. That brought Gale, in particular, into focus with Sperlich and Iacocca, both of whom were impressed with the young designer's credibility and his broad knowledge of all aspects of business.

Sperlich had never really liked DeLaRossa, a feeling that went back to Ford and a time when their offices stood next to each other. Sperlich now, as at Ford, watched DeLaRossa come back from long lunches and viewed Gale as a welcome relief. Iacocca and DeLaRossa, of course, went way back, but the more Iacocca saw Gale in action, the better he liked him.

The California Connection

All U.S. automakers and many from overseas now maintain design studios in California. Most were set up initially to generate advanced concepts. Today they contribute ideas and designs to their parent companies and still turn out show and concept vehicles.

The first major automaker to recognize a need for west-coast styling inputs was Toyota. Toyota set up Calty Design Research in 1973 in El Segundo, California. The name Calty blended the words *California* and *Toyota,* and the original design team included Noritsuna Watanabe, manager, and David J. Stollery III, chief designer. Following Toyota's lead,

Honda set up a similar California studio in 1975, Mazda in 1978, Nissan in 1980 and Mitsubishi in 1982. Calty moved to larger facilities in Newport Beach in 1980, and as other west-coast studios turned more to production design, they also expanded their quarters and staffs.

The first U.S. carmaker to establish a California beach head was Chrysler Pacifica in Aug. 1983. Design v.p. Don DeLaRossa organized this satellite studio with encouragement from Lee Iacocca. Most of the projects from Chrysler Pacifica that have been revealed to the public are showcars: the Aviat, the latter-day Chrysler 300 and Thunderbolt, the Cirrus concept

sedan, Lamborghini Portofino, Eagle Optima, Plymouth Speedster and the Prowler hot rod. The production car most heavily influenced by Chrysler Pacifica was the Dodge Intrepid.

General Motors answered Chrysler with its Advanced Concepts Center in Newbury Park, founded in Sept. 1983. Henry Haga was the original director, and again this facility's more visible products have been showcars: the Chevrolet Express, California Camaro, Sting Ray III and the electric Impact. GM ACC closed down in mid 1996 and sent its staff of six designers, eight modelers and five engineers back to Detroit.

Ford came to California in 1984 but approached the idea a little differently. Designer Richard Hutting contracted with Ford and set up his own private facility in

Created by the Chrysler Pacifica staff in California, Mojave concept coupe bowed at Expo '86 in British Columbia. It started to exhibit the beginnings of cab-forward architecture. The Mojave also represented one of Chrysler's first attempts at computer-aided design. CAD was used to style both the exterior and the interior.

agement—had no idea yet that they were about to lead Chrysler Corp. through its most massive styling revolution since Exner's 1957 models.

The Chrysler roller coaster was still going uphill in 1985, and the company found itself so cash-rich that it started buying businesses worldwide. Iacocca bought Lamborghini, the Italian maker of exotic cars, from the Miram family, then arranged with his friend Alejandro De Tomaso to build bodies for the oft-delayed Maserati TC two-seater convertible. Chrysler also purchased Gulfstream Aerospace, FinanceAmerica, Electrospace Systems and, in 1987, American Motors Corp. Chrysler paid Regie Renault $1.1 billion plus stock for its shares of the near-terminal AMC, but AMC came into Chrysler with one supremely healthy asset: Jeep.

Hardly had Iacocca signed the AMC deal when the roller coaster went over the top and started plunging down again. On Oct. 19,

The K-Car bred variants like rabbits and the L-Cars *looked* like Rabbits: VW Rabbits. All K's and L's were old hat by the late 1980s, outmoded and especially so after the Ford Taurus came out for 1986. Traditional cars like the Dodge Dynasty continued to appeal to a conservative, older minority but they couldn't inspire enough people to part with tight money. What Chrysler clearly needed were new sets of wheels; totally different, non-K lines of automobiles.

Lee Iacocca never liked the Taurus, wasn't impressed with the

Definite cab-forward overtones showed up on 1988 Lamborghini Portofino (left), which in addition boasted swing-up clamshell doors; the 1989 Chrysler Millennium, with its upward sweep at the rear (center); and especially the Eagle Optima. All three took some inspiration from the Ford Taurus and showed Chrysler's future styling direction.

1987, the Dow Jones industrial index fell 508 points and Americans stopped buying cars. Financial soothsayers told of a recession by 1989, and their predictions came true. Suddenly Chrysler found itself cash poor, in debt and facing the 1990s with showrooms and storage lots filled with unsold vehicles.

Excluding the Jeep and the company's captive imports, Chrysler now built all its vehicles on only two platforms: the K and the L.

aero look, and when Taurus sales took off, Iacocca told his people to wait and watch. Give the Taurus three months, he said, and it would crash, same as the AMC Pacer had. As soon as all the kooks bought Tauruses, Iacocca predicted, Ford's grand roll of the dice would come up snake eyes. Middle Americans didn't want jelly-bean cars.

"When that didn't happen with the Taurus," observed Chrysler

1984. He called his company Concept Center California, Inc., and Ford Motor Co. remains his sole client. Hutting's staff of 23 helped design and build, among other cars, prototypes for the 1990 Thunderbird and 1994 Ford Probe. Hutting's studio is in Valencia, California.

The main reason foreign and domestic carmakers set up west-coast design adjuncts has to do with trends. Most automotive trends start in California and migrate east. Californians tend to be more car conscious than the rest of the nation; cars make up a greater part of their culture; west coasters are generally car-nuttier and drive a more mixed variety of foreign, domestic, old, new and oddball vehicles. Pickups, 4x4s and sport utilities became popular in California long before they swept the rest of the country. California incubated

Chrysler Pacifica did mostly sports cars until 1988, when its focus changed to helping develop the 1993 LH sedans.

everything from hot rods and kustoms to low riders, van conversions and mini pickups. Designers feel to some extent that they have to live among trendsetters to be trendsetters.

In 1995, California had 14 auto design

centers operated by specific carmakers. Another four acted as captive design consultants for individual automotive clients. Factory studios are linked electronically to their parent operations, and most have equipment just as sophisticated and modern. Many are housed in nondescript buildings, often in industrial parks, where designers can work unnoticed and undisturbed.

West-coast studios have been known to serve political agendas, too, as when a vice president or chief designer exiles an underling who might threaten his job. But more often Detroit views its California studios as places where strong designers can gain experience and independence to make them better candidates for more responsible future assignments. ◆

Chrysler's cab-forward LH sedans turned the company around. The initial 1993 crop included (L-R) Chrysler Concorde, Eagle Vision and Dodge Intrepid, all built on the same platform and offering the same running gear. For 1994, Chrysler introduced the "Jaguar" C-pillar on the New Yorker (below) and LHS sedans.

Robert A. (Bob) Lutz as a Chrysler executive vice president. Lutz rapidly began ratcheting himself upstairs and, in the process, became more and more involved with design decisions. He took a tremendous interest in styling—perhaps more than any non-designer in the U.S. auto industry at that time. He often confessed that, in his heart of hearts, he was a frustrated car designer himself. On occasion, he did sketch his styling ideas.

The Swiss-born Lutz had been a pilot in the U.S. Marine Corps from 1954 to 1959. He then entered the University of California at Berkeley and earned an MBA with highest honors. After graduating in 1962, he joined Opel in Germany. BMW soon offered him 10 times his Opel salary to become its sales v.p. After three highly successful years with BMW, Lutz went to Ford and served as chairman of Ford of Europe. Bob Lutz was the man who restored the blue oval to European Fords and, after Henry Ford II called him back to the U.S., he installed the blue oval on American Fords, too.

executive designer Neil Walling, "that's when Lee realized he was no longer qualified to pick the designs; that he, in order to have the company succeed, had to delegate that responsibility to those who, in theory, were supposed to make those decisions anyway—the design department." In misjudging the Taurus, then, Iacocca lost some of his personal confidence to choose product.

It was around that time, in June 1986, that Iacocca brought in

Iacocca invited Lutz to join Chrysler at a time when the corporate roller coaster was still going uphill. But by 1988 it was roaring down again at break-neck speed. Chrysler, in fact, to any dispassionate observer, seemed very likely to crash. The situation looked every bit as bad as when Iacocca arrived. K-Cars and K-Car derivatives simply weren't moving anymore. In 1988, both Honda and Toyota sold more cars in the U.S. than Chrysler.

Tom Gale

Thomas C. Gale was born June 18, 1943 in Flint, Michigan and also grew up there. His father worked for Buick as an experimental engineer.

In a recent telephone interview, Tom said he couldn't recall a time in his childhood when he *didn't* draw cars. "One thing I can remember is getting turned on by a particularly terrific art teacher. She was really in the fine arts, painting; it was that teacher who inspired me along the lines that shaped my life. I was always drawing, and she was the one who encouraged that."

Tom had a vague notion in high school that he wanted to become an auto designer, but his counselors weren't aware of Art Center, Pratt and other design colleges, so they recommended he take up mechanical engineering. And when that didn't seem right, they suggested architecture. After exploring on his own, Tom decided to go to Michigan State University to major in indus-

trial design, with minors in engineering and physics. After his undergraduate work, Gale went on to get his master's degree in design and later took an MBA as well, all at MSU.

"As a youngster," observed Gale, "I do remember wrestling with the idea, 'Should I start in engineering or should I start in design,' even though I really wanted to train as a designer.... I just felt that starting out in engineering would be a great basis, even though it kind of set me back a few years in design, but I've never been sorry I did it."

After college, Gale took a job with GM's AC Spark Plug Div., "...in all sorts of engineering and manufacturing capacities, which was just great experience." While still at AC, Tom had the option of going on within GM or moving to Chrysler engineering. In 1967, he decided to take a job at Chrysler as an advanced body engineer, figuring he could always move from engineering into design but not vice-versa.

Gale worked in Chrysler engineering until 1971 and made a good number of lasting friendships there. He then switched to design while Elwood Engel was still v.p. At Chrysler design, he began as a body engi-

neer, then moved on to become a designer, then a senior designer, after which he left design for two years (1976-77) to work as a senior analyst in Chrysler's product planning office. He subsequently returned to design and held a variety of interior and exterior positions.

He began to advance rapidly after Don DeLaRossa arrived at Chrysler in 1980. "I wouldn't be where I am if it weren't for Don," said Gale in a recent interview. "To say that Don was easy to work for would be a misstatement. But those of us, like John [Herlitz] and Neil [Walling] and Trevor [Creed] and me and the others who've spent most of our careers at Chrysler...we really didn't have a good window on the outside world. Don brought that with him. He brought a totally different perspective. After we understood what he was talking about, we'd say, 'Sure, now I see what Lee [Iacocca] and the others expect.' That was very beneficial for us, because it changed the way we operated: changed the way we did things, the way we presented things, the way we interacted."

The big question everyone asks of Gale is: How do you do it? How does Chrysler

The ensuing panic caused Chrysler to start casting off some of its recent acquisitions. It also closed plants, laid off thousands of workers and generally retrenched. At that point it became clear that the only reasonable way to avoid going out of business was to develop a fleet of totally different, good-looking cars as quickly as possible in the hope that Americans would buy them. But what cars?

Iacocca and Lutz didn't agree at first, and a rift soon developed in their relationship. Both had titanic egos, but the Taurus incident had put them on different levels of product confidence. Lutz was sure he knew exactly what sort of cars Americans would buy, but Iacocca now had just a twinge of doubt. According to the book *Comeback: The Fall & Rise of the American Automobile Industry*, Iacocca's vision of the perfect car had been, "...the 1982 Frank Sinatra edition of the Chrysler Imperial. It had wire wheel covers, pillowed velour seats, the initials FS on the front fender and came in just one color—baby blue—to match its namesake's eyes. To Bob Lutz, the car was a bad joke."

Bob Lutz enjoyed talking with Chrysler's four horsemen of styling, particularly with the bright, young Tom Gale and John Herlitz, and as Lutz moved up the corporate ladder, it was he more often than Iacocca who assumed the role of design patron and tastemaker. That's not to say Iacocca abdicated, but Lutz had such a good eye and so much innate interest in design that he began to dominate the product area. And Iacocca now watched that happen. He started resenting Lutz and worked hard to keep Lutz from succeeding him as chairman, but Lutz now began to call the shots in styling.

No one outside the company took much notice of Tom Gale until 1989. That January, Chrysler unveiled the Dodge Viper R/T-10 at the Detroit auto show. The Viper wouldn't save the company, but it did prove a point, one that Lutz considered important to a turnaround. The Viper showed the world that Chrysler could still style an exciting automobile, and credit for the Viper showcar went, reasonably enough, to Tom Gale.

The original Viper sketch was done by a young designer named Craig Durfee, who later went to Audi. The impetus for the car came from a meeting between Lutz, Gale, Carroll Shelby

Like the Viper and LH sedans, the Neon subcompact also had its beginnings in a concept car. The original, shown in 1990, used parallel-opening doors, a 2-stroke experimental Chrysler engine and a full sunroof. The feature the Neon nearly lost on its way into production was its cute, smiling facial expression.

get its designs done without the traditional histrionic fireworks? Gale's answer: "Some of it's generational. But also, it's the corporate culture. I just don't think you can do things the way some of those others [Mitchell, Earl, etc.] did. That's not to fault them in any way, but times change, and sometimes—even today, it sounds like it's all hunkydory and teamwork, but some days things get tough and you have to be tough right along with it.

"However, I've always felt that, in managing the creative process, if you walk in and you've got all the answers, pretty soon the other people will stop trying. And if you've got all the answers, you'd better be pretty darn good. Whereas if you can draw on the expertise of those involved and make everyone feel he or she is contributing, sometimes the sum is a lot greater than the parts—the independent components. That's really the answer: How do you make two plus two equal more than four? That's the approach to management that we've tried to take, and I say 'we' collectively. All of us do it that way. I've always felt we were a great team: John and Trevor and Neil. We really do operate that way.

"At first it was a little rocky. At first there might have been some political things, but I think the more everyone understood that we were sincere with one another, it really became pretty interesting, because our

relationship with the rest of the corporation just kept getting better and better. People would encourage us, listen to us; people would want us to try to do new things. They could see the benefit for themselves and for the product as opposed to us commanding. Because you really can't command. We were several years building up our credibility. Once that was done, though, it really helped. But we have to keep at it all the time."

Gale's diverse background—his hands-on experience in engineering, design, product planning and business—makes him unique in the annals of design administration. No one's ever brought that sort of multi-discipline expertise to a car company before. Tom has been mentioned for even greater responsibilities, a fact based on Chrysler's unprecedented procession of recent trendsetting styling successes. All this bodes well for the legitimacy of auto and truck design in general—not just at Chrysler but in all three American car companies. ◆

The threesome that rounded out Chrysler's design management team were (L-R) Trevor Creed, director of advanced, Jeep/truck and interior design; K. Neil Walling, director of advanced and exterior design; and John Herlitz, vice president of product design.

and a few others. They kicked around the idea of bringing out a Chrysler version of the Shelby Cobra—a car Lutz felt a great deal of attachment to, especially since he owned one. Dodge was developing a huge, eight-liter V-10 truck powerplant at the time, so why not design a modern, Cobra-like Dodge roadster engineered around that monster engine? And that's how the Viper was born. (Texas chili cook Shelby had been a successful race driver early in his career. He developed the Ford Cobra in the 1960s and later helped Chrysler Corp. bring several mini musclecars to market, notably the Dodge Shelby Charger and the Omni GLH. The GLH stands for *Goes Like Hell*.)

Lutz, the former jet pilot who now flew his own helicopter, enjoyed speed. He sometimes borrowed a Lamborghini Countach from the Chrysler engineering garage to enliven his early-morning commutes. On some of those occasions, when traffic was light on the freeway from Ann Arbor, he'd run the Countach up to 140 mph just to wake up. The Viper was intended to have much the same performance capability and aura as the Countach, and that's what Craig Durfee tried to put in his concept sketches.

The Viper showcar proved that Dodge still had an adrenal gland. And the public responded far more eagerly than the company

As Chrysler grew more confident as Detroit's style leader, its cars took on a family resemblance. Cab forward design migrated to the corporation's mid-sized nameplates, including this 1995 Chrysler Cirrus.

anticipated. People started sending in $1000 deposits along with orders for the Viper. Most orders were addressed directly to Lee Iacocca. Chrysler returned all the checks, but the reaction was so overwhelming that, even despite the company's financial plight, Iacocca and Lutz decided to put the Viper into limited production. Chrysler, and especially Dodge, needed a halo car, and the Viper looked perfect.

But there were other, more important products to be developed simultaneously. The most critical were the corporate LH sedans, the 1993 Dodge Intrepid, Chrysler Concorde and Eagle Vision. The company would ultimately stake its entire future on the LH-Cars, just as Ford did with the 1986 Taurus. At the same time, the company needed a new Dodge Ram pickup to compete with Ford's hot-selling F-Series (which Lutz had brought to dominance) and the Chevrolet/GMC C/K pickups. Then, assuming all went well, Chrysler would in time develop the PL (Neon) compact, the JA (Stratus/Cirrus) mid-sized cars, the FJ (Avenger and Sebring) sport coupes and a new minivan. Where all that money would be coming from no one yet knew, but Chrysler's directors assured the platform teams that they'd come up with it somehow. And somehow they did.

The Viper, LHs and Ram pickup would all have to be done concurrently, and they'd have to be done quickly. The old K-Car took some 2000 people to develop. With all its cutbacks and budget constraints, Chrysler couldn't afford that much staff for the LH or any of its other cars. The solution was to adopt Japanese efficiency, and for that an engineering executive named Glenn Gardner came to the rescue.

Gardner had been Chrysler's man at Diamond-Star Motors, the Illinois joint-venture operation with Mitsubishi. He noticed that when Mitsubishi developed a new car, its staff formed a "platform team." This was a self-contained group comprised of all the necessary disciplines: product planners, engineers, cost analysts, designers, marketers and so forth. They worked together in harmony toward a common goal.

This was very unlike the traditional American method of developing a new car, in which each discipline did its job semi-independently, one handing the evolving vehicle along to the next. The way Chrysler and other U.S. automakers typically developed cars: Engineering would hand the package to styling. Styling would come up with the surfaces. Then the cost and manufacturing staffs would "fease out" the entire job, which inevitably meant revisions and compromises. After fease-out and release, the car went into production, whether or not it was truly efficient to produce. And just before Job One, marketing and advertising would get involved.

Diamond-Star, Gardner noted, used an entirely different approach. Not only were Mitsubishi platform teams able to create the car more quickly but it ended up being easier to assemble and needed fewer people. The Diamond-Star plant could turn out cars more quickly than Chrysler, and quality was better. Even more amazing: Mitsubishi didn't have to figure "sliptime" into the development process the way Chrysler did. Sliptime described the delays that inevitably crept into any program due to planning errors, bad communications and handoffs from one discipline to the next.

At a time when the roller coaster was still chugging upward, Glenn Gardner didn't have much luck selling the platform-team concept to Chrysler. But by the late 1980s, when things were already desperate and Iacocca and Lutz realized the company needed to reinvent itself, Gardner's ideas started to make sense. Again, Lutz liked the idea more than Iacocca, but he, too, accepted it.

Chrysler gained confidence in its showcars, too. Chairman Bob Lutz sketched the above on a napkin. It formed basis for 1995 Chrysler Atlantic retro coupe (top). Chrysler Thunderbolt sought a modern interpretation of the 1940 LeBaron concept roadster.

Out of that decision came three platform teams, one for the LHs, another for the Dodge Ram pickup and a third, started in May 1989, for the limited-production Dodge Viper. (Teams were formulated later for the minivan and Jeeps.) The LH team consisted of roughly 750 members (versus 2000 for the K-Car) and a mere 60 for the Viper.

The Viper contained some styling nuances worth mentioning. It had a slightly sinister jack o'lantern face and a very animalistic shape and posture. The entire car—unlike, say, the Corvette—looked alive. Like the Studebaker Avanti, it seemed to crouch, ready to leap. There was also a visually jarring gap at the leading edge of the front door. This discontinuity, where the rear two thirds of the body seemed to slip into the front fender, took inspiration from race-car practice. A number of modern race cars have big, vertical engine-heat outlets behind the front fenders. In the Viper, this gap became a very attention-demanding focal point. The effect was intentionally disconcerting. The two body sections looked at first like they didn't want to fit. The viewer did a doubletake and then concentrated on the break. When it dawned on him that this wasn't a mistake, that the discontinuity was intentional, it came as a relief, like saying, "Hey, you had me going there for a minute."

Tom Gale explained that, "...intersecting wedges have long been a Dodge hallmark, going back to the 1968 Charger. This is also an area where, on other cars, the exhaust headers come out of the body and go into a collector at the rocker sill. So those were some of the thoughts we had in mind when we did [the discontinuity on] the Viper."

The cars on the LH platform (wags said LH stood for "last hope") were packaged under Neil Walling's direction. John Herlitz oversaw the LH exterior designs and Trevor Creed the interiors. The LH capitalized on what Chrysler came to call the "cab-forward" look. Cab forward—that term—was actually used by Ford design v.p. Jack Telnack when he was interviewed by *Ward's Auto World* about the Taurus' success. Asked what he thought the next trend after the aero look would be, Telnack unhesitatingly replied, "Cab forward."

Cab forward went back to mid-engined exoticars of the 1970s. Designers of Ferraris and Panteras pushed the entire passenger compartment ahead on the wheelbase to make room for the powertrain. That look marked a 180° turnaround from past practice, when the traditional sports car had to have a long hood and a short rear deck. Going back to the 1930s, long hoods implied power. The ideal profile of a classic car was a body with the windshield positioned in the center of the wheelbase. That was rarely do-able, but there were sports cars of that era with hoods that stretched from the middle of the wheelbase to the front-axle centerline.

Half a century later, though, designers and auto buffs favored extremely short hoods and steeply raked windshields. Now the ideal *windshield*, not the radiator, rose up from the front-axle centerline. And that's where Chrysler put the windshield base on the LH cars: right above the middle of the front wheels. They also borrowed the race-car practice of moving all four wheels out to the far corners of the body.

The LHs traced their ancestry back to June 1986 and a mid-engined concept sedan done at Chrysler Pacifica called the

Chrysler Corp. has never given up its leadership in the minivan market. For 1996, the company upped the minivan ante again by adding sliding doors on both sides. Chrysler also became the first major automaker to put a street rod into limited production. The 1997 Plymouth Prowler (below) broke new ground and helped establish Chrysler as the company that catered to the young-at-heart. The Prowler, like the Viper, was made possible by Chrysler's good management of cash reserves.

Navajo. The Navajo, brainchild of designer Kevin Verduyn, had minimal overhangs, a relatively short hood and deck, and it maximized cabin space. On his first trip to Chrysler Pacifica, Bob Lutz viewed the Navajo and saw the future in it.

A year or so later, just after Chrysler bought Lamborghini, the decision was made to adapt the Navajo's shape and packaging to a Lamborghini show-car called the Portofino. The Portofino had four swing-up doors, no B-pillars, wheels pushed out to the corners, short overhangs and a long greenhouse. This showcar provided the inspiration for the cab-forward look. And from the Portofino came several theme models, again done at Chrysler Pacifica, for the Dodge Intrepid and the entire line of LH sedans.

Several theme models were trucked from Pacifica to Detroit, and they wowed those who saw them for the first time. "We were all invited to come down to the styling showroom to see the new theme models," recalled Diran Yazejian, a design-office manager. "I walked through the door, and what I saw just blew my mind! There were three LHs, an LX [a rear-drive deriv-ative of the LH], the Optima [showcar] and a production Ford Taurus. The Taurus looked like a shoebox compared to those other cars. At that moment, I *knew* there was hope for Chrysler Corp. In my then-30 years with the company, only the late 1960s and early '70s matched that LH show for excitement."

The LH platform team developed the entire car, from concept to showroom, in less than 39 months (versus 52 months for the K-Car). Ultimately the LH family grew to five nameplates: the Intrepid/Vision/Concorde for 1993 plus the Chrysler New Yorker and Chrysler LHS for 1994. The last two stood out by virtue of their classic C-shaped sail panels, inspired by Bugatti and Jaguar.

The Dodge/Plymouth Neon also had its beginnings in a concept car. The concept Neon and its production cousin were started simultaneously. Both took advantage of the cab-forward configu-ration and, in this instance, the showcar came from a sketch cre-ated by a designer named Joe Dehner. To appeal to a mostly 20- to 40-year-old female audience, Dehner put considerable empha-sis on cuteness. The concept Neon had a playful, smiling, happy facial expression. (The AMC Gremlin and Pacer were also styled to look cute, but the car that overflowed with cuteness—at least in younger minds—was the Volkswagen Beetle.)

One rule of platform teamwork said that management could keep tabs on things but shouldn't tamper. As the Neon design pro-gressed, the team abandoned the showcar face and, for cost rea-

sons, went with Intrepid-like headlights that combined parking and turn-signal lamps. The new face looked like dozens of other cars and lacked the personality of Dehner's Neon showcar.

On a flight back from Pacifica, Lutz, Gale, Walling and several others were talking about the Neon. Someone mentioned that a mistake was being made. The Neon needed its showcar face back. It wasn't cute anymore. Iacocca had already expressed that opin-ion, Lutz had written memos about it to Gale, and now everyone agreed. But to change the Neon at that late date, eight or nine months into tooling, would cost the company some $20 million. This was supposed to be a low-budget program where every penny counted. Besides, management's kibitzing went against all the platform-team rules. Management wasn't supposed to dictate, a fact that left members of the Neon team considerably miffed.

Finally the accountants announced that restoring the Neon's "happy face," with separate round headlights and separate park/turn lamps, would cost $7 million, not the $20 million origi-nally expected. For that price, Gale, Lutz, Iacocca and others thought the showcar face was worth putting back on. Gale asked the PL platform team to trust in his design sense, and ultimately they did.

The team concept homogenized the power of Chrysler's various disciplines. Engineering no longer dominated the corporation. Product planning now played a backup role—very unusual at Chrysler. Observed design manager Jeff Godshall: "Nowadays, when product planning comes over to talk, it's almost with timid-ity. It's amazing and very different from the old way, because product planning used to get whatever it wanted. Under Sperlich, that was where the car was designed. But not anymore. There's a great deal of hands-off now. Design knows what it's doing, and what design wants is usually what goes through."

At Chrysler, designers make up part of each platform team, but design isn't organized on a platform-team basis. Each team borrows designers from a central pool and works with them until they're no longer needed. Just as the platform teams are "lean," so are those from Chrysler's design staff. Says v.p. John Herlitz: "The Design Office serves the platform teams much like a supplier or ad agency serves its clients. This lets our designers help out the teams with the greatest need at any given time. The Design Office commitment says basically, 'We're always there for you.' Our designers call the shots on styling, they debate each design with the platform teams, but in the final analysis, our work has to meet all of the platform team's targets and requirements."

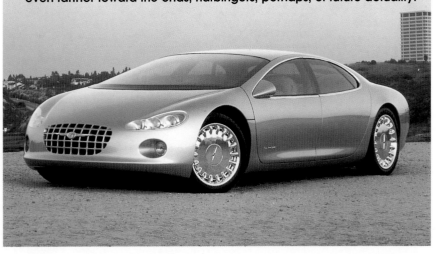

Chrysler's 1996 LHX concept sedan pushed windshield and backlight even farther toward the ends; harbingers, perhaps, of future actuality.

By late 1991, when Gale and his staff moved into Chrysler's new, modern quarters in Auburn Hills, Michigan, the company's team efforts were working beyond Glenn Gardner's rosiest predictions. And by mid 1992, when the first LH sedans began to appear, the corporation had indeed reinvented itself, aesthetically as well as in terms of efficiency and build quality.

And after that revolutionary turnaround, Tom Gale and his staff showed great styling consistency. Chrysler cars now had a corporate look. Even more noticeable: Gale and his colleagues kept batting nothing but home runs season after season. It was clear by the time the Neon arrived that Gale, Herlitz, Walling and Creed had turned Chrysler's design office from its former undistinguished

Dodge Intrepid ESX for '96 demonstrated the eye appeal of short front and long rear overhangs.

self into *the* dominant powerhouse of the American automobile design industry. Chrysler's design partnership now led, and it was Ford and GM who scrambled to follow.

In June 1993, Tom Gale was named Chrysler vice president of product design and international operations, and there was talk within the corporation that he might be in line for even higher office. John Herlitz became a vice president at the same time, of product design in this case. A great deal of credit had to go to Bob Lutz for his patronage and confidence. In the view of Neil Walling, Lutz had become the company's most influential supporter of design. He placed much greater value on it than most.

In 1994, Walling compared Lutz with the recently retired Iacocca. "Where Lee used to take an active part in the design process...would say, 'Yes, we need to make that roof stiffer and do this or that,' as opposed to just choosing a design, Bob is much

more a team player. He'll accept and promote a design but really does want the design group to do the work and tell him which one is right."

Walling also explained what made the styling equation work from the inside. "I think Tom Gale and John Herlitz both fall into the new breed of design executive...strong advocates of design but within an environment of mutual respect for other disciplines. It's a cross-functional environment in which every discipline has to have some knowledge of what the other discipline does and how it's done. Design now has the respect of those other disciplines and respects them in return. Meanwhile, upper management presently assumes the role of coach rather than quarterback, and that makes life a lot easier."

Steven N. Bollinger, formerly with Chrysler and now assistant v.p. of R&D in Honda's west-coast studio, summarized what Gale and Herlitz had done by saying, "They basically created an environment for the designer to design cars. They kept the wolves away. I think the biggest point is that Lutz is the guy who knows cars. He knows a good car when he sees one. He's ahead of you; ahead of the designer. Lutz would come in and look at something and say, 'By God, we've got to do that!' Next thing you know, it's done."

Robert J. (Bob) Eaton replaced corporate chairman Lee Iacocca on New Year's Day 1993. Eaton, previously head of General Motors of Europe, made it known immediately that he would let Chrysler's designers design without his interference. He also announced that he intended to become the first Chrysler chairman who wouldn't have to bring the company back from the brink.

The day of the autocrat seems to be over at Chrysler, and at the other two U.S. automakers as well. As emphasis shifts to the team approach, corporate cooperation appears to be the order of the 21st century. And yet there's a healthy uneasiness at Chrysler.

"When you've got a Dodge Dynasty to replace," Neil Walling reminds himself, "it's pretty easy to be a hero. But when you've got a Dodge Intrepid to replace, it's a heckuva a lot harder. So now comes the tough part. Being successful over time is very, very difficult. There are countless stories of people and companies who've backed away from success; who've been spectacularly successful and then went conservative. We've got to watch ourselves." ◆

GLOSSARY

Airdam: A foil or aerodynamic device, often positioned under the front bumper.

A-pillar: The first set of structural roof supports at either side of the windshield. The next set of pillars, behind the front doors, is called B-pillars, and those behind the rear doors are called C-pillars. Some limousines and station wagons have D-pillars.

Alloy wheel: A wheel cast from alloys of aluminum or magnesium, usually in one piece. (See also "Artillery wheel," "Disc wheel" and "Wire wheel.")

Applied (fender or trim): Fastened onto or stamped into the surface of the body.

Armature: The wooden, metal or hard-foam supporting structure under a clay model.

Artillery wheel: A wooden-spoked wheel with a steel rim. (See also "Alloy wheel," "Disc wheel" and "Wire wheel.")

Axes: In locating points on a car body, designers and draftsmen use the conventional three 3D reference lines: longitudinal, vertical and cross-car. These lines or axes are labeled X-Y-Z. (See also "Zero point.")

Backlight: The rear window opposite the windshield.

Badge engineering: The practice of applying different nameplates to cars with identical or very similar sheetmetal.

Bakeoff: A showdown between design proposals, usually held in the form of a show with clay models from rival studios or designers.

"Banana": The opening between the top of the steering-wheel rim and the hub through which the driver can see the instrument panel.

Bead or beading: A formed, often ornamental molding, usually pliable, sometimes fitted as a sealer ("welting") between two exterior body panels; e.g. between fenders and body. May also be rigid, as in "fender beading". Flexible beading is sometimes used to trim car upholstery.

Bellypan: A partial or full surface, usually of sheetmetal, affixed to the underside of a car body. The bellypan acts as an aerodynamic aid.

Beltline: The horizontal area of the body along the door just below the side-window glass.

Bezel: A shaped, usually ornamental, often bright edging around a functional body component, e.g. lights, gauges, emblems, medallions, etc.

Black metal: The structural, supporting inner sheetmetal of a body, usually painted black.

Blind quarter: A wide sail panel, q.v.

Boattail: The rear of a carbody shaped like the upside-down prow of a boat.

Body in white: The finished but unmounted and unpainted body. It's called "in the white" because the original protective undercoat was white or light yellow.

Body sweeps: (See "Sweeps.")

Bone line: A hard, raised longitudinal peak in the sheetmetal, usually along the side of the car body; more massive than a character line (q.v.).

Boot: (See "Top boot.")

Box, one-, two-, three-: Body morphology is often described in terms of one-box, two-box and three-box. A one-box body usually refers to a van, whose body looks like one big box. A station wagon or something like the VW Rabbit qualifies as a two-box body, the hood being one box and the cabin the second. And a three-box body is usually a conventional sedan or coupe: hood, cabin and trunk. Also called "one-, two- and three-shape."

B-pillar: (See "A-pillar.")

Bridge: An upside-down-U-shaped device that rides on side rails over a clay model. It's used to take reference points and make accurate measurements of the model.

Bridge-truss construction: Body framing that resembles a welded steel bridge, with sheetmetal panels usually welded to the outside and inside. The Chrysler Airflow and Lincoln Zephyr used bridge-truss construction. (See also "Monocoque" and "Unit body.")

Brow: A raised or protruding area above or around an arch, like a headlamp or wheel well.

Buck: (See "Seating buck.")

Bumper: A protective bar or area protruding from the extreme front or rear of a car body.

Bumper pan: Sheetmetal that extends downward from the bumper. (Sometimes called "modesty panel" or "modesty skirt.")

Bustleback: A car body with an attached luggage compartment.

Bulkhead: A large, reinforced, crossbracing sheetmetal panel, typically behind the rear seat of a car body.

Cast (to): To form metal or plastic by pouring the molten substance into a mold and letting it solidify. (See also "Die casting.")

Catalogue custom: A coachbuilt custom body displayed in and sold through an automaker's dealer catalogue. (See also "Series custom.")

Catwalk: The area between the front fender and hood. The word was commonly used for cars of the late 1930s and early 1940s, when catwalks extended from the front bumper to the door cuts.

Centerline: A hypothetical line drawn longitudinally through the center of a developing carbody, also known as the X axis.

Chamfer: The juncture of two angled or beveled flat surfaces.

Channel (to): To lower a car body by cutting out the floor and dropping the body down over the frame rails.

Character line: A raised or indented, creased or peaked line on a smooth surface that adds stronger-than-normal interest to the car's aesthetics.

Chassis: The structural framework of a car but also including the engine, drivetrain, axles, steering apparatus and suspension.

"Cheat" (to): To exaggerate a design feature in a sketch or model in order to improve the car's appearance or proportions, such as stretching the wheelbase and lowering the height of the body.

Chin spoiler: An aerodynamic aid to manage air underneath the front bumper. (See also "Spoiler.")

CHMSL: Center high-mounted stop light (pronounced *Chimsel*).

Chop (to): To lower the top or greenhouse of a car body by cutting out a few inches horizontally and rewelding the pillars and panels.

Clay-milling machine: A machine that can sculpt a clay model in any size based on a mathematical model (q.v.). Modern clay-milling machines are computer-driven, and some are portable so they can be taken from studio to studio.

Coachbuilder: A shop or company, usually from the 1920s and 1930s, that produces custom automobile bodies. (See also "Catalogue custom," "Custom" and "Series custom.")

Cobble (to): To rework or make fit; e.g. to make an existing body fit over a new chassis or new mechanical components.

Coefficient of drag (Cd): A numerical value representing aerodynamic efficiency. The lower the value, the more efficient the shape.

Color sweep: An area, usually on the side of a car body, painted a different color and often outlined by bright moldings. (See also "Sweepspear.")

Composite construction: Wooden body framing skinned with sheetmetal panels, as opposed to all-steel construction.

Concept sketch or concept car: A drawing or model that presents an idea. (See also "Motif" and "Theme sketch.")

Console (or center console): A longitudinal structure between bucket seats. The console often houses a storage compartment, the gearshift lever, ashtray, switches and an armrest. It sometimes sweeps up in front to blend with the instrument panel. If it extends back to the rear seat (rare), it's called a "full-length console".

Coordinate measuring machine: (See "Scanner.")

Couple distance: The distance between the front- and rear-seat

H-points (q.v.); a critical interior packaging dimension.

Coved: Recessed.

Cowl: The surfaced and structural body component at the front of the passenger compartment between the engine hood and the main body back to the windshield. Cowls vary tremendously in detail and construction, but the typical cowl is made up of the firewall and extends back to meet the instrument panel.

C-pillar: (See "A-pillar.")

Crown: A domed area of the hood, fenders or roof. Also a subtle rise or convexity in a surface to make it look straight or flat instead of sunken.

Custom (body): A special or coachbuilt automobile body uniquely designed and fabricated, as opposed to mass-produced bodies. (See also "Catalogue custom" and "Series custom.")

Cutline: The line around an openable body panel; e.g. doors, hood and decklid.

"Dash" (in body engineering): In some car companies, the "dash line" is an all-important measuring marker from which body-length dimensions are taken. During design, the actual "dash" (firewall) is extensively altered to accommodate intrusion by the transmission, ducting, controls, etc., so it rarely coincides with the theoretical "dash" and should never be confused with "Instrument panel," q.v.

Dashboard: In very early cars, an upright wooden or metal panel at the front of the body. This was a holdover from days when the dashboard literally shielded the carriage from the horse and road splash. In more modern cars, the word "dashboard" is sometimes used interchangeably with the more correct term, "instrument panel," q.v.

Dash-to-axle: The distance from the "dash" line or point to the front-axle centerline in side view. This is a crucial dimension in creating interchangeable body programs.

Daylight opening (or DLO): The perimeter of any car window, including the windshield and backlight.

Deauville roof: A carriage or automobile half roof that covers only the rear passengers. The front compartment is open.

Deck: The upper surface of the luggage compartment.

Deck (to): To clear the decklid of ornamentation.

Decklid: The lid of the luggage compartment.

Diecast (to): (See "Cast.")

Diecasting: A part formed by pouring a molten metal alloy, often bronze or zinc, into a mold.

Die model: The master model, traditionally handcarved from mahogany, that served as the final, correct guide for making sheetmetal stamping dies. (See also "Kellering machine.")

Di-Noc: A registered trade name by 3M for a thin, highly flexible, stretchable, paintable plastic film used to cover clay models to give them color and gloss. Di-Noc can be painted after adding an elasticizer. Painted, it's usually soaked in a hot-water solution to make it pliable. The name Di-Noc also refers to an ornamental film used in the 1930s through the early 1950s to bond woodgrain and other ornamental patterns to garnish moldings, instrument panels, station-wagon exteriors, etc.

Disc wheel: A steel wheel whose center is stamped in one piece. (See also "Alloy wheel," "Artillery wheel" and "Wire wheel.")

DLO: Daylight opening, q.v.

Dogleg: An angled bend, often at the trailing edge of a window; also where the rear door curves around the rear wheelhouse of a four-door body style.

D-pillar: (See "A-pillar.")

Draw depth: The depth to which a stamping press can push or fold a metal sheet or panel.

Drip molding: The molding-like, U-shaped trough or gutter at the lower edge of the roof that catches rainwater and carries it away from the windows and doors.

Dutchman: On a sedan or coupe, the sheetmetal surface or panel between the backlight and the top edge of the decklid.

Eggcrate: A geometric, crosshatch pattern of squares or rectangles, usually used in reference to grille texture.

Elevation: As seen in front, rear or side views. A side elevation, for example, is a side view. (The plan or top view is not defined as an elevation.)

Envelope body: A car body whose sides have no visual or actual side-surface interruptions or breaks.

Escutcheon: An ornamental, protective plate or surround, like the bright, raised area around a keyhole.

Extrusion: A part, like a molding, formed by forcing or extruding the material through a shaped orifice.

"Eye envelope": The oval area on an instrument-panel drawing that theoretically shows the range of human vision. The idea is to keep controls and gauges within the eye envelope.

Facelift: Design changes that make a familiar style or ornament look fresh and different.

Fascia: The instrument panel (q.v.); usually British; also a flexible material that covers a bumper.

Fast: A word used to describe the angle or tilt of a windshield or backlight. The "faster" the glass, the more nearly horizontal it is. Its "fastness" is measured between zero degrees (horizontal) and 90° (vertical); i.e. a 57° windshield is faster than one standing more upright at 80°.

Fastback: A body shape in which the roof slopes downward at the rear and blends into the deck or luggage compartment with no notch or visual break.

"Fease out" (to): To determine the feasibility or manufacturability of a design. This is usually an engineering function.

Fender: The panel or area over the wheel that constrains road splash at speed. (See also "Pontoon fender" and "Suitcase fender.")

Fender beading: (See "Beading.")

Fender crown: (See "Crown.")

Fender skirt: A panel or covering, usually of sheetmetal, that covers a wheel arch (q.v.) or fender opening.

Fender valance: (See "Valance.")

Fillet (to): A concave, transitional surface that fills, mates or blends two intersecting surfaces.

Firewall: The vertical wooden or sheetmetal panel that separates the engine compartment from the passenger compartment.

Five-axis (milling machine): A milling machine that can be programmed not only to follow the conventional X-Y-Z axes but which also keeps the milling head perpendicular (normal) to the surface at all times. These additional two "axes" are programmed into the computer as front-to-rear and side-to-side instructions. (The concept of five actual axes is misleading; there are still only three.)

Flag: The triangular area of a car's front door, just above the beltline and behind the A-pillar, to which the outside rearview mirror is often attached. The flag also shortens the front-door glass, allowing it to lower completely into the door.

Flange: A collar, rim or other body component that adds strength or provides a means of attaching another part.

Fome-Cor: A trade name for a material used in the designing of interior bucks and mockups. Fome-Cor typically consists of a 1/8- to 1/4-inch sheet of Styrofoam sandwiched between two layers of heavy, white paper.

Frame-integral: Another term for "unitized body," q.v.

Full-sized draft or layout: An accurate drawing of an automobile body in final scale. Such drafts were usually done on huge sheets of prepared paper, blackboards or white-painted aluminum sheets.

Garnish molding (or garnish rail): Trim moldings on doors, usually to ornament interior window frames.

Greenhouse: That part of the car body above the beltline that includes the roof, pillars and glass.

Grille: A perforated panel or area, usually ornamented. (See also "Radiator grille.")

Ground clearance: The distance from the lowest point on the chassis, excluding wheels, to a level road surface.

Gutter: (See "drip molding.")

Halo car: An automobile intended to stimulate interest in or lend prestige to an automobile line. Example: The Viper is a halo car for Dodge.

Hard points: Specific locations, usually called out on a full-sized body draft, of points that have to be adhered to when designing surfaces. Hard points include axle centerlines, seats, pedal locations, roof and sill heights, luggage-compartment dimensions, etc.

Hardtop or hardtop convertible: A body style that lacks B-pillars so that, although the roof is rigid (usually steel), it has the configuration of a convertible.

Header: The horizontal beam or structural member above the windshield.

Headliner or headlining: The inner trim lining of a car roof, usually made from cloth and suspended by stiff, hidden wires. Late-model headliners are often molded from foam or cardboard and faced with fabric.

Heel-hard: A point on the car floor where the driver's heel normally rests; used to help determine seating position and set dimensions.

Highlight: Light that bounces noticeably off a peak or line or convex surface.

Hinge pillar: A body pillar to which door hinges are attached.

Hood: The openable covering over the engine compartment in a front-engined car, usually made of sheetmetal and hinged at the front, rear or sides.

H-point: The point, usually called out on a full-sized, side-view body draft, where the driver's hip socket rests near the junction of the front-seat cushion and the seatback.

Hubcap: An ornamental, protective, metal covering over the hub of a wheel. Early types were screw-on; later hubcaps were held on by friction. (See also "Wheelcover.")

Instrument panel (also "i.p."): The board or metal panel ahead of the front seat that houses the gauges, controls and glove compartments. (See also "Dash" and "Dashboard.")

Kellering machine: A very precise machine that can reproduce, with the aid of sensors and grinders, three-dimensional surfaces in solid steel, the purpose being ultimately to form stamping dies. The master that guides a Kellering machine is the "die model," q.v.

Kick panel: The protective interior panel ahead of the front door.

Line drawing: An outline sketch without shading or color.

Lip molding (also "wheel-lip molding"): Ornamental bright trim that outlines and visually reinforces a fender wheel cut.

Louver: A slit or narrow opening to let air, light or water in or out. Some louvers are hinged and adjustable.

Mathematical (or "math") model: A computer model, based on an X-Y-Z coordinate system, of a surface or surfaces. (See also "Scanner" and "Clay-milling machine.")

Metalflake paint: Paint that has tiny flakes, usually of bright aluminum, suspended in the liquid.

Mockup: A representation, usually of the final shape of a styled or engineered body. Can be made of wood, fiberglass, metal or any combination.

Modesty panel: (See "Bumper pan.")

Molding: An applied, raised strip, sometimes to cover a joint between body panels, or in later cars pressed in for ornamentation.

Monochromatic: Of a single color.

Monocoque: A type of body construction in which the skins are stressed to form part of the supporting structure.

Motif: A repeated pattern or theme.

Mule: A prototype car, usually built with new mechanicals under an old, cobbled body.

Notchback: A body style in which a relatively upright backlight joins a more horizontal rear deck, the joint forming a notch.

Offsets: A numerical system of locating points (q.v.) along X-Y-Z axes (q.v.) on a 3D body surface.

Ogee: Any S-shaped curve.

One-off: A one-of-a-kind car, body style or body type.

"Oscar": The name given by car designers to the 90th-percentile human form that determines standard interior and seating

dimensions. Oscar can take the form either of an articulated plastic mannequin or a line-defined drawing in the CAD computer.

Overcrown (to): To raise above the surrounding crowned surface.

Overhang: The amount of body/chassis structure, including bumpers, as seen in side view ahead of the front axle centerline and behind the rear axle centerline.

"Package" (the): A drawing or series of specifications that tell where a car's "hard points" (q.v.) are: locations of axles, running gear, seats, instrument panel, roof height, door sills, etc. The package is often determined by engineering, and the design staff has to make surface details conform to the parameters called for.

Peak: A sharp ridge stamped into a body surface, usually directed upward (see also "Windsplit.")

Pillar: An upright, usually structural body member that separates doors or windows.

Pinstripe: A narrow applied or painted stripe, usually in a bright, contrasting color.

Plan view: As seen from the top.

Platform: The engineering basis for a car. The word is used both for the theoretical car during its planning stages and for the finished car as built.

Platform-team concept: The idea of developing a new car or car line by an multi-disciplinary product team. Instead of having each discipline (design, engineering, marketing, manufacturing, advertising, etc.) work separately and sequentially, the platform team comes together at the beginning and sees the car through from concept to showroom. The idea has long been used in Japan. Among the advantages: greater speed of development, better communications, fewer procedural mistakes.

Points: Specific surface locations on an automobile body's X-Y-Z axes, designated numerically. (See "Hard points.")

Point taker: (See "Scanner.")

Pontoon fenders: Rounded, tapered, teardrop-shaped fenders popular during the 1930s.

Potmetal: An alloy of zinc, tin and other metals, often plated and commonly used in the 1920s through 1960s for cast trim items.

Prismacolor: A trade name for colored pencils commonly used by auto designers.

Prototype: In automobile design, a realistic, sometimes running full-sized, three-dimensional representation of an entire car, usually made of wood, fiberglass, metal or a combination.

Proveout model: A model made to confirm that a drawing or numerical model appears as expected.

Pull cup: A handle or area of the door inner trim panel, often recessed into the armrest, used to pull the door shut.

Quarter panel: That part of a car bodyside comprising the rear fender from the rear door opening back.

Quarter window: A small, usually movable glass pane next to a larger window that allows the directing of air into or out of the cabin. Technically, the quarter window is in or behind the rear door, but the term is also used to refer to the front ventipane (q.v.).

R&D: Research and development.

Radiator grille: The protective, often ornamented area or structure ahead of the engine radiator, usually at the front center of the body.

Radiator shell: An ornamental, conforming case that ensheaths the radiator. It's often plated and has some form of grille or mesh over the front.

Rake (windshield or glass): (See "Fast.")

Ramp angle: The angle of a driveway or ramp that can affect body overhang (q.v.). Overhang that's too long or too low will scrape a sharply angled ramp when the car passes over it.

Rendering: A drawing or illustration that includes shading and detail.

Restrike: A term used in metalstamping. After a body part like a hood or fender has been pressed, a restrike--an additional stamping action--can change the original part so that it looks different or fits a different car.

Reveal: (See "Window reveal.")

Reveal molding: The molding or trim surrounding or incorporated into a window reveal.

Rocker (also "rocker panel"): The longitudinal sill along the bottom of the body, beneath the doors. On cars with running-boards, the rocker area covered the chassis frame. On more modern cars, it finishes the area below the doors.

Rocker molding: Ornamental trim fastened to the rocker panel.

Sail panel: The solid areas at the rear of the greenhouse that cover the C- or D-pillars and join the rear side windows to the backlight.

Scanner: An electronic machine that can take and record precise measurements of three-dimensional surfaces. Typically, a scanner has an articulated arm with a probe at the end that either physically touches the surface or "scans" it with a laser probe. The scanner, by assigning digitized numbers based on an X-Y-Z coordinate system and a zero point, forms a point-by-point mathematical model of the surface. (Also called "point taker" and "coordinate measuring machine.")

Scoop: An open-fronted area of the body designed to let in air.

Seating buck: An accurate representation of the interior of a car, including seats, pedals, instruments, steering wheel, doors and floor. Some seating bucks are created to evaluate style; others can be used to prove out ergonomics, comfort, door openings, etc.

Section (to): To lower a car body by cutting a horizontal strip out of the sheetmetal all the way around and then rewelding the remated surfaces.

Section (in diagram form): A representation of a body or part of a body as if it were cut and viewed at 90°.

Series custom: Custom bodies made up in small batches, usually ranging from five to 25. Also called "semi custom."

Sightlines: Theoretical lines from the driver's eyes to objects inside the car (instruments and controls) and also beyond or outside the car windows.

Sill: The longitudinal body rail below in the door openings and above the rocker (q.v.).

Speed streaks: Pressed-in body moldings that represent trails of water swept back by the rush of wind at speed.

Spinner: The ornamental, usually raised or projecting center of a wheel, wheel covering or radiator grille.

Spline: A gently curved or arched surface. The word also refers to a long metal or wooden strip used to form a curve or arch.

Spoiler: A low wing, usually fixed to the top rear surface of the decklid. Its function on race cars is to reduce aerodynamic lift. In most production cars, the spoiler is ornamental. (See also "Chin spoiler.")

Subframe: A chassis structure bolted or welded to the front or rear underside of a unitized body (q.v.) that carries the engine and/or suspension.

Suitcase fender: A fender with a basically rectangular shape, although usually rounded along the leading edge. The suitcase fender was popular in the late 1930s.

Surface plate: A large, precisely machined steel or granite plate that forms the base for making accurate dimensional body measurements.

Swage: A raised molding or windsplit (q.v.) used to stiffen a large panel of sheetmetal.

Sweeps: Long templates, usually made of wood, metal or plastic, used for laying in different curvatures or radii to a full-sized drawing or clay model. Standard sweeps are numbered 1 through 100. Each sweep number represents a 1/8-inch rise in a 60-inch arc. (Example: a #8 sweep has an 8/8 or one-inch rise.) So-called "favorite sweeps" are also designated A through U. All sweeps are based on a chordal length of five feet.

Sweepspear: A typically horizontal body ornamentation, usually with a kickup, often consisting of a bright, applied molding but sometimes also having a contrasting paint color outlined by and contained inside bright trim. (See also "Color sweep.")

"Sweeten" (to): In design, to smooth and improve the aesthetic flow of a surface or line.

Tape drawing: Full-sized "drawings" of side and end car-body elevations made with long, thin strips of flexible adhesive tape. The tape--usually in rolls, black and about 1/8 inch wide--can be repositioned, so it's handier than drawing with pencil or pen.

Template: A hard, cut-out representation of a body surface at a certain section. Taken vertically, templates are made on one side of a clay model to accurately reproduce sections either on the other side of the model or in a drawing.

Theme: A loose design idea, usually in sketch or model form, that captures the essence of a project goal; that inspires and points toward further development.

Through fender: A front fender that flows back onto the door and sometimes beyond it, often to blend into or touch the applied (q.v.) rear fender.

Top boot: A covering over the lowered convertible top. Can be flexible (canvas or vinyl) or rigid (fiberglass or metal).

Track: (See "Tread.")

Tread: The distance, center to center, between both front or both rear tires (or wheels) of a car. Also called "track."

Trim buck: Same as a "seating buck" (q.v.) but trimmed in fabric.

Tumblehome: The inward tilt or angle of the roof from the beltline up as seen in front or rear view.

Turn-under: The inward curvature of a car body below roughly mid door as seen in front or rear view.

Unitized body: A type of construction in which the frame and body form a single unit; also called "frame-integral". (See also "Bridge-truss" and "Monocoque.")

Valance: A front-fender extension hanging down behind the wheel, intended to hide the undersurface and chassis.

Vee or vee angle: An angle shaped like the letter V.

Ventipane or vent pane: The small, hinged, front window behind the A-pillar that allows air to be directed into the passenger compartment. (See also "Quarter window.")

Wheel arch: The fender cutout to the outside of each wheel.

Wheelbase: The distance between the front and rear axle centerlines.

Wheelcover: An ornamental, protective metal disc that covers an entire wheel, as opposed to a hubcap which covers only the center. (See also "Hubcap.")

Wheelhouse: The bottom surface of a fender or the sheetmetal or plastic pan inside a fender.

Window regulator: The door mechanism that raises and lowers the glass.

Window reveal: An enframed window area in the door, usually recessed and often stepped, surrounding the side glass. (See also "Reveal" and "Reveal molding.")

Windshield rake or angle: (See "Fast.")

Windsplit: A raised crease that runs longitudinally along a body surface, typically in the center of the hood, decklid or fender top. A windsplit is lower than a fin.

Windwing: Same as "quarter window," q.v.

Wire wheel: A wheel with multiple, interlaced wire spokes and a steel rim. (See also "Alloy wheel," "Artillery wheel" and "Disc wheel.")

Working drawings: The mechanical drawings used to complete the body engineering drafts.

Wraparound: A window or molding or surface that stretches partially around the body surface.

Zero line (horizontal): A locating line at the top of the chassis frame as seen in side view. Also called "waterline" and "datum line."

Zero line (vertical): A locating line established at the front of the dashboard.

Zero point: A point that serves to locate all other parts and surfaces of the body. The zero point is often at the very center of the theoretical front axle, but it can also be ahead of the car to prevent minus numbers ◆

ACKNOWLEDGEMENT & APPRECIATION

The authors thank and acknowledge the following individuals and institutions: Don Adams; E.G. (Bud) Adams; Fred Adickes; James W. Alexander; American Automobile Manufacturers Association; Amesbury Public Library; Milt Antonick; C. Edson Armi; Art Center College of Design; Auburn-Cord-Duesenberg Museum; *Automotive Industries*; Bennie S. Bailey; Robert Barit; George Barris and Barris Kustom Industries; Lee Beck; Maria Grazia Bergagna; David W. Bird II; John A. Bird; Gene Bordinat Jr.; Kent K. Bordinat; Philip Bordinat; Robert E. Bourke; Harry B. Bradley; Peter Brock; Dan Brooks; Jerry Brochstein; Philip C. and Susan M. Brooks; Arch A. Brown; Roy A. Brown; David Brownell; Bill Brownlie; Laura C. Buckley; The Budd Co.; Mrs. Gordon (Kay) Buehrig; Ann Burnham; Gregg J. Buttermore; G.R. Cairns; Carl A. Cameron; F.L. Campanale; William A. Cannon; Bob Casey; Carriage Museum of America; Cass Technical High School Alumni Assn.; Center for Creative Studies; Roy D. Chapin Jr.; Wayne K. Cherry; Harry E. Chesebrough; John R. Chevedden; G.T. Christiansen; Chrysler Historical Foundation; Classic Car Club of America; The Color Council; John Conde; Steve Coonan; Vincent R. Courtnay; Ross Cousins; Terrence Q. Cressy; David R. Crippen; Dave Cummins; Jonathan Day; John W. DeCampi; Mark L. Dees; Don DeLaRossa; Guiseppi D'Elena; Detroit Public Library; Marion Dietrich; Bill Dobson; The Dodge Club; Henry Dominguez; Edward J. Donnelly; Doubleday & Co. Inc.; Todd L. Duhnke; Ralph H. Dunwoodie; DuPont Automotive; Peggy Dusman; James F. Dworschack; James Milton Earl; Jerome Courtney Earl; Robert R. Ebert; John W. Ebstein; Randy Ema; Judith Endelman; Sally Engel; Marguerite Engel; Thomas G. Ernst; Joseph W. Eskridge; John W. Evermon; Virgil M. Exner Jr.; Nancy E. Fago; Merri Ferrell; Arthur M. Fitzpatrick; Russell Flinchum; Ford Design Center; Ford & Earl Associates Inc.; Henry Ford Museum & Greenfield Village Reference Center; *Fortune* Magazine (a registered trademark of Time Inc.); John Barclay Foster; Patrick R. Foster; Fred K. Fox; H.H. Franklin Foundation; Free Library of Philadelphia; Barbara Fronczak; Thomas C. Gale; Gene Garfinkle; Edwin S. Getner; Ghia S.p.A.; Billy F. Gibbons; Stan Gilliland; Luke Gilliland-Swetland; Gizmochine Inc.; Jeffrey I. Godshall; Jon A. Goedde; Albert J. Gonas; Walter E. Gosden; Ron Grantz; Gray, Maine Historical Society; Susan Green; Carol W. Greene; Marcie Greenfield; Eugene T. Gregorie; A.B. Grisinger; Karl H. Grote; John Gunnell; Hagley Museum & Library; Haysum Hahn; Arthur (Bud) Hall; George L. Hamlin; Steve Hamp; Jessica Hatchigan; Jerry Heasley; Don Hedger; Dwight Heinmuller; Terry R. Henline; John Herlitz; Ron Hill; Fred Hoadley; Allen A. Hogle; Michael C. Holmes; Gary Hoonsbeen; Tim Howley; John A. Hull; Helen V. Hutchings; Charles K. Hyde; Ronald B. Irwin; William S. Jackson; Floyd Joliet; Robert B. (Robin) Jones; Charles M. Jordan; Wayne A. Kady; Lucy M. Karash; D.J. Kava; Tom Kellogg; Beverly Rae Kimes; Dan Kirchner; Ken Koroncey; Krause Publications Inc.; Louis G. Helverson; Franklin Quick Hershey; Homer LaGassey; Tom Land; Richard M. Langworth; Donald C. Lasky; Henry deS. Lauve; Peter Leach; Denise Le Moix; C.A. Leslie Jr.; Maryanne Levinstein; David Lanier Lewis; Paul Lienert; Clark Lincoln; Nathan R. Lipfert; Charles Liskow; Ray Litt; Edward Macauley; Clare MacKichan; Strother MacMinn; Maine Maritime Museum; Patrick M. Malone; Samuel F. Manning; Maritime Museum of Monterey; Linda Martin-Schaff; Randy Mason; Jim McElroy; Robert C. McLellan; Marjorie G. McNinch; Glenn D. Miller; Jack Miller; Rhys Miller; E. Frank Moelich; George E. Moon; Betty Morrison; Vincent Muniga; Elliott L. Myerson; Myrin Library Archives, Ursinus College; Museums at Stony Brook; John Najjar; National Automotive History Collection; National Motor Museum, Beaulieu; Colin Neale; Anthony Nethercott; Jack Nethercutt, Nethercutt Collection; Jan P. & Margaret Norbye; David R. North; John E. Northup; Norton Equipment Corp.; John Okolowicz; Pierre Ollier; Byron D. Olsen; Carl Olsen; Joe & Betty Oros; Edward J. Ostrowski Jr.; Lowell C. Paddock; Jerry P. Palmer; Stanley F. Parker; Howard E. Payne; Gene Perry; George Petsch; Harold Philpot; Pierce-Arrow Society; George Pisani; Charles Pohlmann; Juanita Pomante; Pontiac Motor Div.; Promostyl; E.L. Pruitt; Marc A. Ralston; Cynthia Read-Miller; Edward Reavie; William Reithard; Lloyd E.A. Reuss; Estelle Macauley Ritter; Virginia Rhoads; Ralph S. Roberts; William E. Robinson; Frederick D. Roe; Rolls-Royce Owners Club; Brandt Rosenbusch; Bourke Runton; Irvin W. Rybicki; James T. Sandoro; Margaret C. Sawyer; Richard P. Scharchburg; James J. Schild; Donald J. Schwarz; John E. Schwarz; Tom Scott; William D. Scott; Roger Sherman; John Shettler; Larry Shinoda; Matthew S. Short; Paul O. Sichert Jr.; Ellen Sideri; Jim Sitz; William S. Snyder; Ken Sowles; Adrian Gil Spear Jr.; *Special Interest Autos* Magazine; Jim Sponseller; Jane Macauley Spratt; Rosalie Stapleton; Catherine Stein; Mary Geo Caleal Stephenson; Brooks Stevens; Jeffrey A. Stevens; Richard Stoey; Gerald J. St. Pierre; Thomas M. Stone; Richard H. Stout; Studebaker National Museum; Caroline Sutton; Robert A. Sutton; Willard Sweetser; Jack Telnack; Robert M. Thomas; Jonathan Thompson; Joseph D. Thompson; Frank Tickle; Pat Tobin; Jack Triplett; Pat Tunsky; Dave Turner; John E. Vanous; John R. Velliky; Clifford C. Voss; Bernard J. Weis; Dale K. Wells; Lynn Mitchell Werner; Stanley R. Wilen; Roger B. White; Jill Witzenburg; Donald F. Wood; James A. Wren; Diran Yazejian; Charles Richard Yeaton; Karl S. Zahm. ◆

Index